The SPACES of POSTMODERNITY

The SPACES of POSTMODERNITY

Readings in Human Geography

EDITORS

MICHAEL J. DEAR
AND STEVEN FLUSTY

University of Southern California

Copyright © Blackwell Publishers Ltd 2002
Editorial matter and arrangement © Michael J. Dear and Steven Flusty 2002

The moral right of Michael J. Dear and Steven Flusty to be identified as authors of the editorial material
has been asserted in accordance with the Copyright, Designs and Patents Act 1988.

First published 2002

2 4 6 8 10 9 7 5 3 1

Blackwell Publishers Ltd
108 Cowley Road
Oxford OX4 1JF
UK

Blackwell Publishers Inc.
350 Main Street
Malden, Massachusetts 02148
USA

British Library Cataloguing in Publication Data

A CIP catalogue record for this book is available from the British Library.

Library of Congress Cataloging-in-Publication Data has been applied for.

ISBN 0–631–21781–9 (hbk)
ISBN 0–631–21782–7 (pbk)

Typeset in Sabon on 10/12 pt
by Kolam Information Services, Pvt. Ltd, Pondicherry, India
Printed in Great Britain by TJ International, Padstow, Cornwall

This book is printed on acid-free paper.

Contents

Preface

This Reader documents the emergence and impact of postmodern thought in human geography. It is intended as a companion volume to Michael Dear's *The Postmodern Urban Condition* (Blackwell, 2000). Its narrative engages what has been, since 1965, the most invigorating intellectual roller coaster in the history of human geography, the discipline that seeks to explain the spatial evolution of human beliefs, behaviors, and societies. This book represents a vital piece of human geography's intellectual history, but its contents are also necessary reading for all those interested in the status and prospects of space in contemporary social theory.

Our account has all the ingredients of a first-class academic mystery novel: painstaking protagonists laboring late into the night over some arcane proof; vitriolic personal and ideological clashes; and endless, sometimes even reckless shifts in academic allegiance. By the time you finish this book, we hope you will share at least some of our sense of exhilaration – of a discipline in wild pursuit of its identity, gobbling up intellectual delicacies strewn across its path, all the time driven by a deep desire to influence debates about the burning issues that affect our lives.

This is not a tale for the faint of heart. To arrive at its denouement requires careful attention to character and motivation, clues and false leads, heroines and villains. The extracts that follow have been chosen, above all, for their intensely personal engagement with the task of understanding society and space. Many of the essays also possess a certain intensity, even rawness, as their authors chip away at the edges of geographical knowledge. All of them demonstrate the writers' willingness to go out on a limb, and their courage is often bounteously rewarded. The personal and scholarly journeys that comprise this volume are nothing short of breathtaking: that such changes could occur over a short space of 25 years! Even when the excerpts are scratchy, tentative, or downright belligerent, you should close this book with a sense of vibrancy, discovery, and insight.

But: how to begin? Like all good mystery novels, we open with a puzzle...

They sought it with thimbles, they sought it with care;
They pursued it with forks and hope;
They threatened its life with a railway-share;
They charmed it with smiles and soap.

(Lewis Carroll, *The Hunting of the Snark*)

Lewis Carroll was a master practitioner of deconstruction more than a century before the term was invented. He excelled at turning language and mathematics against themselves, revealing the oft-contradictory concepts and conventions underpinning what had otherwise been blithely regarded as the way things were. In his mock-epic poem *The Hunting of the Snark* (1876), Carroll attains a high-water mark in socially barbed absurdity. This poem, subtitled "An Agony in Eight Fits,"

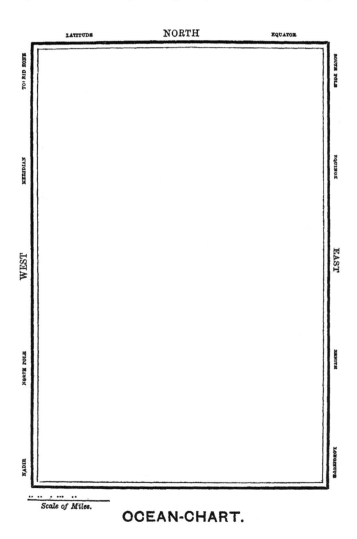

OCEAN-CHART.

narrates the tale of how a motley crew sets sail on a hunting expedition. The crew navigates by a map "representing the sea, without the least vestige of land," because equators, meridians, and the like "are merely conventional signs." Each member of the crew possesses a specialized skill that is largely useless to the task at hand (including a barrister, a billiard-maker, and a beaver with a penchant for knitting lace). Each sets their respective skill to the task of survival while stalking the beast in question. That beast is the Snark, a creature never directly described but only signified by "unmistakable marks," including an aesthetic fondness for placing bathing machines in the landscape, and a tendency to rise so late as to have breakfast during 5 o'clock tea.

Carroll's sign-obsessed hunt for a creature described only by its tangential qualities, by people armed with a blank map and a hodgepodge of inappropriate talents, somehow captures the daunting challenge facing the reader who confronts postmodernism for the first time. So, let's try to clear some ground.

Postmodernism, for all its apparent complexity, can usually be understood as dealing with three related issues, though not always at the same time:

• a series of distinctive cultural and stylistic practices that are in and of themselves intrinsically interesting;
• the totality of such practices, viewed as a cultural ensemble characteristic of the contemporary epoch (generally referred to as postmodernity); and
• a set of philosophical and methodological discourses that are antagonistic to the legacies of Englightenment thought, most particularly the hegemony of any single grand theory.

Needless to say, this simplification does not settle the matter; it merely provides an initial orientation. So, how exactly do we track down a human geography that can be characterized as stylistic, methodological, and epochal, or some unspecified combination thereof? Like Carroll's poem, this work may indeed cause a certain amount of agony, so (following his lead) we have divided our investigation into two "fits."

To give you a first dose of agony, let us assert that we regard *postmodernism as an ontology of radical but principled uncertainty*. Don't worry if this idea seems a bit obscure right now. An "ontology" basically describes someone's "world-view," or the principles and assumptions they bring to knowing the world around them. Ontologies are not the same as "epistemologies," which refer to the different kinds of specific knowledge that are available to us when we get round to explaining that world. For example, let's say that person A believes in God, i.e., a spiritual being guiding our lives and destinies; person B is an atheist, disavowing the existence of such a being. The two people have radically different world views, or ontologies; that is, they have totally contrasting assumptions about our being, here on this planet. Now, let's add that persons A, C, and D are all religious people (they've decided that ontological position): let A be a Jew, C a Christian, and D a Buddhist. Their different religions are akin to alternative epistemologies; i.e., while they have already decided that God exists, they have also selected different ways to know him/her/it.

As you can probably guess, an exactly analogous range of issues confront theorists, scientists, philosophers, and others when they come to select an ontology and epistemology to explain the world about them. What theory should I espouse? Do I prefer Marxism or poststructuralism? Science or a hermeneutic approach? How on earth am I supposed to choose? We *on principle* are not going to choose among these options, preferring to maintain a critical openness. So you, as readers are going to have to live with this uncertainty/ambiguity, at least until much later in the hunt when you'll want to make up your own minds about what all this means.

Just as Lewis Carroll's Snark left traces of its presence to tantalize the hunters, you will discover pieces of our ontology as you proceed. It is, for instance, critical of single rationalities, and of history/time seen as both a linear and progressive process; it pleads for the recovery of the personal, the body, and individual experience as part of our problematic; and it launches a withering investigation into the social con-structedness of supposedly "natural" facts and categorizations (whether of material or symbolic phenomena). Perhaps most notably, our ontology tends towards rela-tionalism, or relativism if you prefer – the notion that a thing becomes what it is not by reason of some inherent essence in the thing itself, but by reason of its relation-ships to other things around it. In this sense, the individual explorers who are brought together as contributors to this volume are, in retrospect, not so disjoint after all. While many of our cotravelers would not willingly identify as postmodern-ists (some would vehemently reject such an appellation!), their writings wrestle with manifestly postmodern themes, and together they presage distinctly postmodern methodological and analytical approaches.

We have done our utmost to equip you, on your exploration into the postmodern, with maps more useful than one without any vestiges of land or meridians. (That would be far too perverse, even for us.) Thus, the volume is divided in two fits. The first is a telling of the emergence of postmodernism in human geography as a factual narrative in linear time (a distinctly modernist conceit, let it be admitted). We excavate the origins, arrival, and spectacular consequences of the advent of post-modernism in human geography. The second fit constitutes the sort of radical break of which Jacques Derrida is so fond, where we outline a cartography of a future postmodern human geography, arranged around contingently defined increments of spatial scale. We move from the most intimate to the most global of spaces; from the individual body to planetary biological and communications systems; and then back again. All scales are copresent in any given place.

But if we provide a map, it is up to you to navigate your path through it. Maps lie. Our choice of extracts, their numbering, *everything about this book*, reflect a series of choices made and choices foregone. We urge you to rail against this sequencing, while we and you are inevitably bound by it. You may equally well read the last sections first, or jump from section to section at will. Readers will ultimately have to find their own ways of reconstructing the deconstruction in these pages. In the meantime, you had best regard this book as an incendiary device. Stuff it in your pocket, and hope it explodes! In fact our strategy is deliberately to place literary land-mines in your path as you navigate through the text. At many points, for instance, we have included at least one distinctly nonacademic extract. This is to dislodge you from comfortable and comforting presuppositions and expectations. The selections are also fun to read. Postmodernism is, after all, in no small part about putting "dancing" back into the revolution (the phrase is Emma Goldman's), through the recovery of desire, pleasure, and play. Other devices of dislocation include the editorial comments that introduce each extract. In these, we deliberately avoid telling you what you should think about the piece, emphasizing instead the subversive nature of each text – and remember, even the ancient scrolls from decades ago were revolutionary in their times! We also draw specific attention to the intellectual dexterity that characterizes all these pieces.

One last thing: in keeping with the metaphors of mystery, subversion, and materiel, this Reader concludes not with a nutshell encapsulation of what, following our expedition, we now "know" things to be. Rather, it ends with a dialogue intended to question and reinterpret the volume's contents, evoking possibilities for what could come next, assuming we choose to make it happen. Hence, we forego a "Conclusion" for an "Inconclusion," refusing even to contemplate a closure that, like so many previous (anti)climaxes, would function only to suppress different ways of knowing. At the end of Lewis Carroll's Snark hunt, the Baker finally met the Snark (or was it a Boojum?); but the Baker disappeared, leaving behind "Not a button, a feather, or mark." We, by contrast, would like to end up with the same number of readers as we began.

REFERENCE

Carroll, L: (Gasson, R. [ed.]). *The Illustrated Lewis Carroll*. Jupiter Books: London 1978, pp. 225–58.

Acknowledgments

We would like to offer special thanks to Django Sibley, who helped immeasurably toward the completion of this volume. He labored with the editing of extracts, contributed an essay of his own, and checked the entire manuscript.

Dallas Dishman assisted in compiling the images used in the book. Important editorial and administrative support was offered by Elina Abedi, Fernando Llamas, Richard Parks, Charisse Smith, and Clare Walker.

Sincere thanks to all those at Blackwell who put their considerable energies and talents into this project, especially Sarah Falkus (a persuasive, patient commissioning editor), Joanna Pyke (a peerless editorial controller), and Brian Johnson (a brilliant book designer). The project was first suggested to us by Jill Landeryou. The Blackwell people who sought the necessary permissions deserve a medal.

We are very grateful to Bill Viola for permission to use the cover image.

And we applaud all the contributors to this volume for the audacious intellectual adventures they have undertaken. We exclude ourselves from this accolade, of course; we are simply glad to be in their company.

We are grateful to authors and publishers for permission to reproduce extracts from the following works:

TEXT

Aksoy, A., and Robins, K., "Exterminating Angels: Morality, Violence and Technology in the Gulf War" from (eds. H. Mowlana, G. Gerbner, and H. I. Schiller)

Triumph of the Image: The Media's War in the Persian Gulf – a Global Perspective (Westview Press, 1992).

Cohen, S., "Sounding out of the City" from (eds. A. Leyshon, D. Matless, and G. Revill) *The Place of Music* (Guilford Press, New York, 1998).

Cox, K. R., and Golledge, R. G., "Behavioral Models in Geography" from *Behavioral Problems in Geography: A Symposium* (Northwestern University, Evanston, 1969).

Dear, M. J., "Postmodernism and Planning" first published in *Environment and Planning D: Society and Space* 4, 1986, reprinted by permission of Pion Limited, London.

Dear, M. J., and Flusty, S., "Postmodern Urbanism" from *Annals of American Geographers* 88(1), 1998, reprinted by permission of the American Geographers Association and Blackwell Publishers, Oxford.

Dimendberg, E., "From Berlin to Bunker Hill: Urban Space, Late Modernity and Film Noir in Fritz Lang's and Joseph Losey's M," *Wide Angle* 19:4 (1997) 69, 71–93 © Ohio University: Athens Center for Film and Video. Reprinted by permission of the Johns Hopkins University Press.

Donnelly, K., "A Ramble through the Margins of the Cityscape" from (eds. J. Dowson and S. Earnshaw) *Postmodern Subjects/Postmodern Texts* (*Postmodern Studies* 13) (Editions Rodopi B.V. Amsterdam, 1995).

Elder, G., Wolch, J., and Emel, J., "La Pratique Sauvage" from *Animal Geographies: Place, Politics and Identity in the Nature-Culture Borderlands* (Verso, London, 1998).

Ellison, H., *Repent, Harlequin: Said the Ticktockman* (Underwood Books, Grass Valley, CA, 1997).

Flusty, S., "Thrashing Downtown: Play as Resistance to the Spatial and Representational Regulation of Los Angeles" reprinted from *Cities* 17(2), 2000, pp. 149, 151–8, with permission from Elsevier Science.

Forté-Escamilla, K., from *The Storyteller with Nike Airs, and Other Barrio Stories* © 1994, by Kleya Forté-Escamilla. Reprinted by permission of Aunt Lute Books.

Friedberg, A., *Window Shopping: Cinema and the Postmodern*, pp. 109–25. Copyright © 1993 The Regents of the University of California (University of California Press, Berkeley, 1993).

Graham, J., "Anti-Essentialism and Overdetermination: A Response to Dick Peet," *Antipode* 24(2) 1992, Blackwell Publishers, Oxford.

Gray, A., *Unlikely Stories, Mostly* (Penguin Books Ltd, Harmondsworth, 1984, reprinted by permission of Cannongate Books Ltd, Edinburgh).

Gregory, D., *Ideology, Science and Human Geography* (Hutchinson, London, 1978).

Gurnah, A., "Elvis in Zanzibar" from (ed. A. Scott) *The Limits of Globalization* (Routledge, London, 1997).

Haggett, P., *Locational Analysis in Human Geography* (Edward Arnold Publishers, London, 1965).

Harley, J. B., "Deconstructing the Map," *Cartographica* 26(2) 1989, reprinted by permission of University of Toronto Press Incorporated.

Harvey, D., *Explanation in Human Geography* (St Martin's Press, New York, 1969).

Harvey, D., *Social Justice and the City*, pp. 1–18, 116–18, 150–2. © 1973 The Johns Hopkins University Press. Reprinted with permission of The Johns Hopkins University Press.

Harvey, D., "The Argument" from *The Condition of Postmodernity: An Inquiry into the Origins of Cultural Change* (Blackwell Publishers, Oxford, 1989).

Hemmings, C., "From Landmarks to Spaces" from (eds. G. B. Ingram, A. M. Bouthillette and Y. Retter) *Queers in Space* (Bay Press, Seattle, 1997).

Jacobs, J. M., "(Post)Colonial Spaces" from *Edge of Empire: Postcolonialism and the City* (Routledge, London, 1996).

Jameson, F., *The Cultural Logic of Late Capitalism/Postmodernism, or The Cultural Logic of Late Capitalism*. Copyright 1991, Duke University Press. All rights reserved. Reprinted with permission.

King, L. J., "Alternatives to a Positive Economic Geography," *Annals of the Association of American Geographers* 66(2), 1976, copyright the Association of American Geographers, published Blackwell Publishers.

Law, J., and Hetherington, K., "Materialities, Spatialities, Globalities" online paper from (ed. J Bryson et al) *Knowledge Space Economy* (Routledge, London, 2000).

Lefebvre, H., *The Production of Space* (Blackwell Publishers, Oxford, 1991).

Ley, D., "Social Geography and Social Action" from Ley, D., and Samuels, M. S., *Humanistic Geography: Prospects and Problems* (Maaroufa Press, Chicago, 1978).

Ley, D., and Mills, C., "Can there be a Postmodernism of Resistance in the Urban Landscape?" from (ed. P. L. Knox) *The Restless Urban Landscape* (Prentice-Hall, Engelwood Cliffs, NJ, 1993).

McDowell, L., "Towards an Understanding of the Gender Division of Urban Space" first published in *Environment and Planning D: Society and Space* 1, 1983, reprinted by permission of Pion Limited, London.

Marcos, Subcommandante, *Shadows of Tender Fury* (Monthly Review Press, New York, 1995).

Olsson, G., *Eggs in Bird* (Pion Limited, London, 1980).

Peet, R., "The Development of Radical Geography in the United States" from *Radical Geography: Alternative Viewpoints on Contemporary Social Issues* (Maaroufa Press, Chicago, 1977).

Pickles, J., "Toward an Economy of Electronic Representation and the Virtual Sign" from *Ground Truth: The Social Implications of Geographic Information Systems* (Guilford Press, New York, 1995).

Rose, G., *Feminism and Geography* (Polity Press and University of Minnesota Press, 1993).

Rushdie, S., from *East, West: Stories by Salman Rushdie*, copyright © 1994 by Salman Rushdie. Used by permission of Pantheon Books, a division of Random House, Inc., and Wylie Agency, New York.

Scott, A. J., and Storper, M., "The Geographical Foundations and Social Regulation of Flexible Production Complexes" from (eds. J. Wolch and M. Dear) *The Power of Geography* (Routledge, London, 1989).

Soja, E., "Taking Los Angeles Apart: Towards a Postmodern Geography" first published in *Environment and Planning D: Society and Space* 4, 1986, reprinted by permission of Pion Limited, London.

Soja, E., and Hooper, B., "The Spaces that Difference Makes" from (eds. M. Keith and S. Pile) *Place and the Politics of Identity* (Routledge, London and New York, 1993).

Stephenson, N., *Snow Crash*. Copyright © 1992 by Neal Stephenson. Used by permission of Bantam Books, a division of Random House, Inc.

Thrift, N. J., "On the Determination of Social Action in Space and Time" first published in *Environment and Planning D: Society and Space* 1, 1983, reprinted by permission of Pion Limited, London.

Tuathail, Gearóid Ó., *Critical Geopolitics: The Politics of Writing Global Space* (Routledge and University of Minnesota Press, 1996).

Turkle, S., *Life on the Screen: Identity in the Age of the Internet* (Simon & Schuster Inc, 1995, reprinted with the permission of Simon & Schuster from LIFE ON THE SCREEN by Sherry Turkle. Copyright © 1995 by Sherry Turkle and Brockman Inc., New York.

Wolch, J., "Zoöpolis," *Capitalism, Nature, Socialism* 7(2) June 1996, reprinted by permission of Guilford Press.

FIGURES

pp. 416–18 Boucq, F. *Pioneers of the Human Adventure* (Catalan Communications plc., New York, 1989).

p. 21 Calvin and Hobbes "Oh no! Everything has suddenly turned Neo-Cubist!" Calvin and Hobbes © 1990 Watterson. Reprinted with permission of Universal Press Syndicate. All rights reserved.

p. 29 Figure 2 "A Model for Models" from R. J. Chorley "Geography and analogue theory" *Annals of the Association of American Geographers* 54, 1964. Association of American Geographers, published Blackwell Publishers.

p. 32 Figure 3 "A comparative historical geography of two railnets: Columbia basin and South Australia" from D. W. Meinig, *Annals of the Association of American Geographers* 52, 1962. Association of American Geographers, published Blackwell Publishers.

HALFTONES

p. 298 Figure 4, "Bunker Hill" from *M*, 1951, Columbia/The Kobal Collection.

p. 445 Figure 1 "Europa Boulevard," 1992. Reproduced by courtesy of Anne Friedberg, Program in Film Studies/PhD Program in Visual Studies, University of California at Irvine.

p. 448 Figure 2 "Dawn of the Dead," 1979, Museum of Modern Art, New York.

Introduction
How to Map a Radical Break

When it becomes possible for people to describe as "postmodern" the décor of a room, the design of a building, the diegesis of a film, the construction of a record, or a scratch video, a television commercial, or an arts documentary, or the intertextual relations between them, the layout of a page in a fashion magazine or critical journal, an anti-teleological tendency within epistemology, the attack on the metaphysics of presence, a general attenuation of feeling, the collective chagrin and morbid projections of a post-war generation of baby boomers confronting disillusioned middle age, the "predica-ment" of reflexivity, a group of rhetorical tropes, a proliferation of surfaces, a new phase in commodity fetishism, a fascination for images, codes and styles, a process of cultural, political or existential fragmentation and/or crisis, the "decentring" of the subject, an "incredulity towards meta-narratives," the replacement of unitary power axes by a plurality of power/discourse formations, the "implosion of meaning," the collapse of cultural hierarchies, the dread engendered by the threat of nuclear self-destruction, the decline of the University, the functioning and effects of the new miniaturized technologies, broad societal and economic shifts into a "media," "con-sumer" or "multinational" phase, a sense . . . of placelessness . . . or the abandonment of placelessness . . . or (even) a generalized substitution of spatial for temporal co-ordinates – when it becomes possible to describe all these things as "postmodern" . . . then it's clear that we are in the presence of a buzzword.

Dick Hebdige, "A Report on the Western Front: Postmodernism and the 'Politics' of Style"

Most detective work starts from the blisteringly obvious, whether you're Sherlock Holmes or Inspector Maigret, Philip Marlowe or George Smiley. So, if we are trying to demonstrate that there has been a radical break in human geographical thought, we must first gumshoe it over to the archives to collect the clues. In this introduction, we intend to establish what human geography is, what postmodernism is about, and then provide a tentative overview of the story of postmodern human geography.

The Geography

Human geography is that part of social theory concerned to explain the spatial patterns and processes that enable and constrain the structures and actions of everyday life. It provides an account of the ways in which complex sociocultural, economic, and political processes act through time and space. What are the main precepts of such an inquiry?

Assume that time and space define two axes of a "fabric" (or "tapestry") upon which are inscribed the processes and patterns of human existence, including political, socio-cultural, and economic activities. At issue is exactly how we conceptualize the structuring of human life on that tapestry. Contemporary social theory invokes two basic emphases in understanding how the human tapestry evolves: *structure* and *agency* (see, for example, Giddens, 1984). To these, we want to add *space*.

Human landscapes are created by knowledgeable actors (or agents) operating within a specific social context (or structure). The linkage between the two, the structure – agency relationship, is conceived as being mediated by a series of institutional arrangements, which both enable and constrain human action. Hence, three "levels of analysis" can be identified: structures, institutions, and agents. To make sure this is clear, let us define:

- *structures* (S) as the long-term, deep-seated social practices that govern daily life, such as law, state, and family (these are often taken for granted, and may even be hidden from consciousness);
- *institutions* (I) the phenomenal forms of structures, including (for example) the apparatus of government; and
- *human agents* (A) the voluntaristic actions of individuals and groups in determining the observable outcomes of social process.

Any narrative about landscape is necessarily an account of the reciprocal relationship between relatively long-term structural forces and short-term routine practices of individual human agents, as mediated by institutional forms (represented graphically as the S-I-A triad in figure 1). It is impossible to predict the exact outcome of the interactions among structure, institution, and agency because, while individual activities are framed within a particular structural context, they can also transform that context. In particular, economic, political, and sociocultural history is *place-specific* in that such relationships unfold in recognizable locales according to a (sometimes opaque) logic of spatial diffusion; it is also *time-specific* in the sense that the relationships evolve at different temporal rates.

As society evolves, so does its geographical expression; but, by the same token, the material form itself has repercussions for the social forces that shape it. This reflexive impact of space on society, and society on space, is realized in many different ways. In the simplest terms, social relations are:

- *constituted* through space (as in the industrial organization of extraction and production in resource-based environments);

- *constrained* by space (such as the inertia imposed by the built environment, or the limits imposed by natural hazards); or
- *mediated* through space (including the development of ideology and belief systems within geographically confined regions or locales).

The consequent landscapes may be said to be a product of the *sociospatial dialectic*.

Interaction through space is complicated by the various *scales* over which it takes place. Geographical regions, or locales, are defined by physical and/or human boundaries that delimit fields of process and interaction. In general terms, the processes of social life operate at macro, meso, or microscales (figure 1); in concrete terms, we could observe such scalar differences become manifest as local, regional, and national effects. The structure–institution–agency triad will be replicated (in different ways) at each scale. So, for instance, national urban structure may be the result of the interaction between global capital and labor relations (e.g, the rise of Pacific Rim cities); but local outcomes may also be influenced by labor relations operating in peculiar ways at the community level (as, for instance, in the specific pattern of plant closures, or traditions governing single-industry communities).

Any *locale* is, therefore, at once a complex synthesis of objects, patterns, and processes, derived from the simultaneous interaction of different levels of social process operating at varying geographical scales. Many levels and scales of process are distilled or crystallized into a single locale; it is as though a multitiered sequence of multiply determined events had been telescoped onto a single plane. Just as importantly, over time, the various horizons of each locale accumulate like sediments over earlier planes of human activity. The locale is thus a complex amalgam of past, present, and newly forming archaeologies that coexist simultaneously in the landscape. The intellectual challenge posed by what we refer to as the "geographical puzzle" is to unravel a locale's complexity into its constitutive elements. *Therefore, in a most fundamental sense, the focal concern in human geography is to understand the simultaneity of time and space in structuring social behaviors. Human geography is the study of the contemporaneity of social process and spatial pattern over time and space.*

One further elaboration is necessary. "Social process" is a phrase that carries multiple meanings. We shall define it loosely to include the generic processes that structure the time–space fabric. In no particular order of priority, these are: political, economic, and sociocultural. They refer respectively to the mechanisms of conflict, production and exchange, and human interaction that characterize every society to varying degrees. The exact manner in which sociocultural, political, and economic processes become operational in any locale is a matter for empirical determination. In a capitalist society, for example, they might be equivalent to (respectively) structures of class, state, and capital. These can be further described in terms of their institutional forms (say, social movements, state apparatuses, and fractions of capital); and ultimately, equivalent categories of human agency (such as neighborhood organizations, municipal government, and local chambers of commerce). Different operational forms would be invoked if we considered noncapitalist social formations, either historical or contemporary. So, hunter/gatherer societies might require appeal to kinship and caste systems to explain social organization. In this

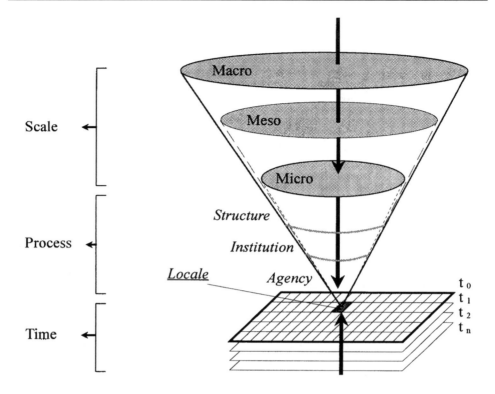

Figure 1.   The geographical puzzle.

case, economic, political, and sociocultural processes may become operationalized through "exchange," "caste," and "matriarchy" (instead of capital, class, and state).

Postmodernism/Postmodernity

Postmodernity is everywhere, from literature, design, and philosophy, to MTV, ice cream, and underwear. This seeming ubiquity only aggravates the difficulties of grasping its meaning. Postmodern discourse seems capable of instant adaptation in response to context and choice of interlocutors. We can cut to the heart of the matter by identifying three principal constructs in postmodernism: style, epoch, and method.

The contemporary explosion of interest in postmodern thought may be traced to the emergence of new *styles* of literature and literary criticism in the 1960s and 1970s. Postmodern cultural sensitivities quickly spread to other artistic endeavors, including design, painting, and photography. The example of architecture is particularly revealing. Here, the search for the new was associated with a revolt against the formalism and austerity of the modern style, epitomized by the unadorned office tower. However, while architecture's departure from modernism was loudly broadcast, the profession's destination remained vague. The burgeoning postmodern architecture was disturbingly divorced from any broad philosophical underpinnings, taking the form of an apparently random cannibalizing of existing architectural archetypes, and combining them into an ironic collage (or pastiche) of previous styles. Called "memory architecture" by its detractors, postmodernism's obituary was published embarrasingly soon after its birth, testimony to the vacuousness of treating it solely as a matter of aesthetics. In other fields (such as cultural studies and literary theory), the divorce between substance and philosophy never materialized, and postmodern inquiry flourishes.

The notion of postmodernism as *epoch* is founded in the contention that a "radical break" with past societal trends is underway, and that the sum of present-day changes is sufficiently apocalyptic as to warrant the definition of a separate culture with identifiable historical limits. The term *postmodernity* tends to be used by those wishing to describe the epoch following modernity. The hypothesis of a postmodern epoch (even in such provisional forms as "post-Fordism," etc.) involves grappling with the problem of theorizing contemporaneity, i.e., the task of making sense out of a plethora of concurrent societal realities. Any landscape is simultaneously composed of obsolete, current, and emergent artifacts; but how do we begin to codify and understand this variety? And at what point is the accumulated evidence sufficient to announce a radical break with the past? The idea that we are living in new times is seductive, but there are no clear answers to these questions. Postmodern culture may yet prove to be an extension of past trends, or the barometer of some more catastrophic changes. In any event, the volume and speed of contemporary world adjustments are surely sufficient to caution against subsuming them too readily into existing theories and presuppositions.

The third version of postmodernism, as *philosophy* or *method*, is basically a revolt against the rationality of modernism, a deliberate attack on the foundational character of much modernist thought. As Huyssen (1984, p. 25) warned, there can be little doubt that the classics of modernism are great works, but problems arise: "when their greatness is used as [an] unsurpassable model and appealed to in order to stifle contemporary artistic production." Postmodern philosophers eschew the notion of universal truth and the search for metanarratives (i.e, grand theoretical frameworks designed to explain the Meaning of Everything). They especially renounce the authority that implicity or explicity bolsters the privilege of one theory over another (as in: mine is good science/hard science; yours is not, hence it is inferior). Such hegemonic claims, postmodernists hold, are ultimately undecidable, and even the attempt to reconcile or resolve the tensions among competing theories should a priori be resisted. Such claims are evidenced in many schools of thought; for instance, Isaiah Berlin (1998) argued many legitimate human values cannot necessarily be ranked or reconciled.

At the core of this epistemological stand off lie the imponderables of language, identity, difference, and subjectivity. Since Wittgenstein, it has been clear that we can never master the language we employ; its effects always go beyond what we can control. The *deconstruction* movement, which may be viewed as part of the postmodern turn, has demonstrated that the use and intentionality of language is intimately bound up with the different subjectivities that guide our inquiries. Hence, we must inevitably fail in the task of representation (i.e., the "objective" reporting of our research "findings"), and in attempts to reconcile conflicting interpretations. In sum, postmodernism undermines the modernist belief that theory can mirror reality, and replaces it with a partial, relativistic viewpoint emphasizing the contingent, mediated nature of theory building. Metatheories and foundational thoughts are rejected in favor of microexplanations and undecidability. More than most thinkers, postmodernists learn to contextualize, to tolerate relativism, and to be conscious always of difference.

The philosophical origins of the postmodern movement have been traced to the nineteenth century, although the term itself began to be employed more freely during the 1930s. At minimum, its complex genealogy encompasses Nietzsche, Heidegger, the French poststructuralists (including Foucault, Derrida, and Lyotard) and American pragmatists (such as Rorty). It should therefore come as no surprise that we lack a unified theory of the postmodern. Instead, theory becomes a constant process of conversation, a discourse in which meaning and representation are subject to continuous negotiation. Critics have seized on this relativism to attack postmodernism's credibility. For instance, Ellis (1989, p. 159) asserts that deconstruction is "inherently antitheoretical," and that what is needed now is: "the development of some check and control on the indigestible, chaotic flow of critical writing through reflection on what is and what is not in principle worthwhile – that is, through genuine, rather than illusory, theoretical reflection." Part of the antirelativists' complaint is undoubtedly motivated by a need to preserve the legitimacy of their own scientific and political projects in the face of a babel of burgeoning discourses. The threat to existing hegemonies seems to be especially keenly felt by Marxists, but it also underlies the defense of Western cultural traditions and the rise of the term *political correctness* as an epithet of scorn amongst neo-conservatives.

Other groups, who initially benefited from postmodernism's antihegemonic stance, have also begun to distance themselves from its precepts. The case of feminism is perhaps the most notorious; once empowered by the critical openness to "different" voices, many feminists now claim that postmodernism's ambiguities run counter to a feminist political agenda. Critics from other persuasions have launched a strong defense of the project of modernity, including Jürgen Habermas, or have claimed that postmodernism cannot escape from the contradiction that it too is a metanarrative.

Much of the furor engulfing postmodernism is undoubtedly political in nature, both within the academy as well as society as a whole (think of the current "culture wars"). Everywhere, the dispute is about who controls the discourse and, hence, holds power. Critics on the left and the right who bemoan the political passivity or political correctness allegedly inherent in postmodernism are fooling only themselves; because like all theories, postmodernism can be enlisted to suit any political purpose. In recognition of the slippery surfaces of theory, many have distinguished between a positive/affirmative and a negative/skeptical perspective on postmodernism. The former allows that a politically progressive agenda is possible within postmodernism; the latter holds that postmodernism is inherently, inevitably conservative. This distinction is encapsulated by Foster (1985), who recognized a postmodernism of *resistance* and a postmodernism of *reaction*. This distinction clarifies what we take to be axiomatic: that in our shifting world, postmodern thought has not removed the necessity for political and moral judgements; what it has done is to question the basis for such judgements.

Postmodern Human Geography: A Premature History

Human geographers took up the postmodern challenge during the mid-1980s. This was partly a consequence of the prominence afforded to *space* in a seminal essay on postmodern culture by Jameson (1984). One of his most audacious claims was that existing time–space systems of societal organization and perception have been fundamentally altered to accommodate the emergent realms of a global capitalism; consequently, a new postmodern "hyperspace" has emerged, the time–space coordinates of which we can so far only dimly perceive. Since Jameson's article was published, an impressive roster of postmodern geographical writing has been compiled.

Two of the earliest geographical articles dealing explicitly with postmodernism were published by Dear (1986) and Soja (1986). The former dealt with urban planning and the production of a postmodern urbanism; the latter was an exuberant deconstruction of Los Angeles by an unrepentant postmodernist. Between 1986 and 1994, over 50 major articles and an equivalent number of critical commentaries appeared in prominent geography journals including especially *Society and Space*, but also the *Annals of the Association of American Geographers*, the *Canadian Geographer*, and the *Transactions of the Institute of British Geographers*.

Postmodern traces

With the benefit of hindsight, traces of a postmodern consciousness can, of course, be uncovered in geographical writings prior to 1986. The principal historical reasons for the absorption of postmodern thought into geography are properly to be found in the resurgence of Marxist social theory in the late 1960 and 1970s. It was out of a broadly based poststructuralist response to the perceived obsolescence of Marxism that impetus was imparted to the postmodern turn. In geography, this trend was instrumental in the renaissance of a more general interest in social theory, and in reconnecting the discipline to a broad spectrum of socioeconomic and political debates. Few of the contributors to these developments identified themselves as postmodernists. Of particular consequence were the substantive emphases on the urban question, and the role of space in economic development and sociospatial relations. The high levels of scholarly productivity in these areas rendered them particularly susceptible to innovation and rapid evolution.

It was not long before the neo-Marxist revival fell under scrutiny, and something like a "golden age" of theoretical/philosophical efflorescence occured in human geographical thought. For instance, in 1978 Gregory published his influential *Science, Ideology and Human Geography*, drawing attention in particular to the work of critical theorists such as Habermas. In the same year, Dear and Clark (1978) began their reappraisal of the theory of the state, with a neo-Marxian emphasis on the structures and language of legitimacy. A humanist geography also developed to counter the Marxian emphasis on structural explanation (Ley and Samuels, 1978). And, during this period, very deliberate attempts were launched to investigate the ontological and epistemological bases of geographical knowledge. The burgeoning connections between geography and social theory were given concrete expression in

1983, with the appearance of the journal *Society and Space* as part of the *Environment and Planning* series. The first issue included Thrift's (1983) wide-ranging reformulation of the problematic of time and space (which reflected his earlier work with Pred on time geography), and McDowell's (1983) fundamental paper on the gender division of urban space.

The 1986 papers by Soja and Dear may thus have crystallized a pervasive turbulence on geography's theoretical discourse and provided a platform for the next stages in the conversation. However, these essays were not so much theoretical departures, but more the culmination of a decade's engagement with the central issues of social theory.

Postmodern consciousness

Jameson's identification of architecture as the "privileged aesthetic" of a postmodern culture made it easy for geographers to adapt his insights to their agenda. Early studies by Relph (1987) and Ley (1987) drew attention to the built environment and the landscapes of postmodernity. These and other studies were instrumental in provoking an uninterrupted sequence of research on postmodern culture, emphasizing place and place-making, spectacle and carnival, and consumption. Given postmodernism's special emphasis on culture, it was inevitable that cultural geographers would be drawn to it.

Another, independent line of geographical inquiry in the late 1980s centered on the processes of contemporary economic restructuring, particularly the move toward flexible specialization (what some call flexible accumulation). Economic geographers were attempting to analyze the emergent dynamics of post-Fordist, flexible industrial systems and their concomitant spatial organization. Although few if any of these inquiries were explicitly postmodern in nature, they inevitably intersected with the problematic of periodization, i.e., whether or not a radical break had occurred to signal the arrival of a post-Fordist or postmodern society.

A third source of fertile intellectual discord concerned the emergent status of social theory in human geography. The validity of a social–theoretical approach was rarely at issue; more usually, the debate took the form of sometimes vitriolic exchanges among competing orthodoxies, the details of which need not detain us here. A temporary truce established two broad positions: one coalition favored maintaining the hegemony of their preferred theory (whatever that happened to be); a second advocated a theoretical pluralism that may properly be viewed as a precursor of postmodern sensibilities.

The point that these trends establish is that a postmodern consciousness emerged in human geography not from some orchestrated plot, but instead from a diversity of separate perspectives – including the cultural landscape, emergent economic geographies, and theoretical stand offs. Each trend had a life of its own before it intersected with postmodernism, but each was irrevocably altered as a consequence of this engagement. By 1988, Dear was able to argue for the relative coherence of what he styled the "postmodern challenge" to human geography. His plea was premised on the significance of space in postmodern thought and the potential of geography's contribution to a rapidly evolving field of social inquiry.

The postmodern wave

The year 1989 saw the publication of two geography books with postmodernism as a central theme. Soja's *Postmodern Geographies: The Reassertion of Space in Critical Social Theory* was a celebration of postmodernism and its challenges; but Harvey's *The Condition of Postmodernity: An Inquiry into the Origins of Cultural Change* was an openly hostile critique of postmodernism that attempted to subsume it within the explanatory rubric of Marxism. A year later, Cooke's *Back to the Future: Modernity, Postmodernity and Locality* appeared – a perspective of the "localities" project in Great Britain that was sympathetic to the claims on postmodernism. Whatever their respective merits, these books and their authors concentrated a discipline's attention on the postmodern question. But truth be told, the wave had already gathered an unstoppable momentum. The roster of publications in 1989 and subsequent years reveals a significant postmodern consciousness in the three topical areas previously identified:

1 *cultural landscapes and place-making*, with an increasing emphasis on the *urban*;
2 *economic landscapes of post-Fordism and flexible specialization*, with particular interest in *global–local* connections and the *spatial division of labor*; and
3 continuing *philosophical and theoretical disputes*, especially those relating to *space* and the problems of *language*.

There was also an explosion of interest in the application of postmodernism to other topical areas, representing a deepening appreciation of the extent of postmodernism's reach and relevance. In summary form, the many themes that became manifest by the mid-1990s may be grouped under four broad rubrics:

1 *problems of representation in geographical/ethnographic writing*, in *cartography*, and in *art*;
2 the *politics of postmodernity*, including both historical and contemporary, *feminist geography*'s discontent with postmodernism, *orientalism and postcolonialism*, and the *law* and critical legal studies;
3 an emphasis on the *construction of the individual and the boundaries of self*, including *human psychology and sexuality*; and
4 a reassertion of *nature and the environmental question*, which has taken many forms, including a fresh look at the relationships between *place* and *health*.

In pedagogic terms, too, postmodernism's emphases on difference and diversity were having profound implications (Graff, 1987). The presences and absences in the typical curriculum confirm that there has been no single canon of geographical thought. Instead, there is merely a series of unresolved, often unacknowledged, conflicts that are usually kept out of the classroom. In private, faculty members customarily adopt a "field-coverage" approach to the subject, believing that innovation and contradiction can least messily be accommodated by adding one more unit to the curriculum. The implicit assumption is that so long as students are exposed to the curricular grid, the subject will teach itself; and any synthesis or contradiction will somehow be resolved in the mind of the student (even though teachers themselves have not assailed these connections). However, it seems more likely that a disabling incoherence will ensure. In any event, wisdom does not derive from the imposition of some false consensus on the "basics" of the geographical canon. A much more defensible alternative is to *teach the differences* in the subject; i.e., to apply a postmodern consciousness to our pedagogy as well as our research.

Postmodern contentions

Needless to say, the introduction of postmodernism into human geography was not without dissent. The most common complaints echo those already current in the intellectual marketplace: that postmodernism's extreme relativism renders it politically incoherent, and hence useless as a guide for social action; that it is (ironically) just one more metanarrative; and that the project of modernity is still relevant, even though there is little agreement about exactly which pieces are worth salvaging.

At a superficial though certainly nontrivial level, many geographer critics simply lost patience with the promiscuous way in which the term was bandied about; if it could be applied to everything, then it probably meant nothing and was simply not worth the effort. Others were upset that they and their work were invoked to support a movement for which they had no sympathy. In one such case, Allan Pred (1992, p. 305) angrily distanced himself with these words: "I have never chosen to label myself as 'postmodern' ... I regard 'postmodern' as an inaccurate, uncritical, deceptive, and thereby politically dangerous 'epochal' labeling of the contemporary world ... [which is] best depicted as modernity magnified, as modernity accentuated and sped up, as *hyper*modern, not *post*modern." Behind these sentiments lies an unequivocal rejection of the postmodern if not everything that postmodernism represents, even though Pred's work is clearly implicated in the rise of postmodernism in geography.

The most sustained rejection of the postmodern turn in geography was undoubtedly that of David Harvey (1989). *The Condition of Postmodernity* is perhaps best understood as a defense of Marxism in light of the postmodern assault. Given Harvey's unassailable reputation within and beyond the discipline, the book was widely read. But, while broadly acknowledged, the book did little to stall the production of postmodern geographical scholarship, which (as we have seen) increased dramatically in subsequent years. The fact that the book met with some stinging rebuttals may have muted its influence within the discipline. In addition, Harvey's orthodoxy might have posed problems for fellow Marxists who had begun the long and arduous task of rewriting their social theory to account for changing conditions.

A different critical geographical literature was less concerned with outright rejection of postmodernism and more directed toward a constructive engagement with its problematic. Most commonly, this work explored the genealogy of postmodern thought, its broad links with the modern era, and the persistence of modernist themes in the present discourse. For instance, Julie Graham (1992) perceptively examined the consequences of postmodernism for a progressive politics. And, in a much-needed corollary, postmodern thought invigorated an effort to define the parameters of modernity itself.

Postmodern consequences

Whether or not we approve or are even aware of it, the postmodern wave had flooded geographical thought by the early 1990s. Some geographers chose to ride the wave; others ducked, hoping it would pass. So, what does the balance sheet on the postmodern turn look like? On the plus side, postmodernity has *enfranchised and empowered* those outside the traditional centers of scholastic authority (especially those beyond the so-called hard sciences); *difference* has been legitimized, no matter what its source (e.g., gender, sexual preference, (dis)ability, race, and ethnicity); and as a consequence, the *hegemony* of existing power centers has been emphatically undermined. Postmodernity, in a word, has been *liberating*. On the negative side, many rue the *loss of rationality*, especially as a basis for individual and collective action; they object to the *cacophony of voices* now crying out to be heard; and have attacked what they see as the essential *conservatism* of a philosophy that, if it espouses anything at all, seems to embrace an open-ended pluralism.

Remember that one does not have to *be* a postmodernist to engage the challenge of postmodern thought. Simply stated, we live in an era of postmodern consciousness; there is no choice in this matter, unless we are prepared to declare in favor of ignorance or the status quo. Beginning in 1984, a revolution of sorts occurred in geographical thinking. Since that time, we have witnessed:

- a truly unprecedented increase in quality scholarship devoted to the relationship between space and society;
- a reassertion of the significance and role of space in social theory and social process;
- an effective reintegration of human geography with mainstream social science and philosophy;
- the establishment of theory and philosophy as the *sine qua non* for the discipline's identity and survival;
- a new appreciation of diversity and difference, and a consequent diversification of theoretical and empirical interests; and
- a self-conscious questioning of the relationship between geographical knowledge and social action.

Some or all of these events may have occurred without the advent of postmodernism; but we doubt it, at least not with the same intensity and consequences.

Looking ahead, we are both optimistic and pessimistic. In one respect, Ellis (1989) was correct in his critique of deconstructionism: that it appealed not because it was a radical departure from entrenched attitudes, but because it fitted the already prevailing climate of intellectual pluralism and lent that climate a new legitimacy. Yet Ellis found himself unable to live with the consequent "chaotic flow" of critical writing, and pleaded for a return to "standards" of intelligent criticism. This is easier said than done. Postmodernism is exactly about standards, concomitant choices, and the exercise of power. Postmodernism places the construction of meaning at the core of geography's problematic. The key issue here is authority; and postmodernism has served notice on all those who seek to assert or preserve their authority in the academic and everyday world. And yet geographers, like everyone else, cling tenaciously to their beliefs. Knowledge is, after all, power, and we are all loathe to relinquish the bases for our claims to legitimacy. But is a critical openness too much to ask for? In the simplest and most profound terms, such openness is exactly what this Reader aims toward.

REFERENCES

Berlin, I.: *The Proper Study of Mankind*. Farrar, Strauss, and Giroux: New York 1998.

Cooke, P.: *Back to the Future: Modernity, Postmodernity and Locality*. Unwin Hyman: London 1990.

Dear, M.: Postmodernism and Planning. *Environment and Planning D: Society and Space* 4, 1986, 367–84.

Dear, M.: The Postmodern Challenge: Reconstructing Human Geography. *Trans. Inst. Br. Geogr. N.S.* 13, 1988, 262–74.

Dear, M. & Clark, G.: The State and Geographic Process. *Environment and Planning A* 10, 1978, 173–83.

Ellis, J. M.: *Against Deconstruction*. Princeton University Press: Princeton 1989.

Foster, H. (ed.): *Postmodern Culture*. Pluto Press: London 1985.

Giddens, A.: *The Constitution of Society*. Polity Press: Oxford 1984.

Graff, G.: *Professing Literature*. University of Chicago Press: Chicago 1987.

Graham, J.: Anti-essentialism and Overdetermination: a response to Dick Peet. *Antipode*, 24, 1992, 141–53.

Gregory, D.: *Science, Ideology and Human Geography*. Hutchinson: London 1978.

Harvey, D.: *The Limits to Capital*. Blackwell: Oxford 1982.

Harvey, D.: *The Condition of Postmodernity*. Blackwell: Oxford 1989.

Hebdige, Dick: A Report on the Western Front: Postmodernism and the "Politics" of Style. *Block* 12, 1986–7, 4–26.

Huyssen, A.: Mapping the Postmodern. *New German Critique* 33, 1984, 5–52.

Jameson, F.: Postmodernism, or the Cultural Logic of Late Capitalism. *New Left Review* 146, 1984, 59–92.

Ley, D.: Styles of the Times: Liberal and Neo-Conservative Landscapes in Inner Vancouver, 1968–1986. *Journal of Historical Geography* 13, 1987, 40–56.

Ley, D. and Samuels, M. S.: *Humanistic Geography: Prospects and Problems*. Maaroufa Press, Chicago 1978.

McDowell, L.: Toward an Understanding of the Gender Division of Urban Space. *Environment and Planning D: Society and Space* 1, 1983, 59–72.

Pred, A.: Commentary: On "Postmodernism, Language and the Strains of Postmodernism", by Curry. *Annals of the Association of American Geographers* 82(2), 1992, 305–8.

Relph, E.: *The Modern Urban Landscape*. The Johns Hopkins University Press: Baltimore 1987.

Soja, E.: Taking Los Angeles Apart. *Environment and Planning D: Society and Space* 4, 1986, 255–72.

Soja, E.: *Postmodern Geographies: The Reassertion of Space in Critical Social Theory*. Verso: New York 1989.

Thrift, N. J.: On the Determination of Social Action in Space and Time. *Environment and Planning D: Society and Space* 1, 1983, 23–58.

FIT THE FIRST

Excavating the Postmodern

● ● ● ● ● ● ● ● ● ● ● ● ● ● ● ● ● ● ● ●

1965–83: Pre-Postmodern Geographies

How do we know what we profess to know? This is the key question driving our academic mystery. There are manifestly different ways of knowing, and oftentimes they are incommensurable, irreconcilable. For instance, creationists understand the universe and its creatures as a sublime design by a celestial being usually called God. Evolutionists view human life as a slow, creative process of adaptation by diverse life forms in response to natural laws. The former appeals to the logic of a deity; the latter to the laws of nature. Both have erected impressive (ontological) edifices to buttress their claims, and neither side shows any sign of working out an accommodation with the other. Without choosing sides, we can infer immediately that an a priori insistence on the superiority of one explanation over another can only be purchased by silencing the other. In the bad old days, people could be executed for heretical thought. Today, they are simply denied tenure, or otherwise ostracized.

During the 1930s, C. P. Snow drew attention to the way human inquiry had tended to fall into two discrete camps that rarely spoke to each other. These "two cultures" were embodied in the fields of science and the humanities. The former proceeded by experimentation to discover truths and rules, even laws about the physical and human worlds. Its methods were rigorous and consistent, setting high standards relating to empirical verifiability, replicability, and so on. The latter proceeded by argumentation, proposal and counter proposal, and relied on rhetoric and the art of persuasion. Its method was more dialectical, and its outcome was more interpretive than concerned with formal derivation of behavioral or physical laws. Instead of truth, discourse in the humanities was more likely to end up with temporary accord (at best), and intellectual standoff (at worst).

Analogous disputes have arisen about how human knowledge is accumulated. For example, in his famous treatise, *The Structure of Scientific Revolutions*, Thomas Kuhn characterized the progress of science as a series of "paradigm" transitions. Science progressed, he observed, as one set of concepts, practices, and puzzles (the paradigm of "normal science") became manifestly outmoded, unable to explain emerging contradictions in the way we understood the world. Sooner or later, Kuhn asserted, a "scientific revolution" would occur, in which the obsolete way of knowing was displaced by a new paradigm capable of better explaining our observations. Yet, in another important study, *Against Method*, Paul Feyerabend railed against the prison house that paradigms became as they established institutionalized rules and procedures that tolerated no variations in scientific practice. Instead of the stultifying conformity of paradigms, Feyerabend recommended that science was better served by an anarchic free-for-all, which ultimately would inspire greater human creativity. A different kind of criticism of Kuhn's orderly march of science is to be found in sociologist Irwin Sperber's *Fashions in Science* (1990). In this book, Sperber likens the practice of science to a popularity contest in which the intrinsic merits of various theories matter less than the personal charisma of the respective proponents. Far from being a disinterested, painstaking accumulation of knowledge, science is instead fueled by personal ambition and animosity, and any honorifics depend on who you know as much as what you profess!

Of course, there is merit in all these characterizations: that much of science proceeds as a series of contradictory puzzles, and criteria such as verifiability and replicability have sorted out much sense from nonsense about knowledge of our world; that scientists would benefit if they were (periodically at least) shaken loose from their paradigm's moorings and encouraged to think outside the limits of normal science; and that knowledge is as much about human personality as it is about stuff. But even these positions assume that some kind of order exists in the world, and the ways we know it. What would happen if there were no such order?

In the popular nonsense verse of Lewis Carroll, illogicality rules. A belief in order, common sense, and linear narrative is suspended in favor of happenstance, inventiveness, and inconsequentiality. And, curiously enough, we gain intense pleasure, even insight from such diversions. Yet how can something that is profoundly, intentionally obfuscatory contrive to manufacture understanding? And what does non-sense tell us about the alternative ways in which human beings demonstrably think?

Postmodernism is interested in the way we know things: What is a *fact*? What is *truth*? How are some facts and truths admissible while others are not? Who decides? It already seems a big mistake to insist on a single way of knowing things, since history is replete with examples of radical revolutions in how we see the world. Would it be helpful to understand the transition from modernity to postmodernity within this broader historical perspective? Two historians and philosophers, Stephen Toulmin and Charlene Spretnak, stand ready to help us with this task.

According to Stephen Toulmin, "The very project of Modernity... seems to have lost momentum, and we need to fashion a successor program" (Toulmin, 1990, p. 3). With commendable clarity, Toulmin determines that the modern world began in the 1630s, and that its problems were caused by the lust for certainty and stability that obsessed those who had suffered through the earlier war-torn eras. Before that, in the late Renaissance, the generations of Erasmus, Rabelais and Montaigne had fostered an intellectual openness, a tolerance of diversity, and an uneasiness with assertions of definitive truth. Montaigne, for example, regarded attempts to reach theoretical consensus as presumptuous and self-deceptive.

The mid-seventeenth-century's economic depression brought prosperity to a skidding halt. It was also a time when printing opened up the classical traditions to lay readers, and the emergence of nation-states permitted new loyalties. Religious fanaticism and war had driven Europe to the edge of chaos, and as a consequence, certainty and stability came to be prized above skepticism and tolerance. Following 1600, the indeterminate dissolved in a few quick decades when scholars "condemned as irrational *confusion* what others welcomed as intellectual *profusion*" (Toulmin, 1990, p. 27). For the next three centuries, the "modernity" represented by Descartes, Galileo, and Newton dominated scholarship, and encased our intellects in bonds that we are only now beginning to unravel.

Instead of expanding the scope for rational debate, seventeenth-century scientists narrowed it. Instead of grounding their debates in the real world, seventeenth-century philosophers sought to render their questions independent of context. In Toulmin's felicitous phrases, the consequent intellectual narrowing may be understood as a shift:

- *from oral to written* (formal logic and proof were approved; rhetoric and argument were rejected);
- *from particular to universal* (general principles were favored over particular cases);
- *from local to general* (concrete diversity was rejected, abstract axioms preferred); and
- *from timely to timeless* (the permanent was foregrounded at the expense of the ephemeral or transitory).

In sum, theirs was a move from a practical philosophy toward a theoretical philosophy (Toulmin, 1990, pp. 30–5).

Charlene Spretnak (1997) pieces together the next steps in the intellectual history of Western thought. The development of what we now understand as the precepts of modernism relied in fact on four historical moments: the Renaissance, the Reformation, the Scientific Revolution, and the Enlightenment. Each may have been a well-intentioned reaction against the church–state monopoly on power and knowledge in the medieval world, yet all had internal contradictions that ultimately would lead to the present crisis of modernity. The *Renaissance* represented a rebirth of classical learning that eventually led to the establishment of secular education based on humanist values; it contrasted a Christian view of humans as weak and prone to sin with a neoclassical sense of Rational Man's unbounded potential. The *Reformation* was a rationalization of religious belief and practice that shifted the emphasis from sacramental experiences to study of the word and text. The Protestant rebellion also advanced private judgment and autonomy against monolithic institutional authority, and established a focus on internal subjectivity that was to become a core feature of modern thought. Spretnak observes that the Reformation doctrine of God's absolute sovereignty precluded revelation through contemplation of the natural world, and thus prepared the ground for the idea of the passivity of nature that was central to the *Scientific Revolution*. As church authority declined, a growing uncertainty about truth, valid knowledge, and reality was ultimately replaced by the precepts of the Scientific Revolution that located truth in what could be measured (e.g., quantitative data, mathematical formulation, and the laws of physics). Finally, the last of four movements that created the modern worldview, the *Enlightenment*, extended the search for laws and truth to all aspects of human behavior. The task of the Age of Reason was to affect radical "social engineering" by designing institutions and practices to reflect natural laws. The Enlightenment was a scientific reforming of society as a whole.

But ... as many have observed, modernist thought overreached itself, becoming as rigid and intolerant as what it sought to replace. In the name of order and stability, Enlightenment thought went on to condone social injustice, and punish claims that cast doubt on its veracity. The science that was so extravagantly admired as pure and impartial was actually place- and time-bound, but its advocates chose to forget that it was only one epistemological variant among many. Yet so effective were they in their advocacy that subsequent centuries have effectively been held hostage by the desire for order that stemmed from the conflicts of the sixteenth and seventeenth centuries. As a result, the open-mindedness and adaptability of (for instance) the generation of Montaigne were erased from collective memory. Only now have postmodernists begun to reclaim this heritage. In Toulmin's acid wit: "The surgery imposed on European thought by the seventeenth-century zealots and perfectionists was so drastic that convalescence was unavoidably slow" (Toulmin, 1990, p. xxx).

Postmodernism begins by emphasizing that there are different ways of knowing, and the study of *epistemology* is concerned with such differing perspectives. But when we ask about how we know things, to make judgments on the conditions of existence (or being) in these diverse perspectives, then we enter the realm of *ontology*. In postmodernism, the *conditions* of knowing became an integral part of the problematic of science. Postmodernism is thus best understood as an ontological stance, a kind of radical undecidability, which posits that all theories are partial and incomplete, even as they each possess some intrinsic merit. Postmodernism also takes nourishment from the gnawing doubt, deep inside, that even if it were possible to add all our theories together, we *still* would not understand everything about human existence. Simply stated, there is no Grand Theory of Everything. Postmodernism adopts this deliberately relativistic stance with respect to all ways of knowing; it is profoundly antihegemonic in its vision; and it approaches knowledge-seeking with a deep humility founded in the inevitability of human frailty. To put it bluntly, we needed postmodernism; and now that we have it, we cannot not use it. The genie is out of the bottle.

***

In the first section of this archeological excavation, we consider how human geography got engaged with postmodernism in the first place. How, in just under 20 years (1965–84) did human geography move from the splendid certainties of science to the yawning abysses of postmodern ambiguity?

It all began quite peaceably, with the birth of the quantitative revolution in human geography (see Readings 1 and 2 below). Once upon a time, many geographers in the USA had been messing around with statistics in a leisurely manner, but by the mid-1960s geographers on both sides of the Atlantic took up the cause of quantitative methods with gusto. The rigors of mathematics and statistics breathed new life into a discipline that could fairly be described as directionless, languishing, or at the very least in need of a loud wake-up call. And, truth be told, the quantitative geographers responded admirably to the alarums. Attracted by the precision and promise of a scientific geography, they produced an enduring legacy of vitally important work. In a few short years, they irrevocably altered the practice of human geography.

The first cracks in the solid edifice of quantitative human geography appeared quite early. Complaints were heard from inside the guild of scientific geography as well as from outside. In Reading 3, for example, Cox and Golledge called for a greater realism in model building, to take account of the observable diversity of human behaviors. At this time (1969), they were fully confident that their new tools could and would rise to the challenges they posed.

During the late 1960s, a more fundamental critique of quantitative geography was being prepared by radical geographers steeped in Marxian traditions. A large part of their dissatisfaction can be traced to what was perceived as the excessive abstractionism of human geographical science. Instead, they advocated a discipline that was more engaged, more relevant to people's everyday needs. As Peet's history (Reading 4) of the radical movement emphasizes, the tumultuous public events of the 1960s also played their part in the rapid resurgence of Marxian thought at this time. Everywhere in academe, the corridors of power and learning echoed with the call for "Relevance!" in what was being studied. One of the most interesting conversions that occurred during this period was that of David Harvey. In 1969, Harvey had published *Explanation in Geography*, a how-to compendium in scientific human geography (Reading 2); yet by 1973, he published *Social Justice and the City*, which became a manifesto of the radical geographers (Reading 5). A number of other quantitative geographers were to beat their own paths to neo-Marxism at this time, including Doreen Massey, Allen Scott, Eric Sheppard, and Michael Webber. Perhaps it was not so hard to switch from one rigorous method of thought to another – from a scientific geography to a scientific Marxism?

The rediscovery of Marx was instrumental in opening geography's door to a wide range of alternative schools of thought. A cohort of humanist geographers emerged early, under the guidance of Anne Buttimer, David Ley, Yi-fu Tuan, and others. In Reading 6, Ley blasts the Marxists for ignoring the role of human agency in sociospatial process. This particular complaint has had a lasting impact, albeit in various manifestations, because it imported into geography one of the central questions in contemporary social theory, viz., the relationship between structure and agency. Or, to put it less cryptically, how individual human actions (agency) related to the broader matrix of social institutions and conventions (structures).

A few quantitative geographers were beginning their own assessment of the legacies of human geography's flirtation with science. Les King steered a path between what he called "recreational mathematics" and the high theory of Marxism to uncover a "middle way" that relied more on storytelling to encompass conflicts of human values in geographical analysis (Reading 7). An early piece by Gunnar Olsson revealed the acute limitations of formal mathematical theorizing as a way of understanding human behavior, and (echoing Feyerabend) called for an intellectual anarchy (Reading 8). One of the single most influential texts that drew together many critics' complaints, and accomplished the shift toward a *critical* human geography, was Derek Gregory's *Ideology, Science and Human Geography*, published in 1978 (Reading 9). Gregory's text secured geography's link to the greener pastures of social theory and philosophy, encompassing works by Anthony Giddens, Jürgen Habermas, and the French philosophers. As in the case of earlier intellectual shifts after the quantitative revolution, geography's engagement with issues in social theory and philosophy had the effect of reconnecting the discipline with the mainstreams of social science, and vice versa.

A self-confident and mature published expression of geography's relevance to mainstream debates in social theory was Nigel Thrift's meditation on social action in space and time (Reading 10). This article originally appeared in the very first issue of *Society and Space (Environment and Planning D)* in 1983, a journal established specifically to embrace questions of social theory in human geography. That same issue contained Linda McDowell's pivotal essay on a feminist understanding of urban space, another key taproot in the fertile garden of geographical thought (Reading 11).

What these selections reveal is that between the mid-1960s and the mid-1980s, human geography experienced an almost bewildering succession of rapid intellectual earthquakes, which all piled up against and over each other, like huge tsunamis breaking on a steeply shelving shore. In the exhilarating confusions left behind in the wake of these intellectual tides, the ship of postmodernism was about to come in.

REFERENCES

Feyerabend, P. K.: *Against Method: Outline of an Anarchistic Theory of Knowledge*. Humanities Press: Atlantic Heights 1975.

Kuhn, T.: *The Structure of Scientific Revolutions*. University of Chicago Press: Chicago 1962.

Toulmin, S.: *Cosmopolis: The Hidden Agenda of Modernity*. The Free Press: New York 1990.

Sperber, I.: *Fashions in Science: Opinion Leaders and Collective Behavior in the Social Sciences*. University of Minnesota Press: Minneapolis 1990.

Spretnak, C.: *The Resurgence of the Real: Body, Nature and Place in the Hypermodern World*. Addison-Wesley: Reading, MA 1997.

CALVIN & HOBBES

BY WATTERSON

Locational Analysis in Human Geography

Peter Haggett

Peter Haggett's *Locational Analysis and Human Geography* (1965) is one of the landmarks of the quantitative revolution. It was published alongside a flurry of other books that announced an intellectual sea-change in geography, including *Models in Geography*, a compendium of quantitative applications in both human and physical geography edited by Haggett and Dick Chorley. There is a delightful, if now somewhat arcane, precision and certainty about this text, reflected even in the numbering systems for sections and subheadings (e.g., 1.111.1a). Haggett swiftly sketches the history of the locational analysis/location theory school, and develops a comprehensive schema (based on Chorley's "model for models") for understanding the problematic of geographical analysis. Drawing heavily on general systems theory, Haggett puts modeling at the core of geography's search for order, and emphasizes the role of probabilistic explanation in geography. This latter emphasis is especially interesting, because (despite his contagious optimism) Haggett is careful to warn of the impossibility of rigidly applying mechanistic models to complex human systems, and of the essential indeterminacy that governs the outcomes of human decision making. Too many of his cohorts overlooked this particular piece of wisdom, and the uncritical application of quantitative methods was soon to create a backlash among those who were unimpressed by the elegant abstractions of the scientific geographers.

I. On the Search for Order

Most of the fundamental questions in human geography have no single answer. If we ask of a given region whether its settlements are arranged in some predictable sequence, or its land-use zones are concentric, or its growth cyclical, then the answer largely depends on what we are prepared to look for and what accept as *order*. Order and chaos are not part of nature but part of the human mind: in Sigwart's words "That there is more order in the world than appears at first sight is not discovered *till the order is looked for*" (Hanson, 1958, p. 204). Chorley (1962) has drawn attention to Postan's lively illustration of this problem as it afflicted Newton, newly struck on the head by an apple: "Had he asked himself the obvious question: why did that particular apple choose that unrepeatable instant to fall on that unique head, he might have written the history of an apple. Instead of which he asked himself why apples fell and produced the theory of gravitation. The decision was not the apple's but Newton's" (Postan, 1948, p. 406).

The convincing psychological demonstrations (for example by Köhler's famous goblet-or-faces drawing) that order depends not on the geometry of the object we see but on the organizational framework into which we place it, has enormous significance for geography. For geography of all sciences has traditionally placed emphasis on "seeing". In how many field classes have we been asked to "see" an erosion level or "recognize" a type of settlement pattern. The "seeing eye" beloved of the late S. W. Wooldridge, is a necessary part of our scientific equipment in that pattern and order exist in knowing what to look for, and how to look.[...]

I. Geography: the internal dialogue

Certain geographers or groups of geographers have conceived the field of geography in different terms at various stages of its evolution. The most widely held view is probably that put forward by Hartshorne as the traditional position of geography – *areal differentiation*. There are however a number of "deviations" from this view; the view of geography as the science of the earth's surface; the view of geography as the study of the relationships between man and his natural environment; and the view of geography as the study of the location of phenomena on the earth's surface. These three major departures are termed here the *landscape* school, the *ecological* school, and the *locational* school.

a. Areal differentiation: the traditional view.

Geography has had separate and recognizable existence as an academic subject for over two thousand years. Even before its formal teaching by the Greeks, the basic curiosity of man to know what lay "over the hill" must have led to a passing on of experience and conjecture on the form of the earth's surface. The subsequent history of geography with the widening knowledge of the Great Age of Discovery, the nineteenth century with the growth of the great exploring societies (like the Royal Geographical Society founded in London in 1833, and other parallel societies in Paris, Berlin, and New York), the present century with its emphasis on rapid and precise survey techniques; these have all been part of the basic need for organized knowledge about the earth's surface. Hartshorne has explicitly stated the historical role in the following definition: "Geography is concerned to provide accurate, orderly, and rational description and interpretation of the variable character of the earth surface" (Hartshorne, 1959, p. 21). In order to perform this considerable task, Hartshorne argues that geographers are primarily concerned with region construction, with what he terms the *areal differentiation* of the earth's surface.

There is little doubt that Hartshorne's definition represents one of the common denominators that runs through the greater part of geographical work from the Greeks onward. But one of the most interesting and explosive of internal debates within geography today is not over the accuracy of Hartshorne's view of the past nature of geography; but rather, whether this past should govern the nature of geography in the future. Hartshorne argued cogently that only by subjugating our personal idiosyncrasies to the great weight of geographic work over the centuries could we hope to achieve a balanced and consistent view: "...If we wish to keep on the track ... we must first look back of us to see in what direction the track had led" (Hartshorne, 1939, p. 31). By careful textual criticism he was able to show both the enormous range in views of scholars over their lifetime, and the need to distinguish what geographers claimed to be doing from what they actually did.

One of the strongest dissents from this approach has come from Bunge (1962). His approach is to try logically to deduce the nature of geography from a series of assumptions. Like Lösch (1954), he is concerned with what should be, rather than what is. In his approach, the statements by the great geographers of the past are pointedly ignored because "...the great men of our past might now, in view of more recent events, hold opinions different from those they then held" (Bunge, 1962, p. 1). In fact neither Hartshorne nor Bunge hold the inductive or deductive approach in its pure form; each extends his work by reference to empirical example or logical argument.

b. Deviations: the landscape school.   The concept of "landscape" has long been obscured by the double meaning attached in common German usage to the apparently parallel term *Landschaft*. Much of the thinking in this "deviationist" school has been derived from German literature and confusion has apparently arisen from the meaning of *Landschaft* as either (a) the landscape in the sense of the general appearance of a section of the earth's visible surface or (b) a restricted region of the earth's surface. In the first meaning, the terms *Landschaft* and landscape are synonyms; in the second the appropriate English synonym must be "region". Hartshorne (1939, pp. 149–58) has expertly exposed the confusion in the original German literature – for example the different uses of the same term by Passarge and Schlüter – and the inevitable take-over of some of this confusion into American literature, particularly through the important essay by Carl Sauer on the morphology of landscape (Sauer, 1925).

Sauer argued that it was possible to break down the landscape of an area into two separate components: the "natural landscape" (*Urlandschaft*) and the "cultural landscape" (*Kulturlandschaft*). He conceived as natural landscape the original landscape of the area before the entry of man; as cultural landscape, that landscape transformed by man. The most important effect of Sauer's essay was in urging that the same morphological methods so fruitful in the analysis of the physical landscape could be transferred to the study of the cultural, a message taken up by Miller (1949). Before Sauer's 1925 essay the role of man as a morphological agent had been recognized, notably by George Perkins Marsh (1864), but it was in the "Berkeley" school (described by Clark, in James, Jones, and Wright, 1954, p. 86) that Sauer gathered together a group of scholars who like Broek (*The Santa Clara Valley*, 1932) organized their work around the theme of landscape change. *Man's role in changing the earth* (Thomas, 1956), an international symposium in which Sauer played a leading part, gives the clearest picture of the strength and vitality of this important theme in the development of human geography.

c. Deviations: the ecological school.   The idea of geography as a study of the relationship between the earth and man has long held a central position in its teaching in both colleges and schools in England. Paradoxically, its origins may be thought to lie in a country where it subsequently played a very small part in the development of geographic thinking, i.e. Germany. Friedrich Ratzel's views on "anthropogeography" appear to have had an indirect but important effect both on Vidal de la Blache in France and more particularly on Ellen Semple in the United States. Her *Influences of geographical environment* (1911) had a decisive effect in spreading the idea of the study of "geographic influences", as a major goal in geographic study, throughout the English-speaking world.

A separate and less extreme branch of this environmental school evolved around H. H. Barrows at the University of Chicago. His view of geography was as "human ecology" (Barrows, 1923); a study in which physical geography is largely eliminated from the field and in which geography becomes a social science concerned with the relationships of human society and its physical environment. Hartshorne (1939, p. 123) suggests that under this view geography stands in relation to the social sciences in an exactly similar location as does plant ecology to the biological sciences. Certainly the dividing line between this view of human geography and the work of sociologists like McKenzie (1933) and Hawley (1950) is very finely drawn, and recent reviews of human ecology (like that of Theodorson, 1961) contain contributions from both sociologists and geographers. The convergence of sociological and geographical lines of thought in Britain have been shown by Pahl (in Chorley and Haggett, 1965B, Chap. 5) while Stoddart (1965) has traced the very wide application of biological-ecological concepts (e.g. that of *ecosystems*) throughout geography.

It is perhaps in France however that the ecological view of human geography has had the most important influence. Two of the most decisive studies of human geography yet produced, the *Géographie humaine* of Jean Brunhes (1925) and the *Principes de géographie humaine* of Vidal de la Blache (1922) show a strongly environmental approach to the "essential facts" of man's occupation of the earth's surface; and Max Sorre in his *Fondements de la géographie humaine* (1947–52, 1961) has followed this trend. For their detailed treatment of an abundance of regional examples and for their broad philosophy of man as part of a closely knit environmental syndrome, these three scholars – Brunhes, Vidal de la Blache, Sorre – may be regarded as corner-stones on which much of the discipline of human geography has been built.

d. Deviations: the locational school.   The view that geography is essentially a distributional science is a third recurrent theme. Bunge (1962, 1964) has recently emphasized the strong dependence of geography on the concepts of geometry and topological mathematics; but nearly a century ago Marthe (1878) described the field of geography as the study of "the where of things". Certainly a central concern for location and distribution is a hallmark of all geographical writing and a recurrent theme in methodological reviews (e.g. de Geer, 1923) and inaugural addresses (e.g. Watson, 1955).

The strongest development of locational "theory" has come from one of the social sciences, economics, rather than from within human geography. Both the early classics of locational theory, von Thünen (1875) on agricultural location, and Weber (1909) on industrial location, were concerned essentially with economic location; and the object of both contemporary and subsequent workers, Launhardt, Predöhl, Ohlin, Palander, Hoover, Lösch, and Isard, has been largely "... to improve the spatial and regional frameworks of the social sciences, especially economics" (Isard, 1956, p. viii). Nevertheless the excellent reviews of economic-location literature, available from both English (Hoover, 1948; Isard, 1956), German (Boustedt and Ranz, 1957), and French scholars (Ponsard, 1955), have served as spurs to the application, development, and refinement of spatial concepts by geographers. Bunge's *Theoretical geography* (1962) shows how far this stimulating process has gone. [...]

III. On Systems and Models

I. Human geography and general systems theory

During the last decade there has been a remarkable growth of interest in the biological and behavioural sciences in *general systems* theory (von Bertalanffy, 1951). Some attempts have been made (notably by Chorley, 1962) to introduce its concepts into geomorphology and physical geography, and there seems no good reason why the concept of systems could not be further extended into human geography. In this section we explore the possibilities.

a. Nature of systems.   What is a system? One loose definition, cited by Chorley, describes it as "... a set of objects together with relationships between the objects and their attributes" (Hall and Fagen, 1956, p. 18). In everyday plumbing parlance we speak of a "hot-water system" in which the set of objects (stove, pipes, cylinders, etc.) are related through circulating water with inputs of energy in the form of heat. In geomorphology we may speak of an "erosional system" in which the set of objects (watersheds, slopes, streams) are related through the circulation of water and sediment with inputs of energy in the form of rainstorms.

In human geography, our nearest equivalent is probably the nodal region in which the set of objects (towns, villages, farms, etc.) are related through circulating movements (money, migrants, freight, etc.) and the energy inputs come through the biological and social needs of the community. This idea is implicit in most central-place theory, though in only a few statements (notably that of Vining, 1953, and Curry, 1964) is the description couched in 'system' terms.

Clearly then, systems are arbitrarily demarcated sections of the real world which have some common functional connections. Von Bertalanffy (1951) distinguishes two separate frameworks: the *closed system* and the *open system*. Closed systems have definable boundaries across which no exchange of energy occurs, but since they are likely, by this definition, to be rather rare in geographical studies (except in the limiting case of a world-wide study) they are not considered here.

b. Nodal regions as open systems.   The view taken in the first half of this book is that we may regard nodal regions as open systems (Philbrick, 1957; Nystuen and Dacey, 1961). Indeed the organization of the chapters shows the build-up of such a system;

viz., the study of *movements* leads on to a consideration of the channels along which movement occurs, the *network* to the *nodes* on that network and their organization as a *hierarchy* with a final integration of the interstitial zones viewed as *surfaces*. This progression, from energy flows to recognizable landforms, may be seen more clearly from Figure 1, in which more familiar geographical forms may be substituted for their abstract geometrical equivalents, i.e. roads, settlements, the urban hierarchy, and land-use zones. If the sceptic still regards the nodal region as a purely mental construct, then Dickinson (1964, pp. 227–434) has provided a detailed review of city-regions within the United States and western Europe, while Caesar (1955; 1964) has shown strong nodal organization within regions as unlike in scale as the communist block in eastern Europe and northeast England.

If we wish to view nodal regions as open systems we must first look at the typical characteristics of such systems and check their existence in the regional system. Chorley (1962, pp. 3–8) suggests that open systems have some of the following six characteristics: (i) the need for an energy supply for the system's maintenance and preservation, together with, the capacity to (ii) attain a "steady-state" in which the import and export of energy and material is met by form adjustments, (iii) regulate itself by homeostatic adjustments, (iv) maintain optimum magnitudes over periods of time; (v) maintain its organization and form over time rather than trending (as do closed systems) towards maximum entropy, and (vi) behave "equifinally", in the sense that different initial conditions may lead to similar end results.

In our regional systems we certainly find some of these six characteristics. Regional organization needs a constant movement of people, goods, money, information to maintain it; an excess of inward movements may be met by form changes (city expansion and urban sprawl) just as decreased movement may lead to contraction and ghost cities. The first two conditions are clearly met. Similarly, on

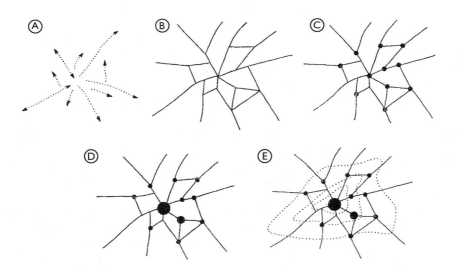

Figure 1.   Stages in the analysis of regional systems. *A* movements. *B* Networks. *C* Nodes. *D* Hierarchies. *E* Surfaces.

the third condition the urban region follows Le Châtelier's Principle in that its hinterland may expand or contract to meet increased or decreased flows. Berry and Garrison (1958) would also suggest that it meets the fourth and fifth requirements in that the form of the urban rank–size relationships tends to be relatively constant over both space and time. Finally, the growing convergence of the form of the major cities in different continents suggests that the urban open system is capable of behaving equifinally.

The advantages of viewing the region as an open system are that it directs our attention towards the links between process and form, and places human geography alongside other biological and social sciences that are organizing their thinking in this manner. Exchanges between students of "ecosystems" at all scale levels should prove rewarding (e.g. Thomas, 1956, pp. 677–806).

2. Model building in human geography

In everyday language the term "model" has at least three different usages. As a noun, model implies a representation; as an adjective, model implies ideal; as a verb, to model means to demonstrate. We are aware that when we refer to a model railway or a model husband we use the term in different senses. In scientific usage Ackoff (Ackoff, Gupta, and Minas, 1962) has suggested that we incorporate part of all three meanings; in model building we create an idealized representation of reality in order to demonstrate certain of its properties.

Models are made necessary by the complexity of reality. They are a conceptual prop to our understanding and as such provide for the teacher a simplified and apparently rational picture for the classroom, and for the researcher a source of working hypotheses to test against reality. Models convey not the whole truth but a useful and comprehensible part of it (Society for Experimental Biology, 1960).

a. Types of models.   A simple three-stage breakdown has been suggested by Ackoff (Ackoff et al., 1962) into *iconic*, *analogue*, and *symbolic* models, in which each stage represents a higher degree of abstraction than the last. Iconic models represent properties at a different scale; analogue models represent one property by another; symbolic models represent properties by symbols. A very simple analogy is with the road system of a region where air photographs might represent the first stage of abstraction (iconic); maps, with roads on the ground represented by lines of different width and colour on the map, represent the second stage of abstraction (analogue); a mathematical expression, road density, represents the third stage of abstraction (symbolic). At each stage information is lost and the model becomes more abstract but more general.

Chorley (1964) carried this classification process further and created a "model of models" (Figure 2), illustrating it with examples from both physical and human geography. His model consists of a flow diagram in which a series of *steps* (A_1 to A_6) are linked by *transformations* (T_1 to T_6). Each step contains some aspect of the real world, model, observation or conclusion; each transformation connects these by some process (idealization, mathematical argument, statistical interpretation, etc.) which advances or checks on the reasoning process.

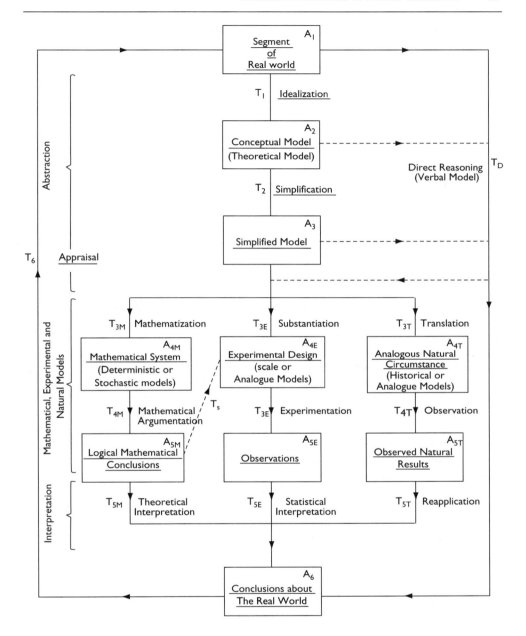

Figure 2. A model for models.

Source: Chorley, 1964, p. 129.

The first section of Figure 2 is concerned with the "abstraction" process in which the complexities of the real world are so simplified that they may become more comprehensible. Chorley argues that this process is difficult largely because as huge amounts of information are lost, extraneous "noise" is introduced; a Cézanne painting represents an abstracted model of a landscape in which the noise level (brush-marks, etc.) is high, while a Van Ruysdael is less simplified but considerably less noisy (Chorley, 1964, p. 132). Successful models are those which manage a considerable amount of simplification without introducing extraneous noise.

The second section of Figure 2 breaks into the three main stems of mathematical, experimental, and natural models. *Mathematical models* might be represented in human geography by Isard's distance-inputs equations (Isard, 1956) or Beckmann's "equation of continuity" (Beckmann, 1952) in which features of the system being studied are replaced by abstract symbols and subjected to mathematical argument. *Experimental models* might be represented by Hotelling's use of a heat-flow analogue in migration theory (Hotelling, 1921; cited by Bunge, 1962, p. 115) or Weber's weight and pulley machine in industrial location (Weber, 1909) where tangible structures are used to simulate certain aspects of reality. Finally *natural models* might be represented by the Garrison ice-cap analogy of city growth (cited by Chorley, 1964, p. 136), where some analogous natural circumstance which is believed to be simpler or more readily available is substituted for reality. The problem in each case is to translate the circumstances being studied into some analogous form in which it is either simpler, or more accessible, or more easily controlled and measured; to study it in this analogue or model form; and to reapply the results of this study to the original system. Models then represent idealized parts of systems, just as systems represent an arbitrarily separated segment of the real world.

b. Approaches to model building.   In economic geography, model building has proceeded along two distinct and complementary paths. In the first, the builder has "sneaked up" on a problem by beginning with very simple postulates and gradually introducing more complexity, all the time getting recognizably nearer to real life. This was the approach of von Thünen (1875) in his model of land use in *Der Isolierte Staat*. In this "isolated state" he begins by assuming a single city, a flat uniform plain, a single transport media, and like simplicities and in this simple situation is able to derive simple rent gradients which yield a satisfying alternation of land use "rings". But von Thünen then disturbs this picture by reintroducing the very things that he originally assumed inert and brings back soil differences, alternative markets and different transport media. With their introduction, the annular symmetry of the original pattern gives way to an irregular mosaic far more like the pattern we observe in our land-use surveys. Nevertheless, Thünen's model has served its point; in Ackoff's terminology it has "demonstrated certain properties" of the economic landscape.

The second method is to "move down" from reality by making a series of simplifying generalizations. This is the approach of Taaffe (Taaffe, Morrill, and Gould, 1963) in his model of route development. The study begins with a detailed empirical account of the development of routes in Ghana over the period of colonial exploitation. From the Ghanaian pattern a series of successive stages is recognized. In the first, a scatter of unconnected coastal trading posts; in the last, an interconnected phase with both high-priority and general links established. This Ghanaian sequence is finally formalized as a four-stage sequence, common to other developing countries like Nigeria, East Africa, Malaya, and Brazil.

Not all such models have developed inductively from observations within geography. Some of the most successful have come from borrowing ideas from related fields, especially the field of physics. Thus Zipf (1949) attempted to extend New-ton's "divine elastic" of gravitation to social phenomena and his P_iP_j/d_{ij} formula for the interaction between two cities of "mass" P_i and P_j at a distance d_{ij} is a direct extension of Newtonian physics. When modified by Isard's refined concept of distance (Isard et al., 1960) and Stouffer's addition of intervening opportunity (Stouffer, 1962) it has proved a very powerful predictive tool in the study of traffic generation between points. A less widely known borrowing was used by Lösch (1954, p. 184). He has related the "bending" of transport routes across landscapes of varying resistance and profitability to the sine formula for the refraction of light and sound. While such borrowing may have its dangers, it is a most fruitful source of hypotheses that can be soberly tested for their relevance to the problems of economic geography. A book like D'Arcy Thompson's *On growth and form* (1917) illustrates how many subjects find common ground in the study of morphology; there is inspiration still to be found in his treatment of crystal structures or honeycomb formation as Bunge (1964) has illustrated.

c. Role of models.   In his *Novum Organum*, Bacon describes scientific theory as consisting of "anticipations, rash and premature". Certainly we might argue that most of the models put forward in the first half of this book fit this description admirably: all are crude, all full of exceptions, all easier to refute than to defend. Why then, we must ask, do we bother to create models rather than study directly the "facts" of human geography? The answer lies in the inevitability, the economy, and the stimulation of model building:

(1)   Model building is inevitable because there is no fixed dividing line between facts and beliefs; in Skilling's terms ". . . belief in a universe of real things is merely a belief . . . a belief with high probability certainly, but a belief none the less" (1964, p. 394A). Models are theories, laws, equations, or hunches which state our beliefs about the universe we think we see.

(2)   Model building is economical because it allows us to pass on generalized information in a highly compressed form. Like rules for the plurals of French adjectives there may be exceptions but the rule is none the less an important ladder in learning the language. This use of models as teaching aids is discussed by Chorley and Haggett (1965–A, pp. 360–4).

(3)   Model building is stimulating in that, through its very over-generalizations, it makes clear those areas where improvement is necessary. The building and testing of models is as important to geography as aeronautics; the test flight of a hypothesis, no less exciting, nor much less dangerous, than the test flight of a prototype "Comet". Each leads on to further research and modifications.

In short the role of models in geography is to codify what has gone before and excite fresh inquiry. To be sure the present stock of models may be unprepossess-ing enough, but as Lösch asked ". . . does not the path of science include many precarious emergency bridges over which we have all been willing to pass provided they would help us forward on our road"; certainly his hope that his work on regions would open ". . . a path into a rich but almost unknown country" (Lösch, 1954, p. 100) has been richly fulfilled.

IV. On Deterministic and Probabilistic Explanation

1. The retreat from determinism in human geography

In the spirit of optimism that seized science after Newton's triumphant demonstration of the laws of gravitation there was much nonsense dreamed about scientific prediction. It was the French mathematician, Laplace, who suggested that it was conceptually possible to forecast the fate of every atom of the universe both forwards and backwards through time. Although all doubted that the technical possibility lay remotely far in the future it served as a goal towards which science might slowly progress. In geography this optimism had its expression in the ideas of *environmental determinism* in which human behaviour was seen to be predictable in terms of the physical environment. The excessive claims, the burnt fingers, the debate over "possibilism" is part of the history of geographical development (see Hartshorne 1939, pp. 56–60) which reflects little credit on our powers of observation, let alone discrimination.

Reactions to the period of excessive environmentalism in geography were both negative and positive. On the negative side, the retreat led to an almost complete rejection of any kind of theory, so that our literature became at once more accurate but infinitely less exciting. Description was substituted for hypothesis, repetition for debate. On the positive side, geographers approached the intricate regional systems wary of any simple cause-and-effect keys. Meinig (1962) in an analysis of the railway network of the Columbia basin in the northwestern United States is a case in point. Figure 3B shows the railways built by the Northern Pacific Railroad in the second half of the nineteenth century. Viewed in relation to present conditions they yield a satisfying logic in which terrain and cities serve as either barriers or magnets to shape the twisting geometry of the network. However as Meinig stresses, such logic is largely illusory. Most of the cities were the subsequent products of the railway, rather than its antecedent causes. As for the rigorous influence of terrain, the map of projected routes constructed from the files of the railway's consulting engineers (Figure 3A) shows a cordon of routes, *all* of which on purely technical

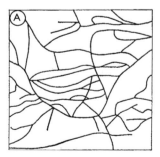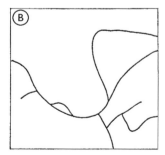

Figure 3.   Contrast between routes which were proposed (A) and actually built (B) by the Northern Pacific Railroad Company in a sector of the northwestern United States (*G=3.7*). Source: Meinig, 1962, p. 413.

grounds were serious contenders for the railway route. Meinig's point is that in order to "explain" the reason why one route was chosen, another abandoned, would involve nothing short of a psychological analysis of board-room decisions. Indeed, the detailed examination of most aspects of human behaviour of interest to human geography (e.g. migration, industrial location, choice of land use) tend to ". . . leave one stranded in the thickets of the decision-making process" (Meinig, 1962, p. 413).

Meinig's view is reinforced by Morrill (1963) in a study of town location in central Sweden, where it is suggested that man is not always able to distinguish between equally good choices, nor can he always recognize optimum locations should these exist. There are, Morrill contends, basic uncertainties in the pattern of human behaviour that we simply cannot wish away. These difficulties are compounded by two further sources of indeterminacy: first, the multiplicity of equal choices, and second, the inability to take into account the myriad of very small effects from many small sources. There are far more potential town sites than towns in central Sweden, so that no unique locational significance springs from site alone; there is instead a multiplicity of factors that enter into urban growth, each factor linking with the other in a labyrinth of small-scale causal links. If Newton was right in principle that an alighting butterfly shifts the earth, it is equally true that the net effect of such infinitesimal causes may be considered random. Unless we wish to follow Aquinas in the metaphysics of the "First Cause" we can hope only to disentangle some of the main threads in any situation, the rest we can only regard as a sort of background noise, a Brownian motion.

2. Normative and probabilistic laws

a. Impact of the uncertainty principle.

One of the fundamental doubts cast on the possibility of extending cause-and-effect interpretations into the world of human behaviour came from the field of small-scale or quantum physics. Once Max Planck had discovered in 1900 that energy, like matter, is not continuous but appears in small groups or quanta, both the theoretical and empirical study of this branch of physics ran into increasing problems. It proved impossible to apply rigid mechanistic laws to these tiny particles and it was a German physicist, Heisenberg, who in 1927 put this problem into a formal principle: the *uncertainty principle*. This stated in effect that all our observations of the natural world contain some final and essential uncertainty. If we try to measure location more accurately, we must sacrifice some aspect of its precise time; in estimating its speed more accurately, we are less sure of its position.

Despite later revision of Heisenberg's physical experiments, this principle, together with the spread of the concepts of Francis Galton and Karl Pearson on statistical probability, had a dramatic effect on the metaphysical battle over determinacy. The replacement of *normative* laws (latin *norma* = a rule) by the idea of probabilistic trends allowed a totally new view of human behaviour in which both "free will" and "determinacy" could be accommodated. Indeed both extreme views may be based on a misunderstanding of scale, for Bronowski (1960, p. 93) would argue that ". . . a society moves under material pressure like a stream of gas; and on the average, its individuals obey the pressure; but at any instance, any individual may, like an atom of gas, be moving across or against the stream".

This realization that physical laws were not deterministic but only statistical approximations of very high probability based on immense – but finite – populations, seeped rather slowly into the social sciences. As Kates (1962) in a study of floodplain hazards has argued, neither Freud's vision of man driven by inner and largely unknown impulses, nor the rigid principles of classical economics (with its vision of *Homo economicus* bending to every flicker in the stock market) give a satisfactory framework within which to study locational behaviour. Both views were attacked from within and look in retrospect "... as mistaken as the attempts of the early physicists to explain everything in terms of four elements, or of the early physicians to explain temperament in terms of four humours" (Kendall, 1960, p. 7).

Simon (1957, pp. 196–200) has drawn attention to two alternative models of individual behaviour, the *optimizer* and *satisficer* models. The optimizer concept has been tacitly introduced into human geography through the assumption of models like those of von Thünen, Weber, Christaller, and Lösch that individuals or groups would arrange themselves spatially so as to optimize the given set of resources and demands. Simon has argued, and Wolpert (1964) has demonstrated, that the optimizer model is rather unsatisfactory. Optimization requires information and decision processes at the highest capacity of the individual or group, and as individuals and as groups there is plentiful evidence that we simply do not operate nor indeed can we operate (because of *time* uncertainties) at that level. Simon would replace this with a satisficer model which postulates that (i) we rank all the alternative courses of action of which we are aware along a preference scale and (ii) select from this set the course that will satisfy a set of needs. Clearly our choice is often sub-optimal, since "... to optimize requires processes several orders of magnitude more complex than those required to satisfice" (March and Simon, 1958, p. 140).

b. **Emergence of stochastic models.** Demonstration of the insufficiency of classic normative models of human behaviour, and the replacement of this with the idea of the "bounded rationality" of man, stimulated the search for alternative kinds of behavioural models. The break-through came in economics with World War II. Here the fusion of mathematics, economics, and logistics led to the appearance of game theory in general, and in particular to a remarkable book *The theory of games and economic behaviour* (Von Neumann and Morgenstern, 1944). In this, the uncertainty principle was formally introduced into economics through the mathematical theory of games. The formalism of supply, demand, and perfect knowledge was replaced by a more robust and yet mathematically more elegant *probability* theory in which uncertainties (e.g. of market, price, and production) were the only constants. This is of course the world which as individuals we know: a world which is neither wholly rational nor wholly chaotic, but a probabilistic amalgam of choice, calculation, and chance.

REFERENCES

Ackoff, R. L., S. K. Gupta, and J. S. Minas (1962). *Scientific method: optimizing applied research decisions*. New York.

Barrows, H. H. (1923). Geography as human ecology. *Annals of the Association of American Geographers*, 13, 1–14.

Beckmann, M. J. (1952). A continuous model of transportation. *Econometrica*, **20**, 643–60.

Berry, B. J. L. and W. L. Garrison (1958). Alternate explanations of urban rank size relationships. *Annals of the Association of American Geographers*, **48**, 83–91.

Bertalanffy, L. Von (1951). An outline of general system theory. *British Journal of the Philosophy of Science*, **1**, 134–65.

Boustedt, O. and H. Ranz (1957). *Regionale Struktur- und Wirtschaftsforschung*. Bremen.

Broek, J. O. M. (1932). *The Santa Clara Valley, California: a study in landscape changes*. Utrecht.

Bronowski, J. (1960). *The common sense of science*. London.

Brunhes, J. (1925). *La géographie humaine*. Two volumes. Paris.

Bunge, W. (1962). Theoretical geography. *Lund Studies in Geography, Series C, General and Mathematical Geography*, **1**.

Bunge, W. (1964). Patterns of location. *Michigan Inter-University Community of Mathematical Geographers, Discussion Papers*, **3**.

Caesar, A. A. L. (1955). On the economic organization of eastern Europe. *Geographical Journal*, **121**, 451–69.

Caesar, A. A. L. (1964). Planning and the geography of Great Britain. *Advancement of Science*, **21**, 230–40.

Chorley, R. J. (1962). Geomorphology and general systems theory. *United States, Geological Survey, Professional Paper*, **500-B**.

Chorley, R. J. (1964). Geography and analogue theory. *Annals of the Association of American Geographers*, **54**, 127–37.

Chorley, R. J. and P. Haggett, Editors (1965–A). *Frontiers in geographical teaching: the Madingley lectures for 1963*. London.

Chorley, R. J. and P. Haggett. Editors. (1965–B) *Models in geography: the Madingley lectures for 1965*. London.

Curry, L. (1964). Landscape as system. *Geographical Review*, **54**, 121–4.

Dickinson, R. E. (1964). *City and region: a geographical interpretation*. London.

Geer, S. De (1923). On the definition, method and classification of geography. *Geografiska Annaler*, **5**, 1–37.

Hall, A. D. and R. E. Fagen (1956). Definition of system. *General Systems Yearbook*, **1**, 18–28.

Hanson, N. R. (1958). *Patterns of discovery*. Cambridge.

Hartshorne, R. (1939). *The nature of geography: a critical survey of current thought in the light of the past*. Lancaster.

Hartshorne, R. (1959). *Perspective on the nature of geography*. London.

Hawley, A. H. (1950). *Human ecology*. New York.

Hoover, E. M. (1948). *The location of economic activity*. New York.

Hotelling, H. (1921). A mathematical theory of migration. *University of Washington, M.A. Thesis*.

Isard, W. (1956). *Location and space-economy: a general theory relating to industrial location, market areas, land use, trade and urban structure*. New York.

Isard, W., D. F. Bramhall, G. A. P. Carrothers, J. H. Cumberland, L. N. Moses, D. O. Price, and E. W. Schooler (1960). *Methods of regional analysis: an introduction to regional science*. New York.

James, P. E., C. F. Jones, and J. K. Wright, Editors (1954). *American geography: inventory and prospect*. Syracuse.

Kates, R. W. (1962). Hazard and choice perception in flood plain management. *University of Chicago, Department of Geography, Research Papers*, **78**.

Kendall, M. G. (1960). New prospects in economic analysis. *Stamp Memorial Lecture*, 1960.

Lösch, A. (1954). *The economics of location*. New Haven.

McKenzie, R. D. (1933). *The metropolitan community*. New York.

March, J. G. and H. A. Simon (1958). *Organizations*. New York.

Marsh, G. P. (1864). *Man and nature; or physical geography as modified by human action.* New York.

Marthe, F. (1878). Begriff, Ziel und Methode der Geographie. *Geographisches Jahrbuch*, 7, 628.

Meinig, D. W. (1962). A comparative historical geography of two railnets: Columbia basin and South Australia. *Annals of the Association of American Geographers*, 52, 394–413.

Miller, A. A. (1949). The dissection and analysis of maps. *Institute of British Geographers, Publications*, 14, 1–13.

Morrill, R. L. (1963). The development and spatial distribution of towns in Sweden: an historical-predictive approach. *Annals of the Association of American Geographers*, 53, 1–14.

Neumann, J. Von and O. Morgenstern (1944). *Theory of games and economic behaviour.* Princeton.

Nystuen, J. D. and M. F. Dacey (1961). A graph theory interpretation of nodal regions. *Regional Science Association, Papers and Proceedings*, 7, 29–42.

Philbrick, A. K. (1957). Principles of areal functional organization in regional human geography. *Economic Geography*, 33, 299–336.

Ponsard, C. (1955). *Economie et éspace: essai d'intégration du facteur spatial dans l'analyse économique.* Paris.

Postan, M. (1948). The revulsion from thought. *Cambridge Journal*, 1, 395–408.

Sauer, C. O. (1925). The morphology of landscape. *University of California, Publications in Geography*, 2, 19–53.

Semple, E. C. (1911). *Influences of geographic environment on the basis of Ratzel's system of anthropo-geography.* New York.

Simon, H. A. (1957). *Models of man.* New York.

Skilling, H. (1964). An operational view. *American Scientist*, 52, 388A–396A.

Society for Experimental Biology (1960). *Models and analogues in biology.* Cambridge.

Sorre, M. (1947–52). *Les Fondements de la géographie humaine.* Three volumes. Paris.

Sorre, M. (1961). *L'homme sur la terre.* Paris.

Stoddart, D. R. (1965). Geography and the ecological approach: the ecosystem as a geographic principle and method. *Geography*, 50.

Stouffer. S. A. (1962). *Social research to test ideas.* New York.

Taaffe, E. J., R. L. Morrill, and P. R. Gould (1963). Transport expansion in underdeveloped countries: a comparative analysis. *Geographical Review*, 53, 503–29.

Theodorson, G. A., Editor (1961). *Studies in human ecology.* Evanston.

Thomas, W. L., Jr., Editor (1956). *Man's role in changing the face of the earth.* Chicago.

Thompson, D'Arcy W. (1917; abrid. edit. 1961). *On growth and form.* Cambridge.

Thünen, J. H. Von (1875). *Der Isolierte Staat in Beziehung auf Landwirtschaft und Nationalökonomie.* Hamburg.

Vidal de la Blache, P. (1922). *Principes de géographie humaine.* Paris.

Vining, R. (1953). Delimitation of economic areas: statistical conceptions in the study of the spatial structure of an economic system. *Journal of the American Statistical Association*, 18, 44–64.

Watson, J. W. (1955). Geography: a discipline in distance. *Scottish Geographical Magazine*, 71, 1–13.

Weber, A. (1909). *Über den Standort der Industrien.* Tübingen.

Wolpert, J. (1964). The decision process in spatial context. *Annals of the Association of American Geographers*, 54, 537–58.

Zipf, G. K. (1949). *Human behaviour and the principle of least effort.* Cambridge.

2 Explanation in Human Geography

David Harvey

David Harvey's *Explanation in Geography* (1969) was an ambitious effort to synthesize the explosion of work in quantitative geography that had occurred during the 1960s. In it, he set out to define an overarching framework for quantitative analysis. Two things are of special interest in the following extracts. The first is Harvey's account of his personal encounter with quantitative geography. He clearly values the multiple ways of seeing that characterize geography, but his pilgrimage reveals just how seductive were the intellectual pleasures that derived from rigorous analysis. There is a sense that geographers were undertaking a crusade on behalf of Science (with a capital S), and that it would involve a progressive accumulation of useful knowledge that would better the human condition. Second, our reprinting of the Table of Contents from *Explanation* (on pages 40–5) is very revealing of the quantitative geographers' mind-set, and the range of intellectual obsessions encompassed by the quantitative revolution. Look carefully at this Table of Contents, and understand how firmly the philosophies of science undergirded the approach; how theories, laws, and hypotheses structured the methodology; how mathematics, geometry, and probability theory provided particular ways of seeing; and how data collection and model building were regarded as the foundations of the geographical enterprise.

The so-called "quantitative revolution" with its innovation centre in the University of Washington diffused slowly throughout the geographic community and by the early 1960s it became fashionable among the avant-garde to compute correlation coefficients, run "t" tests, and the like. Not wishing to be left behind, I naturally indulged in this fashion, but found to my consternation that I only managed to accumulate a drawer full of unpublished and unpublishable papers. I have to acknowledge my debt to several perceptive (or perhaps they were prejudiced) editors who by refusing to publish these papers undoubtedly saved my academic reputation from premature destruction! I also found to my further consternation that often I could not interpret the results of my own analyses. Initially I put this down to my lack of command of statistics and mathematics (a lamentable state of affairs that stemmed from a strong "Arts" background at school and University). This lack of an adequate training undoubtedly did account for the many technical blemishes on my work (the most celebrated published example being a regression equation estimated the wrong way round – I did not realise that if X was regressed on Y it yielded a different result from Y regressed on X!). But the more I brushed up on my techniques (a neverending process it seems), the more I became convinced that something more was involved. I therefore decided to devote some time to a systematic investigation of the quantitative revolution and its implications . . . Out of this investigation came a central and to me vital conclusion. The quantitative revolution implied a philosophical revolution. If I did not adjust my philosophy, the process of quantification would simply lead me into a cul-de-sac. My own lack of success with the new methodology was simply the result of trying to pour new wine into old bottles. I was forcing my philosophical attitudes into an alien methodology. I then had to decide whether to abandon my philosophical attitudes (steadily accumulated from six years of indoctrination in what I can only call "traditional" geography at Cambridge), or whether to abandon quantification. I examined this question very carefully and found, to my surprise, that I could retain much of the philosophical outlook which I valued, while venturing down the path of quantification. Those aspects of my geographical philosophy which had to be abandoned turned out to be those which I could most easily dispense with on other grounds. The assumption (often hidden and vague as it was) that things really are unique, or that human behaviour cannot be measured, and so on, turned out to be inhibiting and not very meaningful when subjected to critical thought. I also found that I was often misinterpreting the assumptions upon which statistical methods were necessarily based and that once these misinterpretations were removed the conflict between much of my geographical philosophy and the new methodology was also removed. When I sought to bring together the positive aspects of traditional geographical thought and the philosophy implied by quantification, I was amazed to observe how much more vigorous and vital the whole philosophy of geography became. It opened up a whole new world of thought in which we were not afraid to think theoretically and analytically, in which we could talk of individuals and populations in the same sentence, in which we could generalise about pattern and particularise about locations in the same context. There seemed to me to be nothing wrong with the aims and objectives of traditional geography (indeed they are to be prized and cherished), but as an academic enterprise it had managed somehow or other to hedge itself about with so many inhibiting taboos and restrictions that it could not hope to realise the aims and objectives it had set itself. In particular, geographers were failing, by and large, to take advantage of the fantastic power of the scientific method. And it was the philosophy of the scientific method which was implicit in quantification.

Some people may flinch at the term "scientific method", so let me make it clear that I interpret this in a very broad sense to mean the setting up and observing of decent intellectual standards for rational argument. Now it is obvious that we can observe these standards without indulging in quantification. Good geographers have always observed them. But the curious thing was that it took quantification to demonstrate to me how extraordinarily lax my own standards were – hence all those unpublishable papers. I believe that the most important effect of quantification has been to force us to think logically and consistently where we had not done so before. This conclusion led me to change the emphasis of my approach. Although it was no accident that quantification was forcing us to up-grade our standards of argument, we could, if we so wished, up-grade those standards without any mention of quantification. The issue of quantification *per se* therefore faded into the background and I became much more interested in the general issue of the standards and norms of logical argument and inference which geographers ought to accept in the course of research. These standards could not be divorced from those of science as a whole. In short, I became interested in the role of scientific method (however conceived) in geography. Now there are many who have been nurtured so long in the ways of science that they appear to need no formal instruction in its method. To instruct such people seems like formalising what they already intuitively know. But there are many geographers who need formal instruction because, like me, they were not raised in the ways of science. But even those geographers who possess a fair intuitive grasp of scientific method cannot afford to ignore the formal analysis of it. An intuitive grasp arises from teaching by precept and example. Such a grasp is usually sufficient to handle routine work (and most of science is routine). But it cannot always handle the new questions, the problems for which there are no precedents. At this point it is often necessary to understand the philosophical underpinnings of scientific method as a whole.

Science provides us with very sharp tools. But as any craftsman will tell you it is the sharp tools which can do most damage when misapplied. The sharpest tools are those provided by mathematics and statistics. The former provides us with a means for formulating arguments rigorously and simply, while the latter provides us with the tools for data analysis and hypothesis testing with respect to data. I believe that these tools have often been misapplied or misunderstood in geography. I certainly plead guilty in this respect. If we are to control the use of these sharp tools in research we must understand the philosophical and methodological assumptions upon which their use necessarily rests. These assumptions are, of course, built up explicitly through an analysis of scientific method. But we have to ensure that the assumptions which we accept with respect to these particular tools of science do not conflict with the broader assumptions which we employ in setting up standards for rational argument and inference. The problem of adequate method is therefore doubly emphasised at the point where quantitative techniques and ordinary rational argument and inference come together. Hence the importance of quantification. We must, therefore, reconcile our assumptions at all levels in geographical research. What started for me as a quest to understand the nature of certain powerful tools of science, thus ended as a quest for an understanding of the totality of the process which leads to the acquisition and codification of geographical understanding.

Contents

3 Behavioral Models in Geography

Kevin R. Cox and Reginald G. Golledge

Some of the very best quantitative geographers (including many who continue this tradition up to the present) were quick to develop a critique of their own enterprise. In this extract from *Behavioral Problems in Geography: A Symposium* (1969), Kevin Cox and Reg Golledge claim that in order to understand spatial structure, we need to know something about the "antecedent decisions and behaviors" that arrange spatial phenomena. This text, published as one of the Northwestern University's Studies in Geography, was one of the first skirmishes in what came to be called "behavioral geography," which did much to focus attention on mental maps, perceptual studies, and survey research. There is a wonderful scratchy optimism about the symposium, which relishes the challenge of introducing behavioral "postulates" into model building (thus reflecting behavioral geography's origins in geographical science). It is also noteworthy that *Symposium* was published during the same year as Harvey's *Explanation* – a fundamental critique appearing contemporaneously with a systematization of the field! – reflecting the fearless energy with which the quantitative revolutionaries threw themselves into their intellectual endeavors. These were exciting times in geography!

Introduction

[...] Contributions to this volume vary a great deal in their emphasis ranging from philosophy and review, to theorizing and operationalization. Each paper, however, recognizes the importance of examining the behavioral basis of spatial activity. This is not new of itself, for many exisiting theories and models in geography have at least an implicit behavioral element in their structure. What is new is the deliberate attempt to unpack and identify these elements, to examine their specific effects on spatial activity, and to operationalize some of the concepts previously used in a subjective and descriptive manner. All papers, therefore, are united by a common concern for the building of geographic theory on the basis of postulates regarding human behavior. The aim of this brief editorial comment is to fit the papers into this general context by pointing out the role of behavioral models in contemporary geography, the types of behavioral model which are relevant, the sources of behavioral postulates and the implications of such models for the operational procedures of the geographer.

The Role of Behavioral Models

In order to anticipate questions regarding the need for the approach adopted in this volume, an initial comment concerning the role of behavioral models in geography is necessary. At a time when geography is undergoing very rapid change in both theory and technique it seems only reasonable to challenge the relevance and necessity of each emerging research theme. Recent papers by Harvey,[1] and Olsson and Gale,[2] and a monograph by Pred,[3] have attempted to answer the questions of need and relevance. For example as Harvey has recently stated, the postulates of geographic theory are in part indigenous and in part derivative: "Indigenous geographic theory may be regarded ... as an attempt to state the laws of spatial form in the specialized languages of geometry or topology, or in the more general form of spatial statistics."[4] He also points out however, that such laws tell one little or nothing about processes, and for this geographic theory must turn to the other social sciences and the postulates about human behavior which they can provide. In order to understand spatial structure, therefore, we must know something of the antecedent decisions and behaviors which arrange phenomena over space. This is the viewpoint stressed in this volume.

Types of Behavioral Models for Geographic Research

A large number of behavioral mechanisms have spatial correlates. This is particularly evident, for example, in those studies which make use of the concept of information flow, where the sender and receiver of the information can be identified as to location and where the efficacy of the mechanism can be related to relative location.[5] It is also evident that there is a growing number of studies in geography which focus upon the mental storage of spatial information.[6] Mental map studies and action space studies, for example, have implicit within them some relationship to the movements and activities which produce spatial structure, and spatial structure cannot be understood without some knowledge of the perception of spatial reality that is retained in the human mind. Hence the emphasis of several papers in this volume is upon social and psychological mechanisms which have explicit spatial correlates and/or spatial structural implications. In this sense the work differs from some of the work done in geography upon environmental perception where the interest has been less in behavioral mechanisms having spatial correlates and more upon the measurement of attitudes toward environmental stimuli.[7]

Preliminary analyses of behavior in space have indicated two distinct but complementary levels of research. The basic level consists of a search for relevant postulates
and models to describe behavioral processes irrespective of the spatial structure in
which the behaviors are found. In other words this search is for the rules of choice,
movement, and interaction which are independent of the spatial system in which
they are to operate. Such rules, rather than descriptive statistics of actual behavior in
a system, should provide the basis for future theorizing. A second level relates
parameters describing actual behavior in an area to specified spatial structures in
the same area. An excellent example of this level is seen in Hägerstrand's use of mean
information fields, where the parameters of the field are based upon actual interaction data for the spatial system in question.[8] Such parameters, as Rushton has
suggested elsewhere, are most likely related to the spatial structure of interaction
opportunities in the specific spatial system.[9] Under such circumstances, behavior in
space is constrained by the existing spatial structure and should not be used to
explain that structure.

We regard this distinction as a crucial one which must be borne carefully in mind
when reviewing progress in this emerging research theme. This does not mean to say,
however, that the first level should be developed to the exclusion of the second level.
Certainly Hägerstrand's work on the diffusion of innovations was based upon a
careful and apparently realistic evaluation of the processes generating the observed
spatial structures in his study areas. In this way he provided a very important
foundation for other studies in which the interpersonal contacts over space which
ignite the spatial diffusion process, can be predicted independently of existing spatial
structure. Furthermore studies at the second level, particularly when carried out in
several very different spatial contexts, underline the fact that behavioral processes –
regardless of the level of research at which they are discovered – must eventually be
used in conjunction with spatial postulates to produce meaningful theory.[10]

Sources of Postulates

If theoretically and operationally convincing models of spatial behavior are to be
developed however, a large program of work lies ahead for geographers in terms of a
careful scrutiny of relevant bodies of theory in associated fields. It will be obvious to
the reader that, in his current attempts to examine the behavioral basis of spatial
activity, the geographer has already drawn heavily on the literature of economics,
psychology, and sociology. This cross-fertilization is but further evidence of an
increasing cooperation among social and behavioral scientists that has given considerable returns in other fields of study. While it is expected that this co-operative
trend will continue, we must not hope for too much in the way of immediate and
substantial returns, for as Harvey so chasteningly points out, the required scrutiny of
other sciences for relevant material will be long and arduous. However a start must
be made; the papers in this volume provide evidence that some researchers have
already delved deep enough to find interesting and significant contributions.

At present, the behavioral postulates employed in geographic research can be
primarily related to three fields of inquiry; economics, sociology, and psychology.
Of these, the longest and most enduring influence has been exerted by economics.

This influence is reflected in the essay on migration and place utility by Brown and Longbrake, who employ a linear programming model with classic system minimization criteria in order to allocate migrants to locations in a competitive housing market. However, as with other papers, the authors draw on more than just the one field. The linear programming model is used to operationalize the concept of place utility – a concept originally developed from joint knowledge of psychology, geography, and economics. Similarly, Rushton takes the ideas of revealed preference from micro-economics and uses scaling models developed by psychologists to give the concept a spatial interpretation in terms of visits by dispersed rural consumers to urban places. Golledge's examples of possible uses of learning theory in geography also draw on both economic and psychological concepts of consumer behavior in an attempt to understand spatial choice and movement.

Sociology has contributed only slightly less than economics to the behavioral mechanisms employed in geographic research. The pioneer in self-conscious resort to the postulates of sociology and sociometry was Hägerstrand who, in the 1950s, worked upon the relationships between informal social relationships on the one hand and the spatial diffusion of innovations and migration on the other hand.[11] Examination of social relationships over space has also allowed the explication of discrepancies between distributions predicted by assumptions of economic man and real world distributions.[12]

The use of sociological postulates, however, while explaining some of the discrepancies between the real world and a spatial theory based on economic man assumptions, is bound to be less than perfect in the sense that information is rarely received in the same form in which it is transmitted. Intervening between the sending of information and the decision to locate are *perceptions* of information. This was possibly realized in the work of geographers on map transformation.[13] It is only more recently however that emphasis has switched from assumptions of perceptual distortion of information to actual inquiry into the nature of perceptual distortion of space and the way in which it affects locational decision making. On a more limited scale, recourse has also been made to psychological research on nonmetric measurement and learning theory for assistance in explaining spatial behavior. Examples of this trend are noted in the papers by Rushton and Golledge.

While singling out economics, sociology, and psychology as having made significant contributions to the papers in this volume, however, it is to be hoped that geographers will examine all the behavioral sciences in order to obtain meaningful concepts and postulates for the refashioning of geographic theory. Clearly such theory will need to be constantly revised to accommodate revisions made by researchers in other fields. [...]

Concluding Comments

Clearly the data and model considerations discussed in the latter part of this introductory note cannot be divorced from those theoretical aims of behavioral work in geography which we discussed earlier. A recent paper by Coleman[14] has attempted to place the relationships between theory, data, and operational models in perspective and the points which he makes have important implications for future work in geography. Coleman draws a contrast between two types of approach in the building of models of social behavior. On the one hand there are those models in which the theoretical basis is relatively meager and in which the analysis must supply the missing information about behavioral parameters; such models require heavy inputs of data in order to say anything useful about the system to which their data pertain and due to their reliance upon system-specific data their degree of generality is often weak. On the other hand, there are models which have a rich theoretical basis and which therefore require little real-world data to describe behavioral propensities; instead such propensities are dictated by the theory. Data input for these models is correspondingly small and the general applicability of the model is greatly enhanced. As Coleman himself states: "What is necessary...is a more economical model: one which can derive the probabilities of action *in particular circumstances* (our italics) from a more general principle. Only in this way is it possible to escape from the enormous appetite for data that a model for a complex system has. Not surprisingly this aim of economy of data is the justification for theory in any area. And the introduction of a general principle from which an individual's action can be derived is exactly the introduction of theory."[15]

Coleman's comment is an apt point at which to terminate these introductory comments underlining as it does the significance of studies of the first level which we defined earlier: i.e. studies involving the identification of postulates and models to describe behavioral processes, irrespective of the spatial structure in which the behaviors are found. Not only are such studies economical of individual data but only with such an ultimate focus can geographers hope to produce theory with the degree of generality to which they aspire.

NOTES

1   David W. Harvey, "Behavioral Postulates and the Construction of Theory in Human Geography," *Bristol Seminar Paper* Series A, No. 6 (1967), (to be published in *Geographica Polonica*, 1969).

2   Gunnar Olsson and Stephen Gale, "Spatial Theory and Human Behavior," *Papers and Proceedings of the Regional Science Association*, Vol. XXI (1968), 229–242.

3   Allan Pred, *Behavior and Location. Foundations for a Geographic and Dynamic Location Theory, Part I.* (Lund: Gleerup, 1967).

4   Harvey, *op. cit.*

5   The spatial diffusion literature contains numerous examples of such models: see, for example: (i) Torsten Hägerstrand, "On the Monte Carlo Simulation of Diffusion," *European Journal of Sociology*, Vol. VI (1965), 43–67; (ii) Lawrence A. Brown, *Diffusion Dynamics: A Review and Revision of the Quantitative Theory of the Spatial Diffusion of Innovation* (Lund: Gleerup, 1968a).

6   The mental-map literature is an outstanding case of such studies: see, for instance, Peter R. Gould, "On Mental Maps," *Michigan Inter-University Community of Mathematical Geographers*, Discussion Paper No. 9 (1966).

7   Consider, for example: (i) Robert W. Kates, *Hazard and Choice Perception in Flood Plain Management.* University Chicago: Department of Geography, Research Paper No. 78

(1962); (ii) Thomas F. Saarinen, *Perception of Drought Hazard on the Great Plains*. University of Chicago: Department of Geography, Research Paper No. 106 (1966).

8 Hägerstrand, *op. cit.*

9 Gerard Rushton, "Analysis of Spatial Behavior by Revealed Space Preference," *Annals of the Association of American Geographers*, Vol. 59 (1969).

10 See, for example: (i) Leslie J. King, "The Analysis of Spatial Form and its Relation to Geographic Theory," *Annals of the Association of American Geographers*, (1969) (ii) Harvey, *op. cit.*

11 Hägerstrand, *op. cit.*; also Torsten Hägerstrand, "Migration and Area," in David Hannerberg, Torsten Hägerstrand, Bruno Odeving (eds.), *Migration in Sweden* (Lund: Gleerup, 1957).

12 An interesting example of this can be found in Julian Wolpert, "The Decision Process in a Spatial Context," *Annals of the Association of American Geographers*, Vol. 54 (1964), 537–558.

13 See Waldo R. Tobler, "Geographic Data and Map Projections," *Geographical Review*, Vol. 53 (1963), 59–78; also see Hügerstrand (1957), *op. cit.*

14 James S. Coleman, "The Use of Electronic Computers in the Study of Social Organization," *European Journal of Sociology*, Vol. 6, No. 1 (1965), 89–107.

15 Coleman, *op. cit.* p. 98.

4 The Development of Radical Geography in the United States

Richard Peet

"Radical geography" spread like wildfire through Anglo-American geography during the early 1970s. In his history of the movement, Dick Peet reveals the impact of the social and political climate of the 1960s on the growth of radical consciousness in universities. The radicalizing process, including the struggles over civil rights and against the war in Vietnam, spilled over into geography. Vociferous demands were made for a more socially relevant research and teaching, and a commitment to advocacy in a radical practice of geography. Even though you might disagree with the politics of radical geography, or be a bit put off by the whiff of disdain in Peet's critique of non-Marxian approaches, there can be no doubt that radical geography had lasting effects on the discipline. Most notably, it directly injected into geography the real-world concerns of class, race/ethnicity, poverty, etc., and encouraged active political engagement with these issues; it provided a stark alternative (and challenge) to the hegemony of quantitative geography; and it opened up geography to the heritage of Marxist thought and (very importantly) to adjacent critiques in social theory. This opening later turned into a tidal wave of new ideas that almost drowned the quantifiers and the Marxists alike, foreshadowing the enormous efflorescence of intellectual activity that was to prepare the ground for geography's postmodern turn in the mid-1980s.

This essay recounts the main events in the recent development of a radical movement in geography in the United States, indicates some of the currents of theoretical emphasis within radical geography, and sets the movement into the context of the material events which originally stimulated its growth and have subsequently provoked change. Two assumptions are implicit in my argument: first, and most obviously, that there is no such thing as objective, value-free and politically neutral science, indeed all science, and especially social science, serves some political purpose; second, that it is the function of conventional, established science to serve the established, conventional social system and, in fact, to enable it to survive. Science does this in two main ways: by providing partial, within-the-system "solutions" to problems thrown up by capitalism's erupting contradictions; and by "explaining away" unsolvable problems, blaming victim groups or special circumstances of the time, or otherwise diverting attention from inherent systemic contradiction. As societal problems deepen, and their solutions become increasingly impossible, the second more obviously ideological function assumes greater importance. Scientists play a leading role in laying down ideological strata which disguise the causal processes behind societal problems. They provide the "scientific underpinnings" of a cultural climate which makes decent people able to function complacently while the economic and social system falls apart around them.

Radical science, and radical geography within it, aims at exposing this "false culture" for what it is – a device for the protection of the social and economic system against the rise of revolutionary consciousness among its own people. Radical science strips away diversions, exposes existing explanations to criticism, provides alternative explanations which trace the relationship between "social problems" at the surface and deep societal causes, and encourages people to engage in their own theory construction. On the foundation of the resulting alternative explanations, a radical political program for restructuring society is erected, while around this program develops a culture which reflects the experience and the yearnings of a reawakened people. Radical science is thus the conscious agent of revolutionary political change. And radical geography is one part of it, sharing the same aims, using the same methods, but specializing on a certain set of the relationships from which society is made.

Radical science in general and radical geography in particular are, at least in North America, of fairly recent origin. They are largely the product of the events of the 1960s; it is with the events of that decade that we should begin our analysis.

General Reactions to Contradiction in the 1960s

The 1960s was a momentous decade for the development, or redevelopment, of political radicalism in the United States. It was a time of mass demonstrations against government policies; uprisings in the cities; the resurgence of previously defunct socialist parties; and, within academic science, a decade in which vigorous radical movements sprang up in virtually every field. Obviously something must have happened to shake people out of their previous political complacency; what were the key events to which we were reacting?

In the United States, the main political events of the 1960s were, undoubtedly, the Civil Rights movement and the Vietnam War. Both resulted from the maturing state of contradiction into which capitalism was moving: the first from capitalism's inherent tendency to produce social inequality and social strife (revealed in the U.S. case as racial inequality and interracial strife); the second from late capitalism's dependence on imperialistic domination and exploitation for its continued functioning and the inevitable reaction (in the form of liberation struggles) against this domination in the Third World. Why both contradictions surfaced almost simultaneously as a sequence of sharpened political events is far more difficult to explain, and beyond the scope of this essay. We can say, however, that bare patches had long been showing in the ideological "explanations" for inequality and racism and that this contributed a healthy dose of popular skepticism when the state tried to disguise the

Vietnam War as "necessary for the protection of freedom" (an explanation which had worked well enough during the Korean War). For the purposes of this essay it *is* necessary to analyze the U.S. reaction to the war in Vietnam, to point out the consequences in terms of political radicalization, and to show how radicalization in the sciences, and in geography in particular, was part of this more general reaction.

Resistance to the war had three types, or levels, of effect on the political consciousness of those involved. For the majority of people opposed merely to United States involvement because it was lasting too long, or costing too much, the war had little political effect. For a second, smaller group opposed to the war on moral grounds, the experience led to a questioning of the values inherent in U.S. involvement, to dissatisfaction with the direction in which the society was moving, and to a liberal-reform politics which culminated in the McGovern presidential campaign of 1972. For a third group U.S. involvement was either further proof, or the final convincing element in proving, that the USA, was the leading imperialist power, world capitalism's military guardian against an insurgent socialism. For this last group opposition to the war became but one part of a more general, revolutionary political movement aimed eventually at the substitution of socialism for capitalism in the United States. At the beginning of mass opposition to the war the revolutionaries numbered no more than a few thousand people. During and after the war, individuals and small groups of people broke off the issue-oriented liberal campaigns (antiwar, environment, appropriate technology, women's liberation, consumers, etc.) and moved toward a deeper, more philosophical, radical politics. By the middle seventies, revolutionary theory and action groups had become quite common in the universities and in certain tenants', minority and union movements, and support had grown to several hundreds of thousands of people.

The process of "breaking off" from liberalism was an extremely important aspect of the wartime and post-Vietnam War radicalization process in politics in general, but also in the simultaneously developing radical movements in U.S. science. "Breaking off" involved, essentially, a shift from one politico-scientific paradigm to another. The starting point was the liberal political and social scientific paradigm, based on the belief that societal problems can be solved, or at least significantly ameliorated, within the context of a modified capitalism. A corollary of this belief is the advocacy of pragmatism – better to be involved in partial solutions than in futile efforts at revolution. Radicalization in the political arena involved, as its first step, rejecting the point of view that one more policy change, one more "new face," would make any difference. Radicalization in the social sciences involved a similar first step of rejecting the notion that another squeeze of old theory, the grafting on of yet another fragment of theory, or a dose of new methodology, would lead to dramatic changes in the insights or results obtained. In both the general political, and the more particular academic case, systemic contradictions revealed themselves in problems so deep and widespread as to put into serious question support of the current (policy or theoretical) efforts made to contain them. The general state of societal contradiction generated a sequence of more particular contradictions in the branches of scientific theory, which in turn set off contradictions in the intellectual efforts of those individuals immersed in, and acting on behalf of, those theories. The result, for those people able and willing to recognize it, was a state of personal crisis, disenchantment, and disillusionment with the existing political and scientific paradigms, a breaking off from liberalism and thus a state of potential radicalization. [...]

The Radicalizing Process in Geography

What was, in general, a complex political situation was made even more complicated by the particular history of academic geography. In the nineteenth and early twentieth centuries geography, as a science of exploration and resource inventory, was extremely important in the expanding, imperialistic countries. But, as the focus of the capitalist system's needs changed from geographic exploration to an internal expansion of the frontiers of psycho-cultural domination (of already discovered people), geography lost prominence to the more obviously social and psychological sciences. This increasingly backwater status did not generate a desire to change the discipline; rather the old preoccupations continued in various new guises, and the mood of the discipline gradually collapsed into a crotchety eclecticism, especially in the United States where geography had scarcely been established before changing conditions undercut its development. Then in the late 1950s in the United States, somewhat later elsewhere, spatial theory and scientific methods were combined into the "new geography" under the influence of society's needs for spatial efficiency and regional planning. Geographers responded to the call for spatial decision makers like old soldiers returning to a long lost army. Geography was again a functioning science.

Yet this very functionalism became a source of radicalization for certain geographers. Many young academics moved readily into the well-heeled ranks of "the quantifiers." But other young geographers, propelled into a heightened state of social awareness by the events of the middle 1960s, noticed that the fine new methodology was being used only to analyze such socially ephemeral matters as shopping behavior and the location of service centers (Peet, 1972; Smith, 1972). Out of the tension between the mundane focal interests of the "new geography" and the urgent need for social relevancy and political involvement came the first stumbling moves toward a "radical" geography.

In Search of a Radical Perspective

It is relatively easy to realize that "something is wrong" with an academic discipline. Such a realization is forced on even the passive observer by the march of events, and remarks that "some kind of change is needed" are commonplace in journals and at academic meetings. Realizing what that "something" is or, rather, tracing a whole series of "somethings" to their common origin, is far more difficult: a wide channel of questioning and doubt separate the two stages of consciousness.

This channel was particularly difficult to cross in geography. In the more obviously functional social sciences students, as part of their usual training, had to be inculcated with the "philosophy" of their science as revealed by its established practitioners; of course, this philosophy did not usually include the critical insights of Marxism. But what students received did give them a certain awareness of, and ability to handle, political-philosophical questions. By contrast the relative non-functionalism of geography dictated that young geographers *not* be trained in the techniques of philosophical inquiry, perhaps for fear of what they might find about the nature of their discipline, and the idea of a critical, Marx-based geography was (and still is) utterly beyond the comprehension of the leading scholars of the field. So we, incipiently radical geographers, arrived at the side of the philosophical sea with handkerchiefs on our heads and our pants rolled up ready to wade, when what we needed was the arduous training of the cross-channel swimmer. It took several years for even the beginnings of a new philosophy to develop.

We can trace the development of a critical comprehension in the pages of *Antipode*, where most of the published discussion of radical geography has appeared. *Antipode* was founded as a journal of radical geography by a group of faculty and students at Clark University in Worcester, Massachusetts, in 1969. As expressed by the editor in the first issue, the aim of the journal was "to ask value questions within geography, question existing institutions concerning their rates and qualities of change, and question the individual concerning his own commitments" (Wisner, 1969, p. iii). What emerged from the practice of radical geography was an interest in two types of issues: among academically oriented geographers an effort to change the focus of the discipline, from what were seen as eclectic irrelevancies, to the study of urgent social problems; among action-oriented geographers, the search for organizational models for promoting social change.

"Social Relevancy"

By the middle to late sixties two streams of thought dominated human geography: an old school, using traditional descriptive methods, concerned itself with an esoteric variety of regional, environmental and economic questions – the particular topic of inquiry depending more on quirk of interest or convenience ("The Goldfish Industry of Martinsville, West Virginia," etc.) than the urgency of the problem; and the "new geography," based in location theory and using quantitative methods, but either focused on non-vital issues (like the distribution of central places) or obviously wedded to industrial and commercial interests (the "optimal" location of industry, supermarket location, etc.). Rivalry between the two groups, fear on the one side, disdain on the other, and competition within the latter group (keeping up with the latest technique), kept the field of geography in a perpetual state of "dynamism" (Hurst, 1973). And then the central cities of the United States erupted and all over the world massive anti-war marches began. The battle cry became "relevancy" – which meant changing the topical focus of the discipline yet retaining the existing research methodology. From 1967 onwards meetings were held at Association of American Geographers conventions urging a more relevant geography (similar meetings were held at Institute of British Geographers meetings) and from the middle sixties papers began to appear in the journals dealing with the obviously geographic aspects of social issues – in particular the location and expansion of the black ghetto in North American cities (Morrill, 1966; Albaum, 1973). [. . .]

"Expeditions" and "advocacy"

A discipline involved in a liberal analysis of society's problems obviously needs ways it can intervene in the social and political process, and especially how it can affect the existing structure of ameliorative government programs. Academic people newly involved in social problem analysis needed intervention methods which allow immediate action and would yield observable "results."

So it was in the early days of radical geography. In 1968 William Bunge founded the Society for Human Exploration calling for the rediscovery of the long forgotten skill of exploration and its use for new purposes. In a typical passage Bunge argued that "the tyranny of fact compels that geographers go into a state of rationally controlled frenzy about the exploration of the human condition" (1969, p. 3). Geographers should form expeditions to the poorest and most blighted areas of the country, contributing rather than taking resources, planning *with* people rather than planning *for* them, incorporating local people rather than excluding them in an elitist way. By becoming a person *of* regions of exploration the geographer would, by experience, find out what kinds of work were needed and would then address her-or himself to the problem. Local people would be trained in geographic skills so they could become part of the solution to their problems and could continue the fight when the expedition moved on. Bunge's proposal was thus a bold reversal of the usual academic priorities and methods. [...]

In a sense the idea of the academic acting as an advocate for the poorest and powerless groups in society, which was emphasized in *Antipode* articles in the early 1970s (e.g., Corey, 1972), was the concept of expeditions write large. Expeditions provided an alternative source of information and planning skills to help low-income communities bargain for power over their own affairs. Likewise, advocate geographers and planners offered their professional expertise to disenfranchised groups to help them deal with powerful institutions and eventually to shift power to the presently powerless. Both were mainly involved in short-term, reactive planning – stopping or delaying urban renewal plans, helping to prevent large institutions from taking inner-city land, and so on (Ernst et al., 1974). But beyond this the problem with the advocacy idea was that its relationship with a deeper and more all-embracing revolutionary movement was always tenuous at best, while at worst advocacy might be considered a liberal diversion of political effort. The expeditionary and advocacy movements were still not *radical* geography (Breitbart and Peet, 1974). [...]

REFERENCES

Albaum, M. 1973. *Geography and contemporary issues: Studies of relevant problems.* New York: John Wiley.

Breitbart, M., and Peet, R. 1974. A critique of advocacy planning. In *Community participation and the spatial order of the city*, ed. D. Ley. pp. 97–107. Vancouver: Tantalus.

Bunge, W. 1969. The first years of the Detroit Geographical Expedition: A personal report. *Field Notes*, discussion paper no. 1.

Corey, K. 1972. Advocacy in planning: A reflective analysis. *Antipode* 4, no. 2: 42–63.

Ernst, R., Hugg, L., Crooker, R., and Ayotte, R. 1974. Competition and conflict over land use change in the inner-city: Institution versus community. *Antipode* 6, no. 2:70–97.

Hurst, M. E. 1973. Establishment geography: Or how to be irrelevant in three easy lessons. *Antipode* 5, no. 2:40–59.

Morrill, R. 1966. The negro ghetto: Alternatives and consequences. *Geographical Review* 55:339–62.

Peet, R. 1972. Some issues in the social geography of American poverty. In *Geographical perspectives on American poverty*, ed. R. Peet, Antipode Monograph in Social Geography, no. 1, Worcester, Massachusetts.

Smith, D. 1972. Towards a geography of social well-being: Inter-state variations in the United States. In *Geographical perspectives on American poverty*, ed. R. Peet, Antipode Monograph in Social Geography. no. 1. Worcester, Massachusetts.

Wisner, B. 1969. "Editor's Note." *Antipode* 1, no. 1:iii.

5 Social Justice and the City

David Harvey

Only four years after *Explanation in Geography*, David Harvey published another highly influential book, *Social Justice and the City* (1973), which explicitly rejected many of the scientific methods espoused in his earlier book, replacing them with a scientific Marxism instead. In these extracts, we focus again on Harvey's account of his personal odyssey toward Marxism – through "liberal formulations" about social justice, to "socialist formulations" based in Marx. In many ways, Harvey's was a riveting transformation, told with a principled energy and a passionate commitment. Other extracts from the same text illustrate how Harvey derived "territorial social justice" from liberal principles; and how his later socialist formulations altered his academic and political missions. One thing that becomes increasingly evident as *Social Justice* unfolds is that Harvey's logic imposed powerful restrictions on the way he approached theory. For instance, he distinguished among *status quo* theory, *counterrevolutionary* theory, and *revolutionary* theory. In favoring the last category, Harvey explicitly devalued status quo and counterrevolutionary theories. Although he defends these choices, his strategy is exactly analogous to the exclusionism of the quantitative geographers, who excised those theories that did not live up to their call for rigor. Such exclusionary behavior is indicative of an "intellectual terrorism" that flourished during these transformative decades; it somehow became fashionable and/or necessary to totally discredit that which you sought to displace. In retrospect, this strategy squandered much that was valuable in earlier and adjacent intellectual traditions, and it introduced into intellectual debate a gladiatorial odor, a strident antagonism. Both these legacies persist into the present day, and we are collectively poorer as a consequence.

Introduction

After completing a study of methodological problems in geography, which was published under the title *Explanation in Geography*, I began to explore certain philosophical issues which had deliberately been neglected in that book. In particular,

I felt it important and appropriate to explore how ideas in social and moral philosophy – ideas that are customarily regarded as distinctive and separate avenues of enquiry from the philosophy of science which had hitherto held my attention – could be related to geographical enquiry and to those fields of intellectual endeavour, such as planning and regional science, with which geography has much in common. It seemed a reasonable starting assumption, for example, that principles of social justice had some relevance for the application of spatial and geographical principles to urban and regional planning. Since I could find scarcely any literature on this topic it seemed important to try to provide something, however inadequate it might turn out to be. In the course of pursuing this general aim it quickly became apparent that it ought not to be pursued in abstraction. I therefore determined to pursue it in a context with which I could become familiar at first hand and yet which was broad enough to provide material examples and a fund of experience upon which to draw whenever necessary. [...]

The interaction between the exploration of "ideas for ideas sake" and the results of material investigation and experience provoked an evolution in my general conception of urbanism and urban problems as well as in my views on such disparate topics as the nature of space, the nature of theory, and, indeed, the nature of knowledge and scientific enquiry in general. The essays assembled in this volume were written at various points along an evolutionary path and therefore represent the history of an evolving viewpoint. [...]

The nature of theory

The initial view of theory stems from an artificial separation of methodology from philosophy. I have never regarded this separation as anything more than a matter of convenience, but it is amazing how far convenience can lure. From this separation flows a tendency to regard facts as separate from values, objects as independent of subjects, "things" as possessing an identity independent of human perception and action, and the "private" process of discovery as separate from the "public" process of communicating the results. All these tendencies are clearly exhibited in *Explanation in Geography* and may be seen in action in the first two chapters in this volume. I now reject these distinctions as injurious to analysis even in their apparently harmless form of a separation of convenience. Initially I also held to the view that the construction of theory requires the manufacture of an adequate and proper language, with fixed definitions and meanings, that could be used to "talk about" phenomena in a logically consistent way. I recognized that definitions could dictate conclusions and that a system of thought erected on fixed definitions and fixed categories and relationships could inhibit rather than enhance our ability to comprehend the world. But these seemed minor problems inherent in the process of scientific enquiry as a whole. I now argue that acts of categorization are quite fundamental: it is vital to understand how categories are established and in particular how they take on meaning and are transformed through and in use. There is a tendency, therefore, to argue in Part 2 for contextually and relationally established meanings – meanings, in other words, which are regarded as moveable, not in some random or arbitrary way, but as a part of the process through which society embraces certain lines of thought in order to rationalize certain lines of action in preference to others.

There is a parallel evolution in the approach to verification. From an initial position in which verification is viewed as a matter of establishing (by some generally accepted means) the empirical relevance and applicability of abstract propositions, I progress to the view that it cannot be separated from social practice in general. There are various types of theory with distinct functions to perform in a social context and each type has particular verification procedures attached to it. The general distinction between *status quo*, *revolutionary* and *counter-revolutionary* theory provides some insight into the question of verification. Verification is achieved through practice which means that theory *is* practice in a very important sense. When theory becomes practice through use then and only then is it really verified. Underlying this view, and indeed underlying the whole evolution in the conception of theory contained in these essays, is, of course, a shift away from philosophical idealism towards a materialist interpretation of ideas as they arise in particular historical contexts.

The nature of space

There are various ways in which we can think about space. It is crucial to formulate a proper conception of it if we are to understand urban phenomena and society in general; yet the nature of space has remained something mysterious to social enquiry. If we regard space as absolute it becomes a "thing in itself" with an existence independent of matter. It then posesses a structure which we can use to pigeon-hole or to individuate phenomena. The view of relative space proposes that it be understood as a relationship *between* objects which exists only because objects exist and relate to each other. There is another sense in which space can be viewed as relative and I choose to call this relational space – space regarded, in the fashion of Leibniz, as being contained *in* objects in the sense that an object can be said to exist only insofar as it contains and represents within itself relationships to other objects. In the first of the essays contained in this volume the case for a relative view of space is put forward. But this case is also argued in a particular way. The argument is ontological, seeking to resolve the question "what is space?" Furthermore, this philosophical question is thought to have a philosophical or linguistic solution independent of everything else. The approach taken is that once we have discovered what space is and have discovered ways of representing it, then we can proceed with our analysis of urban phenomena by fitting our understanding of human behaviour into some general conception of space. This approach fades into insignificance in the later essays and space becomes whatever we make of it during the process of analysis rather than prior to it. Further, space is neither absolute, relative or relational *in itself*, but it can become one or all simultaneously depending on the circumstances. The problem of the proper conceptualization of space is resolved through human practice with respect to it. In other words, there are no philosophical answers to philosophical questions that arise over the nature of space – the answers lie in human practice. The question "what is space?" is therefore replaced by the question "how is it that different human practices create and make use of distinctive conceptualizations of space?" The property relationship, for example, creates absolute spaces within which monopoly control can operate. The movement of people, goods, services and information takes place in a relative space because it takes money, time, energy, and the like, to overcome the friction of distance. Parcels of land also capture benefits because they contain relationships with other parcels; the forces of demographic, market and retail potential are real enough within an urban system and in the form of rent relational space comes into its own as an important aspect of human social practice. An understanding of urbanism and of the social-process–spatial-form theme requires that we understand how human activity creates the need for specific spatial concepts and how daily social practice solves with consummate ease seemingly deep philosophical mysteries concerning the nature of space and the relationships between social processes and spatial forms.

The nature of social justice

Questions of social justice are initially approached as if social and moral philosophy is a distinct field of enquiry through which absolute ethical principles can be laid down with the full force of moral law. These principles, once established, can then be used, it is supposed, to evaluate events and activities in the urban context. Implicit in this approach is a distinction between observation on the one hand and the values on the basis of which we place the stamp of moral approval or disapproval on the other. This distinction between fact and value (which is consistent with the distinction between methodology and philosophy) is one of the innumerable dualisms which, as many philosophers have remarked, pervade post-Renaissance western philosophy. These dualisms can either be accepted as a fact of life or they can be reconciled in some fashion. Kant, for example, constructed an elaborate system of thought designed to link the dualisms into a coherent philosophy, but in the process was forced to resort to the doctrine of the *a priori*. Marx, however collapses the distinctions and thereby proclaims the end to all philosophy (since there is not much left to philosophize about in the usual sense of the term). Philosophy has proceeded unabated subsequent to Marx's analysis, but I am now inclined to accept Marx's view of the matter. This is not to say that ethics are redundant, for there is a Marxian ethics of sorts. But it deals with how concepts of social justice and morality relate to and stem from human practice rather than with arguments about the eternal truths to be attached to these concepts. For Marx, the act of observing *is* the act of evaluation and to separate them is to force a distinction on human practice that does not in reality exist.

A further aspect to this problem is worth elaborating on for it demonstrates nicely the evolution of ideas in these essays. In chapter 2 the forces governing the redistribution of real income in an urban system are examined in detail. Throughout this chapter the question of distribution is examined as if it is entirely independent of the question of production. This is an approach typical of liberalism (hence the title for Part I as "Liberal Formulations"). A contemporary representative of this approach is John Rawls whose voluminous work on *A Theory of Justice* (1971) contains an explicit statement on the nature of distributive justice without mentioning production: this, it is assumed, will be taken care of, presumably through the workings of the market mechanism. Rawls's views are the subject of explicit discussion in chapter 3, but this essay is transitional in the sense that it is there recognized that production and distribution are related to each other and that efficiency in the one is related to equity in the other. But not until chapter 6 is it accepted that production *is* distribution and that efficiency *is* equity in distribution. Here too it is finally recognized that the definition of income (which is what distributive justice is concerned with) is itself defined by production. The forcing of consumption through need-creation and the like is then viewed as part of the process whereby an effective demand for products is ensured.

The collapse of the distinction between production and distribution, between efficiency and social justice, is a part of that general collapse of all dualisms of this sort accomplished through accepting Marx's approach and technique of analysis. The evolution that occurs in these essays is from a liberal to a socialist (Marxist) conception of the problem. I move from a predisposition to regard social justice as a matter of eternal justice and morality to regard it as something contingent upon the social processes operating in society as a whole. This is not to say that social justice is to be regarded as a merely pragmatic concept which can be shifted at will to meet the requirements of any situation. The sense of justice is a deeply held belief in the minds of many (including mine). But Marx posed the question, "why these beliefs?" And this is a disturbing but perfectly valid question. The answer to it cannot be fashioned out of abstractions. As with the question of space, there can be no philosophical answer to a philosophical question – only an answer fashioned out of the study of human practice.

The nature of urbanism

The concept of urbanism undergoes considerable change throughout these essays. Initially urbanism is regarded as a "thing in itself" which can be understood as such (provided we can overcome the barriers posed by disciplinary fragmentation and academic imperialism with respect to its analysis). In chapter 6 urbanism appears as a vantage point from which to capture some salient features in the social processes operating in society as a whole – it becomes, as it were, a mirror in which other aspects of society can be reflected. This transformation occurs partly because urbanism comes to be defined relationally. The urban centre, for example, is regarded as "containing" a periphery, for there can be no centre without a periphery and each helps to define the other. The collapse of the distinction between production and distribution likewise has an impact upon the way in which urbanism is viewed. An initial concern with urbanism as a "thing in itself" thus fades into a concern with all facets of man, society, nature, thought, ideology, production, and so on, built around the concept of a relationally defined urbanism. Urbanism then provides a thread of an argument which serves to pin important but seemingly disparate topics together. The complexity of urbanism is not to be attributed to the inherent complexity of the phenomena in itself but reflects merely our ability to weave an intricate woof of argument around the urbanism concept. It follows from this that we cannot promote an understanding of urbanism through interdisciplinary research, but that we can promote an understanding of disciplinary contributions through a study of urbanism. Urbanism and the social and spatial transformations embedded in its evolution form the hard testing ground for socio-geographic theory. And, as chapter 5 demonstrates, many of our theories do not perform too well in such a fierce environment. An analysis of urbanism has, therefore, to be paralleled by an analysis of urban theory.

It bears repeating that the four themes outlined here do not evolve independently of each other. There are similarities and interactions between the evolutions described. The changes in the conception of space and of social justice are consistent with the change in the approach to theory. Space, social justice and urbanism are all initially viewed as topics "in themselves" which can be explored in abstraction – once it has been established what space is, once it has been established what social justice is, then, it is presumed, we can proceed to the analysis of urbanism. The recognition that these topics cannot be understood in isolation from each other and that the pervasive dualisms implicit in western thought cannot be bridged, only collapsed, leads to a simultaneous evolution of thought on all fronts. And it is, of course, the power of Marx's analysis that it promotes such a reconciliation among disparate topics and the collapse of dualisms without losing control over the analysis. The emergence of Marx's analysis as a guide to enquiry (by which token I suppose I am likely to be categorized as a "Marxist" of sorts) requires some further comment. I do not turn to it out of some *a priori* sense of its inherent superiority (although I find myself naturally in tune with its general presupposition of and commitment to change), but because I can find no other way of accomplishing what I set out to do or of understanding what has to be understood. Chapters 1 and 2, for example, are still adequate statements in certain respects, but in both chapters seemingly insoluble problems arise. The approach to the question of space in chapter 1 poses an irreconcilable dilemma that degenerates into a helpless, formless relativism. The approach to urban society in chapter 2 provides a useful framework for understanding certain important mechanisms which operate within "the urban process", but the distinction between fact and value as it affects the concept of income as "command over resources" again allows important questions to be swamped in a helpless formless relativism to which no solution, apart from opinionated moral exhortation, appears possible. Chapter 3 contains a struggle to bring the question of social justice and space into focus, but insofar as solutions emerge they rest upon an arbitrary characterization of the nature of social justice. Chapter 4 marks a liberation from the old approach and in a crude but exuberant way begins the process of reformulating problems as solutions and solutions as problems. Chapters 5 and 6 seek to consolidate the evolving framework making explicit use of Marx's analysis wherever it seems appropriate. It is in these last three chapters that some fundamental lines of thought and ways of thinking are opened up. [...]

Liberal Formulations

A just distribution justly achieved: territorial social justice

From this examination of the principles of social justice we can arrive at the sense of *territorial social justice* as follows:

1   The distribution of income should be such that (a) the needs of the population within each territory are met, (b) resources are so allocated to maximize inter-territorial multiplier effects, and (c) extra resources are allocated to help over-come special difficulties stemming from the physical and social environment.
2   The mechanisms (institutional, organizational, political and economic) should be such that the prospects of the least advantaged territory are as great as they possibly can be.

If these conditions are fulfilled there will be just distribution justly arrived at.

I recognize that this general characterization of the principles of territorial social justice leaves much to be desired and that it will take a much more detailed examination of these principles before we are in a position to build some kind of theory of location and regional allocation around them. It took many years and an incredible application of intellectual resources to get to even a satisfactory beginning point for specifying a location theory based on efficiency and there is still no general theory of location – indeed we do not even known what it means to say that we are "maximizing the spatial organization of the city" for there is no way to maximize on the multiplicity of objectives contained in potential city forms. In the examination of distribution, therefore, we can anticipate breaking down the objectives into com-ponent parts. The component parts are as follows:

1   How do we specify need in a set of territories in accord with socially just principles, and how do we calculate the degree of need fulfilment in an existing system with an existing allocation of resources?
2   How can we identify interregional multipliers and spread effects (a topic which has already some theoretical base)?
3   How do we assess social and physical environment difficulty and when is it socially just to respond to it in some way?
4   How do we regionalize to maximize social justice?
5   What kinds of allocative mechanisms are there to ensure that the prospects of the poorest region are maximized and how do the various existing mechanisms perform in this respect?
6   What kinds of rules should govern the pattern of interterritorial negotiation, the pattern of territorial political power, and so on, so that the prospects of the poorest area are as great as they can be?

These are the sorts of questions which we can begin to work on in some kind of single-minded way. To work on them will undoubtedly involve us in making difficult ethical and moral decisions concerning the rights and wrongs of certain principles for justifying claims upon the scarce product of society. We cannot afford to ignore these questions for to do so amounts to one of those strategic non-decisions, so prevalent in politics, by which we achieve a tacit endorsement of the *status quo*. Not to decide on these issues is to decide. The single-minded exploration of efficiency has at best amounted to a tacit endorsement of the *status quo* in distribution. To criticize those who have pursued efficiency for this reason is not to deny the importance of analysis based on efficiency itself. As I indicated at the beginning of this chapter, we need to explore efficiency and distribution jointly. But to do so we first need a detailed exploration of those questions of distribution which have for so long been left in limbo. [. . .]

My appeal for a revolution in geographic thought must therefore be interpreted as an appeal for a reformulation of geographic theory designed to "bring us up to date" with the realities we seek to understand, as well as to help with the broader social task of stimulating a political awareness in that segment of the population called "geographers". [. . .]

Socialist Formulations

I contend that there are a number of positive tasks to be performed *within* our discipline. We have to clear away the counter-revolutionary clutter that surrounds us. We also have to recognize the *status quo* apologetic quality of the rest of our theory. These two tasks can in fact be derived by setting out a number of propositions about the nature of theory. Let me set these down as well as I can:

1   Each discipline locates problems and solutions through a study of real conditions mediated through a theoretical framework consisting of categorizations, propositions, suggested relationships and general conclusions.

2   There are three kinds of theory:

(a) *Status quo theory* – a theory which is grounded in the reality it seeks to portray and which accurately represents the phenomena with which it deals at a particular moment in time. But, by having ascribed a universal truth status to the propositions it contains, it is capable of yielding prescriptive policies which can result only in the perpetuation of the *status quo*.

(b) *Counter-revolutionary theory* – a theory which may or may not *appear* grounded in the reality it seeks to portray, but which obscures, be-clouds and generally obfuscates (either by design or accident) our ability to comprehend that reality. Such a theory is usually attractive and hence gains general currency because it is logically coherent, easily manipulable, aesthetically appealing, or just new and fashionable; but it is in some way quite divorced from the reality it purports to represent. A counter-revolutionary theory automatically frustrates either the creation or the implementation of viable policies. It is therefore a perfect device for non-decision making, for it diverts attention from fundamental issues to superficial or non-existent issues. It can also function as spurious support and legitimization for counter-revolutionary actions designed to frustrate needed change.

(c) *Revolutionary theory* – a theory which is firmly grounded in the reality it seeks to represent, the individual propositions of which are ascribed a contingent truth status (they are in the process of becoming true or false dependent upon the circumstances). A revolutionary theory is dialectically formulated and it can encompass conflict and contradiction within itself. A revolutionary theory offers real choices for future moments in the social process by identifying immanent choices in an existing situation. The implementation of these choices serves to validate the theory and to provide the grounds for the formulation of new theory. A revolutionary theory consequently holds out the prospect for creating truth rather than finding it.

3   Individual propositions and, indeed, whole theoretical structures are not necessarily *in themselves* in any one of the above categories. They only enter a category in the process of use in a particular social situation. Otherwise propositions and theories remain abstracted, idealized and ethereal formulations which possess form but not content (they are words and symbols merely). Counter-revolutionary formulations are frequently kept permanently in this content-less state.

4   A theoretical formulation can, as circumstances change and depending upon its application, move or be moved from one category to another. This suggests two dangers which must be avoided:

(a)   *Counter-revolutionary cooptation* – the perversion of a theory from a revolutionary to a counter-revolutionary state.

(b)   *Counter-revolutionary stagnation* – the stagnation of a revolutionary theory through failure to reformulate it in the light of new circumstances and situations – by this means a revolutionary theory may become a *status quo* theory.

But there are also two important revolutionary tasks:

(c)   *Revolutionary negation* – taking counter-revolutionary theory and exposing it for what if really is.

(d)   *Revolutionary reformulation* – taking *status quo* or *counter-revolutionary* formulations, setting them into motion or providing them with real content, and using them to identify real choices immanent in the present.

5   These tasks can be pursued and these dangers can be avoided only if the counter-revolutionary posture of the organized pursuit of knowledge (and in particular disciplinary division) is recognized and reality is confronted directly.

6 Social Geography and Social Action

David Ley

It was not long before dissenting voices reacted against radical geography, in the never-ending dialectic of proposal and counterproposal. One of the earliest complaints came from a loose coalition of humanistic geographers intent on recovering the voice of individual human agents. In their introduction to a collection of essays entitled *Humanistic Geography* (1978), David Ley and Marwyn Samuels highlighted the essentially *relative* nature of human cognitive capacities – that each of us see things differently. With roots in philosophy, especially existentialism and phenomenology, humanistic geographers turned away from a positivist quantitative ethos which they understood as rejecting the "self-understanding that is at the core of being human." In the extract that follows, movement leader David Ley launches a withering attack on conventions of contemporary geographical inquiry, particularly structural Marxism. He points toward a place-based analysis that incorporates both human intentionality and structural factors. Although a strong tradition of humanistic geography did not develop in the discipline, it was an integral force in returning human agency to the forefront of geographical work, and in obliging geographers to confront an even more diverse set of philosophical traditions, especially those concerned with relativism and difference.

In his book *The Idea of History*, R. G. Collingwood develops the argument that "an action is the unity of the outside and inside of an event."[1] This is a message that has been taken seriously of late by human geographers and has led to considerable criticism of research traditions in geography that have remained at the level of form or pattern, preoccupied with the external expression and neglecting the internal expresser. As a result, the 1970s are rapidly acquiring the reputation of the decade of the debunkers. The confident revolution of the 1960s, which was supposed to bring the subject within the scientific fold, has been assailed over the past five years on many fronts. Surprisingly, few of these are substantive or technical, though such commentaries will no doubt appear. No, the assault is not primarily directed at matters such as a sample design or a query over the constancy of a parameter but at issues altogether more fundamental, issues of epistemology and philosophy that challenge the status of the whole enterprise and its entrepreneurs. These assaults range from the severe, if sincere, polemics of Zelinsky's presidential address, to the careful finesse of Olsson's important and equally devastating argument that has been emerging since 1974. Unfortunately, however, the power of the critique is not yet matched by the power of the reconstruction. Zelinsky, for example, concludes his essay fatalistically with a Micawber-like wistfulness that perhaps something will turn up;[2] Olsson, despite his intellectual dexterity, does not at present have a workable counter-proposal, arguing at the conclusion of his most recent papers that maybe there is inspiration to be found in the surrealist school of literature and painting.[3] But as yet this emerging new phoenix has not escaped from the realm of consciousness to take on concrete form.

The epistemological vacuum is proving particularly frustrating in the area of social geography. The 1960s ended with a plethora of enthusiastic review papers optimistic that work would finally move beyond the details of morphology and descriptive spatial analysis to the understanding of prior and consequent social action.[4] Now that the necessary groundwork was covered, now that the last metropolitan area had its factorial ecology and its dot map of crime statistics, the *meaning* of these descriptive patterns could be examined and perhaps laid bare. Until this finally happens, however, the intellectual harvest of social geography will remain meager. In the recently published debate over research on the geography of crime, for example, it is tempting to side with parts of Peet's socialist interpretation, despite its excesses, that much current research has been preoccupied with epiphenomena: with symptoms, not causes.[5] Indeed a less charitable view might level a charge of ideological obscurantism, for in its preoccupation with the map and spatial distributions, subsequent analysis, commonly using correlation and factor analysis, always overidentifies local variables at the expense of overarching ones. The demonstrable map correlation between the incidence of crime and the distribution of group X is used to make the inferential transition from r-value to causal reasoning with distressing ease. But if group X "causes" crime here, why is it that they do not "cause" crime in other locations? Why is it that the same urban neighborhoods now occupied by group X also tended to be high crime areas a generation ago, when they were occupied by group Y? Clearly statistical or cartographic analysis alone is not sufficient to provide an understanding of the social action behind the map of crime, though it may well be a useful first step; such variables, though convenient for the interests of the researcher, are not always as demonstrably salient for the interests of the research.

There is a partiality about such analysis. What is lacking is a sense of history, or at least of biography, and a sense also of the tiers of social context ranging from the innermost and immediate linkages of family and peer group to the outermost but no less pervasive realms of ideology and *Weltanschauung*, the global outlook and dominant ideas of the period.[6] This argument is not entirely new, for prior to the rise of scientism over the past forty years there was considerable sensitivity to at least some of the contexts mentioned above. In the case of juvenile delinquency, for example, it is difficult to see any signal advance in understanding criminal acts since Frederic Thrasher's massive field research in Chicago in the 1920s;[7] certainly much of the research of his successors invites C. Wright Mills' harsh designation of "abstracted empiricism,"[8] research that is so fully withdrawn from a context of human concern that it has little to say to existing social reality.

One preliminary conclusion might therefore be that a socialist critique of present social geography as being preoccupied with epiphenomena is simply not radical enough. In bracketing out the different tiers of the social context of action from understanding and explanation, surely a quintessential focus, it might be said that social geography at present has a limited claim to any separate existence at all.

Two Candidates

Before being more explicit about the identification and analysis of these social contexts, it is worth looking more closely at the intellectual climate of our day, for it offers both positive and negative lessons from which a new synthesis may emerge. It is not, of course, true to claim that there are no emerging paradigms for contemporary social geography; but it is true that there is none that as yet is preeminent. Two major candidates for this status are a structural marxism with a materialist epistemology that emphasizes functional economic relations, and a so-called humanist posture derived variously from existential, phenomenological, and pragmatist philosophers offering a more anthropocentric view incorporating the creativity of human values and perception. These two positions may be caricatured by quoting from influential writers of each persuasion. Consider again Harvey's famous solution to the ghetto problem:

> Our objective is to eliminate ghettos... The mechanism in this case is very simple – competitive bidding for the use of the land. If we eliminate this mechanism, we will presumably eliminate the result. This is immediately suggestive of a policy for eliminating ghettos.[9]

Contrast with it the comment of another observer of the city of the Eastern seaboard, Jean-Paul Sartre: "It was a Sunday in January, 1945, a deserted Sunday. I was looking for New York and couldn't find it."[10]

What a contrast! On the one hand, confidence, certainty, a clear vision, a manifesto at a supra-individual scale tied in to economic relations, the material basis of production. On the other hand, a personal, even solitary, quest for rudimentary understanding, an immanent world where the clarity of material form masks an existential ambiguity. Which epistemology to follow? That of the provocateur or the raconteur, the man of manifestoes or the man of reflection, the way of "materialism" or the way of "ideas"?[11]

Idealism and Social Geography

For better or for worse, the humanist geographer has become associated by critics with the way of reflection, the way of ideas.[12] In part this is not a surprising association in light of the major preoccupation with perception and the subjective meaning contexts of actors in everyday life. But there are also forces pressing humanist geography to a more extreme position like the recent, premature call for a purely idealist perspective in geography – though it might be added that this argument, following Collingwood, does also make the important separation between natural science and the human sciences and also urges inquiry to proceed beyond events to actions, beyond facts to the intent of an actor behind them.[13] In addition to this explicit association are a series of critiques of humanism in geography that are beginning to appear, all of which mistakenly cast the humanist perspective in an excessively idealist mold.[14] These essays have inappropriately overassociated phenomenology with Husserl's transcendental idealism, not recognizing that contemporary phenomenologists in the social sciences draw their inspiration not from Husserl but rather from philosophers with an eye to social science such as Schutz and Merleau-Ponty, who were not prepared to sacrifice existence for essence, for whom perceptions were always considered in context, in the concrete world of everyday life.[15] But most damaging of all in the gradual identification of humanist geography with an excessive idealism has been the drift of some humanist geographers themselves. There is a risk of passing from the revelation of ambiguity to a celebration of ambiguity. Quoting from Apollinaire, one recent paper concludes: "All is quiet. There are only two of us in the cell: I and my mind."[16] The danger is clear: the ideas being uncovered may no longer be those of men in context but the lonely reflections of the researcher himself.[...]

An overly idealist position is forever in danger of pursuing straws in the wind, vague entities that always just elude the grasp. To the extent that humanist positions in geography have moved toward an extreme idealism, they have been frustrated from discovering real substance, stable empirical problems. One repeated suggestion has been to uncover the ambience of location, the sense of place; but this has too often been cast in obscurantist terms, either parrotting the expression of artists or else consisting in loosely connected anecdotes, where the mood is uppermost, but the message is rarely lingering. There is too much concern with cognitive process, too little concern with concrete effects. There is no real content for there is no real problem, and the result is that such work tends to be nonincremental, simply encountering the reader *en passant*, rather than leading to generalization or incipient theory.[17][...]

Imbedded within the criticism of the noncumulative nature of idealistically oriented research is the added charge that such work is simply a negation of an existing orthodoxy, a critique that does not have a countervailing case of its own to develop. This is a common argument used in the already cited criticisms in geography and also in a polemical essay in sociology that concluded that phenomenology and related positions had only a debunking role to play and, as such, had assumed an essentially parasitic relationship with mainstream sociology.[18]

This is by no means a heartening finale to those of us who have been advocating humanistic perspectives in geography, but I feel it is inevitable as long as there might be an overassociation with idealist modes of thought. Both in appearance and in substance such work would abandon the original phenomenological credo of an object for every subject and a subject for every object; the mesh of fact and value would then become simply a starting point for an inquiry pursuing an overly Husserlian or even Hegelian path toward consciousness. The end result of this progression can be whimsy, indulgence, and even solipsism.[19]

Structural Marxism and Social Geography

At first blush the conflicting paradigm of marxist materialism appears attractive. As introduced in geographical writing, it incorporates a central concern with material and structural relationships and the distribution of power, contexts that are more peripheral, though not absent (as is often claimed) in idealist explanation.[20] But the position of values and ideas is now reduced to the stature of epiphenomenon, derivative of a substructure encompassing the mode of production and its consequent power relations. [...]

There are two major attractions that a marxist epistemology might hold for the social geographer. First, its vision is synthetic, not atomistic, holistic rather than piecemeal. It abjures the petty specialisms of bourgeois social science, the division of knowledge that, like the division of labor, it regards as an indicator of fragmented and alienated thought and experience. Its vistas are broad and ambitious, its style optimistic and self-confident... Within this sweeping vision, the neglected variable of power is properly reinstated. Rather than a society predicated upon harmony and consensus (as the marginal economists and structural functionalists in sociology have long pretended), the reality of conflict, potential and actual, structural as well as temporary, is acknowledged and indeed insisted upon.

The second attraction of marxist analysis to the social geographer is that it deals with questions that matter. In an age where, as Sartre tells us, man is anxiety, a secular religion promising not only the accurate diagnosis of contemporary alienation but also its dissolution in experience cannot help but excite curiosity and commitment. Its manifesto is the more compelling when matched against so much social science that appears to be dutifully playing out its counter-revolutionary role of attending to business that so patently does not matter. [...]

Toward a Reconstruction

The conclusion, of course, is that marxism deals in categories that are only imperfect reflections of the world of everyday life. As such it is an abstraction, and it remains a moot point as to the degree of correspondence between the categories of the marxist engineer and the mundane world that he and we naively know in our natural attitude. As this essay now draws away from critique toward reconstruction, it is time to identify what might be some building blocks for the social geographer in approaching reflexively this world of action, experience, and place.

The first building block, it would seem to me, is the fundamental lesson of humanism, the pervasive presence of anthropocentrism, an anthropocentrism that is purposefully, if often unself-consciously, *for* a subject. The world of everyday life is, as Berger and Luckmann assert, riveted "around the 'here' of my body and the 'now' of my present."[21] My consciousness of space, time, and society is irrevocably partial, colored by my own biographical situation and interests at hand. Every time I make a phone call or open a book, I am confirming this partiality; I have selected this number from the multitude the phone book offers, I have chosen this book now in order to pursue my present interests. This integration between fact and value,

between object and subject, between outside and inside is what recent phenomenologists, among others, see in action; this may seem a self-evident truth, but it is one
insisted upon only by a humanist paradigm that gives consciousness, the intent of a
subject, a significant position in its theorizing.

The second construct is the inherently social nature of experience. Here social
geography begins to discover its distinctive character. Intersubjectivity, the sharing
of meaning contexts, intimates our social nature, that we are individuals amid like-
minded others to whom we selectively attend and with whom we selectively associate. Social life is a sequence of distancing from certain associations and entering into
relationships in others with whom we share aspects of biography and particular
interests.[22] Social geographers have for some time documented segregation patterns
by residential area, but it is clear that residence is only one form of segregation and
that other forms, such as the homogeneity of informal cliques and occupational
groupings, may be even more pervasive and significant within the lifeworld. Intersubjective meaning contexts may place greater constraints on our perception than
we are conscious of; thus, the black sociologist Andrew Billingsley has made the
cryptic assessment that in their research on the black family "[white] American
social scientists are much more American than social and much more social than
scientific."[23]

Intersubjectivity has not been a well-articulated building block of the humanist
geographer, who seems to have found the lonely wastelands of existential man more
genial. Yet neither is this position sufficiently reflexive, for there are few existentialists insensitive in their own writing to the judgments of peers. Perhaps Kierkegaard
was one of the few existential men for whom hell really was other people[24] –
remember he asked that his epitaph be simply that of "the individual" – and yet
who could argue the enormous role that Kierkegaard's audience in Copenhagen
played, immensely hostile though it was, to both the quickening and the publication
of his thought?[25]

The circumstances of Kierkegaard's biography, his temporal, spatial, societal, and
intellectual context, including the structures he encountered, such as the lethargic
state church and the superficial world of mass culture, provided the template for his
thought and action. The accidents of biography, those contextual influences inherited by the individual and beyond his everyday control or even awareness,
provide a third building block for the social geographer, identifying as they do the
interchange between a subject and a multidimensional environment. Without an
environment we have only consciousness, albeit collective consciousness, expressing
its will in a flaccid world relieved of the brute reality of material existence. To some
extent this building block may be contentious, for it challenges in part the traditional
geographic concept of the environment. Merleau-Ponty has stated that history is
other people, but as Max Sorre realized, in metropolitan society geography, too, has
become other people; increasingly the effective environment for action is interpersonal. We need to add external contingencies, the reactive "because of" motives, to
the creative "in order to" motives that together determine the action of the subject.[26]
At a social level the environmental contexts of the individual range from the
promptings of an immediate reference group to more distant authority groupings,
including the influence of the *Weltanschauung* of the given era.[27] There are here a
whole range of social contexts, local and over-arching, self-conscious and hidden;

and all introduce varying degrees of influence and authority relations to the ongoing emergence of action.

Thus any action or the product of an action, such as a landscape, intimates several levels of meaning. Like a work of art, it can be interpreted first at face value, second as an expression of the intent of its creator, and third as an indicator of more overarching themes in society.[28] One of the most revealing artifacts is the map, whose selectivity highlights the concerns of its author and age. Consider, for example, the unself-conscious imperial geographies of the turn of the century with their maps of colonies, maps itemizing export commodities and railways but in the text representing the natives only under the category "miscellaneous."[29] The objective map is a testimony to both the intersubjective intent and the power relations of imperialism.

To the geographer one of the most interesting constraints on action is place itself. Yi-Fu Tuan and others have shown the human content of place, that it is indeed an object for a subject.[30] But in the same way place acts back on man; in Marcel's apparently outrageous words, a man is his place. This dialectical interchange between place and identity, where both evolve in partnership, might offer some extremely interesting research directions for the social geographer. So too with all social worlds; though they are the product of human creativity and have a certain autonomy, their autonomy is always contingent. They are never context free. It is here that a synthesis may perhaps be forged between divergent positions, a synthesis that appropriately links man and environment, human intentionality and structural factors. Such an integration "requires a systematic accounting of the dialectical relation between the structural realities and the human enterprise of constructing reality – in history."[31]

NOTES

1 R. G. Collingwood, *The Idea of History* (New York: Oxford University Press, 1956), p. 213.
2 Wilbur Zelinsky, "The Demigod's Dilemma," *Annals of the Association of American Geographers* 65 (1975): 123–43.
3 Gunnar Olsson, *Birds in Egg*, University of Michigan Geographical Publication no. 15 (Ann Arbor, 1975); idem, "Social Science and Human Action: On Hitting Your Head Against the Ceiling of Language" (unpublished paper, University of Michigan Department of Geography, 1976).
4 Ray Pahl, "Trends in Social Geography," in R. Chorley and P. Haggett, eds., *Frontiers in Geographical Teaching* (London: Methuen, 1965), pp. 81–100; Anne Buttimer, "Social Geography," in D. Sills, ed., *International Encyclopedia of the Social Sciences*, vol. 6 (New York: Macmillan, 1968), pp. 134–45.
5 For Peet's critique and its rejoinders, see *The Professional Geographer* 27 (1975): 277–85; ibid., 28 (1976): 96–103.
6 For a beginning to a geographical study of delinquency in these terms, see David Ley, "The Street Gang in Its Milieu," in G. Gappert and H. Rose, eds., *The Social Economy of Cities* (Beverly Hills, Calif.: Sage, 1975), pp. 247–73; *The Black Inner City as Frontier Outpost: Images and Behavior of a Philadelphia Neighborhood*. Association of American

Geographers Monograph Series no. 7 (Washington, D.C.: Association of American Geographers, 1974); David Herbert, "The Study of Delinquency Areas," *Transactions, Institute of British Geographers* ns 1 (1976): 472–92.

7   Frederic Thrasher, *The Gang*, reprinted. (1927; Chicago: University of Chicago Press, 1963).

8   C. Wright Mills, *The Sociological Imagination* (New York: Oxford University Press, 1959), ch. 3.

9   David Harvey, *Social Justice and the City* (London: Edward Arnold, 1973), p. 137.

10 Jean-Paul Sartre, *Literary and Philosophical Essays* (London: Rider, 1955), p. 118.

11 These terms are qualified, for upon closer scrutiny they may no longer appear as fixed as they first seem. As we will see, structural marxism is largely a debate over *ideas*, whereas existential writers are far more concerned with individual action in *concrete* situations.

12 The use of generic terms such as *idealism is* fraught with difficulty in light of their diverse and even divergent use in different philosophical traditions. Here I am using idealism in its broadest sense to denote modes of argument ultimately traceable to consciousness. Compare the definition in the *Dictionary of Philosophy*, R. D. Runes, ed., (Totowa, N. J.: Littlefield, Adams, 1975), p. 136: " . . . any theoretical or practical view emphasizing mind [soul, spirit, life] or what is characteristically of pre-eminent value or significance to it. Negatively, the alternative to Materialism."

13 Leonard Guelke, "An Idealist Alternative in Human Geography," *Annals of the Association of American Geographers* 64 (1974): 193–202.

14 J. N. Entrikin, "Contemporary Humanism in Geography," *Annals of the Association of American Geographers* 66 (1976): 615–32.

15 Ley, "Social Geography and the Taken for-Granted World," *Transactions Institute of British Geographers* ns2, no. 4 (1977): 498–512.

16 Olsson, "Social Science and Human Action," p. 35.

17 Duncan Timms, *The Urban Mosaic* (Cambridge: Cambridge University Press, 1971), p. 74.

18 S. G. McNall and J. C. Johnson, "The New Conservatives: Ethnomethodologists, Phenomenologists, and Symbolic Interactionists," *The Insurgent Sociologist 5* (summer 1975): 49–65.

19 John Rex, *Discovering Sociology* (London: Routledge & Kegan Paul, 1973), p. 192.

20 Marxism is capable of as many definitions as idealism. In this essay I will confine my discussion to the structural and even functionalist forms that have been introduced to geography by David Harvey, Manuel Castells, and Richard Peet.

21 Peter Berger and Thomas Luckmann, *The Social Construction of Reality* (New York: Anchor, 1967), p. 22.

22 Martin Buber, "Distance and Relation," *Psychiatry* 20 (May 1957): 97–104.

23 Andrew Billingsley, "Black Families and White Social Science," *Journal of Social Issues* 26 (1970): 127–42.

24 The line occurs in Jean-Paul Sartre, *No Exit.*

25 Robert Bretall, ed., *A Kierkegaard Anthology* (Princeton: Princeton University Press, 1946).

26 Alfred Schutz, *On Phenomenology and Social Relations*, H. Wagner ed., (Chicago: University of Chicago Press, 1970).

27 Berger and Luckmann, *Social Construction of Reality.*

28 Karl Mannheim, *Essays on the Sociology of Knowledge* (London: Routledge & Kegan Paul, 1952).

29 See, for example, Gill's *Imperial Geography* (London, c. 1900). I am grateful to Deryck Holdsworth for this reference.

30   Yi-Fu Tuan, *Topophilia* (Englewood Cliffs, N.J.: Prentice-Hall, 1974); *Space and Place* (Minneapolis: University of Minnesota Press, 1977).

31   Berger and Luckmann, *Social Construction of Reality*, p. 186; for a similar position see Joseph Scimecca, "Paying Homage to the Father: C. Wright Mills and Radical Sociology," *Sociological Quarterly 17* (spring 1976): 180–96.

7 Alternatives to a Positive Economic Geography

Leslie J. King

In another emphatic departure from the traditions of quantitative geography on which he was raised, Les King examined (in 1976) the legacy of his own positivism in the light of the promises and pitfalls of radical geography. Recognizing a need to incorporate human values (including the subjectivity of the observer) and political differences into a policy-relevant geography, King steers a "middle course" between positivism and Marxism. He invites geographers to concentrate on building operational models that are truly useful in public decision making, and not to be distracted by the abstract pleasures of recreational mathematics. He draws on Martin Rein's "value-critical" approach to social planning, and suggests "storytelling," or scenario construction, as ways of imagining alternative futures. Drawing on the traditions of behavioral geographers such as Julian Wolpert, King's essay is especially prescient if it is read as a harbinger of a broadly based, action-oriented, critical human geography. Present also is a shift from quantitative to qualitative, from numbers to words, and toward the traditions of textual analysis in geographical theory and practice.

Thus far I have used the term "positivism" loosely in describing an approach to the quest for knowledge that is characteristic of various lines of quantitative-theoretic work in economic geography, although admittedly more so in some than in others. Given the wide variation in meaning that is attached to this term in the literature of philosophy and social science, it seems difficult to establish the meaning of the word other than with reference to particular circumstances. In the present context, therefore, the positivistic approach is defined by three suppositions.[1]

1   That the methodological procedures of natural science may be adapted directly to human geography. This implies that the phenomena studied in economic and urban geography may be treated in the same way as objects in the natural world, notwithstanding the subjectivity, volition, and will of the persons involved in economic and social processes. This supposition implies a particular stance concerning the social scientist as an observer of social reality.

2   That the outcome or end-results of geographic investigations can be formulated in the same manner as those of natural science. In other words, the goal of analysis in economic and urban geography can and must be to derive laws and theories such as have been formulated in the natural sciences. This supposition implies a definite view of the social scientist as an "analyst or interpreter of his subject-matter."[2]

3   That geography as a social science has a technical character and generates knowledge which is supposedly free of any implications for the pursuit of values. The social scientist in this context asserts always his "neutrality" and insists upon the "value-free" character of his research. To the extent that he is, or seeks to become, practically involved in social planning then it is always with the belief that his analysis is "objective" by virtue of its neutrality. This third supposition has drawn more criticism than the first two.

My characterization of positivism is less formal than is usually ascribed to the school of "logical positivism" in philosophy, but it is a fair reflection of what is generally meant by the word in the social sciences.[3] [...]

[There are] two unfortunate tendencies in the positivistic approach to social science research. The first is that the quest for a "theoretically acceptable" model often carries the theorist past the point of increasing marginal returns; beyond this point theoretical work begins to feed upon itself and not upon further observations of the real world. Roberts, a critic of the economists' theorizing, expresses the concern thus:[4]

> Consider the now quite fashionable work devoted to proving the existence of an equilibrium in various highly general models of the economy. As the techniques employed have become more elegant, the point of the exercise has become less evident.

The second tendency is a corollary of the first; it relates to the pursuit of mathematical elegance as an end in itself. The advantages of mathematical reasoning, especially as it has been used in the physical sciences, are well known. What is often overlooked is the fact that the phenomena dealt with in the physical sciences are sharply differentiated, and may be categorized in such a way that there is no overlap between the categories and maximum homogeneity within them. In human geography this lack of ambiguity is difficult to achieve unless, as in some of the earlier theorizing on city settlement patterns, the phenomena are reduced to points or other such abstractions. Furthermore, the theorists who apply the mathematics of probability theory to physical science are dealing with very, very large numbers of phenomena in comparison to the usual situation in social science research. Mathematics must be used cautiously in social science research, or theory development may degenerate simply into a form of "recreational mathematics."[5]

Social Planning and Values

One of my more important premises is that social science must contribute to social policy and to the shaping of social change. The nature of this contribution has to be considered.

Yeates and Garner have expressed the optimistic view that "there is no doubt that geographers are becoming increasingly involved in solving... kinds of applied problems, particularly in the context of urban and regional planning, and will continue to do so in the future."[6] Many of these same attempts at applied analysis have been damned by Harvey as consisting of "an attachment to the 'liberal virtue of objectivity' in an ideological world, of a faith in technocratic 'scientific' solutions, and of a naive optimism."[7]

The debate over the nature and role of social science as an applied field of knowledge has been going on for many decades. The major schools of thought in the debate may be identified by their handling of the central issue of the place of human values in fashioning social science knowledge and in shaping social policy.

If "values" are thought of as the moral assumptions and normative suppositions that underlie human behavior, the positivistic tradition insisted upon a sharp separation between values and facts. Values may influence the choice of research problems or the particular paths of analysis that are followed, but the analysis itself is considered free of any such considerations. Only factual statements such as "the regional distribution of unemployment will become more variable" are considered verifiable. Value judgements such as "I regard this tendency as good" cannot be the subject of scientific inquiry since this judgement is merely a matter of personal taste. On the other hand if an objective function is defined, which may be consistent with such personal values, then one can determine the effectiveness of different policies in meeting this objective. The consequences of this insistence upon a sharp separation of facts and values can be seen in geographic research on the spatial structure of urban areas. Spatial equilibrium where households differ only by income implies that households with higher incomes occupy larger parcels of land than those with lower incomes, but the ethical content of this conclusion is seen as outside of the domain of analysis. Similarly, the assumption of a particular distribution of incomes allows for no statements concerning the equity of this distribution.

Consider in a different context how the values of the observer affect the character of the analysis. When using unemployment insurance registration data in Canada I may judge unemployment to be bad, and hence I will evaluate social policies in terms of how well they reduce the levels of unemployment. What is the basis of my judgement that unemployment is bad? Certainly it does not lie in any profound Christian belief in the virtue of labor, nor can I be convinced that "unemployed" persons drawing government insurance benefits are less happy than I am, but I do know that the costs of such programs are a charge to me as a taxpayer, and I reject this form of equalization policy. My views of the problem and my approach to it are certainly going to differ from those of a person who holds a different set of values in regard to my liability as a taxpayer. The Marxist scholar obviously would view the problem in a still different manner. Joan Robinson summarizes the issue well:[8]

it is not possible to describe a system without moral judgements creeping in. For to look at a system from the outside implies that it is not the only possible system; in describing it we compare it (openly or tacitly) with other actual or imagined systems. Differences imply choices, and choices imply judgements. We cannot escape from making judgements and the judgements that we make arise from the ethical preconceptions that have soaked into our view of life.

One important consequence of the separation of fact and value in the positivist approach is the difficulty in reconciling the need for normative statements, as the basis for planning and policy, with the scientific emphasis upon statements of fact. This gap between the "ought" and "is" propositions in the positivist approach has been the subject of much philosophical debate, especially in German sociology, and somewhat more recently in geography.[9] For the moment, however, I will ignore these philosophical considerations and examine the procedures whereby this gap has been bridged by social scientists concerned with policy. Rein has suggested that three techniques have been used.[10] The first is *mapping*, which requires the establishment of laws or law-like statements of cause and effect relationships (the domain of social science), and the specification of certain means and ends (the domain of policy making). These two elements, the "means-ends" and the "cause and effect" relationships, are then considered to be in close correspondence, and the policy ends should be attainable by manipulating the causes. Rein points out that:[11]

> if the known causes ... cannot be manipulated by policy, then they are of little practical application; but even if they can be manipulated, they may also be morally offensive and hence politically unacceptable. On the other hand, the causes may be both manipulable and ethically neutral, and yet in some cases their implementation may conflict with other ends of public policy.

The second technique is *code harmonization*, whereby conflicts "between the feeling of what is morally right and what the legal code prescribes" are corrected by changing the legal code.[12] Finally, *feedback* is a technique whereby research "aids policy by measuring the gap between ideals and practice (evaluation) and by examining alternative programmatic means for more effectively and efficiently narrowing the gap (experimentation)."[13]

Rein does not accept the positivist interpretation of applied social science which encompasses these three techniques. He rejects it mainly because he sees all three techniques as depending upon the development of laws and theories of social science, but he insists:[14]

> there are no general laws in social science that are consistent over time and independent of the context in which they are imbedded. The search for law-like generalization of cause and effect relationships is an illusion. Any particular patterning of events will not remain stable for very long, and generalization about them cannot provide a firm theoretical basis for intervention.

This particular line of criticism is familiar in the social sciences, including geography.[15] Rein also argues that mapping as a technique is plagued by the fact that most policy situations involve more than one simple aim or "end," and tradeoffs inevitably have to be made among them. In such situations, Rein would argue, it is impossible to map onto these competing "ends" the "effects" of social science theories that are, at best, incomplete and partial. Events over the past several years in urban transportation planning have certainly illustrated this point. The competing goals of transportation efficiency, preservation of neighborhood communities, and environmental protection all have had to be balanced in the real world, and no model or theoretical structure seems to have been able to incorporate this feature.

Similarly, code harmonization is limited by the many inconsistencies and unavoidable conflicts between codes. Finally, Rein sees the feedback technique as extremely frustrating because it demands social experimentation which is inevitably affected in all of its phases – definition, design, and interpretation – by the values of those social scientists cast in the roles of the technicians.

The separation of fact and value, wherein lies the essence of the positivist approach, is not acknowledged in the schools of philosophy known as phenomenology and existentialism. These lines of thought have had little impact upon geography, although of late some thoughtful discussions of their philosophical positions have appeared in the geography literature.[16] The distinctive features of the two philosophies have been reviewed and even debated.[17] What emerges is a consensus that inasmuch as these philosophies are concerned with "the nature of experience and with the meaning of being human," they are relevant to those fields of geography such as historical, cultural, and behavioral which focus on man's existence.[18] Less clear is the view these philosophies have of the social scientist as one involved in shaping and directing social change. Buttimer has suggested a partial answer by noting in regard to the phenomenological position:[19]

> that the social scientist's role is neither to choose or decide for people, nor even to formulate the alternatives for choice but rather, through the models of his discipline, to enlarge their horizons of consciousness to the point where both the articulation of alternatives and the choice of direction could be theirs.

This surely suggests that social scientists have some awareness of which models are worth discussing in relation to what issues. The very elegant mathematical models of urban spatial structure or the persuasively stated verbal theories of regional economic development might well enlarge the horizons of consciousness while describing ideal worlds that are unattainable. Besides, the problems of mapping still remain.

To the extent that phenomenology emphasizes a deep sensitivity to issues of the human condition, of human aspirations and feelings, then its message must be heeded by the applied social scientist, but it is difficult to resist the conclusion that the world described by the phenomenologists and existentialists is one in which self-reflection is esteemed above all else. Planning at the societal level demands that decisions be made for groups, often quite large groups, and self-reflection may provide an inadequate guide for balancing the competing claims and aspirations that inevitably are involved. [...]

A Middle Course

I have now reached the point of asking whether there is a middle course between the straits of pure positivism and scientific socialism. What might be suggested to accommodate requests for a new type of social science, one that is not based on the physical sciences paradigm, that considers values along with facts, and that allows for applied social science to contribute to the development of policy paradigms.[20] [...]

Rein has suggested a "value critical" approach as an alternative to the positivist approach.[21] Values and goals themselves become subject to analysis and debate in this framework, which assumes that a social science divorced from action is indefensible. The different consequences of alternative end values, for example of income equalization or lower unemployment goals in regional planning, would be explored and analyzed and choices would be made only after both the ends and their possible consequences had been fully considered. [...]

Research and policy formulation that addresses questions of regional development needs an awareness of the competing goals, an understanding of the consequences of programs tailored to meet these goals, and a sensitive yet critical assessment of the alternatives. "Research within the value critical framework does try to discern patterns but it seeks general principles that take account of the context and comingle facts and values."[22] Using these research findings, the social scientist is then able to communicate with the policy-maker by what Rein calls "story-telling" based on metaphors. The strategy is not unfamiliar in geography; Wolpert used story-telling (scenarios) in describing the role of community groups in neighborhood change.[23] The scenario points up the interactions of forces which affect a community's life cycle and allows for the playing out of fantasies. Geographers have also used metaphors in describing social and economic processes. Tobler's analogy between spatial interaction patterns and winds might be useful to a social scientist advising the policy-maker on controlling the flows of new immigrants within a country.[24] Perhaps the metaphor might suggest ways of devising "windbreaks." The geographer speaks of ideas and changes diffusing over space either as a wave or by progression through the branches of a tree. In the diffusion of adverse economic effects, such as the wage inflation discussed by Weissbrod, it might be possible to discuss policy alternatives in terms of providing protection to the branches of the tree or injecting "correctives" into the trunk. The use of the metaphor allows the social scientist:[25]

> to bring two separate domains into cognitive and emotional relation by using language directly appropriate to the one as a lens for seeing the other; the implications, suggestions, and supporting values entwined with the literal use of the metamorphical expression enable (him) to see a new subject matter in a new way.

In devising his story and metaphors the social scientist must face some vexing issues. He must, for instance, admit his biases in interpreting society if he is to integrate fact and values. They may well be determined by matters of personal style but only up to a point, and more substantively they will reflect the value screen which the observer uses in seeking his explanations.[26] Does he view social issues in terms of the "malfunctioning of institutions and organization," the "failure of people to cope," the "importance of power," or is his perspective a synthesis of elements of these ideologies? Having admitted his biases, how does he maintain objectivity, avoid moral conflicts, and legitimatize his role? These are questions which urban and economic geographers must address if they wish to be social scientists.

Much current formal theoretical work in economic and urban geography appears to be heading in the wrong direction; at a time when more and more questions are being asked about the appropriate institutional forms for the functioning of our modern societies in all their political, economic, and social complexities, these theories continue to regard the institutional frameworks as fixed and given. When welfare criteria as fixed and given. When welfare criteria are discussed, if at all, they are considered something imposed on the system from outside, usually by a benevolent government assumed to be the guardian of the "public interest." Recent widespread labor disputes and strikes in the public sector have brought into sharp focus the question of what indeed is the public interest, who defines it, and who guards it? These are value-laden questions that obviously have policy implications, and if geographers are to say something useful about the shaping of society they cannot ignore such questions. The work of Wolpert and his colleagues on the location of public facilities has made a start on redirecting geographers' attention away from the private to the public sector, and this new emphasis should be reinforced. Land use in our cities of the future, for example, is probably going to be shaped as much by public land ownership policies, and by public housing and environmental protection agencies and the like, as by private entrepreneurs. Rent controls rather than bid-rents may be the more important mechanisms, and geographers should have something to say about such possibilities.

The current research of Hägerstrand and his colleagues on human activity patterns, which is both theoretical and applied, has demonstrated a sensitivity to the human condition and life that too frequently is overlooked in theorectical formulations. The emphasis in economic and urban geography should be shifted from the formal analysis of sterile propositions relating to abstract competitive economic settings to less formal, but still rigorous, analysis of real world situations in which values, conflict, power, the public sector, and the individual are given greater prominence.

This paper began with a discussion of the quantitative revolution in geography and it is appropriate to end with a comment on the role of quantitative analysis in this suggested new plan. It is assumed that the need for quantitative analysis will increase rather than decrease in the future. The story-telling mentioned above will draw upon whatever evidence is available and in the sorting and arrangement of these facts, both for the present and for the future, there will be a requirement for quantitative as well as verbal skills. The argument that runs throughout this discussion, however, is that we should lower our mathematical sights and aim at the target of developing operationally useful models rather than at that of formally proving existence theorems and the like.

NOTES

1   These suppositions are discussed in relation to sociology in A. Giddens, ed., *Positivism and Sociology* (London: Heinemann, 1974)

2   Giddens, op. cit., footnote 1, p. 4.

3   For example, M. Brodbeck, ed., *Readings in the Philosophy of the Social Sciences* (New York: The Macmillan Co., 1968).

4   M. J. Roberts, "On the Nature and Condition of Social Science," *Daedalus*, Vol. 103 (1974), p. 60.

5   Roberts, op. cit., footnote 4, p. 53; and G. Nyrdal *Against the Stream: Critical Essays on Economics* (New York: Pantheon Books, 1973), Chapter 7.

6   M. L. Yeates and B. J. Garner, *The North American City* (New York: Harper and Row, 1971).

7   D. Harvey, "Review of B. J. L. Berry, *The Human Consequences of Urbanization*," *Annals, Association of American Geographers*, Vol. 65 (1975), p. 1.

8   J. Robinson, *Economic Philosophy* (London: A Pelican Book, reprinted 1970), p. 19.

9   The debate in German sociology is discussed in Giddens, op. cit., footnote 1, pp. 17–21, Chapter 8 by H. Albert and Chapter 9 by J. Habermas; in geography by Anne Buttimer, *Values in Geography*, Commission on College Geography Resource Paper No. 24 (Washington: Association of American Geographers, 1974), p. 29; and by D. Harvey, *Social Justice and the City* (London: Edward Arnold, 1973), pp. 14–16.

10 M. Rein, *The Fact-Value Dilemma*. Working Paper No. 28 (Cambridge: Joint Center for Urban Studies of the Massachusetts Institute of Technology and Harvard University, 1974), pp. 8–21.

11 Rein, op. cit., footnote 10, p. 11.

12 Rein, op. cit., footnote 10, pp. 12–13.

13 Rein, op. cit., footnote 10, p. 16.

14 Rein, op. cit., footnote 10, p. 22.

15 For example, the reasoning of L. Guelke, "Problems of Scientific Explanation in Geography," *The Canadian Geographer*, Vol. 15 (1971), pp. 38–53; or the rhetoric of W. Zelinsky. "The Demigod's Dilemma," *Annals, Association of American Geographers*, Vol. 65 (1975), pp. 123–43.

16 Yi-Fu Tuan, "Geography, Phenomenology, and the Study of Human Nature," *The Canadian Geographer*, Vol. 15 (1971), pp. 181–192: idem. *Man and Nature*, Commission on College Geography Resource Paper No. 10 (Washington: Association of American Geographers, 1971); Buttimer, op. cit., footnote 9, and D. J. Walmsley, "Positivism and Phenomenology in Human Geography," *The Canadian Geographer*, Vol. 18 (1974), pp. 95–108.

17 Buttimer, op. cit., footnote 9, pp. 44–58.

18 The quotation is from Tuan (1971), op. cit., footnote 16, p. 191.

19 Buttimer, op. cit., footnote 9, p. 29.

20 The notion of a policy paradigm is developed in M. Rein, *Values, Social Science, and Social Policy*. Working Paper No. 21 (Cambridge: Joint Center for Urban Studies of the Massachusetts Institute of Technology and Harvard University, 1973).

21 Rein, op. cit., footnote 10, pp. 44–72.

22 Rein, op. cit., footnote 10, p. 48.

23 J. Wolpert, A. Mumphrey, and J. Seley, *Metropolitan Neighborhoods: Participation and Conflict over Change*. Commission on College Geography Resource Paper No. 16 (Washington: Association of American Geographers, 1972).

24 Canada has discussed restricting the movement of new immigrants to the three largest metropolitan areas.

25 M. Black, *Models and Metaphors* (Ithaca, New York: Cornell University Press, 1962), pp. 236–37.

26 Rein, op. cit., footnote 10, pp. 54–60.

8 Eggs in Bird

Gunnar Olsson

Gunnar Olsson played an important role in the development of the quantitative revolution, but swiftly moved to begin a more personal (some would say idiosyncratic) exploration in the philosophy of geography. In this extract (originally published in 1978), we witness a poignant moment in the evolution of Olsson's thinking, as he examines the bias (or, in his terms, "mythology") inherent in the negative exponential function, which provided the backbone of much quantitative geographical reasoning. The article is especially noteworthy for its early engagement with the work of deconstructionist Jacques Derrida, and for revealing the inherently political, ideo-logical, and value-laden nature of social-scientific constructs. In his inimitable, quirky writing style, Olsson invites us to confront the demons lurking behind each individual's geographical imagination, and to sign up for his excursion into "intellectual anarchy."

On the Mythology of the Negative Exponential

Towards the end of the 1950s, when I began my university studies, it was thought that the social sciences had an important role to play in the development of a better world. There was an urge to employ optimizing models as blueprints for the building of a new society, more efficient and more just than any before. In the naive minds of brave new students was an idea of social engineering, whose main task was to specify reliable models, estimate their parameters, and on that basis construct an optimal world. There was an image of future geographic engineers engaged in measurements of spatial location and interaction somewhat like aviation engineers performing endurance tests on airplane wings.

There is of course a long tradition both for and against this utility approach to the social sciences. Had my own generation been taught more about it twenty years ago, then there may have been less of the neoromantic reaction today. (See e.g. L Marx (1978) on the critique of contemporary science in general and Gregory (1978) on the special case of geography.) But perhaps there was too much to do about the future for anyone to think about the past.

Time revolved, however. At the wake of 1968 there was consequently much discussion of the efficacy of spatial mathematical models as tools in urban and regional planning. (See e.g. Harvey, 1973; Friedmann, 1973; Brookfield, 1975; Jantsch, 1975; as well as several papers in the special issue of the *Annals of the Association of American Geographers*, 1979.) The break with the established approach was quite clear, even though there are now signs of renewed pragmatism. Under the threat of disciplinary extinction there is even a choir of hollow voices echoing Berry's (1970, page 22) warning that "if we, as geographers, fail to perform in policy-relevant terms, we will cease to be called on to perform at all".

But the key to understanding Berry's plea is not in the verb "to perform" but in the collusion "to be called on". Perhaps the mistake was not in performing, but in listening too obediently to those who did the calling. Perhaps the responsibility of independent intellectuals is not to stand with hat in hand, but to be jesters, sometimes performing and sometimes not. But at whose mercy is that jester who cuts too closely to the truth he is supposed to suggest but never tell?

To substantiate this programmatic plea for intellectual anarchy, I begin by recalling that most spatial plans involve some variant of the social gravity formulation all of which are special cases of the negative exponential; the general function

$$I_{ij} = \mathrm{f}(d_{ij})$$

is consequently specified as

$$I_{ij} = k \ \exp[-b\mathrm{f}(d_{ij})],$$

which in the Wilsonian model becomes

$$T_{ij} = A_i B_j O_i D_j \ \exp(-\lambda C_{ij}).$$

My intention now is not to dwell on the formal derivations of the negative exponential proposed by Wilson (1972), Smith (1975; 1978) and others. Thus, I am not out to prove anything, merely to convince and persuade. As a consequence, I shall pick my intellectual tools from both logic and rhetoric, for whereas logic ties thought down to predefined categories, rhetoric moves through the breaking of established patterns; while logic imposes order on chaos, rhetoric blows adventure into the stale. Both traditions are equally needed, for the constructed must be broken and the broken restructed. Deconstruction is the name of this game which Derrida (1976) adapted from Heidegger and Nietzsche. What I will search for is that particular mythology of thought-and-action of which the negative exponential is a convenient example.

Unveiling the negative exponential is to grasp how a model can present itself as a means not only for understanding the world but for changing it as well. Put differently, my aim is to lay bare the silent rules of the game we have been playing and to argue that the outcomes have depended less on the players than on the play itself; the players have done what the playing demands, which is why we talk about the rules of the game and not about the rules of the players. When I ask "Who speaks in the negative exponential and in the plans derived from it?" then the answer consequently is that it is neither a group of objective researchers nor the phenomenon of spatial interaction. The speaker is nothing but the negative exponential itself. And as it talks, it obeys only itself and its own rules.

But asking why we put order into chaos in one way rather than another is to ask about the power which one logic or one world of tacit knowledge has over another. Perhaps the answer is that plans and scientific constructs are mental products which would be unthinkable if they did not form part of the currently dominant ideology. A major characteristic of this particular mythology is that it is anchored in the dual concept of presence and signification; we place a high degree of trust in what currently is, especially if our descriptions correspond to physical phenomena.

In the interface of geography and planning, the negative exponential currently furnishes the most accurate and most sophisticated description of human behavior. At present, it is this model which provides the best account of what we think we know both about spatial interaction and about optimal spatial arrangements (Batty, 1978). But our enthusiasm must not blind us to the fact that there is always a relation between knowing and knowing what has been, on the one hand, and between knowing and knowing what will be, on the other.

I raise these issues of logic and positivism to remind myself of the fact that both Descartes and Galileo taught that knowledge is neither more nor less than the power to manipulate the world according to the principles inherent in the particular model used. It follows that the structure of knowledge is not in the known or the knowable but in the form which the knowing assumes (Romanowski, 1974). In Nietzsche's head this idea took the shape that "rational thought is interpretation according to a scheme that we cannot throw off" (Nietzsche, 1967, page 261). Accordingly, it was he who drew attention to the conceptual pairs of description-and-knowledge on the one hand and action-and-value on the other; whereas knowledge asks of everything "What is this?" value asks "What is this for me?". It was nevertheless one of our own contemporaries (Spencer Brown, 1972, page v), who wrote that "the universe cannot be distinguished from how we act upon it". Since "planning is about social action applied on abstract structure" (Papageorgiou, 1977, page 1329), it is difficult to say anything much more profound on the matter of thought-and-action, science-and-planning.

But without difficulties there is no challenge. And without challenge there is no meaning. So continue I must.

From these beginnings, I shall now extend Nietzsche's ideas into the realm of the negative exponential. My experiments will remind some of Habermas (1971; 1973; 1975). But these affinities have less to do with direct influence than with the Prussian impact on Swedish thought-and-action and thereby with the fact that culture is a product of culture (Bernstein, 1976). I nevertheless share the aim of critical theory to penetrate:

"beneath the surface grammar of a 'language-game' to uncover the quasi-natural forces embodied in its depth-grammatical relationships and rules; by spelling them out it wants to break their spell. Its internal *telos* is to enhance the autonomy of individuals and to abolish social domination and repression; it aims at communication free of domination. Such a critical theory, consequently, can become 'practical' in a genuine sense only by initiating processes of self-reflection – a self-reflection which would be the first step on the road toward practical emancipation" (Wellmer, 1976, page 258).

Put differently, I believe that "the first step to understanding of men is the bringing to consciousness of the model or models that dominate and penetrate their thought and action" (Berlin, 1962, page 19).

It is for these reasons that I take our social scientific constructs to be profoundly political documents. This politicalness, however, is not essentially in the particular phenomenon which a model is talking *about* but in the deep structure of the language it is talking *in*. So-called analytical investigations may therefore reveal more of the categorial frameworks from which they derive their meaning than of the phenomena to which they allegedly refer. This relation between structure and event is nevertheless peculiar, for in its very mentioning I begin to break it; the hermeneutic circle spins around its center point of language.

I have been led to this viewpoint by following many different routes. Some of them have been trodden before by people like Rimbaud, Mallarmé, Lobachevsky, Łukasiewicz, Bohr, Gödel, Joyce, and Duchamp. Good company! But the entrance to the prisonhouse of the negative exponential was opened when I realized that all political and social scientific theories at bottom concern one issue and one issue only. This is the relation of society and individual, which in other contexts is called the relation between the desire of the self as the same and the desire of the self as other.

Once our models are fitted into this framework of the double, then their language-based bias immediately reveals itself. For to translate a phenomenon like spatial interaction into the terminology of the negative exponential is to render it as it appears from the viewpoint of society at large. It is to describe human behavior in the aggregate and it is to reason by invocation of the law of large numbers. But this is the traditional perspective of bureaucrats, planners, and politicians. It is within this tradition of phallogocentrism that people who obey the dicta of the negative exponential appear to behave in a cost-efficient manner (Smith, 1978).

The trouble with such society-based descriptions is of course that efficiency is in constant conflict with freedom and justice. Thus it does not take many mornings in rush-hour traffic or many visits to the play-grounds of modern apartment complexes to experience that what may well appear as cost-efficient to the analytical planner is an insult and an indecency to the participating individual. And it is exactly in this confluence of Gödel and Arrow that the ideological and political rub is coming. For when we now proceed to action based on those observed and analyzed regularities, then we are effectively perpetuating an attitude which is for the collective and against its individual members.

I take this bias to endanger our very survival as a species. For there are many indications that the creativity inherent in the human condition gets its nourishment exactly from a balanced and dialectical interplay between the two forces of society and individual, of public and private, of macrocosm and microcosm. It follows that when we design our planning efforts to favor one of these forces over the other, then we are effectively cutting into the very heart of both social and individual change. I would even suggest that what a formulation like the negative exponential actually describes is not the free interactions of free people exerting their free choices. What it reflects is rather the structure of the semiotic prison of fetishized communication. From the impenetrable walls of that bulwork few can escape because the human creature is at the same time both individual and social.

It should now be easier to discern the structure of the myth within which I take the majority of social analysts and planners to be operating. The fundamental doctrine is that any conflict between individual and society be resolved to the latter's advantage. Mythology, ideology, and culture itself is indeed often defined as the process by which we assign meaning to our symbols and symbols to our meaning. This process is one of ontological transformations in which things turn into relations and relations into things, visible into invisible, invisible into visible. Sometimes these transformations are communicated in a poem, sometimes in a political slogan, sometimes in a glance, sometimes in an equation. Sometimes they are in a tear, in a fist, in a laugh, in a touch, in a pair of pants. Indeed they are in everything to which we impute meaning, for understanding meaning is impossible without understanding ontological transformations. Occasionally they have even been discussed in the more explicit terms of efficiency, justice, state, and individual (Sen, 1970; Rawls, 1971; Nozick, 1974). And yet it is crucial never to forget that modern czar, who once justified himself by saying that whereas the death of an individual is a tragedy, the death of a million is statistics. The Law of Large Numbers as interpreted in the Highest Court of Supreme Power! The examples multiply. And as they do, they become statistics of their own.

It is in this authoritarian thought pattern of the Law of Large Numbers that I see an important aspect of the currently dominant ideology. Like all other ideologies, it is an ideology of exchange, for all ideologies concern power and all power relations involve exchange relations (Ekeh, 1974, page 182). In our present world, however, many of the most important exchanges do not occur in the currency of conventional Marxian commodities but through complex codes of signs of dress and food (Sahlins, 1976), equations and professional jargon. On their own accord, these codes rationalize and regulate our thoughts-and-actions such that we now subsist in a world in which the distinction between commodities and signs has become artificial (Baudrillard, 1973; Derrida, 1974; 1976; Kristeva, 1977; Barthes, 1977; Coward and Ellis, 1977). In Gramsci's words, "the democratic bureaucratic system has given rise to a great mass of functions which are not at all necessitated by the social necessities of production" (Gramsci, 1971, page 131).

Fetishism transmuted! It is in the signs that things turn into relations and relations into things. As in myth itself, this process of understanding is now on the verge of returning us to those identities and distinctions which are symbolized by the circle, by mandalas, by serpents biting thier own tail, by tales telling their own tale. Perhaps our accumulation of paradoxes will lead to a recognition of self-reference. Perhaps logic will be forced to accept its long-rejected child and thereby itself become truly dialectical. If so, it is appropriate to recall Lenin's words that it was "Hegel who brilliantly divined the dialectics of things in the dialectics of concepts" (Lenin, 1972, page 196). And Hegel, of course, wrote much on tragedy and little on statistics. Only some will understand the connection.

It is when I interpret the negative exponential as an expression of the currently dominant ideology of exchange and communication, that I begin to discern yet another issue. Its name is *power*. But "power" is merely a word for a set of relations. Like other relations, its meaning is context-dependent.

What I now would like to understand about power is how subsisting entities like society function to exert it in the name of the collective good and how individuals strive to counter it with the same motivation; even the most individualistic ideologies tend to be phrased in terms of collective utility. To understand in this context may well be to learn that our most powerful words, concepts, and relations are ontologically double-faced. One of the faces carries the firm features of material existence, while the other is characterized by the ambiguity of mental subsistence. It is a requirement of those who have power that they can play on this opposition by revealing one of the faces and at the same time concealing the other. But to grasp power is to see how the two sides are intrinsically tied together and to use one's knowledge that signs and symbols embody both thing and meaning, both material and social.

One of the first to penetrate this doubling aspect of thought-and-action was Karl Marx, especially in his treatment of the fetishism of commodities and his reference to the unequal relations of use-value and exchange-value; use-value is primarily in the material relations of existing things, while exchange-value is essentially in the subsisting social relations. Bertrand Russell tried to grapple with the same issue through his definitions of proper names and definite descriptions, while Ludwig Wittgenstein drew on the concepts of internal and external relations. Structuralists of various persuasions have focussed on the dialectics of signifier and signified, of word and object.

When the negative exponential is fitted into the analytical framework of the double, it serves to illuminate the intricate relations between human behavior as concrete experience on the one hand, and statistical functions as abstract description on the other. And yet we are never ruled by our things directly, only by the meaning through which we give them life; as Freud knew and Lacan (1966) learned, the aim of psychotherapy is to recover the shared meanings of-and-in our symbols. This is the reason why we should pay less heed to the Law of Large Numbers and more to the Law of the Double, because it is the latter which governs how thought gives rise to symbol and symbol to thought. It is in fact only through the play of doubles that relations are materialized into things and things are spiritualized into thought. But even though symbols are on one side and myths on the other, they are nevertheless linked together in a set of internal relations. Social scientists label them internally consistent belief systems. Theologians call for "God". In both cases the attempt is to name the unnameable.

It is through the Law of the Double that the negative exponential becomes a tool of power and authoritarian manipulation. Perhaps it is both an indication and an explanation of the privileged status I share with my readership that most of us possess both the ability and the opportunity to arrange our own lives in such a way that we do not have to behave as the negative exponential says we should. As with most academicians it is within our power to engage in temporal and spatial interaction patterns which are far more flexible (i.e. individual) than those of the population at large.

As an example of the other (collective) side of the negative exponential, it was recently reported that 55% of the rush-hour commuters cannot find a seat on the train. Instead of sitting comfortably, they are transported between home and work place hanging like monkeys from the straps in the ceiling. It is furthermore projected that the trains of 1990 will be too full even for those who are willing to stand. No one can get on. The train passes by. Inequality climbs.

What makes this example so interesting is that it is not from New York or Tokyo but from Stockholm. And this capital is in a country where the trains are not only state-owned but where they run on time, where housing construction is essentially state-financed and highly regulated, where a large portion of the jobs are in the public sector. Here then is an interaction system in which all variables are essentially government-controlled and open to considerable engineering. But is the system efficient and equitable? And more important, is it creative and therefore human? In turn, these questions once again raise the issues of Weber, Gramsci, Habermas, and others. For if it was possible forty-five years ago to blame the conventional capitalist and his system, who does a Swede blame now? Who do I ask, when I wish to know whether those spatial interaction patterns we describe so well with the negative exponential represent free choice or manipulation?

Perhaps there is nobody to ask but ourselves. Perhaps the serpent snatching its own tail actually is a good symbol for the human condition in the postcapitalist state. Is it such that the main function of the current ideology of planning offices, political parties, and corporate organizations is to fulfill utopian and fetishistic needs for those who think-and-act within its confines? Are Marx and Freud really doubles of each other? If so, can Wittgenstein and Jung alone serve as their mediators or must they be supported by deconstructive artists like James Joyce and Marcel Duchamp? Is it in these constellations that we will find the key to the code in which individual and society converse with each other?

Perhaps it is these questions that carry the answer to what power is. Perhaps real power is in the ability and opportunity of breaking rather than of obeying the laws, of living as anarchists in adventure rather than as conservatives in the Order of Security. Perhaps creative power is not in being average but in placing oneself some standard deviations away from the mean and thereby affecting it most. Perhaps power is in punishing and disciplining others for their own good, while at the same time milking them to the limit. Perhaps the will to order is the will to power, for it was Nietzsche (1967, page 277) who taught that order is logic and that understanding logic is to realize that "the will to equality is the will to power".

But both logic and power are thoroughly dialectical. As a consequence, they are themselves subject to the Law of the Double. Identity and distinction merge as Hegel said they should. The relations of power and authority are therefore too ambivalent to be caught in the well-defined categories of conventional social science, even though social relations are material relations and material relations are social relations. And so it is that the most insightful modern treatments of power, ideology, and planning may not be in our professional journals but in the surrealistic images of writers like Elias Canetti, Gabriel García Márquez, and György Konrád. But perhaps the tradition is already dead, for it is now being dissected by academia itself (Brown, 1977; Jonsson, 1978).

Questions are posed with answers in mind. But when the answers are phrased as perhapses, then the questions themselves become elliptic. Hence the discussion is once again back where it started, albeit at another level. As in life itself, beginnings never reach their end. And yet the question remains: How can I grasp that particular mythology which expresses itself not only in the model I have written *about*, but also in the words I have written *in*? What do they mean, those ordering commands we obey without hearing them? How does suppression keep itself alive constantly changing yet always remaining the same?

My suspicion is that the silent commands are powerful because they reside in internal relations; in Blake's (1977, page 185) aphorism, "Truth can never be told so as to be understood, and not be believ'd". Inherent in the truth of the negative exponential is consequently the authoritarian belief that society is always right, an observation which may make it easier to understand those forces which try to whip us all into the same thoughts-and actions. But who are the masters of the formal axioms? And who are the slaves of the theorems? Does the cognitive order of thoughts become the order of things because the axioms are condensations of conventional truths? Is a language of extreme precision by necessity a language of extreme suppression because conventions without domination are as impossible as obligations without sanction? But is it the few over the many, or the many over the few? You or I, I or You? They! Dialectics again!

I take it as a foreboding of closing times that even though this chapter began in the formalism of the negative exponential, it has moved from proofs and verifications to questions and perhapses. The musings are no longer limited to professional philosophers and social scientists but relate to human beings in general. The questions are updated versions of old ones – murky reflections of their own time and place. There is no choice, because truths are beliefs and beliefs are expressions of internal relations. Tied together like embracing lovers they hide behind the historically specific masks of external relations; as communicated in the word-symbols of Lévi-Strauss (1969, page 20), the important task is not "to show how men think in myths, but how myths think in men, unbeknownst to them".

At this moment, it seems to be in the various forms of language that the I and the world meet, unbeknownst to either. This is my own interpretation of the theories, models, and plans of which the negative exponential provides a convenient example. In Friedrich Schleiermacher's spirit, I have tried to understand those works and their authors better than they have understood themselves. Whether I have succeeded is a question I no longer dare to entertain, for just as those people are caught within their incestuous ideology, so I am caught within mine. And to the mythical veil of *that* ideology, I am so close that I can neither see it nor understand it. Whether changing it is the point or merely our Western heritage, I do not know.

There are nevertheless suggestions about the next unveiling. Paul Ricoeur (1965) may have pointed in the right direction by nothing that there are two types of hermeneutics. One he called a hermeneutics of belief, the other a hermeneutics of suspicion. Among the prophets of the latter camp he included people like Marx, Nietzsche, and Freud. What they all had in common was the aim of exposing the masked motives of our thoughts-and-actions; while Nietzsche and Freud tried to reach this goal by forging a consciousness which kept an eye on the hidden side of things, Marx attempted the same by focussing on the interplay of social and material relations. As with a sandglass, one thought is turned on its head when another is put on its feet.

Perhaps our own time is ripe for engaging these traditions of existence and subsistence in a rhythmic and dialectical fertility dance. Perhaps the place where the beat of that dance is heard most engagingly is on the strange barricades of intellectual Paris. For some time now, Michel Foucault (1975; 1976) has used the prison and the madhouse as a paradigm of social institutions, while Jacques Derrida (1976) conceives of change as words put under the eraser. Thus, through that metaphoric device of crossing out, he tries to symbolize the fact that even what we try to erase always leaves a trace; difference is deferred into differance. Perhaps it is in these French fluctuations of being and nonbeing that the currently dominant ideology now is in the process of sneaking behind yet another mask of obfuscation. Perhaps the features of that mask are in what art critics call the modern tradition of the new, in that movement which was spearheaded by Mallarmé's search for holes in the wall.

Holes through which we may catch a glimpse of the lonely freedom which lies outside of the collective prisonhouse of communication.

Holes which open and close merely by being mentioned.

And so it is that throughout this piece, I have tried to uphold the Nietzschean vision of truth which contains error. "Not the error which has been overcome in a new truth, not the error which those who lie to themselves accept, but the inescapable error which is present even in the new truth" (Wilcox, 1974, page 170). When 1984 comes around, I must therefore not be surprised to learn that a budding scholar has made a frequency analysis of the words of these very pages. Most likely he will discover that they follow the negative exponential. And who am I to judge whether such a find adds to our knowledge; as Kafka knew, judges easily turn into defendents. Yet, if the chance happened, she would be sensitive enough to turn her knowledge into a Joycean instrument, by which she could penetrate the emptiness between Marx and Freud. And she would come. And a new social science would be born.

REFERENCES

Annals of the Association of American Geographers, 1979 **69**(1) special issue

Barthes Roland, 1977 *Fragments d'un Discours Amoureux* (Seuil, Paris)

Batty Michael, 1978 "Reilly's challenge: new laws of retail gravitation which define systems of central places" *Environment and Planning A* **10** 185–219

Baudrillard Jean, 1973 *Le Miroir de la Production* (Casterman, Paris)

Berlin Isaiah, 1962 "Does political theory still exist" in *Philosophy, Politics and Society* Eds P Laslett, W G Runciman (Blackwell, Oxford)

Bernstein Richard J, 1976 *The Restructing of Social and Political Theory* (Harcourt Brace Jovanovich, New York)

Berry Brian J L, 1970 "The geography of the United States in the year 2000" *Transactions of the Institute of British Geographers* **51** 21–53

Blake William, 1977 *The Complete Poems* (Penguin Books, Harmondsworth, Middx)

Brookfield Harold C, 1975 *Interdependent Development* (Methuen, London)

Brown Richard H, 1977 *A Poetic for Sociology* (Cambridge University Press, London)

Coward Rosalind, Ellis John, 1977 *Language and Materialism* (Routledge and Kegan Paul, London)

Derrida Jacques, 1974 *Glas* (Galilée, Paris)

Derrida Jacques, 1976 *Of Grammatology* (Johns Hopkins University Press, Baltimore)

Ekeh P, 1974 *Social Exchange Theory* (Heinemann, London)

Foucault Michel, 1975 *Surveiller et Punir: Naissance de la Prison* (Gallimard, Paris)

Foucault Michel, 1976 *La Volonté de Savoir. 1. Histoire de la Sexualité* (Gallimard, Paris)

Friedman John, 1973 *Retracking America* (Doubleday-Anchor, Garden City, NY)

Gramsci Antonio, 1971 *Selections from the Prison Notebooks* (International Publishers, New York)

Gregory Derek, 1978 *Ideology, Science and Human Geography* (Hutchinson, London)

Habermas Jürgen, 1971 *Knowledge and Human Interests* (Beacon Press, Boston)

Habermas Jürgen, 1973 *Theory and Practice* (Beacon Press, Boston)

Habermas Jürgen, 1975 *Legitimation Crisis* (Beacon Press, Boston)

Harvey David, 1973 *Social Justice and the City* (Edward Arnold, London)

Jantsch Erich, 1975 *Design for Evolution* (George Braziller, New York)

Jonsson Inge, 1978 *Maktens verktyg* (Liber, Stockholm)

Kristeva Julia, 1977 *Polylogue* (Seuil, Paris)

Lacan Jacques, 1966 *Ecrits* (Seuil, Paris)

Lenin VI, 1972 *Philosophical Note-Books. Collected Works* volume 38 (Lawrence and Wishart, London)

Lévi-Strauss Claude, 1969 *The Raw and the Cooked* (Harper and Row, New York)

Marx Leo, 1978 "Reflections on the neo-romantic critique of science" *Daedalus* **107** (2) 61–74

Nietzsche Friedrich, 1967 *The Will to Power* Ed. W Kaufmann (Vintage Books, New York)

Nozick Robert, 1974 *Anarchy, State and Utopia* (Basic Books, New York)

Papageorgiou George J, 1977 "Fundamental problems of theoretical planning" *Environment and Planning A* **9** 1329–1356

Rawls John A, 1971 *A Theory of Justice* (Harvard University Press, Cambridge, Mass)

Ricoeur Paul, 1965 *Freud and Philosophy* (Yale University Press, New Haven, Conn.)

Romanowski Sylvie, 1974 *L'Illusion chez Descartes: La Structure du Discours Cartésien* (Klincksieck, Paris)

Sahlins Marshall, 1976 *Culture and Practical Reason* (University of Chicago Press, Chicago)

Sen Amartya K, 1970 *Collective Choice and Social Welfare* (Holden-Day, San Francisco)

Smith Tony E, 1975 "An axiomatic theory of spatial discounting behavior" *Papers and Proceedings of the Regional Science Association* **34** 31–44

Smith Tony E, 1978 "A cost-efficiency principle of spatial interaction behavior" in *Spatial Interaction Theory and Planning Models* Eds A Karlqvist, L Lundquist, F Snickars, J Weibull (North-Holland, Amsterdam) pp 97–118

Spencer Brown G, 1972 *Laws of Form* (Bantam Books, London)

Wellmer Albrecht, 1976 "Communications and emancipation: reflections on the linguistic turn in critical theory" in *On Critical Theory* Ed. J O'Neil (Heinemann, London) pp 231–263

Wilcox John T, 1974 *Truth and Value in Nietzsche* (University of Michigan Press, Ann Arbor)

Wilson Alan G, 1972 *Papers in Urban and Regional Analysis* (Pion, London)

9 Ideology, Science and Human Geography

Derek Gregory

Along with Peter Haggett's *Locational Analysis* (1965) and David Harvey's *Social Justice* (1973), Derek Gregory's *Ideology, Science and Human Geography* (1978) represents one of the canonical moments of the latter half of the twentieth century. In it, Gregory takes up so many of the loose ends left lying about by the intellectual "bovver boys" of previous generations (the quantifiers, Marxists, humanists, behaviorists, etc.), and welds them into something completely original. Breathtaking in its command of philosophy and social theory, Gregory's work announced the arrival of a committed, *critical* human geography, based largely in the enterprise of the Frankfurt School, most especially the work of Jürgen Habermas. Gregory's book represented, at that time, the most powerful single statement linking social theory with human geography, a conjoining that went on to become a dominant focus in the discipline for the remainder of the twentieth century. Because of its intricate embroidery on a tapestry of diverse philosophical outlooks, Gregory's book should also be read as an important precursor of postmodern sensibilities in geography.

Critical social science involves:

1 *structural explanation*: a form of inquiry which locates explanatory structures outside the domain of immediate experience and which problematizes the relationship between theory and observation;
2 *reflexive explanation*: a form of inquiry which mediates between different frames of reference and which problematizes their self-sufficiency;
3 *committed explanation*: a form of inquiry which specifies its cognitive interest and which problematizes its legitimation.

All of these are in fact different dimensions of a single proposition, namely that the function of social science is to problematize what we conventionally regard as self-evident. The phrasing is Max Weber's, but the intention behind it is a much wider one than his sociology might indicate. In its simplest form, it suggests that what makes science necessary, what distinguishes it from commonsense understanding, is the existence of constraints and meanings on and in our actions which we typically take for granted. Their disclosure thus requires a conscious and deliberate effort on our part. The implication of my characterization of science, therefore, is not so much that ideology, by contrast, is *a*-structural, *ir*reflexive and *un*committed, but that it fails to *problematize* the issues set out above; it was in this sense that I referred to it earlier as an "unexamined discourse". [...]

Committed Explanation in Geography

From Horkheimer to Habermas

The "Frankfurt School" is, as Slater (1977, 26) says, a loose label applied retrospectively. But if the school never achieved any real coherence, let alone sustained an orthodoxy (Lenhardt 1976, 34), it was nevertheless distinctive enough to be widely regarded as one of the most significant intellectual movements to come out of Weimar Germany. Its members preferred to be identified by what they called "the critical theory of society" rather than through any corporate affiliation, but this is still far from providing a more precise appellation inasmuch as it conceals what Connerton (1976, 15) calls their multiple allegiance.

Critique as they used it had at least three meanings. The first of these was derived from the Enlightenment. This has already been described as the age of reason, and critique in this sense was its "essential activity", the subjection of all spheres of life – including, at last, the state itself – to a rational and public scrutiny which strengthened "the long-established claims of reason as a means of knowing natural law" (Hawthorn 1976, 9). This is not to ignore the way in which the rhetoric of the Enlightenment "was sedimented with a layer of class and elite interests" lying beneath its claims to be a universal public discourse (Gouldner 1976, 227), of which the Frankfurt School was profoundly aware, but rather to note a comparable commitment to critique as an activity of "unveiling" or "debunking" (Connerton 1976, 16–17).

The other two meanings of critique were more precise than this one, but they were closely related to it. They were derived from Kant and from Hegel.

The Kantian legacy was concerned with "the proper problem of pure reason", and although it owed much to the earlier contributions of Hume and Rousseau it amounted to much more than a joint account. Thus while Kant agreed with Hume that experience was inscribed in knowledge he also maintained that the latter could not be directly grounded in the former: if this were the case, then "our sense impressions would remain sense impressions and we should not be able to organise them into propositions". Instead, therefore, these abstract concepts had to be located in the "thinking subject" itself, the "I" which actively constitutes the experienced world, and since reason was held to operate with *universal* categories then what Rousseau had described as this "salutary organ of the will" could, in principle, disclose *universal* directives to action which, given their unconditional application to all men, would of necessity be morally binding (Hawthorn 1976, 33–4). Kant remained sceptical about the likelihood of such an historical disclosure being realized, particularly when he saw how his critique was taken up by those claiming to share it, let alone by those who openly rejected it, but nevertheless he continued to try to clarify the grounds on which it was at least *possible*. Critique in this sense, then, came to mean "the rational reconstruction of the conditions which make language, cognition and action possible" (Connerton 1976, 18).

The Hegelian tradition, which developed partly as a reaction to Kant, was concerned with the dialectic of reason and its birthplace was the *Phenomenology of Mind*. Hegel's progression of thesis–antithesis–synthesis presupposed that the logical structure of the present carried within itself the logical structure of the future. This meant that if the world were moved by the Hegelian Spirit, critical reflection on the historically specific forms which it assumed would enable man to free himself from the illusion of their permanence. Critique in this sense was a reflection on and hence a transcendence of the evanescent structures which constrained human action, and as such necessarily entailed a conception of emancipation (Connerton 1976, 20).

All three meanings of critique can be found in the work of the Frankfurt School, but their transparent idealism was transformed through a deliberate encounter with Marx's materialism. The Institute's first Director, Carl Grünberg, who had left his post at the University of Vienna for a Chair of Economics and Social Science at Frankfurt, made it clear in his inaugural lecture that "the method taught as the key to solving our problems will be the Marxist method" and although, as Jay (1973, 12) observes, his understanding of what precisely this involved was later to be questioned – and even abandoned – by the younger members of the Institute, it was nevertheless to prove a lasting declaration of principle. Only four years after his appointment Grünberg suffered a stroke and in 1931, at the age of thirty-five, Max Horkheimer assumed the Directorship. He moved the Institute away from the somewhat mechanical – "unimaginative" (Jay 1973, 12) – concerns of his predecessor and towards what, very early on, he described as the "relation between the various areas of material and mental culture" (Slater 1977, 14).

This is in fact the very intellectual topography which was mapped, in a rough and ready way, into Bartels's discussion of rationality in geography. Its contours can be fixed more precisely through an examination of Horkheimer's programmatic essay on "Traditional and Critical Theory", published in 1937. (This was, incidentally, written in exile: as Jay (1973, 29) says, once Hitler came to power in 1933 "the future of an avowedly Marxist organization, staffed almost exclusively by men of Jewish descent – at least by Nazi standards – was obviously bleak" and the Institute was closed within a matter of months for "tendencies hostile to the state".)

In his essay Horkheimer characterized traditional theory as a scientific activity which claims a determined autonomy or detachment for itself: "the construction and validation of theory are activities carried on without regard for the purposes which it will serve" (Lewis and Melville 1977), with the result that science is elevated above any sectional interest. It follows from this that "the scholarly specialist 'as' scientist regards social reality and its products as extrinsic to him, and 'as' citizen exercises his interest in them through political articles, membership in political parties or social service organizations, and participation in elections. *But he does not unify these two activities*" (Horkheimer 1972, 209–10; italics added). The virginity of science thus depends on whole legions of Dukes of York marching up to the top of the hill and marching down again, moving from (and distinguishing between) their responsibilities as scholars above and as citizens below. It is, of course, this sort of fairy-tale image which has been projected on to the debate about "relevance" in geography from its inception but, to continue the analogy, it is unlikely – to say the least – that the maidenhood of science can be preserved in the midst of military manoeuvres. [. . .]

Horkheimer concluded from this that so-called "common sense" is regarded as a court of appeal "for which there are no mysteries" not because it somehow corresponds to a domain of immanent truth but because "the world of objects to be judged is in large measure produced by an activity that is itself determined by the very ideas which help the individual to recognize that world and to grasp it conceptually". And this uniformity is achieved not through an anonymous Kantian subject, nor through an absolute Hegelian Spirit, but through the structuration of the mode of production. The scientific activity of any society, according to Horkheimer, is but "a moment in the continuous transformation and development of the material foundations of that society" (Horkheimer 1972, 194) and even if, as Lewis and Melville (1977) suggest, he is using the concept in a restricted sense here, it is nevertheless this relation to the mode of production or, better, the social formation, which allows and obliges us to speak of the *formation* of science.

It must follow from this, however, that what Horkheimer (1972, 206) called "critical activity" also emerges from the social structure; and yet at the same time he insisted that "its purpose is not, either in its conscious intention or in its objective significance, the better functioning of any element in the structure". For this to be possible, Horkheimer had to claim that critical theorists "interpret the economic categories of work, value and productivity exactly as they are interpreted in the existing order, and they regard any other interpretation as pure idealism. But at the same time they consider it rank dishonesty simply to accept the interpretation; *the critical acceptance of the categories which rule social life contains simultaneously their condemnation*" (italics added). This notion of science as examined discourse ought, by now, to be a familiar one, but its importance is not simply in its "explicit recognition of the connection of knowledge and interest" (Bernstein 1976, 180), and neither does it reside wholly in its dialectical, transcendent motion, its vision of "a transcended, reconstructed world" (Agger 1977, 13). It also obliges the critical theorist to speak *directly* to those involved, to use and move beyond their *own* categories and cognitions: and in fact Horkheimer (in Connerton 1976, 224) was convinced that critical theory could become "an essential element in the historical effort to create a world which satisfies the needs and powers of men" *only* to the extent that it was able to engage its subjects in this way.

Even so, it has to be admitted that in real terms the project met with only limited success. There were several reasons for this, not least among them being a spectacular failure to speak in a language which *could* be understood outside a narrow circle of *cognoscenti*. But over and above this Bernstein (1976, 184) believes that the really major weakness of the Frankfurt School was its lack of "a sustained argument that move[d] from traditional to critical theory. Such an argument requires showing how the conflicts and contradictions inherent in traditional theory force us to move beyond it. Otherwise we face an impasse where one is in effect being told, 'Here I stand and there you stand'". And in many ways this has been the most serious deficiency of the radical resurgence in geography as well. It has allowed some geographers to claim to be standing here on some occasions and there on others:

so, for example, Chisholm (1975, 175) contends that it is a mistake "to suppose that because one paradigm (the 'scientific' [positivist] paradigm) is inadequate to solve *all* our problems it is *altogether* useless". To some, of course, even this admission might appear as a strategic victory; but to abandon the struggle as a result of it would be to deflect the full force of the Frankfurt School's critique. While its members certainly registered their objections to closed philosophical systems, and indeed developed their ideas through close interactions with other schools of thought (Jay 1973, 41), they just as clearly resisted any eclecticism which threatened to attenuate their critical intentions. In other words, there is a danger that attempts to assimilate critical insights into the corpus of traditional geography will leave its foundations undisturbed and its primary allegiances unchallenged: negation can follow hard on the heels of recognition, no matter how elaborate the ceremony, and the possibility ought not to be taken lightly.

But having said that, arguments like Chisholm's can be given a radically new edge by turning to the philosophical anthropology of Jürgen Habermas. To connect the two of them in this way will perhaps seem mischievous, but my reason for doing so is simply that in recognizing the limited applicability of what, returning to my earlier usage, I will now call the *empirical–analytic* sciences and, by extension, presumably upholding the (co-equal?) claims of the *historical–hermeneutic* sciences, Chisholm must, if Habermas's discussion of knowledge-constitutive interests is correct, accept the imperatives of the *critical* sciences, which involve the conjunction of the other two. To say this is evidently to initiate an ambitious project, and in trying to provide such a grounding for critical theory – the trajectory missing from Horkheimer's contribution – Habermas moves outside the confines of the Frankfurt School. It is impossible to pursue him very closely here, particularly since his project is still provisional and programmatic, but the concept of central importance to our present discussion is clearly that of "interest".

I have already said that Habermas recognizes an interest in *technical control* in the empirical–analytical sciences, an interest in *mutual understanding* in the historical–hermeneutic sciences (the "practical" interest), and an interest in *emancipation* in the critical sciences. The epistemological status of these three knowledge-constitutive interests is, as Bernstein (1976, 192) observes, one of the most problematic features of Habermas's work, and this is certainly not the place to attempt a clarification of the "quasi-transcendental" status which he originally ascribed to them. He himself now admits that the formula was "a product of an embarrassment which points to more problems than it solves" (Habermas 1974, 14). It arose out of the need to find a way of identifying the interests which would locate them neither in a transcendental subjectivity (which would put them beyond the reach of history) nor in a contingent empiricism (which would allow them to be determined by individual intentions). Instead, they were to represent "general cognitive strategies of the action-related organization of experience" (Habermas 1974, 21). The consequences of this are of more immediate significance to us, since the claim I have made for the imperatives of the critical sciences rests on an equivalence between the three interests, and their connection with domains of action will enable us to sort out what is involved much more clearly.

Habermas ties the first two interests to *production* and *interaction* respectively, and even if it is difficult to prise the one from the other as cleanly as perhaps he would wish it is at least plausible to regard them as the primary levels of social action which he requires them to be, and possible to see how they might determine different objects of study and establish different criteria for making valid statements about them. But he ties the third interest to *power* which, although lending renewed force to Hägerstrand's vision of the core of a new human geography, appears to introduce a basic asymmetry into the scheme. Whereas the first two seem to specify only the form which knowledge must take, the emancipatory interest seems to dictate its content as well (Bernstein 1976, 209). Habermas needs to show, therefore, that the specification of an emancipatory interest is not an arbitrary, normative impulse on his part but one which, just like the technical and the practical, *is necessarily grounded in the existing structure of social action*. He tries to establish the equivalence of all three interests in this way by making what has come to be known as the "linguistic turn", into a theory of communicative competence.

His strategy is to maintain that any successful form of communication depends on a mutual presupposition that four different "validity claims" (*Geltungsansprüche*) are met. These are:

1   that the statement is comprehensible;
2   that the propositions in it are true;
3   that the speaker is in a position to make the statement;
4   that the speaker means what he says.

This "background consensus" can be fundamentally disrupted by calling any one of these claims into question, and there is then no obvious way of re-establishing it, because any attempt to justify the disputed validity claim through renewed argument must necessarily involve and rely upon the consensus which has just been disturbed. The only way out of this – and Habermas insists that it is a way which we all take, whether we realize it or not – is to assume that the consensus is tied to an *ideal speech situation*, one which is so free from internal and external constraints that the force of the better argument must necessarily prevail (McCarthy 1973, 153). That such a guarantee of rationality is intrinsically empty is beside the point. All Habermas is seeking to show is that, as he put it in his inaugural lecture, "our first sentence expresses unequivocally the *intention* of universal and unconstrained consensus" (italics added): that the ideal speech situation must be anticipated in any "language-game". It is then a small step to conclude that this must at the same time presuppose an ideal form of social life.

Habermas's analysis, which is much more intricate than this simple sketch can suggest, raises many questions, particularly when we descend from its metatheoretical heights to ask whether it is possible to specify the relationships between critical science and the ideal form of social life in any more concrete form. Habermas's own answer is extremely cautious, and in fact he seemed so evasive and equivocal in the face of the struggles of the late 1960s that he earned the bitter condemnation of the student Left. The reason for their impatience is not hard to see, and in what follows – and bearing in mind that there are many other facets of his project that deserve comment – I will concentrate on Habermas's view of the relationship between theory and practice, and try to relate it more specifically to the conduct of a committed geography.

To anticipate the argument: the theory of communicative competence may provide some sort of warrant for the emancipatory interest, but it cannot legitimize the various courses of action which promise to realize the ideal form of social life. In particular, Habermas (1974, 32) is adamant that "there can be no meaningful theory which per se, and regardless of the circumstances, obligates one to militancy". To claim that positions like Chisholm's involve accepting the imperatives of critical science, therefore, is to claim that they involve accepting a conception of social science as critique – no more. The distinctions between this view and the traditional one should not be minimized, but if it is hardly surprising that such a conception should appear excessive to the traditionalists (who regard it as ideologically motivated), then it is no more surprising that it should appear insufficient to the activists (who regard it as politically bankrupt). It will be clear by now that the first of these reactions is misplaced. The three interests are not barriers to the objectivity of knowledge (as the traditional belief in "pure theory" presupposes), but the very *conditions* of objective knowledge, and this is as true of the emancipatory interest as it is of the technical and the practical. We can turn, therefore, to the second reaction.

Theory and practice in geography

Wellmer (1976, 258) describes Habermas's conception of social theory as a critique which

> penetrates beneath the surface grammar of a "language-game" to uncover the quasi-natural forces embodied in its depth-grammatical relationships and rules; by spelling them out it wants to break their spell. Its internal *telos* is to enhance the autonomy of individuals and to abolish social domination and repression; it aims at communication free of domination. Such a critical theory, consequently, can become "practical" in a genuine sense only by initiating processes of self-reflection – a self-reflection which would be the first step on the road toward practical emancipation.

The extent to which critical theorems can successfully initiate (and be sustained by) these processes of self-reflection is dependent on the extent to which empirical–analytic and historical–hermeneutic forms of science can effectively be brought into conjunction.

In describing the project like this Wellmer is relying on Habermas's debt to structural linguistics, and especially on the connection between the theory of communicative competence and Chomsky's model of linguistic competence. This inevitably distances Habermas from the narrowly positivist interpretations of the empirical–analytic sciences which often seem to be present, particularly in his early work, in so far as it dissociates him from the traditionalists' closure of inquiry around the phenomenal level. At the same time, however, it invites the suspicion of activists, who reject purely linguistic solutions as counter-revolutionary stratagems (and are right to do so). But it is important to realize that Habermas is in fact seeking to "concretize" the conception of critique which he advocates: in other words, to turn the advances made in linguistic philosophy *back* upon themselves, and so *transcend* the categories of existing theoretical structures (Frankel 1974). In this sense his critical intention is the same as Horkheimer's (although obviously given a different expression), and for substantially the same reason: the need to engage the subjects of critical theory in its formation.

The first attempts to end modern geography's cultural isolation through deliberate engagements of this sort were sporadic and short-lived, and it would be idle to pretend that they owed anything to Habermas. Most of them took the form of "geographical expeditions" whose rationales emerged gradually in the course of encounters with the local, typically urban, community. (I am excluding earlier ventures, like Mackinder's famous Extension lectures or the even earlier promulgation of geography through the classes of the Mechanics Institutes, since they were all founded on a traditional pedagogic model and can hardly be described as critical in either conception or execution.) [...]

Dialogical action is committed to liberation (emancipation) in such a total sense that it has to struggle against being subverted by strategies which, appearances to the contrary notwithstanding, are committed to domination. It is for much the same reason that Habermas rejects any prior guarantees for critical theory:

> Decisions for the political struggle cannot at the outset be justified theoretically and then carried out organizationally. The sole possible justification at this level is consensus, aimed at in practical discourse, among the participants, who, in the consciousness of their common interests and their knowledge of the circumstances, of the predictable consequences and secondary consequences, are the only ones who can know what risks they are willing to undergo, and with what expectations. There can be no theory which at the outset can assure a world-historical mission in return for the potential sacrifices [Habermas 1974, 33].

To deny the hermeneutic encounter, then, would necessarily circumscribe the effectivity of critical theory because it would reduce its strategies to narrowly technical ones of manipulation and control. Similarly, Friere (1972, 108–9) points out that strategies like this are predicated on a "necessity for conquest", through which the conqueror "imposes his own contours on the vanquished, who internalise this shape and become ambiguous beings 'housing' another". The most obvious way in which this is done, he suggests, is by "precluding any presentation of the world as a problem and showing it rather as a fixed entity, as something given – something to which men, as mere spectators, must adapt". A critical science realizes its self-image in its response to this, of course, but it must ensure that its problematization does not substitute a revolutionary teleology to which men, as mere instruments, must be bent. "Revolutionary praxis is a unity", warns Friere (1972, 97), "and the leaders cannot treat the oppressed as their possession": if they do, they betray the hope of emancipation and restore the panoply of domination.

But this is not the only way in which self-reflection can be compromised. A critical science cannot afford to let its problematization be devalued through relying on "a *focalized* view of problems rather than on seeing them as dimensions of a *totality*" (Friere 1972, 11). Again, Habermas makes much the same point. This sort of problem-orientation has found its way into most social sciences in recent years, and it carries with it an open invitation to co-optation. The style of research which defines a concern with misery, hunger and oppression as a concern with a world somehow more "real" than the kind of experiences which have traditionally constituted the domain of academic inquiry is only its most strident expression. *It has no place in a genuinely critical science* in so far as it directs attention towards focalized solutions which obscure and ultimately reinforce the basic structures of society. It has this effect because the distinction it makes between "more real" and "less real" worlds is one which readily assumes that assaults on the one need not (and even must not) penetrate the other; that the relationship between them is sufficiently contingent for the warts and blemishes to be removed by a skin-deep surgery which leaves the complexion untouched. As Colenutt (1976, 85) puts it, as long as someone is working on the "more real" world, as long as our understanding of the totality remains fragmented, then the basic structures of society and the forms of knowledge they legitimize remain unexamined. In the end they are built into social engineering designs as fundamentally sound platforms from which to launch individual reforms, and the much-vaunted problem-orientated geography becomes just another expression of "the reforming ideology of contemporary capitalism".

Harvey (1973, 152) suggests that there are two important revolutionary tasks in theory formation, and both of them can be connected to these preliminary considerations. One is *negation*, which involves taking the compromised formulation "and exposing it for what it is", and the other is *reformulation*, which involves transcending the existing theories "and using them to identify real choices immanent in the present". The success of these tasks, I suggest, depends on the ability of a theory of communicative competence to explain how "the structure of communication allows some issues to be seen and spoken, while diverting attention from still others" (Gouldner 1976, 146). Habermas (1974, 12) has in fact recognized this, saying that he wants to develop the theory of communicative competence in historically specific terms and to construct a theory of "systematically distorted communication" consonant with the "fundamental assumptions of historical materialism". [...]

The start is admittedly still only a rudimentary one, but it is nevertheless sufficiently complete for two conclusions to be drawn from it. *First*, if critical theory is not to surrender its political relevance it "needs an emphasis on the institutions connecting the state and language" (Gouldner 1976, 149). It is simply not enough to construct metatheoretical frameworks, important though they are; critical theory has to provide an understanding of the structure of *specific* theoretical systems and of *specific* social mediations. In so far as it is possible to isolate one discipline's contribution to what is effectively a programme of ideology-critique, we can clarify the role of geography. Gouldner (1976, 152) suggests that "the central semiotic effort of modern politics is the capturing and evocation of a symbolism of freedom and/or equality". If this is accepted, then geography's part in the critique of such an effort is likely to consist of (i) a critique of the concepts through which the discipline has sustained its image of the world; and (ii) a critique of the processes through which the social formation has sustained its relations of production. The difficulty of speaking within the existing fragmentation of inquiry is at once revealed, however, because neither of these tasks can be accomplished until the traditional barriers between disciplines are removed. (Not that this is the only condition of success.) Most of the concepts used in geography are derived from other disciplines, and a focus on narrowly "geographical" processes – even supposing that we could agree on what they were – could only partially disclose the structure of the totality. To draw back from the barriers, therefore, is to disengage from the struggle. This assumes all the more force once the close connections between the two tasks are fully recognized. Marx's critique of political economy put it succinctly: only by transcending the theoretical domain in which "rule freedom, equality, property and Bentham" is it possible to show how the process of exchange described there is but "the phenomenon of a process taking place behind it" and to reconstruct the relations of production which constitute the practical domain. To repeat, then, "there are no short-cuts if the potential of geography is to be realized *within an integrated framework*. It requires a thorough critique of existing geography, which is at the same time a critique of the geography of objective reality" (Anderson 1973, 5). And since neither of these are likely to emerge unscathed it is perhaps not surprising that Friere (1972, 99) should proclaim that "critical reflection is also action".

To some, no doubt, this will seem a grotesque prostitution of what action ought to entail, and this brings us abruptly to the second conclusion. If we stay within the programme of ideology-critique set out by Habermas, we can say that geography's major response so far (and there have been others) has been (i) to develop a sustained critique of the concept of rent and, through this, (ii) to show how residential differentiation acts as "an integrating mediating influence in the processes whereby class relationships and social differentiations are produced and sustained" (Harvey 1975, 368). Both of these efforts were initiated by David Harvey and, to speak with Habermas, they expose the manipulation of the background consensus and the suppression of generalizable interests. The way in which the first of these projects resists the systematic distortion of communication ought to be obvious; the effect of the second is to expose the way in which residential differentiation fragments class consciousness into a "community consciousness" which, if not exactly a culture of collaboration, is at least a culture of consolation which is not readily transformed into effective praxis (Stedman Jones 1974; Harvey 1975). [...]

Habermas (and Gouldner) may well be wrong, their arguments flawed and their concerns misplaced, but the only authentic response which can hold out the hope of a different solution with any integrity is one which takes their conclusion seriously: which explores the theory from which it derives and the practice to which it appeals.

Geography has always lived in the shadows between these two domains, hiding from open encounters with the theories which direct it or the practices which sustain it. These pervasive timidities will not easily be overcome, and to expect geography to welcome intruders like this, from within or without, is to expect too much. But, fortunately, this does not matter: like any form of inquiry, geography is balanced on what Griffiths calls "the essential connective imperative"; no matter how hard it tries it will not be able to snap it. And in the end it will be unable to resist its exposure. Its outward detachment will be overcome and its inner commitment revealed.

REFERENCES

Agger, B. (1977), "On happiness and the damaged life", in J. O'Neill (ed.), *On Critical Theory*, London: Heinemann, pp. 12–33

Anderson, J. (1973), "Ideology in geography: an introduction", *Antipode*, vol. 5, no. 3, pp. 1–6

Bernstein, R. J. (1976), *The Restructuring of Social and Political Theory*, Oxford: Basil Blackwell

Chisholm, M. (1975), *Human Geography: Evolution or Revolution?*, Harmondsworth: Penguin

Colenutt, R. (1976), "Comment on 'To what extent is the geographer's world the "real" world?'", *Area*, vol. 8, pp. 84–5

Connerton, P. (ed.) (1976), *Critical Sociology*, Harmondsworth: Penguin

Frankel, B. (1974), "Habermas talking: an interview", *Theory and Society*, vol. 1, pp. 37–58

Friere, P. (1972), *Pedagogy of the Oppressed*, Harmondsworth: Penguin

Gouldner, A. (1976), *The Dialectic of Ideology and Technology: The Origins, Grammar and Future of Ideology*, London: Macmillan

Habermas, J. (1974), *Theory and Practice*, London: Heinemann

Harvey, D. (1973), *Social Justice and the City*, London: Edward Arnold

Harvey, D. (1975), "Class structure in a capitalist society and the theory of residential differentiation", in R. Peel, P. Haggett and M. Chisholm (eds), *Processes in Physical and Human Geography: Bristol Essays*, London: Heinemann

Hawthorn, G. (1976), *Enlightenment and Despair: A History of Sociology*, Cambridge: Cambridge University Press

Horkheimer, M. (1972), *Critical Theory*, New York: Seabury Press

Jay, M. (1973), *The Dialectical Imagination*, London: Heinemann

Lenhardt, C. (1976), "The wanderings of enlightenment", in J. O'Neill (ed.), *On Critical Theory*, London: Heinemann

Lewis, J. and Melville, B. (1977), "The politics of epistemology in regional science", in P. W. J. Batey (ed.), *Theory and Method in Urban and Regional Analysis*, London: Pion

McCarthy, T. A. (1973), "A theory of communicative competence", *Philosophy of the Social Sciences*, vol. 3, pp. 135–56

Slater, P. (1977) *Origin and Significance of the Frankfurt School: a Marxist Perspective.* Frankfurt am Main: Institut für Social forschung

Steadman Jones, G. (1974), "Working-class culture and working-class politics in London, 1870–1900; notes on the remaking of a working class", *Journal of Social History*, vol. 7, pp. 460–508

Wellmer, A. (1976), "Communications and emancipation: reflections on the linguistic turn in critical theory", in J. O'Neill (ed.), *On Critical Theory*, London: Heinemann

10

On the Determination of Social Action in Space and Time

Nigel J. Thrift

In the early 1980s, a new journal began publication, devoted to social theory and human geography. Entitled *Society and Space*, it was published as part of Pion's *Environment and Planning* series, a far-sighted enterprise founded more than a decade earlier by publisher John Ashby. (*Environment and Planning A*, under the editorship of Alan Wilson, was one of the flagships on behalf of the quantitative revolution.) One of *Society and Space's* cofounders was Nigel Thrift who, in the journal's introductory issue (1983), laid out a profoundly important agenda for research on social action in space and time. As sweeping in its purview as Derek Gregory's *Ideology*, Thrift's manifesto addressed that most pervasive (and daunting) of problems in contemporary social theory – the linking of structure and human agency. In developing this problematic, Thrift drew heavily on the structuration theory of sociologist Anthony Giddens, but also incorporated elements of humanistic geography, critical theory, Marxism, and phenomenology. If Thrift did not resolve all the issues raised in his essay, he significantly extended the purview of a critical human geography, foreshadowing the necessity for the cacophony of theoretical voices that postmodernism would encompass.

Introduction: The Problem of Translation

In the last ten years or so, human geographers have become more and more involved with social theory. This involvement has ranged from the extreme determinism of some structural Marxist approaches, which hope to read off the specifics of places through the general laws or tendencies of capitalism, through to the extreme voluntarism of most "humanistic" geography which hopes to capture the general features of place through the specifics of human interaction. But I think it is true to say that, because of the nature of human-geographical subject matter, extant social theory has proved very difficult for human geographers to handle. The reason for this is quite simple. It is very difficult to relate what are usually very abstract generalizations about social phenomena to the features of a particular place at a particular time and to the actions of "individuals" (as discussed later, this is a difficult and problematic term to use) within that place. Of course, this is not a problem peculiar to human geography. Social historians have been having something of the same problem as the focus of their subject has moved from "the circumstances surrounding man to man in circumstance" (Stone, 1979, page 23); in particular, as this subject has moved to the use of selective examples of "individuals" to illustrate the "thinking in-acting out" of *mentalité*.

How is this problem of *translation* to be overcome; indeed, can it be overcome? Conventionally, the problem is now represented in human geography as a polarization between social structure and human agency, a polarization that is also known in the guise of the debates on the relative importance to be given to economy and culture or to determinism and free will. Certainly, at present, words like "agency" and "experience" are virtual talismans in human geography. Their mention provokes knowing nods around the seminar room, perhaps because these terms seem to suggest an almost self-explanatory criticism of social theory as presently constituted. But, in fact, there are at least four major strands to this outwardly homogenous reaction to the problem of the relation of structure to agency. At the limit, the implication is that altogether too much ground has been ceded to structural social theory. This is a proposition that appeals, naturally enough, to empiricists, who deal only in the given as it gives itself and who continually mistake a minute description of some regularity for theory. But it also finds allies amongst humanists, who pine for an anthropological philosophy with the category "man" at its heart. [It is interesting to note that in *The Poverty of Theory and Other Essays*, E P Thompson (1978), at points, actually makes *both* these mistakes.] A second response, one favoured by certain jumbo Marxists, is that social theory was never meant to be applied to the small scale and the unique. An either/or situation is assumed to exist. The choice is either general theory or unique description. No doubt, this reaction is partly due to a reductionism that characterizes some Marxist analyses, both of the concrete to the merely abstract and of social science to philosophy. But perhaps it is also partly linked to a view of social theory that is still wedded to a conception of (social) science and scientific statements as merely being generalizations about social phenomena. [This paper, therefore, is "realist" in intent (compare Sayer, 1981).] It is an unintended consequence of this view that "consideration of the possibility of coming to terms with the unique aspects of situations (as against their common characteristics) within a generalizing frame of reference is neglected because of the seeming refractoriness of the problem to the conventional canons of scientific analysis" (Layder, 1981, page 49). The significance of small-scale human interaction is therefore bound to be minimized. A third view is that a major shift is required in the theoretical centre of gravity of social science that will lead towards a new "structurationist" problematic based upon a theory *of* social action (or practice) that complements theories *about* social action (Dawe, 1979). This is a view that has gained considerable support in human geography (for example, see Carlstein, 1981; Gregory, 1981; Pred, 1981; Thrift and Pred, 1981) and is now being put forward as the touchstone of recent developments in other subjects, for instance in historical sociology (Abrams, 1980; 1982) and in administrative science (Ranson et al, 1980).

A fourth view, the one to which I shall subscribe in this paper, is that is possible to produce general knowledge about unique events, but that this is best achieved through the interpenetration of these structurationist concerns with existing, specifically Marxist, social theory, because Marxism, for all its very definite sins and omissions, has a strong notion of *determination*. No doubt such an extension will prove anathema to many Marxists, but, to foreshadow the argument,

> it is unclear why a preoccupation with the material practices of everyday life – or for that matter the structure of popular belief – is either Utopian or undesirable from a Marxist point of view. Nor is there any reason to counterpose the personal and familial with global and overall views (Samuel, 1981, page xxi).

This does not mean, however, that I am in favour of the "rambling impressionism" (Abrams, 1982, page 328) which it is possible to find in certain texts that have been concerned with, for example, daily life in the past. Rather, I am looking for a theoretically structured approach to the "real world of real human beings", which is not "held at a safe distance by [the] extreme forms of idealist abstraction" (Selbourne, 1980, page 158) that are so characteristic of a substantial proportion of the Marxist tradition. [. . .]

The Two Responses to the Problem of Structure and Agency: Determinism and Voluntarism

Most social theory is not reflexive. It does not consider its own origin in the theoretical and practical thought of a period, as this is determined by the prevailing social and economic conditions. Thus it does not consider what there is to be thought and, in particular, what material is present that can provide the simple metaphorical equivalence on which human "language-thought" is based (compare Bourdieu, 1977; Keesing, 1981; Lakoff and Johnson, 1980; and see Thrift, 1979). Yet no social theorist can, other than very partially, escape thinking in terms of the society she is socialized into. Why, otherwise, was Marxism, an admittedly determinist set of theories, born under the crushing economic imperatives of the nineteenth century (*and* the labour unrest that accompanied it). Similarly, it is quite impossible to believe that there is no connection between the pessimistic view of society of the Frankfurt School and the Weimar and National Socialist Germanies of the 1920s and 1930s. Theories as diverse in their content and aims as the various forms of Marxism or phenomenology are all bound both by the limits of the knowledge they can utilize and by the ways they can combine this knowledge in theories which are imposed upon them as a result of being children of the same society at a particular time. In particular, social theory born under capitalism must reflect many of the features of capitalism and, in particular, the basic contradictions of this system.

Since the Enlightenment, and the intellectual vacuum caused by the gradual dwindling away of notions of cosmic order, humankind has been beset by two tendencies, partly causes of and partly the result of capitalism. The first has been the tendency towards the seemingly ever-greater scale and extent at which the production and reproduction of society takes place: a tendency marked off by such indicators as the continuing concentration and centralization of capital (Marx), the dramatic increase in and concentration of population (Malthus), the growth of the State and the penetration of its bureaucracy into every corner of our lives (Weber, the Frankfurt School), rapid time–space convergence, and the formation of all those "masses" – mass audiences, mass consumption, mass culture, and so on (Arnold, Veblen, the Frankfurt School). The experience of these phenomena is now commonplace in our daily lives. But for the nineteenth-century middle and upper classes, from which so many significant social theorists were drawn, these were *new* experiences that were conceived as real and immediate problems. To give but one example, domestic and foreign visitors to Manchester in the early nineteenth century constantly remarked upon the vast and noisy working-class crowds, whether these crowds were celebrating at a fair or a wake, demonstrating at a Chartist rally, shopping at night, or even travelling to and from work. There was a general sigh of relief as the workers filed into the factories and workshops where they could be neatly closeted away for the day (Storch, 1977). It is therefore not surprising that for the nineteenth-century middle class the problem of scale was above all perceived as centering around words like "order" and "control" and around the question of how social order could come about or was possible in such rapidly changing circumstances.

To deal with the changed situation, new practical and theoretical categories are formulated and old categories are revised. The idea of a population to be counted out and analyzed, the idea of a moral topography, and the whole semantic field of political economy (containing such terminology as "manufacture", "industry", "factory", "class", "capital", "labor" and, finally, "industrial revolution") gradually all come into being (Bezanson, 1922; Briggs, 1979; Foucault, 1977; Jones and Williamson, 1979; Tribe, 1978; 1981; Williams, 1976). Above all, the medical metaphor of the anatomy of society leads to a concern with "structural" explanation (Ginzburg, 1979; 1980).

This tendency was reinforced by the one that grew up beside it. The conception of the individual had gradually and decisively changed – to its precise antithesis. In medieval times "individual" meant inseparable or indivisible (Williams, 1961; 1976; Weintraub, 1978). A "single individual" would have had no meaning. The relatively closed and static medieval community was one founded on a minimal division of labour and the sharing of many tasks. The system was based on the control of social interaction in order to limit interactions to members of the known social world. Everyone therefore knew everyone else and there was no need for a particularly developed system of control and surveillance. It could be local (compare Giddens, 1981). This system gradually gave way, for a variety of interrelated reasons that eventually lead to capitalism – the increasing division of labour, the rise of wage labour, the rise of a calculative rationality, the increase in urban populations, and so on – to a strong *individuality* based upon the concept of human rather than divine will, on the idea that a human being had a choice over the form of self that might be sought, and to self-control (Weintraub, 1978). The connection between individuality and the problem of social control is once more a strong one. The idea of the individual acquires its modern secularized meaning in relation to the State (rather than the Church) (Foucault, 1977; Elias, 1978; 1982). Through all number of new institutions like the civil service and the police, the State gradually builds up a "grid of intelligibility". Everyday life is brought into scientific discourse (Smart, 1982). Individuality is linked with identification; as a concept, individuality now pertains to specific social groups and to the idea of an individual as a set of developing attributes describing a "career" over time (Ginzburg, 1979). The individual is made an operational concept, the object of scientific knowledge (Foucault, 1972). The underlying epistemology is again medical, but it is now based on the diagnosis of *symptoms*. It leads directly to the deciphering of signs, as in semiotics, and to Freud.

In capitalism these two tendencies come together as a major contradiction between socialized production and private appropriation. Capitalist societies are both collectivist and individualistic. On the one hand, each individual lives in a highly socialized world; on the other, each individual lives in a privatized world (Brittan, 1977). The position is uneasy and ambiguous. This tension, I submit, is as obvious in social theory as it is in everyday life (Dawe, 1979). These two contradictory tendencies, pulling either one way or the other, are therefore found in most nineteenth- and twentieth-century social theory. Thus each particular social theory tends to stray, in varying degrees, towards either the determinism of capitalist society or to the voluntarism of capitalist individuality. Thus there are "two" sociologies (Dawe, 1970; 1979), "two" anthropologies (Sahlins, 1976), "two" Marxisms (Albrow, 1974; Veltmeyer, 1978; Gouldner, 1980; Hall, 1980), and so on and so forth. In reality, of course, such a distinction is a simplification of the highest order. Most social theories, and variants thereof, put forward by particular "individuals", are an admixture of both dimensions, and are best represented as points on a continuum between the two polarities. This is what figure 1 tries to do, in a *very* crude fashion, for a number of recent debates in the social sciences. The theoretical positions of particular individuals on the axes in figure 1 are made to appear more simple than is actually the case because of the reduction in dimensionality that is necessary to present such a diagram. [...]

In a related and important way, social theory tends towards either the *compositional* or the *contextual* (Hägerstrand, 1974). [Simpson (1963) and Kennedy (1979) make a similar distinction between *immanent* and *configurational* approaches.] In the compositional approach, which reaches its apogee in the "structural–genetic" method of Marx (Sayer, 1979; Zeleny, 1980), human activity is split up into a set of broad structural categories founded on the property of "alikeness" and derived via a formal–logical method based on the tool of abstraction. These categories are then recombined as an explanation of society or, at least, of parts of it. In the contextual approach, *elements* of which can be found in Schutz's phenomenology, in Berger and Luckmann's phenomenological–dialectical approach, in Goffman's frame analysis, in Harré's architectonics, and in Hägerstrand's time-geography, human activity is treated as a social event in its immediate spatial and temporal setting and the categories so derived are based on a property of "togetherness" that must not be split asunder. Too often, of course, such attempts to construct a contextual explanation have ended in nominalism or monism or, paradoxically, have only pointed yet more forcefully to the power of social structure (compare Abercrombie, 1980, page 170). But that such attempts have ended in failure does not necessarily alter the terms of their critique or lead to the conclusion that the critique has no force. In contrast to the compositional approach, and in many cases in reaction to it, the

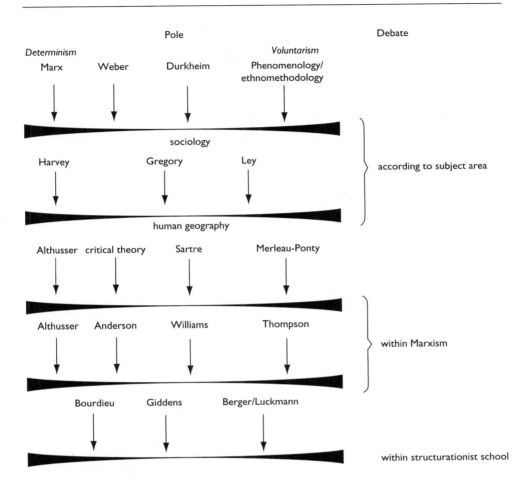

Figure 1. Determinism and voluntarism in various social theorists and subject areas – an approximation.

contextual approach is an attempt to recapture the *flow of human agency* as a series of situated events in space and time. Once again this distinction between compositional and contextual approaches is a simplification – most social theories can be located somewhere on a continuum between these two polarities – but it has important implications for the argument that follows.

The Structurationist School: Towards a Nonfunctionalist Social Science

[...] In the section above I tried to show, albeit briefly, that a basic duality, one that can partly be traced to capitalism, lies at the heart of modern social theory between determinist and voluntarist approaches and between their versions of human agency, respectively, "plastic" and "autonomous" man (Hollis, 1977). Can this duality be recast in such a way that it dialectically recombines social structure and human agency? Certainly this is the hypothesis of a number of authors who espouse, in one form or another, a theory of "*structuration*", elements of which were first put forward by Berger and Luckmann (1966), but which has now reached maturity with the more sophisticated "recursive" or "transformational" model proposed by Giddens (1976; 1977; 1979; 1981), Bhaskar (1979), and Bourdieu (1977). It is important to emphasize that the theories put forward by these three individuals have strong differences, but the similarities are, I think, still sufficiently great for these authors to be described as belonging to a structurationist "school".

Four common concerns unite these authors. First, they are (explicitly or implicitly) antifunctionalist. That is, they recognise that functionalist "explanation" is simply an evasion. At one point, Giddens (1979, page 7) likens his project to "*show[ing] what a non-functionalist social science actually involves*" (my emphasis), and this might well be taken to be the motto of the structurationist school, for each of the other three shared concerns flow into and out of this node.

The second concern is a common message, that neither a structural–determinist (objectivist) nor a voluntarist (subjectivist) approach is satisfactory, joined to a common goal, to link these two approaches together in a dialectical synthesis. Structural–determinist approaches are criticized because they treat human practices as being mechanical and devoid of creativity, what Castoriadis (1975) and others have called "alterity", the quality of newness. Voluntarist approaches, on the other hand, are equally problematic because, in concentrating on interaction, they become blind to the fact that

> interpersonal relations are never, except in appearance, individual-to-individual rela-tionships ... the truth of the interaction is never entirely contained in the interaction. This is what social psychology and interactionism or ethnomethodology forget when reducing the objective structure of the relationship between the individuals to the conjunctural structure of their interaction in a particular situation or group (Bourdieu, 1977, page 81).

No, social structures are characterized by their *duality*. They are both constituted by human practices, and yet at the same time they are the very medium of this consti-tution. Through the processes of socialization, the extant physical environment, and so on, individuals draw upon social structure. But at each moment they do this they must also reconstitute that structure through the production or the reproduction of the conditions of production and reproduction. They therefore have the possibility, as, in some sense, capable and knowing agents, of reconstituting or even *transforming* that structure. Hence, the "transformational" model (Bhaskar, 1979). Social life is there-fore fundamentally *recursive* (Giddens, 1979) and expresses the mutual dependence of structure and agency. Social structure cannot exist independently of motivated (but not necessarily reasoned) activity, but neither is it simply the product of such activity.

However, by far the more important problem is how to forge a nonfunctionalist link between structure and agency. Here individual members of the structurationist school differ in their approach (see figure 2), but no doubt each would concur with Bhaskar (1979, page 51) that we need a system of mediating concepts...designating the "slots", as it were, in the social structure into which active subjects must slip in order to reproduce it; that is, a system of concepts designating the "point contact" between human agency and social structures.

What these Sartrean *mediating concepts* are differs from author to author. Bourdieu's (1977) answer is to insert a third "dialectical" level between social structure and human practices, a "semistructure" called "habitus" consisting of cognitive, motivating ("reason-giving") structures that confer certain objective conditions and predefined dispositions on actors based on the objective life-chances which are incorporated into the strategies involved in particular interactions, these interactions being improvisations regulated by the habitus. Thus each class, for instance, has a particular habitus that results from a common set of material conditions and, therefore, expectations (Pinçon, 1978; Garnham and Williams, 1980; Acciaoli, 1981). Each mode of production has, so to speak, its own modes of perception. Giddens (1979), by contrast, refines existing concepts. For example, structure is limited in its meaning to rules and resources, to particular structural properties. An essentially new concept of "system" is then added as reproduced and regular social practices. Institutions are the basic building blocks of these social systems. Finally Bhaskar (1979, page 51) offers the rather more general concept of a position–practice system; he argues that

it is clear that the mediating system we need is that of *positions* (places, functions, rules, tasks, duties, rights, etc.) occupied (filled, assumed, enacted, etc.) by individuals, and of the *practices* (activities, etc.) in which in virtue of their occupancy of these positions (and vice versa) they engage.

A third major tenet of the structurationist position is the lack of a theory of (practical) action (Giddens), of the acting subject, of a theory of practice (Bourdieu) in most of social theory. [Such a theory should not be confused with sociological theories of individual action (for a review of which see Lazarsfeld, 1972).] There is, therefore, a need for an explicit theory of practical reason and practical consciousness that can account for human intentionality and motivation. This project is vital for three reasons. First, as already pointed out, there is no direct connection between human action and social structure in social theory. Indeed the properties possessed by social forms are often very different from those possessed by the individuals upon whose activity they depend. Thus motivation and intentionality may characterize human activity, but they do not have to characterize social structure or transformations in it. Second, it is also obvious that ordinary people do not spend their whole time reflecting upon their social situation and how to change it. Indeed much of their thinking is bent towards actually carrying out preassigned tasks with no definite goals in mind. And third, there is no reason to believe that when an actress does rationalize an act it will necessarily be the real reason that she is doing it (Wright Mills, 1959). Thus

...people in their conscious activity, for the most part unconsciously reproduce (and occasionally transform) the structures governing their substantive activities of production. Thus people do not marry to reproduce the nuclear family or work to sustain the

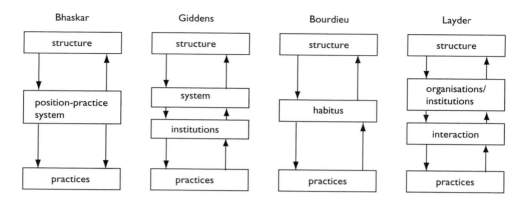

Figure 2. Mediating concepts in the schemas of various members of the structurationist school.

capitalist economy. Yet it is nevertheless the unintended consequence (and inexorable result) of, as it is also a necessary condition for, their activity. Moreover, when social forms change, the explanation will not normally lie in the desires of agents to change them that way, though as a very important theoretical and political limit it *may* do so (Bhaskar, 1979, page 44).

It is therefore important to make a distinction between *practical* and *reflexive* (or discursive) consciousness and reason. Practical activity is not theorized reflexively. Practical consciousness is "tacit knowledge that is skilfully applied in the enactment of courses of conduct, but which the actor is not able to formulate discursively" (Giddens, 1979, page 57). The reasons an actor gives for an action are not necessarily the real ones – which *may* operate outside the understanding of an agent. They are part of a set of "reason-givings", which must, of course, relate to the real reasons, but which can be refracted or even reflected back as their inverse.

The fourth major component of the structurationist case, one that is necessarily related to the third, is that time and space are central to the construction of all social interaction and, therefore, to the constitution of social theory. This does not just mean that social theory must be historically and geographically specific. More importantly, social theory must be about the time–space constitution of social structure *right from the start*. Thus, for Giddens (1979, page 54), "social theory must acknowledge, as it has not done previously, time–space intersections as essentially involved in all social existence". Such a viewpoint has a number of important consequences. Social structure, for example, cannot be divorced from spatial and temporal structure. The two have to be theorized conjointly (see Giddens, 1981; Gregory, 1982), not as the impact of one upon the other. Further, human agency must be seen for what it is, a continuous flow of conduct in time and space constantly interpellating social structure. Such a view of human agency is necessarily *contextual*. As Bourdieu (1977, page 9) puts it: "practices are defined by the fact that their temporal structure, direction and rhythm are constitutive of their meaning". The point is that human action takes place in time as a continual time- (and space-) budgeting process and as an irreversible sequence of actions. There is no doubt that social theory, which has a time that is only partly that of practice, has tended to forget this. Yet it is the ad hoc improvisatory strategy imposed on people's practices by the fact that they have a limited time in which to carry out particular activities (and a limited time in which to decide to do them) that is a crucial part of practice, practical consciousness, and practical meaning. Practice, therefore, is always situated in time and space. This is one link to structure for the structurationists, since the places at which activity is situated are the result of institutions which themselves reflect structure – home, work, school, and so on. These institutions form nodes in time and space around which human activity is concentrated. As Giddens (1979) points out, this is an area that human geographers, through the study of "time-geography", have been particularly involved in for the last ten years or so (Hägerstrand, 1970; 1973; Thrift, 1977; Thrift and Pred, 1981). In this paper, I have tried to show, albeit briefly, that it is possible to conjoin a theory about social action, that of Marx, to the structurationist analysis of social action, utilizing the richness and the importance of what Marx called the "active life process" as it *must* take place in space and time, but retaining the crucial element of determination. I have no doubt that it is the lack of a theory of social action that has disabled Marxism, both practically and theoretically, and that has led to it becoming, in practice, a force for emancipation *and* a force for great oppression (Dawe, 1979; Giddens, 1981). A more *human* (not humanist) Marxism is needed, one that can give *theoretical* respectability to the practical "problems of motivating people to behave in altruistic and considerate, dignified, and conscientious ways without transcendental goals. This is not a matter of 'ideals' or 'morals' but of a daily practical mechanism of conduct, keyed-in to practices and institutions" (Hirst and Woolley, 1982, page 139).

The position I have outlined in this paper is very much a first approximation, open to revision as further work is carried out; comparatively little is yet known about so many of the issues that have been raised. But, whatever the problems, there is little doubt that it is becoming increasingly rare to find social action in space and time treated by social theorists as simply an afterthought or as the mere imprint of social structure or as belonging, in some way, to an autonomous realm of existence. Space and time are always and everywhere social. Society is always and everywhere spatial and temporal. Easy enough concepts, perhaps, but the implications are only now being thought through.

REFERENCES

Abercrombie N, 1980 *Class, Structure and Knowledge* (Basil Blackwell, Oxford)

Abrams P, 1980, "History, sociology and historical sociology" *Past and Present* 87, 3–16

Abrams P, 1982, *Historical Sociology* (Open Books, Shepton Mallet, Somerset)

Acciaoli G L, 1981, "Knowing what you're doing. A review of Pierre Bourdieu's *Outline of a Theory of Practice*" *Canberra Anthropology* 4 23–51

Albrow M, 1974, "Dialectical and categorical paradigms of a science of society" *Sociological Review* 22 183–201

Berger P, Luckmann T, 1966 *The Social Construction of Reality. A Treatise in the Sociology of Knowledge* (Penguin Books, Hardmondsworth, Middx)

Bertaux D, Bertaux-Wiaume I, 1981a. "Artisanal bakery in France: how it lives and why it survives" in *The Petite Bourgeoisie. Comparative Studies of the Uneasy Stratum* Eds F Bechhofer, B Elliott (Macmillan, London) pp 155–181

Bertaux D, Bertaux-Wiaume, I, 1981b, "Life stories in the baker's trade" in *Biography and Society* Ed. D. Bertaux (Sage, Beverley Hills, CA) pp 169–189

Bertaux-Wiaume I, 1977, "The life-history approach to migration" *Oral History* 7 26–32

Bettelheim B, 1969 *The Children of the Dream* (Macmillan, New York)

Bezanson A, 1922, "The early use of the term 'industrial revolution'" *Quarterly Journal of Economics* 36 343–349

Bhaskar R. 1979 *The Possibility of Naturalism. A Philosophical Critique of the Contemporary Human Sciences* (Harvester Press, Hassocks, Sussex)

Bleitrach D, Chenu A, 1981, "Modes of domination and everyday life: some notes on recent research" in *City, Class and Capital. New Developments in the Political Economy of Cities and Regions* Eds M Harloe, E Lebas (Edward Arnold, London) pp 105–114

Bourdieu P. 1977 *Outline of a Theory of Practice* (Cambridge University Press, Cambridge)

Briggs A, 1979, "The language of mass and masses in nineteenth century England" in *Ideology and the Labour Movement* Eds D Martin, D Rubinstein (Croom Helm, Beckenham, Kent)

Brittan A, 1977 *The Privatised World* (Routledge and Kegan Paul, Henley-on-Thames, Oxon)

Burnett J (Ed.), 1974 *Useful Toil: Autobiographies of Working People from the 1820s to the 1920s* (Allen Lane, London)

Carlstein T, 1981, "The sociology of structuration in time and space: a time–geographic assessment of Giddens's theory" *Svensk Geografisk Arsbok* 57 41–57

Castoriadis C, 1975 *L'Institution Imaginaire de la Société* third edition (Editions du Seuil, Paris)

Dawe A, 1970, "The two sociologies" *British Journal of Sociology* 21 207–218

Dawe A, 1979, "Theories of social action" in *A History of Sociological Analysis* Eds T Bottomore, R Nisbet (Heinemann Educational Books, London) pp 362–417

Delaney P, 1976, *The Puritan Experience* (Routledge and Kegan Paul, Henley-on-Thames, Oxon)

Elias N, 1978 *The Civilizing Process. The History of Manners* (Basil Blackwell, Oxford)

Elias N, 1982 *The Civilizing Process. State Formation and Civilization* (Basil Blackwell, Oxford)

Faraday A, Plummer K, 1979, "Doing life histories" *Sociological Review* 27 773–798

Foucault M, 1972 *The Archaeology of Knowledge* (Tavistock Publications, Andover, Hants)

Foucault M, 1977 *Discipline and Punish* (Allen Lane, London)

Fraser R, 1979 *Blood of Spain: The Experience of Civil War, 1936–1939* (Allen Lane, London)

Garnham N, Williams R, 1980, "Pierre Bourdieu and the sociology of culture: an introduction" *Media, Culture and Society* 2 209–223

Giddens A, 1976 *New Rules of Sociological Method* (Hutchinson, London)

Giddens A, 1977 *Studies in Social and Political Theory* (Macmillan, London)

Giddens A, 1979 *Central Problems in Social Theory, Action, Structure and Contradiction in Social Analyses* (University of California Press, Berkeley, CA)

Giddens A, 1981 *A Contemporary Critique of Historical Materialism* (Macmillan, London)

Ginzburg C, 1979, "Clues, Roots of a scientific paradigm" *Theory and Society* 7 273–288

Ginzburg C, 1980, "Morelli, Freud and Sherlock Holmes: clues and scientific method" *History Workshop* 9 5–36

Gouldner A W, 1980 *The Two Marxisms. Contradictions and Anomalies in the Development of Theory* (Macmillan, London)

Gregory D, 1981, "Human agency and human geography" *Transactions of the Institute of British Geographers* new series 6 1–18

Gregory D, 1982, "Solid geometry: notes on the recovery of spatial structure" in *A Search for Common Ground* Eds. P Gould, G Olsson (Pion, London) pp 187–219

Hägerstrand T, 1970, "What about people in regional science?" *Papers of the Regional Science Association* **24** 7–21

Hägerstrand T, 1973, "The domain of human geography" in *Directions in Geography* Ed. R J Chorley (Methuen, Andover, Hants) pp 67–87

Hägerstrand T, 1974, "Tidgeografisk beskrivning–syfte och postulat" *Svensk Geografisk Arsbok* **50** 86–94

Hall S, 1980, "Cultural studies: two paradigms" *Media, Culture and Society* **2** 57–72

Hareven T K, 1975, "Family time and industrial time. Family and work in a planned corporation town, 1900–1924" *Journal of Urban History* **1** 365–389

Hareven T K, 1982 *Family Time and Industrial Time. The Relationship between the Family and Work in a New England Industrial Community* (Cambridge University Press, Cambridge)

Hareven T K, Langenbach R, 1978 *Amoskeag. Life and Work in an American Factory-City* (Pantheon Books, New York)

Hey D G, 1974 *An English Rural Community. Myddle under the Tudors and Stuarts* (Leicester University Press, Leicester)

Hirst P, Woolley P, 1982 *Social Relations and Human Attributes* (Tavistock Publications, Andover, Hants)

Hollis M, 1977 *Models of Man* (Cambridge University Press, Cambridge)

Jones K, Williamson K, 1979, "The birth of the schoolroom. A study of the transformation in the discursive conditions of English popular education in the first half of the nineteenth century" *Ideology and Consciousness* Autumn issue, 58–110

Keesing R M, 1981, "Literal metaphors and anthropological metaphysics: the problematic of cultural translation" available as a mimeograph from Department of Anthropology, Research School of Pacific Studies, Australian National University, Canberra, Australia

Kennedy B A, 1979, "A naughty world" *Transactions of the Institute of British Geographers* **4** 550–558

Lakoff G, Johnson M, 1980 *Metaphors We Live By* (Chicago University Press, Chicago, IL)

Layder D, 1981 *Structure, Interaction and Social Theory* (Routledge and Kegan Paul, Henley-on-Thames, Oxon)

Lazarsfeld P, 1972, "Historical notes on the empirical study of action: an intellectual odyssey" in *Qualitative Analysis. Historical and Critical Essays* Ed. P Lazarsfeld (Allyn and Bacon, Boston, MA) pp 53–105

Lowenstein W, 1978 *Weevils in the Flour. An Oral Record of the 1930s Depression in Australia* (Hyland House, Melbourne)

Macfarlane A, 1970 *The Family Life of Ralph Josselin, a Seventeenth Century Clergyman. An Essay in Historical Anthropology* (Cambridge University Press, Cambridge)

Niehammer L (Ed.), 1980 *Lebensfahrung und kollektives Gedächtnis die Praxis der "Oral History"* (Syndikat, Frankfurt)

Pinçon M, 1978 *Besoins et Habitus. Critique de la Notion de Besoin et Théorie de la Pratique* (Centre de Sociologie Urbaine, Paris)

Pred A, 1981 "Social reproduction and the time–geography of everyday life" *Geografisker Annaler* **63** series B. 5–22

Ranson S, Hinings B, Greenwood R, 1980, "The structuring of organisational structures" *Administrative Science Quarterly* **25** 1–17

Sahlins M, 1976 *Culture and Practical Reason* (Chicago University Press, Chicago, IL)

Samuel R, 1981, "People's history" in *People's History and Socialist Theory* Ed. R Samuel (Routledge and Kegan Paul, Henley-on-Thames, Oxon) pp xiv–xxxvii

Sayer A. 1981, "Abstraction: a realist interpretation" *Radical Philosophy* **28** 6–16

Sayer D. 1979 *Marx's Method. Ideology, Science and Critique in Capital* (Harvester Press, Hassocks, Sussex)

Selbourne D, 1980, "On the methods of *History Workshop*" *History Workshop* 9 150–161

Sennett R, Cobb J, 1972 *The Hidden Injuries of Class* (Cambridge University Press, Cambridge)

Simpson G G, 1963, "Historical science" in *The Fabric of Geology* Ed. C C Albritton (Stanford University Press, Stanford, CA) pp 24–48

Smart B, 1982, "Foucault, sociology and the problem of human agency" *Theory and Society* 11 121–141

Spufford M, 1974 *Contrasting Communities. English Villagers in the Sixteenth and Seventeenth Centuries* (Cambridge University Press, Cambridge)

Stone L, 1979, "The revival of narrative" *Past and Present* 85 3–24

Storch R D, 1977, "The problem of working-class leisure. Some roots of middle-class moral reform in the industrial north: 1825–1880" in *Social Control in Nineteenth Century Britain* Ed. A P Donajgrodski (Croom Helm, London) pp 138–162

Thompson E P, 1978 *The Poverty of Theory and Other Essays* (Merlin Press, London)

Thompson P, 1978 *The Voice of the Past. Oral History* (Oxford University Press, London)

Thompson P, 1981, "The new oral history in France" in *People's History and Socialist Theory* Ed. R Samuel (Routledge and Kegan Paul, Henley-on-Thames, Oxon) pp 567–577

Thompson T, 1980 *Edwardian Childhoods* (Routledge and Kegan Paul, Henley-on-Thames, Oxon) pp 567–577

Thrift N J, 1977 *An Introduction to Time-Geography. Concepts and Techniques in Modern Geography* 13 (Geo-Abstracts, Norwich)

Thrift N J, 1979, "Limits to knowledge in social theory: towards a theory of human practice" available as a mimeograph from Department of Human Geography, Australian National University, Canberra, Australia

Thrift N J, 1980, "Reviews of various books on local history" *Environment and Planning A* 12 855–862

Thrift N J, Pred A R, 1981, "Time-geography: a new beginning" *Progress in Human Geography* 5 277–286

Tribe K, 1978 *Land, Labour and Economic Discourse* (Routledge and Kegan Paul, Henley-on-Thames, Oxon)

Tribe K, 1981 *Genealogies of Capitalism* (Routledge and Kegan Paul, Henley-on-Thames, Oxon)

Veltmeyer H, 1978, "Marx's two methods of sociological analysis" *Sociological Inquiry* 48 101–112

Vincent D (Ed.), 1977 *Testaments of Radicalism* (Europa, London)

Vincent D, 1980, "Love and death and the nineteenth century working-class" *Social History* 5 223–247

Vincent D, 1981, *Bread, Knowledge and Freedom. A Study of Nineteenth-Century Working-Class Autobiography* (Europa, London)

Weintraub K J, 1978 *The Value of the Individual. Self and Circumstance in Autobiography* (Chicago University Press, Chicago, IL)

White J, 1980 *Rothschild Buildings: Life in an East End Tenement Block 1887–1920* (Routledge and Kegan Paul, Henley-on-Thames, Oxon)

White J, 1981, "Beyond autobiography" in *People's History and Socialist Theory* Ed. R Samuel (Routledge and Kegan Paul, Henley-on-Thames, Oxon) pp 33–42

Williams R, 1961 *The Long Revolution* (Chatto and Windus, London)

Williams R, 1976 *Key Words. A Vocabulary of Culture and Society* (Fontana Books, London)

Worpole K, 1981, "A ghostly pavement: the political implications of local working-class history" in *People's History and Socialist Theory* Ed. R Samuel (Routledge and Kegan Paul, Henley-on-Thames, Oxon) pp 22–32

Wright Mills C, 1959 *The Sociological Imagination* (Oxford University Press, London)

Yeo S, 1981, "The politics of community publications" in *People's History and Socialist Theory* Ed. R Samuel (Routledge and Kegan Paul, Henley-on-Thames, Oxon) pp 42–48

Zeleny J, 1980 *The Logic of Marx* (Basil Blackwell, Oxford)

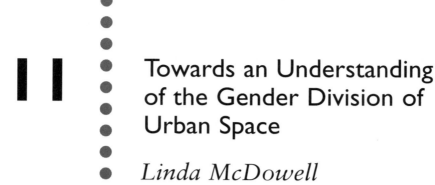

Towards an Understanding of the Gender Division of Urban Space

Linda McDowell

In the same issue of *Society and Space* (1983) that contained Nigel Thrift's essay on social action in time-space (Reading 10), Linda McDowell contributed an enduring argument for a feminist perspective in geographical analysis. Her focus on the question of the gender division of urban space is a report of work-in-progress from a then-emergent field. By explicitly linking Marxist and feminist thought, McDowell drove home the argument in favor of a multiplicity of voices in geographical analysis. Feminist geography thus became another important presence at the birth of postmodern geographical thought.

Women and Space

Although women, as distinct from men, have only recently been considered in urban studies, there is a large body of evidence from a number of disciplinary areas to show that men and women's conception, experience, and use of space is different. Child psychologists have documented differences in the spatial abilities of infant boys and girls (Piaget and Inhelder, 1956), which apparently are reflected later on in subject choice and scholastic ability. There also seems to be a more general awareness that women's reactions to spatial structure are different from those of men. Morris (1974), for example, who became a woman after forty years of being a man, wrote in her autobiography *Conundrum* that she no longer focused on general urban perspectives but on "the interiors of houses...polished knockers, the detail of architrave or nameplate. I look at the place more intimately, perhaps because I feel myself integral to the city's life at last...I am at one with it, linked by an eager empathy with the homelier things about it...." (Morris, 1974, pages 157–158).

Many women resent, rather than enjoy, their restriction to "homelier things" (Tivers, 1977). However, there are strong pressures exerted on women to physically restrict themselves to the domestic aspects of cities and urban life. These range from ways of restricting their mobility (from corsets and high heels to jokes about women drivers) to an ideology which encourages women to consider themselves physically frail. This is not to deny the real problems that arise from vulnerability to rape, which influence how women use space. London women, for example, had to campaign to "reclaim the streets" in part of the capital. Indeed the ideology that a "woman's place is in the home" is so strong that in the recent summing up of a rape case the judge implied that rape was a woman's own fault if she were out alone at night, in this particular case in a rural area with infrequent public transport services (*New Society*, 1982).

Gender divisions of space are common in many societies. In a recent collection of papers by the Women's Studies Committee of the University of Oxford, a group of anthropologists have shown how the patterning of space by gender and the restriction of women to "private" domains is a feature of rural and urban, capitalist and socialist, societies (Ardener, 1981). The definition of privacy, however, is culturally specific.

In conventional urban theory, habitual and almost unthinking distinctions abound: between the public and the private sectors, the city and the suburbs, work and home, production and reproduction. The latter worlds and locations, usually assumed to be uniquely those of women, typically have been ignored, but the former, often falsely equated with those of men, have been the subject matter for theory and analysis. If home-based activities or domestic decisions are considered at all, it is on the basis of an aggregate stereotypical household unit headed by an employed male, despite the shrinking number of households who conform to this ideal (Stapleton, 1980). The internal hierarchical structure of power and the often conflicting interests of individual household members are not viewed as relevant study areas by these theorists.

The "new" urban theory has partly remedied the neglect of the sphere of reproduction. Castells (1978), for example, in the passage below, clearly recognises the vital importance of unpaid domestic labour in maintaining the structure of capitalist cities:

> In the end, if the system still "works" it is because women guarantee unpaid transportation . . . ., because they repair their homes, because they make meals when there are no canteens, because they spend more time shopping around, because they look after others' children when there are no nurseries, and because they offer "free entertainment" to the producers when there is a social vacuum and an absence of cultural creativity. If these women who "do nothing" ever stopped to do "only that", the whole urban structure as we know it would become completely incapable of maintaining its functions. (Castells, 1978, pages 177–178)

However, by defining "the urban" as the sphere of collective consumption, Castells then proceeds to ignore the significance of domestic labour. His focus on collective rather than privatised consumption or, more generally, on the social relations of the reproduction of labour power means that the city itself tends to be seen as the agent of reproduction. Consequently, the role of the family and of patriarchy is neglected Indeed, so gender blind are the majority of urban theorists that they seem unaware of the importance of the shifting boundaries between collectively provided and individually provided goods and services. The current cuts, in Britain and elsewhere in "welfare" services, for example, have implications both for relations between men and women within the family and for women's participation in the labour market. Not only do women service their immediate family but they also form the majority of workers in many of the state-provided consumption services (Cockburn, 1977; Lentell, 1982; Wilson, 1977).

Women and Urban Research

Some of the criticisms of urban studies are gradually becoming invalid. The long absence of women from the urban landscape is being counterbalanced by an explosion of published work documenting certain aspects of women's lives and women's behaviour in Western capitalist cities. This research, which may be loosely classified as "urban", seems to fall into one of four main categories. First, there is a growing number of books, articles, and reports documenting women's unequal access to urban goods and services and the constraints on their spatial behaviour. Although seldom explicitly located in theory, this work tends to fit into the neo-Weberian or "welfare geography" tradition. In the area of housing, for example, there are now published data illustrating women's unequal access to public and private housing in the UK (Austerberry and Watson, 1981; Brion and Tinker, 1980); women's problems in obtaining mortgage finance in the USA (Shalala and McGeorge, 1981); the unmet needs of particular subgroups of women, such as single parents (Anderson-Khleif, 1981); and the costs and benefits of spatial segregation (Ettore, 1978). Other work includes women's use of transportation facilities (Coutras and Fagnani, 1978; Pickup, 1982); shopping behaviour (Bowlby, 1981); access to childcare facilities (Fodor, 1978; Tivers, 1977); more general studies of spatial and temporal activity patterns (Hanson and Hanson, 1980; Palm and Pred, 1978); and the disjunction or lack of fit between women's needs and behaviour on the one hand and the environments of the home and the local neighbourhood, especially in the suburbs and planned communities, on the other (Duncan, 1981; Fava, 1980; Kaplan, 1981; Keller, 1981; Rothblatt et al, 1979).

A second group of work focuses on women and urban design, reporting the impact of a small number of influential women on, for example, the design of urban parks (Cranz, 1981); on the internal layout of dwellings (Hayden, 1978; 1980a; 1981); and on the architecture profession more generally (Torre, 1977). A second strand of this work concentrates on the absence, rather than the presence, of women from the design professions (Leavitt, 1980), and also from academia (Zelinsky, 1973a; 1973b; McDowell, 1979; Momsen, 1980). Many of these authors appear to be suggesting a direct link between the unmet needs of women in the built environment and male domination in the design professions, ignoring the wider social structures that also contribute to women's oppression. In a prescriptive way, a third and related set of papers takes up the theme of the second group and speculates on the form of a nonsexist city (Hayden, 1980b). By stretching the definition of urban, the work of writers such as Le Guin (1971) and Piercy (1978) might be included here. A small number of papers that record women's struggles to change their environment (Mayo, 1977; Movimento di Lotta Femminile, 1972; Rose, 1978) also conveniently fall into this category.

Despite the eclecticism of the research reviewed above, in the issues covered and the approach adopted, they are united, with the possible exception of the transportation studies, by their common focus on the "private" sphere of women's lives. The segregation of male and female roles and women's isolation in the family tends to be taken for granted and is described rather than explained. There is a fourth and growing body of work, however, predominantly undertaken from a Marxist perspective and/or by socialist feminists, which is developing an historical analysis of the origins of women's current oppression and the privatisation of family life in capitalist industrialisation. During the nineteenth century in Britain, the segregation of production and reproduction and the allocation of gender-specific roles was virtually completed. Industrial production became a male-dominated sector, and from the late nineteenth century a belief in the home as the centre of social, not working, life became predominant. Delmar (1976) has characterised this as the period of the "domestification of the working class" (page 283), whereas Davidoff et al (1976) have adopted the phrase "the beau ideal" to refer to the interlinking between an idealisation of rural life and the home as haven, which found a specific expression in British design and layout. Mackenzie and Rose (1983) have begun to draw out more general relationships between urban structure and nineteenth-century changes in the social organisation of production and reproduction, using empirical material from Toronto, Canada (Mackenzie, 1980) and from London, England (Rose, 1981).

Work within this tradition in urban studies, however, concentrating as it does on various aspects of the relations of reproduction, still tends to focus on one side of the private/public dichotomy. Feminist economists, however, using a similar conceptual framework, have linked the specific form of the sexual division of labour to the development of industrial capitalism in order to analyse women's domestic labour and their position in the labour market. Beechey (1977; 1978) has shown how the patriarchal organisation of domestic labour determines the context of women's waged labour. Women, because of the social relations of production within the home, are relatively powerless in the labour market and are concentrated in poorly paid sectors of the economy. There is also a voluminous literature demonstrating that domestic labour is part of the capitalist mode of production and not a separate mode [Gardiner, 1976; Harrison, 1973; Himmelweit and Mohun, 1977; Molyneux, 1979; but see Delphy (1980) for a counterargument].

The relationship between women's domestic labour and women's waged labour, however, is neither unchanging nor unproblematic, but is a source of internal contradictions for capitalism and an arena of actual and potential struggles as women are drawn into and expelled from the labour market. The growing strength of the domestic ideal in the nineteenth century tends to conceal the fact that almost a third of all women in Great Britain have been in paid employment since 1881. This percentage remained almost constant (apart from the war years) until 1951, when it began to rise. The middle-class ideal of the leisured wife, for example, depended on the labour of her working-class sisters. Further, some socialisation of domestic labour has always been necessary to facilitate the entry of women into the labour market. An understanding of patriarchy and the organisation of domestic labour thus allows questions about why and which areas of reproduction became socialised and which remained privatised to become "the urban question" rather than the exclusive focus on collective consumption suggested by Castells (1977). It also provides a more satisfactory focus than the oversimple dichotomy between the public and the private sectors, work and home, that is common in much feminist urban analysis. Thus, I would argue that the focus of Marxist and feminist urban studies must be the inter-relationship of production and reproduction *as part of a single process.*

Production, Reproduction, and Space

It is now generally recognised that space is socially constructed and in its turn, once bounded and shaped, influences social relations. As Urry (1981) has recently argued, spatial relations "are themselves social, socially produced and socially reproducing" (page 458). Thus, the division of urban space both reflects and influences the sexual division of labour, women's role in the family, and the separation of home life from work that developed in the period of capitalist industrialisation. Gender divisions are made concrete and further strengthened by land-use policies that segregate "non-conforming" uses. However, the particular form of these divisions and the consequences for social relations between men and women are neither inevitable nor constant. The relations between production and reproduction vary over time and in space, as does the social construction of gender and patriarchal domination. [...]

REFERENCES

Anderson-Khleif S, 1981, "The housing needs of single-parent mothers" in *Building for Women* Ed. S Keller (Lexington Books, Lexington, MA) pp 21–38

Ardener S (Ed.), 1981 *Women and Space* (Croom Helm, London)

Austerberry H, Watson H, 1981, "A woman's place: a feminist approach to housing in Britain" *Feminist Review* 8 49–62

Beechey V, 1977, "Some notes on female wage labour in capitalist production" *Capital and Class* 3 autumn issue, 45–66

Beechey V, 1978, "Women and production: a critical analysis of some sociological theories of women's work" in *Feminism and Materialism* Eds A Kuhn, A Wolpe (Routledge and Kegan Paul, Henley-on-Thames, Oxon) pp 157–197

Bowlby S, 1981, "Shopping policy and women as consumers" in *Perspectives on Feminism and Geography* proceedings of the IBG Women and Geography Study Group Meeting held September 1981, University College London, pp 24–27; proceedings available in mimeograph form from Department of Geography, University of Reading, Reading, England

Brion M, Tinker A, 1980 *Women in Housing* Housing Centre Trust, London

Castells M, 1977 *The Urban Question* (Edward Arnold, London)

Castells M, 1978 *City, Class and Power* (Macmillan, London)

Cockburn C, 1977 *The Local State* (Pluto Press, London)

Coutras J, Fagnani J, 1978, "Femmes et transports en milieu urbain" *International Journal of Urban and Regional Research* 2(3) 432–439

Cranz G, 1981, "Women and urban parks" in *Building for Women* Ed. S Keller (Lexington Books, Lexington, MA) pp 151–171

Davidoff L, L'Esperance J, Newby H, 1976, "Landscape with figures: home and community in English society" in *The Rights and Wrongs of Women* Eds J Mitchell, A Oakley (Penguin Books, Harmondsworth, Middx) pp 139–175

Delmar R, 1976, "Looking again at Engels' origins of the family" in *The Rights and Wrongs of Women* Eds J Mitchell, A Oakley (Penguin Books, Harmondsworth, Middx) pp 271–287

Delphy C, 1980, "A materialist feminism is possible?" *Feminist Review* 4 79–105

Duncan J S (Ed.), 1981 *Housing and Identity: Cross Cultural Perspectives* (Croom Helm, London)

Ettore E M, 1978, "Women, urban social movements and the lesbian ghetto" *International Journal of Urban and Regional Research* 2(3) 499–520

Fava S, 1980, "Women's place in the new suburbia" in *New Spaces for Women* Eds G Wekerle, R Peterson, D Morley (Westview, Boulder, CO) pp 129–149

Fodor R, 1978, "Day care policy in France and its consequences for women" *International Journal of Urban and Regional Research* 2(3) 463–481

Gardiner J, 1976, "Political economy of domestic labour in capitalist society" in *Dependence and Exploitation in Work and Marriage* Eds D Barker, S Allen (Longman, Harlow, Essex) pp 109–120

Hanson S, Hanson P, 1980, "Gender and urban activity patterns in Uppsala, Sweden" *Geographical Review* 70(3) 291–299

Harrison J, 1973, "The political economy of housework" Bulletin of the Conference of Socialist Economists, London; copy available in mimeograph form from B Fine, Department of Economics, Birkbeck College, London

Hayden D, 1978, "Melusina Fay Peirce and cooperative housekeeping" *International Journal of Urban and Regional Studies* 2 404–420

Hayden D, 1980a, "Redesigning the domestic workplace" in *New space for women* Eds G Wekerle, R Peterson, D Morley (Westview,) Boulder, Co) pp. 101–121

Hayden D, 1980b, "What would a non-sexist city be like?" *Signs* 5 supplement to issue 3, special issue on "Women and the American city", 170–187

Hayden D, 1981, "Two Utopian feminists and their campaigns for kitchenless houses" in *Building for Women* Ed. S Keller (Lexington Books, Lexington, MA) pp 3–20

Himmelweit S, Mohun S, 1977, "Domestic labour and capital" *Cambridge Journal of Economics* 1 15–31

Kaplan I, 1981, "Family life cycle and women's evaluations of community facilities" in *Building for Women* Ed. S Keller (Lexington Books, Lexington, MA) pp 77–92

Keller S, 1981, "Women and children in a planned community" in *Building for Women* Ed. S Keller (Lexington Books, Lexington, MA) pp 67–76

Leavitt J, 1980, "There's more to affirmative action than gaining access: the case of female planners" in *New Space for Women* Eds G Wekerle, R Peterson, D Morley (Westview, Boulder, CO) pp 219–234

Le Guin U, 1971 *City of Illusions* (Victor Gollancz, London)

Lentell H, 1982, "Gender and class" *Social Sciences: A Foundation Course (D102). Unit 12* Open University Press, Milton Keynes

McDowell L, 1979, "Women in British geography" *Area* 11(2) 151–154

Mackenzie S, 1980, "Women and the reproduction of labour power in the industrial city" WP-23, Urban and Regional Studies, University of Sussex, Falmer, Brighton, England

Mackenzie S, Rose D, 1983, "Industrial change, the domestic economy and home life" in *Relict Spaces? Social Change and Industrial Decline in Cities and Regions* Eds J Anderson, S Duncan, R Hudson (Academic Press, London)

Mayo M (Ed.), 1977 *Women in the Community* (Routledge and Kegan Paul, Henley-on-Thames, Oxon)

Molyneux M, 1979, "Beyond the housework debate" *New Left Review* 116 3–28

Momsen J, 1980, "Women in Canadian geography" *The Canadian Geographer* 24(2) 177–182

Morris J, 1974 *Conundrum* (Harcourt Brace Jovanvich, New York)

Movimento di Lotta Femminile, 1972, "Programmatic manifesto for the struggle of housewives in the neighbourhood" *Socialist Revolution* 9 85–90

New Society, 1982, "Woman's place" editorial in *New Society*, 13 January issue, 4

Palm R, Pred A, 1978, "The status of women: a time-geographic view" in *An Invitation to Geography* Eds D A Lanegran, R Palm (McGraw-Hill, New York) pp 99–109

Piaget J, Inhelder B, 1956 *The Child's Conception of Space* (Routledge and Kegan Paul, Henley-on-Thames, Oxon)

Pickup L, 1982, "Combining family and work roles – a time-geographic perspective on women's job chances" paper prepared for the IBG 1982 Annual Conference Session on the Institutionalisation of Gender Differences (available from S Bowlby, Department of Geography, University of Reading, Reading, England)

Piercy M, 1978 *Women on the Edge of Time* (Women's Press, London)

Rose D, 1981, "Accumulation versus reproduction in the inner city: the recurrent crisis of London revisited" in *Urbanization and Urban Planning in a Capitalist Society* Eds M Dear, A Scott (Methuen, Andover, Hants) pp 339–381

Rose H, 1978, "In practice supported, in theory denied: an account of an invisible urban movement" *International Journal of Urban and Regional Research* 2(3) 521–537

Rothblatt D, Garr D, Sprague J, 1979 *The Suburban Environment and Women* (Holt, Rinehart and Winston, New York)

Shalala D, McGeorge J, 1981, "The women and mortgage credit project: a government response to the housing problems of women" in *Building for Women* Ed. S Keller (Lexington Books, Lexington, MA) pp 39–46

Stapleton C, 1980, "Reformulation of the family life-cycle concept: implications for residential mobility" *Environment and Planning A* 12 1103–1118

Tivers J, 1977, "Constraints on spatial activity patterns: women with young children" OP-6, Department of Geography, Kings College, University of London, London

Torre S (Ed.), 1977 *Women and American Architecture: A Historic and Contemporary Perspective* (Whitney, New York)

Urry J, 1981, "Localities, regions and social class" *International Journal of Urban and Regional Research* 5(4) 455–473

Wilson E, 1977 *Women and the Welfare State* (Tavistock Publications, Andover, Hants)

Zelinsky W, 1973a, "The strange case of the missing female geographer" *The Professional Geographer* 25(2) 101–105

Zelinsky W, 1973b, "Women in geography: a brief factual account" *The Professional Geographer* 25(2) 151–165

1984–9: Postmodern Geographies

It's always fun, but seldom easy, to try pinpointing the exact time and place when a new idea or trend first surfaced. There is, for example, a delightful, playful precision in the way architectural historian Charles Jencks dated the death of modern architecture as July 15, 1972, when the public housing blocks of Pruitt-Igoe (in St. Louis, Missouri) were detonated, having been erected barely twenty years earlier.

A different kind of explosion occurred in human geography in 1984, after *New Left Review* published Fredric Jameson's "Postmodernism, or the Cultural Logic of Late Capitalism" (Reading 13). Jameson's packed, densely-argued piece focuses on cultural production in an era of "late capitalism" (a term borrowed from Mandel, but not favored by Jameson). As his title suggests, Jameson was looking at postmodern culture as an expression of the contemporary capitalist era. His overview quickly marshaled sympathetic ears in geography because of his emphasis on space and spatiality as particular characteristics of postmodern ways of knowing. Particularly provocative was his suggestion that we were observing the emergence of a "postmodern hyperspace," the time-space coordinates of which had yet to be established. These speculations were like catnip to a cadre of geographers whose minds had just recently been exposed to the heady promises of a critical social theory.

Jameson is a professor of comparative literature who writes from a neo-Marxist perspective. Not surprisingly, he was influenced by the precepts of the Marxian paradigm, which include the notion that the economic relations of class (manifest in the conflict between capital and labor) are the primary determinants of social relations under capitalism. It's the economic *base* that has primacy, then, and that's what determines the characteristics of the *superstructure*, including cultural life, education, legal systems, etc. In the late 1960s and early 1970s, especially in France, "poststructural" philosophers (including Michel Foucault and Jacques Derrida) began to overturn this traditional logic, emphasizing that the superstructure was as important as the economic base, and indeed was even capable of transforming the economic base. In essence, poststructuralist thinking completely overturned conventional notions of causality in Marxist thought. This was an important breach in conventional continental European thought, and through it flooded a postmodern revolution.

Now, postmodernism is *not* the same as poststructuralism. The specific intellectual correction introduced by poststructuralists (that the superstructure is not slavishly subordinate to the economic base) soon became conflated with postmodernism, even though the latter contained a much broader set of philosophical concerns, many of which had preceded the poststructural turn. Therefore, it may be helpful to understand Jameson's intervention as inspired (i) by the logic of poststructuralism; and (ii) the broader cultural concerns of postmodernism, what Jameson characterized as the "cultural logic" of late capitalism.

Jameson traces his interest in space back to the work of Henri Lefebvre, a French Marxist philosopher who has influenced many geographers involved in the postmodern turn. Lefebvre was, without doubt, the principal twentieth-century philosopher who worried about space and the spatial organization of human activities. He was a prolific author who wore his Marxism lightly, and was unafraid of charging into the polemics of the political left, right, or center. His ideas retain a remarkable vitality and relevance. Sensitive to difference, Lefebvre understood Marxism as *one* of many ways of seeing the world; he foresaw the need to theorize the body in a global–local context; and he returned *space* to a central position in contemporary philosophy (Reading 12).

Two of the earliest sustained encounters with postmodernism by geographers were published in a 1986 issue of the journal *Society and Space*, which was devoted entirely to the emergent urbanisms of Los Angeles. Ed Soja's paper was an exuberant trip around LA, understood as the harbinger of the postmodern city (Reading 14); and Michael Dear's inquiry on contemporary urban planning emphasized the altered rationalities characteristic of postmodern urban geography (Reading 15). Soja's article was reprinted in his highly influential book, entitled *Postmodern Geographies: The Reassertion of Space in Critical Social Theory* (1989), which considerably expanded his purview on postmodern geography. That same year, David Harvey published *The Condition of Postmodernity: an Inquiry into the Origins of Cultural Change*, a polemic against postmodernism, which while conceding that important global and local changes were underway, insisted on interpreting them through a Marxian lens of "capitalism-as-usual" (Reading 16). Many agreed with Harvey's critique, or simply wished postmodernism would fade away. However, by then, the groundwork laid between 1965 and 1984 had prepared human geography for the efflorescence of postmodern thought.

"Repent, Harlequin!" Said the Ticktockman

the classic story by
Harlan Ellison

illustrated by
Rick Berry

designed by
Arnie Fenner

High above the third level of the city, he crouched on the humming aluminum-frame platform of the air-boat (foof! air-boat, indeed! swizzleskid is what it was, with a tow-rack jerry-rigged) and he stared down at the neat Mondrian arrangement of the buildings.

Somewhere nearby, he could hear the metronomic left-right-left of the 2:47 PM shift, entering the Timkin roller-bearing plant in their sneakers. A minute later, precisely, he heard the softer right-left-right of the 5:00 AM formation, going home.

An elfin grin spread across his tanned features, and his dimples appeared for a moment. Then, scratching at his thatch of auburn hair, he shrugged within his motley, as though girding himself for what came next, and threw the joystick forward, and bent into the wind as the air-boat dropped. He skimmed over a slidewalk, purposely dropping a few feet to crease the tassels of the ladies of fashion, and – inserting thumbs in large ears – he stuck out his tongue, rolled his eyes and went wugga-wugga-wugga. It was a minor diversion. One pedestrian skittered and tumbled, sending parcels every-whichway, another wet herself, a third keeled slantwise and the walk was stopped automatically by the servitors till she could be resuscitated. It was a minor diversion.

Then he swirled away on a vagrant breeze, and was gone. Hi-ho.

As he rounded the cornice of the Time-Motion Study Building, he saw the shift, just boarding the slidewalk. With practiced motion and an absolute conservation of move-ment, they sidestepped up onto the slow-strip and (in a chorus line reminiscent of a Busby Berkeley film of the antediluvian 1930s) advanced across the strips ostrich-walking till they were lined up on the expresstrip.

Once more, in anticipation, the elfin grin spread, and there was a tooth missing back there on the left side. He dipped, skimmed, and swooped over them; and then, scrunching about on the air-boat, he released the holding pins that fastened shut the ends of the homemade pouring troughs that kept his cargo from dumping prematurely. And as he pulled the trough-pins, the air-boat slid over the factory workers and one hundred and fifty thousand dollars' worth of jelly beans cascaded down on the express-strip.

Jelly beans! Millions and billions of purples and yellows and greens and licorice and grape and raspberry and mint and round and smooth and crunchy outside and soft-mealy inside and sugary and bouncing jouncing tumbling clittering clattering skittering fell on the heads and shoulders and hardhats and carapaces of the Timkin workers, tinkling on the slidewalk and bouncing away and rolling about underfoot and filling the sky on their way down with all the colors of joy and childhood and holidays, coming down in a steady rain, a solid wash, a torrent of color and sweetness out of the sky from above, and entering a universe of sanity and metronomic order with quite-mad coocoo newness. Jelly beans!

The shift workers howled and laughed and were pelted, and broke ranks, and the jelly beans managed to work their way into the mechanism of the slidewalks after which there was a hideous scraping as the sound of a million fingernails rasped down a quarter of a million blackboards, followed by a coughing and a sputtering, and then the slide-walks all stopped and everyone was dumped this away and that away in a jackstraw tumble, still laughing and popping little jelly bean eggs of childish color into their mouths. It was a holiday, and a jollity, an absolute insanity, a giggle. But ...

The shift was delayed seven minutes.

They did not get home for seven minutes.

The master schedule was thrown off by seven minutes.

Quotas were delayed by inoperative slidewalks for seven minutes.

He had tapped the first domino in the line, and one after another, like chik chik chik, the others had fallen.

The System had been seven minutes' worth of disrupted. It was a tiny matter, one hardly worthy of note, but in a society where the single driving force was order and unity and equality and promptness and clocklike precision and attention to the clock, reverence of the gods of the passage of time, it was a disaster of major importance.

So he was ordered to appear before the Ticktockman. It was broadcast across every channel of the communications web. He was ordered to be *there* at 7:00 dammit on time. And they waited, and they waited, but he didn't show up till almost ten-thirty, at which time he merely sang a little song about moonlight in a place no one had ever heard of, called Vermont, and vanished once again. But they had all been waiting since seven, and it wrecked *hell* with their schedules. So the question remained: Who is the Harlequin?

12 The Production of Space

Henri Lefebvre

Henri Lefebvre's *Production de l'espace* was originally published in 1974, and intermittently found its way into Anglo-American geographical discourse. However, since its English-language translation as *The Production of Space* in 1991, the book's influence has become pervasive. It is not an easy book to grasp in a single reading. Its argument is often dense and prolix; it digresses easily into sometimes arcane squabbles that have frequently fallen into disuse; and its pages promiscuously loop back to previously encountered concepts. Nevertheless, it remains a touchstone of contemporary thinking, and is indeed one of the most sustained meditations on space by a twentieth-century philosopher. In addition, it is permeated by insights that can be read as harbingers of postmodern thought (though some would dispute this claim). The extracts that follow are taken from the early sections of *The Production of Space*, where Lefebvre sets out the structure of his spatial problematic, what he initially refers to as a "science of space." One of the most innovative aspects of this presentation is Lefebvre's insistence that space is never "innocent." It always contains traces of the processes that produced it, and subsequently is acted upon by a variety of material and mental processes to provide the context through which we know things. Space, in this sense, is *constitutive* of our ontologies and epistemologies; and, space itself is a social product. From such beginnings, Lefebvre weaves an impressive, engaging tapestry about the "conceptual triad" of spatial practices, representations of space, and representational spaces, particularly as these relate to the production of urban space. Such concepts bring into question the way we "decode" space, which is a fundamental piece of the postmodern sensibilities of Fredric Jameson, Edward Soja, Michael Dear, and David Harvey (Readings 13–16).

IV

Epistemologico-philosophical thinking has failed to furnish the basis for a science which has been struggling to emerge for a very long time, as witness an immense accumulation of research and publication. That science is – or would be – a *science of space.* To date, work in this area has produced either mere descriptions which never achieve analytical, much less theoretical, status, or else fragments and cross-sections of space. There are plenty of reasons for thinking that descriptions and cross-sections of this kind, though they may well supply inventories of what *exists in* space, or even generate a *discourse on* space, cannot ever give rise to a *knowledge of* space. And, without such a knowledge, we are bound to transfer onto the level of discourse, of language *per se* – i.e. the level of mental space – a large portion of the attributes and "properties" of what is actually social space. [...]

V

Few people today would reject the idea that capital and capitalism "influence" practical matters relating to space, from the construction of buildings to the distribution of investments and the worldwide division of labour. But it is not so clear what is meant exactly by "capitalism" and "influence". What some have in mind is "money" and its powers of intervention, or commercial exchange, the commodity and its generalization, in that "everything" can be brought and sold. Others are concerned rather with the actors in these dramas: companies national and multinational, banks, financiers, government agencies, and so on. In either case both the unity and the diversity – and hence the contradictions – of capitalism are put in brackets. It is seen either as a mere aggregate of separate activities or else as an already constituted and closed system which derives its coherence from the fact that it endures – and solely from that fact. Actually capitalism has many facets: landed capital, commercial capital, finance capital – all play a part in practice according to their varying capabilities, and as opportunity affords; conflicts between capitalists of the same kind, or of different kinds, are an inevitable part of the process. These diverse breeds of capital, and of capitalists, along with a variety of overlapping markets – commodities, labour, knowledge, capital itself, land – are what together constitute capitalism.

Many people are inclined to forget that capitalism has yet another aspect, one which is certainly bound up with the functioning of money, with the various markets, and with the social relations of production, but which is distinct from these precisely because it is dominant. This aspect is the *hegemony* of one class. The concept of hegemony was introduced by Gramsci in order to describe the future role of the working class in the building of a new society, but it is also useful for analysing the action of the bourgeoisie, especially in relation to space. The notion is a refinement of the somewhat cruder concept of the "dictatorship" first of the bourgeoisie and then of the proletariat. Hegemony implies more than an influence, more even than the permanent use of repressive violence. It is exercised over society as a whole, culture and knowledge included, and generally via human mediation: policies, political leaders, parties, as also a good many intellectuals and experts. It is exercised, therefore, over both institutions and ideas. The ruling class seeks to maintain its hegemony by all available means, and knowledge is one such means. The connection between knowledge (*savoir*) and power is thus made manifest, although this in no way interdicts a critical and subversive form of knowledge (*connaissance*); on the contrary, it points up the antagonism between a knowledge which serves power and a form of knowing which refuses to acknowledge power.

It is conceivable that the exercise of hegemony might leave space untouched? Could space be nothing more than the passive locus of social relations, the milieu in which their combination takes on body, or the aggregate of the procedures employed in their removal? The answer must be no. Later on I shall demonstrate the active – the operational or instrumental – role of space, as knowledge and action, in the existing mode of production. I shall show how space serves, and how hegemony makes use of it, in the establishment, on the basis of an underlying logic and with the help of knowledge and technical expertise, of a "system". Does this imply the coming into being of a clearly defined space – a capitalist space (the world market) thoroughly purged of contradictions? Once again, the answer is no. Otherwise, the "system" would have a legitimate claim to immortality. Some over-systematic thinkers oscillate between loud denunciations of capitalism and the bourgeoisie and their repressive institutions on the one hand, and fascination and unrestrained admiration on the other. They make society into the "object" of a systematization which must be "closed" to be complete; they thus bestow a cohesiveness it utterly lacks upon a totality which is in fact decidedly open – so open, indeed, that it must rely on violence to endure. The position of these systematizers is in any case self-contradictory: even if their claims had some validity they would be reduced to nonsense by the fact that the terms and concepts used to define the system must necessarily be mere tools of that system itself.

VI

The theory we need, which fails to come together because the necessary critical moment does not occur, and which therefore falls back into the state of mere bits and pieces of knowledge, might well be called, by analogy, a "unitary theory": the aim is to discover or construct a theoretical unity between "fields" which are apprehended separately, just as molecular, electromagnetic and gravitational forces are in physics. The fields we are concerned with are, first, the *physical* – nature, the Cosmos; secondly, the *mental*, including logical and formal abstractions; and, thirdly, the *social*. In other words, we are concerned with logico-epistemological space, the space of social practice, the space occupied by sensory phenomena, including products of the imagination such as projects and projections, symbols and utopias.

The need for unity may be expressed in other ways too, ways that serve to underscore its importance. Reflection sometimes conflates and sometimes draws distinctions between those "levels" which social practice establishes, in the process raising the question of their interrelationships. Thus housing, habitation – the human "habitat", so to speak – are the concern of architecture. Towns, cities – urban space – are the bailiwick of the discipline of urbanism. As for larger, territorial spaces, regional, national, continental or worldwide, these are the responsibility of planners and economists. At times these "specializations" are telescoped into one another under the auspices of that privileged actor, the politician. At other times their respective domains fail to overlap at all, so that neither common projects nor theoretical continuity are possible.

This state of affairs, of which the foregoing remarks do not claim to be a full critical analysis, would be brought to an end if a truly unitary theory were to be developed.

Our knowledge of the material world is based on concepts defined in terms of the broadest generality and the greatest scientific (i.e. having a content) abstraction. Even if the links between these concepts and the physical realities to which they correspond are not always clearly established, we do know that such links exist, and that the concepts or theories they imply – energy, space, time – can be neither conflated nor separated from one another. What common parlance refers to as "matter", "nature" or "physical reality" – that reality within which even the crudest analysis must discern and separate different moments – has thus obviously achieved a certain unity. The "substance" (to use the old vocabulary of philosophy) of this cosmos or "world", to which humanity with its consciousness belongs, has properties that can be adequately summed up by means of the three terms mentioned above. When we evoke "energy", we must immediately note that energy has to be deployed within a space. When we evoke "space", we must immediately indicate what occupies that space and how it does so: the deployment of energy in relation to "points" and within a time frame. When we evoke "time", we must immediately say what it is that moves or changes therein. Space considered in isolation is an empty abstraction; likewise energy and time. Although in one sense this "substance" is hard to conceive of, most of all at the cosmic level, it is also true to say that evidence of its existence stares us in the face: our senses and our thoughts apprehend nothing else.

Might it not be possible, then, to found our knowledge of social practice, and the general science of so-called human reality, on a model borrowed from physics? Unfortunately not. For one thing, this kind of approach has always failed in the past. Secondly, following the physical model would prevent a theory of societies from using a number of useful procedures, notably the separation of levels, domains and regions. Physical theory's search for unity puts all the emphasis on the bringing-together of disparate elements. It might therefore serve as a guardrail, but never as a paradigm.

The search for a unitary theory in no way rules out conflicts within knowledge itself, and controversy and polemics are inevitable. This goes for physics, and mathematics too, for that matter; sciences that philosophers deem "pure" precisely because they have purged them of dialectical moments are not thereby immunized against internal conflicts.

It seems to be well established that physical space has no "reality" without the energy that is deployed within it. The modalities of this deployment, however, along with the physical relationships between central points, nuclei or condensations on the one hand and peripheries on the other are still matters for conjecture. A simple expanding-universe theory assumes an original dense core of matter and a primordial explosion. This notion of an original unity of the cosmos has given rise to many objections by reason of its quasi-theological or theogonic character. In opposition to it, Fred Hoyle has proposed a much more complex theory, according to which energy, whether at the level of the ultra-small or at that of the ultra-large, travels in every direction. On this view a single centre of the universe, whether original or final, is inconceivable. Energy/space–time condenses at an indefinite number of points (local space–times).

To the extent that the theory of supposedly human space can be linked at all to a physical theory, perhaps Hoyle's is the one which best fits the bill. Hoyle looks upon space as the product of energy. Energy cannot therefore be compared to a content filling an empty container. Causalism and teleology, inevitably shot through with metaphysical abstraction, are both ruled out. The universe is seen as offering a multiplicity of particular spaces, yet this diversity is accounted for by a unitary theory, namely cosmology.

This analogy has its limits, however. There is no reason to assume an isomorphism between social energies and physical energies, or between "human" and physical fields of force. This is one form of reductionism among others which I shall have occasion explicitly to reject. All the same, human societies, like living organisms human or extra-human, cannot be conceived of independently of the universe (or of the "world"); nor may cosmology, which cannot annex knowledge of those societies, leave them out of its picture altogether, like a state within the state. [...]

VIII

Everyone knows what is meant when we speak of a "room" in an apartment, the "corner" of the street, a "marketplace", a shopping or cultural "centre", a public "place", and so on. These terms of everyday discourse serve to distinguish, but not to isolate, particular spaces, and in general to describe a social space. They correspond to a specific use of that space, and hence to a spatial practice that they express and constitute. Their interrelationships are ordered in a specific way. Might it not be a good idea, therefore, first to make an inventory of them, and then to try and ascertain what paradigm gives them their meaning, what syntax governs their organization?

There are two possibilities here: either these words make up an unrecognized code which we can reconstitute and explain by means of thought; alternatively, reflection will enable us, on the basis of the words themselves and the operations that are performed upon them, to construct a *spatial code*. In either event, the result of our thinking would be the construction of a "system of space". Now, we know from precise scientific experiments that a system of this kind is applicable only indirectly to its "object", and indeed that it really only applies to a *discourse* on that object. The project I am outlining, however, does not aim to produce a (or *the*) discourse on space, but rather to expose the actual production of space by bringing the various kinds of space and the modalities of their genesis together within a single theory.

These brief remarks can only hint at a solution to a problem that we shall have to examine carefully later on in order to determine whether it is a *bona fide* issue or merely the expression of an obscure question about origins. This problem is: does language – logically, epistemologically or genetically speaking – precede, accompany or follow social space? Is it a precondition of social space or merely a formulation of it? The priority-of-language thesis has certainly not been established. Indeed, a good case can be made for according logical and epistemological precedence over highly articulated languages with strict rules to those activities which mark the earth, leaving traces and organizing gestures and work performed in common. Perhaps what have to be uncovered are as-yet concealed relations between space and language: perhaps the "logicalness" intrinsic to articulated language operated from the start as a spatiality capable of bringing order to the qualitative chaos (the practico-sensory realm) presented by the perception of things.

To what extent may *a* space be read or decoded? A satisfactory answer to this question is certainly not just around the corner. As I noted earlier, without as yet adducing supporting arguments or proof, the notions of message, code, information and so on cannot help us trace the genesis of a space; the fact remains, however, that an already produced space can be decoded, can be *read*. Such a space implies a process of signification. And even if there is no general code of space, inherent to language or to all languages, there may have existed specific codes, established at specific historical periods and varying in their effects. If so, interested "subjects", as members of a particular society, would have acceded by this means at once to *their* space and to their status as "subjects" acting within that space and (in the broadest sense of the word) comprehending it.

If, roughly from the sixteenth century to the nineteenth, a coded language may be said to have existed on the practical basis of a specific relationship between town, country and political territory, a language founded on classical perspective and Euclidean space, why and how did this coded system collapse? Should an attempt be made to reconstruct that language, which was common to the various groups making up the society – to users and inhabitants, to the authorities and to the technicians (architects, urbanists, planners)?

A theory can only take form, and be formulated, at the level of a "supercode". Knowledge cannot rightly be assimilated to a "well-designed" language, because it operates at the conceptual level. It is thus not a privileged language, nor a metalanguage, even if these notions may be appropriate for the "science of language" as such. Knowledge of space cannot be limited from the outset by categories of this kind. Are we looking, then, for a "code of codes"? Perhaps so, but this "meta" function of theory does not in itself explain a great deal. If indeed spatial codes have existed, each characterizing a particular spatial/social practice, and if these codifications have been *produced* along with the space corresponding to them, then the job of theory is to elucidate their rise, their role, and their demise. The shift I am proposing in analytic orientation relative to the work of specialists in this area ought by now to be clear: instead of emphasizing the rigorously formal aspect of codes, I shall instead be putting the stress on their dialectical character. Codes will be seen as part of a practical relationship, as part of an interaction between "subjects" and their space and surroundings. I shall attempt to trace the coming-into-being and disappearance of codings/decodings. My aim will be to highlight *contents* – i.e. the social (spatial) practices inherent to the forms under consideration. [...]

XII

(Social) space is a (social) product. This proposition might appear to border on the tautologous, and hence on the obvious. There is good reason, however, to examine it carefully, to consider its implications and consequences before accepting it. Many people will find it hard to endorse the notion that space has taken on, within the present mode of production, within society as it actually is, a sort of reality of its own, a reality clearly distinct from, yet much like, those assumed in the same global process by commodities, money and capital. Many people, finding this claim paradoxical, will want proof. The more so in view of the further claim that the space thus

produced also serves as a tool of thought and of action; that in addition to being a means of production it is also a means of control, and hence of domination, of power; yet that, as such, it escapes in part from those who would make use of it. The social and political (state) forces which engendered this space now seek, but fail, to master it completely; the very agency that has forced spatial reality towards a sort of uncontrollable autonomy now strives to run it into the ground, then shackle and enslave it. Is this space an abstract one? Yes, but it is also "real" in the sense in which concrete abstractions such as commodities and money are real. Is it then concrete? Yes, though not in the sense that an object or product is concrete. Is it instrumental? Undoubtedly, but, like knowledge, it extends beyond instrumentality. Can it be reduced to a projection – to an "objectification" of knowledge? Yes and no: knowledge objectified in a product is no longer coextensive with knowledge in its theoretical state. If space embodies social relationships, how and why does it do so? And what relationships are they?

It is because of all these questions that a thoroughgoing analysis and a full overall exposition are called for. This must involve the introduction of new ideas – in the first place the idea of a diversity or multiplicity of spaces quite distinct from that multiplicity which results from segmenting and cross-sectioning space *ad infinitum*. Such new ideas must then be inserted into the context of what is generally known as "history", which will consequently itself emerge in a new light.

Social space will be revealed in its particularity to the extent that it ceases to be indistinguishable from mental space (as defined by the philosophers and mathematicians) on the one hand, and physical space (as defined by practico-sensory activity and the perception of "nature") on the other. What I shall be seeking to demonstrate is that such a social space is constituted neither by a collection of things or an aggregate of (sensory) data, nor by a void packed like a parcel with various contents, and that it is irreducible to a "form" imposed upon phenomena, upon things, upon physical materiality. If I am successful, the social character of space, here posited as a preliminary hypothesis, will be confirmed as we go along. [...]

XIV· ·

As a programmatic foretaste of the topics I shall be dealing with later, I shall now review some of the implications and consequences of our initial proposition – namely, that (social) space is a (social) product.

The first implication is that (physical) natural space is disappearing. Granted, natural space was – and it remains – the common point of departure: the origin, and the original model, of the social process – perhaps even the basis of all "originality". Granted, too, that natural space has not vanished purely and simply from the scene. It is still the background of the picture; as decor, and more than decor, it persists everywhere, and every natural detail, every natural object is valued even more as it takes on symbolic weight (the most insignificant animal, trees, grass, and so on). As source and as resource, nature obsesses us, as do childhood and spontaneity, via the filter of memory. Everyone wants to protect and save nature; nobody wants to stand in the way of an attempt to retrieve its authenticity. Yet at the same time everything conspires to harm it. The fact is that natural space will soon be lost to view. Anyone so inclined may look over their shoulder and see it sinking below the horizon behind us. Nature is also becoming lost to *thought*. For what is nature? How can we form a picture of it as it was before the intervention of humans with their ravaging tools? Even the powerful myth of nature is being transformed into a mere fiction, a negative utopia: nature is now seen as merely the raw material out of which the productive forces of a variety of social systems have forged their particular spaces. True, nature is resistant, and infinite in its depth, but it has been defeated, and now waits only for its ultimate voidance and destruction.

XV

A second implication is that every society – and hence every mode of production with its subvariants (i.e. all those societies which exemplify the general concept – produces a space, its own space. The city of the ancient world cannot be understood as a collection of people and things in space; nor can it be visualized solely on the basis of a number of texts and treatises on the subject of space, even though some of these, as for example Plato's *Critias* and *Timaeus* or Aristotle's *Metaphysics A*, may be irreplaceable sources of knowledge. For the ancient city had its own spatial practice: it forged its own – *appropriated* – space. Whence the need for a study of that space which is able to apprehend it as such, in its genesis and its form, with its own specific time or times (the rhythm of daily life), and its particular centres and polycentrism (agora, temple, stadium, etc.).

The Greek city is cited here only as an example – as one step along the way. Schematically speaking, each society offers up its own peculiar space, as it were, as an "object" for analysis and overall theoretical explication. I say each society, but it would be more accurate to say each mode of production, along with its specific relations of production; any such mode of production may subsume significant variant forms, and this makes for a number of theoretical difficulties, many of which we shall run into later in the shape of inconsistencies, gaps and blanks in our general picture. How much can we really learn, for instance, confined as we are to Western conceptual tools, about the Asiatic mode of production, its space, its towns, or the relationship it embodies between town and country – a relationship reputedly represented figuratively or ideographically by the Chinese characters?

More generally, the very notion of social space resists analysis because of its novelty and because of the real and formal complexity that it connotes. Social space contains – and assigns (more or less) appropriate places to (i) the *social relations of reproduction*, i.e. the bio-physiological relations between the sexes and between age groups, along with the specific organization of the family; and (ii) the *relations of production*, i.e. the division of labour and its organization in the form of hierarchical social functions. These two sets of relations, production and reproduction, are inextricably bound up with one another: the division of labour has repercussions upon the family and is of a piece with it; conversely, the organization of the family interferes with the division of labour. Yet social space must discriminate between the two – not always successfully, be it said – in order to "localize" them.

To refine this scheme somewhat, it should be pointed out that in precapitalist societies the two interlocking levels of biological reproduction and socio-economic production together constituted social reproduction – that is to say, the reproduction of society as it perpetuated itself generation after generation, conflict, feud, strife, crisis and war notwithstanding. That a decisive part is played by space in this continuity is something I shall be attempting to demonstrate below.

The advent of capitalism, and more particularly "modern" neocapitalism, has rendered this state of affairs considerably more complex. Here *three* interrelated levels must be taken into account: (i) *biological reproduction* (the family); (ii) the *reproduction of labour power* (the working class *per se*); and (iii) the *reproduction of the social relations of production* – that is, of those relations which are constitutive of capitalism and which are increasingly (and increasingly effectively) sought and imposed as such. The role of space in this tripartite ordering of things will need to be examined in its specificity.

To make things even more complicated, social space also contains specific representations of this double or triple interaction between the social relations of production and reproduction. Symbolic representation serves to maintain these social relations in a state of coexistence and cohesion. It displays them while displacing them – and thus concealing them in symbolic fashion – with the help of, and onto the backdrop of, nature. Representations of the relations of reproduction are sexual symbols, symbols of male and female, sometimes accompanied, sometimes not, by symbols of age – of youth and of old age. This is a symbolism which conceals more than it reveals, the more so since the relations of reproduction are divided into frontal, public, overt – and hence coded – relations on the one hand, and, on the other, covert, clandestine and repressed relations which, precisely because they are repressed, characterize transgressions related not so much to sex *per se* as to sexual pleasure, its preconditions and consequences.

Thus space may be said to embrace a multitude of intersections, each with its assigned location. As for representations of the relations of production, which subsume power relations, these too occur in space: space contains them in the form of buildings, monuments and works of art. Such frontal (and hence brutal) expressions of these relations do not completely crowd out their more clandestine or underground aspects; all power must have its accomplices – and its police.

A conceptual triad has now emerged from our discussion, a triad to which we shall be returning over and over again.

1 *Spatial practice*, which embraces production and reproduction, and the particular locations and spatial sets characteristic of each social formation. Spatial practice ensures continuity and some degree of cohesion. In terms of social space, and of each member of a given society's relationship to that space, this cohesion implies a guaranteed level of *competence* and a specific level of *performance*.

2 *Representations of space*, which are tied to the relations of production and to the "order" which those relations impose, and hence to knowledge, to signs, to codes, and to "frontal" relations.

3 *Representational spaces*, embodying complex symbolisms, sometimes coded, sometimes not, linked to the clandestine or underground side of social life, as also to art (which may come eventually to be defined less as a code of space than as a code of representational spaces). [...]

XVII

The third implication of our initial hypothesis will take an even greater effort to elaborate on. If space is a product, our knowledge of it must be expected to reproduce and expound the process of production. The "object" of interest must be expected to shift from *things in space* to the actual *production of space*, but this formulation itself calls for much additional explanation. Both partial products located *in space* – that is, things – and discourse *on space* can henceforth do no more than supply clues to, and testimony about, this productive process – a process which subsumes signifying processes without being reducible to them. It is no longer a matter of the space of this or the space of that: rather, it is space in its totality or global aspect that needs not only to be subjected to analytic scrutiny (a procedure which is liable to furnish merely an infinite series of fragments and cross-sections subordinate to the analytic project), but also to be *engendered* by and within theoretical understanding. Theory *reproduces* the generative process – by means of a concatenation of concepts, to be sure, but in a very strong sense of the word: from within, not just from without (descriptively), and globally – that is, moving continually back and forth between past and present. The historical and its consequences, the "diachronic", the "etymology" of locations in the sense of what happened at a particular spot or place and thereby changed it – all of this becomes inscribed in space. The past leaves its traces; time has its own script. Yet this space is always, now and formerly, a *present* space, given as an immediate whole, complete with its associations and connections in their actuality. Thus production process and product present themselves as two inseparable aspects, not as two separable ideas. [...]

To follow this up further, let us return to the three concepts introduced earlier.

1 *Spatial practice*: The spatial practice of a society secretes that society's space; it propounds and presupposes it, in a dialectical interaction; it produces it slowly and surely as it masters and appropriates it. From the analytic standpoint, the spatial practice of a society is revealed through the deciphering of its space.

What is spatial practice under neocapitalism? It embodies a close association, within perceived space, between daily reality (daily routine) and urban reality (the routes and networks which link up the places set aside for work, "private" life and leisure). This association is a paradoxical one, because it includes the most extreme separation between the places it links together. The specific spatial competence and performance of every society member can only be evaluated empirically. "Modern" spatial practice might thus be defined – to take an extreme but significant case – by the daily life of a tenant in a government-subsidized high-rise housing project. Which should not be taken to mean that motorways or the politics of air transport can be left out of the picture. A spatial practice must have a certain cohesiveness, but this does not imply that it is coherent (in the sense of intellectually worked out or logically conceived).

2 *Representations of space*: conceptualized space, the space of scientists, planners, urbanists, technocratic subdividers and social engineers, as of a certain type of artist with a scientific bent – all of whom identify what is lived and what is perceived with what is conceived. (Arcane speculation about Numbers, with its talk of the

golden number, moduli and "canons", tends to perpetuate this view of matters.) This is the dominant space in any society (or mode of production). Conceptions of space tend, with certain exceptions to which I shall return, towards a system of verbal (and therefore intellectually worked out) signs.

3 *Representational spaces*:   space as directly *lived* through its associated images and symbols, and hence the space of "inhabitants" and "users", but also of some artists and perhaps of those, such as a few writers and philosophers, who *describe* and aspire to do no more than describe. This is the dominated – and hence passively experienced – space which the imagination seeks to change and appropriate. It overlays physical space, making symbolic use of its objects. Thus representational spaces may be said, though again with certain exceptions, to tend towards more or less coherent systems of non-verbal symbols and signs.

The (relative) autonomy achieved by space *qua* "reality" during a long process which has occurred especially under capitalism or neocapitalism has brought new contradictions into play. The contradictions within space itself will be explored later. For the moment I merely wish to point up the dialectical relationship which exists within the triad of the perceived, the conceived, and the lived.

13 Postmodernism, or, The Cultural Logic of Late Capitalism

Fredric Jameson

A pivotal moment in the genesis of postmodern human geography was the 1984 publication of Fredric Jameson's "Postmodernism, or the cultural logic of late capitalism." This long essay ranged widely over architecture, literature, art, video, Marxism, and cultural practices. But, for geographers, it was Jameson's emphasis on *space*, as a vital trope of postmodernism, that attracted most attention. There is much to reflect on in Jameson's rich meditations, most notably the notion that postmodernity represented a "radical break" in the social history and social practices of capitalist society, and his assertion that postmodernism (or postmodern theory) constituted a "new discursive genre." Taking his commitments from Lefebvre and Marxist theory, Jameson yet manages to identify the merits of antifoundationalist ways of thinking, with roots in poststructuralism as well as Jean-François Lyotard's *The Postmodern Condition* (1984). In the extract that follows, Jameson traces the origins of postmodern society, both as a "periodizing hypothesis" and a "cultural dominant." His theory of space, if it amounts to such, is scattered widely throughout the text, and geographers have carefully mined this essay for the elements that compose Jameson's putative "postmodern hyperspace." These include: a new depthlessness, a waning of affect, a decentering of the subject, and pastiche/collage. Our extract focuses on Jameson's bold interpretation of one "full-blown postmodern building" – John Portman's Bonaventure Hotel in Los Angeles – a bewildering edifice that Jameson uses as a formal metaphor for our immersion in the ambiguities of postmodernity. Cognitive mapping becomes, for Jameson, a key to understanding the putative postmodern hyperspace; he places particular emphasis on the language of architecture because of its "virtually unmediated" relationship with the capitalist political economy.

Introduction

As for *postmodernism* itself, I have not tried to systematize a usage or to impose any conveniently coherent thumbnail meaning, for the concept is not merely contested, it is also internally conflicted and contradictory. I will argue that, for good or ill, we cannot not use it. But my argument should also be taken to imply that every time it is used, we are under the obligation to rehearse those inner contradictions and to stage those representational inconsistencies and dilemmas; we have to work all that through every time around. *Postmodernism* is not something we can settle once and for all and then use with a clear conscience. The concept, if there is one, has to come at the end, and not at the beginning, of our discussions of it. Those are the conditions – the only ones, I think, that prevent the mischief of premature clarification – under which this term can productively continue to be used.[...]

The Cultural Logic of Late Capitalism

The last few years have been marked by an inverted millenarianism in which premonitions of the future, catastrophic or redemptive, have been replaced by senses of the end of this or that (the end of ideology, art, or social class; the "crisis" of Leninism, social democracy, or the welfare state, etc., etc.); taken together, all of these perhaps constitute what is increasingly called postmodernism. The case for its existence depends on the hypothesis of some radical break or *coupure*, generally traced back to the end of the 1950s or the early 1960s.

As the word itself suggests, this break is most often related to notions of the waning or extinction of the hundred-year-old modern movement (or to its ideological or aesthetic repudiation). Thus abstract expressionism in painting, existentialism in philosophy, the final forms of representation in the novel, the films of the great *auteurs*, or the modernist school of poetry (as institutionalized and canonized in the works of Wallace Stevens) all are now seen as the final, extraordinary flowering of a high-modernist impulse which is spent and exhausted with them. The enumeration of what follows, then, at once becomes empirical, chaotic, and heterogeneous: Andy Warhol and pop art, but also photorealism, and beyond it, the "new expressionism"; the moment, in music, of John Cage, but also the synthesis of classical and "popular" styles found in composers like Phil Glass and Terry Riley, and also punk and new wave rock (the Beatles and the Stones now standing as the high-modernist moment of that more recent and rapidly evolving tradition); in film, Godard, post-Godard, and experimental cinema and video, but also a whole new type of commercial film (about which more below); Burroughs, Pynchon, or Ishmael Reed, on the one hand, and the French *nouveau roman* and its succession, on the other, along with alarming new kinds of literary criticism based on some new aesthetic of textuality or *écriture*... The list might be extended indefinitely; but does it imply any more fundamental change or break than the periodic style and fashion changes determined by an older high-modernist imperative of stylistic innovation?

It is in the realm of architecture, however, that modifications in aesthetic production are most dramatically visible, and that their theoretical problems have been most centrally raised and articulated; it was indeed from architectural debates that my own conception of postmodernism – as it will be outlined in the following pages – initially began to emerge. More decisively than in the other arts or media, postmodernist positions in architecture have been inseparable from an implacable critique of architectural high modernism and of Frank Lloyd Wright or the so-called international style (Le Corbusier, Mies, etc), where formal criticism and analysis (of the high-modernist transformation of the building into a virtual sculpture, or monumental "duck," as Robert Venturi puts it[1] are at one with reconsiderations on the level of urbanism and of the aesthetic institution. High modernism is thus credited with the destruction of the fabric of the traditional city and its older neighborhood culture (by way of the radical disjunction of the new Utopian high-modernist building from its surrounding context), while the prophetic elitism and authoritarianism of the modern movement are remorselessly identified in the imperious gesture of the charismatic Master.

Postmodernism in architecture will then logically enough stage itself as a kind of aesthetic populism, as the very title of Venturi's influential manifesto, *Learning from Las Vegas*, suggests. However we may ultimately wish to evaluate this populist rhetoric, it has at least the merit of drawing our attention to one fundamental feature of all the postmodernisms enumerated above: namely, the effacement in them of the older (essentially high-modernist) frontier between high culture and so-called mass or commercial culture, and the emergence of new kinds of texts infused with the forms, categories, and contents of that very culture industry so passionately denounced by all the ideologues of the modern, from Leavis and the American New Criticism all the way to Adorno and the Frankfurt School. The postmodernisms have, in fact, been fascinated precisely by this whole "degraded" landscape of schlock and kitsch, of TV series and *Reader's Digest* culture, of advertising and motels, of the late show and the grade-B Hollywood film, of so-called paraliterature, with its airport paperback categories of the gothic and the romance, the popular biography, the murder mystery, and the science fiction or fantasy novel: materials they no longer simply "quote," as a Joyce or a Mahler might have done, but incorporate into their very substance.

Nor should the break in question be thought of as a purely cultural affair: indeed, theories of the postmodern – whether celebratory or couched in the language of moral revulsion and denunciation – bear a strong family resemblance to all those more ambitious sociological generalizations which, at much the same time, bring us the news of the arrival and inauguration of a whole new type of society, most famously baptized "postindustrial society" (Daniel Bell) but often also designated consumer society, media society, information society, electronic society or high tech, and the like. Such theories have the obvious ideological mission of demonstrating, to their own relief, that the new social formation in question no longer obeys the laws of classical capitalism, namely, the primacy of industrial production and the omnipresence of class struggle. The Marxist tradition has therefore resisted them with vehemence, with the signal exception of the economist Ernest Mandel, whose book *Late Capitalism* sets out not merely to anatomize the historic originality of this new society (which he sees as a third stage or moment in the evolution of capital) but also to demonstrate that it is, if anything, a *purer* stage of capitalism than any of the moments that preceded it. I will return to this argument later; suffice it for the moment to anticipate that every position on postmodernism in culture – whether apologia or stigmatization – is also at one and the same time, and *necessarily*, an implicitly or explicitly political stance on the nature of multinational capitalism today.

A last preliminary word on method: what follows is not to be read as stylistic description, as the account of one cultural style or movement among others. I have rather meant to offer a periodizing hypothesis, and that at a moment in which the very conception of historical periodization has come to seem most problematical indeed. I have argued elsewhere that all isolated or discrete cultural analysis always involves a buried or repressed theory of historical periodization; in any case, the conception of the "genealogy" largely lays to rest traditional theoretical worries about so-called linear history, theories of "stages," and teleological historiography. In the present context, however, lengthier theoretical discussion of such (very real) issues can perhaps be replaced by a few substantive remarks.

One of the concerns frequently aroused by periodizing hypotheses is that these tend to obliterate difference and to project an idea of the historical period as massive homogeneity (bounded on either side by inexplicable chronological metamorphoses and punctuation marks). This is, however, precisely why it seems to me essential to grasp postmodernism not as a style but rather as a cultural dominant: a conception which allows for the presence and coexistence of a range of very different, yet subordinate, features. [. . .]

V

· ·

Now I want to sketch an analysis of a full-blown postmodern building – a work which is in many ways uncharacteristic of that postmodern architecture whose principal proponents are Robert Venturi, Charles Moore, Michael Graves, and, more recently, Frank Gehry, but which to my mind offers some very striking lessons about the originality of postmodernist space. Let me amplify the figure which has run through the preceding remarks and make it even more explicit: I am proposing the notion that we are here in the presence of something like a mutation in built space itself. My implication is that we ourselves, the human subjects who happen into this new space, have not kept pace with that evolution; there has been a mutation in the object unaccompanied as yet by any equivalent mutation in the subject. We do not yet possess the perceptual equipment to match this new hyper-space, as I will call it, in part because our perceptual habits were formed in that older kind of space I have called the space of high modernism. The newer architecture therefore – like many of the other cultural products I have evoked in the preceding remarks – stands as something like an imperative to grow new organs, to expand our sensorium and our body to some new, yet unimaginable, perhaps ultimately impossible, dimensions.

The building whose features I will very rapidly enumerate is the Westin Bonaventure Hotel, built in the new Los Angeles downtown by the architect and developer John Portman, whose other works include the various Hyatt Regencies, the Peachtree Center in Atlanta, and the Renaissance Center in Detroit. I have mentioned the populist aspect of the rhetorical defense of postmodernism against the elite (and

Utopian) austerities of the great architectural modernisms: it is generally affirmed, in other words, that these newer buildings are popular works, on the one hand, and that they respect the vernacular of the American city fabric, on the other; that is to say, they no longer attempt, as did the masterworks and monuments of high modernism, to insert a different, a distinct, an elevated, a new Utopian language into the tawdry and commercial sign system of the surrounding city, but rather they seek to speak that very language, using its lexicon and syntax as that has been emblematically "learned from Las Vegas."

On the first of these counts Portman's Bonaventure fully confirms the claim: it is a popular building, visited with enthusiasm by locals and tourists alike (although Portman's other buildings are even more successful in this respect). The populist insertion into the city fabric is, however, another matter, and it is with this that we will begin. There are three entrances to the Bonaventure, one from Figueroa and the other two by way of elevated gardens on the other side of the hotel, which is built into the remaining slope of the former Bunker Hill. None of these is anything like the old hotel marquee, or the monumental porte cochere with which the sumptuous buildings of yesteryear were wont to stage your passage from city street to the interior. The entryways of the Bonaventure are, as it were, lateral and rather back-door affairs: the gardens in the back admit you to the sixth floor of the towers, and even there you must walk down one flight to find the elevator by which you gain access to the lobby. Meanwhile, what one is still tempted to think of as the front entry, on Figueroa, admits you, baggage and all, onto the second-story shopping balcony, from which you must take an escalator down to the main registration desk. What I first want to suggest about these curiously unmarked ways in is that they seem to have been imposed by some new category of closure governing the inner space of the hotel itself (and this over and above the material constraints under which Portman had to work). I believe that, with a certain number of other characteristic postmodern buildings, such as the Beaubourg in Paris or the Eaton Centre in Toronto, the Bonaventure aspires to being a total space, a complete world, a kind of miniature city; to this new total space, meanwhile, corresponds a new collective practice, a new mode in which individuals move and congregate, something like the practice of a new and historically original kind of hypercrowd. In this sense, then, ideally the minicity of Portman's Bonaventure ought not to have entrances at all, since the entryway is always the seam that links the building to the rest of the city that surrounds it: for it does not wish to be a part of the city but rather its equivalent and replacement or substitute. That is obviously not possible, whence the downplaying of the entrance to its bare minimum. But this disjunction from the surrounding city is different from that of the monuments of the International Style, in which the act of disjunction was violent, visible, and had a very real symbolic significance – as in Le Corbusier's great *pilotis*, whose gesture radically separates the new Utopian space of the modern from the degraded and fallen city fabric which it thereby explicitly repudiates (although the gamble of the modern was that this new Utopian space, in the virulence of its novum, would fan out and eventually transform its surroundings by the very power of its new spatial language). The Bonaventure, however, is content to "let the fallen city fabric continue to be in its being" (to parody Heidegger); no further effects, no larger protopolitical Utopian transformation, is either expected or desired.

Figure 1. Los Angeles' Bonaventure Hotel.

This diagnosis is confirmed by the great reflective glass skin of the Bonaventure, whose function I will now interpret rather differently than I did a moment ago when I saw the phenomenon of reflection generally as developing a thematics of reproductive technology (the two readings are, however, not incompatible). Now one would want rather to stress the way in which the glass skin repels the city outside, a repulsion for which we have analogies in those reflector sunglasses which make it impossible for your interlocutor to see your own eyes and thereby achieve a certain aggressivity toward and power over the Other. In a similar way, the glass skin achieves a peculiar and placeless dissociation of the Bonaventure from its neighborhood: it is not even an exterior, inasmuch as when you seek to look at the hotel's outer walls you cannot see the hotel itself but only the distorted images of everything that surrounds it.

Now consider the escalators and elevators. Given their very real pleasures in Portman, particularly the latter, which the artist has termed "gigantic kinetic sculptures" and which certainly account for much of the spectacle and excitement of the hotel interior – particularly in the Hyatts, where like great Japanese lanterns or gondolas they ceaselessly rise and fall – given such a deliberate marking and foregrounding in their own right, I believe one has to see such "people movers" (Portman's own term, adapted from Disney) as somewhat more significant than mere functions and engineering components. We know in any case that recent architectural theory has begun to borrow from narrative analysis in other fields and to attempt to see our physical trajectories through such buildings as virtual narratives or stories, as dynamic paths and narrative paradigms which we as visitors are asked to fulfill and to complete with our own bodies and movements. In the Bonaventure, however, we find a dialectical heightening of this process: it seems to me that the escalators and elevators here henceforth replace movement but also, and above all, designate themselves as new reflexive signs and emblems of movement proper (something which will become evident when we come to the question of what remains of older forms of movement in this building, most notably walking itself). Here the narrative stroll has been underscored, symbolized, reified, and replaced by a transportation machine which becomes the allegorical signifier of that older promenade we are no longer allowed to conduct on our own: and this is a dialectical intensification of the autoreferentiality of all modern culture, which tends to turn upon itself and designate its own cultural production as its content.

I am more at a loss when it comes to conveying the thing itself, the experience of space you undergo when you step off such allegorical devices into the lobby or atrium, with its great central column surrounded by a miniature lake, the whole positioned between the four symmetrical residential towers with their elevators, and surrounded by rising balconies capped by a kind of greenhouse roof at the sixth level. I am tempted to say that such space makes it impossible for us to use the language of volume or volumes any longer, since these are impossible to seize. Hanging streamers indeed suffuse this empty space in such a way as to distract systematically and deliberately from whatever form it might be supposed to have, while a constant busyness gives the feeling that *emptiness is here absolutely packed*, that it is an element within which you yourself are immersed, without any of that distance that formerly enabled the perception of perspective or volume. You are in this hyperspace up to your eyes and your body; and if it seemed before that that suppression of depth I spoke of in postmodern painting or literature would necessarily be difficult to achieve in architecture itself, perhaps this bewildering immersion may now serve as the formal equivalent in the new medium.[. . .]

So I come finally to my principal point here, that this latest mutation in space – postmodern hyperspace – has finally succeeded in transcending the capacities of the individual human body to locate itself, to organize its immediate surroundings perceptually, and cognitively to map its position in a mappable external world. It may now be suggested that this alarming disjunction point between the body and its built environment – which is to the initial bewilderment of the older modernism as the velocities of spacecraft to those of the automobile – can itself stand as the symbol and analogon of that even sharper dilemma which is the incapacity of our minds, at least at present, to map the great global multinational and decentered communicational network in which we find ourselves caught as individual subjects.

NOTE

1   Robert Venturi and Denise Scott-Brown, *Learning from Las Vegas*, (Cambridge, Mass. 1972).

14

Taking Los Angeles Apart: Some Fragments of a Critical Human Geography

Edward W. Soja

In 1986, in the same issue of *Society and Space*, the first sustained engagements between geography and postmodernism were published by Ed Soja and Michael Dear (Reading 15). In his contribution, Ed Soja invited us to plunge into postmodernity, and relish the insights and pure pleasure that result from indulging in new ways of seeing. His perambulation through Los Angeles (viewed the quintessential postmodern city) is a *tour-de-force*. In his decoding of the texts of the urban, *à la* Lefebvre and Jameson, Soja is simultaneously exuberant and outrageous, witty and perceptive. His voyage around the city is easy to understand, irresistible. This essay changed the way we see, think, and write about cities.

Los Angeles is tough-to-track, peculiarly resistant to conventional description. It is difficult to grasp persuasively in a temporal narrative, for it generates too many conflicting images, confounding historicization, always seeming to extend laterally instead of sequentially. At the same time, its spatiality challenges orthodox analysis and interpretation, for it too seems limitless and constantly in motion, never still enough to encompass. Looking at Los Angeles from the inside, one tends to see only fragments and immediacies, fixed islands of myopic understanding generalized to represent the whole. To the more far-sighted outsider, the visible aggregate, the whole of Los Angeles, churns so confusingly that it induces little more than stereotype and illusion, if it is seen at all.

What is this place? Even knowing where to focus, to find a starting point, is not easy, for perhaps more than any other place Los Angeles is *everywhere*. It is global in the fullest senses of the word. Nowhere is this more evident than in its cultural projection and ideological reach, its almost ubiquitous screening of itself as Dream Machine to the world. Los Angeles broadcasts its imagery so widely that probably more people have seen this place – or at least fragments of it – than any other on the planet. As a result, the seers of Los Angeles have become countless, even more so as the progressive globalization of its urban political economy flows along similar channels, making Los Angeles perhaps the epitomizing World-City, *une ville deve-nue monde*.

Everywhere seems also to be *in* Los Angeles. To it flows the bulk of the transpa-cific trade of the United States of America, a cargo which currently surpasses that of the smaller ocean to the east. Global currents of people, information, and ideas accompany the trade. Once dubbed Iowa's seaport, today Los Angeles has become an entrepôt to the world, a true pivot of the four quarters, a congeries of East and West, North and South. And from the teeming shores of every quarter has poured a pool of cultures so diverse that contemporary Los Angeles re-presents the world in urban microcosms, reproducing in situ the customs and ceremonies, the conflicts and confrontations, of a hundred homelands. [...]

A round around Los Angeles

Circumspection

Securing the Pacific rim has been the manifest destiny of Los Angeles, a theme which defines its urbanization perhaps more than any other analytical construct. Efforts to secure the Pacific signpost the history of Los Angeles from its smoky inception as El Pueblo de Nuestra Señora la Reina de Los Angeles de Porciuncula in 1781, through its heated competition for commercial and financial hegemony with San Francisco, to the unfolding sequence of Pacific wars that marked the past forty-five years. It is not always easy to see the imprint of this imperial history on the empirical land-scape, but a cruise directly above the contemporary circumference of the Sixty-Mile Circle can be unusually revealing.

The Circle cuts the south coast at the border between Orange and San Diego Counties, near one of the key checkpoints regularly set up to intercept the northward flow of undocumented migrants and not far from the San Clemente "White House" of Richard Nixon and the San Onofre nuclear power station. The first rampart to watch, however, is Camp Pendleton Marine Corps Base, the largest military base in California in terms of personnel, the freed spouses of whom have helped to build a growing high-technology complex in northern San Diego County (figure 1). After cruising over Camp Pendleton, the Cleveland National Forest, and the vital Color-ado River Aqueduct draining in from the east we can land directly on rampart number 2, March Air Force Base, adjacent to the City of Riverside. The insides of March are a major outpost for the Strategic Air Command.

Another quick hop over Sunnymead, the Box Spring Mountains, and Redlands takes us to rampart number 3, Norton Air Force Base, next to the city of San Bernardino and just south of the San Manuel Indian Reservation. The guide books tell us that the primary mission of Norton is military airlifts. To move on we must rise higher to pass over the ski-sloped peaks of the San Bernardino Mountains and National Forest, through Cajon Pass, and past the old Santa Fe Trail, into the Mojave Desert. Near Victorville is rampart number 4, George Air Force Base, specializing in air defense and interception. Almost the same distance away – our stops seem remarkably evenly spaced thus far – takes us by dry Mirage Lake to sprawling Edwards Air Force Base, rampart number 5, site of NASA (National

Aeronautics and Space Administration) and USAF (US Air Force) research and development activities and a landing field for the Space Shuttle. Stretching to the south is an important aerospace corridor through Lancaster, to Palmdale Airport and Air Force Plant 42, which serves the key historical function of Edwards as testing ground for advanced fighters and bombers.

The next leg is longer and more serene: over the Antelope Valley and the Los Angeles Aqueduct (tapping the Los Angeles-owned segments of the Owens River

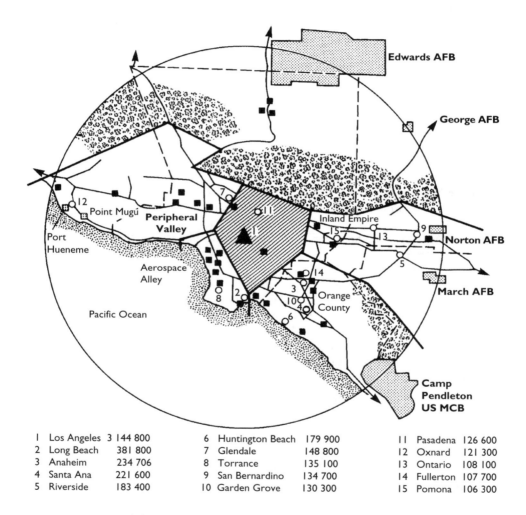

1	Los Angeles	3 144 800	6	Huntington Beach	179 900	11	Pasadena	126 600
2	Long Beach	381 800	7	Glendale	148 800	12	Oxnard	121 300
3	Anaheim	234 706	8	Torrance	135 100	13	Ontario	108 100
4	Santa Ana	221 600	9	San Bernardino	134 700	14	Fullerton	107 700
5	Riverside	183 400	10	Garden Grove	130 300	15	Pomona	106 300

Figure 1. A view of the outer spaces of Los Angeles. The urban core is outlined in the shape of a pentagon, with the Central city denoted by the black triangle. The major military bases on the perimeter of the Sixty-Mile circle are identified and the black squares are the sites of the largest defense contractors in the region. Also shown are the county boundaries, the freeway system outside the central pentagon, and the location of all cities with more than 1 000 000 inhabitants (small open circles).

Valley two hundred miles further away); across Interstate 5 (the main freeway corridor to the north), a long stretch of Los Padres National Forest and the Wild Condor Refuge, to the idyll-ized town of Ojai, and then to the Pacific again at the Mission of San Buenaventura, in Ventura County. A few miles away (the Sixty-Mile Circle actually cut right through the others) is rampart number 6, a complex consisting of a now inactive Air Force Base at Oxnard, the Naval Construction Battalion Center of Port Hueneme, and, above all, the longsighted Naval Air Missile Center at Point Mugu. If we wished, we could complete the full circle of coincidence over the Pacific, picking up almost directly below us the US Naval Facilities on San Nicolas and San Clemente Islands.

It is startling how much of the circumference is owned by the Federal Government in one way or another. Premeditation may be impossible to ascribe, but postmeditation on the circumscriptive federal presence is certainly in order.

Enclosures

What in the world lies behind this Herculean wall? What appears to need such formidable protection? In essence, we return to the same question with which we began: what is this place? There is, of course, the far-reaching Dream Machine and its launching pads, transmitting visual images and evocative sounds of that "good life" announced on the facade of City Hall. But the "entertainment" industry is itself a facade and significant though it may be, there is much more being screened behind it, much more that has developed within the Sixty-Mile Circle that demands to be protected.

If there has emerged a compelling focus to the recent academic literature on Los Angeles, it is the discovery of extraordinary industrial production, a eureka so contrary to popular cognition of Los Angeles that its explorers are often compelled to exaggerate to keep their lines of vision open and clear. Yet it is no exaggeration to claim that the Sixty-Mile Circle contains the premier industrial growth pole of the 20th century, at least within the advanced capitalist countries. Oil, agriculture, films, and flying set the scene at the beginning of the century and tend to remain fixed in many contemporary images of industrious, but not industrial, Los Angeles. Since 1930, however, Los Angeles has probably led all other major metropolitan areas in the USA, decade by decade, in the accumulation of new manufacturing employment. Around 250 000 manufacturing jobs were added in the 1940s, nearly 400 000 in the 1950s, another 200 000 in the 1960s and, during a decade when the net increase for the entire country was not more than a million, an estimated 225 000 in the 1970s. There has been somewhat of a slowdown in the 1980s, but not enough to prevent the Sixty-Mile Circle from finally surpassing the twenty-six-county Greater New York Area in total manufacturing employment. [. . .]

Apparently invisible, hidden from view, was not only one of the historical source regions for advanced technology in aerospace and electronics, but also what may well be the largest concentration of high-technology industry and employment in the country if not the world, the foremost Silicon Landscape.

Even excluding aerospace, the generative core of the region's high-technology sector, Los Angeles County alone today employs over 250 000 people in the Bureau of Labor Statistics "Group 3" category, a widely used definition of "high tech", versus about 160 000 in Santa Clara County, heart of the image-fixing Silicon Valley. With aerospace included, the Sixty-Mile Circle had *added* during the 1970s an employment pool in high-technology industries almost equivalent to that of the entire Silicon Valley at the end of the decade.

Still partially hidden behind these statistics are the primary generative agencies, the intricate processes producing this preeminent production complex. One key link, however, is abundantly clear. Over the past half century, no other area has been so pumped with federal money as Los Angeles, via the Department of Defense to be sure, but also through numerous federal programs subsidizing suburban consumption (suburbsidizing?) and the development of housing, transportation, and water delivery systems. From the last Great Depression to the present, Los Angeles has been the prototypical Keynesian state-city, a federalized metro-sea of state-rescued capitalism enjoying its place in the sun, demonstrating decade by decade its redoubtable ability to go first and multiply the public seed money invested in its promising economic landscape. No wonder it remains so protected. In it are embedded many of the crown jewels of advanced industrial capitalism.

If anything, the federal flow is accelerating today, under the aegis of the military Keynesianism of the Reagan Administration and the permanent arms economy. At Hughes Aircraft Company in El Segundo, engineers have already used some of the $60 million in prime Star Wars contracts to mock up a giant infrared sensor so acute that it can pick up the warmth of a human body at a distance of a thousand miles in space, part of their experimentation with "kinetic" weapons systems. Nearby, TRW Inc. ($84 million) and Rockwell International's Rocketdyne division ($32 million) competitively search for more powerful space lasers, capable it seems of incinerating whole cities if necessary, under such project code-names as Miracl, Alpha, and Rachel. Research houses such as the Rand Corporation, just to the north in Santa Monica, jockey for more strategic positions, eager to claim part of what could potentially reach a total of $1.5 trillion (Sanger, 1985). Today, not only the Pacific is being secured and watched over from inside the Sixty-Mile Circle.

Outer spaces

The effulgent Star Wars colony currently blooming around Los Angeles International Airport (LAX) is part of a much larger "Outer City" which has taken shape along the Pacific slope of Los Angeles County. In the context of this landscape, through the story line of the aerospace industry, can be read the explosive history and geography of the National Security State and what Davis (1984) has called the "Californianization" of Late-Imperial America.

If there is a single birthplace for this Californianization, it can be found at old Douglas Field in Santa Monica, today close by an important transit-point for President Reagan's frequent West Coast trips. From this spot fifty years ago the first DC-3 took off to begin a career of military accomplishment in war after war after war. Spinning off in its tracks has been an intricate tracery of links, from defense and space-related expenditures on research and development, and the associated formation of the aerospace industry in the wake of civilian aircraft manufacturing; to the instigation of computerized electronics and modern information-processing technology, building upon an ancillary network of suppliers and demanders of goods and services which stretches out to virtually every sector of the contemporary economy and society. Over half a million people now live in this "Aerospace Alley", as it has come to be called. During working hours, perhaps 800 000 are present to sustain its preeminence. Many millions more lie within its orbit.

Attached around the axes of production are the representative locales of the industrialized Outer City: the busy international airport; corridors filled with new office buildings, hotels, and global shopping malls; neatly packaged playgrounds and leisure villages; specialized and master-planned residential communities for the high technocracy; armed and guarded housing estates for top professionals and executives; residual communities of low-pay service workers living in overpriced homes; and the accessible enclaves and ghettoes which provide dependable flows of the cheapest labor power to the bottom bulge of the bimodal local labor market (specialized scientists and engineers filling the smaller bulge at the top). The LAX-City compage reproduces the segmentation and segregation of the Inner City based on race, class, and ethnicity, but manages to break it down still further to fragment residential communities according to specific occupational categories, household composition, and a broad range of individual attributes, affinities, and intended life-styles.

This extraordinary differentiation, fragmentation, and social control over specialized pools of labor is expensive. Housing prices and rental costs in the Outer City are easily among the highest in the country and the provision of appropriate housing increasingly absorbs the energy not only of the army of real estate agents but of local corporate and community planners as well, often at the expense of long-time residents fighting to maintain their foothold. From the give and take of this competition have emerged peculiarly intensified urban landscapes. Along the shores of the South Bay, for example, part of what Banham (1971) once called "Surfurbia", there has developed the largest and most homogenous residential enclave of scientists and engineers in the world. Coincidentally, this beachhead of the high technocracy is also the most formidable racial redoubt in the region. Although just a few miles away, across the fortifying boundary of the San Diego Freeway, is the edge of the largest and most tightly segregated concentration of blacks west of Chicago, the sun-belted beach communities stretching south from the airport have remained almost 100% white.

The Sixty-Mile Circle is ringed with a series of these Outer Cities at varying stages of development, each a laboratory for exploring the contemporaneity of capitalist urbanization. At least two are combined in Orange County, meshing together into the largest and probably fastest growing Outer City compage in the country. The key nucleus here is the industrial complex embedded in the land empire of the Irvine Company, which owns one sixth of the entire county. Arrayed around it is a remarkable accretion of master-planned New Towns which paradigmatically evince the global cultural inspirations of the Outer City imposed atop local visions of the experimental community of tomorrow. [...]

The Orange County compage has also been the focus for detailed research into the high-technology industrial complexes which have been recentralizing the urban fabric of the Los Angeles region and inducing the florescence of master-planned New Towns. The pioneering work of Scott, for example, has helped us see more clearly the transactional web of industrial linkages which draw out and geographically cluster specialized networks of firms, feed off the flow of federal contracts, and spill over to precipitate a supportive local space economy (Scott, 1986). What has been provided is a revealing glimpse into the generative processes behind the urbanization of Orange County and, through this window, into the deeper historical interplay between industrialization and urbanization that has defined the development of the capitalist city wherever it is found.

There are other Outer Cities fringing the older urbanized core. One has taken shape in the Ventura Corridor through the west San Fernando Valley into Ventura County (now being called the "Peripheral Valley", with its primary cores in "Gallium Gulch" and the Chatsworth area). Another is being promoted (although not yet achieved) in the "Inland Empire" stretching eastward from Pomona (General Dynamics is there) through Ontario (with Lockheed and a growing international airport and free trade zone) to the county seats of San Bernardino and Riverside, hard by their military ramparts (see figure 1).

As Scott's work in particular has helped us see, these new compages seem to be turning the industrial city inside out, recentering the urban to transform the metropolitan periphery into the core region of advanced industrial production. Decentralization from the Inner City has been taking place selectively for at least a century all over the world, but only recently has the peripheral condensation become sufficiently dense to challenge the older urban cores as centers of industrial production, employment nodality, and urbanism. This restructuring process is far from being completed, but it is beginning to have some profound repercussions on the way we think about the city, on the words we use to describe urban forms and functions, and on the language of urban theory.

Back to the Center

To see more of Los Angeles, it is necessary to move in from the periphery and return, literally and figuratively, to the center of things, to the still adhesive core of the urbanized landscape. In Los Angeles, as in every city, the nodality of the center defines and gives substance to the *specificity* of the urban, its distinctive social and spatial meaning. Urbanization and the spatial divisions of labor associated with it revolve around a socially constructed pattern of nodality and the power of the occupied centers to both cluster and disperse, to centralize and decentralize, to structure spatially all that is social and socially produced. Nodality *situates* and *contextualizes* urban society by giving material form to essential social relations.

It is easy to overlook the tendential processes of urban structuration that emanate from the center, especially in the late-modern capitalist city. Indeed, in contemporary societies the authoritative and allocative power of the center is purposefully obscured or, alternatively, detached from place, ripped out of context, and given the appearance of democratic ubiquity. In addition, as we have seen, the historical development of urbanization of the past century has been marked by a selective dispersal and decentralization, emptying the center of many of the activities and populations which once aggregated densely around it. For some, this has signalled a negation of nodality, an age of peripheral urbanization, the submergence of the power of place.

Yet the centers *hold*. Even as some things fall apart, dissipate, new nodalities form and old ones are reinforced. The centrifuge is always spinning, but centripetal nodality never disappears. And it is the persistent residual of political power which continues to precipitate, specify, and contextualize the urban. Cities originated with the simultaneous concentration of commanding symbolic forms, *civic* centers designed to ceremonialize, administer, acculturate, and control. In and around the institutionalized locale of the *citadel* adhered people and their ordered social relations, creating a *civil* society and an accordingly built environment which were urbanized and regionalized through the interplay between two interactive processes, *surveillance* and *adherence*, looking out from and in towards the center. To be urbanized still means to adhere, to be made an adherent, a believer in a specified ideology rooted in extensions of *polis* (politics, policy, polity, police) and *civitas* (civil, civic, citizen, civilian, civilization). To maintain adhesiveness, the civic center has always served as a key surveillant node of the state, supervising locales of production, consumption, and exchange. It still continues to do so, even after centuries of urban recomposition and restructuring. It is not production or consumption or exchange in themselves that specify the urban, but rather their collective surveillance, supervision, and anticipated control within the powerful context of nodality.

This does not mean that a mechanical determinism is assigned to nodality in the specification of the urban. Adherence is a sticky notion and is not automatically enacted by location in an urbanized landscape; nor is it always awarely expressed in practical consciousness. Surveillance too is problematic, for it can exist without being embracingly effective. There is always room for resistance, rejection, and redirection in the nonetheless structured arena of the urban, creating an active politics of nodal spatiality, struggles for place, space, and position within the regionalized urban landscape. Adherence and surveillance are thus unevenly developed in their geographical manifestations, their regionalization. Simultaneously, this patterned differentiation, this immediate superstructure of the urban spatial division of labor, becomes a critical arena in which the human geography of the city is shaped.

Recentralization

The Downtown core of the City of Los Angeles – signs call it Central City – is the agglomerative and symbolic nucleus of the Sixty-Mile Circle, certainly the oldest but in other ways also the newest major node in the region. Given what is contained within the Circle, the physical size and appearance of Downtown Los Angeles seem modest, even today after a period of enormous expansion. As usual, however, appearances can be deceptive.

Perhaps more than ever before, Downtown serves in ways no other place can as a strategic vantage point, an urban panopticon counterposed to the encirclement of watchful military ramparts and militarized Outer Cities. Like the central well in Bentham's eminently utilitarian design for a circular prison, the original panopticon,

Downtown can be seen (when visibility permits) by each separate individual, from each territorial cell, within its orbit. Only from the advantageous outlook of the center, however, can the surveillant see everyone collectively, disembedded but interconnected. Not surprisingly, from its origin, the Central City has been an aggregation of overseers, a primary locale for social control, political administration, cultural codification, ideological surveillance and the incumbent regionalization of its adherent hinterland. [...]

What stands out from a hard look at the Inner City seems almost like an obverse (and perverse) reflection of the Outer City, an agglomerative compage of dilapidated and overcrowded housing, low-technology workshops, relics and residuals of an older urbanization, a sprinkling of niches for recentered professionals and supervisors, and above all the largest concentration of cheap, culturally splintered, occupationally manipulable Third World immigrant labor to be found so tangibly available in any First World urban region. Here then is another of the manufactured crown jewels of Los Angeles, carefully watched over, maintained, and reproduced to service the continued development of the region.

The degree and persistence of simultaneous concentration here in Downtown Los Angeles cannot be ignored either by participants or by observers. The industrialization of the periphery may be turning the production space of the region inside out, but the old center is more than holding its own as the preeminent political and economic citadel. [...]

Lateral Extensions

Population densities do mound up around the centers of cities, even in the polycentric archipelago of Los Angeles (where there may be several dozen such mounds, although the most pronouned still falls off from the Central City). There is also an accompanying concentric residential rhythm associated with the family life cycle and the relative premiums placed on access to the dense peaks versus the availability of living space in the sparseness of the valleys for those who can afford such freedoms of choice. Land values (when they can be accurately calculated) and some job densities also tend to follow in diminishing peaks outward from the center, reminiscent of those tented webs of the urban geography textbooks.

Adding direction to the decadence of distance reduces the Euclidian elegance of concentric gradations, and many of the most mathematical of urban theoreticians have accordingly refused to follow this path. But direction does induce another fit, by pointing out the emanation of fortuitous wedges or sectors out from the center. The sectoral wedges of Los Angeles are especially pronounced once you leave the inner circle around Downtown.

The Wilshire Corridor extends the citadels of the Central City almost twenty miles westwards to the Pacific, picking up several other prominent but smaller downtowns en route (the Miracle Mile which initiated this extension, Beverly Hills, Century City, Westwood, Brentwood, Santa Monica). Watching above it is an even lengthier wedge of the wealthiest residences, running with almost staggering homogeneities to the Pacific Palisades and the privatized beaches of Malibu, sprinkled with announcements of armed responsiveness and signs which say that "trespassers will be shot".

As if in counterbalance, on the other side of the tracks east of Downtown is the salient of the largest Latino *barrio* in Anglo-America, where many of those who might be shot are carefully imprisoned. And there is at least one more prominent wedge, stretching southward from Downtown to the twin ports of Los Angeles–Long Beach and reputed to be one of the largest consistently industrial urban sectors in the world. This is the primary axis of Ruhral Los Angeles.

A third ecological order perturbs the geometrical neatness still further, punching wholes into the monocentric gradients and wedges based on the segregation of races and ethnicities. Segregation is so noisy that it overloads the conventional statistical methods of urban factorial ecology with scores of tiny but "significant" components. In Los Angeles, arguably the most segregated city in the country, these components are so numerous that they operate statistically to obscure the spatiality of social class relations deeply embedded in the zones and wedges of the urban landscape, as if they needed to be obscured any further. [...]

Deconstruction

Back in the center, shining from its circular turrets of bronzed glass, stands the Bonaventure Hotel, an amazingly storeyed architectural symbol of the splintered labyrinth that stretches sixty miles around it. Like many other Portman-teaus which dot the eyes of urban citadels in New York and San Francisco, Atlanta and Detroit, the Bonaventure has become a concentrated representation of the restructured spatiality of the Late Capitalist city: fragmented and fragmenting, homogeneous and homogenizing, divertingly packaged yet curiously incomprehensible, seemingly open in presenting itself to view but constantly pressing to enclose, to compartmentalize, to circumscribe. Everything imaginable appears to be available in this micro-urb, but real places are difficult to find, its spaces confuse an effective cognitive mapping, its pastiche of superficial reflections bewilder coordination and encourage submission instead. Entry by land is forbidding to those who walk but do not drive, but entrance is nevertheless encouraged at many different levels, from the truly pedestrian skyways above to the bunker-like inlets below. Once in, however, it becomes daunting to get out again without assistance. In so many ways, architecture recapitulates and reflects the sprawling manufactured environments of Los Angeles.

There has been no conspiracy of design behind the building of the Bonaventure or the socially constructed spatiality of the New World Cities. Both designs have been conjunctural, reflecting the specifications and exigencies of time and place, of period and region. Thus the Bonaventure both simulates the restructured landscape of Los Angeles and is simulated by it. From this interpretive interplay emerges an alternative way of looking at the human geography of contemporary Los Angeles.

From the center to the periphery, in both Inner and Outer Cities, the Sixty-Mile Circle today encloses a shattered metro-sea of fragmented yet homogenized communities, cultures, and economies confusingly arranged into a contingently ordered spatial division of labor. As is true for so much of the patterning of 20th century urbanization, Los Angeles both sets the historical pace and most vividly epitomizes the extremes of contemporary expression. Municipal boundary-making and territorial incorporation, for example, have produced the most extraordinary crazy quilt of opportunism to be found in any metropolitan area. Tiny enclaves of country land and whole cities such as Beverly Hills, West Hollywood, and Santa Monica pockmark the "Westside" bulk of the incorporated City of Los Angeles, and thin slivers of City land reach out like tentacles to grab onto the key seaside outlets of the port at San Pedro and Los Angeles International Airport Nearly half the population of the City, however, lives in the quintessentially suburban San Fernando Valley, one and a half million people who statistically are counted as part of the Central City of the Los Angeles–Long Beach SMSA (Standard Metropolitan Statistical Area). Few other places make such a mockery of the standard classifications of urban, suburban, and exurban. [...]

For at least fifty years, Los Angeles has been defying conventional categorical description of the urban, of what is city and what is suburb, of what can be identified as community or neighbourhood, of what copresence means in the urban context. It has in effect deconstructed the urban into a confusing collage of signs which advertise what are often little more than nominal communities and outlandish representations of urban location. There remain an economic order, a nodal structure, an essentially exploitative spatial division of labor, and this spatially organized urban system has for the past half century been more continuosly productive than almost any other. But it is increasingly obscured from view, imaginatively mystified in an environment more specialized in the production of encompassing mystifications than practically any other. And as so often has been the case in the USA, deconstruction is accompanied by a numbing depoliticization of fundamental class relations and conflicts when all that is seen is so fragmented and filled with whimsy.

With exquisite irony, contemporary Los Angeles has come to resemble more than ever before a gigantic agglomeration of theme parks, a region comprised of Disney-worlds divided into showcases of global cultures and mimetic American landscapes, all-embracing shopping malls and main streets, corporation-sponsored magic kingdoms, high-technology-based experimental prototype communities of tomorrow, attractively packaged places for rest and recreation, all cleverly hiding the buzzing workstations and labor processes which help to keep it together. Like the original "Happiest Place on Earth", the enclosed spaces are subtly but tightly controlled by overseers, despite the open appearance of fantastic freedoms of choice. The experience of living here can be extremely diverting and exceptionally enjoyable, especially for those who can afford to remain inside for a sufficient length of time. And, of course, the enterprise has been enormously profitable over the years. After all, it was built on what began as relatively cheap land, has been sustained by a constantly replenishing army of even cheaper imported labor, is filled with the most modern technological gadgetry, enjoys extraordinary levels of protection and surveillance, and runs under the smooth aggression of the most efficient management systems, almost always capable of delivering what is promised just in time.

Synthesis?

I have looked at Los Angeles from many different points of view and each in part assists in sorting out the interjacent medley of the subject landscape. The perspectives explored are purposeful, eclectic, fragmentary, incomplete, and frequently contradictory, but so too is Los Angeles and, indeed, the experienced historical geography of every urban landscape. Totalizing visions, attractive though they may be, can never capture all the meanings and significations of the urban when the landscape is critically read as a fulsome geographical text. There are too many *auteurs* to identify, the *literalité* (materiality?) of the manufactured environment is too multilayered to be allowed to speak for itself, and the countervailing metaphors and metonyms frequently clash like discordant symbols drowing out the underlying themes. More seriously, we still know too little about the grammar and syntax of human geographies, the phonemes and epistemes of spatial interpretation. We are constrained by language much more than we know: what we can see in Los Angeles and in the spatiality of social life is stubbornly simultaneous, but what we write down is successive, because language is successive.

There is hope nonetheless. The critical and theoretical reading of geographical landscapes has recently expanded into realms that functionally had been spatially illiterate for most of the 20th century. New readers abound as never before, many are directly attuned to the specificity of the urban, and several have significantly turned their eyes to Los Angeles. Moreover, many practiced readers of surface geographies have begun to see through the alternatively myopic and hypermetropic distortions of past perspectives to bring new insight to spatial analysis and social theory (Soja, 1985). Here too Los Angeles has attracted observant readers after a history of neglect and misapprehension, for it insistently presents itself as palimpsest and paradigm of 20th century urban-industrial development and popular consciousness.

REFERENCES

Banham R, 1971 *Los Angeles: The Architecture of Four Ecologies* (Harper and Row, New York)

Davis M, 1984, "The political economy of Late Imperial America" *New Left Review* **143**, 6–38

Sanger D, 1985, "Star Wars industry rises" *New York Times* 19 November, Business Day, pp 25, 32

Scheer R, 1983, "California wedded to military economy but bliss is shaky" *Los Angeles Times* 10 July, part VI, pp 13, 14

Scott A, 1986, "High technology industry and territorial development: the rise of the Orange County Complex, 1955–1984" *Urban Geography* 7 3–45

Soja E W, 1985, "The spatiality of social life: towards a transformative retheorization" in *Social Relations and Spatial Structures* Eds D Gregory, J Urry (Macmillan, London) pp 90–127

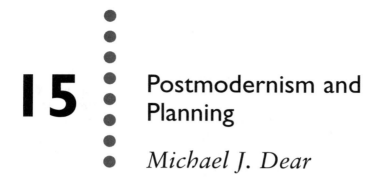

15 Postmodernism and Planning

Michael J. Dear

Michael Dear's 1986 essay on postmodern planning appeared in the same issue of *Society and Space* alongside Soja's excursion in Los Angeles (Reading 14). It was here that Dear first spelled out his understanding of postmodernism as style, epoch, and philosophy/method (a distinction that is explained in more detail on pages 4–6 of this Reader.) Like Soja, Dear wanted to show how the precepts of post-modern thought could change the way we read cities. In deconstructing city-making ideologies of the latter part of the twentieth century, he uncovered the changing intentionalities behind public intervention in the urban process, thereby foreshadowing the altered rationalities of a distinctly "postmodern urbanism" (Reading 21).

Deconstructing Planning

We can begin to conquer the complexity and opacity of contemporary planning by deconstructing its primary texts: the city, theory, and practice. In the scope of this paper. I can only encompass the texts of theory. [See Soja (1986) for a textual analysis of Los Angeles.] How do we begin to judge discourse in planning theory? We can follow Derrida's contention "that thought can break with its delusive prehistory only by constantly and actively rehearsing that break" (Norris, 1982, page 127).

In this section, I outline a cognitive map of planning knowledge for the period 1945–85. This social history focuses on the broad experiences of the USA, Britain, and Canada during this period (Figure 1).

A cognitive map of planning knowledge

1945–60: Postwar reconstruction and the preeminence of physical land-use planning The period following World War 2 was one of massive physical and social reconstruction.

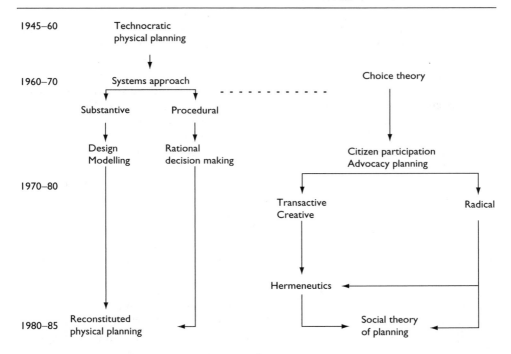

Figure 1.   A social history of planning knowledge 1945–85.

In Western Europe, extensive war damage meant that nations were necessarily preoccupied with the rebuilding efforts. It was this period that spawned, for example, the British new town legislation which was to provide an important model for controlled urban growth for the next four decades of development in Western Europe. In Canada, cities such as Toronto tentatively moved toward large-scale comprehensive metropolitan plans. In the USA, which had not suffered significant physical destruction through war, new federal initiatives were undertaken especially in the field of housing. In short, the early postwar years were a period in which an extensive (renewed) mandate was granted for state intervention in the land and property development process. In North America, it was time when the incipient planning profession consolidated its physical land-use planning identity.

1960–70: The new scientism and the rise of popular planning   The decade of the 1960s was a time of remarkable ferment in planning. Two major philosophies were to impact the discipline: first, a new scientism which suggested that planning could and should take on the methodologies of the natural sciences; and, second, a new concern with populism in planning, which arose largely out of a worldwide surge in participatory democratic politics, and the consequent crisis in the profession's sense of legitimacy.

The new scientism which shook most social sciences in the 1960s was represented in planning as a commitment to systems theory. It provoked a fundamental shift toward rationality and was the initial impetus toward the substantive–procedural rift in planning. The substantive focus (on the objects being planned) served to propel the existing practice of land-use planning toward a more "scientific" approach akin to the rationality of engineering or architectural building methods. The rational substantive approach received a strong reinforcement and consolidation through the advent of mathematical model-building in planning. The use of quantitative methods in computer-based, large-scale land-use and transportation models was particularly prominent in the USA. It provided a considerable legitimacy for believers in the scientific method of planning. This was further reinforced by the spillover from computer-assisted methods of architectural design.

The movement toward scientific planning was accelerated by what was initially perceived as a competing theoretical domain. Procedural theories of planning also derived from rational systems models. However, as applied to planning, they laid emphasis on the administrative and managerial context of planning decisions. They sought to establish rules of rational decisionmaking and to pursue the reasons for irrationality in the practice of planning. Although many writers later pointed to the damaging effects of the procedural–substantive dichotomy, and the ultimate need for both in planning, the dichotomy had a strong appeal for protagonists in each camp. Its legacy persists to the present day.

As well as being a decade of scientific optimism, the 1960s was also a highly charged political decade. In planning, this took the form of growing citizens' involvement in planning decisions within the general context of an increasingly participatory democratic politics. Very importantly, at the same time, professional planners began a deep search for their sources of legitimacy. A loose coalition of essentially liberal-minded planners rallied under the banner of a "choice theory" of planning. This somewhat ill-defined theory emphasized the significance of citizen choice in, and even control over, planning decisions. As it became obvious that citizen participation did not significantly alter the balance of power in development decisions, advocacy planning enjoyed a relatively brief vogue as a means of enfranchising citizen groups. The net effect of 1960s populism was to place planning irrevocably on the political agenda. Perhaps in no period since has the structure of political power been so rawly exposed as in these early community battles.

1970–80: The emergence of a critical left   The optimism and prosperity of the 1960s spilled over into the early years of the next decade. In this more committed, relatively tolerant climate, two overtly ideological concepts of planning emerged. The first was the movement toward transactive or creative planning: the second was a more radical critique – a firestorm of criticism ignited by a rejection of both the transactive philosophy and the studied apoliticism of the rationalists. The transactive–creative approach in planning emphasized "mutual learning", a creative use of a community's intelligence and planners' skills to invent the urban future. The lineage of this approach can be directly traced to an underlying belief in rationality and a commitment to involving communities in planning their futures. Transactive–creative planning was essentially an atheoretical view of planning, and as such, it was uncomfortable for those who did not share its essentially liberal-democratic ideology.

The radical critique which resurfaced in the mid-1970s was largely provoked by the perceived inadequacy of the theoretical bases for the new planning. Critics argued for a social theory of planning which would specifically incorporate is political economic setting. Deriving impetus initially from a neo-Marxist or materialist philosophy, they emphasized the essentially subordinate role of planning in the context of capitalist urbanization. The radical critique provided a new way of thinking about planning. However, the debate was generally conducted at such a high level of abstraction that practitioners and theoreticians alike had difficulty in linking it to everyday practice. Moreover, many of its supporters themselves seemed incapable or unwilling to dig themselves out of the trap of "structuralist inactivity" into which their view of planning had led them.

Then, in the late 1970s, a potential resolution of the liberal–radical split was plucked from the social theory of the Frankfurt School, and of Habermas in particular. The phenomenological and hermeneutic schools of thought became influential for two reasons. First, hermeneutics offered a firm theoretical basis for the essentially dialectical or interpretive method which was implicit in transactive–creative planning. Second, it provided the option for a new alliance with the radical left without the need to espouse Marxism. In short, hermeneutics provided a new theoretical and practical legitimacy where it was urgently needed.

1980–85: A frenzy of discourse and the retreat to origins   The recession-ridden 1980s have been accompanied by an increasing frenzy of discourse on planning. Doubts and uncertainties began to assail the left, and an increasingly "bullish" center-right coalition began to reassert itself. The net effects have been a retreat from context and a rediscovery of function in planning.

In the first place, the sparkling promise of hermeneutics did not translate readily into practice, nor was its theoretical promise being realized. Second, radical critics became quiescent. For some, the increasingly strident political conservatism was cause enough for retreat; others were absorbed into the search for a wider social theory of planning. Whatever political commitment remained seems to have become somewhat diluted. Kiernan's (1983) "politics of positive discrimination" (for instance) builds a new planning from the social context of Marx, plus Weberian notions of key bureaucrats, and guides the systems with Rawlsian notions of justice.

In the vacuum left by the apparent retreat of the social theorists, and in a conservative economic and political culture, a new attempt now appears to be underway to recapture the center ground in planning. Planning is being defined again as land-use planning. This retreat to the traditional core of the discipline is undoubtedly an effort to reaffirm the identity of planning and to demarcate clearly its professional "turf". The core movement reveals itself in many ways, as (for instance) in direct attacks on social theories of planning which are perceived as harming the professional credibility of planning. It is also evident from a new emphasis on "public – private partnerships" in the land-development process.

But the strongest evidence for a revitalization of traditional land-use planning lies in (i) the rejection of what is perceived to be "practice-irrelevant" theory, and (ii) the rebirth of physical planning theory. This trend (the two themes are surely manifestations of but a single event) is well represented in Breheny's revealingly entitled article "A practical view of planning theory". Breheny (1983, page 106) seems to identify with those: "who are concerned to pin down the essential features of planning *before* proceeding with the task of theory building" (emphasis added).

Not surprisingly, he is led to conclude that: "Land-use ... planning is concerned with government intervention in the private land-development process. . . . The role of planners is to assist in the administration of this activity and in helping governments make and implement decisions".

The ascendancy of pastiche

Postmodern planning appears as a *pastiche of practices*. "Planning theory" has been isolated as a babel of languages, most of which are voluntarily ignored by practitioners. "Planning practice" has developed into a ritualized choreography of routines. One dimension of practice has been deeply embedded in the apparatus of the state. There it is highly insulated and free from capture or influence. In essence, planning serves to legitimize the actions of the state. The second dimension of practice is part of land and property development interests. It is equally insulated, a passive tool capable of only the most muted social criticism. In this case, planning serves to legitimize the actions of capital. In its roles as legitimator of state and capital, planning resembles architecture. (But note one crucial and inexplicable difference: architecture has always sought to rationalize or to conceal its subordinate role by wider appeals to art, philosophy, history; planning, in contrast, has studiously rejected such engagement, including even a link to social sciences.)

The notion of a pastiche of practice is intended to convey the ensemble of free-floating, unsystematized "theories" illustrated in figure 1. Discourse around planning theory is essentially splintered. Since each approach has its advocate, pastiche is in the ascendancy. Paradoxically, however, the dominant focus of discourse in all narratives is increasingly being restricted. For instance, the long heritage of utopian concerns has been excised from our vocabulary. In addition, the ideological commitment of the 1960s and 1970s has lost much of its power of persuasion, having retreated into its own version of pastiche (a little bit of Marx, a touch of Weber, stir with Rawls).

The preeminent discourse in the future planning pastiche is likely to be that which best supports the evolving postmodern hyperspace. So we need to consider the time–space coordinates of this putative space. Its fundamental characteristic is that time and space have been stretched to create a new global political economy. Over much of the world, capitalist exchange relations predominate; production and distribution systems are organized on a global scale; world politics is dominated by the nuclear survival issue. Social relations in everyday life are equally impacted. A culture of (predominantly US) commercialism dominates taste, culture, and fashion. Traditional social organizations and belief systems are usurped and distorted. Communities atrophy, and social networks shrink. Life becomes a ritualized choreography of signs, symbols, and expectations led by and mirrored in the media (especially advertising).

Postmodernism is a political economy of social dislocation. Time and space are now ordered differently and no longer exert the influence to which we are accustomed. The diverse spaces which we inhabit no longer intersect neatly: social space, political space, economic space, and physical space are increasingly out of fit. Few have the resources or the ability to overcome this dislocation of spheres. Jameson (1985) argued that we are unable even to grasp the coordinates of these spheres at this moment.

Pursuing this logic, the postmodern city should be an atomized city – a world pastiche of built environments in unsynchronized, aesthetic–functional disharmony. The example which comes immediately to mind is that of the classic downtown renewal schemes: Bunker Hill in Los Angeles, with its string of modern baubles hung indelicately across a landscape of enduring inner-city networks; the Renaissance center in Detroit: and the Eaton Center in Toronto. These examples find their suburban analog in the vast expanses of prepackaged life-styles and physical settings in Orange County (Mission Viejo, for example), and – somewhat downmarket – in the Inland Empire. Davis (1985) has suggested that the postmodern city is fuelled by international capital and spatial differentiation. But it seems to me that the seeds of postmodernism were planted by the state-sponsored urban renewal schemes of the 1960s. As public funds dried up, a voracious finance capital crossed the world in search of profit. The institutionalized profession of planning was coopted by the state to support urban renewal, and remained in position as private capital moved in. So, cities no longer grow "organically", that is, as a result of a myriad public–private tensions. The postmodern city is a deliberate mutation engendered by a bureaucratic state and a corporate civil society. Both spheres are driven by economic return, in fiscal or in profit forms. The postmodern city has become a mutant money machine, driven by the twin engines of (state) penetration and (corporate) commodification.

The planning that is now developing is intended to support this machine. Planners are increasingly being pressed to legitimate actions by state and civil society in the mutation of the built environment. The planning role ultimately may be reduced to that of a facilitator; the planning process reduced to commodified "bits" susceptible to an instrumental logic. (It is in this sense that we can speak of a new depthlessness in planning.) Already planners are operating special areas where regular zoning restrictions have been suspended; already there are courses in "public–private" enterprise in planning schools. We are poised, it seems, to create a truly postmodern planning – a planning of filigree, of decoration. The profession may yet be canonized as the fig leaf which discreetly covers the enterprises of state and civil society.

What might we expect to happen to discourse in postmodern planning? Two scenarios might be drawn. First, let us assume that we have entered a long period of recession or no-growth. Under such circumstances, the retrenchment which we are currently experiencing in planning is likely to accelerate. Planning will survive purely as a subordinate technocracy, in which discourse on what we currently call substantive planning will predominate. The "development planner" will be the dominant species. Second, let us assume economic recovery. I would then anticipate a relatively long but slow period of expansion during which a chastened profession will seek to retain its credibility and its roots. The planning discourse is likely to be one in which pastiche is tolerated. We would be doomed to relive the expansionary experiences of the past two decades. By the year 2000, we should essentially be in the same spot as we are today. The pastiche of practice will likely be as confusing then as it seems now.

REFERENCES

Breheny M J, 1983 "A practical view of planning theory" *Environment and Planning B: Planning and Design* **10** 101–115

Davis M. 1985, "Urban renaissance and the spirit of post-modernism" *New Left Review* **151** 106–113

Jameson F, 1985, "Postmodernism and consumer society" in *Postmodern Culture* Ed. H Foster (Pluto Press, London) pp 111–125

Kiernan M J, 1983, "Ideology, politics, and planning: reflections on the theory and practice of urban planning" *Environment and Planning B: Planning and Design* **10** 71–87

Norris C, 1982 *Deconstruction: Theory and Practice* (Methuen, Andover, Hants)

Soja E, 1986, "Taking Los Angeles apart: some fragments of a critical human geography" *Environment and Planning D: Society and Space* **4** 255–272

16 The Condition of Postmodernity

David Harvey

If geography's marriage with postmodernism was announced in 1986, their honeymoon ended abruptly in 1989 with the publication of David Harvey's *The Condition of Postmodernity*. Harvey makes clear that he doesn't like postmodernism. His principal complaints are: that postmodernism's relativism is obfuscatory, and detracts from the political agenda of Marxism; that the putative emergence of a postmodern society is best understood as simply a blip in the long march of capitalism; and that the only way to make use of postmodernism's insights is to bring them back to the Marxian framework. Harvey's attack might have stopped postmodern human geography dead in its tracks, but it didn't. The very fact that a scholar of Harvey's pre-eminence would devote a book-length treatment to the topic stood, in some perverse way, as testimony to the power of the postmodern turn.

The Argument

There has been a sea-change in cultural as well as in political–economic practices since around 1972.

This sea-change is bound up with the emergence of new dominant ways in which we experience space and time.

While simultaneity in the shifting dimensions of time and space is no proof of necessary or causal connection, strong a priori grounds can be adduced for the proposition that there is some kind of necessary relation between the rise of postmodernist cultural forms, the emergence of more flexible modes of capital accumulation, and a new round of "time–space compression" in the organization of capitalism.

But these changes, when set against the basic rules of capitalistic accumulation, appear more as shifts in surface appearance rather than as signs of the emergence of some entirely new postcapitalist or even postindustrial society.

POSTmodernISM or postMODERNism?

How, then, should postmodernism in general be evaluated? My preliminary assessment would be this. That in its concern for difference, for the difficulties of communication, for the complexity and nuances of interests, cultures, places, and the like, it exercises a positive influence. The meta-languages, meta-theories, and meta-narratives of modernism (particularly in its later manifestations) did tend to gloss over important differences, and failed to pay attention to important disjunctions and details. Postmodernism has been particularly important in acknowledging "the multiple forms of otherness as they emerge from differences in subjectivity, gender and sexuality, race and class, temporal (configurations of sensibility) and spatial geographic locations and dislocations" (Huyssen, 1984, 50). It is this aspect of postmodernist thought that gives it a radical edge, so much so that traditional neo-conservatives, such as Daniel Bell, fear rather than welcome its accommodations with individualism, commercialism, and entrepreneuralism. Such neo-conservatives would, after all, hardly welcome Lyotard's (1980, 66) assertion that "the temporary contract is in practice supplanting permanent institutions in the professional, emotional, sexual, cultural, family, and international domains, as well as in political affairs." Daniel Bell plainly regrets the collapse of solid bourgeois values, the erosion of the work ethic in the working class, and sees contemporary trends less as a turn towards a vibrant postmodernist future and more as an exhaustion of modernism that surely harbingers a social and political crisis in years to come.

Postmodernism also ought to be looked at as mimetic of the social, economic, and political practices in society. But since it is mimetic of different facets of those practices it appears in very different guises. The superimposition of different worlds in many a postmodern novel, worlds between which an uncommunicative "otherness" prevails in a space of coexistence, bears an uncanny relationship to the increasing ghettoization, disempowerment, and isolation of poverty and minority populations in the inner cities of both Britain and the United States. It is not hard to read a postmodern novel as a metaphorical transect across the fragmenting social landscape, the sub-cultures and local modes of communication, in London, Chicago, New York, or Los Angeles. Since most social indicators suggest a strong increase in actual ghettoization since 1970, it is useful to think of postmodern fiction as perhaps mimetic of that fact.

But the increasing affluence, power, and authority emerging at the other end of the social scale produces an entirely different ethos. For while it is hard to see that working in the postmodern AT&T building by Philip Johnson is any different from working in the modernist Seagram building by Mies van der Rohe, the image projected to the outside is different. "AT&T insisted they wanted something other than just another glass box," said the architect. "We were looking for something that projected the company's image of nobility and strength. No material does that better than granite" (even though it was double the cost of glass). With luxury housing and corporate headquarters, aesthetic twists become an expression of class power. Crimp (1987) takes it further:

> The present condition of architecture is one in which architects debate academic, abstract aesthetics while they are in fact in the thrall of the real-estate developers who

are ruining our cities and turning working class people out of their homes.... Philip Johnson's new skyscraper... is a developer building, with a few applied geegaws, thrust upon a neighborhood that is not particularly in need of another skyscraper.

Invoking the memory of Hitler's architect Albert Speer, Crimp goes on to attack the postmodernist mask of what he sees as a new authoritarianism in the direction of city forms.

I have chosen these two examples to illustrate how important it is to think through exactly what kinds of social practice, what sets of social relations, are being reflected in different aesthetic movements. Yet this account is surely incomplete because we have yet to establish exactly what postmodernism might be mimetic of. Furthermore, it is just as surely dangerous to presuppose that postmodernism is solely mimetic rather than an aesthetic intervention in politics, economy, and social life in its own right. The strong injection of *fiction* as well as *function* into common sensibility, for example, must have consequences, perhaps unforeseen, for social action. Even Marx insisted, after all, that what distinguishes the worst of architects from the best of bees is that the architect erects structures in the imagination before giving them material form. Changes in the way we imagine, think, plan, and rationalize are bound to have material consequences. Only in these very broad terms of the conjoining of mimesis and aesthetic intervention can the broad range of postmodernism make sense.

Yet postmodernism sees itself rather more simply: for the most part as a wilful and rather chaotic movement to overcome all the supposed ills of modernism. But in this regard I think postmodernists exaggerate when they depict the modern as grossly as they do, either caricaturing the whole modernist movement to the point where, as even Jencks admits, "modern architecture bashing has become a form of sadism that is getting far too easy," or isolating one wing of modernism for criticism (Althusserianism, modern brutalism, or whatever) as if that was all there was. There were, after all, many cross-currents within modernism, and postmodernists echo some of them quite explicitly (Jencks, for example, looks back to the period 1870–1914, even to the confusions of the 1920s, while including Le Corbusier's monastery at Ronchamp as an important precursor of one aspect of postmodernism). The meta-narratives that the postmodernists decry (Marx, Freud, and even later figures like Althusser) were much more open, nuanced, and sophisticated than the critics admit. Marx and many of the Marxists (I think of Benjamin, Thompson, Anderson, as diverse examples) have an eye for detail, fragmentation, and disjunction that is often caricatured out of existence in postmodern polemics. Marx's account of modernization is exceedingly rich in insights into the roots of modernist as well as postmodernist sensibility.

It is equally wrong to write off the material achievements of modernist practices so easily. Modernists found a way to control and contain an explosive capitalist condition. They were effective for example, in the organization of urban life and the capacity to build space in such a way as to contain the intersecting processes that have made for a rapid urban change in twentieth-century capitalism. If there is a crisis implicit in all of that, it is by no means clear that it is the modernists, rather than the capitalists, who are to blame. There are, indeed, some extraordinary successes in the modernist pantheon (I note the British school building and design programme in the early 1960s that solved some of the acute housing problems of education within tight budget constraints). While some housing projects were indeed dismal failures, others were not, particularly when compared with the slum conditions from which many people came. And it turns out that the social conditions in Pruitt–Igoe – that great symbol of modernist failure – were much more at the heart of the problem than pure architectural form. The blaming of physical form for social ills has to rest on the most vulgar kind of environmental determinism that few would be prepared to accept in other circumstances (though I note with distress that another member of Prince Charles's "kitchen cabinet" is the geographer Alice Coleman, who regularly mistakes correlation between bad design and anti-social behaviour with causation). It is interesting to note, therefore, how the tenant population in Le Corbusier's "habitat for living" at Firminy-le-Vert has organized into a social movement to prevent its destruction (not, I should add, out of any particular loyalty to Le Corbusier but more simply because it happens to be their home). As even Jencks admits, postmodernists have taken over all of the great achievements of the modernists in architectural design, though they have certainly altered aesthetics and appearances in at least superficial ways.

I also conclude that there is much more continuity than difference between the broad history of modernism and the movement called postmodernism. It seems more sensible to me to see the latter as a particular kind of crisis within the former, one that emphasizes the fragmentary, the ephemeral, and the chaotic side of Baudelaire's formulation (that side which Marx so admirably dissects as integral to the capitalist mode of production) while expressing a deep scepticism as to any particular prescriptions as to how the eternal and immutable should be conceived of, represented, or expressed.

But postmodernism, with its emphasis upon the ephemerality of *jouissance*, its insistence upon the impenetrability of the other, its concentration on the text rather than the work, its penchant for deconstruction bordering on nihilism, its preference for aesthetics over ethics, takes matters too far. It takes them beyond the point where any coherent politics are left, while that wing of it that seeks a shameless accommodation with the market puts it firmly in the tracks of an entrepreneurial culture that is the hallmark of reactionary neoconservativism. Postmodernist philosophers tell us not only to accept but even to revel in the fragmentations and the cacophony of voices through which the dilemmas of the modern world are understood. Obsessed with deconstructing and delegitimating every form of argument they encounter, they can end only in condemning their own validity claims to the point where nothing remains of any basis for reasoned action. Postmodernism has us accepting the reifications and partitionings, actually celebrating the activity of masking and cover-up, all the fetishisms of locality, place, or social grouping, while denying that kind of meta-theory which can grasp the political–economic processes (money flows, international divisions of labour, financial markets, and the like) that are becoming ever more universalizing in their depth, intensity, reach and power over daily life.

Worst of all, while it opens up a radical prospect by acknowledging the authenticity of other voices, postmodernist thinking immediately shuts off those other voices from access to more universal sources of power by ghettoizing them within an opaque otherness, the specificity of this or that language game. It thereby disempowers those voices (of women, ethnic and racial minorities, colonized peoples, the unemployed, youth, etc.) in a world of lop-sided power relations. The language game of a cabal of international bankers may be impenetrable to us, but that does not put it on a par with the equally impenetrable language of inner-city blacks from the standpoint of power relations.

The rhetoric of postmodernism is dangerous for it avoids confronting the realities of political economy and the circumstances of global power. The silliness of Lyotard's "radical proposal" that opening up the data banks to everyone as a prologue to radical reform (as if we would all have equal power to use that opportunity) is instructive, because it indicates how even the most resolute of postmodernists is faced in the end with either making some universalizing gesture (like Lyotard's appeal to some pristine concept of justice) or lapsing, like Derrida, into total political silence. Meta-theory cannot be dispensed with. The postmodernists simply push it underground where it continues to function as a "now unconcious effectivity" (Jameson 1984).

I find myself agreeing, therefore, with Eagleton's repudiation of Lyotard, for whom "there can be no difference between truth, authority and rhetorical seductiveness; he who has the smoothest tongue or the raciest story has the power." The eight-year reign of a charismatic story-teller in the White House suggests that there is more than a little continuity to that political problem, and that postmodernism comes dangerously close to complicity with the aestheticizing of politics upon which it is based. This takes us back to a very basic question. If both modernity and postmodernity derive their aesthetic from some kind of struggle with the *fact* of fragmentation, ephemerality, and chaotic flux, it is, I would suggest, very important to establish why such a fact should have been so pervasive an aspect of modern experience for so long a period of time, and why the intensity of that experience seems to have picked up so powerfully since 1970. If the only thing certain about modernity is uncertainty, then we should, surely, pay considerable attention to the social forces that produce such a condition. It is to these social forces that I now turn. [...]

Postmodernism as the Mirror of Mirrors

One of the prime conditions of postmodernity is that no one can or should discuss it as a historical–geographical condition. It is never easy, of course, to construct a critical assessment of a condition that is overwhelmingly present. The terms of debate, description, and representation are often so circumscribed that there seems to be no escape from evaluations that are anything other than self-referential. It is conventional these days, for example, to dismiss out of hand any suggestion that the "economy" (however that vague word is understood) might be determinant of cultural life even in (as Engels and later Althusser suggested) "the last instance." The odd thing about postmodern cultural production is how much sheer profit-seeking is determinant in the first instance.

Postmodernism has come of age in the midst of this climate of voodoo economics, of political image construction and deployment, and of new social class formation. That there is some connection between this postmodernist burst and the image-making of Ronald Reagan, the attempt to deconstruct traditional institutions of working-class power (the trade unions and the political parties of the left), the masking of the social effects of the economic politics of privilege, ought to be evident enough. A rhetoric that justifies homelessness, unemployment, increasing impoverishment, disempowerment, and the like by appeal to supposedly traditional values of self-reliance and entrepreneurialism will just as freely laud the shift from ethics to aesthetics as its dominant value system. The street scenes of impoverishment, disempowerment, graffiti and decay become grist for the cultural producers' mill, not, as Deutsche and Ryan (1984) point out, in the muckraking reformist style of the late nineteenth century, but as a quaint and swirling backdrop (as in *Blade Runner*) upon which no social commentary is to be made. "Once the poor become aestheticized, poverty itself moves out of our field of social vision", except as a passive depiction of otherness, alienation and contingency within the human condition. When "poverty and homelessness are served up for aesthetic pleasure", then ethics is indeed submerged by aesthetics, inviting, thereby, the bitter harvest of charismatic politics and ideological extremism.

If there is *a meta-theory* with which to embrace all these gyrations of postmodern thinking and cultural production, then why should we not deploy it? [...]

The Crisis of Historical Materialism

The odd thing is how radical some of these diverse responses appeared, and how difficult it has been for the left, as opposed to the right, to cope with them. On reflection, the oddity disappears easily enough. A mode of thought that is anti-authoritarian and iconoclastic, that insists on the authenticity of other voices, that celebrates difference, decentralization, and democratization of taste, as well as the power of imagination over materiality, has to have a radical cutting edge even when indiscriminately used. In the hands of its more responsible practitioners, the whole baggage of ideas associated with postmodernism could be deployed to radical ends, and thereby be seen as part of a fundamental drive towards a more liberatory politics in exactly the same way that the turn to more flexible labour processes could be seen as an opening to a new era of democratic and highly decentralized labour relations and co-operative endeavours.

From the standpoint of the traditionalist right, the excesses of the 1960s and the violence of 1968 appeared subversive in the extreme. Perhaps for that reason, Daniel Bell's description in *The cultural contradictions of capitalism*, though launched entirely from a right-wing perspective that sought the restoration of respect for authority, was probably more accurate than many of the left attempts to grasp what was happening. Other writers, like Toffler and even McLuhan, saw the significance of time–space compression and the confusions it generated in ways that the left could not see, precisely because it was so deeply embroiled in creating the confusion. Only recently has the left come to terms with some of these issues, and I think it significant that Berman's book, published in 1982, recuperates some of these themes only by treating Marx as the first great modernist writer rather than as a Marxist who could see through what modernism was all about.

The New Left was preoccupied with a struggle to liberate itself from the dual shackles of old left politics (particularly as represented by traditional communist parties and "orthodox" Marxism) and the repressive powers of corporate capital and bureaucratized institutions (the state, the universities, the unions, etc.). It saw itself from the very outset as a cultural as well as a political–economic force, and helped force the turn to aesthetics that postmodernism has been about.

But there were unintended consequences of such a line of action. The push into cultural politics connected better with anarchism and libertarianism than with traditional Marxism, and set the New Left against traditional working-class attitudes and institutions. The New Left embraced the new social movements which were themselves agents of fragmentation of old left politics. To the degree that the latter were at best passive, and at worst reactionary, in their treatment of race and gender issues, of difference, and of the problems of colonized peoples and repressed minorities, of ecological and aesthetic issues, some kind of political shift of the sort that the New Left proposed was surely justified. But in making its move, the New Left tended to abandon its faith both in the proletariat as an instrument of progressive change and in historical materialism as a mode of analysis. André Gorz proclaimed farewell to the working class, and Aronowitz announced the crisis of historical materialism.

The New Left thereby cut itself off from its own ability to have a critical perspective on itself or on the social processes of transformation that underlay the surge into postmodernist ways of thought. In insisting that it was culture and politics that mattered, and that it was neither reasonable nor proper to invoke economic determination even in the last instance (let alone invoke theories of capital circulation and accumulation, or of necessary class relations in production), it was unable to stop its own drift into ideological positions that were weak in contest with the new-found strength of the neo-conservatives, and which forced it to compete on the same terrain of image production, aesthetics, and ideological power when the means of communication lay in its opponents' hands. In a 1983 symposium, *Marxism and the interpretation of culture*, for example, most of the authors paid far more attention to Foucault and Derrida than they did to Marx (Nelson and Grossberg, 1988). Ironically, it was an old left figure (noticeably absent from that symposium), Raymond Williams, a long-time student of working-class cultural forms and values, who crossed the tracks of the New Left and tried to re-establish the material groundings of what cultural practices might be about. Williams not only rejected modernism as a valid category but, by extension, saw postmodernism as itself a mask for the deeper transformations in the culture of capitalism which he sought to identify.

The interrogation of "orthodox" Marxian formulations (by writers in the tradition of Fanon or Simone de Beauvoir as well as by the deconstructionists) was both necessary and positive in its implications. Important transitions were indeed afoot in political economy, in the nature of state functions, in cultural practices, and in the time–space dimension across which social relations had to be assessed (the relation between, say, apartheid in South Africa and working-class movements in Europe or North America became even more significant as a political issue than it had been at the high point of direct imperialism). It took a properly dynamic rather than static conception of both theory and historical materialism to grasp the significance of these shifts. Of the areas of greatest development I would list four:

1   The treatment of difference and "otherness" not as something to be added on to more fundamental Marxist categories (like class and productive forces), but as

something that should be omni-present from the very beginning in any attempt to grasp the dialectics of social change. The importance of recuperating such aspects of social organization as race, gender, religion, within the overall frame of historical materialist enquiry (with its emphasis upon the power of money and capital circulation) and class politics (with its emphasis upon the unity of the emancipatory struggle) cannot be overestimated.

2   A recognition that the production of images and of discourses is an important facet of activity that has to be analysed as part and parcel of the reproduction and transformation of any symbolic order. Aesthetic and cultural practices matter, and the conditions of their production deserve the closest attention

3   A recognition that the dimensions of space and time matter, and that there are real geographies of social action, real as well as metaphorical territories and spaces of power that become vital as organizing forces in the geopolitics of capitalism, at the same time as they are the sites of innumerable differences and othernesses that have to be understood both in their own right and within the overall logic of capitalist development. Historical materialism is finally beginning to take its geography seriously.

4   Historical–geographical materialism is an open-ended and dialectical mode of enquiry rather than a closed and fixed body of understandings. Meta-theory is not a statement of total truth but an attempt to come to terms with the historical and geographical truths that characterize capitalism both in general as well as in its present phase.

REFERENCES

Aronowitz, S. (1981): *The crisis of historical materialism*. New York.

Bell, D. (1978): *The cultural contradictions of capitalism*. New York.

Berman, M. (1982): *All that is solid melts into air*. New York.

Crimp, D. (1987): "Art in the 80s: the myth of autonomy." *PRECIS* 6, 83–91.

Deutsche, R. and Ryan, C. (1984): "The fine art of gentrification." *October*, 31, 91–111.

Eagleton, T. (1987): "Awakening from modernity." *Times Literary Supplement*, 20 February 1987.

Huyssen, A. (1984): "Mapping the post-modern." *New German Critique*, 33, 5–52.

Jameson, F. (1984): "Postmodernism, or the cultural logic of late capitalism." *New Left Review*, 146, 53–92.

Jencks, C. (1984): *The language of post-modern architecture*. London.

Lyotard, J. (1984): *The postmodern condition*. Manchester.

Nelson, C. and Grossberg, L. (eds) (1988): *Marxism and the interpretation of culture*. Urbana, Ill.

1990–2000: The Altered Spaces of Postmodernity

By the early 1990s, postmodernism was an established part of the discourse in human geography. It remained, needless to say, a highly contested concept, but its influence was demonstrable across many diverse fields, from cultural to economic geography, and from feminist thought to postcolonialism. Postmodernism, in a few short years, had introduced new ways of seeing into geography. It had liberated geographers from antiquated (if not obsolete) paradigms; it bestowed a new legitimacy on the study of space/place; and it connected geography and geographers to key debates in philosophy, social theory, and the humanities. It would be an invidious task to attempt to summarize the voluminous outpourings of postmodern human geography that occurred between 1990 and the year 2000. Instead, in this section, we provide an abbreviated overview of just a few of the remarkable consequences that derived from the intersection of postmodernism and human geography.

Julie Graham provides a perceptive, witty cartography of human geography's diverse intellectual landscape after postmodernism (Reading 17). Jane Jacobs explores the postcolonial spaces that postmodernism helped to pry open (Reading 18). Jennifer Wolch's "zoöpolis" is nothing less than a complete reorientation of the field of biogeography, bringing the nonhuman animal world back into geography (Reading 19). Michael Storper and Allen Scott begin rewriting economic geography by examining the evidence for a post-Fordist regime of "flexible accumulation" and its associated modes of social regulation (Reading 20). Dear and Flusty revise long-held conventions about urban geography, and devise a program for investigating a "postmodern urbanism" (Reading 21). John Pickles boldly applies one of postmodernism's key puzzles (the problem of representation) to the technological world of GIS or geographical information systems (Reading 22). And finally, Gearóid Ó Tuathail examines postmodernism's impact on geopolitical discourse (Reading 23).

Although these contributions are presented as exemplars of the riches that flow when geographers confront the postmodern challenge, it bears repeating that their authors may or may not regard themselves as postmodernists. Some don't even mention the P word in their essays. Yet, no matter what their personal beliefs, each extract demonstrates the wisdom of a new adage that warrants constant repetition: one does not have to *be* a postmodernist to engage fruitfully with the tenets of postmodern thought.

Snow Crash

Neal Stephenson

Hiro Protagonist and Vitaly Chernobyl, roommates, are chilling out in their home, a spacious 20-by-30 in a U-Stor-It in Inglewood, California. The room has a concrete slab floor, corrugated steel walls separating it from the neighboring units, and – this is a mark of distinction and luxury – a roll-up steel door that faces northwest, giving them a few red rays at times like this, when the sun is setting over LAX. From time to time, a 777 or a Sukhoi/Kawasaki Hypersonic Transport will taxi in front of the sun and block the sunset with its rudder, or just mangle the red light with its jet exhaust, braiding the parallel rays into a dappled pattern on the wall.

But there are worse places to live. There are much worse places right here in this U-Stor-It. Only the big units like this one have their own doors. Most of them are accessed via a communal loading dock that leads to a maze of wide corrugated-steel hallways and freight elevators. These are slum housing, 5-by-10s and 10-by-10s where Yanoama tribespersons cook beans and parboil fistfuls of coca leaves over heaps of burning lottery tickets.

It is whispered that in the old days, when the U-Stor-It was actually used for its intended purpose (namely, providing cheap extra storage space to Californians with too many material goods), certain entrepreneurs came to the front office, rented out 10-by-10s using fake IDs, filled them up with steel drums full of toxic chemical waste, and then abandoned them, leaving the problem for the U-Stor-It Corporation to handle. According to these rumors, U-Stor-It just padlocked those units and wrote them off. Now, the immigrants claim, certain units remain haunted by this chemical specter. It is a story they tell their children, to keep them from trying to break into padlocked units.

No one has ever tried to break into Hiro and Vitaly's unit because there's nothing in there to steal, and at this point in their lives, neither one of them is important enough to kill, kidnap, or interrogate. Hiro owns a couple of nice Nipponese swords, but he always wears them, and the whole idea of stealing fantastically dangerous weapons presents the would-be perp with inherent dangers and contradictions: When you are wrestling for possession of a sword, the man with the handle always wins. Hiro also has a pretty nice computer that he usually takes with him when he goes anywhere. Vitaly owns half a carton of Lucky Strikes, an electric guitar, and a hangover.

At the moment, Vitaly Chernobyl is stretched out on a futon, quiescent, and Hiro Protagonist is sitting cross-legged at a low table, Nipponese style, consisting of a cargo pallet set on cinderblocks.

As the sun sets, its red light is supplanted by the light of many neon logos emanating from the franchise ghetto that constitutes this U-Stor-It's natural habitat. This light, known as loglo, fills in the shadowy corners of the unit with seedy, oversaturated colors.

Hiro has a house cappuccino skin and spiky, truncated dreadlocks. His hair does not cover as much of his head as it used to, but he is a young man, by no means bald or balding, and the slight retreat of his hairline only makes more of his high cheekbones. He is wearing shiny goggles that wrap halfway around his head; the bows of the goggles have little earphones that are plugged into his outer ears.

The earphones have some built-in noise cancellation features. This sort of thing works best on steady noise. When jumbo jets make their takeoff runs on the runway across the street, the sound is reduced to a low doodling hum. But when Vitaly Chernobyl thrashes out an experimental guitar solo, it still hurts Hiro's ears.

The goggles throw a light, smoky haze across his eyes and reflect a distorted wide-angle view of a brilliantly lit boulevard that stretches off into an infinite blackness. This boulevard does not really exist; it is a computer-rendered view of an imaginary place.

Beneath this image, it is possible to see Hiro's eyes, which look Asian. They are from his mother, who is Korean by way of Nippon. The rest of him looks more like his father, who was African by way of Texas by way of the Army – back in the days before it got split up into a number of competing organizations such as General Jim's Defense System and Admiral Bob's National Security.

Four things are on the cargo pallet: a bottle of expensive beer from the Puget Sound area, which Hiro cannot really afford; a long sword known in Nippon as a *katana* and a short sword known as a *wakizashi* – Hiro's father looted these from Japan after World War II went atomic – and a computer.

The computer is a featureless black wedge. It does not have a power cord, but there is a narrow translucent plastic tube emerging from a hatch on the rear, spiraling across the cargo pallet and the floor, and plugged into a crudely installed fiber-optics socket above the head of the sleeping Vitaly Chernobyl. In the center of the plastic tube is a hair-thin fiber-optic cable. The cable is carrying a lot of information back and forth between Hiro's computer and the rest of the world. In order to transmit the same amount of information on paper, they would have to arrange for a 747 cargo freighter packed with telephone books and encyclopedias to power-dive into their unit every couple of minutes, forever.

Hiro can't really afford the computer either, but he has to have one. It is a tool of his trade. In the worldwide community of hackers, Hiro is a talented drifter. This is the kind of lifestyle that sounded romantic to him as recently as five years ago. But in the bleak light of full adulthood, which is to one's early twenties as Sunday morning is to Saturday night, he can clearly see what it really amounts to: He's broke and un-employed. And a few short weeks ago, his tenure as a pizza deliverer – the only pointless dead-end job he really enjoys – came to an end. Since then, he's been putting a lot more emphasis on his auxiliary emergency backup job: freelance stringer for the CIC, the Central Intelligence Corporation of Langley, Virginia.

The business is a simple one. Hiro gets information. It may be gossip, videotape, audiotape, a fragment of a computer disk, a xerox of a document. It can even be a joke based on the latest highly publicized disaster.

He uploads it to the CIC database – the Library, formerly the Library of Congress, but no one calls it that anymore. Most people are not entirely clear on what the word "congress" means. And even the word "library" is getting hazy. It used to be a place full of books, mostly old ones. Then they began to include videotapes, records, and maga-zines. Then all of the information got converted into machine-readable form, which is to say, ones and zeroes. And as the number of media grew, the material became more up to date, and the methods for searching the Library became more and more sophisticated, it approached the point where there was no substantive difference between the Library of Congress and the Central Intelligence Agency. Fortuitously, this happened just as the government was falling apart anyway. So they merged and kicked out a big fat stock offering.

Millions of other CIC stringers are uploading millions of other fragments at the same time. CIC's clients, mostly large corporations and Sovereigns, rifle through the Library looking for useful information, and if they find a use for something that Hiro put into it, Hiro gets paid.

A year ago, he uploaded an entire first-draft film script that he stole from an agent's wastebasket in Burbank. Half a dozen studios wanted to see it. He ate and vacationed off of that one for six months.

Since then, times have been leaner. He has been learning the hard way that 99 percent of the information in the Library never gets used at all.[. . .]

So Hiro's not actually here at all. He's in a computer-generated universe that his computer is drawing onto his goggles and pumping into his earphones. In the lingo, this imaginary place is known as the Metaverse. Hiro spends a lot of time in the Metaverse. It beats the shit out of the U-Stor-It.

Hiro is approaching the Street. It is the Broadway, the Champs Élysées of the Metaverse. It is the brilliantly lit boulevard that can be seen, miniaturized and backward, reflected in the lenses of his goggles. It does not really exist. But right now, millions of people are walking up and down it.

The dimensions of the Street are fixed by a protocol, hammered out by the computer-graphics ninja overlords of the Association for Computing Machinery's Global Multimedia Protocol Group. The Street seems to be a grand boulevard going all the way around the equator of a black sphere with a radius of a bit more than ten thousand kilometers. That makes it 65,536 kilometers around, which is considerably bigger than Earth. [. . .]

Like any place in Reality, the Street is subject to development. Developers can build their own small streets feeding off of the main one. They can build buildings, parks, signs, as well as things that do not exist in Reality, such as vast hovering overhead light shows, special neighborhoods where the rules of three-dimensional spacetime are ignored, and free-combat zones where people can go to hunt and kill each other.

The only difference is that since the Street does not really exist – it's just a computer-graphics protocol written down on a piece of paper somewhere – none of these things is being physically built. They are, rather, pieces of software, made available to the public over the worldwide fiber-optics network. When Hiro goes into the Metaverse and looks down the Street and sees buildings and electric signs stretching off into the darkness, disappearing over the curve of the globe, he is actually staring at the graphic representations – the user interfaces – of a myriad different pieces of software that have been engineered by major corporations. In order to place these things on the Street, they have had to get approval from the Global Multimedia Protocol Group, have had to buy frontage on the Street, get zoning approval, obtain permits, bribe inspectors, the whole bit. The money these corporations pay to build things on the Street all goes into a trust fund owned and operated by the GMPG, which pays for developing and expanding the machinery that enables the Street to exist.

Hiro has a house in a neighborhood just off the busiest part of the Street. It is a very old neighborhood by Street standards. About ten years ago, when the Street protocol was first written, Hiro and some of his buddies pooled their money and bought one of the first development licenses, created a little neighborhood of hackers. At the time, it was just a little patchwork of light amid a vast blackness. Back then, the Street was just a necklace of streetlights around a black ball in space.

Since then, the neighborhood hasn't changed much, but the Street has. By getting in on it early, Hiro's buddies got a head start on the whole business. Some of them even got very rich off of it.

That's why Hiro has a nice big house in the Metaverse but has to share a 20-by-30 in Reality. Real estate acumen does not always extend across universes.

The sky and the ground are black, like a computer screen that hasn't had anything drawn into it yet; it is always nighttime in the Metaverse, and the Street is always garish and brilliant, like Las Vegas freed from constraints of physics and finance. But people in Hiro's neighborhood are very good programmers, so it's tasteful. The houses look like real houses. There are a couple of Frank Lloyd Wright reproductions and some fancy Victoriana.

So it's always a shock to step out onto the Street, where everything seems to be a mile high. This is Downtown, the most heavily developed area. If you go a couple of hundred kilometers in either direction, the development will taper down to almost nothing, just a thin chain of streetlights casting white pools on the black velvet ground. But Downtown is a dozen Manhattans, embroidered with neon and stacked on top of each other.

In the real world – planet Earth, Reality – there are somewhere between six and ten billion people. At any given time, most of them are making mud bricks or field-stripping their AK-47s. Perhaps a billion of them have enough money to own a computer; these people have more money than all of the others put together. Of these billion potential computer owners, maybe a quarter of them actually bother to own computers, and a quarter of these have machines that are powerful enough to handle the Street protocol. That makes for about sixty million people who can be on the Street at any given time. Add in another sixty million or so who can't really afford it but go there anyway, by using public machines, or machines owned by their school or their employer, and at any given time the Street is occupied by twice the population of New York City.

That's why the damn place is so overdeveloped. Put in a sign or a building on the Street and the hundred million richest, hippest, best-connected people on earth will see it every day of their lives.

It is a hundred meters wide, with a narrow monorail track running down the middle. The monorail is a free piece of public utility software that enables users to change their location on the Street rapidly and smoothly. A lot of people just ride back and forth on it, looking at the sights. When Hiro first saw this place, ten years ago, the monorail hadn't been written yet; he and his buddies had to write car and motorcycle software in order to get around. They would take their software out and race it in the black desert of the electronic night.

17 Anti-Essentialism and Overdetermination

Julie Graham

Watch for the ways in which Julie Graham situates her feminist post-Marxism in a postmodern intellectual climate. She pressures conventional Marxist/radical geographers (in this case, Dick Peet; see Reading 5) to understand that Marxism is only one way to understand the world – a message propounded by Henri Lefebvre in 1974 (Reading 12). Graham's imaginative cartography of the contemporaneous world of human geographical thought is worth a lot of your attention. Also noteworthy is the striking clarity in Graham's presentation of complex issues, plus the strength of her commitment to a radical practice of geography in a postmodern world that many regard as bereft of politics.

Essentialism or Overdetermination?

An essentialist approach to social theory assumes that complex social phenomena can be understood as manifestations or expressions of simpler realities at their core. Thus a humanist essentialism might theorize social processes and events as reflections of certain basic human qualities, such as the need for community or the desire for power, whereas a structuralist essentialism might theorize the same processes and events as manifesting the causal efficacy of certain stable and enduring social relations.

Within the extensive and varied Marxist tradition, the economy has often played the role of social essence. Economic relations and processes are frequently given preeminence in social causation or privileged in some other way. Even when they are not invoked in a particular theoretical formulation or social analysis, they may be understood as determinant in the "last instance" or as structures with causal powers that are unrealized in a particular setting. They may even share the stage with certain non-economic processes that are similarly privileged, such as racial and gender oppression or political power of various sorts.

From an anti-essentialist theoretical perspective, no aspect of the social or natural world merits such special ontological status. Every aspect of reality participates in constituting the world and, more specifically, in constituting every other aspect. This mutual constitutivity is what is meant by the term "overdetermination," used in the sense put forward by Resnick and Wolff (see, for example, 1987).

The notion of mutual constitution provides an alternative to mechanistic conceptions of cause and effect, in which independent and static entities are sporadically set into motion. It also provides an alternative to dualistic notions of dialectical interaction and interpenetration. An overdetermined site or process is complexly constituted by an infinite multiplicity of conditions; it changes continually as those conditions change; and it is pushed and pulled in contradictory directions as its myriad conditions change at different rates and in different ways. It has no essence, no stable core, no central contradiction. Instead it is decentered, existing in complex contradiction and continual change.

In a recent interview, Marc Schell captured aphoristically the meaning of overdetermination for social explanation: "(n)othing less than everything is a sufficient explanation for anything" (1991: 9). There is no social or natural process that is truly independent of any other. The context of any event constitutes and specifies it, and every aspect of life makes up that context. To understand a process or event involves theorizing the way in which every other process contributes to its contradictory development.

Where does this leave social analysts who are unable to evaluate the contribution of an infinity of constituent "causes" to the objects of their studies? It seems that they must make a choice. They must focus on one or several processes that they find interesting or important (for some overdetermined autobiographical reason). If they are pursuing their analysis within the context of Marxism, for example, they may choose to focus on the production, appropriation and distribution of surplus labor and the ways in which this class process conditions the existence of other events and processes. They may also examine the complex and various conditions that constitute the process of class.

If they understand their choice in essentialist terms, they may justify their focus on class by arguing that it is one of the most important or fundamental relations in social life. If, on the other hand, they take an anti-essentialist view, they may see themselves as unable to examine the full range of constituents of a complex phenomenon and as therefore unable to say which one or several are the most important. They may then explain their choice of focus as overdetermined by a wide range of factors and experiences.

Unlike some of their essentialist counterparts, the overdeterminist researchers will never be able to say that they have conducted complete or definitive analyses. Instead they will view their work as partial and particular. They will be careful, then, not to claim that they have found the singular and universal truth about, or the best explanation of, the object at hand. From their perspective, they have produced analyses that differ from and conflict with other analyses, ones that start with different interests and concerns. This is what makes their analyses special and important, not the identification of fundamental causes and constituents to which complex phenomena can be reduced. [. . .]

Out of Touch or Overdetermined?

> [Graham provides]...a recipe for the theorization process which...loses all touch with the world. (Peet, 1992: 123)

According to Peet, I know how to lose touch with the world and I can teach the rest of you how to do it, if only you will follow my "recipe."

Unfortunately, I think he overestimates me here. I am quite incapable of losing touch with the world, through theory or through any other (non-fatal) device. Sometimes this distresses me but mostly I accept my fate.

What he correctly detects, but mistakenly identifies, is a conception of knowledge which is different from his own. In his conception, knowledge is always in danger of losing touch with the world. As knowledge develops, it requires continual adjustment to ensure that it "capture(s)" and "replicate(s)" reality (p. 124). In my conception, knowledge is inevitably in touch with the world but it can never replicate or capture it. How did we get to this impasse?

To answer this question, I have provided a fictionalized autobiographical map (see figure 1). Starting with Richard Rorty, a somewhat arbitrary point of departure, I take a short road through postmodern feminist theories of knowledge and end up in the anti-essentialist Marxist territory where I currently reside.

The landscape of this region is very different from that of classical Marxism where Dick Peet dwells. The institutions and rules are different as well. Over the years, the differences between the two regions have contributed to a variety of misunderstandings and even outright battles between their inhabitants. None of these battles has been decisive, leading to the suppression or annexation of the foe. Nevertheless, it is my impression that Peet's region is losing population while mine is experiencing a small but significant gain.

As figure 1 shows, a major barrier between the two regions is the epistemological divide, which bifurcates the landscape of social theory. Though many have participated in the (social) construction of this topographical feature, the philosopher, Richard Rorty, is perhaps the most well-known. For this reason, I will start with him.

Rorty (1979) wants philosophers to "set aside" the epistemological project of providing the foundations of knowledge. He rejects the goal (and disbelieves in the possibility) of creating a knowledge which can assist in distinguishing true knowledges from their cultural inferiors in some objective and universally appropriate way.

Modern epistemology is the study of the conditions under which true knowledge can be produced or detected. As a philosophical project it developed in part to defend a fledgling natural Science against religious forms of knowledge. Today, when Science itself has become the paradigm of knowledge, epistemology is an isolated and irrelevant cultural practice. The "rest of culture" does not need a profession which adjudicates its claims to truth. Increasingly the pretensions of philosophers to know the essence of knowing are seen as attempts to convince themselves and others that they have something important to do (Rorty, 1979: 392).

In his effort to entice philosophy from its epistemological *cul de sac*, Rorty reveals the historical origins of its transhistorical pretensions. He focuses particularly on

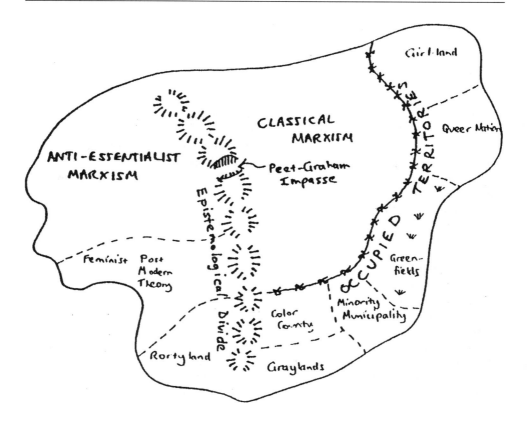

Figure I.   Map.

concepts and images of mind that have prevailed in Western culture and, especially, since the seventeenth century. One of the major intellectual preconditions of modern epistemology is the notion of mind as an inner space in which certain processes produce knowledge of an external world. It is the separation of mind and world that presents the epistemological problem of trying to reconcile them (Graham and St. Martin, 1990).

Reinforcing and refining the image of separation is the extended metaphor of mind as mirror and of knowledge as reflection in a glass. This imagery has fostered the prevalent conception of knowledge as representation, and the related concern with adjudicating between more and less accurate representations of the real. Rorty's goal is to undermine the metaphor of reflection and its companion image of the knowing mind. To the extent that he succeeds, some of the infrastructure supporting the debilitating distinctions between knowledge and reality, thought and action, will be "set aside" or left behind.

As an alternative to knowledge as representation, Rorty proposes the metaphor of conversation. Perhaps, he says, we could understand people as "saying things, better or worse things, without seeing them as externalizing inner representations of reality" (1979: 371). Stripped of its grounding metaphors of reflection and inner mental space, the epistemological problem dissolves and disappears. In its place is a postmodern image of knowledge as an ongoing and contradictory process of social interaction rather than the authoritative repository of accurate representations. This alternative conception accords with Rorty's liberal hope for an open and pluralistic culture.

Feminist Anti-foundationalism

Many feminists share Rorty's conception of knowledge as grounded in social and personal experience rather than in universal protocols for adjudicating truth (see Nicholson, 1990). They are less likely, however, to invoke the metaphor of conversation. From the perspective of most feminists, knowledge is a social process but that process is one of political struggle. The image of the conversation is too tame and bloodless, too confident and urbane.

What many feminists do have in common with Rorty is a postmodern skepticism about the possibility of a singular truth which encapsulates the essence of the world. They question the authority of knowledges that pretend to universality, showing the ways in which these knowledges participate in the suppression of other voices and perspectives. They challenge the "God's-eye view" of the knower who transcends space and time, locating him squarely in the modern era and patriarchal tradition. To the modernist "view from nowhere," they counterpose the postmodern acknowledgment of historical and geographical location. Knowledges are produced in particular contexts, not in a transcendent or universal "situation."

For some feminists, however, the association with postmodernism is problematic as well as liberating. Postmodernist deconstruction exposes the view from nowhere as an attempt to escape from the limits of subjective location, but it provides an alternative means of escape. "New images of disembodiment" are available to those who seek transcendence of the body's time and space – images of multiple and shifting identity; of "inexhaustible vantage points" floating across time. The modern view from nowhere may have been exposed and discredited but in its place we find the postmodern view from everywhere – equally, though differently, context-free (Bordo, 1990: 142–145).

The alienated mind or the overdetermined knower?

The fear that postmodern knowledges and knowers will escape from reality is also expressed by Peet, who invokes the image of "fantastic, free-floating theories" traveling in "outer space" (p. 128). Although it is different in many ways from feminist concerns, his expression of suspicion seems founded in a similar presumption. It preserves the modern separation, the ultimate disjuncture between mind and world. This separation creates the possibility of knowledge that is "close" to reality and the counter-possibility of knowledge that is free-floating, out of touch with the universal or personal real. It is what requires us to ground knowledge in experience, or on meta-experiential foundations. It constrains us to polish our mirrors, until the image is indistinguishable from the object it reflects.

None of these problems or solutions could exist except under conditions of mental alienation, in which the mind is an inner space not fully contiguous with an external world. The divorce between mind and world is the precondition for their reconciliation, and it seems to generate a longing for that state. Knowledge touches the world at the point of truth, and separation is overcome.

There is, of course, another possible response to the problem of separation and the frustrations it presents. As Rorty suggests, we could simply set the problem aside. We could participate in alternative discursive formations with other problems and solutions.

In a discursive setting where mind did not exist – or at least not as an internal counterpart to an external world – the problem of knowledges being out of touch would not arise. Such an alternative setting is provided by an anti-essentialist Marxism in which the concept of overdetermination plays a prominent role. Overdetermination posits the mutual constitution of all social and natural processes. It provides a radical conceptual alternative to forms of determinism, or causal essentialism, and to all other attempts to reduce complex realities to simpler essences at their core.

Rather than confronting the distinction between mind and world, the concept of overdetermination circumvents it. As a concept which presumes integration, it leaves no theoretical space for separated realms of existence which operate independently and relate to each other in problematic ways. This is why I find it difficult to meet Peet's criticisms head on. What is a problem for him does not arise, cannot be conceptualized in my terms.

In an overdeterminist theoretical setting, knowledge is a social process which is constituted by all other social and natural processes and which in turn participates in their constitution. Fully embedded in social and natural life, it cannot lose touch with other aspects of the world. Knowledges have no existence except as overdetermined sites, no being except at the intersection of their many determinations.

An overdetermined knowledge is a process without an essence. It has no *a priori* or essential motive, no abstract vocation to represent the world. Its purposes, like its content, change as other social and natural processes change. Specific and partial and existing in change, knowledges cannot mirror the world in thought any more than construction projects can mirror it in masonry and steel. They are not pieces in a grand puzzle, or participants in a unified project of representation. Taken together they diverge and contradict rather than coalesce and cohere.

Why choose overdetermination?

For me, perhaps the most compelling thing about an overdeterminist conception is the efficacy it confers. Intimations of potency are absent from traditional conceptions of knowledge and muted in Rorty's metaphor of conversation. Overdetermination theory, on the other hand, explicitly constructs knowledge as a cause among causes rather than as simply an effect. Knowledge is not a passive reflection but a social process with an effectivity of its own.

An overdeterminist approach to knowledge dispels not only the metaphor of reflection but also a range of related conceptions that disable the process of knowing. It undermines the distinction between thought and action which incapacitates thought. It refuses to sanction the gap between knowledge and reality which segregates knowledge in some second-order reality or in the realm of the unreal. In circumventing the dualities of subject and object, of mind and world, it withdraws a crucial support from the myth of the spectator-knower (Benhabib, 1990).

In the context of overdetermination, knowledge is not only divorced from debilitating connotations of impotence and subservience but has lost the basis of its exclusiveness as well. For too long the view of knowledge as the singular true representation of the world has contributed to the suppression of left and feminist discourses in academic settings. Outside the academy on the left, similar proscriptions have prevailed. Most potently, perhaps, the designation of a form of classical Marxism as the "science of history" has circumscribed leftist visions of political opportunity and confined leftist activity within the bounds of "correct" theory and "objective" historical fact.

Feminism, anti-essentialist Marxism and a number of other postmodern approaches have pried open these exclusive domains. In a variety of settings, postmodern conceptions of knowledge have undermined traditional conceptions. They have challenged the dominance of particular knowledges and released all knowledges from their subordinate representational role. For me, this has meant that I can now envision the contribution of fully effective knowledges to a revitalized politics on the left.

I am aided in this vision by the example of feminism, which has reshaped the way that many of us think about and experience the world. In recent years, feminist knowledges have opened up a whole new social and cultural territory, previously uncharted and largely unexplored. In the process, they have unavoidably participated in constituting a politics of gender of a new and challenging sort.

With others, I hope to do for class and exploitation what feminism has done for gender. I would like to make the production and appropriation of surplus labor visible as a process which affects all aspects of social and natural life. By creating a knowledge of exploitation which does not make exploitation the essence (or central determinant) of social existence, I hope to participate in creating a novel and diverse politics of class transformation.

I pursue these goals within an anti-essentialist Marxism which challenges the dominance of classical Marxism, rejecting its economism and its claim to accurate representation. From this theoretical vantage, I understand knowledge as effective (rather than reflective) and social life as decentered and infinitely complex. In contradictory ways that I cannot envision, the knowledge I produce will have political effects and other kinds of consequences as well. Assessing the contribution of this non-essentialist class knowledge to a reinvigorated politics of class transformation, perhaps someone someday will pay it one of the compliments that Rorty recommends. Perhaps, if I'm lucky, they will call it valid and true. [...]

To Be a Geographer

Peet finds it unsatisfactory that I do not articulate a way forward for a non-essentialist Marxist geography (p. 124). In the face of my silence, he suggests that "environment, space, or place" are the "obvious examples" of geographical entry points into social analysis (p. 124). He argues that "the main aim of a geo-materialist Marxism in the next years should be to outline the crisis relations between world society and the global and regional environments" (p. 127).

As a Marxist geographer reading these claims, I am struck by the fact that they have little connection to my current and previous work or to my future plans. They suggest a future for Marxist geography which builds on the work that Peet has done but which would require a complete reorientation for me. In the face of Peet's presumption of a uniformity of interests based on a shared academic and theoretical location, I find it necessary – or more accommodating to my existence – to theorize geography as a heterogeneous collection of discourses, and Marxism as a discursive formation marked by conflict and difference rather than by a dominant topical or methodological orientation.

Within geography, as well as within the other academic fields in which I actively participate, I work on the topic of women and industrial policy in a variety of industrial and national settings. I also work on plant closings and the ways in which, in a number of U.S. communities they have given rise to an alternative discourse of worker and community rights (and, in particular, rights to industrial property). Both of these research areas, as well as others in which I am involved, are connected to my interest in promoting a politics of class. They both derive in part from my long-standing participation in regional development discourses, some of which are pre-eminently geographic. They are also related to my history as a feminist activist and shaped by the productionism of the Marxism that I first encountered, and reproduced, when I entered the Ph.D. program at Clark. I could go on with the overdetermined reasons for my research orientation but perhaps it is time for me to make my point.

Dick Peet sees geography as in some sense a unity which is manifest in geographers' shared topics and perspectives. Though I recognize the basis of his vision of cohesion, I tend rather to see geography as a zone of great cultural diversity. My discursive affinity with Marxists, feminists and postmodernists in other disciplines seems to me much greater than my discursive affinity with the climatologist in my department or, for that matter, the specialists in resource management and cartographic methods (though in non-discursive areas we have a lot in common).

For me a distinctive and unifying thing about geography is the extraordinary difficulty that geographers have in defining the basis of its presumed unity and disciplinarity. Unfortunately for non-geographers (and in particular Marxists and feminists in other fields), this difficulty is not so marked in other disciplines. In economics, for example, it has been possible for some schools of thought to exclude others from universities and other institutional settings by prescribing a limited set of questions and methods as quintessentially economic (Amariglio et al., 1990). Geography, on the other hand, is self-consciously decentered. And it is the renowned inability of geographers to agree upon central geographic procedures and questions that makes me feel at home in this particular academic field. The openness that Peet deplores as giving rise to "latest-thing-itis" is what I see as allowing feminism, postmodernism and Marxism to thrive. If you like these things, and the interactions among them, geography is an exciting place to be.

REFERENCES

Amariglio, J., S. Resnick, and R. Wolff. (1990) Division and difference in the "discipline" of economics. *Critical Inquiry* 17 (Autumn): 108–137.

Benhabib, S. (1990) Epistemologies of postmodernism: a rejoinder to Jean-François Lyotard. In L. J. Nicholson (Ed.) *Feminism/Postmodernism*. New York: Routledge, pp. 107–130.

Bordo, S. (1990) Feminism, postmodernism and gender-scepticism. In L. J. Nicholson (Ed.) *Feminism/Postmodernism*. New York: Routledge, pp. 133–156.

Graham, J. and K. St. Martin. (1990) Knowledge and the "localities" debate: meditations on a theme by Cox and Mair. *Antipode* 22: 168–174.

Nicholson, L. J., ed. (1990) *Feminism/Postmodernism*. New York: Routledge.

Peet, R. (1992) Some critical questions for anti-essentialism. *Antipode* 24: 113–130.

Resnick, S. and R. Wolff. (1987) *Knowledge and Class*. Chicago: University of Chicago Press.

Rorty, R. (1979) *Philosophy and the Mirror of Nature*. Princeton: Princeton University Press.

Schell, M. (1991) Interview. *Massachusetts* 2,3 (Spring): 9.

18 (Post)Colonial Spaces

Jane M. Jacobs

Jane Jacobs ties geography to postcolonial ways of understanding the world. She slices unambiguously through the difficult terrains of colonialism, imperialism, space, and postcolonialism, showing how their concerns have productively "cross-fertilized" with postmodern theory. In its merging of these diverse interests, plus its engagement with feminism, cultural geography, urban geography, and geo-politics, Jacobs' essay is a beautifully executed proof of the value of multiple ways of seeing.

In recent years imperialism and postcolonialism have attracted unprecedented academic attention. The emphasis of much of this new work is decidedly cultural, emerging as it does from literary studies, but its effect has reached into a wide range of disciplinary fields. There is little doubt that Edward Said's *Orientalism* (1978) established a template for studies alert to the "culture" of imperialism. As Williams and Chrisman (1993: 5) suggest, Said's approach "inaugurated" the field of study which has come to be known as colonial discourse analysis. Such studies show the ways in which discursive formations worked to create a complex field of values, meanings and practices through which the European Self is positioned as superior and non-Europeans are placed as an inferior, but necessary, Other to the constitution of that Self. Such metropolitan constructs of Self and Other were integral to the territorial, military, political and economic extensions of European power across the globe, the processes known as colonialism and imperialism. As Said (1995: 332) emphasises, processes of social construction of identity are not simply "mental exercises", but also "urgent social contests involving...concrete political issues" such as territory, violence, law and policy. Social constructs and the meanings and practices they generate are at the very heart of the uneven material and political terrains of imperial worlds.

As the work on the nexus of power and identity within the imperial process has been elaborated, so many of the conceptual binaries that were seen as fundamental to its architecture of power have been problematised. Binary couplets like core/ periphery, inside/outside, Self/Other, First World/Third World, North/South have given way to tropes such as hybridity, diaspora, creolisation, transculturation, border. James Clifford (1994: 303) refers to this proliferation of a new analytic language as an "unruly crowd of...terms". This new language is associated with what has come to be known as a postcolonial perspective and owes much to those writing from and about "the margins" and the vigilantly deconstructive potential of poststructuralism. Such terms provide the conceptual frames for interpreting a range of new (or newly found) phenomena which might be loosely described as counter-acting or unsettling imperialism. But they also offer the means for rethinking familiar imperialist structures of domination whose complexities were once obscured by neat binary classifications. The postcolonial critique has mobilised a new conceptual framework which, while not denying the efficacy of imperialist structures of domination, uncovers their often anxious contingency and internal variability. This is not to deny that binary notions of Self/Other did not, inhabit the imperial imagination, but rather to show that this was an intensely unstable arrangement in which these notions of Self and Other, as Derrida (1982) puts it, always "solicited" each other and produced decidedly distruptive effects (Gelder and Jacobs 1995: 153). [...]

While it is enticing to think of the present as somehow already postcolonial, this "postcoloniality", as the term itself suggests, is still deeply entwined with colonial formations. Colonial constructs not only belong to a past that is being worked against in the present, but also to a past that is being nostalgically reworked and inventively adapted in the present. Just as postcolonialist tendencies have always been produced by colonialism, so colonialist tendencies necessarily inhabit often optimistically designated postcolonial formations. [...]

Colonialism and Imperialism

Confusions commonly surround the terms colonialism and imperialism and what may be registered as their contemporary variants, such as neo-colonialism. Edward Said (1993: 8) provides a useful distinction between colonialism and imperialism. Imperialism he defines as the practice, the theory and the attitudes of a dominating metropolitan centre ruling a distant territory. Colonialism, by his definition, is a specific articulation of imperialism associated with territorial invasions and settlements. Williams and Chrisman (1993: 2) also propose that colonialism is a phase within a more persistent process of capitalist imperialism, spanning until the present. Like Said, they define colonialism as that phase of imperialism in which the expansion of the accumulative capacities of capitalism was realised through the conquest and possession of other people's land and labour in the service of the metropolitan core. Colonialism, then, entails the establishment and maintenance of domination over a separate group of people, who are viewed as subordinate, and their territories, which are presumed to be available for exploitation. This is clearly expressed in nineteenth-century British imperialism in which territorial expansion ensured that raw materials were supplied to the metropolis and new markets were created for manufactured goods (King 1990: 49).

There is, then, an implied chronological ordering in the terms colonialism and imperialism. Said (1993: 8) proposes that "direct colonialism has largely ended" but "imperialism . . . lingers where it has always been, in a kind of general cultural sphere as well as in specific political, ideological, economic, and social practices". In part Said is referring to the tenacious persistence of the ideologies, practices and economies of high colonialism in the present moment of formal decolonisation. He is also alluding to various cultural and economic expansions which have continued well beyond the territorial appropriation associated with the colonial period. [. . .]

Imperialism and Space

Already this general discussion of imperialism and colonialism has unavoidably implicated considerations of space. In Edward Said's afterword to the 1995 reprint of *Orientalism*, he proposes that the task for the critical scholar of imperialism is to connect the "struggles of history and social meaning" with the "overpowering materiality" of the "struggle for control over territory" (1995: 331–332). Imperialism for Said (1993: 271) is "an act of geographical violence through which virtually every space in the world is explored, charted, and finally brought under control". Imperial expansions established specific spatial arrangements in which the imaginative geographies of desire hardened into material spatialities of political connection, economic dependency, architectural imposition and landscape transformation.

The role of the spatial imaginary in the imperial project is perhaps most clearly evident in the spatial practices of mapping and naming. Harley has demonstrated the convincing relationship between cartographic practices and the production of "known" space in imperial projects. The quest to map may well be undertaken as an "innocent" cartographic science, but the maps produced never simply replicate the environment. They are part of the "territorial imperatives of a particular political system", most notably that of imperialism (1988: 278). They are, as Harley (ibid.: 283) notes, "the currency of political 'bargains' . . . the force of the law in the landscape". As Huggan (1991) suggests, the cartographic exercise within the colonisation process depended upon a technique (and a hope) of representing a stable and knowable reality in what were unknown lands inhabited by unknown people.

The map has in a sense become the over-determined signifier of the spatiality of the imperial imagination. But the intersection of imaginary and material spatialities was present in other areas of the colonial project and no more so than in the making of cities. The successful exploitation of colonial resources required cities to be built in the colonies. These functioned as centres for colonial administration, sites of local production and consumption, and conduits for the flow of goods and services. There has been a long tradition of studying the colonial and the Third World city in the historical formation of imperialism (see, for overview, Simon 1984; Yeoh 1991; Alsayyad 1992; King 1992). One theme within this broad and theoretically diverse field is the transfer of European architectural styles and planning practices as part of the project of colonial domination (for example, Ross and Telkamp 1985; King 1990). Other work, drawing on Wallerstein's world-system theory, has been concerned with describing the role of the colonial/Third World city in the emergence of a broader capitalist system of dependency (Friedmann 1966; and more recently Timberlake 1985). Anthony King (1976, 1990), for example, has proposed a theory of colonial urban development to explain the political, economic and cultural processes that gave rise to new cities in colonised territories. Colonial cities were, according to King, important sites in the transfer of modern capitalist culture to new worlds. This can be seen in the architectural form and planning of such cities which regularly mimicked the cities of the imperial home. Colonial cities also operated as important sites in the deployment of the technologies of power through which indigenous populations were categorised and controlled. Here town planning became the mechanism by which colonial adjudications of cleanliness, civility and modernity were realised quite literally on the ground. Not least, it was in the name of the ideal city that many of the most comprehensive colonial territorialisations and displacements occurred and the most rigid policies of segregation were implemented (King 1990: 9).

Colonialism did not simply involve the transfer of metropolitan processes of urbanisation to the colonies; there was reverse movement as well. As King (ibid.: 7) argues, "urbanism and urbanisation in the metropole cannot be understood separately from development in the colonial periphery". This involves more than the process that brought exoticised fads to the architecture of imperial cities or saw monuments made to the triumphs of empire. The use of peripheral territories for primary production and resource extraction facilitated, indeed necessitated, the growth of industrialised and commercialised urban centres in the imperial core. [. . .]

The Limits of the Postcolonial

Just as there is confusion around the terms colonialism and imperialism, so there is a proliferation of uses and implied meanings pinned to the term postcolonialism. The term refers not only to formal political status, but also to certain subject positions, political processes, cultural articulations and critical perspectives. Paradoxically, the process of decolonisation after the Second World War, which released former colonies from nineteenth-century colonial arrangements, is perhaps the least meaningful signifier of what might be thought of as postcoloniality. The move to formal independence is shot through with imperialism itself. Formal postcolonial status is a product of imperial cores conceding power over colonised territories. More often than not structures of neo-colonialism provided the very preconditions for such gestures of decolonisation (R. Young 1990: 122). Contemporary resettlements and reterritorialisations undo the geographies of colonialism. Yet diasporic groups, citizens of newly independent nations and indigenous peoples still face the force of neo-colonial formations and live lives shaped by the ideologies of domination and the practices of prejudice established by imperialism. Historically speaking, postcolonialism implies a liberation frequently beyond the limits of existing power relations.

The equivocal nature of postcolonialism as a formal political and historical condition is well demonstrated by nation-states like Australia. Australia might best be described as a "break-away settler colony" which was founded on the principle of transferring imperial power, with little change, from the core to the colony itself (McClintock 1992: 89). Australia is not part of the Third World; it is a reasonably successful western nation which is, relatively speaking, economically independent of dominant core countries. Australia's historical and economic development, and its place in global capitalist relations as an advanced or First World nation, means that it is as much metropolitan as it is (post)colonial (Williams and Chrisman 1993: 4). Yet while Australia has always had tendencies which have moved it away from its colonial maker, it is still a member of the Commonwealth and the British Queen is still officially the head of state. Indeed as Australia struggles with the idea of becoming a republic, of finally realising a more complete and formal state of independence, it is evermore apparent that it is a nation deeply marked by forms of internal colonialism. This is clearly evident in the fact that Australia has a Fourth World, Aboriginal Australia, within its First World boundaries.

For the indigenous peoples of Australia, the "post" of postcolonialism is still a long way off. Indeed in self-consciously multicultural nations like Australia, the original political nexus of coloniser and colonised relations is being decentred by the presence of a range of migrant settlers from around the world: Asia, Africa, South America, the Middle East and elsewhere. These new settlers are not without their own experiences of colonialism, but they are as often as not removed from the specificities of the British colonisation of Australia. "Post" colonial politics in Australia is practised within a nation-state which joyously moves towards multiculturalism: where the often irreconcilable responsibilities produced by the colonialist violence of dispossession compete with the seductive promise of a more worldly and most appetising (for food is one of its great markers) multicultural Australia. It is in the fact of the displacing force of multiculturalism that the claim of being indigenous, *not a settler of any sort*, has gained in importance in First Nation/Fourth World political movements in nation-states like Australia and Canada. The claim of habitation, of not having arrived, becomes the means by which indigenous struggles gain distinction in an increasingly diasporic present (Clifford 1994: 308). Australia, then, is the sort of nation that may be visioned as postcolonial by some but feels decidedly colonial to others. It is the type of ex-colonial territory that points to the formal limits of the historical condition called postcolonialism and the fantastic optimism of the "post" in postcolonialism. [. . .]

Postcolonialism may be better conceptualised as an historically dispersed set of formations which negotiate the ideological, social and material structures of power established under colonialism. Ashcroft et al (1995: 7) go so far as to say that there can be no postcolonialism without the historical precondition called colonialism. They are, in a sense, stating the obvious: one is, of course, the determining condition of the other – one is always already "contaminated" by the other (Hutcheon 1995: 134). From the beginnings of colonial encounters to the contemporary moment of a disseminated global imperialism, there have been counter-colonial movements and outcomes which unsettle colonialism. These may be registered as anti-colonial nationalisms but also as more fractured forms of opposition and destabilisation. [. . .]

Postmodern Space and the (Post)Colonial

Williams and Chrisman (1993: 13–14) note that the much-debated relationship between postcolonialism and postmodernism still requires "lengthy and careful delineation". This nexus is of particular relevance to this volume which takes as its empirical focus not the colonial past but an urban present which is so often read as a paradigmatic site of the "condition of postmodernity" (for example, Harvey 1989; Soja 1989). There is little doubt that postcolonial theoretical revisions have productively cross-fertilised with postmodern theory. The postmodern projects of deconstructing Master narratives, unsettling binaries and admitting marginalised knowledges, follow closely the objectives of the postcolonial critical project. Similarly, these various perspectives are conjoined in their attention to the relationship between discourse and power, the socially constituted and fragmented subject and the unruly politics of signification – the workings of irony, parody, mimicry (Ashcroft et al. 1995: 117). As theories, postmodernism and postcolonialism appear to be one and the same, with postcolonialism perhaps distinguishing itself by the primary concern it has with the processes associated with the condition called colonialism, as feminism has with patriarchy. This overlap between postmodern and postcolonial theoretical perspectives has produced its own discourse of differentiation in which claims are made as to which came first, which has the "real" politics, and what one does to the other. [. . .]

It is undeniable that the condition of postmodernity has meant that even the most recalcitrant Marxists have admitted culture, if not a cultural politics, into their understanding of the workings of capitalism. Culture is, as Jameson tells us, the "new logic" of capitalism. Late Capitalism has produced, we are told, a uniquely "semiotic" society which is "regulated" by a combination of the material and the representational (Lash 1990). For Jameson there is hardly an area of life (not Nature, not the Unconscious, not Culture) untouched by the prodigious expansion of capital (Jameson 1991: 48–49). Within Jameson's narrative, a formerly autonomous cultural sphere is appropriated into the service of capital's accumulative logic and, once entrapped, delivered as an inauthentic culture of pastiche, simulacrum and commodification. Culture, at least in the First World of Jameson, serves not the processes by which identity is articulated or negotiated, but the (now) semiotic motor of capital accumulation.

Jameson depicts a deactivated cultural sphere in which difference is subsumed with the seamless homogeneity of "hyperspace" (R. Young 1990: 204 n. 49). But his notion of homogenisation at the hands of a predatory capitalism is deeply problematic. In other accounts of postmodernity, late capitalism is depicted as being in a complex and contradictory arrangement with the local. It is undeniable that globalisation is occurring but, in a seemingly paradoxical reverberation, place specificity and social difference are being articulated as strongly as ever. Michael Watts (1991: 10) proposes that globalisation does not "signal the erasure of difference" but rather the reconstitution and revalidation of "place, locality and difference". So, for example, recent economic restructurings regularly cohere around specific cultural differences in labour markets (see, as an example, Massey 1984). Similarly, different localities often elaborate distinctive self-images as place-selling strategies (see, as examples, Sorkin 1992; Kearns and Philo 1993 and Urry 1995). Such examples point to the way postmodernity manufactures difference in the service of its own consuming passions (see Urry 1995). This is not a productive politics of difference.

The inability of these hyperspaced versions of postmodernity to accommodate an activated cultural politics may well rest in their nostalgia for the uncontaminated Other and for its role in a revolutionary displacement of capitalism. But as Arjun Appadurai (1990) argues, globalisation is not predatory in a simple sense. Products brought into the Third and Fourth Worlds are regularly indigenised, whereas indigenous products that spiral out of their local sites of production and into international markets as often as not perform a constructive role in counter-imperial articulations, allowing them to be amplified in the global context (ibid.: 15). Appadurai is proposing not only that globalisation does not obliterate the local but that it may also help to establish new globalised conditions for the expression of difference. His postcolonial account of postmodernity serves to illustrate that if an activated politics of cultural production and identity articulation were factored into accounts of the condition of postmodernity, slightly different stories would then begin to be told.

REFERENCES

Alsayyad, N. (1992) "Urbanism and the dominance equation", in N. Alsayyad (ed.) *Forms of Dominance: On the Architecture and Urbanism of the Colonial Enterprise*, Aldershot: Avebury, 1–26.

Appadurai, A. (1990) "Disjuncture and difference in the global cultural economy", *Public Culture* 2, 2: 1–32.

Ashcroft, B., Griffiths, G. and Tiffin, H. (1995) "Introduction: issues and debates", in B. Ashcroft, G. Griffiths and H. Tiffin (eds) *The Post-colonial Studies Reader*, London and New York: Routledge, 7–11.

Clifford, J. (1994) "Diasporas", *Cultural Anthropology* 9, 3: 302–338.

Derrida, J. (1982) *Margins of Philosophy*, Chicago: University of Chicago Press.

Friedmann, J. (1966) "The World City hypothesis", *Development and Change* 17, 1: 69–83.

Gelder, K. and Jacobs, J. M. (1995) "'Talking out of place': authorizing the Aboriginal sacred in postcolonial Australia", *Cultural Studies* 9, 1: 150–160.

Harley, J. B. (1988) "Maps, knowledge and power", in D. Cosgrove and S. Daniels (eds) *The Iconography of Landscape*, Cambridge: Cambridge University Press, 277–312.

Harvey, D. (1989) *The Condition of Postmodernity*, Oxford: Blackwell.

Huggan, G. (1991) "Decolonising the map: post-colonialism, post-structuralism and the cartographic connection", in I. Adam and H. Tiffin (eds) *Past the Last Post: Theorizing Post-Colonialism and Post-Modernism*, New York: Harvester-Wheatsheaf.

Hutcheon, L. (1995) "Circling the downspout of empire: post-colonialism and postmodernism", in B. Ashcroft, G. Griffiths and H. Tiffin (eds) *The Post-colonial Studies Reader*, London and New York: Routledge, 130–135.

Jameson, F. (1991) *Postmodernism, or, The Cultural Logic of Late Capitalism*, Durham, NC: Duke University Press.

Kearns, G. and Philo, C. (eds) (1993) *Selling Places: The City as Cultural Capital. Past and Present*, Oxford: Pergamon.

King, A. D. (1976) *Colonial Urban Development: Culture, Social Power and Environment*, London: Routledge and Kegan Paul.

King, A. D. (1990) *Urbanism, Colonialism and the World-Economy*, London and New York: Routledge.

King, A. D. (1992) "Rethinking colonialism: an epilogue", in N. Alsayyad (ed.) *Forms of Dominance: On the Architecture and Urbanism of the Colonial Enterprise*, Aldershot: Avebury, 339–355.

Lash, S. (1990) *Sociology of Postmodernism*, London: Routledge.

McClintock, A. (1992) "The angel of progress: pitfalls of the term 'post-colonialism'", *Social Text* 10, 2 and 3: 84–98.

Massey, D. (1984) *Spatial Divisions of Labour: Social Structures and the Geography of Production*, London: Macmillan.

Ross, R. and Telkamp, G. (eds) (1985) *Colonial Cities: Essays on Urbanism in a Colonial Context*, Dordrecht: Martinus Nijhoff.

Said, E. W. (1978) *Orientalism*, London: Routledge and Kegan Paul.

Said, E. W. (1993) *Culture and Imperialism*, London: Chatto and Windus.

Said, E. W. (1995) "Afterword to the 1995 printing", in *Orientalism*, London: Penguin, 329–354.

Simon, D. (1984) "Third world colonial cities in context", *Progress in Human Geography* 8, 4: 493–514.

Soja, E. (1989) *Postmodern Geographies*, London: Verso.

Sorkin, M. (ed.) (1992) *Variations on a Theme Park: The New American City and the End of Public Space*, New York: The Noonday Press.

Timberlake, M. (ed.) (1985) *Urbanization in the World-Economy*, Orlando: Academic Press.

Urry, J. (1995) *Consuming Places*, London and New York: Routledge.

Watts, M. J. (1991) "Mapping meaning, denoting difference, imagining identity: dialectical images and postmodern geographies", *Geografiska Annaler* 73B: 7–16.

Williams, P. and Chrisman, L. (1993) "Colonial discourse and post-colonial theory: an introduction", in P. Williams and L. Chrisman (eds) *Colonial Discourse and Post-Colonial Theory: A Reader*, New York: Columbia University Press, 1–26.

Yeoh, B. (1991) "Municipal Control, Asian Agency and the Urban Built Environment in Colonial Singapore, 1880–1929". Unpublished D.Phil., Oxford University.

Young, R. (1990) *White Mythologies: Writing History and the West*, London and New York: Routledge.

19 Zoöpolis

Jennifer Wolch

Jennifer Wolch's *zoöpolis* invites us to bring animals back into human geography. Her programmatic outline for a "transspecies urban theory," at least in this early version (1996), is not overtly postmodern, yet postmodern sensitivies are evident in her multiple ways of seeing, her incorporation of diversity and difference, and her consideration of an "animal standpoint." This is another essay to relish for its willingness to grapple with an almost bewildering variety of epistemologies, and come out at the end with a totally original vision of a geography that matters. (Compare Reading 37).

Introduction

Urbanization in the west was based historically on a notion of progress rooted in the conquest and exploitation of nature by culture. The moral compass of city-builders pointed toward the virtues of reason, progress, and profit, leaving wild lands and wild things – as well as people deemed to be wild or "savage" – beyond the scope of their reckoning. Today, the logic of capitalist urbanization still proceeds without regard to nonhuman animal life, except as cash-on-the-hoof headed for slaughter on the "disassembly" line or commodities used to further the cycle of accumulation. Development may be slowed by laws protecting endangered species but you will rarely see the bulldozers stopping to gently place rabbits or reptiles out of harm's way.

Paralleling this disregard for nonhuman life, you will find no mention of animals in contemporary urban theory – whether mainstream or Marxist, neoclassical or feminist. The lexicon of mainstream theory, for example, reveals a deep-seated anthropocentrism. Urbanization transforms "empty" land through a process called "development," to produce "improved land" whose developers are exhorted (at least in neoclassical theory) to dedicate it to the "highest and best use." Such language reflects a peculiar perversion of our thinking: wildlands are not "empty" but teeming with nonhuman life; "development" involves a through denaturalization of the environment; "improved land" is invariably impoverished in terms of soil quality, drainage, and vegetation; and judgments of "highest and best use" reflect profit-centered values and interests of humans alone, ignoring not only wild or feral animals but captives such as pets, lab animals, and livestock who live and die in urban space shared with people. Marxian varieties of urban theory are also anthropocentric, setting "the urban" as a human stage for capitalist production, social reproduction of labor, and capital circulation and accumulation. Similarly, feminist urban theory, when grounded primarily in socialist and liberal feminisms (rather than ecofeminism), avoids questions of how patriarchy and gendered social practices shape the fate of animals in the city.

Our theories and practices of urbanization have contributed to disastrous ecological effects. Wildlife habitat is being destroyed at record rates as the urban front advances worldwide, driven in the First World by suburbanization and edge-city development, and in the Second and Third Worlds by pursuit of a "catching-up" development model which produces vast rural to urban migration flows and sprawling squatter landscapes. Entire ecosystems and species are threatened, while individual animals crowded out of their homes (or dumped) must risk entry into urban areas in search of food or water, where they encounter people, vehicles and other dangers. The substitution of pets for wild nature in the city has driven an explosion of the urban pet population, polluting urban waterways as well as leading to mass killings of dogs and cats. Isolation of urban people from the domestic animals they eat has distanced them from the horrors and ecological harms of factory farming, and the escalating destruction of rangelands and forests driven by the market's efforts to create/satisfy a lust for meat. For most free creatures, as well as staggering numbers of captives such as pets and livestock, cities imply suffering, death, or extinction.

The aim of this paper is to foreground an urban theory that takes nonhumans seriously. In the first part, I clarify what I mean by "humans" and "animals," and provide a series of arguments suggesting that a *transspecies urban theory* is necessary to the development of an eco-socialist, feminist, anti-racist urban praxis. Then, in the second part, I argue that current considerations of animals and people in the capitalist city (based on U.S. experience) are strictly limited, and suggest that a transspecies urban theory must be grounded in contemporary theoretical debates regarding urbanization, nature and culture, ecology, and urban environmental action.

Why Animals Matter (Even in Cities)

The rationale for considering animals in the context of urban environmentalism is not transparent. Urban environmental issues traditionally center around the pollution of the city conceived as human habitat, not animal habitat. Thus the various wings of the urban progressive environmental movement have avoided thinking about nonhumans, and have left the ethical as well as pragmatic ecological, political and economic questions regarding animals to be dealt with by those involved in the defense of endangered species or animal welfare. Such a division of labor privileges the rare and the tame, and ignores the lives and living spaces of the large number and variety of animals who dwell in cities. In this section, I argue that even common, everyday animals should matter.

The human-animal divide: a definition

At the outset, it is imperative to clarify what we mean when we talk about "animals" or "nonhumans" on the one hand, and "people" or "humans" on the other. Where does one draw the line between the two, and upon what criteria? This is probably humankind's Ur-question, since the biological, social and psychological construction of what is human depends unequivocally on what is animal. At various times and places particular answers to this Ur-question have gained hegemony. In many parts of the world beliefs in transmogrification or transmigration of souls provide a basis for beliefs in human-animal continuity (or even coincidence). But in the western world animals have for many centuries been defined as fundamentally different and ontologically separate from humans. This is despite the fact that the explicit criteria for establishing the human-animal difference have changed over time (have they souls? can they reason? talk? suffer?). All such criteria have routinely used humans as the standard for judgment. The concern is, can animals do what humans do? rather than can humans do what animals do (breathe in water, simultaneously distinguish 30 different odors, etc.)? Thus judged, animals are inferior beings. Such convictions were widely popularized by Thomas Aquinas and René Descartes among others. And although the Darwinian revolution declared a fundamental continuity among species, humans (or rather white men) still stood firmly astride the apex of the evolutionary chain. Lacking souls or reason, and below humans on the evolutionary scale, animals could still be readily separated from people, objectified and used instrumentally for food, clothes, transportation, company or spare body parts.

Agreement about the human/animal divide has recently collapsed. Critiques of post-Enlightenment science have undermined claims of human-animal discontinuity, and exposed the deeply anthropocentric and androcentric roots of modernist science. Greater understanding of animal thinking and capabilities now reveals the astonishing range and complexity of animal behavior and social life, while studies of human biology and behavior emphasize the similarity of humans to other animals. Claims about human uniqueness have thus been rendered deeply suspicious. Debates about the human-animal divide have also raged as a result of sociobiological discourses about the biological bases for human social organization and behavior, and feminist and anti-racist arguments about the social bases for human differences claimed to be biological. Long held beliefs in the human as social subject and the animal as biological object have thus been destabilized.

My position on the human/animal divide is similar to that of Noske, who like Haraway, Plumwood, and others, argues that "animals do indeed resemble us a great deal" but that their "otherness" must also be recognized by people. This otherness is not simply the result of obvious morphological differences as emphasized by the life sciences; such an emphasis essentializes animals by reducing them to their biological traits alone. This is an unforgivable tactic when directed toward specific categories of people (e.g., women) but somehow deemed perfectly acceptable for animals, despite the misleading conclusions that result. Those who minimize human-animal discontinuity also obliterate animal otherness through the denial of difference. Both extremes are anthropocentric, and deny the possibility that animals as well as people socially construct their worlds and influence each other's worlds; the resulting "animal constructs are likely to be markedly different from ours but may be no less real." Animals have their own realities, their own worldviews – in short, they are *subjects* not objects.

This position is rarely reflected in eco-socialist, feminist and antiracist practices which have conceptualized "the environment" in one of three ways: (i) as set of scientifically defined biological, geophysical and geochemical assemblages or systems, e.g., biosphere, lithosphere, ecosystem, etc.; (ii) as a stock of "natural resources," the essential medium for human life and source of economic well-being whose quality must therefore (and only therefore) be protected; or (iii) as an active but somehow unitary subject that responds in both predictable and unpredictable (often uncooperative) ways to human interference and exploitation and which must be respected as an independent force with inherent value. The first scientific approach, which denies any subjectivity to nature, is covertly anthropocentric; it predominates in mainstream, managerial environmentalism but also lies at the base of many progressive analyses of urban environmental problems. The second resourcist line of thinking, often embedded in the first approach as a rationale for looking at the urban environment in the first place, is blatantly anthropocentric; it is common not only among reform environmentalists but also in more radical elements of environmentalism including the environmental justice movement. The third approach, often framed in explicitly ecocentric terms, seems an improvement (and in many ways is). But in emphasizing ecological holism it backgrounds interspecific differences among animals (human and nonhuman), as well as the differences between animate and inanimate nature, the latter having subjectivity only in the metaphoric sense or perhaps at the level of atomic particles and other diverse quanta. This view prevails in many strands of green thought offered by deep ecologists scientific Gaians, and environmental historians (reacting to the perceived postmodern relegation of landscape to socially-constructed text). Thus, in most forms of progressive environmentalism, animals have been either objectified and/ or backgrounded.

Thinking like a bat: the question of animal standpoints

The recovery of animal subjectivity implies an ethical and political obligation to redefine the urban problematic and to consider strategies for urban praxis from the standpoints of animals. Granting animals subjectivity at a conceptual level is a first step. Even this is apt to be hotly contested by human social groups who have been marginalized and devalued by claims that they are "closer to animals" and hence less intelligent, worthy, or evolved than, say, white males. It may also run counter to those who interpret the granting of subjectivity as synonymous with a granting of rights, and object either to rights-type arguments in general or to animal rights specifically. (A recovery of the animal subject does not imply that animals have rights although the rights argument does hinge on the conviction that animals are subjects of a life.) A more difficult step must be taken if the revalorization of animal subjectivity is to be meaningful in terms of day-to-day practice. We not only have to "think like a mountain" but also to "think like a bat" – somehow overcoming Nagel's classic objection that because bat sonar is not similar to any human sense, it is humanly impossible to answer a question such as "what it is like to be a bat?"

Is it impossible to think like a bat? There is a parallel here with the problems raised by standpoint (or multipositionality) theories of knowledge that assert that a variety of individual human differences (such as race, class or gender) so strongly shape experience and thus interpretations of the world, that any suggestion of a single position marginalizes others. For example, the essentialist category "woman" silences differences of race, and in so doing allows the dominant group to create its own master narrative, define a political agenda, and maintain power. Such polyvocality may lead to a nihilistic relativism and a paralysis of political action. But the response cannot be to return to practices of radical exclusion and denial of difference. Instead, we must recognize that individual humans are embedded in social relations and networks with people similar or different, and upon whom their welfare depends. This realization allows for a recognition of kinship but also of difference, since identities are defined not only through seeing that we are similar to others, but that we are also different from them. Using what Haraway terms a "cyborg vision" that allows "partial, locatable, critical knowledge sustaining the possibility of webs of connection called solidarity," we can embrace kinship as well as difference and encourage the emergence of an ethic of respect and mutuality, caring and friendship.

The webs of kinships and differences that shape individual identity involve both humans and animals. It is easy to accept in the abstract that humans depend upon a rich ecology of animal organisms. But there is also a large volume of archeological, paleoanthropological, and psychological evidence suggesting that concrete interactions and interdependence with animal others are indispensable to the development of human cognition, identity and consciousness, and to a maturity which accepts ambiguity, difference and lack of control. In short, animals are not only "good to think" (to borrow a phrase from Lévi-Strauss) but indispensable to learning how to think in the first place, and how to relate to other people.

Who are the relevant animal others? Unlike Shepard, who maintains that only wild animals play a role in human ontology, I argue that many sorts of animals matter, including domesticated animals. Domestication has profoundly altered the intelligence, senses, and life ways of creatures such as dogs, cows, sheep and horses, so as to drastically diminish their otherness. So denaturalized, they have come to be seen as part of human culture. But wild animals have been appropriated and denaturalized by people too. This is evidenced by the myriad ways wildlife is commercialized and incorporated into human culture. And like domestic animals, wild animals can be profoundly impacted by human actions, often leading to significant behavioral adaptations. Ultimately, the division between wild and domestic must be seen as a permeable social construct; it may be better to conceive of a *matrix* of animals who vary with respect to the extent of physical or behavioral modification due to human intervention, and types of interaction with people. In such a matrix, animals range from those whose bodies and lifeways remain unaffected by humans and who have no contact with people (a dwindling number of species), to those who are "built-to-suit" and sleep with us under the bedclothes at night. In other cells of the matrix are a host of more ambiguous and complex cases – livestock, feral animals, lab animals, the genetically engineered, "pet" lizards, turtles or tarantulas, and trout from the fish farm.

Our ontological dependency on animals seems to have characterized us as a species since the Pleistocene. Human needs for dietary protein, desires for spiritual inspiration and companionship, and the ever-present possibility of ending up as somebody's dinner required thinking like an animal. This role of animals in human development can be used as an (anthropomorphic) argument in defense of wildlife conservation or pet-keeping. But my concern is how human dependency on animals was played out in terms of the patterns of human-animal interactions it precipitated. Did ontological dependency on animals create an interspecies ethic of caring and webs of friendship? Without resurrecting a 1990s version of the Noble Savage – an essentialized indigenous person living in spiritual and material harmony with nature – it is clear that for most of (pre)history, people ate wild animals, tamed them, and kept them captive, but also respected them as kin, friends, teachers, spirits, or gods. Their value lay both in their similarities with and differences from humans. Not coincidentally, most wild animal habitats were also sustained.

Re-enchanting the city: an agenda to bring the animals back in

How can animals play their integral role in human ontology today? How can ethical responses and political practices engendered by the recognition of human-animal kinship and difference be fostered? How can this develop in urban settings where everyday interaction with so many kinds of animals has been eliminated? In the west, many of us interact with or experience animals only by keeping captives of a restricted variety or eating "food" animals sliced into steak, chop and roast. We get a sense of wild animals only by watching *Wild Kingdom* re-runs or going to Sea World to see the latest in a long string of short-lived "Shamus." In our apparent mastery of urban nature, we are seemingly protected from all nature's dangers but chance losing any sense of wonder and awe for the non-human world. The loss of both humility and the dignity of risk results in a widespread belief in the banality of day-to-day survival.

To allow for the emergence of an ethic, practice and politics of caring for animals and nature, we need to renaturalize cities and invite the animals back in – and in the process re-enchant the city.

I call this renaturalized, re-enchanted city *zoöpolis*. The reintegration of people with animals and nature in zoöpolis can provide urban dwellers with the local, situated everyday knowledge of animal life required to grasp animal standpoints or ways of being in the world, interact with them accordingly in particular contexts, and motivate political action necessary to protect their autonomy as subjects and their life spaces. Such knowledge would stimulate a thorough rethinking of a wide range of urban daily life practices: not only animal regulation and control practices, but landscaping, development rates and design, roadway and transportation decisions, use of energy, industrial toxics and bioengineering – in short, all practices that impact animals and nature in its diverse forms (e.g., climate, plant life, landforms, etc.).

And, at the most personal level, we might rethink eating habits, since factory farms are so environmentally destructive *in situ*, and the western meat habit radically increases the rate at which wild habitat is converted to agricultural land worldwide (to say nothing of how one feels about eating cows, pigs, chickens or fishes once they are embraced as kin).

While based in everyday practice like the bioregional paradigm, the zoöpolis model differs in including animals and nature in the metropolis rather than relying on an anti-urban spatial fix like small-scale communalism. It also accepts the reality of global interdependence rather than opting for autarky. Moreover, unlike deep ecological visions epistemically tied to a psychologized individualism and lacking in political-economic critique, urban renaturalization is motivated not only by a conviction that animals are central to human ontology in ways that enable the development of webs of kinship and caring with animal subjects, but that our alienation from animals results from specific political-economic structures, social relations, and institutions operative at several spatial scales. Such structures, relations and institutions will not magically change once individuals recognize animal subjectivity, but will only be altered through political engagement and struggle against oppression based on class, race, gender and species.

Beyond the city, the zoöpolis model serves as a powerful curb on the contradictory and colonizing environmental politics of the west as practiced both in the west itself

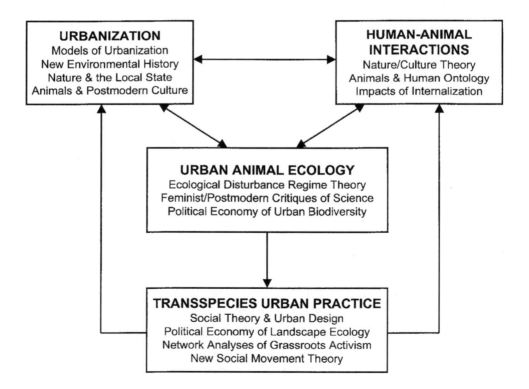

Figure I. A trans-species urban theory.

and as inflicted on other parts of the world. For example, wildlife reserves are vital to prevent species extinction. But because they are "out there," remote from urban life, reserves can do nothing to alter entrenched modes of economic organization and associated consumption practices that hinge on continual growth and make reserves necessary in the first place. The only modes of life that the reserves change are those of subsistence peoples who suddenly find themselves alienated from their traditional economic base and further immiserated. But an interspecific ethic of caring replaces dominionism to create urban regions where animals are neither incarcerated, killed, nor sent off to live in wildlife prisons but instead are valued neighbors and partners in survival. This ethic links urban residents with peoples elsewhere in the world who have evolved ways of both surviving and sustaining the forests, streams, and diversity of animal lives, and enjoins their struggles. The western myth of a pristine arcadian wilderness, imposed with imperial impunity on those places held hostage to the International Monetary Fund and World Bank in league with powerful international environmental organizations, is trumped by a post-colonial politics and practice that begins at home with animals in the city.

Ways of Thinking Animals in the City

An agenda for renaturalizing the city and bringing animals back in should be developed with an awareness of the impacts of urbanization on animals in the capitalist city, how urban residents think about and behave toward animal life, the ecological adaptations made by animals to urban conditions, and current practices and politics arising around urban animals. The goal is to understand capitalist urbanization in a globalizing economy and what it means for animal life; how and why patterns of human-animal interactions change over time and space; urban animal ecology as science, social discourse, and political economy; and transspecies urban practice shaped by managerial plans and grassroots activism. Figure 1 lays out a metatheoretical heuristic device that links together the disparate discourses of the transpecies urban problematic.

20 The Geographical Foundations and Social Regulation of Flexible Production Complexes

Michael Storper and Allen J. Scott

In recent decades, economic geographers have been tremendously busy, attempting to keep up with the rapid pace of global economic change, including (for instance) deindustrialization, post-Fordism, globalization, and the rise of an information society. In the 1980s, Michael Storper, Allen Scott, and many others began a painstaking inquiry into the terms and conditions of contemporary economic restructuring. One crucially important piece of their conceptual apparatus was the notion that we had moved from a "Fordist" to a "post-Fordist" mode of production. In this early statement (1989), Storper and Scott explore the notion of a "radical break" in global economic geography, without once mentioning the P word.

The Turning Point

In all of the advanced capitalist countries, problems of deindustrialization have commanded considerable attention for some time now. Since the late 1960s, in many of the core industrial cities and regions of Britain, France, Italy, West Germany and the USA, there have been steep declines in output and employment in the mass production industries that served as the propulsive engines of economic growth in the post-war period. These declines accelerated in the early 1980s and have now become visible even in Japan. As production was restructured over this period (by plant closure, technical rationalization or decentralization) the resulting business cutbacks and job losses in core regions frequently engendered deep fiscal crises of local government and much community distress. In the face of these problems, a large literature on deindustrialization and its local effects in both the US and Western Europe has come into being (Bluestone & Harrison 1982, Massey & Meegan 1984, Markusen 1985, Stoffaës 1978).

At the very time when the deindustrialization of core regions was reaching its peak in the late 1970s and early 1980s, however, a number of other areas were experiencing rapid growth of industrial output and employment. This growth, moreover, has in many cases been posited on the development of alternative ways of organizing production systems and local labor markets. Indeed, it now seems that a new, hegemonic model of industrialization, urbanization, and regional development has been making its historical appearance in the US and Western Europe, based on a four-fold shift from the model that dominated over much of the post-war period. The shift may be characterized in the following terms:

1   The *central sectors* of the production system are no longer focused to the same degree as previously on the production of consumer durables and associated capital goods. They consist, rather, of ensembles of flexible production sectors such as (a) selected high technology industries, (b) revitalized craft specialty production, and (c) producer and financial services. These ensembles are becoming increasingly central in the sense that they account for a steadily rising share of employment and output growth in the North American and Western European economies.

2   In all these sectors, *flexible production methods* constitute a basic principle of organization in contrast with the Fordist mass production methods of the preceding hegemonic model (cf. Piore & Sabel 1984). Note, however, that despite the recent tendency of the Fordist model to break down, it has far from disappeared altogether and it remains still a significant way of organizing production in many sectors.

3   The *geographical foundations* of industrial growth have been shifting, in some cases quite radically. Many flexible production sectors have been locating in places that are often far removed from the old centers of Fordist mass production. At these places, moreover, there has been a definite re-creation of the process of spatial agglomeration. We might say, indeed, that a new set of core industrial regions is beginning to take shape on the landscape of contemporary capitalism.

4   Every dominant model of industrialization is associated with a distinctive set of broader social institutions. In the post-war period, for example, mass production was coupled to Keynesian welfare-statist institutions designed to stimulate mass consumption and to maintain broad social order. As such, these institutions helped to regulate macroeconomic accumulation over the long-run. The transition to flexible production is beginning to bring with it wide ranging changes in social organization in North America and Western Europe. New forms of *collective social and institutional order* are now appearing in the specific locales of flexible production, as well as in the body politic at large. [...]

Two Technological-institutional Models of Production

Capitalist production apparatuses may assume many alternative technological and institutional configurations, ranging, for example, from the early putting out system through classical factory methods to Fordist mass production, and so on. Each particular configuration consists in a historically determinate technological-institutional model of production comprising a web of production techniques, employment relations, methods of organizing the intra-and inter-firm division of labor, managerial and entrepreneurial relations, and so on. Each such model is also roughly equivalent to what theorists of the French Regulationist School call a *regime of accumulation* and a *mode of social regulation* (cf. Aglietta 1976, Boyer 1986, Lipietz 1986), i.e., a structure governing the production, appropriation and reinvestment of the economic surplus. Two-contrasting technological-institutional models of production are of particular relevance in North America and Western Europe at the present time, namely, the aging model of Fordist mass production and an ascending model of flexible production organization. [...]

Fordist mass production

The Fordist model of production was decisively installed in the major capitalist economies in the inter-war years. It flourished through a period of high Fordism corresponding more or less to the long post-war boom after which, in the 1970s and 1980s, it entered into an extended period of crisis, restructuring, and spatial reorganization that is still far from over. Fordism was based essentially on mass production, though we should keep in mind that other species of productive activity (such as small-scale batch production and skilled artisanal industry) continued to prosper throughout the Fordist period. In its classical guise, Fordism was underpinned by large and highly capitalized units of production consisting of either (i) continuous flow processes, as in the cases of petrochemicals or steel production, or (ii) assembly line processes (and deep technical divisions of labor), as in the cases of cars, electrical appliances or machinery. Production was geared to an insistent search for internal economies of scale via increasing standardization of outputs, routinization of processes, and rigidly dedicated capital equipment. There was, as a consequence, a tendency for both physical output per plant and productivity per worker to rise steadily over time. Major plants in leading sectors were, and are, located at the center of networks of upstream producers providing necessary physical inputs and services, sometimes on the basis of non-Fordist artisanal labor processes. As selected production activities within the Fordist system reached technological maturity, they tended to become embodied in branch plants and then to decentralize to cheap labor sites in national and international peripheries.

These physical features of Fordism were matched in institutional terms by the emergence of oligopolistic multi-establishment corporations and big industry-wide labor unions. A basic division of labor also appeared between white-collar managerial workers who planned and directed production, and blue-collar manual workers caught up in a deepening dynamic of task fragmentation and deskilling. Through their union representatives, blue-collar workers secured contractual codification of job categories, seniority rules, and productivity-based wage-setting practices. The rigidities brought into being by these contractual arrangements were then typically matched by countervailing lay-off and recall processes as the mechanism by which producers attempted to adjust their demand for labor to changes in the economic cycle (rather than adjustment by means of wage rate variations or the re-allocation of labor on the shop floor).

The entire Fordist system tended generally to expand over time, despite cyclical downswings and periodic economic depressions. In the effort to regulate the system and to stabilize its overall growth path, a series of governmental measures inspired by Keynesian welfare-statist conceptions of economic and social control made their appearance after the 1930s in all the major capitalist nations. These measures differed in detail from country to country, but they were all nonetheless generally (and at first successfully) directed to attempts (i) to mitigate recessionary conditions and rising unemployment by means of deficit spending and subsidized consumption as well as (ii) to maintain a social and industrial peace by means of redistributive legislation in matters of unemployment insurance, housing, public welfare, and so on.

Flexible production and accumulation

In spite of the dominating position of Fordist mass production over much of the 20th century, more flexible patterns of industrial organization were – as we have already, suggested – always present, and even preceded the historical emergence of Fordism (cf. Sabel & Zeitlin 1985). However, the specific forms of flexible production that are now shifting into an increasingly central position in the advanced capitalist economies have their origins in the period following World War 2, and have grown to major economic prominence only since about the end of the 1960s.

When we speak of flexible production systems we refer to forms of production characterized by a well developed ability both to shift promptly from one process and/or product configuration to another, and to adjust quantities of output rapidly up or down over the short run without any strongly deleterious effects on levels of efficiency. Both of these types of flexibility are achieved through a variety of intersecting strategies. Within the firm, flexibility may be attained through the use of general purpose, non-dedicated equipment and machinery (often programable) and/or craft labor processes. There is also a tendency within the flexible firm for job descriptions to break down into a restricted number of broadly-ranging categories, and for concomitant extensions to occur in the redeployability of labor on the shop floor. In the domain of inter-firm relations, flexibility is achieved by extensions of the social division of labor facilitating rapid changes in combinations of vertical and horizontal linkage between producers, thus leading to intensification of external economies of scale in the production system as a whole. In addition, the labor markets associated with flexible production systems tend to be typified by high rates of turnover, and by the proliferation of part-time and temporary work as well as homework.

As a consequence of these proclivities, individual units of production in flexible production systems are usually less specialized and smaller in size than mass production units. They are technologically capable of achieving great flexibility of production within their own spheres of operation and, at the same time, this flexibility is multiplied by the system effects of the social division of labor, which permits the formation and re-formation of interdependent combinations of producers. Product differentiation increases as a result, and markets become increasingly competitive. Flexibility is yet further enhanced by a certain tendency for a super-structural tier of firms to emerge involving specialists in system coordinating and marketing functions, like the celebrated *impannatori* of Prato in Italy (Becattini 1987).

The rise of the new flexible technological-institutional model of production has coincidentally been accompanied in the majority of the advanced capitalist countries by the electoral success of governments committed in varying degrees to attempts to dismantle the apparatus of Keynesian welfare-statism. Backed up by resurgent neoconservative ideologies, these governments are attempting to install new policies putatively designed to reinforce economic competition, entrepreneurialism, privatization, and self-reliance. [...]

The Politics of Place in Flexible Production Complexes

By the politics of place we mean to suggest processes of the formation and appropriation of systems of place-bound norms integral to the functioning of any locale as a center of economic and social life. These norms emerge in part from the historical geography of each given place and they are also an object of efforts on the part of various groups and factions to shape them actively to serve their interests. For example, in an earlier era of industrialization in the USA, attempts were made by elite groups to enhance the efficient operation of the dominant centers of growth through political movements such as Progressivism (and its manifestations in the City Beautiful and the City Efficient movements) and Boosterism. As the Fordist regime of accumulation deepened and as high Fordism came on to the scene in the post-war years, the politics of place came to center on a consumerist representation of urban life as manifest in ideals about the nuclear family, suburban residence, and private car ownership. This indeed is what in part kept Fordism going as a macro-economic phenomenon (Walker 1981). This representation was accompanied by increasingly rigid practices, rules, and norms governing the interrelations between business and labor in the workplace, in the labor market, and in the municipal environment. One consequence, we have shown, was a dynamic of continually rising wage levels, and this in turn fed upon and helped to intensify the consumerist ideology of high Fordism. With the weakening of Fordism after the late 1960s, the accumulated culture and traditions of mass production centers reinforced the crisis and prompted producers in new production ensembles to seek out alternative locations where accumulation could be reconstructed unhindered by a Fordist politics of place.

Thus, as the window of locational opportunity (to which we alluded earlier) opened in the late 1950s and early 1960s, producers in many of the new flexible production ensembles actively took advantage of it in an attempt to maximize their geographical and social distance from established centers of Fordist production. High technology industry aggressively pioneered new production locations on the extensive margins of industrialization, as did some of the new artisanal industries. However, in many cases artisanal production together with burgeoning service industries tended to grow at sites where there was already some pre-existing activity of the same type, for these antecedent activities were already well insulated from Fordist labor markets. In all of these places, a new post-Fordist politics of place has been constructed, though with considerable variation from industry to industry and from location to location. Three examples may be invoked in illustration of these remarks.

First, new high technology growth centers in the US Sunbelt have developed a politics of place that is, in a sense, an attempt to perfect the model of suburban life that came to be strongly associated with urbanization under Fordism. This phenomenon may be identified partially in terms of low densities of urban development, highly privatized forms of domestic life based on individual homeownership, and abundant recreational opportunities. As we have shown, growth was largely initiated by producers in the new high technology industrial ensemble seeking out places without a prior history of Fordist industrialization, where the relations of production and work could be reconstructed anew. These experiments have turned out so far to be extremely successful, for a politics of place has been instituted and maintained in which neo-conservative attitudes about work and life have become remarkably pervasive (cf. DiLellio 1987). At the same time, these attitudes conform well to the need for high levels of flexibility among producers, for they inhibit precisely the kinds of organizational responses on the part of workers that create dysfunctional forms of inertia and rigidity in the production system. The more experimental and changeable the technology, the more these qualities are important to producers. In addition, local governments have reinforced the process of growth by taking an entrepreneurial stance in which they compete among one another in providing the tangible bases of a good business climate.

Second, in the craft communities of the Third Italy, despite a long tradition of active labor union organization and leftist municipal government, an effective politics of place has been constructed around a social agreement about growth among labor unions, employers, and local governments. Labour unions have helped to mobilize and reproduce craft skills and consciousness among workers (Scarpitti & Trigilia 1987). Employers have combined in order to coordinate local production activities through institutional arrangements. In addition, local governments have taken an active role in the promotion of the small firm sector, in aiding the coordinating activities of firms, and in enhancing local labor market flexibility by providing special unemployment payments and retraining programs (Hatch 1987).

Third, and finally, over the last couple of decades, dense service production complexes have grown in and around the central business districts of major world cities such as New York, London, Paris, and Los Angeles. These developments have been posited upon both massive downtown redevelopment projects and extensive gentrification of inner-city neighborhoods to house the burgeoning white-collar workforce of the central service complex. Downtown office redevelopment has been facilitated by the emergence of growth coalitions which have been able significantly to shape the direction of urban planning and renewal in central cities (cf. Davis 1987). Gentrification has, in its turn, been associated with the rise of active and influential neighborhood and community groups that lobby on behalf of their own interests (neighborhood preservation, continued upward momentum of property values, improved services, and so on). As all of this has come about, the centers of major world cities have been remade, both physically and symbolically, as domains of leisure and self-identification for the new service and managerial fractions, as centers of international taste and culture, and as loci of mass spectacle of the sort described by Debord (1967).

These examples demonstrate the great variety of the politics of place in and around contemporary flexible production agglomerations. The cases we have examined have all thus far developed without encountering major social and political break-downs. This condition is underpinned by the recency of their emergence as modern flexible production agglomerations, for oppositional forms of consciousness and organization – if they are to appear – need time in order to be built. If the history of previous industrial localities is any indication, we may well expect one form or another of organized opposition to materialize, whether it be based on class or community relations. We may also expect that if such opposition should appear, complementary political responses by producers and local government would also come into being, though in some cases (in the USA above all) producers' own neoconservatism and the historically low level of coordination of small business may turn out to be barriers to the formation of such responses. In view of the wayward character of history, we take the precaution of refraining from any attempt to imbue these expectations with further substance.

One final important point needs to be made in this context. In some accounts of new industrial development, and above all in many analyses of high technology industrial location, the observed communal characteristics of Sunbelt growth centers are described unproblematically as signifying a "high quality of life." This, in and of itself, is then said to attract large numbers of technical and scientific workers from other places to these centers. The same accounts frequently go on to the conclusion that the location of high technology industrial enterprises can accordingly be largely accounted for in terms of the prior residential preferences and migratory patterns of these workers. In view of what we have written above about the logic and dynamics of the formation of industrial agglomerations, this conclusion is surely incorrect; indeed, it represents a highly ideological view of things, for it reduces the complex totality of growth center development to a simple set of consumer preferences and behaviors. As we have shown both here and elsewhere (Scott & Storper 1987), we can surely more effectively approach this problem in terms of the intricate interrelations between the technological-institutional bases of production, the dynamics of industrial organization and local labor market development, and processes of local social regulation.

REFERENCES

Aglietta, M. 1976. *A theory of capitalist regulation*. London: New Left Books.

Becattini, G. (ed.) 1987. *Mercato e forze locali: il distretto industriale*. Bologna: Il Mulino.

Bluestone, B. & B. Harrison 1982. *The deindustrialization of America*. New York: Basic Books.

Boyer, R. 1986. *La théorie de la régulation: une analyse critique*. Paris: Editions La Décou-verte.

Davis, M. 1987. Chinatown, part two: the internationalization of downtown Los Angeles. *New Left Review* no. 164, 65–86.

Debord, G. 1967. *La société du spectacle*. Paris: Buchet/Chastel.

DiLellio, A. 1987. Changing citizenship in "High Tech" communities: the case of Dallas (US) and Grenoble (France). Paper presented at the International Conference on Technology, Restructuring and Urban Development, Dubrovnik, Yugoslavia, June 25–30.

Hatch, R. 1987. Manufacturing networks and reindustrialization: strategies for state and local economic development. Newark, N.J.: New Jersey Institute of Technology.

Lipietz, A. 1986. New tendencies in the international division of labor: regimes of accumulation and modes of social regulation. In *Production, work, territory: the geographical anatomy of industrial capitalism*, A. J. Scott & M. Storper (eds), 16–40. Boston: Allen & Unwin.

Markusen, A. 1985. *Profit cycles, oligopoly, and regional development*. Cambridge, Mass.: MIT Press.

Massey, D. & R. Meegan 1984. *Spatial divisions of labour; social structures and the geography of production*. London: Macmillan.

Piore, M. & C. Sabel 1984. *The second industrial divide* New York: Basic Books.

Sabel, C. & J. Zeitlin 1985. Historical alternatives to mass production: politics, markets and technology in nineteenth century industrialization. *Past and Present* **108**, 133–76.

Scarpitti, L. & C. Trigilia 1987. Strategies of flexibility: firms, unions and local governments – the case of Prato. Paper presented to the Conference on New Technologies and Industrial Relations: Adjustment to a Changing Competitive Environment, Endicott House, Dedham, Mass., February.

Scott, A. J. & M. Storper 1987. High technology industry and regional development: a theoretical critique and reconstruction. *International Social Science Review* **112**, 215–32.

Stoffaës, C. 1978. *La grande menace industrielle*. Paris: Calmann-Lévy.

Walker, R. 1981. A theory of suburbanization. In *Urbanization and urban planning in capitalist society*. M. Dear & A. J. Scott (eds). London: Methuen.

21 Postmodern Urbanism

Michael Dear and Steven Flusty

In this essay, your intrepid editors outline a theory of urban structure based on the notion of a "postmodern urbanism." Dear and Flusty claim to recognize a "proto-postmodernism" in the urban landscapes of contemporary Southern California, but subsequently recast this vision to derive a theory of "keno capitalism," a new way of seeing the urban. They overturn one of the most cherished principles of the "Chicago School" of urban structure, which posits that the urban center organizes its hinterland; in a "Los Angeles School," by contrast, it's the hinterlands that organize what's left of the center.

Ways of Seeing: Southern Californian Urbanisms

One of the most prescient visions anticipating a postmodern cognitive mapping of the urban is Jonathan Raban's *Soft City* (1974), a reading of London's cityscapes. Raban divides the city into *hard* and *soft* elements. The former refers to the material fabric of the built environment – the streets and buildings that frame the lives of city dwellers. The latter, by contrast, is an individualized interpretation of the city, a perceptual orientation created in the mind of every urbanite. The relationship between the two is complex and even indeterminate. The newcomer to a city first confronts the hard city, but soon:

> the city goes soft; it awaits the imprint of an identity. For better or worse, it invites you to remake it, to consolidate it into a shape you can live in. You, too. Decide who you are, and the city will again assume a fixed form around you. Decide what it is, and your own identity will be revealed (p. 11).

Raban makes no claims to a postmodern consciousness, yet his invocation of the relationship between the cognitive and the real leads to insights that are unmistakably postmodern in their sensitivities.

Ted Relph (1987) was one of the first geographers to catalogue the built forms that comprise the places of postmodernity. He describes postmodern urbanism as a self-conscious and selective revival of elements of older styles, though he cautions that postmodernism is not simply a style but also a frame of mind (p. 213). He observes how the confluence of many trends – gentrification, heritage conservation, architectural fashion, urban design, and participatory planning – caused the collapse of the modernist vision of a future city filled with skyscrapers and other austere icons of scientific rationalism. The new urbanism is principally distinguishable from the old by its *eclecticism*. Relph's periodization of twentieth-century urbanism involves a premodern transitional period (up to 1940); an era of modernist cityscapes (after 1945); and a period of postmodern townscapes (since 1970). The distinction between *cityscape* and *townscape* is crucial to his diagnosis. Modernist cityscapes, he claims, are characterized by five elements (Relph 1987: 242–50):

1   megastructural bigness (few street entrances to buildings, little architectural detailing, etc.),
2   straight-space / prairie space (city-center canyons, endless suburban vistas),
3   rational order and flexibility (the landscapes of total order, verging on boredom),
4   hardness and opacity (including freeways and the displacement of nature), and
5   discontinuous serial vision (deriving from the dominance of the automobile).

Conversely, postmodern townscapes are more detailed, handcrafted, and intricate. They celebrate difference, polyculturalism, variety, and stylishness (pp. 252–58). Their elements are:

6   quaintspace (a deliberate cuteness),
7   textured facades (for pedestrians, rich in detail, often with an "aged" appearance),
8   sylishness (appealing to the fashionable, chic, and affluent),
9   reconnection with the local (involving deliberate historical/geographical reconstruction), and
10 pedestrian-automobile split (to redress the modernist bias toward the car).

Raban's emphasis on the cognitive and Relph's on the concrete underscore the importance of both dimensions in understanding sociospatial urban process. The pallette of urbanisms that arises from merging the two is thick and multidimensional. We turn now to the task of constructing that palette (what we earlier described as a template) by examining empirical evidence of recent urban developments in Southern California. [. . .]

Edge cities

Joel Garreau noted the central significance of Los Angeles in understanding contemporary metropolitan growth in the U.S. He asserts (1991: 3) that: "Every single American city that *is* growing, is growing in the fashion of Los Angeles," and refers to L.A. as the "great-granddaddy" of edge cities (he claims there are twenty-six of them within a five-county area in Southern California). For Garreau, edge cities represent the crucible of America's urban future. The classic location for contemporary edge cities is at the intersection of an urban beltway and a hub-and-spoke lateral road. The central conditions that have propelled such development are the dominance of the automobile and the associated need for parking, the communications revolution, and the entry of women in large numbers into the labor market. Although Garreau agrees with Robert Fishman that "[a]ll new city forms appear in their early stages to be chaotic" (1991: 9), he is able to identify three basic types of edge city. These are: *uptowns* (peripheral pre-automobile settlements that have subsequently been absorbed by urban sprawl); *boomers* (the classic edge cities, located at freeway intersections); and *greenfields* (the current state-of-the-art, "occurring at the intersection of several thousand acres of farmland and one developer's monumental ego" [p. 116]).

One essential feature of the edge city is that politics is not yet established there. Into the political vacuum moves a "shadow government" – a privatized protogovernment that is essentially a plutocratic alternative to normal politics. Shadow governments can tax, legislate for, and police their communities, but they are rarely accountable, are responsive primarily to wealth (as opposed to numbers of voters), and subject to few constitutional constraints (Garreau 1991: 187). Jennifer Wolch (1990) has described the rise of the shadow state as part of a society-wide trend toward privatization. In edge cities, "community" is scarce, occurring not through propinquity but via telephone, fax, and private mail service. The walls that typically surround such neighborhoods are social boundaries, but they act as community "recognizers," not community "organizers" (pp. 275–81). In the edge-city era, Garreau notes, the term "master-planned" community is little more than a marketing device (p. 301). [...]

Privatopia

Privatopia, perhaps the quintessential edge-city residential form, is a private housing development based in common-interest developments (CIDs) and administered by homeowners' associations. There were fewer than 500 such associations in 1964; by 1992, there were 150,000 associations privately governing approximately 32 million Americans. In 1990, the 11.6 million CID units constituted more than 11 percent of the nation's housing stock (McKenzie 1994: 11). Sustained by an expanding catalogue of covenants, conditions, and restrictions (or CC&Rs, the proscriptive constitutions formalizing CID behavioral and aesthetic norms), privatopia has been fueled by a large dose of privatization, and promoted by an ideology of "hostile privatism" (McKenzie 1994: 19). It has provoked a culture of nonparticipation.

McKenzie warns that far from being a benign or inconsequential trend, CIDs already define a new norm for the mass production of housing in the U.S. Equally important, their organizations are now allied through something called the Community Associations Institute, "whose purposes include the standardizing and professionalizing of CID governance" (1994: 184). McKenzie notes how this "secession of the successful" (the phrase is Robert Reich's) has altered concepts of citizenship, in which "one's duties consist of satisfying one's obligations to private property" (1994:

196). In her futuristic novel of L.A. wars between walled-community dwellers and those beyond the walls (*Parable of the Sower*, 1993), Octavia Butler has envisioned a dystopian privatopian future. It includes a balkanized nation of defended neighborhoods at odds with one another, where entire communities are wiped out for a handful of fresh lemons or a few cups of potable water; where torture and murder of one's enemies is common; and where company-town slavery is attractive to those who are fortunate enough to sell their services to the hyperdefended enclaves of the very rich.

Cultures of heteropolis

One of the most prominent sociocultural tendencies in contemporary Southern California is the rise of minority populations (Ong et al. 1994; Roseman et al. 1996; Waldinger and Bozorgmehr 1996). Provoked to comprehend the causes and implications of the 1992 civil disturbances in Los Angeles, Charles Jencks (1993: 32) zeroes in on the city's *diversity* as the key to L.A.'s emergent urbanism: "Los Angeles is a combination of enclaves with high identity, and multienclaves with mixed identity, and, taken as a whole, it is perhaps the most heterogeneous city in the world." Such ethnic pluralism has given rise to what Jencks calls a *hetero-architecture*, which has demonstrated that: "there is a great virtue, and pleasure, to be had in mixing categories, transgressing boundaries, inverting customs and adopting the marginal usage" (1993: 123). The vigor and imagination underlying these intense cultural dynamics is everywhere evident in the region, from the diversity of ethnic adaptations (Park 1996) through the concentration of cultural producers in the region (Molotch 1996), to the hybrid complexities of emerging cultural forms (Boyd 1996, 1997).

The consequent built environment is characterized by transience, energy, and unplanned vulgarity, in which Hollywood is never far away. Jencks views this improvisational quality as a hopeful sign: "The main point of hetero-architecture is to accept the different voices that create a city, suppress none of them, and make from their interaction some kind of greater dialogue" (1993: 75). This is especially important in a city where *minoritization*, "the typical postmodern phenomenon where most of the population forms the 'other,'" is the order of the day, and where most city dwellers feel distanced from the power structure (Jencks 1993: 84). Despite Jenck's optimism, other analysts have observed that the same Southern California heteropolis has to contend with more than its share of socioeconomic polarization, racism, inequality, homelessness, and social unrest (Anderson 1996; Baldassare 1994; Bullard et al. 1994; Gooding-Williams 1993; Rocco 1996; Wolch and Dear 1993). Yet these characteristics are part of a sociocultural dynamic that is also provoking the search for innovative solutions in labor and community organizing (e.g., Pulido 1996), as well as in interethnic relations (e.g., Abelmann and Lie 1995; Martínez 1993; Yoon 1997).

City as theme park

California in general, and Los Angeles in particular, have often been promoted as places where the American (suburban) Dream is most easily realized. Its oft-noted qualities of optimism and tolerance coupled with a balmy climate have given rise to an architecture and society fostered by a spirit of experimentation, risk taking, and hope. Architectural dreamscapes are readily convertible into marketable commodities, i.e., saleable prepackaged landscapes engineered to satisfy fantasies of suburban living. Many writers have used the "theme park" metaphor to describe the emergence of such variegated cityscapes. For instance, Michael Sorkin, in a collection of essays appropriately entitled *Variations on a Theme Park* (1992), describes theme parks as places of simulation without end, characterized by aspatiality plus technological and physical surveillance and control. The precedents for this model can be traced back to the World's Fairs, but Sorkin insists that something "wholly new" is now emerging. This is because "the 800 telephone number and the piece of plastic have made time and space obsolete," and these instruments of "artificial adjacency" have eviscerated the traditional politics of propinquity (Sorkin 1992: xi). Sorkin observes that the social order has always been legible in urban form; for example, traditional cities have adjudicated conflicts via the relations of public places such as the agora or piazza. In today's "recombinant city," however, he contends that conventional legibilities have been obscured and/or deliberately mutilated. The phone and modem have rendered the street irrelevant, and the new city threatens an "unimagined sameness" characterized by the loosening of ties to any specific space, rising levels of surveillance, manipulation and segregation, and the city as a theme park. Of this last, Disneyland is the archetype – described by Sorkin as a place of "Taylorized fun," the "Holy See of Creative Geography" (1992: 227) What is missing in this new cybernetic suburbia is not a particular building or place, but the spaces between, that is, the connections that make sense of forms (xii). What is missing, then, is connectivity and community.

In extremis, California dreamscapes become simulacra. Ed Soja (1992: 111), in a catalogue of Southern California's urban eccentricities, identified Orange County as a massive simulation of what a city should be. He describes Orange County as: "a structural fake, an enormous advertisement, yet functionally the finest multipurpose facility of its kind in the country." Calling this assemblage "exopolis," or the city without, Soja asserts that "something new is being born here" based on the hyper-realities of more conventional theme parks such as Disneyland (1992: 101). The exopolis is a simulacrum, an exact copy of an original that never existed, within which image and reality are spectacularly confused. In this "politically-numbed" society, conventional politics is dysfunctional. Orange County has become a "scamscape," notable principally as home of massive mail-fraud operations, savings and loan failures, and county-government bankruptcy (1992: 120).

Fortified city

The downside of the Southern Californian dream has, of course, been the subject of countless dystopian visions in histories, movies, and novels. In one powerful account, Mike Davis noted how Southern Californians' obsession with security has transformed the region into a fortress. This shift is accurately manifested in the physical form of the city, which is divided into fortified cells of affluence and places of terror where police battle the criminalized poor. These urban phenomena, according to Davis, have placed Los Angeles "on the hard edge of postmodernity" (Davis 1992a: 155). The dynamics of fortification involve the omnipresent application of high-tech policing methods to the "high-rent security of gated residential developments" and "panopticon malls." It extends to "space policing," including a proposed satellite observation capacity that would create an invisible Haussmannization of Los Angeles. In the consequent "carceral city," the working poor and destitute are spatially sequestered on the "mean streets," and excluded from the affluent "forbidden cities" through "security by design."

Interdictory space

Elaborating upon Davis's fortress urbanism, Steven Flusty observed how various types of fortification have extended a canopy of suppression and surveillance across the entire city. His taxonomy of interdictory spaces (1994: 16–17) identifies how spaces are designed to exclude by a combination of their function and cognitive sensibilities. Some spaces are passively aggressive: space concealed by intervening objects or grade changes is "stealthy"; space that may be reached only by means of interrupted or obfuscated approaches is "slippery." Other spatial configurations are more assertively confrontational: deliberately obstructed "crusty" space surrounded by walls and checkpoints; inhospitable "prickly" spaces featuring unsittable benches in areas devoid of shade; or "jittery" space ostentatiously saturated with surveillance devices. Flusty notes how combinations of interdictory spaces are being introduced "into every facet of the urban environment, generating distinctly unfriendly mutant typologies" (1994: 21–33). Some are indicative of the pervasive infiltration of fear into the home, including the bunker-style "block-home," affluent palisaded "luxury laager" communities, or low-income residential areas converted into "pocket ghettos" by military-style occupation. Other typological forms betray a fear of the public realm, as with the fortification of commercial facilities into "strongpoints of sale," or the self-contained "world citadel" clusters of defensible office towers.

One consequence of the sociospatial differentiation described by Davis and Flusty is an acute fragmentation of the urban landscape. Commentators who remark upon the strict division of residential neighborhoods along race and class lines miss the fact that L.A.'s microgeography is incredibly volatile and varied. In many neighborhoods, simply turning a street corner will lead the pedestrian/driver into totally different social and physical configurations. One very important feature of local neighborhood dynamics in the fortified culture of Southern Californian cities is, of course, the presence of street gangs (Klein 1995; Vigil 1988).

Historical geographies of restructuring

Historical geographies of Southern California are relatively rare, especially when compared with the number of published accounts of Chicago and New York. For reasons that are unclear, Los Angeles remains, in our judgment, the least studied major city in the U.S. Until Mike Davis's *City of Quartz* (1990) brought the urban record up to the present, students of Southern California tended to rely principally on Carey McWilliams's (1973) seminal general history and Fogelson's *The Fragmented Metropolis* (1967), an urban history of L.A. up to 1930.[...]

In his history of Los Angeles between 1965 and 1992, Soja (1996) attempts to link the emergent patterns of urban form with underlying social processes. He identified six kinds of *restructuring*, which together define the region's contemporary urban process. In addition to *Exopolis* (noted above), Soja lists: *Flexcities*, associated with the transition to post-Fordism, especially deindustrialization and the rise of the information economy; and *Cosmopolis*, referring to the globalization of Los Angeles both in terms of its emergent worldcity status and its internal multicultural diversification. According to Soja, peripheralization, post-Fordism, and globalization together define the experience of urban restructuring in Los Angeles. Three specific geographies are consequent upon these dynamics: *Splintered Labyrinth*, which describes the extreme forms of social, economic, and political polarization characteristic of the postmodern city; *Carceral City*, referring to the new "incendiary urban geography" brought about by the amalgam of violence and police surveillance; and *Simcities*, the term Soja uses to describe the new ways of seeing the city that are emerging from the study of Los Angeles – a kind of epistemological restructuring that foregrounds a post-modern perspective.

Fordist versus post-Fordist regimes of accumulation and regulation

Many observers agree that one of the most important underlying shifts in the contemporary political economy is from a Fordist to a post-Fordist industrial organization. In a series of important books, Allen Scott and Michael Storper have portrayed the burgeoning urbanism of Southern California as a consequence of this deep-seated structural change in the capitalist political economy (Scott 1988a, 1988b, 1993; Storper and Walker 1989). For instance, Scott's basic argument is that there have been two major phases of urbanization in the U.S. The first related to an era of Fordist mass production, during which the paradigmatic cities of industrial capitalism (Detroit, Chicago, Pittsburgh, etc.) coalesced around industries that were themselves based upon ideas of mass production. The second phase is associated with the decline of the Fordist era and the rise of a post-Fordist "flexible production." This is a form of industrial activity based on small-size, small-batch units of (typically subcontracted) production that are nevertheless integrated into clusters of economic activity. Such clusters have been observed in two manifestations: labor-intensive craft forms (in Los Angeles, typically garments and jewelry), and high technology (especially the defense and aerospace industries). According to Scott, these so-called "technopoles" until recently constituted the principal geographical loci of contemporary (sub)urbanization in Southern California (a development prefigured in Fishman's description of the "technoburb"; see Fishman 1987; Castells and Hall 1994).

Post-Fordist regimes of accumulation are associated with analogous regimes of regulation, or social control. Perhaps the most prominent manifestation of changes in the regime of regulation has been the retreat from the welfare state. The rise of neoconservatism and the privatization ethos have coincided with a period of economic recession and retrenchment which has led many to the brink of poverty just at the time when the social welfare "safety net" is being withdrawn. In Los Angeles, as in many other cities, an acute socioeconomic polarization has resulted. In 1984, the city was dubbed the "homeless capital" of the U.S. because of the concentration of homeless people there (Wolch and Dear 1993).

Globalization

Needless to say, any consideration of the changing nature of industrial production sooner or later must encompass the globalization question (cf. Knox and Taylor 1995). In his reference to the global context of L.A.'s localisms, Mike Davis (1992b) claims that if L.A. is in any sense paradigmatic, it is because the city condenses the intended and unintended spatial consequences of post-Fordism. He insists that there is no simple master-logic of restructuring, focusing instead on two key localized macro-processes: the overaccumulation in Southern California of bank and real-estate capital, principally from the East Asian trade surplus, and the reflux of low-wage manufacturing and labor-intensive service industries, following upon immigration from Mexico and Central America. For instance, Davis notes how the City of Los Angeles used tax dollars gleaned from international capital investments to subsidize its downtown (Bunker Hill) urban renewal, a process he refers to as "municipalized land speculation" (1992b: 26). Through such connections, what happens today in Asia and Central America will tomorrow have an effect in Los Angeles. This global/local dialectic has already become an important (if somewhat imprecise) *leitmotif* of contemporary urban theory.

Politics of nature

The natural environment of Southern California has been under constant assault since the first colonial settlements. Human habitation on a metropolitan scale has only been possible through a widespread manipulation of nature, especially the control of water resources in the American West (M. L. Davis 1993; Gottleib and FitzSimmons 1991; and Reisner 1993). On one hand, Southern Californians tend to hold a grudging respect for nature, living as they do adjacent to one of the earth's major geological hazards and in a desert environment that is prone to flood, landslide, and fire (see, for instance, McPhee 1989; Darlington 1996). On the other hand, its inhabitants have been energetically, ceaselessly, and sometimes carelessly unrolling the carpet of urbanization over the natural landscape for more than a century. This uninhibited occupation has engendered its own range of environmental problems, most notoriously air pollution, but it also brings forth habitat loss and dangerous encounters between humans and other animals.

The force of nature in Southern California has spawned a literature that attempts to incorporate environmental issues into the urban problematic. The politics of environmental regulation have long been studied in many places, including Los Angeles (e.g., FitzSimmons and Gottleib 1996). The particular combination of circumstances in Southern California has stimulated an especially political view of nature, however, focusing both on its emasculation through human intervention

(Davis 1996) and on its potential for political mobilization by grass-roots movements (Pulido 1996).[...]

Synthesis: protopostmodern urbanism

If these observers of the Southern California scene could talk with each other to resolve their differences and reconcile their terminologies, how might they synthesize their visions? At the risk of misrepresenting their work, we suggest a schematic that is powerful, yet inevitably incomplete. It suggests a "protopostmodern" urban process, driven by a global restructuring that is permeated and balkanized by a series of interdictory networks; whose populations are socially and culturally heterogeneous, but politically and economically polarized; whose residents are educated and persuaded to the consumption of dreamscapes even as the poorest are consigned to carceral cities; whose built environment, reflective of these processes, consists of edge cities, privatopias, and the like; and whose natural environment, also reflective of these processes, is being erased to the point of unlivability while, at the same time, providing a focus for political action.

Postmodern Urbanism

Urban pattern and process

We begin with the assumption that urbanism is made possible by the exercise of instrumental control over both human and nonhuman ecologies (Figure 1). The very

Table I   Elements of a Postmodern Urbanism

GLOBAL LATIFUNDIA
HOLSTEINIZATION
PRAEDATORIANISM
FLEXISM
NEW WORLD BIPOLAR DISORDER
Cybergeoisie
Protosurps
MEMETIC CONTAGION
KENO CAPITALISM
CITISTĀT
Commudities
Cyburbia
Citidel
In–Beyond
Cyberia
POLLYANNARCHY
DISINFORMATION SUPERHIGHWAY

occupation and utilization of space, as well as the production and distribution of commodities, depends upon an anthropocentric reconfiguration of natural processes and their products. As the scope and scale of, and dependency upon, globally integrated consumption increases, institutional action converts complex ecologies into monocultured factors of production by simplifying nature into a *global latifundia*. This process includes both homogenizing interventions, as in California agriculture's reliance upon vast expanses of single crops, and forceful interdiction to sustain that intervention against natural feedbacks, as in the aerial spraying of pesticides to eradicate fruit flies attracted to these vast expanses of single crops. Being part of nature, humanity is subjected to analogous dynamics. *Holsteinization* is the process of monoculturing people as consumers so as to facilitate the harvesting of desires, including the decomposition of communities into isolated family units and individuals in order to supplant social networks of mutual support with consumersheds of dependent customers. Resistance is discouraged by means of *praedatorianism*, i.e., the forceful interdiction by a praedatorian guard with varying degrees of legitimacy.

The global latifundia, holsteinization, and praedatorianism are, in one form or another, as old as the global political economy, but the over-arching dynamic signaling a break with previous manifestations is *flexism*, a pattern of econo-cultural production and consumption characterized by near-instantaneous delivery and rapid

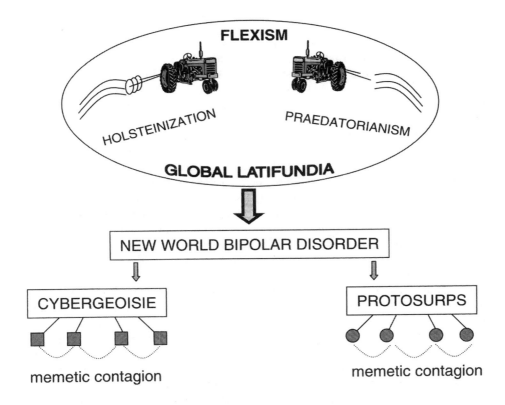

Figure 1. Elements of a postmodern urbanism -1.

redirectability of resource flows. Flexism's fluidity results from cheaper and faster systems of transportation and telecommunications, globalization of capital markets, and concomitant flexibly specialized, just-in-time production processes enabling short product- and production-cycles. These result in highly mobile capital and commodity flows, able to outmaneuver geographically fixed labor markets, communities, and bounded nation states. Globalization and rapidity permit capital to evade long-term commitment to place-based socioeconomies, thus enabling a crucial social dynamic of flexism: whereas, under Fordism, exploitation is exercised through the alienation of labor in the place of production, flexism may require little or no labor at all from a given locale. Simultaneously, local down-waging and capital concentration operate synergistically to supplant locally owned enterprises with national and supranational chains, thereby transferring consumer capital and inventory selection ever farther away from direct local control.

From these exchange asymmetries emerges a new world *bipolar disorder*. This is a globally bifurcated social order, many times more complicated than conventional class structures, in which those overseeing the global latifundia enjoy concentrated power. Those who are dependent upon their command-and-control decisions find themselves in progressively weaker positions, pitted against each other globally, and forced to accept shrinking compensation for their efforts (assuming that compensation is offered in the first place). Of the two groups, the *cybergeoisie* reside in the "big house" of the global latifundia, providing indispensable, presently unautomatable command-and-control functions. They are predominantly stockholders, the core employees of thinned-down corporations, and write-your-own-ticket freelancers (e.g., CEOs, subcontract entrepreneurs, and celebrities). They may also shelter members of marginal creative professions, who comprise a kind of paracybergeoisie. The cybergoisie enjoy perceived socioeconomic security and comparatively long-term horizons in decision making; consequently their anxieties tend toward unforeseen social disruptions such as market fluctuations and crime. Commanding, controlling, and prodigiously enjoying the fruits of a shared global exchange of goods and information, the cybergoisie exercise global coordination functions that predispose them to a similar ideology and, thus, they are relatively heavily holsteinized.

Protosurps, on the other hand, are the share-croppers of the global latifundia. They are increasingly marginalized "surplus" labor providing just-in-time services when called upon by flexist production processes, but otherwise alienated from global systems of production (though not of consumption). Protosurps include temporary or day laborers, fire-at-will service workers, a burgeoning class of intra- and international itinerant laborers specializing in pursuing the migrations of fluid investment. True surpdom is a state of superfluity beyond peonage – a vagrancy that is increasingly criminalized through antihomeless ordinances, welfare-state erosion, and widespread community intolerance (of, for instance, all forms of panhandling). Protosurps are called upon to provide as yet unautomated service functions designed to be performed by anyone. Subjected to high degrees of uncertainty by the omnipresent threat of instant unemployment, protosurps are prone to clustering into affinity groups for support in the face of adversity. These affinity groups, however, are not exclusive, overlapping in both membership and space, resulting in a class of marginalized indigenous populations and peripheral immigrants who are relatively less holsteinized.

The sociocultural collisions and intermeshings of protosurp affinity groups, generated by flexist induced immigration and severe social differentiation, serves to produce wild *memetic contagion*. This is a process by which cultural elements of one individual or group exert crossover influences upon the culture of another, previously unexposed individual/group. Memetic contagion is evidenced in Los Angeles by such hybridized agents and intercultural conflicts as Mexican and Central American practitioners of Afro-Caribbean religion (McGuire and Scrymgeour 1998), blue-bandanna'd Thai Crips, or the adjustments prompted by poor African-Americans' offense at Korean merchants' disinclination to smile casually. Memetic contagion should not be taken for a mere epiphenomenon of an underlying political economic order, generating colorfully chaotic ornamentations for a flexist regime. Rather, it entails the assemblage of novel ways of seeing and being, from whence new identities, cultures, and political alignments emerge. These new social configurations, in turn, may act to force change in existing institutions and structures, and to spawn cognitive conceptions that are incommensurable with, though not necessarily any less valid than, existing models. The inevitable tensions between the anarchic diversification born of memetic contagion and the manipulations of the holsteinization process may yet prove to be the central cultural contradiction of flexism.

With the flexist imposition of global imperatives on local economies and cultures, the spatial logic of Fordism has given way to a new, more dissonant international geographical order. In the absence of conventional communication and transportation imperatives mandating propinquity, the once-standard Chicago School logic has given way to a seemingly haphazard juxtaposition of land uses scattered over the landscape. Worldwide, agricultural lands sprout monocultures of exportable strawberry or broccoli in lieu of diverse staple crops grown for local consumption. Sitting amid these fields, identical assembly lines produce the same brand of automobile, supplied with parts and managed from distant continents. Expensive condominiums appear among squatter slums, indistinguishable in form and occupancy from (and often in direct communication with) luxury housing built atop homeless encampments elsewhere in the world. Yet what in close-up appears to be a fragmentary, collaged polyculture is, from a longer perspective, a geographically disjointed but hyperspatially integrated monoculture, that is, shuffled sames set amid adaptive and persistent local variations. The result is a landscape not unlike that formed by a keno gamecard. The card itself appears as a numbered grid, with some squares being marked during the course of the game and others not, according to some random draw. The process governing this marking ultimately determines which player will achieve a jackpot-winning pattern; it is, however, determined by a rationalized set of procedures beyond the territory of the card itself. Similarly, the apparently random development and redevelopment of urban land may be regarded as the outcome of exogenous investment processes inherent to flexism, thus creating the landscapes of *keno capitalism*.

Keno capitalism's contingent mosaic of variegated monocultures renders discussion of "the city" increasingly reductionist. More holistically, the dispersed net of megalopoles may be viewed as a single integrated urban system, or *Citistät* (Figure 2). Citistät, the collective world city, has emerged from competing urban webs of colonial and postcolonial eras to become a geographically diffuse hub of an omnipresent periphery, drawing labor and materials from readily substitutable locations

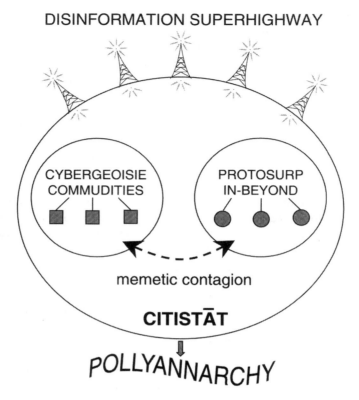

Figure 2.   Elements of a postmodern urbanism - 2.

throughout that periphery. Citistāt is both geographically corporeal, in the sense that urban places exist, and yet ageographically ethereal in the sense that communication systems create a virtual space, permitting coordination across physical space. Both realms reinforce each another while (re)producing the new world bipolar disorder.

Materially, Citistāt consists of *commudities* (centers of command and control), and the in-beyond (internal peripheries simultaneously undergoing but resisting instrumentalization in myriad ways). Virtually, Citistāt consists of *cyburbia*, the collection of state-of-the-art data-transmission, premium pay-per-use, and inter-active services generally reliant upon costly and technologically complex interfaces; and *cyberia*, an electronic outland of rudimentary communications including basic phone service and telegraphy, interwoven with and preceptorally conditioned by the disinformation superhighway (DSH).

Commudities are commodified communities created expressly to satisfy (and profit from) the habitat preferences of the well-recompensed cybergeoisie. They commonly consist of carefully manicured residential and commercial ecologies managed through privatopian self-administration, and maintained against internal and external outlaws by a repertoire of interdictory prohibitions. Increasingly, these prepackaged environments jockey with one another for clientele on the basis of recreational, cultural, security, and educational amenities. Commonly located on difficult-to-access sites like hilltops or urban edges, far from restless populations undergoing conversion to protosurpdom, individual commudities are increasingly teleintegrated to form *cyburbia* (Dewey 1994), the interactive tollways comprising the high-rent district of Citistät's hyperspatial electronic shadow. (This process may soon find a geographical analog in the conversion of automotive freeways linking commudities via exclusive tollways.) Teleintegration is already complete (and de rigeur) for the *citidels*, which are commercial commudities consisting of highrise corporate towers from which the control and coordination of production and distribution in the global latifundia is exercised.

Citistät's internal periphery and repository of cheap on-call labor lies at the *in-beyond*, comprised of a shifting matrix of protosurp affinity clusters. The in-beyond may be envisioned as a patchwork quilt of variously defined interest groups (with differing levels of economic, cultural, and street influence), none of which possesses the wherewithal to achieve hegemonic status or to secede. Secession may occur locally to some degree, as in the cases of the publicly subsidized reconfiguration of L.A.'s Little Tokyo, and the consolidation of Koreatown through the import, adjacent extraction, and community recirculation of capital. The piecemeal diversity of the in-beyond makes it a hotbed of wild memetic contagion. The global connectivity of the in-beyond is considerably less glamorous than that of the cybergeoisie's commudities, but it is no less extensive. Intermittent phone contact and wire-service remittances occur throughout *cyberia* (Rushkoff 1995; also see Knox and Taylor 1995). The pot-holed public streets of Citistät's virtual twin are augmented by extensive networks of snail mail, personal migration, and the hand-to-hand passage of mediated communications (e.g., cassette tapes). Such contacts occasionally diffuse into commudities, as with the conversion of cybergeosie youth to wannabe gangstas.

Political relations in Citistät tend toward polyanarchy, a politics of grudging tolerance of *difference* that emerges from interactions and accommodations within the in-beyond and between commudities, and less frequently, between in-beyond and commudity. Its more pervasive form is *pollyannarchy*, an exaggerated, manufactured optimism that promotes a self-congratulatory awareness and respect for difference and the asymmetries of power. Pollyannarchy is thus a pathological form of polyanarchy, disempowering those who would challenge the controlling beneficiaries of the new world bipolar disorder. Pollyannarchy is evident in the continuing spectacle of electoral politics, or in the citywide unity campaign run by corporate sponsors following the 1992 uprising in Los Angeles.

Wired throughout the body of the Citistät is the *disinformation superhighway* (or DSH), a mass info-tain-mercial media owned by roughly two dozen cybergeoisie institutions. The DSH disseminates holsteinizing ideologies and incentives, creates wants and dreams, and inflates the symbolic value of commodities. At the same time, it serves as the highly filtered sensory organ through which commudities and the in-beyond perceive the world outside their unmediated daily experiences. The DSH is Citistät's "consent factory" (Chomsky and Herman 1988), engineering memetic contagion to encourage participation in a global latifundia that is represented as both inevitable and desirable. But since the DSH is a broadband distributor of information designed primarily to attract and deliver consumers to advertisers, the ultimate reception of messages carried by the DSH is difficult to target and predetermine. Thus the DSH also serves inadvertently as a vector for memetic contagion, e.g., the conversion of cybergeoisie youth to wannabe gangstas via the dissemination of hip-hop culture over commudity boundaries. The DSH serves as a network of preceptoral control, and is thus distinct from the coercive mechanisms of the praedatorian guard. Overlap between the two is increasingly common, however, as in the case of televised disinfotainment programs like America's Most Wanted, in which crimes are dramatically reenacted and viewers invited to call in and betray alleged perpetrators.

As the cybergeoisie increasingly withdraw from the Fordist redistributive triad of big government, big business, and big labor to establish their own micronations, the social support functions of the state disintegrate, along with the survivability of less affluent citizens. The global migrations of work to the lowest-wage locations of the in-beyond, and of consumer capital to the citidels, result in power asymmetries that become so pronounced that even the DSH is at times incapable of obscuring them, leaving protosurps increasingly disinclined to adhere to the remnants of a tattered social contract. This instability in turn creates the potential for violence, pitting Citistāt and cybergeoisie against the protosurp in-beyond, and leading inevitably to a demand for the suppression of protosurp intractibility. The praedatorian guard thus emerges as the principal remaining vestige of the police powers of the state. This increasingly privatized public/private partnership of mercenary sentries, police ex-peditionary forces, and their technological extensions (e.g., video cameras, helicop-ters, criminological data uplinks, etc.) watches over the commudities and minimizes disruptiveness by acting as a force of occupation within the in-beyond. The praeda-torian guard achieves control through coercion, even at the international level where asymmetrical trade relations are reinforced by the military and its clientele. It may only be a matter of time before the local and national praedatorians are adminis-tratively and functionally merged, as exemplified by proposals to deploy military units for policing inner-city streets or the U.S.–Mexico border.

An alternative model of urban structure

We have begun the process of interrogating prior models of urban structure with an alternative model based upon the recent experiences of Los Angeles. We do not pretend to have completed this project, nor claim that the Southern Californian experience is necessarily typical of other metropolitan regions in the U.S. or the world. Still less would we advocate replacing the old models with a new hegemony. But discourse has to start somewhere, and by now it is clear that the most influential of existing urban models is no longer tenable as a guide to contemporary urbanism. In this first sense, our investigation has uncovered an *epistemological radical break* with past practices, which in itself is sufficient justification for something called a Los Angeles School. The concentric ring structure of the Chicago School was essentially a concept of the city as an organic accretion around a central, organizing core. Instead, we have identified a postmodern urban process in which the urban periphery organizes the center within the context of a globalizing capitalism.

The postmodern urban process remains resolutely capitalist, but the nature of that enterprise is changing in very significant ways, especially through (for instance) the telecommunications revolution, the changing nature of work, and globalization. Thus, in this second sense also, we understand that a *radical break* is occurring, this time in the conditions of our *material world*. Contemporary urbanism is a consequence of how local and interlocal flows of material and information (including symbols) intersect in a rapidly converging globally integrated economy driven by the imperatives of flexism. Landscapes and peoples are homogenized to facilitate large-scale production and consumption. Highly mobile capital and commodity flows outmaneuver geographically fixed labor markets, communities, and nation-states, and cause a globally bifurcated polarization. The beneficiaries of this system are the cybergoisie, even as the numbers of permanently marginalized protosurps grow. In the new global order, socioeconomic polarization and massive, sudden population migrations spawn cultural hybrids through the process of memetic contagion. Cities no longer develop as concentrated loci of population and economic activity, but as fragmented parcels within Citistät, the collective world city. Materially, the Citistät consists of commudities (commodified communities) and the in-beyond (the permanently marginalized). Virtually, the Citistät is composed of cyburbia (those hooked into the electronic world) and cyberia (those who are not). Social order is maintained by the ideological apparatus of the DSH, the Citistät consent factory, and by the praedatorian guard, the privatized vestiges of the nation-state's police powers.

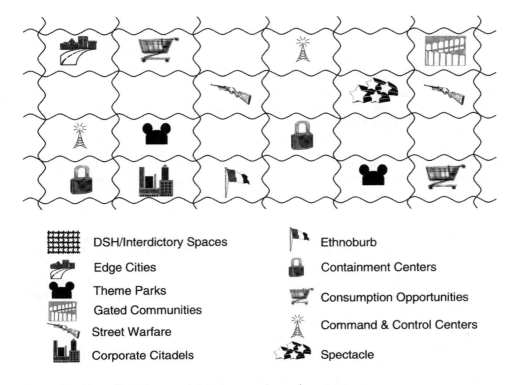

Figure 3. Keno Capitalism: a model of postmodern urban structure.

Keno capitalism is the synoptic term that we have adopted to describe the spatial manifestations of the postmodern urban condition (Figure 3). Urbanization is occurring on a quasi-random field of opportunities. Capital touches down as if by chance on a parcel of land, ignoring the opportunities on intervening lots, thus sparking the development process. The relationship between development of one parcel and nondevelopment of another is a disjointed, seemingly unrelated affair. While not truly a random process, it is evident that the traditional, center-driven agglomeration economies that have guided urban development in the past no longer apply. Conventional city form, Chicago-style, is sacrificed in favor of a noncontiguous collage of parcelized, consumption-oriented landscapes devoid of conventional centers yet wired into electronic propinquity and nominally unified by the mythologies of the disinformation superhighway. Los Angeles may be a mature form of this postmodern metropolis; Las Vegas comes to mind as a youthful example. The consequent urban aggregate is characterized by acute fragmentation and specialization – a partitioned gaming board subject to perverse laws and peculiarly discrete, disjointed urban outcomes. Given the pervasive presence of crime, corruption, and violence in the global city (not to mention geopolitical transitions, as nation-states give way to micro-nationalisms and transnational mafias), the city as gaming board seems an especially appropriate twenty-first century successor to the concentrically ringed city of the early twentieth.

REFERENCES

Abelmann, N., and Lie, J. 1995. *Blue Dreams: Korean Americans and the Los Angeles Riots.* Cambridge: Harvard University Press.

Anderson, S. 1996. A City Called Heaven: Black Enchantment and Despair in Los Angeles. In *The City: Los Angeles & Urban Theory at the End of the Twentieth Century*, ed. A. J. Scott and E. Soja, pp. 336–64. Los Angeles: University of California Press.

Baldassare, M., ed. 1994. *The Los Angeles Riots.* Boulder, CO: Westview Press.

Boyd, T. 1997. *Am I Black Enough for You?* Indianapolis: University of Indiana Press.

Boyd, T. 1996. A Small Introduction to the "G" Funk Era: Gangsta Rap and Black Masculinity in Contemporary Los Angeles. In *Rethinking Los Angeles*, ed. M. Dear, H. E. Schockman, and G. Hise, pp. 127–46. Thousand Oaks, CA: Sage Publications.

Bullard, R. D., Grigsby, J. E., and Lee, C. 1994. *Residential Apartheid.* Los Angeles: UCLA Center for Afro-American Studies.

Butler, O. E. 1993. *Parable of the Sower.* New York: Four Walls Eight Windows.

Castells, M. and Hall, P. 1994. *Technopoles of the World: The Making of the 21st Century Industrial Complexes.* New York: Routledge.

Chomsky, N. and Herman, E. 1988. *Manufacturing Consent.* New York: Pantheon Books.

Darlington, D. 1996. *The Mojave: Portrait of the Definitive American Desert.* New York: Henry Holt.

Davis, M. 1996. How Eden Lost Its Garden: A Political History of the Los Angeles Landscape. In *The City: Los Angeles & Urban Theory at the End of the Twentieth Century*, ed. A. J. Scott and E. Soja, pp. 160–85. Los Angeles: University of California Press.

Davis, M. 1990. *City of Quartz: Excavating the Future in Los Angeles.* New York: Verso.

Davis, M. 1992a. Fortress Los Angeles: The Militarization of Urban Space. In *Variations on a Theme Park*, ed. M. Sorkin, pp. 154–80. New York: Noonday Press.

Davis, M. 1992b. Chinatown Revisited? The Internationalization of Downtown Los Angeles. In *Sex, Death and God in L.A.*, ed. D. Reid, pp. 54–71. New York: Pantheon Books.

Davis, M. 1993. *Rivers in the Desert: William Mulholland and the Inventing of Los Angeles.* New York: Harper Collins.

Dewey, F. 1994. Cyburbia: Los Angeles as the New Frontier, or Grave? Los Angeles Forum for Architecture and Urban Design *Newletter*, May, pp. 6–7.

Fishman, R. 1987. *Bourgeois Utopias: The Rise and Fall of Suburbia.* New York: Basic Books, Inc.

FitzSimmons, M., and Gottlieb, Robert. 1996. Bounding and Binding Metropolitan Space: The Ambiguous Politics of Nature in Los Angeles. In *The City: Los Angeles & Urban Theory at the End of the Twentieth Century*, ed. A. J. Scott and E. Soja, pp. 186–224. Los Angeles: University of California Press.

Flusty, S. 1994. *Building Paranoia: The Proliferation of Interdictory Space and the Erosion of Spatial Justice.* West Hollywood, CA: Los Angeles Forum for Architecture and Urban Design.

Folgelson, R. M. 1967. *The Fragmented Metropolis: Los Angeles 1850–1970.* Berkeley: University of California Press.

Garreau, J. 1991. *Edge City: Life on the New Frontier.* New York: Doubleday.

Gooding-Williams, R., ed. 1993. *Reading Rodney King, Reading Urban Uprising.* New York: Routledge.

Gottlieb, R., and FitzSimmons, M. 1991. *Thirst for Growth: Water Agencies and Hidden Government in California.* Tucson: University of Arizona Press.

Jencks, C. 1993. *Heteropolis: Los Angeles, the Riots and the Strange Beauty of Hetero-Architecture.* London: Academy Editions; Berlin: Ernst & Sohn; New York: St. Martin's Press.

Klein, M. 1995. *The American Street Gang: Its Nature, Prevalence, and Control.* New York: Oxford University Press.

Knox, P., and Taylor, P. J., eds. 1995. *World Cities in a World System.* Cambridge: Cambridge University Press.

McGuire, B., and Scrymgeour, D. 1998. Santeria and Curanderismo in Los Angeles. In *New Trends and Developments in African Religion*, ed. Peter Clarke, pp. 211–14 Westport, CT: Greenwood Publishing.

McKenzie, E. 1994. *Privatopia: Homeowner Associations and the Rise of Residential Private Government.* New Haven: Yale University Press.

McPhee, J. 1989. *The Control of Nature.* New York: Noonday Press.

McWilliams, C. 1973 (first published 1946) *Southern California: An Island on the Land.* Salt Lake City: Peregrine Smith Books.

Martínez, R. 1993. *The Other Side: Notes from the New L.A., Mexico City, and Beyond.* New York: Vintage Books.

Molotch, H. 1996. L.A. as Design Product: How Art Works in a Regional Economy. In *The City: Los Angeles & Urban Theory at the End of the Twentieth Century*, ed. A. J. Scott and E. Soja, pp. 225–75. Los Angeles: University of California Press.

Ong, P., Bonacich, E., and Cheng, L., eds. 1994. *The New Asian Immigration in Los Angeles and Global Restructuring.* Philadelphia: Temple University Press.

Park, E. 1996. Our L.A.? Korean Americans in Los Angeles after the Civil Unrest. In *Rethinking Los Angeles*, ed. M. Dear, H. E. Schockman, and G. Hise, pp. 153–68. Thousand Oaks, CA: Sage Publications.

Pulido, L. 1996. Multiracial Organizing among Environmental Justice Activists in Los Angeles. In *Rethinking Los Angeles*, ed. M. Dear, H. E. Schockman, and G. Hise, pp. 171–89. Thousand Oaks, CA: Sage Publications.

Raban, J. 1974. *Soft City.* New York: E. P. Dutton.

Reisner, M. 1993. *Cadillac Desert: The American West and Its Disappearing Water.* New York: Penguin Books.

Relph, E. C. 1987. *The Modern Urban Landscape.* Baltimore: Johns Hopkins University Press.

Rocco, R. 1996. Latino Los Angeles: Reframing Boundaries/Borders. In *The City: Los Angeles & Urban Theory at the End of the Twentieth Century,* ed. A. J. Scott and E. Soja, pp. 365–89. Los Angeles: University of California Press.

Roseman, C., Laux, H. D., and Thieme, G., eds. 1996 *EthniCity.* Lanham, MD: Rowman and Littlefield.

Rushkoff, D. 1995. *Cyberia: Life in the Trenches of Hyperspace.* New York: Harper and Collins.

Scott, A. J. 1988a. *New Industrial Spaces: Flexible Production Organization and Regional Development in North America and Western Europe.* London: Pion.

Scott, A. J. 1988b. *Metropolis: From the Division of Labor to Urban Form.* Berkeley: University of California Press.

Scott, A. J. 1993. *Technopolis: High-Technology Industry and Regional Development in Southern California.* Berkeley: University of California Press.

Soja, E. 1992. Inside Exopolis: Scenes from Orange County. In *Variation on a Theme Park,* ed. M. Sorkin, pp. 94–122. New York: Noonday Press.

Soja, E. 1996. Los Angeles 1965–1992: The Six Geographies of Urban Restructuring. In *The City: Los Angeles & Urban Theory at the End of the Twentieth Century,* ed. A. J. Scott and E. Soja, pp. 426–62. Los Angeles: University of California Press.

Sorkin, M., ed. 1992. *Variations on a Theme Park: The New American City and the End of Public Space.* New York: Hill and Wang.

Storper, M., and Walker, R. 1989. *The Capitalist Imperative.* Cambridge: Blackwell.

Vigil, J. 1988. *Barrio Gangs: Streetlife and Identity in Southern California.* Austin: University of Texas Press.

Waldinger, R., and Bozorgmehr, M. 1996. *Ethnic Los Angeles.* New York: Russell Sage Foundation.

Wolch, J. 1990. *The Shadow State: Government and Voluntary Sector in Transition.* New York: The Foundation Center.

Wolch, J. and Dear, M. 1993. *Malign Neglect: Homelessness in an American City.* San Francisco: Jossey-Bass.

Yoon, I. 1997. *On My Own: Korean Businesses and Race Relations in America.* Chicago: University of Chicago Press.

22 Toward an Economy of Electronic Representation and the Virtual Sign

John Pickles

Postmodernism and deconstruction have brought into question how we see, under-stand, and write about the subjects/objects of our analysis. How do we decide what to observe, who is important, and what should be included in the report of our experiences? Under which circumstances can we claim that our reports represent (in any sense) the "truth" about what we have seen? Such questions encompass a very thorny issue that lies close to the heart of the radical uncertainties of postmodernism: what authority/legitimacy/authenticity (if any) do our *representations* of reality possess? Each observer, in practice, actually develops his or her own unique way of seeing the world. Indeed, it is something of a miracle that the sensibilities of multiple observers can *ever* translate into a consensus about what is being observed! (But, once again, note in passing that consensus is brought about only through the silencing of difference.) In a highly innovative essay, John Pickles brings together issues of representation with the apparently objective, technology-obsessed world of geographical information systems (GIS). Pickles argues that the multiple layering of GIS images is a far from innocent task, since each layer is a particular abstraction/representation of a complex reality. The merging of these images may indeed be analogous to the synthesis of postmodern ontologies, both suggesting multiple ways of seeing in layered combinations. No matter what your opinions are on this, notice the skill with which Pickles undermines the techno-logical objectivity of GIS, and exposes the value-laden ambiguities at the heart of GIS representations. He also demonstrates how these issues matter, as in the practice of democracy. Neither he, nor we, are saying that GIS is inherently *wrong;* it's simply not as right as it appears to be. In a topic that, on the surface at least, bears no relation to postmodernism, Pickles shows how postmodern eyes can bring powerful new sense to the fields of science.

Digitality and representational technologies (such as GIS) produce new codings and practices, and with them new possible geographies. Whether in the secret labs of the

U.S. Air Force, where new human–machine interfaces are being operationalized; in the studios of innovative television producers, where virtual realities and cyberspace are being "concretized" and rapidly disseminated as "real futures"; in ads for sports shoes, soft drinks, or political parties, where new cultural codings are occurring; in the operating theaters of hospitals, where digital and spectral imaging techniques are combined to produce real-time internal pictures of organs at work; or in planning offices or the lecture rooms of art departments, where students are being challenged to extend the visual powers of cyberart and virtual worlds, technologies of visual representation are challenging our fundamental categories of objectness, clear sight, the seen and the unseen, the obvious, the stable, and the exterior and interior.

The dislocation of universals and of the authority of the text is at the same time an opening up of the intertextuality of all texts. GIS is a system of spatial data handling and representation, and as such incorporates multiply embedded systems of texts (including signs, databases, and representations). All texts are, in this sense, embedded within chains of signification: meaning is dialogic, polyphonic, and multivocal – open to, and demanding of us, a process of ceaseless contextualization and recontextualization. Intertextuality cannot be fused with positivist or more broadly empiricist epistemologies, but requires a thoroughly different understanding of epistemology – a rejection of the univocity of texts (and images), of representation as a mirror of nature, and of a metaphysics of presence (and the foundational claims of positivism) to ground itself unproblematically in the given real world or the immediacy of observation. These implications are devastating for so much of what stands for theory of mapping in contemporary GIS, which is so heavily dominated by what Jameson (1971, p. x) has called the "anti-speculative bias" of the liberal tradition with its "emphasis on the individual fact or item at the expense of the network of relationships in which that item may be embedded" – a bias which keeps people from "drawing otherwise unavoidable conclusions at the political level."

Intertextuality implies a decentering of the author and the reader, and the situating of meaning in the margins between texts and writers – in an illimitable chain of signification, a network that as Heinz Pagels (1989) suggests has "no 'top' or 'bottom' . . . no central executive authority that oversees the system." In this sense, the turn from the text as isolated object to a text embedded in a constantly expanding chain of signification could mean for GIS, in the way it means for Gerard Genette (1982, p. 147, quoted in Landow, 1992, p. 60), an escape from a "sort of idolatry, which is no less serious, and today more dangerous" than the idealization of the author, "namely, the fetishism of the work – conceived of as a closed, complete, absolute object." Moreover, implied in this shift to an understanding of texts as constantly open to interpretation and critique, is a different understanding of what texts are for. Roland Barthes (1975) has called this a change from "readerly texts" (whose purpose is to create readers for already written texts) to "writerly texts" (whose purpose is to see texts as producing an open series of readings, each of which requires that the reader also be in part the author of meaning).

The shift that occurs from the "tactile" (pen and ink) to the "digital" (electronic code) with the adoption of GIS combines fixity and flexibility in new ways (Landow, 1992, p. 19; see also Baudrillard, 1983, 1988; Kellner, 1989). In this sense, "digitality is with us. It is that which haunts all the messages, all the signs of our societies. But this digitality also brings with it a commitment to a binary logic connected to a

particular metaphysical principle: cybernetic control . . . the new *operational* configuration" (Baudrillard, 1983, p. 103). The theorist of GIS sits with two apparently
incommensurable "ontologies" – Derrida and Baudrillard, intertextuality and cybernetic control through simulation – paradoxical strands running through the question
of virtuality and digitality, and requiring of GIS and geography a much fuller
engagement with the theory of signs, dissimulation, and inscription.

Deterritorialization, Delocalization, and "Community" Identity

Decentering of the subject, the pluralization of culture, and GIS object as critically
embedded text must also be seen against a backcloth of increasing monopoly control
over GIS and other electronic technologies. GIS has become an important commodity and (along with hypertext, multimedia, and virtual reality) a very profitable
frontier for investment. In this context of market ideology and monopoly capital,
everything comes under the sway of "information" as an object of counting, measuring, and analysis. Modern technological society even sets up human beings and
nature as objects of manipulation in such ways that "our whole human existence
everywhere sees itself challenged – now playfully and now urgently, now breath-
lessly and now ponderously – to devote itself to the planning and calculating of
everything" (Heidegger, 1957/1969, pp. 34–35). As a consequence, "what could
freedom of information, or even the existence of more than one radio or TV channel,
mean in a world where the norm is the exact reproduction of reality, perfect
objectivity, the complete identity of map and territory?" (Vattimo, 1992, pp. 6–7).

Kroker (1992, pp. 1–2) has gone so far as to suggest that "refusing the pragmatic
account of technology as freedom and eschewing a tragic description of technology
as degeneration, an arc of twentieth century French thinkers, from Jean Baudrillard
and Roland Barthes, to Paul Virilio, Jean-Francois Lyotard, Deleuze and Guattari
and Foucault have presented a description of technology as cynical power. . . . Here,
technological society is described under the sign of possessed individualism: an
invasive power where life is enfolded within the dynamic technological language
of virtual reality."

Certainly, the ways in which new electronic technics create new conditions for
domination and the exercise of power were at the heart of Lyotard's (1984) report
on knowledge in *The Postmodern Condition*:

> Our working hypothesis is that the status of knowledge is altered as societies enter what
> is known as the postindustrial age and cultures enter what is known as the postmodern
> age. This transition has been under way since at least the end of the 1950s . . .
>
>   I will take as my point of departure a single feature, one that immediately defines our
> object of study. Scientific knowledge is a kind of discourse. And it is fair to say that for
> the last forty years the "leading" sciences and technologies have had to do with
> language: phonology and theories of linguistics, problems of communication and
> cybernetics, modern theories of algebra and informatics, computers and their lan-
> guages, problems of translation and the search for areas of compatibility among
> computer languages, problems of information storage and data banks, telematics and
> the perfection of intelligent terminals. (pp. 3–4)

Lyotard (1984) saw the effects of these changes as deep and serious:

> It is reasonable to suppose that the proliferation of information-processing machines is having, and will continue to have, as much of an effect on the circulation of learning as did advancements in human circulation (transportation systems) and later, in the circulation of sounds and visual images (the media). (p. 4)

At the end of his report on the condition of knowledge Lyotard (1984) leaves us with this warning:

> We are finally in a position to understand how the computerization of society affects this problematic. It could become the "dream" instrument for controlling and regulating the market system, extended to include knowledge itself and governed exclusively by the performativity principle. In that case, it would inevitably involve the use of terror. But it could also aid groups discussing metaprescriptives by supplying them with the information they usually lack for making knowledgeable decisions. The line to follow for computerization to take the second of these two paths is, in principle, quite simple: give the public free access to the memory and data banks. Language games would then be games of perfect information at any given moment. But they would also be non-zero-sum games, and by virtue of that fact discussion would never risk fixating in a position of minimax equilibrium because it had exhausted its stakes. For the stakes would be knowledge (or information, if you will), and the reserve of knowledge – language's reserve of possible utterances – is inexhaustible. This sketches the outline of a politics that would respect both the desire for justice and the desire for the unknown. (p. 67)

[...] We need to ask again about the ways in which electronic information and mapping technologies are reconfiguring the contemporary world. As counting machines and typewriters had done earlier, new computerized information systems and artificial neural networks facilitate data entry, capture, and reproduction (Benjamin, 1968). Informatics effect new capacities in speed, efficiency, and the reduction of effort by which we communicate and act (see Virilio & Lotringer, 1983; Virilio, 1986). These new forms of experience correspond in part to the shift from a modernist Fordism to a liberal productivism, postmodernism, and post-Fordism (Lipietz, 1992). They also emerge at the boundary of the Cold War, and here GIS (and related information-handling and imaging systems) functions to create new codes whose liminal futures and new geographies are yet to be written. Mapping techniques extend a rationalistic logic – a universal calculus – to unify space as object, material, and fundament, and earth as exploitable resource, unified community, or commercial logo. A naturalized present is scripted and inscribed within the domains of cultural production, in terms of which new cultural imaginaries of natural (earth, nature, globe) and social identity are being forged, and electronic images of the earth, interactions in cyberspace, conversations on the community net, or concrete engagements with virtual reality represent self and others in new ways, create alternative forms of experience, and establish new forms of social interaction. Fully normalized, the technics of data exchange and representation legitimize new social practices and institutions in ways that we have only begun to recognize and regulate.

Such reconfigurations directly affect the ways in which citizens and democratic practices operate at all scales, and raise important questions about whether we are building an electronic global village, global corporate monopolies, or new civic arenas for citizen action. In the process, democratic polities experience the universalization and freezing in place of particular institutional forms (e.g., representative, liberal democracy), and the power to visualize alternatives gives way to the power to assert the value of a single representation of freedom (Fukuyama, 1992; Peet, 1993a, 1993b). If Benedict Anderson (1983) is correct to point to the role of print capitalism in the emergence of imagined communities of hegemonic national identity, in what ways is electronic/computer capitalism (or to use Ben Agger's [1989] phrase, "fast capitalism") now building an image of militaristic internationalism and corporatist global government? "Living without alternatives" – as Zygmunt Bauman (1992) expresses the contemporary situation – is also living with systems of information gathering, data manipulation, and image production that naturalize the present ideology of commodification, restructuring, and creative destruction.

At home and abroad, governments script and inscribe new versions of state power, in which information imaging systems facilitate military, political, and economic goals simultaneously. Thus, the Persian Gulf War was the first GIS war, although only the latest in a long line of geographical wars (Clarke, 1992). It must be remembered that General Powell was one of the Pentagon's top experts on electronic information systems and smart systems, and Robert Hanke (1992, p. 136) has pointed out how in the Persian Gulf War smart weaponry, GIS technology, and telecommunications (including CNN) were carefully orchestrated and coordinated – a "kind of simulacra game in which the technology of entertainment television and the technology of mass destruction were deployed together as part of U.S. military strategy to both deceive Iraqi military forces and to pre-empt/post-empt the formation of an oppositional public sphere." [...]

New methods of data handling and electronic imaging are producing deep shifts in the ontology of modern life, and specifically changes in the role of the visual in the contemporary world: As Jameson (1992, p. 1) has argued, "All the fights about power and desire have to take place here, between the mastery of the gaze and the illimitable richness of the visual object." And it is precisely here – in the intersection of the mastery of the gaze and the textual malleability of electronic images – that geographic theory remains surprisingly silent, particularly about the ways in which GIS has begun to effect deep-seated changes in the discursive practices of the discipline, the broader economy of information, and the uses to which such imaging techniques are put. [...]

Democratizing Appropriations

The unlimited scope for the "democratization" of the image and information for the masses, and the corresponding adjustment of the masses to this new reality, have important implications for our understanding of the democratic potential of GIS and electronic technology generally. Up to now, the debate about the implications of new electronic technologies has tended to ossify around a comfortable dualism across whose borders insults and occasional mortars are lobbed, but between whose positions little that passes for sustained critique has emerged. On the one side, GIS is claimed to enhance access to information and therefore potentially (and inherently) can be used to enhance democratic practices. On the other side, GIS is seen to foster the interests of particular users and to produce increasingly constrained and controlled public spheres.

Of course, since the social changes taking place are not restricted to the impacts of GIS/electronic/computer technologies, but reflect a broader restructuring of social relations, the debate cannot be limited only to GIS and geography. The issue is one with a much longer history, as Benjamin (1968) has shown us:

> With the increasing extension of the press, which kept placing new political, religious, scientific, professional, and local organs before the readers, an increasing number of readers became writers – at first, occasional ones. It began with the daily press opening to its readers space for "letters to the editor." And today there is hardly a gainfully employed European who could not, in principle, find an opportunity to publish somewhere or other comments on his work, grievances, documentary reports, or that sort of thing. Thus, the distinction between author and public is about to lose its basic character. The difference becomes merely functional; it may vary from case to case. At any moment the reader is ready to turn into a writer. (p. 232)

What are the effects of these changes? On the one hand, the technologies of reproducibility can – in the hands of a Brecht – be turned into critical theater that challenges and destabilizes the categories and arrogance of bourgeois culture and life. Or like the letter writer, the pc user at home has the opportunity to use the edifice of complex information processing and mapping technologies as he or she wishes. The individual engages the system, and molds it to his or her particular needs. On the other hand, technoculture redefines even the notion of who this individual agent is: as, for example, when GIS applications constitute new individual identities based on neighborhood data profiles and aggregate characteristics. These "produced identities" are deemed sufficiently "accurate" insofar as they facilitate "effective" action, a form of instrumentalism that is proliferating in many spheres of GIS use, whether the object is a parcel of land, terrain for military action, or a neighborhood of "like" consumers.

GIS technologies and practices are increasingly being used (along with other abstractive and distancing technologies) to produce collective identities. The consequences can be serious, as Benjamin (1968) has shown us:

> Mass reproduction is aided especially by the reproduction of masses. In big parades and monster rallies, in sports events, and in war, all of which nowadays are captured by camera and sound recording, the masses are brought face to face with themselves. This process, whose significance need not be stressed, is intimately connected with the development of the techniques of reproduction and photography. Mass movements are usually discerned more clearly by a camera than by the naked eye. A bird's-eye view best captures gatherings of hundreds of thousands. And even though such a view may be as accessible to the human eye as it is to the camera, the image received by the eye cannot be enlarged the way a negative is enlarged. This means that mass movements, including war, constitute a form of human behavior which particularly favors mechanical equipment. (p. 251)

According to Benjamin (1968, p. 241), the "proletarianization of modern man and the increasing formation of masses are two aspects of the same process. Fascism attempts to organize the newly created proletarian masses without affecting the property structure which the masses strive to eliminate. Fascism sees its salvation in giving these masses not their right, but instead a chance to express themselves; Fascism seeks to give them an expression while preserving property." The result is the aestheticization of political life and the celebration of ritual values.

> All efforts to render politics aesthetic culminate in one thing: war. War and war only can set a goal for mass movements on the largest scale while respecting the traditional property system. This is the political formula for the situation. The technological formula may be stated as follows: Only war makes it possible to mobilize all of today's technical resources while maintaining the property system. (Benjamin, 1968, p. 241)

Benjamin's discussion of the aestheticization of war under fascism and Marinetti's manifesto on the Ethiopian colonial war have an eerie parallel in the emergence of new technologies of war in the late 20th century. In particular, the incorporation of GIS technologies in the Persian Gulf War "pinpoint" blanket bombing of Iraq, its presentation through television, and its aestheticization in a ritual celebration of national power and virtue, raise important questions about the nature of new information technologies and their claims to foster democratic practices. [...]

To deepen our understanding of the impact of GIS as technology, object, practice, and social relation, it will be necessary to broaden the context within which the disciplinary history is written.... We continue to need a critical theory of social life, and a much stronger debate about democracy, property, individual rights and responsibilities, the limits of state power, and the exercise of competition. As the capacities and applications of spatial data and imaging systems continue to be broadened and deepened by forces of cybernetic capitalism and the celebration of technoscience, these questions remain pressing and open. We are only at the beginning of the process of delimiting and mapping the territory and content of this new currently solidifying terra incognita.

REFERENCES

Agger, B. (1989). *Fast capitalism: A critical theory of significance.* Urbana: University of Illinois Press.

Anderson, B. (1983). *Imagined communities: Reflections on the origins and spread of nationalism.* London: Verso.

Barthes, R., (1975). *S/Z* (R. Miller, Trans.). New York: Hill and Wang.

Baudrillard, J. (1983). *Simulations* (P. Foss, P. Patton, & P. Beitchman, Trans.). New York: Semiotext(e).

Baudrillard, J. (1988). *Jean Baudrillard: Selected writings.* (M. Poster, Ed. & Trans.). Stanford, CA: Stanford University Press.

Bauman, Z. (1992). *Intimations of postmodernity.* New York: Routledge.

Benjamin, W. (1968). The work of art in the age of mechanical reproduction. In H. Arendt (Ed.), *Illuminations: Essays and reflections* (pp. 217–257). New York: Schocken Books. (Original work published 1931)

Clarke, K. C. (1992). Maps and mapping technologies of the Persian Gulf War. *Cartography and Geographic Information Systems, 19*(2), 80–87.

Fukuyama, F. (1992). *The end of history and the last man.* New York: Avon Books.

Genette, G. (1982). Stendhal. In A. Sheridan (Ed.), *Figures of literary discourse.* New York: Columbia University Press.

Hanke, R. (1992). The first casualty? *Public, 6: Violence,* 134–140.

Heidegger, M. (1969). *Identity and difference.* (J. Stambaugh, Trans.). New York: Harper and Row. (Original work published 1957)

Jameson, F. (1971). *Marxism and form: Twentieth century dialectical theories of literature.* Princeton, NJ: Princeton University Press.

Jameson, F. (1992). *Signatures of the visible.* New York: Routledge.

Kellner, D. (1989). Media, simulations and the end of the social. In *Jean Baudrillard: From Marxism to postmodernism and beyond* (pp. 60–92). Stanford, CA: Stanford University Press.

Kroker, A. (1992). *The possessed individual: Technology and the french postmodern.* New York: St. Martin's Press.

Landow, G. P. (1992). *Hypertext: The convergence of contemporary critical theory and technology.* Baltimore: Johns Hopkins University Press.

Lipietz, A. (1992). *Towards a new economic policy.* Oxford: Oxford University Press.

Lyotard, J. F. (1984). *The postmodern condition: A report on knowledge.* (G. Bennington & B. Massumi, Trans.). Minneapolis: University of Minnesota Press.

Pagels, H. R. (1989). *The dreams of reason: The computer and the rise of the sciences of complexity.* New York: Bantam Books.

Peet, R. (1993a). Reading Fukuyama: Politics at the end of history. *Political Geography, 12*(1), 64–78.

Peet, R. (1993b). The end of prehistory and the first man. *Political Geography, 12*(1), 91–95.

Vattimo, G. (1992). *The transparent society.* Baltimore: Johns Hopkins University Press.

Virilio, P. (1986). *Speed and politics: An essay on dromology* (M. Polizzotti, Trans.). New York: Semiotext(e).

Virilio, P., & Lotringer, S. (1983). *Pure war* (M. Polizzotti, Trans.). New York: Semiotext(e).

23 Critical Geopolitics: The Politics of Writing Global Space

Gearóid Ó Tuathail

Modern geopolitics has been described as the study of rivalry and conflict among nation-states. In his study of *Critical Geopolitics* (1996), Ó Tuathail takes a long look at world politics following the end of the Cold War, and outlines a postmodern perspective on "geopolitical discourse" – viewed as "the writing of global space by intellectuals of statecraft." In the absence of the rationalities imposed by the twin superpowers (the USA and the USSR), and in the presence of a multipolar, multi-cultural world, Ó Tuathail invents a new geopolitics capable of dealing with emerging global (ir)rationalities. His vision emphasizes a much more complex way of seeing and understanding the world quite at odds with the imperialist geopolitics of the nineteenth and twentieth centuries.

Constellations of Geo-power at the End of the Twentieth Century

In the maelstrom of the time–space compression of the last fin de siècle, geopolitics congealed as a governmentalized form of geography designed to envision and discipline the spinning globe to a fixed imperial perspective. A floating sign without an essential identity, geopolitics imperfectly named a practice where geographical knowledge was combined with political imperatives by intellectuals of statecraft to envision and script global space in an imperial manner. A century later, a series of new congealments of geography and governmentality are emerging amid an even more intense round of time–space compression, a *fin de* millenium vertigo of informationalization and globalization that is remaking global space and creating new conditions of possibility for its representation by systems of authority. The challenge for critical geopolitics today is to document and deconstruct the institutional, technological, and material forms of these new congealments of geo-power, to problematize how global space is incessantly reimagined and rewritten by centers of power and authority in the late twentieth century. Critical geopolitics needs to confront the overdetermining role now played by the media, technology, and the political economy of globalization in enframing the global. While congealments of geo-power are best studied in their specificity, a few final points on the general problematic at the end of the twentieth century are in order.

First, the creation and consolidation of global media networks by transnational media corporations like Disney–Capital Cities, Time–Warner, and News Corp. over the past decade have transformed how we see and experience global politics. Within the circuits, feeds, and flows of networks like CNN (whose icon is a perpetually spinning globe), global political space is skimmed twenty-four hours a day and produced as a stream of televisual images featuring a terrorist attack here, a currency crisis there, and a natural disaster elsewhere. Global space becomes global pace. Being there live is everything. The local is instantly global, the distant immediately close. Place-specific political struggles become global televisual experiences, experiences structured by an entertainmentized gaze in search of the dramatic and the immediate. Control over the means of televisualizing events (as Ted Turner, Rupert Murdoch, and Silvio Berlusconi well know) is now crucial to the exercise of power and authority in the world. The emissions and power projectionism of the media world a televisual global not only for the masses but also for the new class of rapid reaction global managers whose very jobs depend on their ability to move capital, troops, and technology with the greatest speed possible in response to the latest information. Unlike the situation rooms of old, contemporary situation rooms are full not of maps but of computer screens and television monitors. A considerable part of foreign policy is now preoccupied with the ballistics of televisual projectiles, the trajectory, velocity, and potentially explosive impact of controversial images working their way through media space. Inevitably, geopolitics has itself become a televisual and entertainmentized phenomenon. Mediagenic "wise men" like Henry Kissinger, for example, offer deep thoughts in a sage voice to suitably impressed news anchors while other geopolitical experts war game with studio models and graphic displays. On display here is an important new type of geopolitics, a televisualizing of global politics that deserves careful study by critical geopolitics.

Second, in contemplating the changing nature of geo-power in the late twentieth century, the role of contemporary technoscience in inventing new ways of imaging ourselves and the earth needs to be considered. In radically expanding the range of our vision from the furthest reaches of the galaxy to the smallest fragment of DNA, contemporary corporate technoscience has redefined the limits and dimensions of that which we can now see and map. Military generals who in the past studied maps in order to grasp the length, breadth, and height of the battlefield now study maps of the electromagnetic spectrum. Daily electronic mappings of the surface of the globe are produced by spy satellites, AWACS (Advanced Warning Airborne Command System) planes, stealthy aircraft, and new generations of unmanned aerial vehicles. The organization of the surface of the earth into digitized information stored in geographical information systems (GIS) has technologized geo-power to an unprecedented degree. Places are now digital points, electronic sites made visible by GIS grids and global positioning devices.[1] In the digitized world of cybernetic war machines, everything that can be seen can be destroyed. The challenge is to disappear, to avoid and deflect electromagnetic grids. All of these developments prompted Paul Virilio to proclaim that geopolitics as the management of space has been eclipsed by chronopolitics, the management of time. Space, Virilio provocatively declared, now resides in electronics, not territory.[2] In the military realm, this is indeed the case. Perhaps the most striking example is TERCOM, the terrain contour mapping software brain that guides cruise missiles through hostile territory to their GIS-programmed targets. In this instance, geographical knowledge has come together with governmentality to create a geo-power that is armed, automated, and primed to speed to the kill.

Third, overdetermining the problematic of the writing of global space at the end of the twentieth century is the receding power of the state relative to the global economy in mastering space. Indeed, in many parts of the world, space is no longer mastered by the state at all but by regional warlords and criminal gangs with connections to the global economy. On the African continent, as Robert Kaplan has argued, places like the Sudan, Nigeria, Sierra Leone, Liberia, Zaire, Rwanda, Burundi, and Somalia are nominally states but, in practice, are something else.[3] Most of Angola's diamonds, Cambodia's timber, Peru's cocaine, and Afghanistan's poppy plants are controlled, exploited, and sold to the international market by bandit groups operating beyond the state. Even in industrial and industrializing regions, governmental authority is in retreat in the face of successful contraband economies mediating the global and the local outside the national. In all of the world's states, significant portions of the economy operate outside the law and official statistics. In Russia, for example, organized crime, in partnership with former Communist Party capitalists, controls as much as 40 percent of the turnover in goods and services in the economy.[4] In more affluent regions, global space is also being remastered, as transnational enterprises try to instrumentalize relatively strong states to serve their postnational interests while the wealthy in general try to downsize the state to a self-serving minimalist functionalism. The European Union envisions Europe largely within the terms of a corporatist vision of the Continent as an integrated environment for capital accumulation. In the United States, transnational corporations and their ideologues have successfully rezoned the territory of the United States into a North American free trade region that presently includes Canada and Mexico and will soon incorporate Chile. New transnational corporatist spaces are envisioned for the future. A free trade zone from Alaska to Argentina is promised by the year 2005, while an enormous Pacific Basin free trade zone is projected for the year 2020.

Whatever the nature of new writings of global space by intellectuals of statecraft, all must now take account of the dynamics of informationalization and globalization, of integration and disintegration, in a world where the modern sociospatial triad of the interstate system is in crisis. As already noted, the meaning of state sovereignty is questionable when even the most powerful of states depend upon the goodwill of private financial markets for their economic health and security. Similarly, transcontinental missiles, global satellite television, the Internet, and global warming have rendered territorial integrity a problematic notion. Statist notions of community are also straining, as nominally national but functionally transnational classes use the state to serve their global interests and attempt to secede from common national space by barricading themselves off from the rest in gated enclaves of privilege and affluence. Although somewhat simplistic, the notion of the world being increasingly marked by "wild zones" of poverty and violence, on the one hand, and "tame zones" of wealth and privatized security, on the other hand, is not that farfetched when one considers Washington, D.C., the former capital of the "free world" and current exemplary of a starkly bifurcated world of "haves" and "have nots."[5] The distance between the crack houses and ghettos of the central city, its wild zones of urban poverty and violence, and the master-planned elegance and simulated historic charm of edge cities like Reston, Virginia, the district's outlying postsuburban tame zone where traditional governmental functions like security and zoning are privatized, is only a matter of a few miles, but it is a distance that perhaps foreshadows the spatial structure of twenty-first century transnational corporatist capitalism.[6]

Managing the wild zones of the globe and protecting the security of its tame zones will certainly exercise the minds of the geopoliticians of the future, geopoliticians who will invariably construct their mappings of global space from the standpoint of tame regions and with the agenda of protecting the privileges of the affluent and tame against those who appear to threaten their spatial security and quality of life. Indeed, the recent greening of governmentality marked by the discourse of politicians like Al Gore, the rising influence of think tanks like the aptly named World Watch Institute – a technocratic institution devoted to monitoring the state of the world's environment – and the emergence of a new congealment of geo-power called "environmental security" can be interpreted as a response to the problems that decades of environmental degradation are posing for the rich and powerful, planetary-wide dilemmas involving questions of production, technology, sustainable development, and consumerism that the rich can no longer afford to ignore.[7] Even in their relatively immunized tame zones, the world's richest peoples and ruling classes will be affected. Thus questions of ozone depletion, rainforest cover, biodiversity, global warming, and production using environmentally hazardous materials are the subject of new environmentalist mappings of the global, contemporary acts of geo-power that triangulate global space around the fears and fantasies of the already affluent.

Commenting on these issues, and with Robert Kaplan's vivid description of a coming anarchy in world affairs in mind, President Clinton, in an address to the National Academy of Sciences on sustainable development, revealed a strikingly televisual consciousness of these issues when he remarked that "if you look at what is going on, you could visualize a world in which a few million of us live in such opulence we could all be starring in nightime soaps. And the rest of us look as though we're in one of those Mel Gibson 'Road Warrior' movies."[8] Yet, following the transnational liberalism of his predecessors, President Clinton's plans for embedding the U.S. territorial economy in transnational free trade zones will inevitably hasten this process as significant segments of the U.S. workforce are made redundant by cheaper foreign producers with unimpeded access to the U.S. market. With increasing globalization comes increasing deterritorialization and with increasing deterritorialization comes increasing insecurity. This, in turn, can render the need for the old foundational myths of state, territory, and identity all the greater. In the midst of the unraveling of these old apparent certainties, the will to remythologize them in ever more aesthetic ways can intensify.

Barnet and Cavanagh's declaration that the fundamental political conflict in the opening decades of the new century will not be between nations or even trading blocs but between the forces of globalization and territorially based forces of local survival seeking to preserve and to redefine community – anticipates this. Yet, at the same time, it does not acknowledge how a backlash by certain "territorially based forces of local survival" can territorialize globalization in such a way as to represent it as conflicts between nations, trading blocs, and civilizations. Seemingly anachronistic identities and dormant territorial disputes between states can take on renewed symbolic meanings amid the dislocations of globalization.

Luttwak's and Huntington's acts of geo-power reveal an anxiety at deterritorialization and a will to reterritorialize global political space that make their work both exemplars yet also complicating refutations of Barnet and Cavanagh's claim. Their work is part of a larger culture of anxiety about the disassembling "West," a culture riven by its contradictory commitments to transnational liberalism and to conservative nationalism. Politicians courting opinion-poll popularity are now simultaneously championing open markets yet closed borders. Leaders are now more aware of transnational threats to the planet yet more willing to fall back on neo-isolationist rhetoric and retreat into a neo-Malthusian stance toward the problems of the world.[9] Fears about the restlessness of the non-Western rest abound in campaigns to harden borders, crack down on immigrants, and "retake" mythic homelands from despoiling foreigners. Revanchism and xenophobic nationalism are on the rise in the political cultures of relatively affluent states, largely white masculinist cultures of resentment over lost power and diminishing influence, the more extreme versions of which find expression in racist attacks on foreigners or incidents like the Oklahoma City bombing.

Confronting the operation of all these emergent constellations of geographical knowledge and power is a pressing intellectual and political challenge. In taking up this challenge, we would do well to remember that the general problematic of geopolitical discourse – the writing, global space by intellectuals of statecraft – is a complex and messy one that traverses all four substantive sources of social power identified by Michael Mann in his account of the mutual development of classes and nation-states from the eighteenth century.[10] Geopolitical discourses are inevitably entwined with economic sources of power. The imperialist visions of classical geopoliticians, for example, were all shaped by economic interests, materialist motivations, and commercial aspirations, although the saliency of these factors varied considerably, from the relatively insignificant (Ratzel and Haushofer) to the moderate (Mackinder) and strongly significant (Bowman). Geopolitical discourses are also entwined with ideological sources of power. Religious, racial, nationalist, and patriarchal ideologies of identity and difference have all conditioned geopolitical discourse. Yet, while the politics of identity is important to the functioning of geopolitics as an ideology itself, it is not reducible to questions of identity. Geopolitical discourses are furthermore entwined with the growth in political sources of social power, its founding intellectuals owing their very careers to the expanding infrastructural power of the polymorphous nation-state from the late nineteenth century onward. Finally, and perhaps most significantly, geopolitical discourses are entwined with the military as a distinct source of power in modernity. While the military as an institution monopolized a declining relative share of overall state revenues in the nineteenth and twentieth centuries (exempting wartime), it nevertheless expanded in absolute terms, professionalizing and bureaucratizing itself, all the while accumulating greater and greater destructive power.

If geopolitical discourse is organically connected to one social phenomenon above all others in the twentieth century, it is militarism. Militarism, of course, involves not only the military. It is a state–society crystallization that brings together autocratic bureaucracy, technocratic professionalism, class segments, lethal technology, economic interests, and popular nationalism, a crystallization that interweaves elements of many different sources of social power and is reducible to no single factor. As Mann points out, it is a crystallization historically independent of and powerful over all other state crystallizations.[11] This autonomy proved to be fateful on many occasions in the twentieth century beginning in 1914. Yet, profound as the destructive influence of militarism has been on the twentieth century, contemporary geography and political science rarely give it the attention it deserves.

Therefore, in problematizing the re-envisioning of global space at the end of the twentieth century and in developing an agenda for critical geopolitics in the twenty-first century, let us remember that geopolitics is a complex phenomenon embedded in multiple, overlapping networks of power within contemporary states, a phenomenon with long-standing connections to militarism. Geopolitics, as noted in the introduction, is not a singularity but a multiplicity, a twentieth-century constellation of the more general problematic of geo-power, the entwined development of geographical knowledge with the power apparatuses of the modern state. From the cartographic charts of the Elizabethan war machine in Ireland to the electronic grids of the U.S. war machine in the Persian Gulf, geography has long served as a technology of power enframing space within imperial regimes of truth and visibility. Yet the imposition and smooth unfolding of such imperial orders of space has never been without contestation and resistance (as the unfortunate Bartlett found out). Critical geopolitics is one of many cultures of resistance to Geography as imperial truth, state-capitalized knowledge, and military weapon. It is a small part of a much larger rainbow struggle to decolonize our inherited geographical imagination so that other geo-graphings and other worlds might be possible.

NOTES

1   John Pickles, ed., *Ground Truth: The Social Implications of Geographic Information Systems* (New York: Guilford, 1995).
2   Paul Virilio and Sylvère Lotringer, *Pure War*, trans. Mark Polizzotti (New York: Semiotext[e], 1983), 115.
3   See Robert Kaplan, "The Coming Anarchy," *Atlantic Monthly* 273 (February 2, 1994): 44–76.
4   This estimate is from the Russian Ministry of Internal Affairs and is for the year 1993.
5   The notion of wild and tame zones is discussed at greater length in Ó Tuathail and Luke, "Present at the (Dis)Integration." See also Max Singer and Aaron Wildavsky's *The Real World Order: Zone of Peace/Zones of Turmoil* (Chatham, N.J.: Chatham House, 1993).
6   See Paul L. Knox, "Capital, Material Culture, and Socio-Spatial Differentiation," in *The Restless Urban Landscape*, ed. P. L. Knox (Englewood Cliffs, N.J.: Prentice-Hall, 1993), 1–3; and Knox, "The Stealthy Tyranny of Community Spaces," *Environment and Planning A* 26 (1994): 170–73.

7   See Timothy W. Luke, "Worldwatching at the Limits of Growth," *Capitalism, Nature, Socialism 5*, no. 2 (1995): 43–63; and Simon Dalby, "The Politics of Environmental Security," in *Green Security or Militarized Environment?* ed. J. Kakonen (Aldershot: Dartmouth, 1994), 25–53.

8   President Clinton, "Advancing a Vision of Sustainable Development," *U.S. Department of State Dispatch 5*, no. 29 (July 18, 1994): 477–79.

9   See Paul Kennedy, *Preparing for the Twenty-First Century* (New York, Random House, 1993); "Overpopulation Tilts the Planet," *New Perspectives Quarterly* 11, no. 4 (Fall 1994): 4–6; Matthew Connelly and Paul Kennedy, "Must It Be the Rest against the West?" *Atlantic Monthly* 274 (December 6, 1994): 61–83; and Virginia Abernethy, "Optimism and Over-population," *Atlantic Monthly* 274 (December 6, 1994): 84–111.

10 Mann, *The Sources of Social Power*, vol. 2, *The Rise of Classes and Nation-States*.

11 Ibid., 440.

FIT THE SECOND

Geographies from the Inside-Out

● ● ● ● ● ● ● ● ● ● ● ● ● ● ● ● ● ● ●

The Representation of Space

Postmodern thought is intensely concerned with the epistemological problem of knowledge, and commonly responds to this problem by taking positions that amount to a principled and limited relativism. This position hinges upon ideas of "representation" or, more specifically, the argument that all human conceptions of the world are necessarily abstracted representations of an underlying reality. From a postmodern perspective, this reality can never be fully apprehended, tending only to recede from grasp the more one tries to get a grip on it. Further, any attempt to definitively assert what reality *is* constitutes an imposition upon other ways of seeing and experiencing the world, and may eventually drive those other ways of seeing and being into oblivion. Thus, overarching truths are to be regarded with, at best, suspicion.

To explore this claim in greater depth, consider the diversity of humans engaged in understanding the world. Each of us occupies a particular location in material space at numerous scales: an affluent nation or a deeply indebted one, a major metropolis or an isolated farmstead, a boardroom or a classroom. Simultaneously, we occupy particular locations in social space, influenced by a wide range of factors. Each of us has certain visible characteristics, e.g., a given concentration of melanin per square inch of skin. And we participate in certain practices, e.g., harvesting our own food or purchasing it at a market, engaging in romance with partners of the same or different sexes, praying not at all or once every Sunday or five times a day while facing east. All these located factors carry a range of meanings within their larger, similarly localized social contexts, and this stew of influences gives rise both to us, and to how we see the world. In short, this is the stuff our realities are made of. But given that our realities are made of such differing menus of things, there must be as many potential realities as there are different people. And while many of these differing realities will share enough common features and underlying formative experiences to harmoniously converge, others will be so wildly divergent as to be incommensurable.

This raises critical questions: how many realities are present at any given moment? How do we make them and they, in turn, make us? Which version of reality is the right one? Which ways of seeing and being in the world are correct? Which knowledge of the world is true? Within the framework of modernist thought, roughly speaking, the answer was relatively simple: there is an objective reality *out there*, and by comparing it against different subjective realities we can rationally determine whose reality comes closer to the truth. But is that objective reality *out there*, the one we take for the touchstone of our perceptions, so objective and innocent as we have believed? From a postmodern perspective, the answer is a resounding "no." The world is something we only know through our own representations of it, which we transmit to ourselves and to others. And those representations of the world we collectively hold to be correct are not necessarily true but tend, in fact, to merely be the most popular and/or best legitimized within the logics of their social context. In short, objective representations of the world are not so much right as they are simply big, both in their explanatory scope and popular acceptance. In short, we tend to favor not the "true story" but big stories, or (in the lingo of the field) metanarratives.

Two conclusions may be drawn from this. First, knowledge and truth are inextricably bound up with the limited perception, historical prejudices, predilections, and personal interests of the knower. And second, any authoritative knowledge advancing any single version of "the way things are" must necessarily advance some persons' interests at the (sometimes severe) expense of others holding (or assigned to) differing conceptions of the world.

In her writings on the history of science, Donna Haraway has mobilized geographic metaphors to probe these propositions. She asserts that all knowledge is "situated knowledge," localized by the knower's position in social space. Knowledge is thus a product of varied localized ways of seeing, and each entails a particular perspective that is not necessarily incorrect, but must necessarily be partial and possessed of an internal consistency laden with blindspots. The problem, Haraway claims, emerges when any particular way of seeing attains a place of privilege, claiming a relatively clear and complete view of the world that supersedes alternative perspectives. Such tricks might involve the rationalist's "view from everywhere," or the absolute relativist's "view from nowhere." This "god-trick," Haraway concludes, must be countered by the recognition that all knowledge is local knowledge. Moreover, by adopting strategies of "mobile positioning" that permit individuals to experience multiple local knowledges, dialogues can be established among those various situated knowledges.

The key to understanding what is being attempted in this second fit is that reality is a plural word. It can only be humanely approached in multiple versions. This necessitates a drastic shift in the focus of research. Previously, academic writing concentrated upon constructing knowledge of the world as an *object*. However, this search for objective truth is being augmented, even eclipsed, by concern with how different human *subjects* understand and represent the truths of their worlds. This entails not only highlighting the broad problematic of reality-as-representation, but also a sharpened attention to the sensory and sensual modes through which such representations are experienced and imagined.

Many geographers have undertaken work in postmodern reconstruction by focusing on the subject, adopting their own forms of mobile positioning, and partially inhabiting multiply-situated knowledge systems to address the question of spatial representation in two ways. First, how do different ways of seeing and knowing the world give rise to different concepts of constructs of spaces? And second, how have geographers and others gone about representing the world, and in what ways might assumptions about the truthfulness of these representations be both presumptuous and oppressive to other ways of seeing?

We begin this inquiry with Kleya Forté-Escamilla's narration of an epic quest across a perilous landscape. This adventure is one of symbols made flesh: it takes place amongst menacing characters inhabiting the desertified landscape of a migrant laborer's psyche. The object of the quest is nothing less than the subjective soul of the immigrant herself. We follow this with Sara Cohen's ethnographic investigation into how one man's musical self-representation sculpts a material geography for himself (Reading 24). Next we address the authority concealed beneath the more formal spatial representations we call maps, those supposedly disinterested depictions of space that Brian Harley shows to be riddled with the makers' hidden agendas, partial truths, and tacit prejudices (Reading 25). Finally, we consider how cinematic representations of urban alienation altered during the middle part of the twentieth century (Reading 26).

REFERENCE

Haraway, D.: *Simians, Cyborgs and Women: The Reinvention of Nature.* Routledge, New York 1991.

The Storyteller With Nike Airs

Kleya Forté-Escamilla

By the time Lucia walked out of the Barrio, took the Greyhound bus de Tucson, changed buses in San Diego, changed again to the junky #10 bus to Santa Cruz, hung loose at the Metro with all the punks wearing purple and green hair, who looked more like los juveniles de sombra – the shadow kids – than they looked like themselves, took the Express to Watsonville, got off at the exit to Highway 152, trudged through the dunes, and arrived at a little wooden house sitting in the middle of a stinking brussels sprout field, the women were already crying.

The field worker and the cannery worker were there; the woman from town who worked at the Nopalitos Restaurant was there too. La doctora from the clinica had been there, trying to do something, but there was no point. The patient had not responded to any of her treatments.

Having been raised in a family of folk healers, la doctora trusted her instincts. There was nothing physically wrong with Josefina; it was a spiritual illness, what the old people called daño, the kind of soul damage better left to a curandera to deal with. At least for now, la doctora decided, because – and here her modern medical training obscured her vision – Josefina was not in any life-threatening situation.

The women who were crying knew better. La doctora was right about one thing, though: la curandera alone understood the true nature of the illness. Josefina didn't want to keep breathing because the world she had come to inhabit was a world without life. It was a life in which the earth, La Madre de todos, was dead, or more correctly in Josefina's understanding, La Madre had been murdered. The desert, with its birds and animals and cactus flowers, had retreated all the way to the mountains. She couldn't reach it. To go on living was impossible. The pain was unbearable, and Josefina spun off into imaginary landscapes confirming her perception that the desert was gone, and she was lost, a wanderer through the fields of an alien world.

While the other women were weeping, la curandera was sitting quietly and intently beside Josefina. But she was thinking, La cosa es, Josefina tiene razón. Her desert belongs to the rich, and the day when there is no place left for her fell on her head. Y aquí, la esclava de los files no tiene fin. She can't escape the labor of the fields here, and she has no strength. She is swallowed up. Only one chance is left: Lucia has to make a place for Josefina's life and plant her in it.

That her godchild could accomplish this feat of story telling, la curandera never doubted. Wasn't she the cream of all her students? Hummph! And the one who gave her the most grey hairs too. Lucia's seventeen years were too few for her daring, but there was no time in this world to dance barefoot or sit fanning oneself under a tree. Lucia would have to go through many trials, and it hurt la curandera's heart that she would not be there to help. For that reason, she reminded herself, she had to be strong with Lucia while she could.

So, when Lucia came through the door, la curandera said, quite gruffly, "Hasta que llegastes, it's about time you got here! Ponte fuerte, the matter is urgent!" She gave Lucia a glass of rainwater, blessed by her hand, to drink, and that was all.

The three women stopped sniffling and listened intently. They had never seen or heard a storyteller like Lucia before: a kid with beads hanging in strings from her feathered hair, Levi's with holes in the knees and a faded black leather jacket, and – even more scandalous – pink and lavender high-top tennies with fluorescent green laces.

Lucia laughed, "Chill out, niña!" The women drew in their breath, but Lucia was deep in her teacher's eyes, inside that jolt of recognition that told her who she was. In that moment, Lucia saw her own mother's words from so long ago, carrying the seed of a world inside. "Desde chiquita and a haciendo cuentos. All she does is make stories, but now she's disappearing inside of them. La cosa es serio. Do what you can with her and teach her whatever she can learn." So saying, her mother gave ten-year-old Lucia into the hands of her niña. La curandera began explaining to Lucia the nature of words, how to use them to make a world. And how to bring sick people back to their bodies.

And this was what Lucia was here for now. Her niña was right: Josefina looked deader than dead. Without wasting another second, Lucia started her breath deep in her stomach, clearing the path from heart to head and emptying her body so it could contain only a deep yearning, a desire, a vast and impersonal love needed to make the way to reach Josefina.

When Lucia was prepared, la curandera had covered the windows and turned to her. "Now, remember what I taught you. Don't be in a hurry and you won't get lost. No más, don't stop to hang out at the corner con los juveniles deliquentes, because those shadow kids can make you forget. Your body just sits here and rots if you forget everything."

"Ya, ya, niña," said Lucia. "They're just kids." Here she was, wrecked from traveling all night, and starving, but she couldn't eat anything because it would cloud her body and she wouldn't be able to see clearly. And her niña was already beginning.

First, la curandera placed her hands on Josefina, one at the top of her spine and one at the bottom, letting her own life force circulate through Josefina's body. After some minutes she removed her hands and poured cold water over them up to the elbows. Then the woman from the Nopalitos Restaurant made a circle around Josefina with yerba buena, and she and the other two sat outside it at three points, guarding it. Lucia and la curandera sat inside the circle with the patient.

Lucia felt her everyday self, the rad kid from the Barrio, begin to fade into the background. She knew where to go to open the channel to her power. As fast as an intention, she was back home in the desert, climbing quickly up the eastern mountains above Gate's Pass. As she drew near, the rocky slope turned purple, and in the circle of her personal sacred place the jumping cactus stood in clumps, golden and haloed by the rising sun. Pinpoints of light from a deep pool of water danced like stars in her eyes. She surrendered her fears to the mountain, knowing it would keep her strong, and brought herself, the self with no name, back to the circle.

La curandera was holding the grounding healing energy steady, and Lucia-with-no-name began to listen to Josefina's body. She saw the story the woman's body was telling, and gradually the room faded. All of a sudden Lucia left the circle with a "pop" and was inside Josefina's story, tracking her:

Josefina saw her brothers riding horses at full gallop toward the village and recognized a friend, the boy she'll marry someday, but his face seemed to change as he drew near. When he pulled up the reins in front of her, it wasn't him. The air was filled with angry sweating faces and hoarse shouts and the glint of sunlight on steel.

Josefina tried to run, but she was in an abandoned house which suddenly filled up with young white men fixing things. She realized there was no one there, and she was in a room with walls heating up like the metal insides of a stove. She glanced frantically around the kitchen for something recognizable, but there were only things, white metal things that made buzzing and grumbling noises.

Amid the clutter of old take-out boxes, rotting food and garbage, a baby sat alone in a highchair made out of ironwood. Where there had been a wall only a moment before, there were multiple panes of glass. On the roof of the garage next door she saw the gringo boys with their dogs, black huskies all with the exact same markings. They were milling around in the tight area of the roof, and below them water was backed up and smelled like a sewer.

Josefina ran back through the house, the baby in her arms . . . but no, the baby wasn't in her arms anymore. She didn't know where she herself was, on the street, circling buildings in a panic. She finally saw the boys on the roof, and one of them told her the names of streets, but they were incomprehensible to her. She saw so many jagged streets and crooked houses, but she couldn't tell what they looked like; they were shining so brightly with a blackish shine, like fresh tar . . . not fresh tar . . . blood, as black as the water of a lagoon.

Then the train appeared in front of her standing still, so huge and shining with the same black light, without a sound, motionless and waiting. Josefina walked toward a kind of subway entrance, where a group of schoolgirls stood. She tried to speak their language, but the girls couldn't make sense of what she was saying and quickly lost interest. Just as they were scattering, she thought of the right question to ask, "What place is this? What part?" They were unfamiliar with directions, they conferred. "East, yes, east," one affirmed. Then Josefina saw the land beyond, geometrical, a pattern of unfamiliar shades of green and blue separated by grey or black stripes rolling up and down slick rubbery-looking hills. There were vermilion squares, like linoleum, and red rocks everywhere. Suddenly she knew what was on the hill: a saguaro without any arms, a bare trunk coated in teflon standing in a circle of fake rocks that gleamed like glass. Josefina screamed but she didn't know at what the village, the earth and the bluepurpleyellowgreen of her homeland and blew up in front of her like from the explosion of a bomb. It knocked her on her face. Her teeth were gritty with dust and someone was pressing her down. She held the baby, shielding it with her body. With a shock, she saw the baby's open eyes were blue, a strange flat blue without luster. But she knew it was alive; she felt its beating heart against her breast.

The muscles of Josefina's back jumped convulsively, bare flesh being cut with a razor. Systematically, deliberately, the soldier's blade slashed letters into her back, and then continued, making a cut like a half moon around the baby's eye with the sharp tip of the blade. Neither Josefina nor the baby made a sound, and there was no blood.

But the train loomed above her, wet and glistening black as though it had passed through dying entrails. The teflon desert stretched in front of her, black lines dissecting it in all directions, but there was no blood there either. Josefina heard her own voice, as though her consciousness was burning in a final blazing fire, bright enough to make words: "Si así es, no quiero vivir!"

She spun off from her life into a place that was freezing cold and buried in silence. The only thing she saw, reflected back at her out of the darkness, was her own eyes, and those eyes were blue.

Lucia-with-no-name, tracking Josefina's story as it developed, reached this point just as Josefina disappeared into the jumbled-up streets behind the subway. Lucia had been able to interpret the varying landscapes of Josefina's story correctly, although their jagged edges pierced one another like a broken puzzle of glass. The pieces Josefina had left behind would soon fade without her energy, and Lucia was pissed at herself for not getting there before Josefina had created the teflon desert – that was what took her off the deep end. But God, the train was something else!

Lucia walked around the giant glittering train but it faded out in back, incompletely imaged, like the false fronts at Old Tucson. Still, it was pretty rad for an old lady.

Now Josefina had entered a place of bits and pieces of unreal stories floating in fantasy, without souls. She would be harder to find; it would be harder to sift out the stray sentences and words – or even just letters – to find her.

Thinking of the pale blue eyes she'd seen, and the bloodless wounds, Lucia knew there wasn't much time. Then she saw las juveniles de sombra across the street, flickering on and off. Boy, they wanted to live badly, clinging to the wisps of Josefina's story with what rays they had. The shadow kids were soul punks, souvenirs of every living person's growing-up. They populated the corners of all the stories Lucia had been in. Sometimes they were nice; sometimes they were as mean as cactus thorns in your heel. They weren't important to a story, just fixtures of memory, but sometimes they could make a story or break it.

Lucia-with-no-name took a deep breath: this was one of those times. She had run out of clues; may be they knew where Josefina was.

Lucia sauntered across the street, flashing her lavender and pink Nike Airs. The shadow girls, one wearing Josefina's huaraches, watched Lucia coming with ravenous envy. Desire-to-have leaped out of them in sickening green ooze that barely missed Lucia's feet. The strongest of them, a concoction of the most sangrona bully at school and the sonza who would break your head with the bat for striking her out, leaned toward Lucia out of a vat of something that looked like the swirling Orange Julius sold on South Sixth in the summer. She glared at Lucia and said, "Dame tus Nikes or I'll make you wish you never set foot en Watsonville!"

Pretty smart, thought Lucia, and her estimation of Josefina's creativity went up another notch. As she was thinking about it, she felt her niña yank on the string tying them together – a hard yank that clearly said, "Quit messing around y sigue con el cuento because Josefina's vibes are getting weaker."

Lucia felt a gust of snow beginning to fall in the Sierras and she knew with certainty that Josefina had gone beyond words and was going where neither of them had any business going. The story signs were turning into scratches and mere punctuation marks fluttering in the wind. Only ghosts of memories wandered there, unable to come home. They could all be lost, even the women guarding the circle.

Lucia thought quickly. "Listen," she said, snagging a green streak from the lead shadow girl with her fingernail, "I'll give you my Nikes if you tell me where Josefina is."

"Who?" sneered the lead shadow kid, disdain gleaming in her eye. Lucia was having a tough time following the eye as it twirled around.

"You know who: the reason you have any shoes at all."

The shadow kid's mouth flopped over in a smirk, but the smirk vanished when Lucia took off her Nike Airs and dangled them by their fluorescent green laces.

"Take the old way to the valley," the shadow kid said respectfully. "Then across on the edge of Wolf Ridge. She's in a clump of pines." Lucia handed over the Nikes and the shadow leader, with this added strength, sucked the other shadow girls in with a smack.

Awesome, thought Lucia-with-no-name, pero no vale nada. At least I hope not. She pulled the threads of the story in, tied them to her wrist, and made the words that dropped her on the expert run at Squaw Valley at the edge of darkness. Bitter ragged snow flurries raked her face from the storm level blowing off the ridge. Lucia made up a ton of ski lessons and snapped her boots into a new pair of Rossignol 180s.

"Sierra winter sucks!" growled Lucia. "How the heck does this transplanted India refugee from the desert know this stuff?"

"Good intuition," she felt her niña say through morse coded yanks on their common strings.

"Good thing I read niña's book *Skiing The Killy Way* last year when I was sick."

Lucia pushed off toward a black maw of howling snow-storm. No more cow pucky, meadow muffin crap, she thought. This is it. I've got to get her now or las tortillas se comen el suelo mugroso! The tortillas bite the caca floor!

Meanwhile, in the brussels sprout field on the central coast of California, the little house was shaking like a 5.5. The ping ping of phantom hailstones hit the roof and slid down like clanking chains against the sides of the house. The wallboards creaked and a roar of wind turned into the snuffling slobbering snarl of some gigantic animal trying to eat through the house.

The daño in Josefina's soul, knowing its time was limited, was trying to break into the world. There was a scratching on glass, over and over again, like a blade writing on the window, trying to make the words that would split it open. La curandera cautioned the three women guarding the circle with her eyes, and they held tight, shaking in their calzones with fright.

Back in the Sierras above Squaw Valley, Lucia was struggling to reach Josefina before they both went over the edge of the story into a crevice of pain from which no one would return. Following the steps her spiritual mother taught her, Lucia-with-no-name walked, or rather, skied on the side of nothing, where threads of many stories, living or without soul, drifted like snakes without skins. At last she dropped down on Josefina squatting beneath a gondola, her past and her blank future hanging above her head in the heavy air.

Not bothering with a greeting, Lucia wove her own story into Josefina's. A bubble of warm air expanded around them, a microcosm of Lucia's sacred place. Outside the snow was a blinding fury, but inside the smell of sage mingled with the perfume of wild honeysuckle. Lucia plunged Josefina with her into the desert pool of spring-fed waters, and they floated.

Although she couldn't speak, Josefina's eyes were dark again and her skin warm to the touch. The scars on her back bled at last (the way they had that day the Mexican soldiers destroyed her village). In the water the blood changed to sparks and passed through both of them, as if they were made of air.

When Josefina emerged from the water she saw what was really there: Lucia and the living force of the desert surrounding her life. Lucia drew Josefina into the circle, showing her how to enter and leave, so she could keep this piece of wild desert of the heart to last forever. It would be a place she could go to and be at peace, a real place.

Lucia-with-no-name pulled the ends of their stories tight and put the slack between her teeth. For added insurance, she tied Josefina to her with a string dipped in honey. Then she ended the story with a sound like the whirring of great wings – clearly a convention of her own – and shot back into the little house with a snap so hard the furniture rattled.

A few moments prior, la curandera had lit her sweet grass pipe and was quickly blowing mouthfuls of smoke in all directions, not knowing where they would pop in from. The storyteller, Lucia-with-no-name, arrived coughing madly, waving her arms to clear the smoke. She dumped Josefina unceremoniously into her body. Then she told the guards to open the door. As soon as Josefina opened her eyes, la curandera made her close them again and suggested a deep and peaceful sleep.

"Hasta que llegastes!" her niña exclaimed to Lucia, who had pulled in all of herself from the sacred place and was grinning ear to ear.

"Se te paró el pelo, didn't it?" she laughed at her niña. La curandera's hair had come loose from her hairpins, her long black skirt was turned sideways and her glasses slid down to the edge of her nose. Then Lucia understood, and kissed her niña's wrinkled cheek. "It's okay, I'm okay, niña," she said softly.

"Ya ya, quítate," said her niña with fake gruffness. La curandera dissolved the gathering and sent the guards home. She made almond tea for Lucia and drank a Carta Blanca Dark herself. The old woman and the young woman went outside and had a good laugh. They laughed until their nervous systems had shaken out all the ghost words.

Her niña took out a piece of licorice stick she had in her pocket and gave it to Lucia, who nibbled it, then leaned back comfortably against the wall of the little house and went to sleep in the evening sun.

"She might be a great storyteller some day," mumbled Lucia's niña to herself, "if she would only learn to stop wearing her good shoes to work." La curandera was looking at Lucia's Nike Airs, covered all over with green, shiny, slimy goop.

24

Sounding Out the City: Music and the Sensuous Production of Place

Sara Cohen

One of the central innovations of late-twentieth-century human geography is the idea that space is not a neutral container to be explored or inhabited. Rather, it is something that is brought into being according to how it is used, surveyed, and invested with symbolic significance. Such investigations have tended to focus on the eye and the hand: acts of seeing and manually reconfiguring space. But Sarah Cohen points out that other senses, and a rich sensuality in general, play equally important roles in the subjective production of space. Moreover, she demonstrates that the stimuli and product of these other senses, in this case sound and hearing, need not be concrete and materially enduring to have durably concrete effects. Finally, Cohen shows a keen sensitivity to the importance of recursivity, i.e., the inevitable inter-dependencies linking what spaces produce and the (re)production of space. The music she documents is informed by the social spaces in which it is produced; and in filling those spaces, it reshapes the social relationships of which those spaces are comprised.

Living and Defining Place

Relations of kinship and community

Jack was born in London's East End in 1906. His parents were part of a wave of Jewish immigrants who came to Britain from Eastern Europe in the late 19th century, many of them fleeing the ravages of the Crimean War. The port of Liverpool acted as a staging post for hundreds of thousands of Jews who passed through it on their way westward. Some, however, remained in Liverpool. When Jack moved there with his family at the age of eight, the city's Jewish population had increased to around 11,000, and has created what is generally referred to as a Jewish "quarter" around a street called Brownlow Hill, a name that retains symbolic significance for many Liverpool Jews. Jack's family finally settled in that street after occupying a series of dilapidated apartments in neighboring streets. His sisters ran a milliner's shop on the street.

Jack left school at 14, after which he held 37 different jobs including selling trinkets and other items door-to-door mostly in Jewish neighborhoods, collecting money for Jewish charities, selling advertisements for the local Jewish newspaper, and working on commission for other Jewish organizations. Over the years Jack was also hired by various Jewish tailors whenever work was available. Jack's employment experiences were typical of those of many Jewish immigrants. Throughout the 19th century Liverpool suffered chronic unemployment. Unlike other big industrial towns, such as Manchester, it had little manufacturing industry, and as a port it attracted large numbers of unskilled laborers. Fluctuations in trade made for an unstable labor market, a situation exacerbated by the flood of Irish, Jewish, and other immigrants to the city during the latter half of the 19th century. Most of the Jewish immigrants lived in poverty. About 40% were unskilled, and many of these took to some form of peddling (selling drapery, crockery, furniture, tobacco, stationary, pirated sheet music, etc.). But there also existed within the Brownlow Hill neighborhood a small-scale industrial economy of Jewish tailoring and cabinet-making workshops, many of which were situated in people's homes. (Jack's mother worked as a buttonholer, his father was a tailor, his father-in-law was a cabinet-maker.) There were also quite a few Jewish shops in Brownlow Hill: bakers, butchers, booksellers, and so on. In contrast to Manchester and Leeds, commerce predominated among Liverpool's new immigrant Jews, perhaps largely because of the city's lack of manufacturing industry.

The first generation of immigrants, including Jack's parents, aunts, and uncles, spoke Yiddish and they tended to work, socialize, and worship only with fellow Yiddish-speaking Jews. They established tightly knit social networks based on relations of kinship and fellowship with others from the same country of origin. Together these groups constituted quite an isolated population. As a young boy Jack also associated only with fellow Jews. Later, he and his Jewish peers had Gentile friends but they never visited their houses or entertained the idea of marrying a Gentile. In 1939 Jack, like his sister, entered into an arranged marriage.

The impoverished situation of the new immigrants, and that of Liverpool's laboring classes generally, contrasted greatly with the wealth of the city's elite which included a small established Jewish population. By the beginning of the 19th century there already lived in Liverpool about 1,000 Jews, including a middle class of merchants, bankers, and shopkeepers (largely of German and Dutch origin) that was well integrated into the upper echelons of Liverpool society but, as a minority, was concerned to be seen as well behaved and to fit in with wider society. This highly anglicized Jewish elite lived a few miles outside of the "Jewish quarter" in the large mansions situated around two of Liverpool's finest parks. They had little in common culturally or economically with the new immigrants. In 1906 a lawyer and renowned member of this elite, Bertram B. Benas, gave a presidential address to the Liverpool Jewish Literary Society in which he said:

> A self-imposed ghetto is for the first time in process of formation in our city. Entire streets are being wholly occupied by Russo-Polish immigrants in the Brownlow

Hill district.... The non-Jewish residents are removing to the more distant outskirts....

To see them at prayer is quite a revelation to modern Liverpool Jewry. Their services are full of emphatic, vivid, even uncouth devotion. To listen to their ready and soulful responses, to see the weird swinging of their bodies during their orisons, to hear the loud and earnest sounds of their great Amen, their hearty unison in songs of praise, wanting perhaps in musical culture, yet giving food for inspiration.

Class and other distinctions among Liverpool Jews were reinforced in the popular press. A series of articles entitled "The Liverpool Jew" appeared in the *Liverpool Review* in 1899. The articles were full of anti-Semitic references to Jewish character and culture. Four classes ("specimens") of Liverpool Jew were portrayed, from the uppermost "English Jew," down to the "newly-imported Foreign Jew" based in the "little colony," as the Brownlow Hill neighborhood was referred to, a term that, like "ghetto" or "quarter," implies a position of powerlessness and incarceration. Second-generation immigrants comprised the second class of Liverpool Jew, which was typified as frequenting music and dance halls, "exhibiting his 'light fantastic toe' at cheap cinderellas and dances," while the fourth class, the English Jew, was portrayed as much more "cultured" – artistic, literary, and "Musical – to an acute degree" – found at almost every concert devoted to the classical productions of the world's great composers. Such stereotypes illustrate the way in which music (in this case through writing and verbal discourse) is used to define and distinguish people and places according to class and ethnicity. As Stokes has emphasized,[1] this underlines the importance of turning from "defining the essential and 'authentic' traces of identity 'in' music ... to the question of how music is used by social actors in specific local situations to erect boundaries, to maintain distinctions between us and them."

Musical performance, exchange, and interaction

The consumption and production of music also draws people together and symbolizes their sense of collectivity and place. For the immigrant Jews of Brownlow Hill, music (religious, folk, popular, and classical) played an important role in everyday life and the rituals, routines, and discourses that comprised it. Music was in fact the focus of many social gatherings, helping to establish and strengthen the immigrants' relations with each other or their relationship with God, and music also framed particular events such as wedding ceremonies and religious festivals, setting them apart from other daily activities, heightening their symbolic significance.[2]

Most of the immigrant Jews were indeed very religious, and religious music and practice undoubtedly helped maintain their individual and collective identity in a context of considerable uncertainty and unfamiliarity. The immigrants set up Chevra, societies through which those who had originated in a particular Eastern European town or district met together to worship and socialize, often in someone's house. Gradually they set up their own synagogues which contrasted greatly with the opulence and grandeur of those frequented by the Jewish elite. (They also set up their own welfare organizations, assisted by the Jewish elite for whom charitable activity played an important role, as it has done in many Euro-American Jewish circles, acting as a source of collective cohesion and prestige.)

Within Judaism, particularly its Eastern European traditions, vocal music is believed to provide the closest communication with God, with the Hasidic song or wordless chant possessing "more power than any other prayer; representing pure religious ecstasy"[3]; and embodying the notion that while the life of a text is limited, the melody lives on forever. The chanting is traditionally done by and for men (chazans). Hasidic song has left a strong imprint on Eastern European Jewish music as a whole. Today, synagogue attendance has declined among Liverpool Jews, but the symbolic meanings and ritual imagery of the synagogue are deeply internalized. Jack's stories often incorporate religious references, and synagogue music has great emotional significance for him. "It shows you your place," he explains, "[It is] traditional. They daren't alter it. That music goes on and on and on. Fathers play to sons, and sons play to sons. Always the same. It never alters ... that music is there forever." He thus depicts the music as a timeless (and gendered) tradition representing security and stability.

When Jack was young his parents listened on the family gramophone to recordings of the great chazans imported by a nearby record retailer from a Jewish wholesaler in London. They also listened to recordings of Yiddish folk music. One of Jack's strongest memories of music as a young child is of his mother and aunts sitting together, singing Yiddish songs and weeping to the mournful sounds that reminded them of Poland, their homeland ("der heim"). Such songs typically depict aspects of daily life and work, or tell tales about separation and parting, or focus on the worlds of children and women. Jack said of the women, "They loved to weep, that was their pleasure." Many people maintain a link with their past through attachment to specific places, and music is often used to remember such places. The Yiddish music provoked and structured particular emotions in Jack's female relatives, emotions through which they expressed their feelings about their country of origin and the relations and practices they had left behind. The music brought them together and symbolized their collective identity. Listening to that music today, Jack is reminded of those women and the female domestic space or home that they represented.

Referring to the recordings that his relatives listened to, Jack said, "And somehow those records came around. And one person got hold of one, and it was passed all round.... And bit by bit we used to have records." This description conforms with Jack's depiction of Liverpool Jews as living "in one circle," a spatial metaphor for neighborhood that incorporates Jewish records and songs as part of the circle, and part of the process of defining it. Likewise, there existed for a short period a Liverpool Yiddish book publisher, Ghetto Press, and a regional Yiddish newspaper that Jack also described as being passed around the neighborhood from house to house.

But what Jack talks about most in relation to the past is film and dance music, which he describes as "the whole life and soul of [his] generation." As a young man he attended the cinema on a weekly basis and the films and music he saw and heard there inspired him. He has sung, for example, the songs of Al Jolson's for me, demonstrating through his voice and the movement of his arms the emotional intensity that they evoke. Jolson too was the son of Jewish immigrants struggling to find their place in a new country, and Gabler[4] has written that he was "caught between the old life and the new...of both and of neither." Jolson's on-screen performances often articulated this experience, which is perhaps one reason why his music appealed so strongly to Jack.

Since he left school in 1920, dancing and dance halls have been Jack's major obsession. "Dancing," he told me, "was my life." At one time he went out dancing six nights a week at Jewish functions, at the tailor's club, and at various dance halls in the city. During his early 20s he started running dances himself and acted as Master of ceremonies (MC) in local dance halls. Jack's reminiscences indicate the attraction that dance-hall culture had for him, the sense of excitement and occasion, as well as the anticipation and preparation, that a dance provoked, and the escape that it offered from the worries and routines of everyday life. He describes in vivid detail the women he danced with, their beauty and glamour, and the fashionable dress of them and the men. Sitting on his sofa, he sways his torso and arms, closing his eyes in an expression of blissful engrossment, attempting to convey to me the physical attraction of the dance and the heightened sensuality and pleasure it evoked, displaying a sense of pride in the talents he had as a dancer and the proficiency and skill with which he mastered the various dance steps.

For Jack's bar mitzvah his parents bought him a piano. Although none of his family could play it, there was always someone in the neighborhood who could. Jack remembers social gatherings in his house when people would stand around the piano and sing popular songs of the day (e.g., "Rambling Rose"). Others in the neighborhood played instruments on a semiprofessional basis. During the 1920s and 1930s there were quite a few Jewish dance bands based in the Brownlow Hill neighborhood. Jack was close friends with these musicians, and he refers to them with affection and pride as "local musicians," "local" here meaning not just musicians from the Brownlow Hill neighborhood, but that neighborhood's Jewish musicians (i.e., he is claiming them as the community's own). Similarly, Jack sometimes talks of "Liverpool," or "this town" when he is referring only to its Jewish community. "Local" is, of course, a discursive shifter or variable determined by factors such as ethnicity and class.

Jack yearned to perform in a dance band himself. Later, during the 1940s, he took the plunge and spent all his savings on a saxophone. He joined a band but eventually decided that he wasn't a very good musician. Like many of his peers, he also dreamed of being a professional dancer, but again decided that he wasn't good enough, saying, "The only place to be a professional was London, and all my family was in Liverpool. I wouldn't leave them for the world to go to London." However, the beginnings of the modern British entertainment industry coincided with Jewish immigration from Eastern Europe and that industry did attract may enterprising immigrants. Access was relatively easy compared with entry into other industries due to lower financial barriers and less discrimination. Entertainment was an area not yet dominated by Gentile talent and capital, partly because it was considered risky and disreputable. Consequently, Jews entered the industry at every level. Close inspection of reports and publications on Liverpool's theaters and cinemas, for example, and of local Jewish archives, reveals passing references to Jewish performers, entertainment agents, and owners, managers, and promoters of clubs and cinemas. (This situation was mirrored in other British cities, particularly London,

Manchester, and Birmingham and it was magnified in America). On the music retail side, there have been several Jewish owned music instrument and record shops in Liverpool (hence the Jewishness of the entertainment infrastructure surrounding the Beatles, including clubs, agents, managers, retailers, and solicitors).

Music and the social, cultural, and economic production of place

This account of the social and cultural life of the immigrant Jews of Brownlow Hill has been brief, fragmented, and rather superficial. However, it has promoted a view of music and place not as fixed and bounded texts or things, but as social practice involving relations between people, musical sounds, images and artifacts, and the material environment. It has also highlighted the importance of place in defining Jewish ethnicity, and indicated some of the ways in which music is involved in the social, cultural, economic, and sensual production of place.

Jack is very proud of Liverpool and its history. Explaining why he feels so strongly about the city he said, "I live here. My home's here. My mother and father, my daughter, they're buried here. So where they're buried is my home." Places thus reify or symbolize social relationships, and kinship relations are obviously of particular emotional significance. Although Jack has few living relatives in Liverpool, he is bound to the city through relations with dead kin and relations of affinity with fellow Jews. Music is one means through which such relations of kinship and community are established, maintained, and transformed.

A particular Liverpool neighborhood like Brownlow Hill has been shown to be lived and shaped through music. Musical events, whether involving small family gatherings or grander community rituals, festivals, and celebrations, and musical practices such as the exchange of musical artifacts, illustrate music's role in the social production of that neighborhood. Via performance or through the peddling of sheet music, music was also a means of generating individual income and developing that neighborhood economically and materially. Music was also used to represent the neighborhood, whether through well-known local musicians who came to symbolize it and acted as its ambassadors; or through the use of particular musical genres and styles that evoked a collective past and tradition; or through the musical stereotypes in the local press that used music to present alternative images of the neighborhood.

But music is not just represented and interpreted: it is also heard, felt, and experienced. For Jack it is sound as well as sight and smell that conjures up images, emotions, and memories of Brownlow Hill and its atmosphere. His attempts to demonstrate the physical pleasures of music and the way in which it resonates within the body, stimulating movement and emotion, emphasize the intensity of experience evoked by music and its effectiveness in producing a sense of identity and belonging.

The musical practices and interactions of the immigrant Jews helped to define and shape the particular geographical and material space within the city that they inhabited. At the same time, they invested that space with meaning and a sense of place, thus distinguishing it from other places within the city. Hence neighborhoods, cities, and other places are socially and materially produced as practical settings or contexts for social activity, but through such activity places are also produced as concepts or symbols. To describe places as being "produced" is to emphasize the processes that shape their material, social, and symbolic forms. Music is part of such processes. Music reflects aspects of the place in which it is created (hence "different cities make different noises"),[5] but music also helps to produce place. Hence Appadurai[6] has described locality as both figure and ground.[6]

Comparative material on Liverpool's Irish and black populations emphasizes music's role in the production of place, the spatial politics of everyday life, and the expression of ethnic identity. One musician, for example, describes how in the 1930s a black neighbor would play his records loudly and open all the windows so that the sound would travel and publically proclaim his status as the owner of a gramophone. Mean while, a color bar operated in many of the city's clubs and dance halls, which led to a situation in which black musicians performed in "white" spaces, but the leisure activities of black people were restricted to one particular area of the city. Elsewhere in the city marching concertina bands have acted as a focus and trigger for Irish sectarian conflict, representing an appropriation or invasion of public space and a marker of territory.[7]

In defining a sense of "this place," music also marks relations of kinship, alliance, and affinity with places elsewhere. Yiddish music, for example, was commonly used by the immigrant Jews to maintain relations with Eastern Europe, and from the 1920s onward various Hebrew songs were used to forge relations with another home or promised land and to express Jewish nationalism. Zionism and other political movements have used music to reify particular places in the pursuit of common goals so that those places come to embody the future and alternative ways of living. Many songs of Eretz Israel represent a synthesis of elements from Eastern European and Middle Eastern folksong. They are usually about the land and those who work on it, and many have an assertive, patriotic ring, thus contrasting with the Yiddish songs that conjure up images of everyday life in homelands like Poland. Jack finds it hard to relate to the songs of Eretz Israel, partly, perhaps, because unlike his contemporaries who have established connections with other places (especially London and Israel) through their middle class children and grandchildren, Jack has few such connections. The songs are in a language he can't understand, and he sees them as belonging to another generation. "I don't want to know," he says, "they're not in my era. Once we became a land of our own, a State, the whole thing changed. The youngsters took over... and it was different then." Thus Jack sometimes expresses a sense of alienation from his contemporaries and from the younger middle class Jewish establishment in Liverpool, yet says at the same time "I knew their parents," again expressing a sense of community and belonging through kinship ties.

Relations between Liverpool Jews and Jews in Israel, America, or elsewhere are reinforced via visiting musicians and through other musical exchanges. Jack's reminiscences frequently allude to Liverpool Jews who are now, in his words, "scattered all over the world." Like other Jews of his generation, he discusses the music of Jewish immigrants from Eastern Europe, such as Al Jolson, Irving Berlin, and Sophie Tucker (all based in America), in a manner that suggests a sense of affinity with those sharing similar heritages and experiences. In addition, however, Jack frequently cites Irish songs and songs of black slaves in America, acknowledging through them a sense of unity with other immigrant or oppressed peoples. He said of the latter: "They all had their songs ... they've got their roots here, their roots there ... Nobody wants them. They're a misfit. They get out, but where can you go? They've got no home."

The images and information that Jack has acquired about such people have been largely obtained through popular song and film. He talks with affection about the "black mammy women" from the American South, describing the little spectacles they wore and their warm-heartedness. He also quotes at length from the song "Danny Boy," linking the lyrics to Irish experiences of oppression, and linking that form of oppression to Jewish experience and history, thus suggesting the marking of "families of resemblance" through music.[8]

This highlights the way in which music enables Jack to travel in an imaginary sense to different times and places. Illustrating how music inspires his fantasy, transporting him from one place and immersing him somewhere else, Jack described his Monday afternoons at a Liverpool ballroom during the 1920s. Monday, he explained, was traditionally washing day. The women used to take off their aprons after a hard morning's work, do their hair, put on their finery, and take the bus to the city center, arriving at the ballroom for the 2:30 P.M. start. Jack once danced there to a tune entitled "In a Garden in Italy," and he enthused about how the music made him picture that garden, and how wonderful that experience was. Jack said of music: "It doesn't matter if it's dance music or what, it's there in my radio, and you're in another world. It takes you to a new world." He cited songs with American places-names in their title such as "Back Home in Tennessee," "Chicago," "Memphis Blues," "California Here I Come." He depicted the scene at the Swanny River: "All the women with their wide dresses. The men with their bowler hats. . . . So there you are, that's the Swanny. I don't even know where it is. I don't even know if there is a Swanny River. . . . I used to lie awake at night going through all the districts of the tunes. . . . Marvellous . . . . You'd go off to sleep thinking of them."

Jack began his dancing life in the dance halls based in the Brownlow Hill neighborhood, but as he gradually became more involved with dancing he frequented halls beyond that neighborhood, thus extending his music "pathways"[9] and broadening his knowledge and experience of the city. As a profession, music also offered other Liverpool Jews a "way out" of the neighborhood or city they lived in and the possibility of creating a new place. Gabler,[10] in his portrayal of the Eastern European Jewish immigrants who founded and built Hollywood, argued that the desire of these immigrants to assimilate and achieve status and power led them to a "ferocious, even pathological embrace of America." Through film these Jews created an idealized image of the America that they aspired to. "Prevented from entering the real corridors of power, they created a new country, an empire of their own, and colonized the American imagination to such an extent that the country came largely to be defined by the movies." The same was achieved through song by George Gershwin, Irving Berlin, Jerome Kern, and other Jewish composers. The experience of migration can thus exagerate attachments to romanticized homelands, but also lead migrants to stridently assert an adoptive belonging.[11]

In the biography of Vesta Tilley, a well-known music hall performer and wife of Walter de Frece, a Liverpool Jew and theatrical entrepreneur involved with the music hall business, Maitland[12] suggests certain parallels with the experience of the Hollywood Jews. Walter spearheaded the move to make the music hall more respectable and enhance its appeal to the middle classes. He himself had political and social aspirations that eventually led him and Vesta Tilley to drop their associations with the music hall. Eventually he was awarded a knighthood, and in 1924 he became a member of Parliament and a deputy lieutenant. This suggests that the music hall both helped and hindered Walter's efforts to achieve upward mobility and embody respectable Englishness, and it highlights the ideological significance of music in the production of place.

So far I have discussed music's influence on social relations and activities in particular places, on people's aesthetic experiences of place, and on the economic and material development of place. I have suggested ways in which music is used to represent or symbolize a place, distinguishing it from, or linking it to, other places, and associating it with particular images and meanings. Now I would like to explore the ideological nature of this process.

Representing and transforming place

Music, ideology, and social mobility

Jews like Jack gradually assimilated with wider Liverpool culture not just through interaction with Gentiles at dance halls and elsewhere, but through pressures brought to bear upon them by the Jewish establishment. While Jack's mother and aunts wept to Yiddish music at home, Jack and his peers were singing "Land of Hope and Glory" at school, undergoing a social and educational program instigated by the Jewish elite. The program was designed to anglicize the immigrants, by ridding them of their Yiddish language and culture; to control their leisure, by directing it away from disreputable activities (e.g., gambling and frequently dance halls); and to depoliticize them, by exorcising the socialist, anarchist, and trade union activity that some of them promoted. The elite were motivated by a variety of reasons. They feared, for example, that the foreign ways of the newcomers would threaten their own acquired respectability and standing and promote hostility to the Jewish population as a whole. Alternatively, popular culture has commonly acted as a focus for moral panic and social control, particularly in connection with working-class or immigrant youth. The concern of the Jewish Liverpool elite with anglicization, and with fitting Jewish tradition into the wider culture, can be detected early on in the rapid changes they introduced in their synagogues. A choir was introduced in one Liverpool synagogue at the beginning of the 1840s, for example, and an organ in another during the 1870s. These and other changes have continually reflected and provoked divisions among British Jews regarding processes of assimilation and distinctiveness.

The social and educational program aimed at the new immigrants was instituted via a framework of Jewish societies and clubs, many of which were based upon models in the wider English society. They included a Jewish Working Men's Club that ran classes in English, and a branch of the Jewish Lad's Brigade – a national Jewish cadet force based on the Church Lads' Brigade, whose letter-headed paper states that its object "is to train its members in loyalty, humour, discipline and self respect that they shall become worthy and useful citizens and be a credit to their country and their community." The Brigade was backed by a number of social clubs, including the Jewish Lad's Club, the Jewish Boy Scouts, and the Jewish Girls' Clubs. The process of anglicization was continued in the Hebrew school founded in 1840. Pupils were encouraged to change their names, mark British celebrations, and enter choral competitions and similar events.

These societies and clubs represented leisure and entertainment, but they were also highly politicized, combining both power and pleasure. Music was used to mold particular identities and allegiances, whether it be the military brass band music of the Jewish Lads' Brigade, the choral and orchestral societies of the Jewish Working Men's Club, or songs and anthems that acted as symbols of Englishness and expressions of national loyalty and unity. The program indicates pressures of assimilation, but also the simultaneous concern with maintaining distinctiveness as Jews. Jewish societies, clubs, and dances were regarded as safe contexts in which Jewish people could meet and form suitable friendships with people of their own kind. The program was extremely successful. Within a single generation, Yiddish had practically disappeared from the cultural scene.

Yet the production of national or other place-bound identities is always a contested process, and not all the Jewish immigrants were totally influenced by the social and educational program instigated by the Jewish elite. Many kept to their own more informal leisure activities based around their homes. Some, like Jack, attended organized walks, played football, and participated in other activities organized by Jewish societies, but also went to "outside" functions held at local dance halls frequented by Gentiles and forbidden to many Jewish young people. Meanwhile the Jewish elite patronized different clubs and venues and Jack never mixed with them. They also had their own social and cultural institutions – for example, literary societies – and gradually began to encourage the more up-and-coming of the new immigrants to join their activities until members of this nonveau riche started setting up their own similar organizations. Most such societies organized regular dances, concerts, and gramophone recitals in addition to dramatic, sporting, and fundraising activities, and debates and lectures. According to their minute books, many talks focused on politics and high culture. Debates addressed issues such as the division between established and immigrant Jews, and the generation gap between immigrants and their "English children." These societies gradually died out in the face of growing competition from the newly flourishing entertainment industries.

Music, stability, security

Like many other immigrant Jewish populations, Liverpool's immigrant Jews experienced rapid social and economic advancement. Within two generations a significant transformation of the class position of the immigrants had occurred. This was due to a mixture of social, cultural, and economic factors, including the fact that the city's high rate of unemployment discouraged further Jewish immigration. Most of the pedlars progressed as entrepreneurs. They came into contact with Gentiles because they moved around a lot, and they did better economically than the masses of skilled cabinet makers and tailors who worked long hours in small shops for a fixed wage. However, the latter's occupational structure also eventually shifted, toward clothing, drapery, and furniture businesses, and toward the professions which many were encouraged into as a means of improving themselves and their families.

Biographical information on some of the Jewish individuals and families involved with the Liverpool entertainment industries illustrates the way in which they were able to quickly establish themselves in those industries, but also indicates the cultural transformation that enhanced status and respectability might demand. Mal Levy, for example, had a recording contract in the 1960s and toured the country as a performer until he succumbed to parental pressure and returned to Liverpool to join the family tailoring business. "I think it was 'Don't put your son on the stage,'" says Mal, "You know, the old-fashioned Jewish outlook – it's not a good job, it's not a decent job....They looked down on music in those days." Such attitudes help explain why Liverpool Jews have tended to work in the business-and management-ends of music rather than in the performance end, and why rock and pop music have received such little attention from the city's Jewish institutions.

Brian Epstein came from a respected Liverpool family that ran a lucrative furniture business. Epstein opened a record retail branch within this business before taking up management of the Beatles and setting up his own music management company. According to Coleman,[13] Epstein's father, along with other relatives, wasn't too thrilled about Brian's association with the Beatles ("those yobbos"), and persuaded him to take on his brother Clive as joint director.[14] Although Brian Epstein's success eventually earned him respect from Liverpool's Jewish community, his obituary in the *Jewish Chronicle* stated: "The sad thing is that Brian was never completely au courant with the music that he was so much involved in....His strength of character came from the solidarity of his upbringing and the integrity of his background. It was this strength that he relied on when his artistic judgement failed."[15] During Epstein's funeral in Liverpool, the officiating rabbi ignored his achievements and fame and described him as "a symbol of the malaise of the 60s generation."[16] News of Epstein's death in the *Liverpool Jewish Gazette* was limited to a few short lines in the obituary notices at the back. It began, "Brian Epstein, manager of the Beatles . . ." and went straight on to mention his donations to Jewish charities.

While the first part of this chapter pointed to music as a fundamental part of everyday life, and to its role in the production of identity, belonging, and place, the second part has emphasized the ideological dimension to this process. Particular musical styles and activities come to symbolize particular values, and they can be used as a tool to transform notions of place and identity in order to maintain or challenge a particular hierarchical social order. Music is thus bound up with the struggle for power, prestige, and place. It reflects but also influences the social relations, practices, and material environments through which it is made.

Place, image, status

As the immigrants made their way up the economic and social scale, they gradually moved out of the Brownlow Hill neighborhood. During the 1930s that neighborhood underwent massive slum clearance which hastened the Jewish exodus. By the late 1930s only a small minority of Liverpool's Jews remained in the Brownlow Hill area. The Jews moved along Smithdown Road to settle in the more affluent neighboring suburbs of Allerton, Woolton, and Childwall where the overwhelming majority of Liverpool Jews are now based. As one informant put it, "It is easier to be Jewish when you live with other Jews." During Jack's lifetime a great transformation in Liverpool's Jewish population has thus taken place. It has involved a shift from notions of Russian or Polish Jews to Anglo Jews; from notions of a Jewish "quarter" or "ghetto" to a Jewish "area" or "district"; and from a social split between the elite, more established Jews and the immigrant Jews, to a single unified middle-class Jewish community based in that area or district. Notions of being inside, outside, or "on the fringes" of the community have strengthened as socio-economic homogeneity among the Jewish population intensified, increasing pressures for conformity.

Many young Liverpool Jews describe the community as "incestuous" and "traditional." The head of music at the Jewish school told me that Jewish religious "rules" make it impossible for many of the Jewish children to join in some musical events and activities, and that even if they aren't religious they have to be seen to be. "That's why it's such a close-knit community," she said, "because they make their fun together." When Liverpool's economic situation worsened after the 1960s, young Jews, along with those from other social groups, began to leave the city in search of economic and social opportunities elsewhere. This, along with emigration to Israel, a significant drop in the birthrate, and the high rate of intermarriage, led to a significant decline in the Jewish population. At present there are around 4,000 Jews in Liverpool. The Jewish authorities recently launched a "Come Back to Liverpool" campaign and video to encourage younger people to stay in, or return to, the city. The video emphasizes the uniqueness of the Jewish community and the area in which it is located. The smallness and safeness of the community is also emphasized, pointing out that it is easier to be someone in such a context, rather than be a small fish in a big pool somewhere else. The video features leisure amenities that project an image linked to classical music, emphasizing, for example, longstanding Jewish associations with the Royal Liverpool Philharmonic Orchestra. Hence place, "community," and "Jewishness" have become more commonly defined through so-called high culture.

Embodying Place

Travel and migration

The story of Jewish migration is a familiar one that features strongly in Jewish collective memory. Judaism has been likened by one Liverpool Jew to a "mental map by which we find each other as Jews in every part of the globe."[17] Jack's mental maps of the world, of Britain, of Liverpool, are partly based upon collective knowledge and experience of the geographical global movements of Jewish people, particularly the movement of Jews from Eastern Europe to particular British and American cities, and the movement of Liverpool Jews from the city center to the suburbs.

In contexts of change and mobility the production of place is often intensified. Stokes,[18] writing about Turkish and Irish migrants, points out that place, for many migrant communities, is something constructed through music with an intensity not found elsewhere in their social lives.' Concerning today's global mobility, Stokes wrote that "the discourses in which place is constructed and celebrated in relation to music have never before had to permit such flexibility and ingenuity." Musical sounds and structures reflect but also provoke and shape such movement.[19] Hebrew songs, for example, helped inspire the Zionist movement, while Irish traditional music has developed through continual movement between Ireland (the "home country") and the more distant countries adopted by Irish emigrants. Irish music influenced and blended with different musical styles in America, for example, and some of the resulting hybrid styles and sounds were then reimported to Ireland and treated as authentic, traditional expressions of Irishness.

Many musical compositions address the experience of migration or travel more directly through lyrics or through the culturally specific semiotic coding of musical sounds and structures. American country and blues musicians, for example, frequently write about the experience of being on the road, and Jack sings songs about leaving and returning written by Irish and other migrants. Such songs are prevalent in ports like Liverpool with their mobile and displaced populations, for whom concepts of "home" and "homeland" can evoke strong emotions – although relations with, and notions of, homeland depend on the particular circumstances of those involved, for example whether they emigrated individually or, like the Jews, in family groups. Today in Liverpool, songs from *Fiddler on the Roof* are often played at social gatherings of elderly Jews like Jack, songs that remind them of their collective origins and experiences of homelessness and emigration.

Place is also produced through the shorter journeys, routes, and activities of everyday life. All Jack's stories are about the city and people and places within it. Sitting in his front room he has taken me on a tour of parts of the city, house by house, dance hall by dance hall, street by street, pointing out relevant events, individuals, family and other relationships as we pass by, and transforming my own view of the city. Jack's phenomenal memory of, and emotional investment in, these buildings, locations, and social networks may be partly due to the daily door-to-door journeys he conducted around the city by foot as a traveling salesman. His leisure activities as a dancer, which took him on a nightly basis to various parts of the city, have added to his perspective on the city and its spatial geography. "I've been round this town for the last 70 years," says Jack, "and I know it backwards. I know everybody, and almost everybody knows me, except the growing generation. . . ."

In this sense places can be seen to be literally embodied. Through their bodies and bodily movements (whether through long-distance travel, walking, conversation, etc.) people experience their environment physically. Depending upon the circumstances surrounding them, some movements, such as long-distance journeys, can be quite stressful. Other more repetitive movements, such as the day-to-day journeys involved with work, or the sensual and expressive movements of dance, can be particularly memorable or intense. All can have a deep impact upon individual and collective memory and experiences of place, and upon emotions and identities associated with place.

Bodies, sounds, sentiments

Music can evoke or represent this physical production of place quite well. There is no space here to explore evidence for this in detail, but personal observations supported by the work of several critical musicologists indicate, without essentializing music, the particular way in which music produces place.

First, music is in a sense embodied. Musical performances also represent repetitive physical movements, whether through the fingering of instrumentalists, or the gestures of dancers. Music can move bodies in a way that distinguishes it from everyday speech and action and from the visual arts. Although music is part of everyday life, it can also be perceived as something special, something different from everyday experience.[20] Hence many people in Liverpool and elsewhere have prioritized music, making enormous financial sacrifices so that their children might learn how to read and play it, and even write it.

In addition, we listen to music and hear the presence and movements of the performing musicians. Hence Tagg describes music as an "extremely particular form of interhuman communication"[21] involving "a concerted simultaneity of non-verbal sound events or movements . . . [that makes music] particularly suited to expressing collective messages of affective and corporeal identity of individuals in relation to themselves, each other, and their social, as well as physical, surroundings."[22] Music also creates its own time, space, and motion, taking people out of "ordinary time." Blacking[23] points out that, "we often experience greater intensity of living when our normal time values are upset . . . music may help to generate such experiences." Furthermore, as sound, music fills and structures space within us and around us, inside and outside. Hence, much like our concept of place, music can appear to envelop us, but it can also appear to express our innermost feelings/being. Travel writers or journalists often single music out as representing the essence, soul, or spirit of a place, perhaps because music appears to be "more natural" than visual imagery since its social constructedness/semiotics is less familiar.

The images and experiences engendered by music are, of course, dependent upon the particular circumstances in which the music is performed and heard, and upon the type of musical style and activity involved. But through its embodiment of movement and collectivity, and through the peculiar ambiguity of its symbolic forms, music can appear to act upon and convey emotion in a unique way. It represents an alternative discourse to everyday speech and language, although both are of course ideologically informed and culturally constructed. Hence male, working-class, rock musicians in Liverpool use music to express ideas and sentiment in a manner that may be discouraged in most public settings, or that aren't so easily expressed through other means. Their music is very personal, although it is at the same time created for public performance. This can make music a particularly precious resource in the production of place and local subjectivity. As popular culture, music can be a particularly powerful and accessible resource. For the general listener just one simple musical phrase can simultaneously represent a private world of memory and desire and a collective mood or a soundtrack to particular public events.

For Jack, sitting alone and listening to music on the radio, or simply talking about music, can evoke some of his most intense feelings and experiences. His musical tastes and experiences are individual, reflecting his personal biography. At the same time, however, his reminiscences have been shown to be shaped by the social relations, networks, and collectivities that he has been a part of. All this indicates music's effectiveness in stimulating a sense of identity, in preserving and transmitting cultural memory, and in establishing the sensuous production of place. Individuals can use music as a cultural "map of meaning," drawing upon it to locate "themselves in different imaginary geographies at one and the same time," and to articulate both individual and collective identities.

NOTES

1   Stokes, M. (Ed.). (1994). Place, exchange and meaning: Black Sea musicians in the West of Ireland. *Ethnicity, identity: The musical construction of place*. Oxford: Berg, p. 6.
2   Finnegan, R. (1989). *The hidden musicians: Music-making in an English town*. Cambridge: Cambridge University Press.
3   Werner, E. (1990). Jewish music: Liturgical Ashkenazic tradition. In S. Sadie (Ed.), *The new Grove dictionary of music and musicians* (Vol. 9). London: Macmillan, p. 629.
4   Gabler, N. (1989). *An empire of their own: How the Jews invented Hollywood*. London: W. H. Allen.
5   Street, J. (1993). (Dis)located? rhetoric, politics, meaning and the locality. In W. Straw et al. (Eds.), *Popular music: Style and identity* Montreal: Centre for Research on Canadian Cultural Industries and Institutions.
6   Appadurai, A. (1993). *The production of locality*. Unpublished paper delivered at the decennial conference of the Association of Social Anthropologists, Oxford University.
7   McManus, K. (1994). *Ceilies, jigs, and ballads: Irish music in Liverpool*. Liverpool: Institute of Popular Music, p. 5.
8   Lipsitz, G. (1989). *Time passages: Collective memory and American popular culture*. Minneapolis: University of Minnesota Press, p. 136.
9   Finnegan, *The hidden musicians*.
10   Gabler, *An empire of their own*.
11   Lowenthal, D. (1985). *The past is a foreign country*. New York: Cambridge University Press, p. 42.
12   Maitland, S. (1986). *Vesta Tilley*. London: Virago.
13   Coleman, R. (1989). *Brian Epstein: The man who made the Beatles*. Harmondsworth, U.K.: Viking, p. 83.
14   Ibid., pp. 102–103.
15   Ibid., p. 415.
16   Ibid., p. 410.
17   Kokosolakis, N. (1982). *Ethnic identity and religion: Tradition and change in Liverpool Jewry*. Washington, D.C.: University Press of America, p. 199.
18   Stokes, Place, exchange, and meaning, p. 114.
19   Ibid.
20   Finnegan, *The hidden musicians*, pp. 336–337.
21   Tagg, P. (1981). On the specificity of musical communication: Guidelines for non-musicologists. In *Stencilled papers from Gothenburg University Musicology Department. 8115*. Gothenburg: Gothenburg University Press, p. 1.
22   Tagg, P. (1994). *Introductory notes to music semiotics*. Unpublished paper, p. 18.
23   Blacking, J. (1976). *How musical is man?* London: Faber, p. 51.

25 Deconstructing the Map

J. B. Harley

The notion that space is not an a priori given but a product of diverse uses, experiences and understandings carries devastating implications for our capacity to represent space with singular objectivity. After all, if a space may be any number of things according to one's physical and symbolic position within it, then any univocal claim about the nature of that space must be both partial and an implicit arrogation of descriptive authority on the part of the claimant. If this is the case, then we should expect authoritative representations of space to be laden with concealed exaggerations and omissions serving, intentionally or no, to advance the representer's assumptions and interests at the expense of others'. By critically interrogating those blunt statements of spatial facticity we call maps, J. B. Harley formulates and confirms precisely this hypothesis. Contrary to our long-held assumptions, Harley mobilizes the empirical evidence of cartographic history to reveal how maps are not disinterested depictions of their spatial subjects. Rather, a map is a partisan assertion about the nature of space concealed beneath a veneer of representational veracity, an assertion often deployed to subject space to particular political and commercial interests. Thus, Harley reminds us of the cautionary to never mistake the map for the territory, and extends a warning that while territory may be authoritatively mapped, it can never be truthfully mapped.

The pace of conceptual exploration in the history of cartography – searching for alternative ways of understanding maps – is slow. Some would say that its achievements are largely cosmetic. Applying conceptions of literary history to the history of cartography, it would appear that we are still working largely in either a "premodern," or a "modern" rather than in a "postmodern" climate of thought. A list of individual explorations would, it is true, contain some that sound impressive. Our students can now be directed to writings that draw on the ideas of information theory, linguistics, semiotics, structuralism, phenomenology, developmental theory, hermeneutics, iconology, marxism, and ideology. We can point to the names in our footnotes of (among others) Cassirer, Gombrich, Piaget, Panofsky, Kuhn, Barthes and Eco. Yet despite these symptoms of change, we are still, willingly or unwillingly, the prisoners of our own past.

My basic argument in this essay is that we should encourage an epistemological shift in the way we interpret the nature of cartography. For historians of cartography, I believe a major roadblock to understanding is that we still accept uncritically the broad consensus, with relatively few dissenting voices, of what *cartographers* tell us maps are supposed to be. In particular, we often tend to work from the premise that mappers engage in an unquestionably "scientific" or "objective" form of knowledge creation. Of course, cartographers believe they have to say this to remain credible but historians do not have that obligation. It is better for us to begin from the premise that cartography is seldom what cartographers say it is.

As they embrace computer-assisted methods and Geographical Information Systems, the scientistic rhetoric of map makers is becoming more strident. The "culture of technics" is everywhere rampant. We are told that the journal now named *The American Cartographer* will become *Cartography and Geographical Information Systems*. Or, in a strangely ambivalent gesture toward the nature of maps, the British Cartographic Society proposes that there should be two definitions of cartography, "one for professional cartographers and the other for the public at large." A definition "for use in communication with the general public" would be "Cartography is the art, science and technology of making maps": that for "practicing cartographers" would be "Cartography is the science and technology of analyzing and interpreting geographic relationships, and communicating the results by means of maps."[1] Many may find it surprising that "art" no longer exists in "professional" cartography. In the present context, however, these signs of ontological schizophrenia can also be read as reflecting an urgent need to rethink the nature of maps from different perspectives. The question arises as to whether the notion of a progressive science is a myth partly created by cartographers in the course of their own professional development. I suggest that it has been accepted too uncritically by a wider public and by other scholars who work with maps. For those concerned with the history of maps it is especially timely that we challenge the cartographer's assumptions. Indeed, if the history of cartography is to grow as an interdisciplinary subject among the humanities and social sciences, new ideas are essential.

The question becomes how do we as historians of cartography escape from the normative models of cartography? How do we allow new ideas to come in? . . . In this essay I also adopt a strategy aimed at the deconstruction of the map.

The notion of deconstruction[2] is also a password for the postmodern enterprise. Deconstructionist strategies can now be found not only in philosophy but also in localized disciplines, especially in literature, and in other subjects such as architecture, planning and, more recently, geography. I shall specifically use a deconstructionist tactic to break the assumed link between reality and representation which has dominated cartographic thinking, has led it in the pathway of "normal science" since the Enlightenment, and has also provided a ready-made and "taken for granted" epistemology for the history of cartography. The objective is to suggest that an alternative epistemology, rooted in social theory rather than in scientific positivism, is more appropriate to the history of cartography. It will be shown that even "scientific" maps are a product not only of "the rules of the order of geometry and reason" but also of the "norms and values of the order of social . . . tradition."[3] Our task is to search for the social forces that have structured cartography and to locate the presence of power – and its effects – in all map knowledge.

The ideas in this particular essay owe most to writings by Foucault and Derrida. My approach is deliberately eclectic because in some respects the theoretical positions of these two authors are incompatible. Foucault anchors texts in sociopolitical realities and constructs systems for organizing knowledge of the kind that Derrida loves to dismantle. But even so, by combining different ideas on a new terrain, it may be possible to devise a scheme of social theory with which we can begin to interrogate the hidden agendas of cartography. Such a scheme offers no "solution" to an historical interpretation of the cartographic record, nor a precise method or set of techniques, but as a broad strategy it may help to locate some of the fundamental forces that have driven map-making in both European and non-European societies. From Foucault's writings, the key revelation has been the omnipresence of power in all knowledge, even though that power is invisible or implied, including the particular knowledge encoded in maps and atlases. Derrida's notion of the rhetoricity of all texts has been no less a challenge. It demands a search for metaphor and rhetoric in maps where previously scholars had found only measurement and topography. Its central question is reminiscent of Korzybski's much older dictum "The map is not the territory"[4] but deconstruction goes further to bring the issue of how the map represents place into much sharper focus.

Deconstruction urges us to read between the lines of the map – "in the margins of the text" – and through its tropes to discover the silences and contradictions that challenge the apparent honesty of the image. We begin to learn that cartographic facts are only facts within a specific cultural perspective. We start to understand how maps, like art, far from being "a transparent opening to the world," are but "a particular human way . . . of looking at the world."[5]

In pursuing this strategy I shall develop three threads of argument. First, I shall examine the discourse of cartography in the light of some of Foucault's ideas about the play of rules within discursive formations. Second, drawing on one of Derrida's central positions I will examine the textuality of maps and, in particular, their rhetorical dimension. Third, returning to Foucault, I will consider how maps work in society as a form of power–knowledge.

The Rules of Cartography

One of Foucault's primary units of analysis is the discourse. A discourse has been defined as "a system of possibility for knowledge."[6] Foucault's method was to ask;

> what rules permit certain statements to be made; what rules order these statements; what rules permit us to identify some statements as true and others as false; what rules allow the construction of a map, model or classificatory system . . . what rules are revealed when an object of discourse is modified or transformed . . . Whenever sets of rules of these kinds can be identified, we are dealing with a discursive formation or discourse.[7]

The key question for us then becomes, "What type of rules have governed the development of cartography?" Cartography I define as a body of theoretical and practical knowledge that map-makers employ to construct maps as a distinct mode of visual representation. The question is, of course, historically specific: the rules of cartography vary in different societies. Here I refer particularly to two distinctive sets of rules that underlie and dominate the history of Western cartography since the seventeenth century.[8] One set may be defined as governing the technical production of maps and are made explicit in the cartographic treatises and writings of the period. The other set relates to the cultural production of maps. These must be understood in a broader historical context than either scientific procedure or technique. They are, moreover, rules that are usually ignored by cartographers so that they form a hidden aspect of their discourse.

The first set of cartographic rules can thus be defined in terms of a scientific epistemology. From at least the seventeenth century onward, European map-makers and map users have increasingly promoted a standard scientific model of knowledge and cognition. The object of mapping is to produce a "correct" relational model of the terrain. Its assumptions are that the objects in the world to be mapped are real and objective, and that they enjoy an existence independent of the cartographer; that their reality can be expressed in mathematical terms; that systematic observation and measurement offer the only route to cartographic truth; and that this truth can be independently verified. The procedures of both surveying and map construction came to share strategies similar to those in science in general: cartography also documents a history of more precise instrumentation and measurement; increasingly complex classifications of its knowledge and a proliferation of signs for its representation; and, especially from the nineteenth century onward, the growth of institutions and a "professional" literature designed to monitor the application and propagation of the rules. . . . A "scientific" cartography (so it was believed) would be untainted by social factors. Even today many cartographers are puzzled by the suggestion that political and sociological theory could throw light on their practices. They will probably shudder at the mention of deconstruction.

The acceptance of the map as "a mirror of nature" (to employ Richard Rorty's phrase[9]) also results in a number of other characteristics of cartographic discourse even where these are not made explicit. Most striking is the belief in progress: that, by the application of science ever more precise representations of reality can be produced. The methods of cartography have delivered a "true, probable, progressive, or highly confirmed knowledge."[10] This mimetic bondage has led to a tendency not only to look down on the maps of the past (with a dismissive scientific chauvinism) but also to regard the maps of other non-Western or early cultures (where the rules of mapmaking were different) as inferior to European maps.[11] Similarly, the primary effect of the scientific rules was to create a "standard" – a successful version of "normal science"[12] – that enabled cartographers to build a wall around their citadel of the "true" map. Its central bastions were measurement and standardization and beyond there was a "not cartography" land where lurked an army of inaccurate, heretical, subjective, valuative, and ideologically distorted images. Cartographers developed a "sense of the other" in relation to nonconforming maps. Even maps such as those produced by journalists, where different rules and modes of expressiveness might be appropriate, are evaluated by many cartographers according to standards of "objectivity," "accuracy," and "truthfulness." [...]

In cases where the scientific rules are invisible in the map we can still trace their play in attempting to normalize the discourse. The cartographer's "black box" has to be defended and its social origins suppressed. The hysteria among leading cartographers at the popularity of the Peters' projection,[13] or the recent expressions of piety among Western European and North American map-makers following the Russian admission that they had falsified their topographic maps to confuse the enemy give us a glimpse of how the game is played according to these rules. The implication is that Western maps are value free. According to the spokesman, our maps are not ideological documents, and the condemnation of Russian falsification is as much an echo of Cold War rhetoric as it is a credible cartographic criticism.

This timely example also serves to introduce my second contention that the scientific rules of mapping are, in any case, influenced by a quite different set of rules, those governing the cultural production of the map. To discover these rules, we have to read between the lines of technical procedures or of the map's topographic content. They are related to values, such as those of ethnicity, politics, religion, or social class, and they are also embedded in the map-producing society at large. Cartographic discourse operates a double silence toward this aspect of the possibilities for map knowledge. In the map itself, social structures are often disguised beneath an abstract, instrumental space, or incarcerated in the coordinates of computer mapping. And in the technical literature of cartography they are also ignored, notwithstanding the fact that they may be as important as surveying, compilation, or design in producing the statements that cartography makes about the world and its landscapes. Such an interplay of social and technical rules is a universal feature of cartographic knowledge. In maps it produces the "order" of its features and the "hierarchies of its practices."[14] In Foucault's sense the rules may enable us to define an *episteme* and to trace an archaeology of that knowledge through time.[15]

Two examples of how such rules are manifest in maps will be given to illustrate their force in structuring cartographic representation. The first is the well-known adherence to the "rule of ethnocentricity" in the construction of world maps. This has led many historical societies to place their own territories at the center of their cosmographies or world maps. While it may be dangerous to assume universality, and there are exceptions, such a rule is as evident in cosmic diagrams of pre-Columbian North American Indians as it is in the maps of ancient Babylonia, Greece or China, or in the medieval maps of the Islamic world or Christian Europe. Yet what is also significant in applying Foucault's critique of knowledge to cartography is that the history of the ethnocentric rule does not march in step with the "scientific" history of map-making. [...] It is also arguable that such world maps have in turn helped to codify, to legitimate, and to promote the world views which are prevalent in different periods and places.

A second example is how the "rules of the social order" appear to insert themselves into the smaller codes and spaces of cartographic transcription. The history of European cartography since the seventeenth century provides many examples of this tendency. Pick a printed or manuscript map from the drawer almost at random and what stands out is the unfailing way its text is as much a commentary on the social structure of a particular nation or place as it is on its topography. The map-maker is often as busy recording the contours of feudalism, the shape of a religious hierarchy, or the steps in the tiers of social class, as the topography of the physical and human landscape. [. . .]

Once again, much like "the rule of ethnocentrism," this hierarchicalization of space is not a conscious act of cartographic representation. Rather it is taken for granted in a society that the place of the king is more important than the place of a lesser baron, that a castle is more important than a peasant's house, that the town of an archbishop is more important than that of a minor prelate, or that the estate of a landed gentleman is more worthy of emphasis than that of a plain farmer. Cartography deploys its vocabulary accordingly so that it embodies a systematic social inequality. The distinctions of class and power are engineered, reified and legitimated in the map by means of cartographic signs. The rule seems to be "the more powerful, the more prominent." To those who have strength in the world shall be added strength in the map . . . We can begin to see how maps, like art, become a mechanism "for defining social relationships, sustaining social rules, and strengthening social values."[16]
  In the case of both these examples of rules, the point I am making is that the rules operate both within and beyond the orderly structures of classification and measurement. They go beyond the stated purposes of cartography. Much of the power of the map, as a representation of social geography, is that it operates behind a mask of a seemingly neutral science. It hides and denies its social dimensions at the same time as it legitimates. Yet whichever way we look at it the rules of society will surface. They have ensured that maps are at least as much an image of the social order as they are a measurement of the phenomenal world of objects.

Deconstruction and the Cartographic Text

To move inward from the question of cartographic rules – the social context within which map knowledge is fashioned – we have to turn to the cartographic text itself. The word "text" is deliberately chosen. It is now generally accepted that the model of text can have a much wider application than to literary texts alone. To non-book texts such as musical compositions and architectural structures we can confidently add the graphic texts we call maps. It has been said that "what constitutes a text is not the presence of linguistic elements but the act of construction" so that maps, as "constructions employing a conventional sign system,"[17] become texts. With Barthes we could say they "presuppose a signifying consciousness" that it is our business to uncover.[18] "Text" is certainly a better metaphor for maps than the mirror of nature. Maps are a cultural text. By accepting their textuality we are able to embrace a number of different interpretative possibilities. Instead of just the transparency of clarity we can discover the pregnancy of the opaque. To fact we can add myth, and instead of innocence we may expect duplicity. Rather than working with a formal science of communication, or even a sequence of loosely related technical processes, our concern is redirected to a history and anthropology of the image, and we learn to recognize the narrative qualities of cartographic representation as well as its claim to provide a synchronous picture of the world. All this, moreover, is likely to lead to a rejection of the neutrality of maps, as we come to define their intentions rather than the literal face of representation, and as we begin to accept the social consequences of cartographic practices. I am not suggesting that the direction of textual enquiry offers a simple set of techniques for reading either contemporary or historical maps. In some cases we will have to conclude that there are many aspects of their meaning that are undecidable.

Deconstruction, as discourse analysis in general, demands a closer and deeper reading of the cartographic text than has been the general practice in either cartography or the history of cartography. It may be regarded as a search for alternative meanings.... Our reading has to go beyond the assessment of geometric accuracy, beyond the fixing of location, and beyond the recognition of topographical patterns and geographies. Such interpretation begins from the premise that the map text may contain "unperceived contradictions or duplicitous tensions"[19] that undermine the surface layer of standard objectivity. Maps are slippery customers.... Throughout the history of modern cartography in the West, for example, there have been numerous instances of where maps have been falsified, of where they have been censored or kept secret, or of where they have surreptitiously contradicted the rules of their proclaimed scientific status.[20]

As in the case of these practices, map deconstruction would focus on aspects of maps that many interpreters have glossed over:

> To "deconstruct" a piece of writing is therefore to operate a kind of strategic reversal, seizing on precisely those unregarded details (casual metaphors, footnotes, incidental turns of argument) which are always, and necessarily, passed over by interpreters of a more orthodox persuasion. For it is here, in the margins of the text – the "margins," that is, as defined by a powerful normative consensus – that deconstruction discovers those same unsettling forces at work.[21]

A good example of how we could deconstruct an early map – by beginning with what have hitherto been regarded as its "causal metaphors" and "footnotes" – is provided by recent studies reinterpreting the status of decorative art on the European maps of the seventeenth and eighteenth centuries. Rather than being inconsequential marginalia, the emblems in cartouches and decorative titlepages can be regarded as *basic* to the way they convey their cultural meaning,[22] and they help to demolish the claim of cartography to produce an impartial graphic science. But the possibility of such a revision is not limited to historic "decorative" maps. A recent essay by Wood and Fels on the Official State Highway Map of North Carolina[23] indicates a much wider applicability for a deconstructive strategy by beginning in the "margins" of the contemporary map... It is also clear that the State Highway Map of North Carolina is making other dialogical assertions behind its mask of innocence and transparence. I am not suggesting that these elements hinder the traveler getting from point A to B, but that there is a second text within the map. No map is devoid of an intertextual dimension and, in this case too, the discovery of intertextuality enables us to scan the image as more than a neutral picture of a road network. Its "users" are not only the ordinary motorists but also the State of North Carolina that has appropriated its publication (distributed in millions of copies) as a promotional device. The map has become an instrument of State policy and an instrument of sovereignty.[24] At the same time, it is more than an affirmation of North Carolina's dominion over its territory. It also constructs a mythic geography, a landscape full of "points of interest," with incantations of loyalty to state emblems and to the values of a Christian piety. The hierarchy of towns and the visually dominating highways that connect them have become the legitimate natural order of the world. The map finally insists "that roads really *are* what North Carolina's all about."[25] The map idolizes our love affair with the automobile. The myth is believable.

A cartographer's stock response to this deconstructionist argument might well be to cry "foul." The argument would run like this: "Well after all it's a state highway map. It's designed to be at once popular and useful. We expect it to exaggerate the road network and to show points of interest to motorists. It is a derived rather than a basic map." It is not a scientific map. The appeal to the ultimate scientific map is always the cartographers' last line of defence when seeking to deny the social relations that permeate their technology.

It is at this point that Derrida's strategy can help us to extend such an interpretation to all maps, scientific or non-scientific, basic or derived. Just as in the deconstruction of philosophy Derrida was able to show "how the supposedly literal level is intensively metaphorical"[26] so too we can show how cartographic "fact" is also symbol. In "plain" scientific maps, science itself becomes the metaphor. Such maps contain a dimension of "symbolic realism" which is no less a statement of political authority and control than a coat-of-arms or a portrait of a queen placed at the head of an earlier decorative map. The metaphor has changed. The map has attempted to purge itself of ambiguity and alternative possibility.[27] Accuracy and austerity of design are now the new talismans of authority culminating in our own age with computer mapping. We can trace this process very clearly in the history of Enlightenment mapping in Europe. The topography as shown in maps, increasingly detailed and planimetrically accurate, has become a metaphor for a utilitarian philosophy and its will to power. Cartography inscribes this cultural model upon the paper and we can examine it in many scales and types of maps. Precision of instrument and technique merely serves to reinforce the image, with its encrustation of myth, as a selective perspective on the world. Thus maps of local estates in the European *ancien regime*, though derived from instrumental survey, were a metaphor for a social structure based on landed property. County and regional maps, though founded on scientific triangulation, were an articulation of local values and rights. Maps of the European states, though constructed along arcs of the meridian, served still as a symbolic shorthand for a complex of nationalist ideas. And world maps, though increasingly drawn on mathematically defined projections, nevertheless gave a spiralling twist to the manifest destiny of European overseas conquest and colonization.[28] In each of these examples we can trace the contours of metaphor in a scientific map. This in turn enhances our understanding of how the text works as an instrument operating on social reality.

In deconstructionist theory the play of rhetoric is closely linked to that of metaphor. In concluding this section of the essay I will argue that notwithstanding "scientific" cartography's efforts to convert culture into nature, and to "naturalize" social reality,[29] it has remained an inherently rhetorical discourse. Another of the lessons of Derrida's criticism of philosophy is "that modes of rhetorical analysis, hitherto applied mainly to literary texts, are in fact indispensable for reading *any* kind of discourse."[30] There is nothing revolutionary in the idea that cartography is an art of persuasive communication. It is now commonplace to write about the rhetoric of the human sciences in the classical sense of the word rhetoric. Even cartographers – as well as their critics – are beginning to allude to the notion of a rhetorical cartography but what is still lacking is a rhetorical close-reading of maps.

The issue in contention is not whether some maps are rhetorical, or whether other maps are partly rhetorical, but the extent to which rhetoric is a universal aspect of all cartographic texts. Thus for some cartographers the notion of "rhetoric" would remain a pejorative term. It would be an "empty rhetoric" which was unsubstantiated in the scientific content of a map. "Rhetoric" would be used to refer to the "excesses" of propaganda mapping or advertising cartography or an attempt would be made to confine it to an "artistic" or aesthetic element in maps as opposed to their scientific core. My position is to accept that rhetoric is part of the way all texts work and that all maps are rhetorical texts. Again we ought to dismantle the arbitrary dualism between "propaganda" and "true," and between modes of "artistic" and "scientific" representation as they are found in maps. All maps strive to frame their message in the context of an audience. All maps state an argument about the world and they are propositional in nature. All maps employ the common devices of rhetoric such as invocations of authority (*especially* in "scientific" maps) and appeals to a potential readership through the use of colors, decoration, typography, dedications, or written justifications of their method. Rhetoric may be concealed but it is always present, for there is no description without performance.

The steps in making a map – selection, omission, simplification, classification, the creation of hierarchies, and "symbolization" – are all inherently rhetorical. In their intentions as much as in their applications they signify subjective human purposes rather than reciprocating the workings of some "fundamental law of cartographic generalisation." Indeed, the freedom of rhetorical manoeuvre in cartography is considerable: the mapmaker merely omits those features of the world that lie outside the purpose of the immediate discourse. There have been no limits to the varieties of maps that have been developed historically in response to different purposes of argument, aiming at different rhetorical goals, and embodying different assumptions about what is sound cartographic practice. The style of maps is neither fixed in the past nor is it today. It has been said that "The rhetorical code appropriates to its map the style most advantageous to the myth it intends to propagate."[31] Instead of thinking in terms of rhetorical versus non-rhetorical maps it may be more helpful to think in terms of a theory of cartographic rhetoric which accommodated this fundamental aspect of representation in all types of cartographic text. Thus, I am not concerned to privilege rhetoric over science, but to dissolve the illusory distinction between the two in reading the social purposes as well as the content of maps.

Maps and the Exercise of Power

For the final stage in the argument I return to Foucault. In doing so I am mindful of Foucault's criticism of Derrida that he attempted "to restrict interpretation to a purely syntactic and textual level,"[32] a world where political realities no longer exist. Foucault, on the other hand, sought to uncover "the social practices that the text itself both reflects and employs" and to "reconstruct the technical and material framework in which it arose."[33] Though deconstruction is useful in helping to change the epistemological climate, and in encouraging a rhetorical reading of cartography, my final concern is with its social and political dimensions, and with understanding how the map works in society as a form of power-knowledge. This closes the circle to a context-dependent form of cartographic history.

We have already seen how it is possible to view cartography as a discourse – a system which provides a set of rules for the representation of knowledge embodied in the images we define as maps and atlases. It is not difficult to find for maps – especially those produced and manipulated by the state – a niche in the "power/ knowledge matrix of the modern order."[34] ... Yet to understand how power works through cartographic discourse and the effects of that power in society further dissection is needed. A simple model of domination and subversion is inadequate and I propose to draw a distinction between *external* and *internal* power in cartography. [...]

The most familiar sense of power in cartography is that of power *external* to maps and mapping. This serves to link maps to the centers of political power. Power is exerted *on* cartography. Behind most cartographers there is a patron; in innumerable instances the makers of cartographic texts were responding to external needs. Power is also exercised *with* cartography. Monarchs, ministers, state institutions, the Church, have all initiated programs of mapping for their own ends.... In all these cases maps are linked to what Foucault called the exercise of "juridical power."[35] The map becomes a "juridical territory": it facilitates surveillance and control. Maps are still used to control our lives in innumerable ways. A mapless society, though we may take the map for granted, would now be politically unimaginable. All this is power *with* the help of maps. It is an external power, often centralized and exercised bureaucratically, imposed from above, and manifest in particular acts or phases of deliberate policy.

I come now to the important distinction. What is also central to the effects of maps in society is what may be defined as the power *internal* to cartography. The focus of inquiry therefore shifts from the place of cartography in a juridical system of power to the political effects of what cartographers do when they make maps. Cartographers manufacture power: they create a spatial panopticon. It is a power embedded in the map text. We can talk about the power of the map just as we already talk about the power of the word or about the book as a force for change. In this sense maps have politics.[36] It is a power that intersects and is embedded in knowledge. It is universal.... To catalogue the world is to appropriate it[37] so that all these technical processes represent acts of control over its image which extend beyond the professed uses of cartography. The world is disciplined. The world is normalized. We are prisoners in its spatial matrix. For cartography as much as other forms of knowledge, "All social action flows through boundaries determined by classification schemes."[38] ... The power of the map-maker was not generally exercised over individuals but over the knowledge of the world made available to people in general. Yet this is not consciously done and it transcends the simple categories of "intended" and "unintended" altogether. I am not suggesting that power is deliberately or centrally exercised. It is a local knowledge which at the same time is universal. It usually passes unnoticed. The map is a silent arbiter of power.

What have been the effects of this "logic of the map" upon human consciousness? . . . I believe we have to consider for maps the effects of abstraction, uniformity, repeatability, and visuality in shaping mental structures, and in imparting a sense of the places of the world. It is the disjunction between those senses of place, and many alternative visions of what the world is, or what it might be, that has raised questions about the effect of cartography in society. . . . Consider, for example, the fact that the ordinary road atlas is among the best selling paperback books in the United States[39] and then try to gauge how this may have affected ordinary Americans' perception of their country. What sort of an image of America do these atlases promote? On the one hand, there is a patina of gross simplicity. Once off the interstate highways the landscape dissolves into a generic world of bare essentials that invites no exploration. Context is stripped away and place is no longer important. On the other hand, the maps reveal the ambivalence of all stereotypes. Their silences are also inscribed on the page: where, on the page, is the variety of nature, where is the history of the landscape, and where is the space–time of human experience in such anonymized maps?

The question has now become: do such empty images have their consequences in the way we think about the world? Because all the world is designed to look the same, is it easier to act upon it without realizing the social effects? It is in the posing of such questions that the strategies of Derrida and Foucault appear to clash. For Derrida, if meaning is undecidable so must be, *pari passu*, the measurement of the force of the map as a discourse of symbolic action. In ending, I prefer to align myself with Foucault in seeing all knowledge – and hence cartography – as thoroughly enmeshed with the larger battles which constitute our world. Maps are not external to these struggles to alter power relations. The history of map use suggests that this may be so and that maps embody specific forms of power and authority. . . . While the map is never the reality, it helps to create a different reality. Once embedded in the published text the lines on the map acquire an authority that may be hard to dislodge. Maps are authoritarian images. . . . Sometimes agents of change, they can equally become conservative documents. But in either case the map is never neutral. Where it seems to be neutral it is the sly "rhetoric of neutrality" that is trying to persuade us.

Conclusion

The interpretive act of deconstructing the map can serve three functions in a broad enquiry into the history of cartography. First, it allows us to challenge the epistemological myth (created by cartographers) of the cumulative progress of an objective science always producing better delineations of reality. Second, deconstructionist argument allows us to redefine the historical importance of maps. Rather than invalidating their study, it is enhanced by adding different nuances to our understanding of the power of cartographic representation as a way of building order into our world. If we can accept intertextuality then we can start to read our maps for alternative and sometimes competing discourses. Third, a deconstructive turn of mind may allow map history to take a fuller place in the interdisciplinary study of text and knowledge.... By dismantling we build. The possibilities of discovering meaning in maps and of tracing the social mechanisms of cartographic change are enlarged. Postmodernism offers a challenge to read maps in ways that could reciprocally enrich the reading of other texts.

NOTES

1   Reported in *Cartographic Perspectives: Bulletin of the North American Cartographic Information Society* 1/1, 1989: 4.
2   Deriving from the writings of Jacques Derrida: for exposition see the translator's Preface to Jacques Derrida, *Of Grammatology*, trans. Gayatri Chakratvorty Spivak. Baltimore: The John Hopkins University Press, 1976: ix–lxxxvii; Christopher Norris, *Deconstruction: Theory and Practice*. London: Methuen, 1982; and Christopher Norris, *Derrida*. Cambridge, Mass.: Harvard University Press, 1987.
3   Louis Marin, *Portrait of the King*, trans. Martha M. Houle, *Theory and History of Literature* 57. Minneapolis: University of Minnesota Press, 1988: 173.
4   Alfred Korzybski, *Science and Sanity: An Introduction to Non-Aristotelian Systems and General Semantics*, 3rd ed. with new pref. Lakeville, Connecticut: The International Non-Aristotelian Library Pub. Co., 1948: 58, 247, 498, 750–51.
5   H. G. Blocker, *Philosophy and Art*, New York: Charles Scribner's Sons, 1979: 43.
6   Mark Philip, "Michel Foucault," *In* Skinner, *The Return of Grand Theory*: 69.
7   Ibid.
8   "Western cartography" is defined as the types of survey mapping first fully visible in the European Enlightenment and which then spread to other areas of the world as part of European overseas expansion.
9   Richard Rorty, *Philosophy and the Mirror of Nature*. Princeton, 1979.
10 Larry Laudan, *Progress and Its Problems: Toward a Theory of Scientific Growth*. Berkeley: University of California Press, 1977: 2.
11 For a discussion of these tendencies in the historiography of early maps see J. B. Harley, "L'Histoire de la cartographie comme discours," *Préfaces* 5 December 1987-January 1988: 70–75.
12 In the much-debated sense of Thomas S. Kuhn, *The Structure of Scientific Revolutions*. Chicago: The University of Chicago Press, 1962.
13 Arno Peters, *The New Cartography*, New York: Friendship Press, 1983. The responses included John Loxton, "The Peters Phenomenon," *The Cartographic Journal* 22/2, 1985: 106–8; "The So-called Peters Projection," in ibid., 108–10; A.H. Robinson, "Arno Peters and His New Cartography," *American Cartographer* 12, 1985: 103–11; Phil Porter and Phil Voxland, "Distortion in Maps: The Peters' Projection and Other Devilments," *Focus* 36, 1986: 22–30; and, for a more balanced view, John P. Snyder, "Social Consciousness and World Maps," *The Christian Century*, February 24th, 1988: 190–92.
14 Michel Foucault, *The Order of Things: An Archaeology of the Human Sciences*. A Translation of *Les mots et les choses*. New York: Vintage Books, 1973, xx.
15 Ibid., xxii.
16 Gifford Geertz, "Art as a Cultural System" in *Local Knowledge: Further Essays in Interpretive Anthropology*. New York: Basic Books, 1983, 99.
17 D. McKenzie, *Bibliography and the Sociology of Texts*. London: The British Library, 1986: 35.

18 Roland Barthes, *Mythologies: Selected and Translated from the French by Annette Lavers*. London: Paladin, 1973: 110.

19 Hoy, "Jacques Derrida," In Quentin Skinner, ed., *The Return of Grand Theory in the Human Sciences*. Cambridge: Cambridge University Press, 1985: 540.

20 J.B. Harley, "Silences and Secrecy: The Hidden Agenda of Cartography in Early Modern Europe," *Imago Mundi* 40, 1988: 57–76.

21 Christopher Norris, *Derrida*. Cambridge, Mass.: Harvard University Press, 1987: 19.

22 Most recently, C.N.G. Clarke, "Taking Possession: The Cartouche as Cultural Text in Eighteenth-Century American Maps," *Word and Image* 4/2, 1988: 455–74; also Harley, "Maps, Knowledge, and Power," esp. 296–99 and J.B. Harley, "Meaning and Ambiguity in Tudor Cartography," in *English Map-Making, 1500–1650: Historical Essays*, ed. Sarah Tyacke. London: The British Library Reference Division Publications, 1984: 22–45; and "Power and Legitimation in the English Geographical Atlases of the Eighteenth Century," in *Images of the World: The Atlas Through History*, ed. John A. Wolter, Washington, D.C.: Library of Congress, Center for the Book.

23 Denis Wood and John Fels, "Designs on Signs/Myth and Meaning in Maps," *Cartographica* 23/3, 1986.

24 Ibid., 63.

25 Ibid., 60.

26 Hoy, "Jacques Derrida" In Skinner, *The Return of Grand Theory*, 1985: 44.

27 I derive this thought from Eagelton, *Literary Theory*, 135, writing of the ideas of Roland Barthes.

28 These examples are from Harley, "Maps, Knowledge, and Power", 1988: 300.

29 Terry Eagelton, *Literary Theory: An Introduction*. Minneapolis: University of Minnesota Press, 1983: 135–36.

30 Christopher Norris, *Deconstruction*, 19.

31 Wood and Fels, "Designs on Signs", 1986, 71.

32 Hoy, "Jacques Derrida" In Skinner, *The Return of Grand Theory*, 1985: 60; for further discussion see Norris, *Derrida*, 1987: 213–20.

33 Hoy, "Jacques Derrida": 60.

34 Philip, "Michel Foucault," In Skinner, *The Return of Grand Theory*, 1985: 76.

35 Michel Foucault, *Power/Knowledge: Selected Interviews and Other Writings, 1972–1977*, ed. Colin Gordon, trans. Colin Gordon, Leo Marshall, John Mepham, Kate Sopher. New York, Pantheon Books, 1980, 88; see also Joseph Rouse, *Knowledge and Power: Toward a Political Philosophy of Science*. Ithaca, Cornell University Press, 1987: 209–10.

36 I adapt this idea from Langdon Winner, "Do Artifacts have Politics?", *Daedalus* 109/1, 1980: 121–36.

37 Adapting Roland Barthes, "The Plates of the *Encyclopedia*," in *New Critical Essays*. New York: Hill and Wang, 1980: 27, who writes much like Foucault, "To catalogue is not merely to ascertain, as it appears at first glance, but also to appropriate." Quoted in Wood and Fels, "Designs on Signs", 1986: 72.

38 Robert Darnton, *The Great Cat Massacre and Other Episodes in French Cultural History*. New York: Basic Books, 1984: 192–93.

39 Andrew McNally, "You Can't Get There from Here, with Today's Approach to Geography," *The Professional Geographer* 39, November, 1987: 389–92.

26 From Berlin to Bunker Hill. Urban Space, Late Modernity, and Film Noir in Fritz Lang's and Joseph Losey's *M*

Edward Dimendberg[1]

What is a downtown? A collection of tall buildings and canyon-like streets? A zone for the conduct of commerce and, secondarily, perhaps residence? Neither answer is incorrect, but these answers barely scratch the surface. Edward Dimendberg shows that a downtown is what it is, a place of community and camaraderie, of menace and mayhem, and all of the above by virtue of the responses it evokes in the psyches of its denizens. Such urban sensibilities are evanescent things, embedded in the minds of the perceivers, prone to flux across space and time, and thus difficult to chronicle. Fortunately, urban sensibilities may also be encapsulated and externalized, most notably through the palpable sights and sounds of the cinema. It is in such cinematic representations that Dimendberg gives us entree to time-and-space-bound experiential particularities of urbanity and alienation, to representations of the urban and to an urban human geography of the imaginary.

Film Noir and Late Modernity

From architect Joseph Hudnut to Lewis Mumford to the paintings of Hopper, the newly emerging metropolis of the forties and fifties appeared to many contemporary observers increasingly bereft of its former glories, a site of social and technological alienation, the domain of the "invisible city" ringed by expanding centerless suburbs.[2] This new form of settlement – gutted by urban renewal in its center and surrounded by highways and tract homes on its periphery – must be understood as a vital social content of the film noir cycle (not merely a set of stylistic attributes or backgrounds) that registers the discourses and tensions of postwar American urbanism and removes the still-contested notion of film noir from long, sterile debates about genre and relocates it within American social, urban, and cultural history. But this spatial infrastructure is hardly unified, and presents itself in two discrete, but interrelated types which I will suggest reappear throughout film noir.

The decay of the city center, controversies around downtown urban renewal precipitated by passage of the Housing Act of 1949, public apartment projects, and the growth of pedestrian zones in response to the spread of the automobile define the conditions of what I call "centripetal space" of the postwar American city: the navigable metropolis whose fabric of neighborhoods, public landmarks, and zones of safety, danger, and transgression form an unbroken chain from the nineteenth-century urban fictions of Emile Zola and Arthur Conan Doyle to twentieth century works by Alfred Döblin, Dashiell Hammett, and Raymond Chandler that culminates in film noirs such as *The Naked City* (1948) and *Criss Cross* (1949).

No less significant is the conceptual complement of "centripetal space," the dispersed realm of "centrifugal space": a world of highways, movement, and the replacement of metropolitan density and verticality by suburban sprawl. During the period of 1940 to 1947, sixty million Americans, or almost half of the population, had moved to new homes. And although the urban population grew by forty-five per cent from 1950 to 1960, it doubled the amount of land it occupied.[3] Centrifugal space is organized around speed and the redeployment of surveillance away from tracking the human body in the city toward the automobile and data collection as exemplified in films such as *Plunder Road* (1957) and *City of Fear* (1959). They explore a "post-urban" spatial environment less defined by the movement of pedestrians and increasingly permeated by the circulation of immaterial information.

Joseph Losey's 1951 remake of Fritz Lang's *M* (1931) offers a rich point of entry into the analysis of urban space in film noir, for like the city in which it is set, Los Angeles, the film is constructed on an unstable foundation and occupies a faultline between centripetal and centrifugal space. It allows us to analyze how a key text of the Weimar cinema was remade in a different cultural and spatial setting and suggests how both the original film and the remake respond to and articulate distinct instances of social and political crisis. Losey's *M* represents a significant, if little known, contribution to the film noir cycle that highlights important features of the spatial environment and visual culture of late modernity, many of which were already prefigured in Lang's original. I will begin with a consideration of spatiality in Lang's *M* and then examine the metropolitan environment in Losey's remake.

Skirmishes of Vision and Power: Berlin in Lang's *M* . . . .

A significant characteristic of urban space in Lang's *M* is the permanent tension between the verbal and the visual registers of the centripetal metropolis, presented in his film as a realm that is read *and* seen, a battleground whose combatants are the perceptual modes of reading and seeing. From the very first image of the credit sequence in which the letter "M" is set against the dark silhouette of an ominous figure, the film continually opposes letters to shapes, words to images, and reading to seeing. In its opening minutes the film cuts from a shot of a school to a busy city street where Elsie Beckmann is conducted to the other side by a traffic policeman standing before a school crossing sign. Written language, compared here with an officer of the law, maintains spatial order throughout the film. The advertising column against which Elsie bounces her ball announces the reward for the capture of the murderer, whose menacing shadow looms against the silent text. An empty street is punctuated by the cry "Extra! Extra!" as the urban crowd clamors to purchase the latest issues of the Tabloid *Uhu* at a kiosk. While people read a poster describing the murders, the camera tracks slowly away from the scene and suggests the process of reading as a community activity.

Following the tradition of Jack the Ripper and Weimar serial killer Peter Kürten, the murderer Beckert writes a letter to the newspaper, and hopes to convey his deranged condition to the reading public. Inspector Lohmann corrects a typographical error in a police report on the state of the investigation. Frau Beckmann reads the melodramatic magazines delivered to her door by the letter carrier. The detective reads in his notebook the addresses of former mental patients. And the "lawyer" in the final court sequence administers the law on the basis of the books next to him on the table. Each of these incidents underscores written language as the social tie that binds an isolated individual to larger organizational and social structures.

Verbal discourse is the domain of rationality, the "glue" that holds together the social world of the city. Like the letter "M" that will later be stamped upon his shoulder, these textual signifiers attach the individual body to a larger social body. Unlike earlier avant-garde modernist representations of Berlin such as in Ruttmann's city symphony film, the metropolis in Lang's film is rendered not as a stylized or geometric visual abstraction but as an ensemble of readable messages and visual maps. The urban "conditioning mechanisms" described by Tafuri appear in *M* not to deform and reform space through montage but perform the task of linguistically locating and "addressing" city dwellers.

A striking illustration of this is found in the film's predilection for high angle overhead shots. This suggests the mechanisms of surveillance and "total mobilization" associated with the First World War and proposes *M* as an early precursor of later American urban dragnet and police procedure films of the forties such as *He Walked By Night* (1949). These shots (the urban crowd unjustly accusing an innocent man, the "controlled" space of street intersections, the police marching through the nocturnal city to conduct their manhunt, an underworld member watching the police convoys from a window with binoculars, the blind organ grinder) depict both the police and the underworld. Just as the much discussed cross cutting between these two allegedly distinct groups actually functions to suggest their similarity, the use of high angle shots suggests a common mode of controlled vision that eludes the control of both the law and the criminals.

These elevated views propose photographic and cinematic surveillance as key elements of a late modernity that appropriates earlier avant-garde techniques developed in the aftermath of the First World War. The high overhead angles of these shots recall the visual aesthetic of the "new seeing" ("*das Neue Sehen*") associated with Weimar period photographers such as Moholy-Nagy and Rodchenko. Yet unlike their photographs, the elevated views in *M* never transform the depicted individuals and street scenes into visual abstractions and the resulting images in the film are more analogous to maps or aerial reconnaissance photographs than artworks. No longer a purely aesthetic enterprise, the facility with which the movie camera can adopt multiple standpoints and explore space in all directions appears in *M* to support a more ominous agenda of social control than that suggested in the buoyant rhetoric of the photographers associated with the New Objectivity (*Neue Sachlichkeit*).

Figure 1. High angle shot of the street from Fritz Lang's *M* (1931).

Here in the mobilization of bodies, technology, and surveillance practices in the centripetal metropolis – the controlled space of police maps, elevated reconnaissance vision and burglar alarms – is where we might begin to construct a genealogy of film noir in the cinema and late modern visual culture of Weimar Germany. This would allow us to jettison the long stale deliberations about the influence of expressionist cinematography and continuities in directorial style and approach both Weimar cinematic texts such as *M* and the American film noir cycle as examples of the spatial culture of late modernity. For in its presentation of a systematically organized metropolis where, in the words of Friedrich Kittler, "from the national postal service to the public telephone to the license plate on every registered vehicle, media are at work replacing people with their addresses," *M* explores the relation between legible urban space and social control, the linkage between the rationalization and surveillance of space and the "addressability" and visibility of urban subjects.

Although the accents and dialogue of characters in Lang's film clearly identify Berlin as its setting, the one visual clue that irrefutably confirms this appears in the shot when Schränker studies a map in the course of organizing the beggars and we recognize the shape of Berlin's central park, the Tiergarten. This suggests a metamorphosis in the representation of the metropolis from an ensemble of recognized visualizable neighborhoods or locations (evident in the city films of Ruttmann, Feuillade, or Vertov with their extensive location photography) to a set of discrete spaces which lose their geographic specificity and become mappable entities. We find this idea conveyed in the shot of the police circling the city map with a compass, but also in the enlarged poster of a suspect's fingerprint displayed in the police headquarters. Like the map of the city in the underworld headquarters, the traces of the criminal suspect's finger also have been divided into sections.

M intimates that a paradoxical consequence of increased spatial mastery and surveillance – the very ability to locate and "address" spatial users – might well be the concomitant loss of a city's experienceable identity by those who inhabit it. The anonymous metropolis, unfettered from the historical associations of particular sites of memory and public spatial practices, a realm that Henri Lefebvre calls "abstract space," informs Lang's film.[4] According to Lefebvre, abstract space is dominated by technological mediations, commodification, conceptualizations, and visual stimuli.... Quantitative relations of measurement, exchange, and calculation usurp the place of the body in abstract space and reduce its three dimensions to the domain of maps, blueprints, and the trajectories of spatial users, a tendency evident in the film's enthusiasm for the written word. This reduction of space to linguistic coordinates also manifests itself in the search activities of the police and underworld, most dramatically in the assignment of exact street locations to each beggar.

Traditionally celebrated for its "realism" and ostensibly concerned with protecting the Berlin citizenry from dangerous psychopathic behavior, *M* contains surprisingly few representations of inhabited public urban space. It depicts a mostly studio-fabricated Berlin notably lacking in monumentality and composed of streets

Figure 2.   The map of Berlin dominates the mise-en-scene, from Fritz Lang's *M* (1931).

with little more than display windows. These spatial realms of the knife, toy, and book stores visited by Beckert evoke fascination with the consumer merchandise displayed behind the glass and the luster of consumer objects. They elicit the gaze of Beckert, his potential child victims, and the film spectator, and insinuate the powerful lure of the visual as an erotic force opposed to verbal language, a notion suggested by the effect the balloon and photographs – rather than the spoken language of his interlocutors – exercises upon Beckert in the final trial sequence.

Filmed in full profile tableaux from *inside* the shop facing toward the street as seen from the point of view of the merchandise, these scenes confront the spectator with the space of the city *behind* Beckert and the young girls. They reveal an active urban space visible only to the film viewer. Here the tensions are not between the verbal and visual registers but rather between front and back, the static yet seductive display window opposed to the dynamic street, the restricted gaze of Beckert opposed to the omnipotent vision of the film audience who can see both the merchandise and the city. Mirrors in the window of the knife store and in the doorway of the grocery store (where Beckert discovers himself branded with the letter "M") allow him to see objects behind him.

The reverse shot from the point of view of the merchandise in each of these display window scenes can be contrasted with that in which Beckert stands in front of the bookstore window that displays both paintings *and* reading material. In this scene we see the bookstore only from the point of view of the characters, as if books and the written material on display, unlike other commodities, were incapable of returning the gaze. The rotating spiral and vertically moving arrow visible in the shop window appear as signs of ekphrastic dissonance, a reminder of the ultimate untranslatability of the visual into the verbal. They evoke a tension between the image and the text and highlight Beckert's constitution as a murderer who is seduced by the force of the visual. Paradoxically, his sole knowledge of the crimes he commits comes from reading about them on the posters plastered throughout the city, a suggestion that even the criminal perpetrator requires verbal discourse to learn of his own actions.

Describing his visit to Berlin in July 1930, Antonin Artaud wrote perceptively of the fascination with the spectacle of the display windows evident in its cityscape: "If I did not suffer from my perpetual headaches, I should greatly enjoy the life of Berlin, a city of astonishing luxury and frightening licentiousness. I am constantly amazed by what I see. They carry their obsession with eroticism everywhere, even into shop-windows in which all the dummies thrust their bellies forward."[5] Lang's *M* confirms this characterization of Berlin as a display case that functions as an erotic lure for the gaze of the passerby, especially Beckert. From the 1928 "Berlin im Licht" event that festively illuminated the city streets, to the pervasive concern with store displays and building advertisements among architects, interest in the visual presentation of the city's nocturnal face and potential appeal to consumers was pervasive during the Weimar Republic.

Yet *M* contains little of the New Objectivity architecture and bold neon advertisements widely associated with Berlin's modernity during the Weimar period and thereby anticipates the drab and subdued representations of the post-expressionist metropolis pervasive throughout film noir. Despite its portrayal of the most advanced technology of the day, the city in *M*, like the urban environment that would later manifest itself in film noir, appears spartan and functional, decrepit and almost

Figure 3. Tension between the static yet seductive display window and the dynamic street. Production still from Fritz Lang's *M* (1931).

under repair, as in the shot of the large storm pipe outside of the produce store where Beckert gives Elsie a slice of apple.

The cinematic representation of late modernity in *M* may well hinge less upon the depiction of actual architectural spaces than the presentation of more intangible changes involving the role of technology and urban forms in our perception and experience of the metropolis. Beckert's obsession with viewing objects behind him culminates in the confession during his trial of walking through the endless streets of Berlin and being followed by himself. Yet this very desire to attain the visual mastery enjoyed by the film's spectator emphasizes the ocularcentrism of *M* and the manner in which both pathological and normal urban subjects apprehend an increasingly abstract urban space less through bodily experiences of urban passage and increasingly through visual and verbal mediations.

Bunker Hill and Losey's *M*

In an interview Joseph Losey relates his initial aversion toward the idea of remaking *M*:

[Lang's *M*, E.D.] is and remains a classic, which one doesn't want to compete with, so for a variety of reasons I somewhat reluctantly undertook my version. One was that there was a considerable Hollywood pinch because of political pressures, and I didn't want to go a long time without work. Another was that I was very much interested in David Wayne, whom I thought brilliant and extraordinarily right for the part. And I undertook it with a restriction on the structure and basic story line, because the censorship office wouldn't pass it as a new script, only as a remake of a classic. Therefore my treatment of the central figure came into direct conflict with the whole structure.... All that emerges from the film, really, is a couple of – I think – remarkable sequences, some previously unseen aspects of Los Angeles, and a fantastic performance from Wayne...[6]

A fundamental difference between the two versions of *M* involves the significant role assumed by the television medium in Losey's 1951 remake. Whereas the citizens of Berlin learn about the child murders from the newspaper and the posters plastered on the surrounding walls of the city, the residents of Bunker Hill in Los Angeles primarily obtain their information from television broadcasts they watch together in public. The special report by the chief of police that presents "Five Don'ts" to warn parents how to protect their children is viewed in a television store window by a group of city dwellers. Looking at the static photographs of city neighborhoods, narrated by the law officer, replaces reading as the activity that bonds isolated individuals into a community. Notably, in Losey's film the murderer Harrow never writes to the newspaper, an insinuation that in the social world constituted by television in fifties America communication was increasingly visual and unidirectional.

Live television coverage of news events became an increasing fact of life for Los Angeles residents in the late forties and early fifties.... Losey's film grants the mass media a more prominent role than they possess in Lang's film and presents the newspaper publisher as the third agent of power (together with the police and the underworld) engaged in ruling the city. It insinuates the growing force of television to shape urban experience and community in Los Angeles.

The film's opening sequence on the Angels' Flight funicular railway conveys the spatial separation of its setting, the Bunker Hill neighborhood whose destruction by the agents of urban renewal coincides with Losey's filming. Bunker Hill was one of the oldest neighborhoods in the city, dating back to the nineteenth-century and full of irregularly shaped streets and Victorian-era mansions converted into long shabby rooming houses memorialized by writers such as Raymond Chandler and John Fante. Losey's predilection for this earlier location for films such as of *Act of Violence* and *Criss Cross* (1949), associates his remake with the film noir cycle. Under the aegis of urban renewal, an idea much in vogue after the recent passage of California Community Redevelopment Act of 1948 and the federal Housing Act of 1949, this area would undergo a fundamental transformation during the fifties to reconstruct its spatial identity from a decrepit residential district into the crown of a revitalized downtown.

Sixteen months after Losey completed principal photography of *M* on Bunker Hill, the Community Redevelopment Agency of Los Angeles voted in 1951 to condemn most of the buildings in the neighborhood. The Los Angeles depicted in his film bears witness to the decentralizing dynamic of centrifugal space and the emergence of abstract space of the postwar American metropolis. It suggests an unresolved conflict between the representation of Los Angeles as receptive to the future and "forward-looking" and an ambivalence on the part of many residents toward the history of their built environment.[7] Although ultimately unsuccessful, the efforts to prevent the redevelopment of Bunker Hill and the public outcry against its destruction suggest that the embrace of urban renewal and modernist planning principles was hardly universal.

Like the film noir cycle more generally, Losey's *M* can be approached as a site for the cinematic analysis of this postwar geographic metamorphosis, an opportunity for recording architectural and urban fragments of earlier historical moments before their imminent disappearance. Unlike Lang's studio-filmed *M* in which the urban specificity of Berlin nearly vanishes, Losey's remake emphasizes those older urban forms and ambients that, following Ernst Bloch, I would describe as "non-contemporaneous" elements and "declining remnants" of an unrefurbished past.[8] In an age of rampant suburbanization and spatial deconcentration, urban centrality and a traversable scale could no longer be taken for granted. Produced in the context of the late forties vogue for actual location semi-documentary filmmaking (itself an indirect consequence of the shortage of lumber for film set construction caused by

Figure 4.   Bunker Hill. Angels' Flight funicular tracks and the Third Street Tunnel. Production still from Joseph Losey's *M* (1951).

the boom in suburban house starts!), *M* explores Bunker Hill as an instance of centripetal space displaced in 1951 Los Angeles, a spatial and temporal anomaly. The city attracted its share of prominent visitors after the Second World War, one of whom, Jean-Paul Sartre, described it as follows:

> Los Angeles, in particular, is rather like a big earthworm that might be chopped into twenty pieces without being killed. If you go through this enormous urban cluster, probably the largest in the world, you come upon twenty juxtaposed cities, strictly identical, each with its poor section, its business streets, night-clubs and smart suburb, and you get the impression that a medium-sized urban center has schizogenetically reproduced itself twenty times.[9]

Sartre's description of a decentralized Los Angeles divided into smaller cities echoes the urban planning literature of the period and accurately captures the character of Bunker Hill in Losey's *M* and in other films noir. According to the creed of the postwar planners, each smaller "nucleated" city in Los Angeles would contain commercial and industrial centers and what Sartre calls "survivals" (Bloch's "non-contemporaneous" elements). Surrounded by the encroaching Harbor Freeway and the Third Street Tunnel to the West, Bunker Hill in 1951 was indeed an "island of resistance" and a challenge to the postwar expulsion of residential dwelling units from the city's central business district.

Rapid growth and dispersal frustrated the tradition of spatial monumentality Sartre ascribes to the European metropolis, and it is tempting to hypothesize that to a greater extent than other American cities Los Angeles registers collective memories not in spatial constructions but through cinematic representation. The military metaphors of the bomb attack, the nucleated city, and the island of resistance suggest the relationship in Los Angeles between the aggressive urbanism of the Cold War era and the film noir cycle. "Anything about which one knows that one soon will not have it around becomes an image," as Benjamin presciently noted.[10]

Unlike the concentrated "centripetal" space of Berlin in Fritz Lang's *M*, the space of Los Angeles in Losey's *M* has mutated into an abstract "centrifugal" space organized around the automobile and the mobilized gaze. From the construction of parking structures and streets designed for the automobile to the building of the vast network of freeways, urban form in Los Angeles follows what one 1949 metropolitan theorist calls "the cardinal principle of movement": "all conflict or interference must be removed."[11] The army of beggars mobilized by the underworld in Berlin is replaced by a fleet of radio-networked taxi drivers in Los Angeles. Driving through Bunker Hill, the cab driver surveys the street through the windshield of his car, a clue that the automobilized gaze has supplanted the overhead angle as a constituent element in the perception of abstract space. Unlike Lang's *M*, spatial surveillance in Losey's film substitutes the roving, horizontal view from the automobile and the road for the fixed and vertically elevated perspective in the centripetal metropolis.

The film's appropriation of the Bradbury Building as the site of the manhunt for the child murderer, a Los Angeles landmark associated before its 1982 appearance in *Blade Runner* with films noir such as *D.O.A.* (1950) (also filmed by Losey's cinematographer Ernest Laszlo), and the 1953 *I, the Jury* (filmed by John Alton) evokes the plight of public space and the pedestrian in the postwar American city.

Built in 1893 by mining millionaire Lewis Bradbury, who commissioned an unknown draftsman, George Wyman, to design the structure, the building's open central courtyard remains a prime example of French wrought iron decorative architecture with the trademark glass skylight illumination associated with the typological form of the arcade.

Wyman's design has been apocryphally understood to bear the influence of Edward Bellamy's 1887 utopian novel, *Looking Backward* and the book's description of commercial architecture bathed in light. Once associated by writers and critics such as Emile Zola and Walter Benjamin with the phantasmagoria of capitalist visuality, the iron and glass architecture that appears in *M* in the form of the Bradbury Building is a degraded remnant of this earlier thinking, the "new" of the modern that has long since become antiquated. But its manifestation in a 1951 film set in Los Angeles suggests an earlier mode of urban public space in danger of becoming forgotten.[...]

The Bradbury building functions in *M* as a non-contemporaneous remnant, an unexpected fragment of the past that calls the present into question. Transposed from Europe to Los Angeles, its nineteenth-century grandeur and pedestrian-friendly space is as anomalous in 1951 Los Angeles as were the arcades encountered by Benjamin and the surrealists in Paris during the twenties. It appears in the film without masses of consumers or pedestrians, an uncomfortable hybrid between an interior and exterior realm that is spatially and temporally displaced in the heart of 1951 Los Angeles, a telling comment on the social predicament of the American city in late modernity that would soon be assailed by the bulldozers of urban redevelopment.

Unlike Lang's depiction of the display windows in his *M*, Losey's remake adopts a less enthusiastic stance toward this mode of capitalist visual display. Filmed by daylight on actual Los Angeles streets, the display window scenes exude a less violent and seductive character and emphasize their setting and the point of the view of the characters. This skepticism toward the urban commodity spectacle is most apparent in the scene where members of the underworld search the Bradbury Building for the murderer and destroy its many glass windows. At once a critique of the culture of the phantasmagoria, the surface, and the gaze, Losey's representation of this structure also presents it as a viable public space threatened by the mindless destruction of the capitalist plunderers.

While at the end of the courtroom scene in both films the police seize the child murderer and protect him from the angry crowd, Losey's *M* presents Langley, the underworld lawyer and defender of the rule of law who attains a more prominent role in the remake, as a victim of this process. Filmed in the spring and summer of 1950 during the height of the HUAC witchhunts, Losey's *M* takes the political persecutions of the Hollywood blacklists as its allegorical subtext, a subject of obvious personal interest to a man who joined the American communist party and was subject to intense FBI surveillance in the early forties. The suspension of the rule of law during the American Cold War conflict with communism is alluded to in the film's frequent references to corrupt policemen, victims, and retribution.

That Lang's *M* film was remade at all by Losey is a consequence of both the German and the American versions sharing the same producer, German exile Seymour Nebenzal.... *M* was the last film Nebenzal ever produced, and his decision to remake it with Joseph Losey led Fritz Lang to claim its ownership. Writing in a Los Angeles newspaper at the end of the film's production, Nebenzal offered this account of his fight with Fritz Lang and his motivations for remaking *M*:

> Mr. Lang makes the statement that the old picture was built around the sex criminal being caught and tried by a group of organized beggars in a kangaroo court. He also says that because there is no organized group of beggars in the United States, therefore the premise of the original film is not valid here. I am surprised to hear that the matter of organized beggars should be the premise of the old picture. I always thought, and still think, that the problems connected with a sex criminal of this type, his menace to the community and the treatment of such criminals was the basic premise of the story – a problem which is much more acute today in the United States than the few isolated cases were in Germany in the early 1930s.
>
> Mr. Lang further states that "M" is a classic and it is stupid to try to improve on it. My reasons for making an English version of the picture are the followings (sic):
>
> 1–The German language picture is by now antiquated in its psychological approach to the problem.
>
> 2–As I have already pointed out, the problem is becoming more and more acute.
>
> 3–The German picture was never generally released in the United States, but was shown only in some art houses and by the Museum of Modern Art. Only a very small percentage of theater goers have seen it – and they had to depend on subtitles.[12]

Produced during a short period of political calm between the HUAC hearings that originated in October 1947 and recommenced in March 1951, the decision to remake *M* appears as a canny strategy on the part of Nebenzal and Losey intended to circumvent censorship restrictions and tackle the real problem "becoming more and more acute" in 1950 in Hollywood around the time of *M*'s production. In September 1950, three months after its principal photography was completed, the last of the Hollywood Ten went to jail after their legal appeals proved unsuccessful. As Larry Ceplair and Steven Englund note in their book *The Inquisition in Hollywood*, by 1951 no one without a political clearance approved by the House Un-American Activities could work in the Hollywood film industry.[13] By the time Karen Morley, who plays the murdered Elsie's mother, was called by Losey to act in *M*, she had already been blacklisted for involvement in an UAW documentary against racism. Waldo Salt, the dialogue writer for Losey's film and an unfriendly witness before the Committee in 1947, was once more subpoenaed in March 1951.

Writing of the film's premiere, a newspaper reviewer noted "Many in the cast, whose names have been associated with communistic fronts and activities, brought about a picket line in front of the two theaters, the pickets' signs protesting the use of 'known reds' in the film and therefore urging non-patronage."[14] With their common narratives involving victims, murderers, surveillance, the mass media, lawyers, guilty parties, the desire for retribution, and the reestablishment of legal authority, both *M* films appear as instances of a single cultural narrative about the scapegoat that circulated in German and American societies undergoing political and social crises.

Whether we think of the elaborate security system in the Berlin warehouse or the Bradbury building, the prominence of television and automobile-dominated space in

Losey's remake, or the eradication of an older centripetal space organized around the corporeal experience of pedestrians in both versions of *M*, these films betray a fascination with the new media and perceptual technologies which developed in tandem with cinema. Unlike the visual art or cinema of early modernism, the compelling object of their attention is less the architectural or pictorial facade of the city than the non-cinematic technological mediations through which urban space increasingly is experienced. The culture of late modernity exemplified in *M* and explored throughout the film noir cycle is perhaps best understood as a response to the new experiences of space, time, speed, and social control brought about by the convergence of cinema with television, the automobile, and surveillance technologies. The two versions of *M* remind us of the political stakes of these new perceptual modalities, their continuing ability to organize our experiences of the metropolis, and the growing inextricability of space and representation throughout the course of the twentieth century.

NOTES

1   Edward Dimendberg is International Institute Assistant Professor of Architecture, Film and Video Studies, and German Studies at the University of Michigan.
2   Joseph Hudnut, *Architecture and the Spirit of Man* (Cambridge: Harvard University Press, 1949), 157–68.
3   Cited in John B. Rae, *The Road and the Car in American Life* (Cambridge: MIT Press, 1971), 226–27.
4   Henri Lefebvre, *The Production of Space*, trans. Donald Nicholson-Smith (Cambridge, MA and Oxford: Blackwell, 1991), 306–21. See also Edward Dimendberg, "Henri Lefebvre on Abstract Space," in Andrew Light and Jonathan M. Smith, eds., *Public Space* (Lanham, Maryland: Rowman and Littlefield, 1997).
5   Antonin Artaud, *Oeuvres Completes* 3:193, quoated and translated in Martin Esslin, *Artaud* (London: Fontana, 1976), 34.
6   Tom Milne, *Joseph Losey* (Garden City: Doubleday, 1968), 85.
7   Anastasia Loukaitou-Sideris and Gail Sainsbury, "Lost Streets of Bunker Hill," *California History* 74 (1996), 394.
8   Ernst Bloch, *Heritage of Our Times*, trans. Steven and Neville Plaice (Berkeley and Los Angeles: University of California Press, 1990), 108.
9   Jean-Paul Sartre, "American Cities," (1945) in *Literary and Philosophical Essays*, trans. Annette Michelson (New York: Collier, 1962), 120–22.
10   Walter Benjamin, *Charles Baudelaire: A Lyric Poet in the Era of High Capitalism*, trans. Harry Zohn (London: NLB, 1973), 86–87.
11   Mel Scott, *Metropolitan Los Angeles: One Community* (Los Angeles: The Haynes Foundation, 1949), 94.
12   Quoted in column by Ezra Goodman, *Los Angeles Daily News*, 28 Jun. 1950.
13   Larry Ceplair and Steven Englund, *The Inquisition in Hollywood: Politics in the Film Community, 1930–1960* (Berkeley and Los Angeles, University of California Press, 1983), 387.
14   Lowell E. Redlings, "*M* Remake Genuine Thriller: David Wayne Impressive as Psychopathic Killer," *Citizen News*, 26 Oct. 1951. Clipping in film file in collection of Academy of Motion Picture Arts and Sciences, Beverly Hills, California.

Emplaced Bodies, Embodied Selves

Postmodern human geography has concerned itself to no small extent with the subjectivities of space. But this beggars the question of just what a human subject is. Within the broader arena of postmodern thought, this question has produced a retheoretization of the subject itself, with particular attention to the how subjects are presenced in bodies.

Daniel Dennet argued that the greatest pleasures in life are to be had through "putting things into oneself or into others." It is in these crossings of the boundaries of the individual body, he asserts, that we engage in the continual process of becoming who we are. Michel Foucault would likely add that there is more than pleasure in negotiating body boundaries. The practices of crossing these boundaries entail both the reconstitution of the body and (in bodies' relations to one another) of society as a whole. And Foucault extends his attention to the ways in which bodily boundaries, and that which they contain, are policed. Such policing is a product both of brute action taken against individual bodies (e.g., imprisonment), and of the common social norms underpinning those actions. Discipline and punishment, Foucault maintains, are not only inflicted upon one's body by others, but are also inscribed onto/into the body itself, rendering every active body disciplined and self-disciplining. Of course, the bodily inscription of what is permissible also creates the potential for bodies to transgress such inscriptions. Transgression may either be by choice or by circumstance. Bodies thus become, for Foucault, the nexus at which power is produced through activation and resistance, a process particularly visible in such places as prisons and hospitals for people classified as insane.

In the writings of Michel de Certeau, there is a great deal of congruency with both Foucault and Dennet. He asserts that the meaning of the street, tantamount to what the street *is*, is a product of how embodied persons occupy and utilize that street. Thus, de Certeau foregrounds space as both the constitutive medium of embodiment, and as something constituted by bodily practices. He considers how the relatively powerful employ strategies to define, through repeated enforcement, what spaces "are." Against this, the less powerful may willfully deviate by remaking their spaces through hit-and-run tactics of spatial occupation.

And so, we begin our reconstruction of postmodern human geography at the space of the body. We are our bodies, and our bodies are made by and make places. But at the same time, we are more than just moving meat. Our bodies can be inscribed, and can transgress any inscriptions, because they possess capacities that enable us to retain, react to, and act upon being inscribed. These capacities are memory, creativity, and self-identity. But selves and identities are not so self-evident as Decartes' pronouncement of "I think therefore I am" has led us to believe.

One of the primary functions taken up by an individual is the continuing construction and reconstruction of the boundaries defining the body's integrity. The creation of a self is the device by which this boundedness is established. Returning to Dennett, the self is a protective and enabling web of words and deeds, spun by the brain. Humans, however, don't just extrude this web spider-like from within. Rather, we gather the materials of the self from the surrounding environment, from things, ideas, and behaviors within the realm of the individual human's apprehension, and from this material we organize an encircling "web of discourse." Thus, self is a narrative. It is established by assembling and telling stories about who we are, represented to others by means of "language and gesture, external and internal." Further, this process is largely automatic, in that:

> we ... do not consciously and deliberately figure out what narratives to tell and how to tell them. Our tales are spun, but for the most part we don't spin them, they spin us ... our narrative selfhood is their product, not their source. (Dennett, pp. 417–18)

Implicit in the gathering of material for, and representation of, the self is the assumption that self-spinning is of necessity a collective process. Selves are produced by social processes establishing webs of component relations and beliefs which, should they collapse, would result in the erasure of self.

The suggestion that "selves" are not self-evident finds congruence in the notion of "the death of the subject." Fredric Jameson presents two arguments advocating the end of the subject. One asserts that the idea of the unique individual may well have existed in an era of bourgeois dominance and market competition; but now, with a swelling population absorbed into pervasive mass bureaucracies, the unique individual has become something of an archeological relic. The second argument goes a step further, claiming that the "individual" was a modernist artifact, a construct that was "merely a philosophical and cultural mystification which sought to persuade people that they 'had' individual subjects and possessed this unique personal identity." While the two perspectives differ in their historical perspectives, both indicate "that the old individual or individualist subject is 'dead'; and that one might even describe the concept of the unique individual and the theoretical basis of individualism as ideological." (Jameson, in Caplin, pp. 13–29) And in so dismantling individuality's innateness, both perspectives open space for a different kind of self, one that is simultaneously a social invention and invented through sociability.

In moving from the "politics of difference" to a "politics of recognition," Charles Taylor underscores the collective dimension of self-invention. Our identities are ultimately formed by how we represent ourselves to, and are represented by, "significant others." Self-identity is formed dialogically with others over the course of one's lifetime, producing collective identities that "...provide what we might call scripts: narratives that people can use in shaping their life plans and in telling their life stories." They enable us to fit those life stories into larger social narratives (Taylor, p. 160).

Such options, Appiah warns, are not unlimited. "We do make choices, but we do not determine the options among which we choose" (Appiah in Taylor, p. 155). The narratives defining self become legible to others only in the context of larger narratives of group identity. Group identities serve as "lifescripts," imparting meaning to narratives of self in accordance with the extent to which the self adheres to, or deviates from, that lifescript. In this way, lifescripts serve as templates that, at the level of the individual, can both impart much needed meaning and enforce oppressive standards. The lifescript may function to constitute a collective in opposition to others, providing an ideal type that can be creatively played against, and frequently establishing collective solidarity against hostile social contexts.

The notions that bodies are spatialized entities, and that spaces and bodies reciprocally (re)produce one another, provide an important point of departure in geographical analysis. Such perspectives approach space as a terrain that is continually contested and reforged at multiple scales by even the most intimate of everyday activities. Bodies interacting with other bodies to form selves are situated in space, and form their selfhoods by means of more-or-less locally emplaced experiences. Within this analytical framework, space underpins the collective, dialogical, ongoing negotiation of the construction of self- and group-identities. This applies not only to the invention of the individual self, but for the production of aggregate lifescripts that we know as ethnicity and nationality. Given that the polysemous construction of identity occurs *in situ*, it is no surprise that many geographers have turned their attention towards examining spaces as the sites of the bodily construction of the self.

We begin our reconstruction with a story by Salman Rushdie, in which a host of familiar and impossible selves manipulate spaces, artifacts, and (perhaps most of all) memory by means of extreme, sometimes outlandish, and frequently terrifying bodily practices. Turning to more commonplace identities, Gillian Rose surveys contemporary feminist geography. She highlights how women's experiences of the same space, while copresent with and no less valid than men's experiences of the same space, are often radically different and subject to devaluation (Reading 27). This problematic of spatial marginalization is further explored by Clare Hemmings, who documents how bisexual desire struggles to find a place for itself in a sociospatial context that pre-emptively marks all spaces as *either* straight *or* gay (Reading 28). The marginalized, however, will not always remain tidily confined to the margin. In his study of skaters, poets, and buskers in a downtown financial district, Steven Flusty demonstrates how the bodily practice of playful dissidence not only persists, but eventually commands official accommodation (Reading 29). Finally, Ahmed Gurnah deepens this notion of the assembled self. Gurnah posits that while identities may well be composites of outside influences, those influences come together both with respect to local norms *and* by means of personally creative and pleasurable practices. In an autobiographical analysis of his own coming of age in 1950s Zanzibar, Gurnah negotiates the complex interplay of transgression and conformance while emphasizing the centrality of joy in bringing together the diverse (and globally dispersed) cultural influences that made him what he is – including Elvis Presley (Reading 30)!

REFERENCES

Caplin, E. A. Postmodernism and its Discontents. London: Verso, 1988.

de Certeau, M.: *The Practice of Everyday Life*. University of California Press: Berkeley, 1984.

Dennett, D.: *Consciousness Explained*. Little, Brown and Company: Boston, 1991.

Foucault, M. (Gordon, C., ed.) *Power/Knowldege: Selected Interviews and Other Writings*. Pantheon: New York, 1982.

Taylor, C. (and Gutmann, A. ed.) *Multiculturalism: Examining the Politics of Recognition*. Princeton University Press: Princeton, 1994

East, West Stories

Salman Rushdie

At the Auction of the Ruby Slippers

The bidders who have assembled for the auction of the magic slippers bear little resemblance to your usual saleroom crowd. The Auctioneers have publicised the event widely and are prepared for all comers. People venture out but rarely nowadays; nevertheless, and rightly, the Auctioneers believed this prize would tempt us from our bunkers. High feelings are anticipated. Accordingly, in addition to the standard facilities provided for the comfort and security of the more notable personages, extra-large bronze cuspidors have been placed in the vestibules and toilets, for the use of the physically sick; teams of psychiatrists of varying disciplines have been installed in strategically located neo-Gothic confessional booths, to counsel the sick at heart.

Most of us nowadays are sick.

There are no priests. The Auctioneers have drawn a line. The priests remain in other, nearby buildings, buildings with which they are familiar, hoping to deal with any psychic fall-out, any insanity overspill.

Units of obstetricians and helmeted police s w a t teams wait out of sight in side alleys in case the excitement leads to unexpected births or deaths. Lists of next of kin have been drawn up and their contact numbers recorded. A supply of strait-jackets has been laid in.

See: behind bullet-proof glass, the ruby slippers sparkle. We do not know the limits of their powers. We suspect that these limits may not exist.

Movie stars are here, among the bidders, bringing their glossy, spangled auras to the saleroom. Movie-star auras, developed in collaboration with masters of Applied Psychics, are platinum, golden, silver, bronze. Certain genre actors specialising in villainous rôles are surrounded by auras of evil – livid green, mustard yellow, inky red. When one of us collides with a star's priceless (and fragile) aura, he or she is instantly knocked to the floor by a security team and hustled out to the waiting paddy-wagons. Such incidents slightly reduce the crush in the Grand Saleroom.

The memorabilia junkies are out in predictable force, and now with a ducking movement of the head one of them applies her desperate lips to the slippers' transparent cage, setting off the state-of-the-art defence system whose programmers have neglected to teach it about the relative harmlessness of such a gesture of adoration. The system pumps a hundred thousand volts of electricity into the collagen-implanted lips of the glass-kisser, terminating her interest in the proceedings.

It is an unpleasantly whiffy moment, but it fails to deter a second *aficionado* from the same suicidal act of devotion. When we learn that this moron was the lover of the first fatality, we rather wonder at the mysteries of love, whilst reaching once again for our perfumed handkerchiefs.

The cult of the ruby slippers is at its height. A fancy dress party is in full swing. Wizards, Lions, Scarecrows are in plentiful supply. They jostle crossly for position, stamping on one another's feet. There is a scarcity of Tin Men on account of the particular discomfort of the costume. Witches bide their time on the *balcons* and *galeries* of the Grand Saleroom, living gargoyles with, in many cases, high credit ratings. One corner is occupied entirely by Totos, several of whom are copulating enthusiastically, obliging a rubber-gloved janitor to separate them so as to avoid giving public offence. He does this with great delicacy and taste.

We, the public, are easily, lethally offended. We have come to think of taking offence as a fundamental right. We value very little more highly than our rage, which gives us, in our opinion, the moral high ground. From this high ground we can shoot down at our enemies and inflict heavy fatalities. We take pride in our short fuses. Our anger elevates, transcends.

Around the – let us say – shrine of the ruby-sequinned slippers, pools of saliva have been forming. There are those of us who lack restraint, who drool. The jump-suited Latino janitor moves amongst us, a pail in one hand and a sequeegee mop in the other. We admire and are grateful for his talent for self-effacement. He removes our mouth waters from the floor without causing any loss of face on our part.

Opportunities for encountering the truly miraculous are limited in our Nietzschean, relativistic universe. Behaviourist philosophers and quantum scientists crowd around the magic shoes. They make indecipherable notes.

Exiles, displaced persons of all sorts, even homeless tramps have turned up for a glimpse of the impossible. They have emerged from their subterranean hollows and braved the bazookas, the Uzi-armed gangs high on crack or smack or ice, the smugglers, the emptiers of houses. The tramps wear stenchy jute ponchos and hawk noisily into the giant potted yuccas. They grab fistfuls of canapés from trays borne upon the superb palms of A-list caterers. Sushi is eaten by them with impressive quantities of *wasabi* sauce, to whose inflammatory powers the hoboes' innards seem impervious. SWAT teams are summoned and after a brief battle involving the use of rubber bullets and sedative darts the tramps are removed, clubbed into unconsciousness and driven away. They will be deposited some distance beyond the city limits, out there in that smoking no-man's-land surrounded by giant advertising hoardings into which we venture no more. Wild dogs will gather around them, eager for luncheon. These are uncompromising times.

Political refugees are at the auction: conspirators, deposed monarchs, defeated factions, poets, bandit chieftains. Such figures no longer wear the black berets, the pebble-lensed spectacles and enveloping greatcoats of yesteryear, but strike resplendent attitudes in boxy silken jackets and high-waisted Japanese couture pantaloons. The women sport toreador jackets bearing sequinned representations of great works of art. One beauty parades *Guernica* on her back, while several others wear glittering scenes from the *Disasters of War* sequence by Francisco Goya.

Incandescent as they are in their suits of lights, the female political refugees fail to eclipse the ruby slippers, and huddle with their male comrades in small hissing bunches, periodically hurling imprecations, ink-pellets, spitballs and paper darts across the salon at rival clusters of *émigrés*. The guards at the exits crack their bullwhips idly and the politicals control themselves.

We revere the ruby slippers because we believe they can make us invulnerable to witches (and there are so many sorcerers pursuing us nowadays); because of their powers of reverse metamorphosis, their affirmation of a lost state of normalcy in which we have almost ceased to believe and to which the slippers promise us we can return; and because they shine like the footwear of the gods.

Disapproving critiques of the fetishising of the slippers are offered by religious fundamentalists, who have been allowed to gain entry by virtue of the extreme liberalism of some of the Auctioneers, who argue that a civilised saleroom must be a broad church, open, tolerant. The fundamentalists have openly stated that they are interested in buying the magic footwear only in order to burn it, and this is not, in the view of the liberal Auctioneers, a reprehensible programme. What price tolerance if the intolerant are not tolerated also? "Money insists on democracy," the liberal Auctioneers insist. "Anyone's cash is as good as anyone else's." The fundamentalists fulminate from soapboxes constructed of special, sanctified wood. They are ignored, but some senior figures present speak ominously of the thin end of the wedge.

Orphans arrive, hoping that the ruby slippers might transport them back through time as well as space (for, as our equations prove, all space machines are time machines as well): they hope to be reunited with their deceased parents by the famous shoes.

Men and women of dubious character are present – untouchables, outcasts. The security forces deal brusquely with many of these.

"Home" has become such a scattered, damaged, various concept in our present travails. There is so much to yearn for. There are so few rainbows any more. How hard can we expect even a pair of magic shoes to work? They promised to take us *home*, but are metaphors of homeliness comprehensible to them, are abstractions permissible? Are they literalists, or will they permit us to redefine the blessed word?

Are we asking, hoping for, too much?

As our numberless needs emerge from their redoubts and press in upon the electrified glass, will the shoes, like the Grimms' ancient flatfish, lose patience with our ever-growing demands and return us to the hovels of our discontents?

The presence of imaginary beings in the Saleroom may be the last straw. Children from nineteenth-century Australian paintings are here, whining from their ornate, gilded frames about being lost in the immensity of the Outback. In blue smocks and ankle socks they gaze into rain forests and red deserts, and tremble.

A literary character, condemned to an eternity of reading the works of Dickens to an armed madman in a jungle, has sent in a written bid.

On a television monitor, I notice the frail figure of an alien creature with an illuminated fingertip.

This permeation of the real world by the fictional is a symptom of the moral decay of our post-millennial culture. Heroes step down off cinema screens and marry members of the audience. Will there be no end to it? Should there be more rigorous controls? Is the State employing insufficient violence? We debate such questions often. There can be little doubt that a large majority of us opposes the free, unrestricted migration of imaginary beings into an already damaged reality, whose resources diminish by the day. After all, few of us would choose to travel in the opposite direction (though there are persuasive reports of an increase in such migrations latterly).

I shelve such disputes for the moment. The Auction is about to begin.

It is necessary that I speak about my cousin Gale, and her habit of moaning loudly while making love. Let me be frank: my cousin Gale was and is the love of my life, and even now that we have parted I am easily aroused by the mere memory of her erotic noisiness. I hasten to add that except for this volubility there was nothing abnormal about our love-making, nothing, if I may put it thus, *fictional*. Yet it satisfied me deeply, deeply, especially when she chose to cry out at the moment of penetration: "Home, boy! Home, baby, yes – you've come home!"

One day, sad to relate, I came home to find her in the arms of a hairy escapee from a caveman movie. I moved out the same day, weeping my way down the street with my portrait of Gale in the guise of a tornado cradled in my arms and my collection of old Pat Boone 78 r.p.m. records in a rucksack on my back.

This happened many years ago.

For a time after Gale dumped me I was bitter and would reveal to our social circle that she had lost her virginity at the age of fourteen in an accident involving a defective shooting-stick; but vindictiveness did not satisfy me for long.

Since those days I have dedicated myself to her memory. I have made of myself a candle at her temple.

I am aware that, after all these years of separation and non-communication, the Gale I adore is not entirely a real person. The real Gale has become confused with my re-imaging of her, with my private elaboration of our continuing life together in an alternative universe devoid of ape-men. The real Gale may by now be beyond our grasp, ineffable.

I caught a glimpse of her recently. She was at the far end of a long, dark, subterranean bar-room guarded by freelance commandos bearing battlefield nuclear weapons. There were Polynesian snacks on the counter and beers from the Pacific rim on tap: Kirin, Tsingtao, Swan.

At that time many television channels were devoted to the sad case of the astronaut stranded on Mars without hope of rescue, and with diminishing supplies of food and breathable air. Official spokesmen told us of the persuasive arguments for the abrupt cancellation of the space exploration budget. We found these arguments powerful; influential voices complained of the sentimentality of the images of the dying spaceman. Nevertheless, the cameras inside his marooned craft continued to send us poignant pictures of his slow descent into despair, his low-gravity, weight-reduced death.

I watched my cousin Gale as she watched the bar's TV. She did not see me watching her, did not know that she had become my chosen programme.

The condemned man on another planet – the condemned man *on* TV – began to sing a squawky medley of half-remembered songs. I was reminded of the dying computer, Hal, in the old film *2001: A Space Odyssey*. Hal sang "Daisy, Daisy" as it was being unplugged.

The Martian – for he was now a permanent resident of that planet – offered us his spaced-out renditions of "Swanee", "Show Me the Way to Go Home" and several numbers from *The Wizard of Oz*; and Gale's shoulders began to shake. She was crying.

I did not go across to comfort her.

I first heard about the upcoming auction of the ruby slippers the very next morning, and resolved at once to buy them, whatever the cost. My plan was simple: I would offer the miracle-shoes to Gale in all humility. If she wished, I would say, she could use them to travel to Mars and bring the spaceman back to Earth.

Perhaps I might even click the heels together three times, and win back her heart by murmuring, in soft reminder of our wasted love, *There's no place like home*.

You laugh at my desperation. Ha! Go tell a drowning man not to clutch at straws. Go ask a dying astronaut not to sing. Come here and stand in my shoes. What was it the Cowardly Lion said? Put 'em up. Put 'em uuuuup. I'll fight you with one hand tied behind my back. I'll fight you with my eyes closed.

Scared, huh? Scared?

The Grand Saleroom of the Auctioneers is the beating heart of the earth. If you stand here for long enough all the wonders of the world will pass by. In the Grand Saleroom, in recent years, we have witnessed the auction of the Taj Mahal, the Statue of Liberty, the Alps, the Sphinx. We have assisted at the sale of wives and the purchase of husbands. State secrets have been sold here, openly, to the highest bidder. On one very special occasion, the Auctioneers presided over the sale, to an overheated and inter-denominational bunch of smouldering red demons, of a wide selection of human souls of all classes, qualities, ages, races and creeds.

Everything is for sale, and under the firm yet essentially benevolent supervision of the Auctioneers, their security dogs and SWAT teams, we engage in a battle of wits and wallets, a war of nerves.

There is a purity about our actions here, and also an aesthetically pleasing tension between the vast complexity of the life that turns up, packaged into lots, to go under the hammer, and the equally immense simplicity of our manner of dealing with this life.

We bid, the Auctioneers knock a lot down, we pass on.

All are equal before the justice of the gavels: the pavement artist and Michelangelo, the slave girl and the Queen.

This is the courtroom of demand.

They are bidding for the slippers now. As the price rises, so does my gorge. Panic clutches at me, pulling me down, drowning me. I think of Gale – sweet coz! – and fight back fear, and bid.

Once I was asked by the widower of a world-famous and much-loved pop singer to attend an auction of rock memorabilia on his behalf. He was the sole trustee of her estate, which was worth tens of millions. I treated him with respect.

"There's only one lot I want," he said. "Spend what ever you have to spend."

It was an article of clothing, a pair of edible ricepaper panties in peppermint flavour, purchased long ago in a store on (I think this was the name) Rodeo Drive. My employer's late wife's stage act had included the public removal and consumption of several such pairs. More panties, in a variety of flavours – chocolate chip, knickerbocker glory, cassata – were hurled into the crowd. These, too, were gobbled up in the general excitement of the concert, the lucky recipients being too carried away to consider the future value of what they had caught. Undergarments that had actually been worn by the lady were therefore in short supply, and presently in great demand.

During that auction, bids came in across the video links with Tokyo, Los Angeles, Paris and Milan, bids so rapid and of such size that I lost my nerve. However, when I telephoned my employer to confess my failure he was quite unperturbed, interested only in the final price. I mentioned a five-figure sum, and he laughed. It was the first genuinely joyful laugh I had heard from him since the day his wife died.

"That's all right then," he said. "I've got three hundred thousand of those."

———

It is to the Auctioneers we go to establish the value of our pasts, of our futures, of our lives.

The price for the ruby slippers is rising ever higher. Many of the bidders would appear to be proxies, as I was on the day of the underpants; as I am so often, in so many ways.

Today, however, I am bidding – perhaps literally – for myself.

There's an explosion in the street outside. We hear running feet, sirens, screams. Such things have become commonplace. We stay where we are, absorbed by a higher drama.

The cuspidors are in full employment. Witches keen, movie stars flounce off with tarnished auras. Queues of the disconsolate form at the psychiatrists' booths. There is work for the club-wielding guards, though not, as yet, for the obstetricians. Order is maintained. I am the only person in the Saleroom still in the bidding. My rivals are disembodied heads on video screens, and unheard voices on telephone links. I am doing battle with an invisible world of demons and ghosts, and the prize is my lady's hand.

At the height of an auction, when the money has become no more than a way of keeping score, a thing happens which I am reluctant to admit: one becomes detached from the earth.

There is a loss of gravity, a reduction in weight, a floating in the capsule of the struggle. The ultimate goal crosses a delirious frontier. Its achievement and our own survival become – yes! – fictions.

And fictions, as I have come close to suggesting before, are dangerous.

In fiction's grip, we may mortgage our homes, sell our children, to have whatever it is we crave. Alternatively, in that miasmal ocean, we may simply float away from our desires, and see them anew, from a distance, so that they seem weightless, trivial. We let them go. Like men dying in a blizzard, we lie down in the snow to rest.

So it is that my cousin Gale loses her hold over me in the crucible of the auction. So it is that I drop out of the bidding, go home, and fall asleep.

When I awake I feel refreshed, and free.

Next week there is another auction. Family trees, coats of arms, royal lineages will be up for sale, and into any of these one may insert any name one chooses, one's own, or one's beloved's. Canine and feline pedigrees will be on offer, too: Alsatian, Burmese, Saluki, Siamese, Cairn terrier.

Thanks to the infinite bounty of the Auctioneers, any of us, cat, dog, man, woman, child, can be a blue-blood; can be – as we long to be; and as, cowering in our shelters, we fear we are not – *somebody*.

27

Feminism and Geography: The Limits of Geographical Knowledge

Gillian Rose

Given that you are reading this text (or having it read to you), we feel safe in assuming you have a body. We also assume that your body is emplaced, that you are somewhere. While there is nothing more we can say about you with any certainty, we assert this: much of *what* you are results from how your body's attributes are evaluated within the web of power relations embedded in *where* you are. If your body conforms to your locale's dominant norms, you may never give much thought to either body or place. They simply, unproblematically "are." But if your body diverges from those norms, you are marked as in some way alien, suspicious, perhaps even an object to be studied. And space for you becomes a hostile medium, one that may assault or reject your very existence. Gillian Rose shows this to be the case for the "minority" comprising 53% of humanity: women. But in documenting how women are marked as different by an implicitly male norm, and alienated from tacitly masculinized spaces, Rose goes beyond the supposedly exhaustive binary division of "man" and "woman." She pays close attention to the ways in which women differ from one another, and thus experience spatial marginalization differently. Thus Rose rejects the pyrrhic political task of wresting power from the hegemon, only to pass that hegemony on to some other "Other." Instead she explores ways of moving beyond practices of spatial domination and exclusion.

A Politics of Paradoxical Space

Why think about spaces and the subject of feminism?

An interest in the work performed by spatial images in contemporary theory is not unusual; spatial images are proliferating in social and cultural theory, and Hebdige has suggested two reasons for their popularity.[1] First, he notes the startling geography of contemporary socio-economic shifts, which geographers among others are charting: globalization, time-space compression and localization. Second, Hebdige points to the intellectual influence of Foucault. He suggests that Foucault's rejection of a teleological version of history, and his rescue of space from "the dead, the fixed, the undialectical, the immobile",[2] have encouraged many others to think spatially too. Whether this genealogy is the only one applicable to feminists, however, is questionable. Obviously feminists are responding to the so-called postmodern world, and some have explicit worked with Foucault's ideas (although their interest has focused on his writings on sexuality rather than on space). But I think that feminists' use of such imagery has a trajectory of its own too. This trajectory would also be an intellectual story materially embedded, but with a very different geography from the global economic narratives which are usually constructed to contextualize postmodern thinking. Consider this parable, told by Marilyn Frye to conclude her discussion of anger as a demand for respect and of the limits placed on women's expression of anger:

> No two women live, in a daily and detailed way, in identical spaces created by identical ranges of the concept of Woman . . . For better or for worse, though, in each of our lives, others' concepts of us are revealed by the limits of the intelligibility of our anger. Anger can be an instrument of cartography. By determining where, with whom, about what and in what circumstances one can get angry and get uptake, one can map others' concepts of who and what one is.
>
> One woman took this thought home with her and tried it out. She walked about the apartment she shares, not unhappily, with her young husband, testing in imagination for the viability of her anger – in what situations would it "work", would get uptake. She discovered that the pattern was very simple and clear. It went with the floor plan. She could get angry quite freely in the kitchen and somewhat less freely and about a more limited range of things in the living room. She could not get angry in the bedroom.
>
> Anger. Domain. Respect.[3]

Frye's domestic geography traces that woman's role in patriarchal society: she is expected to be a housewife and therefore in the kitchen, the site of much of her domestic labour, she can challenge her husband, get angry, speak with authority, and be heard, "get uptake". But in the bedroom she has no authority to speak independently. There she is not to speak her mind, but to be eloquent only with her body, for his pleasure. This everyday geography of kitchens and bedrooms – and streets and workplaces and neighbourhoods – is the geography of many women's spatiality, and of feminism too. Feminism, I think, through its awareness of the politics of the everyday, has always had a very keen awareness of the intersection of space and power – and knowledge. As de Lauretis says, there is "the *epistemological* priority which feminism has located in the personal, the subjective, the body, the symptomatic, the quotidian, as the very site of material inscription of the ideological".[4] De Lauretis also locates the struggle for self-representation by the subject of feminism in the everyday and its "constellation or configuration of meaning effects".[5] [. . .]

Some feminists talking about oppressive spaces

When feminists talk about experiences of space, very often they evoke a sense of difficulty. Being in space is not easy. Indeed, at its worst this feeling results in a desire to make ourselves absent from space; it can mean that "we acquiesce in being made invisible, in our occupying no space. We participate in our own erasure".[6] . . . This sense of being confined by space, into spaces, is not the only understanding of space that women have. I examine it here because, as I will argue, it offers a critique of the transparent space of geography by speaking of the costs of its masculinism.

Some experiences of confinement in space   In her discussion of the meaning of oppression, Frye uses a figure of confinement:

> The root of the word "oppression" is in the element "press". *The press of the crowd; pressed into military service; to press a pair of pants; press the button* . . . Something pressed is something caught between or among forces and barriers which are so related to each other that jointly they restrain, restrict or prevent the thing's motion or mobility. Mold. Immobilize. Reduce.[7]

Confinement is a recurring image in women's accounts of their lives. Iris Marion Young has argued that "a space surrounds us in imagination that we are not free to move beyond; the space available to our movement is a constricted one".[8] We often do not gesture and stride, stretch and push to the limits of our physical capabilities. Frances Angela, describing her experience of being a working-class white woman, says:

> . . . if I have to think of one word that could work as a motif for this experience, it is confinement – the shrinking of horizons, the confinements of space, of physical and assertive movements within institutions, the servility that masqueraded as civility, the subjugation of my body, emotions and psyche, the lack of opportunities in employment and education.[9]

For women of colour part of their sense of the difficulty of space is having to look white, and to act right, sometimes to sound right. Here is Rosario Morales, a Puerto Rican woman, describing her negotiation of a "straight", "tidy", "neat", white geography:

> what I do remember is to walk in straight and white into the store and say good morning in my see how white how upper class how refined and kind voice all crisp with consonants bristling with syllables   protective coloring in racist fields looks white and crisp like cabbage   looks tidy like laid out gardens   like white aprons on black dresses like please and thank you and you're welcome   like neat and clean and see I swept and scrubbed and polished   ain't I nice que hay de criticar   will I do   will I pass   will you let me thru   will they let me be   not see me here beneath my skin behind my voice   crouched and quiet and so so still   not see not hear me there where I crouch hiding my eyes   my indian bones my spanish sounds muttering[10]

Discussions about confinement are about a body feeling constrained by a particular gender, class and race position. For some women, as Russo remarks, there is no greater fear than that of making a spectacle of herself: too much rouge, a dingy bra strap showing, a voice too shrill in laughter.[11] Skin colour, class and gender are all social attributes which are inscribed onto bodies; and part of women's sense of oppression, of confinement, is their awareness of that process. I think that much of the buffetting and bruising, the confinement and stumbling, of women's experience of space is part of a self-consciousness about being noticed: women watching themselves being watched and judged.

Women of all kinds are expected to look right, and to look right for a gaze which is masculine. Bordo has noted a history of particularly intense disciplinary moments for the female body.[12] She correlates them with periods when women's actual political, economic and social activities are in conflict with the images of woman-hood offered by the dominant culture. She suggests that the surge of such images in the both the late nineteenth and the late twentieth centuries coincides with moments of feminist activism. Braidotti agrees: "it is as if men could not forgive women for having ceased to play the role of passive mirrors aggrandizing the male ego, and, incapable of looking critically at themselves, turned their gaze outwards, capturing women in images that are just anxious projections about the future of Man-kind".[13] There then occurs a proliferation of images of Woman, so that "in contemporary patriarchal culture, a panoptical male connoisseur resides within the consciousness of most women".[14] Bordo suggests that anorexia can be understood as a denial of the female body which sees that body and its desires in masculinist terms as excessive. Anorexia is an effort to deny the body in the manner of the master subject. It is also an effort to evade entrapment in an oppressive space:

> The anorexic is always convinced she is taking up too much space, eating too much, wanting food too much. I've never felt that way, but I've often felt that I was *too much* – too much emotion, too much need, too loud and demanding, too much *there*, if you know what I mean.[15]

The threatening masculine look materially inscribes its power onto women's bodies by constituting feminine subjects through an intense self-awareness about being seen and about taking up space.

Young has clarified a link between an awareness of embodiment and women's sense of space as not their own.[16] She notes that the threat of being seen and evaluated is one of the most objectifying processes to which the body is submitted, and argues that the constitution of our bodies as objects to be looked at encourages many of us to see ourselves as located in space. Unlike men who believe they can transcend the specificities of their body and see themselves and their intentions as the originating co-ordinate for organizing everyday space, women see their bodies as objects placed in space among other objects. Because our bodies are an object to us, we see ourselves as positioned in a space not our own. And that space can feel like an alien territory. Women's sense of embodiment can make space feel like a thousand piercing eyes; "location is about vulnerability".[17] This produces a sense of space as something tricky, something to be negotiated, a hazardous arena. The space spoken of by the women quoted here is far from being the transparent space of geography, then, and has none of the grandeur of visions of spatial differentiation; it is a space which constitutes women as embodied objects to be looked at. I suggest that these are the voices of women caught in the analytical stare of geography, caught inside spaces, speaking in places, figures in landscapes, telling the costs of geography's architectonic impulse.

Even as they speak its costs, however, these accounts also challenge the masculinist geographical imagination. This sense of space offered by these feminists dissolves the split between the mind and body by thinking through the body, their bodies. This way of thinking also seems to disregard any distinction between metaphorical and real space; spaces are made meaningful through experience and interpretation, which makes feminist spaces resonate with an extraordinary richness of emotion and analysis. Spaces are felt as part of patriarchal power.

Transparent space as the territory of the oppressors   If the costs of not being white, bourgeois, heterosexual and masculine have been described by feminists in spatial terms, so too has masculinism itself. I suggest that many women's difficulty in space can be understood not only in terms of an inscribed embodiment but also of masculinist claims to know which are experienced as a claim to space and territory. This spatialization of the master subject, far from being a mere figure of speech, invokes "the referential suffering of women" and their struggles to resist.[18] I develop the epistemological consequences of this imaginary now because they have implications for the paradoxical spaces imagined by feminists.

For Virginia Woolf, access to particular places as a woman and access to knowledge were directly equivalent. Absorbed by thought in the quad of an Oxbridge college,

> I found myself walking with extreme rapidity across a grass plot. Instantly a man's figure rose to intercept me. Nor did I at first understand that the gesticulations of a curious-looking object, in a cut-away coat and evening shirt, were aimed at me. His face expressed horror and indignation. Instinct rather than reason came to my help; he was a Beadle; I was a woman. This was the turf; there was the path. Only the Fellows and Scholars are allowed here; the gravel is the place for me...As I regained the path the arms of the Beadle sank, his face assumed its usual repose.[19]

Although women now are rarely physically debarred from entering the archives of knowledge, a sense of difficulty still arises in part from a feeling that we are caught within the effects of something strong and powerful which restricts us by claiming to know who women are. We are physically restricted, but there is also a sensation that the limits of what we are and can be have already been mapped by somebody else.[...]

The claims to know of the master subject are often imagined as a claim to territory. June Jordan, for example, talking about why racism continues, says that "once you try to answer that question you find yourself in the *territory* of people who despise you, people who are responsible for the invention of the term racism or sexism".[20] Territory is a kind of property won, historically, often by violence and conquest. Dejean has noted that as the modern nation-state developed, so the subjectivity of its powerful masculine subjects was imagined as structured like a fortress, both for the protection of the self and the exclusion of others;[21] in some key early modern fiction, irrational Others are exiled to a no man's land surrounding the master subject. The establishment of rational masculine identity involves rule over public space, and the violence following the need for that rule [is] continually reasserted. The epistemic closures and exclusions which legitimate that violence have been described as coercive in their claims to territories of knowledge; Braidotti, for example, suggests that "violence is the protective enclosure of rationality, which can only impose itself by processes of exclusion and denial. Violent reason. Reasonable violence".[22] This violence is the guarantee of the Same, because "by means of that exclusion and that seizure, reality can be a quiet place in which to meditate on oneself."[23] Kamuf describes this quiet place as a study:

> . . . the privileged place in question is The Room of One's Own. These capital letters will refer us to the original room, the room properly named, the room of the Cartesian subject, where *Ego sum* is struck as an emblem bearing a proper name, taking up space the limits of which can be delineated and, perhaps most importantly, where the subject becomes one – both singular and whole.[24]

In the study the exhaustiveness of masculinism is asserted. In describing epistemic exclusion then, feminists imagine the space of masculine subjectivity as a territory that is violently defended: as Braidotti says, "the economy of the rational order is basically an economy of war, in which women [among others] have suffered". [25] [. . .]

Women are not only imprisoned in the study as an object of knowledge, then, but also exile themselves from the study, knowing that they are not what the master subject assumes. Prisoners and exiles: the first appearance of what I am calling paradoxical space. No wonder space is so tortuous for so many women.

The paradoxical spaces of the subject of feminism

The violence implicit in the spatial imaginary of the white masculine subject is a major reason why feminists have tried to think about a different subjectivity. We want to be neither the victim nor the perpetrator of the experiences of displacement, exile, imprisonment and erasure. The project of the subject of feminism is to comprehend the "positivity of otherness",[26] and resistance to the exclusions of dominant subjectivities is articulated through spatial images. These images are not used casually; I argue that they are structured in order to resist the territoriality of masculinism. They offer a sense of space which refuses to be a claim to territory and thus allows for radical difference. This section outlines their politicized, complex and paradoxical space.

Geometrics of difference   The subject of feminism is understood as "a site of differences" because of the impact of critiques of dominant forms of feminism from other women over the past decade or so. Women who are not middle class, white, heterosexual and able-bodied have interpreted their experiences and insisted on being heard. Their arguments have enriched the spatial imaginary of feminism; for example, the centrality of the public/private distinction to white feminism has been challenged by the elaboration of very different geographies of work, home and community from black feminisms. The feminist political imaginary has also been diversified by the addition of interpretations of immigration, or of exile, or of certain structures of community, from the feminism of women of colour. What Miller has described as the "geopolitics of a poetics of gender" has created a fragmented and rich geographical imaginary in feminism.[27]

These articulations of different spatial structures have also complicated arguments about claims to know social spaces. For many feminists now, to think of the geography of difference is extremely complex. This geography can no longer simply be a mapping of social power relations onto territorial spaces: masculine and feminine onto public and private, for example. The impact of black and lesbian feminism is evident in the recognition that everywhere all women are subject to constitution not only by gender but by sexuality and by class and by race and by religion, and by a whole range of other social relations; and feminists of colour insist that these relations are always experienced simultaneously.[28] For the subject of feminism, then, "the issue is dispersion".[29] Social space can no longer be imagined simply in terms of a territory of gender. The geography of the master subject and the feminism complicit with him has been ruptured by the diverse spatialities of different women. So, a geographical imagination is emerging in feminism which, in order to indicate the complexity of the subject of feminism, articulates a "plurilocality".[30] In this recognition of difference, two-dimensional social maps are inadequate. Instead, spaces structured over many dimensions are necessary; what Haraway has described as "geometrics of difference and contradiction".[31]

As well as this multiplicity of dimensions, the subject of feminism also depends on a paradoxical geography. Any position is imagined not only as being located in multiple social spaces, but also as at both poles of each dimension. It is this tension which can articulate a sense of an elsewhere beyond the territories of the master subject.

The paradox of occupying both the centre and the margin   I have noted that the territory of the Same is differentiated between the centre of the Same and the margin of the Other. The Other is not outside the discursive territory of the Same. Eve Kosofsky Sedgwick has explored this paradox in the case of the homosexual and the trope of the closet; she suggests that the image of the closet represents homosexuality as an open secret around which a certain knowledgeable ignorance can centre.[32] Diana Fuss has also pointed out the complexity of this doubled position for gay men and lesbian women.[33] Their simultaneous inside-ness and outside-ness produces many unpredictable paradoxes: for example, "to be out, in common gay parlance . . . is really to be in – inside the realm of the visible, the speakable, the culturally intelligible . . . [but] to come out can also work not to situate one on the inside but to jettison one from it".[34] These paradoxes of "inside" and "outside" can painfully disempower those caught within them but, as Fuss also argues, "one can, by using these contested words, use them up, exhaust them, transform them into the historical concepts they are and always have been."[35] Here I examine the subversive potential of this paradoxical position. [. . .]

The destabilization of the Same/Other is also part of paradoxical position described by Patricia Hill Collins.[36] She describes the simultaneous occupation of a position both inside and outside the centre as the "outsider-within stance", and she suggests that it is a position articulated very often by black women because of their role as domestic workers in white homes. There they were on intimate terms with the children of the family in particular, but were also made to know that they did not belong, that they were only employees; they were there but also absent. Collins argues that this gives black feminists a unique insight into the contradictions between the ideology and the practice of the dominant group. It is a location from which the credibility of the master subject can be undermined. Frye suggests a similar subject position for white lesbian and gays, but one which is enabled for different reasons; by acting straight they can be inside but also watch as outsiders.[37]

This simultaneous occupation of centre and margin can critique the authority of masculinism, then. Another kind of paradoxical space helps some feminists to think about both recognizing differences between women and continuing to struggle for change as women. This is evident in some recent discussions about separatism. For those feminists most insistent on the poststructuralist interpretation of subject positioning, essentialist radical feminism and its associated practice of physical separatism are often seen as a passing moment of great importance to feminism, but with a politics that is no longer tenable.[38] The claim that separate women-only spaces enable the recovery of an essentially feminine identity is condemned as a mere reflection of the importance of boundaries to hegemonic subjectivity, with all the violent exclusions that entails. Diamond and Quinby, who wrote one of the epitaphs for separatist feminism, describe separatism as a "reverse discourse" which merely inverts the dominant value system without challenging its fundamental categories.[39] However, separatism of a kind is not dead: it is still advocated by many feminist writers. There are good reasons for separatism: Freedman has argued that in the nineteenth century, it "helped mobilize women and gained political leverage in the larger society"[40] and many women continue to argue that separatism can give women a breathing space to reflect, mediate, gain strength and recover a sense of identity... What women find in contemplation may be a complex and divided self which recognizes the need for alliances in struggle. The difference of others is acknowledged and strategic alliances forged. The spaces of separatism in these discussions, then, is also a space of interrelations – another paradox.

The paradox of being within the Same/Other and also elsewhere   The manipulation of the field of the Same/Other, being both separate and connected, the simultaneous occupation of both the centre and the margin, being at once inside and outside: all these discursive spaces depend on a sense of an "elsewhere" for their resistance. The subject of feminism has to feel that there is something beyond patriarchy in order to adopt these strategies of subversion. Thus the paradoxes described in the previous subsection themselves depend on a paradoxical space which straddles the spaces of representation and unrepresentability. This space of unrepresentability can acknowledge the possibility of radical difference, as de Lauretis argues.

Marilyn Frye describes a space beyond representation, which she calls lesbianism. Frye's defence of separatism argues that it is an effort by women to control men's access to them and its point is to enable women to define more clearly who they are. "When women separate (withdraw, break out, step outside, migrate, say *no*), we are simultaneously controlling access and defining. We are doubly insubordinate, since neither of these is permitted".[41] But she does not prescribe what women will define themselves as; in fact, she goes on to celebrate lesbianism as an existence precisely beyond definition.... Sedgwick too sees lesbian practices as occupying the realm of the non-representable; she suggests that dominant discourses can leave "in the stigma-impregnated space of refused recognition, sometimes also a stimulating aether of the unnamed, the lived experiment".[42]

This notion of a "stimulating aether" is not, it must be emphasized, in any simple sense outside the discourses of gender, race, class or sexuality; it is meaningful only in relation to the absences in those discourses – hence the paradoxicality of its spatial imaginary. This complicity is especially clear in the diasporic politics of many women of colour. Black feminism has spoken of segregated communities, of immigration, of exile, of the diaspora, of a "third world" now found on the streets of New York and London as well as in the southern hemisphere, and speaks of these spaces not as "natural" units which divide social groups but as part of a political consciousness of shared oppression and potential coalition.[43] In a double gesture, diasporic feminist politics both claims the black identity given by white racism as basis for struggle, and also refuses to be interpellated as the white man's Other by rejecting exclusionary, territorial claims to identity. This complex position has also imagined a paradoxical space which simultaneously grounds and denies identity – "a 'pre-post'-erous space"[44] – in order to articulate a politics of resistance.

The subject of feminism, then, depends on a paradoxical geography in order to acknowledge both the power of hegemonic discourses and to insist on the possibility of resistance. This geography describes that subjectivity as that of both prisoner and exile; it allows the subject of feminism to occupy both the centre and the margin, the inside and the outside. It is a geography structured by the dynamic tension between such poles, and it is also a multidimensional geography structured by the simultaneous contradictory diversity of social relations. It is a geography which is as multiple and contradictory and different as the subjectivity imagining it. I have already suggested how some of the founding antinomies of Western geographical thought are negated by this feminist subjectivity: its embodiment which overcomes the distinction between mind and body; its refusal to distinguish between real and metaphorical space; its refusal to separate experience and emotion from the interpretation of places. All these threaten the polarities which structure the dominant geographical imagination. They fragment the dead weight of masculinist space and rupture its exclusions. Above all, they allow for the possibility of a different kind of space through which difference is tolerated rather than erased.

NOTES

1   D. Hebdige, "Subjects in space", *New Formations*, 11 (1990), pp. v–x, p. vii.
2   M. Foucault, "Questions of geography", in *Power/Knowledge*, ed. C. Gordon (Harvester, Brighton, 1980), pp. 63–77, p. 70.
3   M. Frye, *The Politics of Reality: Essays in Feminist Theory* (Crossing Press, Trumansburg, NY, 1983), pp. 93–4.

4   de Lauretis, "Feminist studies/critical studies: issues, terms and contexts" in *Feminist Studies/Critical Studies*, ed. T. de Lauretis (Macmillan, London, 1986), pp. 1–19, p. 11.

5   de Lauretis, *Technologies of Gender: Essays on Theory, Film and Fiction*. (Macmillan, London, 1987), p. 18.

6   Frye, *The Politics of Reality*, p. 2.

7   Frye, *The Politics of Reality*, p. 2.

8   I. M. Young, *Throwing Like a Girl and Other Essays in Feminist Philosophy and Social Theory* (University of Indiana Press, Bloomington, 1990), p. 146.

9   F. Angela, "Confinement", in *Identity: Community, Culture, Difference*, ed. J. Rutherford (Lawrence and Wishart, 1990), pp. 72–87, pp. 72–3.

10 R. Morales, "The other heritage", in *This Bridge Called My Back: Writings by Radical Women of Color*, eds C. Moraga and G. Anzaldúa, second edition (Kitchen Table Press, New York, 1983), pp. 107–108, p. 108.

11 M. Russo, "Female grotesques: carnival and theory", in *Feminist Studies/Critical Studies*, ed. T. de Lauretis (Macmillan, London, 1986), pp. 213–29, p. 213.

12 S. Bordo, "*Anorexia nervosa*: psychopathology as the crystallisation of culture", in I. Diamond and L. Quinby, eds. *Feminism and Foucault: Reflections on Resistance* (Northeastern University Press, Boston, 1988), pp. 87–117.

13 Braidotti, *Patterns of Dissonance: a Study of Women in Contemporary Philosophy* (Polity Press, Cambridge, 1991), p. 135.

14 S. Lee Bartky, "Foucault, femininity, and the modernization of patriarchal power", in *Feminism and Foucault: Reflections on Resistance*, eds I. Diamond and L. Quinby (Northeastern University Press, Boston, 1988), p. 72. See also K. P. Morgan, "Women and the knife: cosmetic surgery and the colonization of women's bodies", *Hypatia* 6 (1991), pp. 25–53.

15 An unnamed student quoted in Bordo, "*Anorexia nervosa*", p. 106.

16 Young, *Throwing Like a Girl*.

17 D. Haraway, *Simians, Cyborgs and Women: The Reinvention of Nature* (Free Press Association, London, 1991), p. 196.

18 N. K. Miller, "The text's heroine: a feminist critic and her fictions", in *Conflicts in Feminism*, eds M. Hirsch and E. Fox Keller (Routledge, New York, 1990), pp. 112–20, p. 114.

19 Woolf, *A Room of One's Own* (Pan Books, London, 1977), pp. 7–8.

20 J. Jordan, quoted in P. Parmar, "Black feminism: the politics of articulation", in *Identity: Community, Culture, Difference*, ed. J. Rutherford (Lawrence and Wishart, London, 1990), pp. 101–26, p. 109, my emphasis.

21 J. Dejean, "No man's land: the novel's first geography", *Yale French Studies* 73 (1987), pp. 175–89.

22 Braidotti, *Patterns of Dissonance*, p. 279.

23 P. Kamuf, "Penelope at work: interruption in *A Room of One's Own*", in *Feminism and Foucault: Reflections on Resistance*, eds I. Diamond and L. Quinby (Northeastern University Press, Boston, 1988), pp. 149–64, p. 158.

24 Kamuf, "Penelope at work", p. 158.

25 Braidotti, *Patterns of Dissonance*, p. 216.

26 Braidotti, *Patterns of Dissonance*, p. 264.

27 N. K. Miller, "Changing the subject", in *Coming To Terms: Feminism, Theory, Politics*, ed. E. Weed (Routledge, London, 1989), pp. 3–16, p. 9.

28 Combahee River Collective, "A Black feminist statement", in *This Bridge Called My Back: Writings by Radical Women of Color*, eds C. Moraga and G. Anzaldúa, second edition (Kitchen Table Press, New York, 1983), pp. 210–18.

29   Haraway, *Simians, Cyborgs, and Women*, p. 170.

30   P. Kamuf, "Replacing feminist criticism", in *Conflicts in Feminism*, eds M. Hirsch and E. Fox Keller (Routledge, New York, 1990), pp. 105–111, p. 111.

31   Haraway, *Simians, Cyborgs, and Women*, p. 170.

32   Sedgwick, *Epistemology of the Closet*. (Harvester Wheatsheer F, Hemel Hempstead, 1991).

33   Fuss, "Inside/Out", in *Inside/Out: Lesbian Theories, Gay, Theories*, ed. D. Fuss (Routledge, New York, 1991) pp. 1–10.

34   Fuss, "Inside/Out", p. 4.

35   Fuss, "Inside/Out", p. 7.

36   P. Hill Collins, *Black Feminist Thought: Knowledge, Consciousness and the Politics of Empowerment* (Harper Collins, London, 1990), p. 11. See also b hooks, *Feminist Theory: From Margin to Center* (South End Press, Boston, 1984).

37   Frye, *The Politics of Reality*, p. 148. See also M. Bruce Pratt, "Identity: skin blood heart", in *Yours in Struggle: Three Feminist Perspectives on Anti-Semitism and Racism*, in E. Bulkin, M. Bruce Pratt and B. Smith (Long Haul Press, New York, 1984), pp. 9–63, p. 20.

38   Braidotti, *Patterns of Dissonance*, p. 207; M. Gatens, *Feminism and Philosophy: Perspectives on Difference and Equality* (Polity Press, Cambridge, 1991), pp. 79–84.

39   I. Diamond and L. Quinby, "Introduction", in I. Diamond and L. Quinby, eds, *Feminism and Foucault: Reflections on Resistance* (Northeastern University Press, Boston, 1988), pp. ix–xx, p. xi.

40   E. Freedman, "Separatism as a strategy: female institution building and American feminism, 1870–1930", *Feminist Studies* 5 (1979), pp. 512–29, p. 513.

41   Frye, *The Politics of Reality*, p. 107.

42   Sedgwick, *Epistemology of the Closet*, p. 63.

43   See, especially, C. T. Mohanty, "Introduction: cartographies of struggle: Third World Women and the politics of feminism," in *Third World Women and the Politics of Feminism* ed. C. T. Mohanty (University of Indiana Press, Bloomington, 1991) pp. 1–47. For the importance of the diaspora to Black politics, see S. Hall, "Cultural identity and diaspora" in *Identity: Community, Culture, Difference*, ed. J. Rutherford (Lawrence and Wishart, London, 1990), pp. 222–37.

44   R. Radhakrishnan, "Ethnic identity and post-structuralist *différance*", *Cultural Critique*, 6 (1987), pp. 199–220, p. 199.

28 From Landmarks to Spaces: Mapping the Territory of a Bisexual Genealogy

Clare Hemmings

If to be banished to the margins is to experience oppression, how much more oppressive must it be to live in exile from the center and its margins? A body's doings are as much a basis for self-formation, and for spatial exclusion, as a body's being. This is particularly true for those whose bodily doings render them "both this *and* that" in discursive and spatial contexts informed by modernist notions where only being "either this *or* that" is possible. Clare Hemmings illustrates this predicament with her analysis of space and bisexuality. She makes clear that such a predicament may be less dire than it sounds. Given the dominant division of sexual desire into heterosexuality and homosexuality, and the resultant partition of space into "straight" and "queer," it would seem that bisexuals simply have no place to be. This in turn suggests that, as a counter to nonexistence, bisexuals must follow the lead of straights and gays by producing distinctly bispaces. In documenting how bisexuals creatively negotiate both straight and queer spaces to their satisfaction, Hemmings shows that partitioning selves into homogeneous categories and providing exclusive spaces to match, is neither necessary nor desirable. Rather, she suggests that the interstices of physical and discursive spaces (sometimes called liminal spaces) can be entirely viable places in which to dwell. By re-imagining place not as the proprietary terrain of particular identity categories, but as a theater for enacting multifarious practices, space can amicably accommodate a wide range of selves simultaneously.

I have been thinking through the possibilities of theorising bisexuality in and through spaces in the last two years and writing about it in the last year, after I went to the Organizing Sexualities Conference in Amsterdam in June 1994. The conference was organised to coincide with EuroPride 1994. For once, academic and activist worlds did not seem completely at variance. Amsterdam was buzzing; the streets were decked with pink triangles and banners; it was warm. Performances, workshops, dance clubs, academic presentations, all jostled for my attention, were all part of the conference experience. The subtitle of the conference was "Gay and Lesbian Movements since the 1960s." I was the only person giving a paper on bisexuality and – as far as I was aware – the only out bisexual delegate at the conference. Although none of the organisers was actively biphobic, bisexual space – both concrete and theoretical – was not part of the conference format. Unsurprisingly, the only space given to bisexuality as a relevant area of concern was created by my presentation or by specific interventions.

One paper at the conference was on the different kinds of spaces in Amsterdam that mark out a young gay male's identity. In the discussion after the paper, the importance of public spaces – streets, parks, backrooms, and baths – in the formation of a contemporary gay and lesbian identity was tentatively explored. At a certain point one participant turned to me – as the holder of all bisexual wisdom – to ask what and where are bisexual spaces? While I was thinking about it, another delegate answered that perhaps both gay and straight spaces are bisexual spaces. This is true in certain respects. Bisexuals certainly occupy both lesbian or gay and straight spaces and may call one or the other or both "home." One might also highlight the fact that both gay and straight spaces – including bars, clubs, restaurants, and "political" spaces – have been partly formed through the intervention and work of bisexual people as well as gay or straight people. But in this conference discussion about gay male spaces, and in many other more general discussions about "queer" spaces, spaces were being viewed as linked to identity. In that sense, neither gay nor straight spaces could be said to be bisexual spaces per se. A bisexual's identity is never the dominant identity being produced, delineated, or contested in either gay or straight spaces. "Bisexual" may be added on, may be seen as included, but it is never seen as inclusive.

This exchange raised a number of issues for me, issues that I thought about after the conference and am still pondering now. If the conclusion is that bisexual space is not both gay and straight but rather neither gay nor straight, what are the implications for a positive bisexual identity or for bisexual theorising? If bisexual identity is not inclusive but rather always partial, if there are no "bisexual spaces" per se, then how do we represent bisexuality, and what is the relationship between bisexuality and space? This is the quandary that faced me a year ago: a sense of my own identity as bisexual, some temporary bisexual spaces such as conferences and support groups but few examples of a bisexual culture that could be read through analysis of particular public spaces at particular times. Add to that the lack of much that could be termed "bisexual theory" to provide alternative models or alternative ways of reading predominantly lesbian and gay or straight spaces, and you begin to get a sense of my frustration. The problem of spaces and bisexuality has kept returning to me, has kept presenting itself as a series of questions to ask about bisexual theorising: What is a bisexual space? How do bisexuals negotiate sexual spaces that do not take their name or confirm their identity?[...]

In this discussion I want to experiment with an imaginative and theoretical move from seeing bisexuality as a sexual identity with a conventional linear narrative and history, to looking at bisexuality as it is produced and negotiated in relation to particular queer sexual spaces. Accompanying this move is another one that focuses on bisexual desire, on bisexual bodies and acts, rather than on bisexual identities. Bisexual desire does not always correlate to a self-identified bisexual subject. To limit my analysis to people who identify as bisexual would be to ignore the complex history of many individuals' desire for more than one sex, for more than one gender, or for a changing gender position. By moving away from a focus on identities, I am not advocating an oppositional emphasis on "performance," on a postmodern disembodied "play." Neither am I advocating a move to distance theory from the experience or politics of individuals or communities. Differences can only be acknowledged by attending to specific bodies, to the shared and different histories of particular queer bodies and their relationships with one another, politically, theoretically, and personally. By focusing on bisexual desire rather than identities, I hope to reemphasise that queer desire takes place in particular spaces at particular times and that desire is enacted through our bodies. It is our bodies that pay the price, our bodies that experience the pleasure.

Primarily, my decision to write about bisexuality in terms of spaces, in terms of desire and bodies, is a response (and I hope not merely a reactive one) to prevalent ways of reading, writing, and articulating sexual identities as boundaried, as separable from one another, as separate. Conventionally bisexuality has not been seen as an identity at all, because it is not structurally consistent in terms of gender of object choice, a gendered subject position, or chronology. Politically bisexuality has also been "denied" legitimacy in terms of sexual identity. Commonly a bisexual woman is understood as "a good example of inauthenticity in a lesbian." Only existing models of sexual identity will do, it seems. As a response to exclusion, most bisexual writers have argued that bisexuality is a valid sexual identity, that it has its own form of consistency, its own coming-out narratives, its own unique culture.

The problem is that, in the courageous effort to grant bisexuality some sense of authenticity, the same identity frameworks are often adopted. Bisexuality becomes separated off as if it were discrete and separate from lesbian and gay or straight identity, from lesbian and gay or straight history. The identity narrative plots the progression of sexuality through identity above all. A bisexual history along these lines sees the emergence of a bisexual identity as more critical than, say, histories of bisexual behaviour and desire that surface unexpectedly without the consciousness of contemporary bisexual meanings. Only a few souls that amount to bisexual tokens and icons can be rescued, those who are created in "our" own image, to show how we progressed to the contemporary moment of awareness or self-identification. Sappho, Oscar Wilde, Virginia Woolf are all being reclaimed as bisexual because of their relationships with more than one biological sex.

Another, relatively recent, way of trying to separate bisexual identity out from other forms of sexual identity is through the use of the term "monosexuality." Bisexuals, both activists and researchers, use the term to distinguish between bisexuals, who desire more than one sex, and "monosexuals," who don't; monosexuals are lesbians, gay men, and heterosexuals. The term has begun to appear, often unquestioned and unclarified, in most recent bisexual publications in the United States, including *Vice Versa, Bi Any Other Name, Closer to Home*, and *Bisexual Politics*. Rather than challenging identity categories, the invention and use of the term monosexual reemphasises the primary significance of sex and gender in the formulation of a sexual identity, while simultaneously attempting to mark out bisexuals as somehow "beyond" sex and gender. In this rubric bisexuals are uniquely oppressed by monosexism and are therefore politically entitled to their own oppressed minority status and identity. By setting up this division, the differences between lesbians and gay men and heterosexuals in terms of power are elided. The politics of identity fade away. It is precisely the fact that bisexual desire blurs the boundaries between heterosexual, gay, and lesbian desire and blurs the separation of heterosexual, gay, and lesbian communities that marks it out as politically and theoretically important at this time.

To return once again to the experience at the Organizing Sexualities Conference in Amsterdam, to the realisation of the lack of what might be called bisexual spaces, the relationship between bisexuals and other sexual identities and communities is key to beginning to theorise bisexuality. Bisexuals never find themselves represented or reflected wholly in gay, lesbian, or straight spaces or communities. We may be part of heterosexual culture in terms of access through a partner and of privilege, however temporary or illusory. We may also be part of lesbian and gay culture, again in terms of relationships and politics. Our histories may be within both heterosexual and gay and lesbian cultures, sometimes sequentially, and sometimes simultaneously. Often it is not our own sexuality that grants us access to a particular community but that of our partner(s) and friends.

Because of bisexual presence – sometimes overt and sometimes not – in what are assumed to be gay, lesbian, or straight spaces, bisexual history is partly lesbian and gay history, and vice versa. Bisexuals are not outside lesbian and gay movements and spaces, banging on the door trying to get in. Bisexuals are already there, are already part of what shapes the particular spaces where sexual identity is grounded, determined, and enacted. For all of us whose sexual behaviour and acts mark us out as "other" to mainstream heterosexual culture, we are closer to one another than we might like to think – even though that closeness is not always comfortable. We share spaces and lives, dance, tred on one another's toes, lose ourselves in each other, find ourselves, cruise, talk, move, eat, mourn. But some of those bodies that I dance, cruise, and fight with write bodies of theory that ask if I should be allowed to share, "that space where I sweated with you, showed fear with you." They are theories that reinscribe sex-gender-sexuality connections and ideas of identity in ways that do not allow me to recognise myself, not even in part.

Let me be clear that I do not think that identity narratives are a "bad" thing, as such. Narratives are what enable us sexual "perverts" to make sense of ourselves in a hostile world. In fact my need for this "re-imagining" is precisely because there is a lack of a clear bisexual narrative, a lack of spaces where my sexuality is "read as" bisexual. We need stories – desperately. My purpose here is to consider ways that bisexual stories and histories can be written that emphasise that familiar sense of partiality that bisexuals commonly experience, rather than looking for narratives that emphasise only individual and community consistency and identity. Bisexual identity narratives and the reclaiming of a unique history serve an important purpose, but they do not make sense of the discontinuities and misrepresentations that also make up my life and are part of bisexual history. If I tell my own past as internally consistent (I always knew I was bisexual; I always found both men and women attractive; once I came out as bisexual I found my identity and community that had always been there) that tells part of the story. But the time I have spent in the lesbian community, my three years as a lesbian separatist, the moments where I am "read as" something else in the present, the always partial sense of "homecoming" – these things also make up my sense of self as bisexual – determine what it means to me to be bisexual, not just whether or not I am bisexual. These experiences are as much a part of my experience of self-identifying as bisexual as is my desiring men and women.

The overlaps between different sexual communities are always going to be an important part of the history of bisexuality. I want to do justice to our histories of being closeted, of exclusion, of misrecognition, or of desire accepted and rejected, as much as I want to be proud of out, visible bisexual identities and communities now. Only a genealogy that focuses on those contradictions can explain where we are now. A chronological history of bisexual identity ends up reading like the coming-out narrative of self that seeks to release or reveal the "true" bisexual story at the expense of our desires, our commitments, both political and personal, and our very bodies. To focus on bisexual desire, on spaces where that desire plays out, is one way to begin documenting that complexity. My desire is to "re-member" a genealogy of bisexuality, not through the lens of a distant past but through the perception of a complex present. I seek to pinpoint the formation of sexual spaces by making the margins of bisexuality the main focus, which does not require other discourses being phased out or being made out of focus. I want to re-member the margins and their relation to the centre and to one another. In that sense I am re-membering a genealogy that already exists in the present, in my body, and in my body's relationship to other bodies.

II

[A]n individual's perception of a landscape changes with the experience of moving through it. It is less obvious but equally true that an apparently unified landscape may actually be composed of several fragmentary ones, some sharing common elements of the larger assemblage. Indeed this may be the only way to make sense of certain landscapes.

D. Upton

For the purposes of this essay I use the notion of space in a number of different ways. Firstly, I am referring to geographically concrete spaces, such as bars, clubs, restaurants, urban/rural areas, individual living spaces, and so on. Secondly, I am referring to what might be called "spaces of articulation." By this I mean the scope and range of meanings that concrete spaces have outside their specific geographical confines, as well as the effect that those meanings have on other spaces. For example, a lesbian and gay culture or subculture may be built up around specific bars and clubs primarily in cities or towns, but the meaning of those spaces within discourses of sexuality will often extend beyond those walls to create a larger sense of "lesbian and gay culture." Lesbian and gay spaces of articulation can also be produced, changed, and discussed in other concrete spaces that may have no direct relation to concrete lesbian and gay spaces per se. Feminists, who may or may not be lesbian, who may or may not occupy lesbian S/M cultural spaces, have discussed, negotiated, and affected the issue of lesbian S/M, but not exclusively in lesbian spaces. Thirdly, I am interested in "performative space," by which I mean temporary spaces where relationships occur between members of the same and different communities, often spontaneously, as well as the new spaces that are created within and outside those relationships. These spaces are, if you like, experiential ones that are formed and negotiated by lovers and friends, which may have an influence on the formation and meanings of larger sexual spaces.

Of course those three senses of space are not discrete. In most cases elements of all three uses are combined. In the rest of this paper I look at some examples of how bisexuality plays out in particular spaces – mixed gay and straight spaces, women-only space, bisexual conference space, lesbian and gay space. My aim is to see whether and how bisexuality might be theorised through those spaces, not as separate and not as a discrete identity, but as one part, a very important part, of queer space and queer meaning.

A bi place to be? a place to be bi?
The North Star, Northampton, Massachusetts

The North Star bar and dance club formerly of Northampton, Massachusetts (it is now The Grotto), is one of the main focal points for queer social interaction in a town known in the popular press as "lesbianville." This lesbian-owned bar is located on the corner of Green Street, at the top of Main Street and close to Smith College. Inside, the bar is on the right and a dance space and a pool area slightly raised and next to the dance floor, are on the left. The North Star Seafood Restaurant and Bar (the restaurant closed in early 1995) has provided a venue for lesbian performance, music, and workshops on anything from teaching to sales management since 1989. The North Star is open more or less daily in the afternoons and evenings, offering weekly special events such as Latin music evenings, with Latin music dance class in the early evening. Friday and Saturday nights are club nights, Friday for eighteen and over. The music is eighties and nineties bop, with the usual smattering of seventies favourites. Although the North Star is lesbian-owned and known as a lesbian bar, it has a wide clientele of nonlesbians including the growing gay male population of Northampton, trendy straight people who like the music and the ambience, bisexuals, and older straight men who appear to turn up by accident or for whom the North Star is the nearest local bar.

Arriving at the North Star on a Saturday night around 11:30 P.M. (it's open until 1 A.M.) a straight doorman takes your $4. The bar is jam-packed, two people deep. The barwomen are curt and overworked. The place is busy, but not so busy that you can't look or move around. The club is on the small side, low lighting but not gloomy. The majority of the men, who are mostly gay in style, stand around in the space between the bar and the dance floor; some are dancing, and these men are mostly in their early twenties or so. The women are spread out over the whole club. The pool area is dominated by butches who are mostly young. But some are older women, probably in their forties, who shoot pool or lean nonchalantly against the walls, drinking bottled beer and smoking, looking at the women dancing, but not really cruising, certainly not hard cruising. Mostly, men talk and dance with other men; women talk and dance with other women. Some men and women talk and dance together – friends, lovers, gay, lesbian, straight, or bi? Butch and femme is common, particularly among the older women, though not exclusively. The predominant style is casual – there are no leather men or dykes – though some femmes are high femme, and some of the butches (if they are butches) are cross-dressed. A lot of people know one another – the atmosphere is intimate and friendly.

It seems that at the North Star people from different communities with different identities coexist fairly easily. Because the club is so small and because Northampton does not have much to offer in the way of places to socialise past midnight, people make room for one another. It appears that everyone has their own piece of territory. But with such mixing, misrecognition and blurring of the boundaries also occurs. Does this mixing of straight and queer make this a bisexual space? [...]

It would seem that the North Star is a mixed space, one that can accommodate a range of sexual orientations and gender positions. But this does not make it a "bisexual space." One is read as gay, lesbian, or straight, even though those identities can mix. What the North Star does provide, though, amongst other things, is a place to be bisexual, a place where bisexual people can dance and cruise with people of either sex and still feel part of queer culture. The North Star is also a place where desire can find expression, even if that desire is misread as signaling an identity that is other than the identity claimed. In relation to the third scenario, for example, the North Star is a space where my lover's and my desire could be expressed safely even though it may be misread, even though we may misread one another in terms of identity. My point is not that people should not be misreading identity but rather that identity is impossible not to misread. Identity always allows itself to be misread. The three examples of reading and/or presenting identities that I have given highlight the ways in which identity is used to maintain a clear sense of boundaries among recognizable sexual identities. "Straight" is used to create distance from lesbian and gay, either in terms of desire, as in the case of the man my friend Alex asked to dance, or in terms of style and association, as in the case of Jane's high femme style and gay male friends. And the choices in terms of reading my and my lover's desire is as straight or lesbian. It is unlikely that we were being read as bisexual femme and FTM, and it is unlikely that we ever would be.

An analysis of places such as the North Star could be used to highlight the complexity of queer social spaces in a number of ways. Although there may not be any bisexual clubs and bars, it is clear that (i) bisexuals currently occupy space within queer and straight spaces, and (ii) that an individual's desire for people of more than one sex (as well as gender) may be expressed in those spaces, even if their identity is "misread." It is not only bisexual desire that gets "misread" as signaling a particular identity. Femme desire, style, and identity, for example, are often also read as "straight," even though femme desire has been a founding part of lesbian culture. Gaps among identity, desire, and style always emerge in sexual spaces and not just when bisexuality is the issue. Those gaps form part of the sexual tension that ebbs and flows in queer sexual spaces – Is she or isn't she? Will she or won't she? It will be interesting to see whether spaces such as the North Star become more "bi-conscious" in the next few years. As bisexuality becomes more visible, as bisexual identity becomes more solidified (if it does), will there be a way of being "read as" bisexual?

REFERENCES

Angelides, S. 1995. The Economy of (Hetero)sexuality. *Melbourne Historical Journal* 23(44).

Bell, D. 1995. Perverse dynamics, sexual citizenship and the transformation of intimacy. In *Mapping Desire: Geographies of sexualities*. London and New York: Routledge.

Bell, D., and G. Valentine, eds. 1995. *Mapping Desire: Geographies of sexualities*. London and New York: Routledge.

Blumstein, P., and P. Schwartz. 1976. Bisexual women. In *The Social Psychology of Sex*. Edited by J. P. Wiseman. New York: Harper and Row.

Bode, J. 1976. *A View from Another Closet: Exploring bisexuality in women*. New York: Hawthorn.

Bowie, M. 1992. Bisexuality. In *Feminism and Psychoanalysis: A critical dictionary*. Edited by E. Wright. Oxford, England: Basil Blackwell.

Bristow, J., and A. Wilson, eds. 1993. *Activating Theory: Lesbian, gay, bisexual politics*. London: Lawrence and Wishart.

Card, C. 1985. Lesbian attitudes and the second sex. *Women's Studies International Forum* 8(3).

Faderman, L. 1985. *Surpassing the Love of Men: Romantic friendship and love between women, from the Renaissance to the present*. London: Women's Press.

Faderman, L. 1991. *Odd Girls and Twilight Lovers: A history of lesbian life in twentieth-century America*. New York: Columbia University Press.

Fast, J., and H. Wells. 1975. *Bisexual Living*. New York: Pocket Books.

Foucault, M. 1971. The discourse on language. In *The Archaeology of Knowledge*. New York: Harper and Row.

Foucault, M. 1978. *The history of sexuality, volume 1: An introduction*. Translated by R. Hurley. London: Penguin Books.

Fraser, M. 1996. Framing contention: Bisexuality displaced. In *RePresenting Bisexualities: Subjects and cultures of fluid desire*. Edited by Donald E. Hall and Maria Pramaggiore. New York: New York University Press.

Freud, S. 1925. Psychogenesis of a case of homosexuality in a woman. In *Collected Papers, Volume II: Clinical Papers, Papers on Technique*. Translated by J. Riviere. London: Hogarth Press.

Freud, S. 1937. The ego and the id. In *The Standard Edition of the Complete Psychological Works of Sigmund Freud*. Translated by J. Strachey. London: The Hogarth Press and the Institute of Psychoanalysis.

Frye, M. 1985. History and responsibility. *Women's Studies International Forum* 8(3).

Garber, M. 1995. *Vice Versa: Bisexuality and the eroticism of everyday life*. New York: Simon and Schuster.

Geller, T., ed. 1990. *Bisexuality: A reader and sourcebook*. Ojai, California: Times Change Press.

George, S. 1993. *Women and Bisexuality*. London: Scarlet Press.

Gregory, D. 1983. The case for a feminist bisexuality. In *Sex and Love: New thoughts on old contradictions*. Edited by S. Cartledge and J. Ryan. London: Women's Press.

Hemmings, C. 1996. From lesbian nation to transgender liberation: A bisexual feminist perspective. *Journal of gay, lesbian, and bisexual identity*. (1)1 (January).

Hutchins, L., and L. Ka'ahumanu, eds. 1991. *Bi Any Other Name: Bisexual people speak out.* Boston: Alyson Publications.

Kermode, F. 1992. Review of *Vice Versa: Bisexuality and the eroticism of everyday life. New York Times Book Review* (July 9).

Kinsey, A. C., W. B. Pomeroy, and C. E. Martin. 1953. *Sexual Behavior in the Human Female.* Philadelphia and London: W. B. Saunders Company.

Klein, F., and T. Wolf, eds. 1985. *Two Lives to Lead: Bisexuality in men and women.* New York: Harrington Park Press.

Masson, ed. and trans. 1985. *Freud S.: The complete letters of Sigmund Freud to Wilhelm Fliess 1887–1904.* Cambridge, Massachusetts: Harvard University Press.

McFarquhar, L. 1994. Review of *Vice Versa: Bisexuality and the eroticism of everyday life. The Nation* (July 24).

Munt, S. 1995. The lesbian *flâneur.* In *Mapping Desire: Geographies of sexualities.* Edited by David Bell and Gill Valentine. London and New York: Routledge.

Off Pink Collective. 1988. *Bisexual Lives.* London: Off Pink Publishing.

Richards, A. ed. 1977. Three essays on the theory of sexuality. In *The Penguin Freud Library Volume 7: On Sexuality.* London: Penguin Books.

Richards, A. ed. 1993. Hysterical phantasies and their relation to bisexuality and A child is being beaten. In *The Penguin Freud Library Volume 10: On Psychopathology.* London: Penguin Books.

Rose, S., and C. Stevens et al, eds. 1994. *Bisexual Horizons.* London: Lawrence and Wishart.

Scott, J. 1992. Experience. In *Feminists theorize the political.* Edited by Judith Butler and Joan Scott. London and New York: Routledge.

Tucker, N., ed. 1995. *Bisexual Politics.* New York: The Haworth Press.

Upton, D. 1988. White and black landscapes in eighteenth-century Virginia. In *Material Life in America, 1600–1860.* Edited by Blair St. George. Boston: Northeastern University Press.

Weise, E. R. ed. 1992. *Closer to Home: Bisexuality and feminism.* Seattle: Seal Press.

Weisser, S. O., and J. Fleischner, eds. 1994. *Feminist Nightmares: Women at odds.* New York: New York University Press.

White, E. 1995. Review of *Vice Versa: Bisexuality and the eroticism of everyday life. New Yorker* (July 17).

29 Thrashing Downtown: Play as Resistance to the Spatial and Representational Regulation of Los Angeles

Steven Flusty

We make our spaces as they make us, and our spaces make us just as we make them. When space excludes and oppresses bodies, it becomes necessary to undertake actions that function to produce alternative spaces that can be both occupied and ultimately sustained. Flusty chronicles how the everyday practices of marginalized, dissident, and disappeared subcultures disregard the authoritative programs of urban space, and appropriate that space for themselves. Not only can such alternative spaces exist, but they are continually being carved out right under our noses. Central to Flusty's belief is that no space is inherently and exclusively a single thing, regardless of proprietary claims to the contrary (cf. Reading 28). Rather, a space is as many different things as there are different visions of what it could be, and as there are embodied selves to perform in those spaces.

Introduction

A single dirt path rises between two vacant lots. One is destined to become a performing arts center. The other, with the manic recovery of the real estate market from the deep recession of the early 1990s, will sprout a block of luxury apartments. This doomed and dusty remnant of upper 2nd Street provides the only ready pedestrian passage up from the remnants of the century-old city center below, through a palisade of concrete parking garages, and into L.A.'s new hilltop compound of multinational corporate finance. Ted hangs out at the top of this path, one of the few homeless people to make the climb up from Skid Row a half-mile to the southwest. He squats on his haunches and makes specific requests of the business-suited passers-by trying to avoid him: a cup of decaf, an herbal tea, a bran muffin perhaps? Ted is health conscious, claims to have no use for money (a claim supported by his rejections of cash offerings), and gestures to the surrounding street as he explains where he may or may not request sustenance. The forbidden zones are clearly marked by a flat, 4-inch wide bronze-tone metal strip bolted to the sidewalk, concretizing the line between public right of way and privately administered plazas. To drive the point home, a fist-sized brass plaque is embedded into the sidewalk before each plaza entrance. Each plaque is embossed with the words:

PRIVATE PROPERTY. RIGHT TO PASS BY PERMISSION, AND SUBJECT TO CONTROL, OF OWNERS sec 1008 CIVIL CODE.

This on-going standoff between Ted and the bronzed manifestation of the surrounding area's dominant social order concisely illustrates what happens when lifeworlds collide. This collision raises the question: What is the city, according to whom? [. . .]

A Fractured Monolith

Bunker Hill is a semi-permeable enclave bristling with the spikes of clustered capital accretion: "A-class" office towers, luxury hotels and corporately leased executive residential suites. Taken as a whole, it is a financial axis mundi saturated with observation cameras and pocked with publicly-assisted private plazas that are intended more as rent-leveraging tenant amenities than as remedies to the area's open space deficit (Flusty, 1994). With no significant population beyond the week-day lunch hour crowd, the (commonly chain) retailers that occupy each tower's plaza level or subterranean mall are, with few exceptions, shuttered by sundown (see Figure 1).

Bunker Hill's target users, in the words of a promotional brochure for one multi-tower development, are "office workers [who] will find outdoor areas for noontime relaxation where they may choose solitude or colorful outdoor cafes and bistros" (Metropolitan Structures n.d.). Such sights, sounds and activities as may be alien to this clientele have been exorcised from Bunker Hill's collective program. This proscriptive dynamic is exacerbated by the need to ensure a businesslike decorum that communicates managerial competence. Thus, urban design, municipal law and private policy conjoin to preclude the potential for unpredictable or "abnormal" behavior in every street and plaza. As a result, Downtown L.A. has become an agglomeration of pretty, homogenized spaces. It is a rarefied monolith of a place, where the individual who appears unable to afford the escalating price of prefabricated recreation has no option other than to be at home, at work, or in transit between the two. This monolith, however, is rife with cracks, enabling a wide and eccentric range of unforeseen, unauthorized actions. Further, it is precisely the centrality and exclusivity of this monolith, both geographically and administratively, that invites these unauthorized acts by highlighting their insubordinate implications.

A Busker's-eye View: the City as Stage

Paul, in his forties, sports chopped salt-and-pepper hair, a bushy beard, a one-man-band harmonica rig on his shoulder that holds a smoldering cigarette, and a utility belt. The utility belt carries a diver's light, a battery pack, a flat plastic tray, a bottle

Figure 1.   Saturated with observation cameras.

of dish washing soap, and another of purified water. These are the tools of Paul's trade.

Paul claims to be one of nine professional bubblemen in the United States and, by his account, a good one. He has been practicing for over a decade, devoting himself to the making of beautiful, ephermeral soap bubble sculptures.

He displays a large repertoire of tricks, which he guards zealously from imitators and photographers. He will blow six bubbles, forming a cube at their intersection. He will then poke a straw into this cube, fill it with cigarette smoke, and highlight the play of iridescent soap sheen against swirling smoke with the beam of his diver's light. He makes flying saucer bubbles, honeycombs of bubbles, miniature rococo bubble filigrees that cling to larger bubbles, even a series of nesting bubbles with a smoke saturated center that, when punctured, gives up its haze and floats to the ground without bursting.

Paul expresses a fondness for working between Bunker Hill's built geometries, although he finds the institutional opposition to bubble blowing downtown discouraging. On humid nights, when increased moisture content in the air keeps the bubbles wet and permits more time for the execution of complex stunts, he blows bubbles 10 to 15 feet across and positions them to be carried many stories aloft by the winds generated between the hill's highrises. On calmer evenings, Paul will blow a series of nested bubbles and push them into the reflecting pool that surrounds the Department of Water and Power headquarters. Then he watches as the external bubble compresses into a hemisphere against the water, while the bubbles contained within careen off one another. Usually, he completes two or three tricks before being ejected from the property by a nightwatchman, with an apology along the lines of "What you're doing is really neat, just not here" (see Figure 2).

Despite "knowing where to find every security camera on Bunker Hill", Paul finds it increasingly difficult to practice his trade in public. He worries that draconian crackdowns on street performers may eventually lead such arts to extinction. Once, Paul attempted a trick in a Bunker Hill plaza before dark, on a Sunday afternoon shortly after a humidifying rain shower. Well before the trick was complete, a blue-blazered security man instructed Paul to leave the premises, a request the bubbleman says he politely declined. Following Paul's physical removal from the property by an additional contingent of security guards, he stood on the sidewalk adjacent to the plaza, gauged wind speed and direction, and blew 15-foot diameter bubbles wafted by the breeze into the plaza. Within moments, L.A. police officers instructed Paul from the cabin of their cruiser to move on or face incarceration for loitering.

To the eyes of Mr. K., a major plaza's event director, the space under his jurisdiction does not suggest a bubble-sculptor's workshop. He offers a variety of reasons a bubbleman would be considered inappropriate. Soap bubbles breaking against 14th-story office windows might necessitate additional expenditures on window washing.

Figure 2. Bunker Hill, a great place for bubble blowing.

Soap bubble residue might cause a passer-by to slip, fall, and launch a personal injury lawsuit against plaza management. A bubbleman may draw attention away from midday events sanctioned by management, consisting largely of mainstream music performances. Most significantly, the unannounced appearance of bubbleman suggests a pass-the-hatter (which Paul sometimes is), just one notch above a pan handler and thus anathema to the image the plaza is intended to present to an upscale professional clientele.

These considerations accord with Mr. K.'s concern for modulating what management calls "user mix", the types of people occupying the plaza at any given moment. The ideal mix is considered to be Bunker Hill employees and residents, with a preponderance of the plaza area's 5,000 tenants preferred. Determination of whether any given individual fits this mix is left to plaza security and, according to guards, is made on the basis of overall appearance and behavior. While the masses of predominantly new immigrant Mexicans and Central Americans who frequent the commercial establishments downslope east of Bunker Hill, and reside across the Harbor Freeway to the west, are not actively excluded, plaza environs and events are seldom programmed to address these potential users or advertised to them. This may be attributable to management's belief that a sizable influx of lower income Mexicans and Central Americans would intimidate those business people who comprise the plaza's target market.

This well-maintained target market is appreciated by plaza retailers, who claim daily earnings of over $1,000 even during less well-attended weekend night events. Profits fluctuate minimally despite the economic tribulations of the late 1980s through early 1990s, as long-term leases have held corporate tenants on Bunker Hill. Further, discomfort with, and lack of, convenient access to the environs of the "down-scale" commercial areas adjacent have kept the hill's employee population a captive market.

From the viewpoint of the Bunker Hill businesspeople, staged events and user mixes are of little relevance. With the entire business community taking a simultaneous 45-minute lunch break, or less as "rightsizing" generates heavier work loads for the remaining staff, employees complain that by the time they emerge from line with their meals there is barely enough time to left to eat before sprinting back to the office. Despite this, there exists a consensus that it is nice to know Bunker Hill boasts landscaped plazas, even if there is insufficient time in the workday's schedule to loiter in them. One security guard believes that the mere presence of such greened places has a calming effect, even for those consistently denied passage over the property line.

Paul, however, remains less than calm when savoring the prospects Downtown's architecture and aerodynamics holds for his craft. Thus, under the occasional cover of a sufficiently humid night, Paul still straps on his utility belt and makes his way downtown to stealthily claim his stage atop Bunker Hill's summit.

A Skater's-eye View: the City as Playground

From deep within the bowels of Bunker Hill, Pablo, Juan, Julio and Bob come rumbling out of the Third Street tunnel. Confronted by a red light and a river of one-way traffic at Hill Street, they kick up the noses of their skateboards in unison and, tails scraping against the sidewalk, come to a dead stop inches from the curb. Dressed in Chinos and baggy knee-length shorts, T-shirts and tanktops emblazoned with skate team and band logos, visored caps askew on their heads, these four comprise the core of Mad Dog Skate. Mad Dog is one of a multitude of loosely constituted amateur skateboard teams. These teams, commonly formed of 13- to 18-year old Latinos (and, very occasionally, Latinas), inhabit the fringes of downtown. They come over the Harbor Freeway from their densely crowded apartments to the west, just past an expanse of dirt lots punctuated by crumbling concrete stairs and foundations. These derelict architectural remnants mark the lacuna of another "blighted" community, razed in the early 1980s for the now stalled development of a high-rise Central City West.

Mad Dog's staple skate turf is in the decrepit warehouse district fringing Little Tokyo, east of Bunker Hill and the old downtown. This area, hard-up against the increasingly disutilized rail yards adjacent to the concrete coated banks of the Los Angeles River, is designated an artists-in-residence district. Artistic presence, however, has been long stunted by the premature mass incursion of real estate speculators, and rents to match. Thus, the area is ripe with such skater's amenities as empty streets, open lots, loading ramps, wide curb cuts and – as continuing deindustrialization begets continual demolition – a fluid inventory of tilted concrete planes and exposed monolithic drainage culverts. Demolition sites make for problematic skating, however, as demo firms (particularly those following the Japanese model) have taken to pulverizing old concrete into mountains of recyclable sand. Sand is a skater's enemy: should it penetrate the inner workings of a skateboard's polymeric wheels, it quickly grinds precision ball bearings into nicked and scored paraboloids. Damaged equipment is no small concern, as a good composite deck with stainless trucks and high grade wheels can cost in excess of $100. Mad Dog does not have that kind of money (see Figure 3).

In time, Mad Dog hopes to enter formal competition with counterpart teams from as far away as the San Fernando Valley and the harbor town of San Pedro. For now, they practice. Even with practice, money is an issue. As with much else in Los Angeles, skating is fast becoming a two-tiered culture. A good competition skater can earn a position on a professional team or superstar status and concomitant product sponsorships, with potential for lines of signature clothing, equipment, videos and assorted merchandising tie-ins shortly thereafter. To attain this level of proficiency, however, a skater must practice relentlessly.

For children of affluent families, practice is relatively attainable. Those few private skate parks that have not closed out of liability concerns charge admission fees, and are located in the suburbs where lower built densities permit such extensive uses of space. Access to far-flung skate facilities and other skateable open spaces is facilitated by the two-parent, single wage earning family, commonly charging one parent with the rôle of chauffeur to younger teens. With a sufficiently large yard and cash outlay, these future champions can construct personal, professional quality obstacles like 11-foot tall, 36-foot long plywood halfpipes and bowls.

Those of Mad Dog's parents who are at present working work long hours at poorly recompensed jobs, earning minimum and sub-minimum wages. They are largely transit-dependent, thus precluding ready transport to and from skate parks.

Figure 3. Warehouse District: rails to nowhere.

They live in apartment buildings wedged onto small sites that leave no space for the installation of large obstacles, even if the required raw materials were affordable. So Mad Dog's members look to the streets and, in the process, have contributed to the evolution of a "street style" of skating.

Increasingly, street skating obstacles are built more of legalese than of wood and concrete. The profusion of "skate-boarding is not a crime" T-shirts and bumper stickers notwithstanding, skate-boarding redefined as trespass or pedestrian endangerment has earned two members of Mad Dog rides in Los Angeles Police Department (LAPD) patrol cars. This happened despite the fact that the incident of "pedestrian endangerment" occurred in a deserted light industrial district long after dusk. Ignoring the assertions of Mad Dog and similar skaters that they're not "jacking people up or using crack, just skating or sometimes tagging or downing some beer," civic authorities have been working at break-neck pace to criminalize skating outside the boundaries of distant and expensive private reserves. Public streets, sidewalks, parks and boardwalks are infested with the red circle-and-bar international symbol for "no", superimposed over a stylized skateboard. Infractions can merit fines, hours of community service and/or short sentences in juvenile detention facilities.

In response, street skaters have evolved into "pavement commandos", developing ever more aggressive hit-and-run tactics to claim the only space available to them, evade capture and, not incidentally, irritate authority. Foremost among Mad Dog's tactics is the late night "blitz" of Bunker Hill.

The hill is "prime 'crete", an agglomeration of low curbs, wide expanses of pavement, flights of gentle steps, and networks of handrails ideal for slides and grinds. The hill is rife with long handicap access ramps for picking up speed, and retaining walls that protrude from plaza surfaces out into open air as the hill falls away beneath. Mad Dog shreds this landscape hard, pummeling the pastel-tinted concrete, waggling their backsides in front of observation cameras and twisting high speed just beyond the reach of security guards. According to Pablo, those team members who come closest to physical contact with plaza security agents, without breaking pace, are accorded tremendous respect. This valorized tweaking of authority's nose, embodied in the persons of uniformed guards, is a particularly clear indication that the opportunities for serious play afforded by Bunker Hill go well beyond its topography (see figure 4).

In a ranking of plaza occupant desirability, Mr. K., the plaza event director, sees skaters as falling well beneath the homeless. Skaters, according to management's perspective, are "noisy", "disruptive", and engage in high velocity maneuvers that physically endanger "legitimate plaza users", again raising the specter of costly personal injury litigation. Most damning, though, is Mr. K.'s allegation

Figure 4. Bunker Hill, "prime 'crete."

that the skateboards' incursions "scar" architectonic surfaces, depositing dark rubber skid-marks across the plaza's face. Although such marks have usually proven impermanent, as Mr. K. sees it, outdoor fixtures and pavement finishes are not there to be transformed into skate-furniture. It is this view that necessitates the exclusion of Mad Dog's members, which further whets their appetites for repeatedly transforming Bunker Hill's plazas into playgrounds.

A Poet's-eye View: the City as Soapbox

With the final dismantling of L.A.'s legendary trolley system in the 1960s, the reappearance of relatively expensive fixed-rail mass transit (also known in local parlance as "serious" mass transit) was considered a utopian prospect. A Los Angeles subway, according to popular belief, was as improbable as the sudden demolition of the Berlin Wall. By the end of 1990, one of the last intact segments of the Berlin Wall was being installed for permanent exhibition immediately northeast of L.A., at Simi Valley's Ronald Reagan Presidential Library. Simultaneously, the L.A. Metro Blue Line light rail had entered service at a terminus buried deep beneath Bunker Hill's southern fringe. Two years later, this Blue Line was spliced onto a Red Line heavy rail subway. Emerging from a hub in the municipal government's Civic Center, the rail-cabs run adjacent to Bunker Hill and, predictably, dogleg around the old city center.

Sitting in one of these cabs, Guillermo's chin rests in his hand, bouncing against his palm in tempo with the train's rhythmic passage over rail cross-ties. A slight man in his early twenties, with slicked back black hair and a small jutting goatee, he sits packed into the train with a score of his associates. Together, they all concentrate on a young man who stands in the aisle while belting out poetry at the top of his lungs. The reader, Marlon, performs a piece composed specifically for this event, the third "impromptu" Blue Line open poetry reading in as many months. Gesticulating wildly, long hair flailing, Marlon employs verse to lambaste L.A.'s Cardinal Roger Mahony for traversing the city in a donated helicopter and then-Mayor Tom Bradley for traveling in a city limousine (a Town Car, in fact) while the common citizen is obliged to ride "the thin blue line":

> The line that the mayor says is the color of me and you. I wonder if he thinks it's the color of him, too? Will he ride, or will he drive? More than likely, he'll just fly while you and I draw big blue lines... streaks across the concrete streets. Take me home, take me home, on the blue line.

Marlon finishes to enthusiastic applause and takes his seat, as the audience chants for another reader. Every member of this audience writes poetry, and each will have read at least one composition by the time the train rounds Long Beach and returns the roughly 18 miles to downtown's Seventh Street "Metro Center" station. Nor is reading restricted to the poets. Occasionally, unsuspecting commuters are dragooned into the role of reader, good-naturedly cajoled into the aisle with a poem pressed into their hands.

Metro Rail's managing authority neither supports nor opposes these monthly poetry readings. This is largely due to the fact that the authority does not know about the readings. Guillermo and a few friends settle on a date and time for a reading in consultation with a Blue Line departure schedule, then pass word through friends and an informal poets' network de-centralized at various metropolitan area coffee houses.

These coffee houses serve as a pseudo-public analog for "living rooms" in neighborhoods where young, downwardly mobile, underemployed professionals (or dumpies) manage rent payments by doubling- and tripling-up in one- or two-bedroom apartments. Thus, with simultaneous rises in rents and declines in average earnings amongst the young, the coffee houses have swollen in number from two to dozens throughout the 1980s and 1990s. Some of them have long-standing presence, others have closed and occasionally reopened under different names and at various locations. Some offer complimentary screenings of rare films and homemade videos, others tabla and pipa players, yet others invite customers to draw on the walls. All but the Johnny-come-lately chain coffee boutiques permit the patron to linger indefinitely for the price of a cappuccino, and provide venues for uncensored and casually scheduled live performances that include poetry and storytelling.

Guillermo and his fellow instigators, however, prefer the train. They see mass transit as an ideal venue for taking live poetry to a broader audience beyond the coffee house "poetry ghetto". The train, Guillermo believes, is inherently exciting by virtue of being in motion. Further, it provides a captive audience, and is readily affordable with round trip tickets for the Blue Line costing just over $1.

The Los Angeles County Sheriffs, entrusted with Metro Rail security, occasionally stumble into the readings. Despite apparent suspicions that something is not right, however, they are unable to determine the precise nature of the infraction and are thus unable to enforce corrective penalties. The poets are careful to provide no excuse for police intervention. They refrain from drinking, smoking, or eating so much as a hard-candy, and keep their tickets with them throughout the trip. One sheriff, after commanding a reader to "keep it down", turns to his partner and comments that he lacks the authority to punish a passenger for public speaking.

"Decent" poetry, Marlon asserts (without engaging the question of how such decency is determined), is immune to suppression in any society with pretensions to civility. As he sees it, this is because the spoken word as artform may "twist the mind", but is incapable of damaging property or "breaking bones". The trouble-free experiences of the Blue Line poets support Marlon's observation, indicating that the reading of poetry, decent or otherwise, does not pose a clear-and-present enough threat to provoke official proscription. Thus, the mass transit readings have continued and proliferated, temporarily refashioning subway cars into soapboxes from whence poets launch aural assaults on commuters and convention alike.

Theory is Good, but . . .

Mike sits hunched on an island of concrete at the furthest southern boundary of downtown, his back pressed against one of the US Interstate 10's massive support columns. Before him is a broad sheet of white paper perched atop a portable stand. At first glance, it might easily be assumed that Mike is one of the city's innumerable (and ill-numerated) homeless. First glances, however, can deceive. Mike's sign is not boldly handlettered to read "WILL WORK FOR FOOD" or, in keeping with more recent trends, "WHY LIE, I NEED A BEER". Rather, its outer face is blank, its obverse printed with bars of musical notation. And Mike's hunching is less a product of hard living than it is an accommodation to the tenor saxophone cradled between his legs. He serenades lanes of traffic to either side, packed with late afternoon commuters vacating the CBD.

Mike asserts that he has explored a variety of practice locations, but found each one problematic. Neighbors vociferously objected to his practicing off the balcony of his apartment. Attempts to play late at night in a nearby parking garage attracted a modest audience of LAPD patrol officers with guns at the ready. Amidst the traffic, however, nobody objects. While the site is not the quietest for his purpose, the ambient noise is well made up for by the resonance of the freeway's underside. Further, the site affords opportunities to riff off fragments of music emanating from the stereos of automobiles queued for the adjacent on-ramp. While these "freeway gigs" were originally an accommodation to resource limitations, Mike has come to cherish how his performances gently startle motorists. In so doing, Mike believes he creates a brief interpersonal connection that "makes life worth living" in a city where spatial diffusion often engenders social alienation.

Mike's efforts to claim a space for himself in the face of systemic neglect and even opposition, like similar efforts by Paul the Bubbleman, the personnel of Mad Dog Skate and the Blue Line poets, could be read as signifying nothing more than the poignant melancholy commonly attendant upon lost causes. More extremely, it could be suggested that to celebrate such ephemeral spatialized tactics of rebellion is to fall prey to a demobilizing romance with the flashy, frivolous, and ultimately futile, while the city at large proceeds with the business of crushing its citizenry en masse. It could be argued that the activities I have narrated show no clearly articulated opposition to (or even consciousness of) capitalism, patriarchy, or hegemonic metanarratives, entail no apparent attempt at mass organization, and certainly do not indicate any sort of revolutionary vanguard. Underpinning such interpretations, however, is the assumption that small deviations average out over time. And, at least in the case of Los Angeles, there is evidence to suggest that such an assumption is mistaken.

The practices I have documented are inarguably those of relatively eccentric individuals and small groups who are engaged primarily in expressing themselves through activities they enjoy. As such, they are engaged not in "serious" oppositional endeavors. Rather, they are engaged in play. Seen in relation to a downtown comprised increasingly of tightly restricted quasi-public spaces, however, this persistent and highly visible play becomes a stark refusal to disappear beneath the imperatives of spatial regulation that favors select target markets. In this refusal to disappear is an insistence on a right to claim, and remake, portions of the city. And in the playing, this right is not merely asserted. It is acted upon in creative and highly visible ways.

Forms of resistance need not be overtly serious, a fact alluded to by Marlon's observation of poetry's relative invulnerability to suppression. Conventional forms of protest in downtown L.A. would draw, and have drawn, a quick response from helicopter-backed riot police. But the playfulness (and even outright absurdity) of bubble-blowing, skating, poetry reading or a saxophone serenade in the face of

Figure 5.   Old Downtown and new watcher.

official censure ensures that attempts to forcibly curtail these activities will ultimately recast authority as an ill-tempered curmudgeon, entailing a loss of face and a corollary degradation of legitimacy. Thus, such resistances are ideally suited to persist, propagate and, eventually, bring about degrees of officially sanctioned coexistence (see Figure 5).

By way of example, the near-criminalization of skateboarding, and the subsequent radicalization of street skaters into pavement commandos, has impelled innumerable skaters to coordinate effective agitation for a right to skate free. Their efforts, carried out in person and across the internet, have to date resulted in the construction of numerous municipal skate parks nationwide, including three in the traditionally working-class, L.A.-adjacent city of Huntington Beach (RC's Skate Shop). L.A.'s buskers have witnessed analogous successes. They have gone beyond simply asserting their presence, and are now central players in creating self-management policies. These policies have successfully secured freely accessible street entertainment venues throughout such open-air pedestrian and shopping areas as Third Street Promenade in Santa Monica, Colorado Boulevard in Pasadena, and Venice Beach

Boardwalk. Similarly, local poets have formed alliances like Hyperpoets which, in conjunction with shoe-string-budget cultural institutions, secure both funding and venues in L.A.'s streets, store windows, and parks. Even Mr. K.'s plaza itself is now the occasional site of edgy after-hours performances that combine poetry with dance and multimedia technologies. Thus, the "soft cities" of the bubbleman, the skater, and the poet establish themselves within the "hard city" of pavement and office-towers, of the real estate financiers and the traffic planners. Subways are trans-formed into soapboxes, plazas viscerally reconstituted as playgrounds, and places of commerce become stages for the display of soap bubble confectionery.

These proliferating, concrete impacts of "soft cities" upon the "hard" suggest that no matter how restrictively space is programmed, no matter how many "armed response" security patrols roam the streets, and no matter how many video cameras keep watch over the plazas, there remain blindspots that await, and even invite, inhabitation by unforeseen and potent alternative practices. Even in a totally rebuilt and totalizing environment like Bunker Hill, panopticism fails. This failure enables resistances to persist and even make themselves at home. The inevitable selectivity and positionality of any surveillant eye's view entails the simultaneous production of blindspots harboring spaces that must remain less well attended to. In Mike's words, "So long as there's a space nobody's paying attention to, I've got a place to play".

As with the material fabric of the city, similarly, there exists no privileged vantage point from which to attain panopticity in representations of the city. Attempts to describe the urban condition exhibit a taste for the "hard" stuff, downplaying the "soft" for the sakes of parsimony and generalizability. As a result, comprehensive visions of the city are advanced that unwittingly await, and even invite, undermining by contradictorily divergent realities that are presumed too insignificant, intimate, eccentric, or mundane to warrant attention.

While what we look for is what we get, this in no way prevents what we did not think to look for from finding ways to exist, thrive, and make its presence felt. Differences persist, despite being unaccounted for in overarching narratives of the city. We ignore this at our peril, and to the extreme detriment of our conceptions of, and discourse about, the city.

REFERENCES

Flusty, S (1994) Building Paranoia: The Proliferation of Interdictory Space and the Erosion of Spatial Justice. Los Angeles Forum for Architecture and Urban Design, West Hollywood, CA.

Metropolitan Structures. California Plaza (Promotional Brochure). Undated.

30 Elvis in Zanzibar

Ahmed Gurnah

"Space," to quote Douglas Adams, "is big. Really big." Big enough to hold a wide array of languages, pictures, beliefs, foods, songs, stories, and cultural materiel from which our selves are assembled. Of course, the spatial embeddedness of bodies ensures that selves can be comprised only of limited subsets of cultural materiel, usually those that by reason of proximity happen to fall within our experiential reach. Still, the selection of materiel that remains within reach is quite varied indeed. And if one defining characteristic of the postmodern condition is the compression of space and time, then our reach is presumably increasing. With so extensive a menu of possible ingredients, how do we choose what to include in our selves? And how do we combine the selected ingredients into constellations that can be personally fulfilling and collectively coherent? Ahmed Gurnah approaches these questions by considering the formative influences upon his own youth. His answers are particularly exciting because they stand much thinking about cultural formation on its head. Gurnah does not present his autobiography as mere anecdote, to be absorbed into some overarching theoretical explanation of cultural formation. Instead, he uses his experiences as a lens through which to *emplace* culture discursively and in space, thus providing a touchstone to evaluate theories of cultural formation, and a framework to open-endedly synthesize them. Through this focus on self as both an absorber and shaper of culture, Gurnah makes clear that selves and cultures are as much the products of individual interest, personal enjoyment, self-empowerment, and the happenstance of geography, as they are the results of any overarching sociostructural logic.

Tales from Malindi

Growing up in Zanzibar in the 1950s, I was lucky from the outset to experience international culture. Zanzibar Town was then a cosmopolitan urban *entrée-port*, which for several centuries handled trade between the Mid and Far East and the eastern seaboard of Africa. From Zanzibar bazaars the smells of cloves, chillies, shark fins, perfume and red piping hot halwa, transported one through the Orient. In the nineteenth century, Sultan Said partially ruled along most of the Indian Ocean coast from Oman to Mozambique and traded with people on the coastal settlements between the two. This "merchant prince" chose Zanzibar as the seat of his government, where several great cultures routinely mixed and exchanged goods and ways of living. If for now we leave aside how it was possible for these cultures to mix, the depth of our core learning experience in the 1950s was, therefore, shaped by African and Arabic cultures, and articulated by Indian, Western and Chinese cultures.

The first sounds I wriggled to as a toddler I heard on Radio Cairo. Every local café tuned into Arabic love songs by Mohammed Abdul-Wahab and Farid El-Atrash before evening prayers. As cups of strong and bitter Arabic coffee were consumed, these singers eulogized about the moon's ability to mend their broken hearts or rescue them from drowning in their own bitter tears. Sometimes men at the cafés became sufficiently moved by a particular taunting phrase to interrupt their game of dominoes or a political controversy, assume a love-pained expression and sing along with the love-bitten poet. In extreme cases, serious men disrespectfully – but maybe not intentionally – articulated their Quranic Stanza with an odd lunar phrase. Women had their sessions too, which included a little dancing, but as a nosy little boy I was dispatched on harmless errands out of the way, and I never suspected the truth.

There was no "bookish" tradition of music in Zanzibar; sound, meaning and performance were the main ways people related to it. In this atmosphere at the age of 6 or 7 I learnt to sing Kiswahili *taarab*; though my immaturity allowed me only a partial understanding of the innuendo and fierce but highly amusing war of words hidden in the lyric of competing music clubs or writers.

As a 9-year-old in the mid-1950s, I stumbled over Harry Belafonte's version of calypso. My older cousin who wanted to go and study in Trinidad bought a record player on which we ceaselessly played and danced to "Hold 'Em Joe". Around the house were also records of the mellifluous Latin bands for Hollywood of Xavier Cugat playing such waist twisters as "Mambo Jumbo", "Linda Mujer", "The Peanut Vendor" and "Mambo Negro". Rock and roll followed OK Jazz and other "Congolese" and Kenyan bands. Elvis was king in our household in Malindi (or was it Sir Cliff?) as much as he was in Iowa or Liverpool. My brother later reneged to the Rolling Stones; unbelievable. In my late teens I listened to American jazz, especially Satchmo, and a little swing, but mercifully held out against Bing Crosby; but at no time was even he "foreign". The grandson of a deposed Sultan three houses away (still in waiting for the British to allow him to resume his crown) used to sing along with Bing. We used to accompany him loudly in distorted voices, which rather provoked him into drunken abuse about us and our whole lineage.

Architecture in Zanzibar Town itself is a testimony to that cultural confluence. There were buildings of Mediterranean Arabic styles in the Stonehouse area, African bungalows in N'gambo, Anglo-Indian hybrids in official buildings and mystical Eastern courtyards for the wealthy. Historical buildings in different states of repair include Arabic, Portuguese and British fortifications from the seventeenth to the nineteenth century.

Not counting the colonial government mobile cinema showing Pathé News and the Three Stooges, I saw the big screen for the first time in 1954 at the age of 7.

Delmer Daves' liberal reinterpretation of Cochise in *Broken Arrow* only left me confused about the routine racist treatment of "Red Indians" and interrupted my sleep for months afterwards. After that I caught many glimpses of other cultures through Indian and Egyptian cinema and Hollywood. We went to the Sunday matinée at *Cine Afrique* or *Majestic* for "one shilling all round"; when we could sit for the same price even in the exclusive boxes usually occupied by the select: the rich, the aristocrats and Europeans. English cinema was largely restricted to our huge appreciation of Terry Thomas, whom everybody inexplicably and immovably believed to be "typically British".

My knowledge of Shakespeare, eighteenth- and nineteenth-century English literature and Enid Blyton grew with my familiarity with the library of our English-speaking King George VI School. Mao Tse Tung, Franz Fanon, Che Guevara and Khame Nkuruma did not feature much here, but became essential reading once the anticolonial/nationalist movement got going. I was introduced to Peter Abrahams, Chinua Achebe, V. S. Naipaul and Raymond Chandler not by my white British teachers, but by a returning Zanzibari student. Of course, long before I engaged with this "English" literature in secondary school, I had been learning Kiswahili sayings, Arabic and the Quran. Our appreciation of Islamic literature, theology and culture was organic and considerable.

Our ability to read these and other literatures in the original is the proof of the competence of many Zanzibaris in English and Arabic, in addition to Kiswahili. In some communities, people also spoke and read Hindi and Urdu. The sense of linguistic plurality was periodically increased by visits of Somali and other African traders and workers who came to Zanzibar during the monsoons for seasonal employment and trade.

This sense of linguistic plurality was topped only by the variety of cuisine easily available on the streets, in cafés and in small shops. It was possible routinely to eat Indian or Arabic food, African – local or from the mainland – or Chinese food. Indian Ocean trade brought in goods from up the coast and from the Mediterranean and the Far East.

Curiously at this time, however, I devoured the British literary material as I have never done since. The latest fashions were in our living rooms only a few months behind London. *Romeo* kept us informed about Eden Kane or Brenda Lee's hairdo, *Valentine* about Ricky Nelson or Bobby Vee. This *was* the stuff of globalization, as significant as the adoption of communism or science. Daniel Bell would have been proud of us: the American dream travelled safely through Liverpool to the tropics. The European teachers in my school in Zanzibar were not so sure. Pleased about the "modernization" (Westernization), they were rather alarmed by our voracious consumption of the rebellious pop and youth culture, particularly when juxtaposed to our growing nationalist views. I guess they must have felt rather like Deborah Kerr did in *The King and I*, when she was seeking to transform a "native boy" (the king) into a colonial parody. Our teachers probably viewed our enthusiasm for rock and roll as part of their "burden".

Equally alarmed were the politicized older Zanzibari folk stuffing snout up their noses. They shuddered in disbelief at the sight of our stiff and curly hair sculptured into teddy styles, but not so very silently. They were equally mystified by our imitations of Yul Bryner (arm extended) saying, "etc., etc., etc." or Marlon Brando nasally muttering "You scum-sucking pig" from *One Eyed Jacks*. Viewing us as spoilt brats seduced by foreign (Western) glitter, they loudly prayed to the amusement of the whole neighbourhood that our deviation from our organic culture was only temporary. A sentiment which no doubt increased their hostility to living under colonialism and strengthened their nationalist resolve. On a visit back to Zanzibar in 1994, dressed and perfumed like an Arab Sheikh, one of these old folks, not having seen me for thirty odd years, sidled up to me at a funeral and checked if I had eventually returned to my culture! They were not so worried about Egyptian or Indian "foreign" cultures because they shared them. Some did later turn against these too as the nationalist struggle hotted up.

I was always in trouble with our copper-moustachioed Welsh headteacher for wearing tan terylene "drain pipes" instead of the stipulated large khaki shorts which he too sported, along with brown leather shoes, woolen leggings and a ribbon! I was on firmer ground here. As a Muslim adult I could legitimately count on common sense and my long suffering parents' support for the need to cover my knees; as it were, cultural manipulation for personal liberty.

The question here is, how was all this possible? It would seem odd that little African girls and boys should get so excited and involved with the image of Elvis in the way we did; yet, from this description it was the most natural thing in the world for us to do. My problems increase if you reject, as I do, essentialist explanations of human communication put forward by Kant, Lévi-Strauss and Habermas (see Gurnah and Scott 1992). Clearly African children in the 1950s were able to acquire other cultures from a very wide range of sources – some old standing and some new. But by what mechanisms were they able to do this? How do we explain the fascination and alienation of our traveller to Morocco? Pointing at colonial influence and imperialism or at the power of popular culture is not sufficient. For that only describes the political background within which all of this takes place and the fact that it happens widely, but does not identify the sociological processes which enable or incline Africans to acquire and later also express effectively through such "foreign" cultures or why these processes succeed at all.

Internationalism or Misspent Youth?

What this proves is that there is a sophisticated selection process going on that brings about intercultural exchange and influences and that cultures around the world are much more open-ended and complex than politicized or functionalist accounts might imply. This also shows that while identifying "communal", "group" or "national" culture, we cannot ignore the individual cultural modalities. My teachers and the old folk in Zanzibar could not both be right. For if we were parodists, culturally we were still Zanzibaris. But if Westernized, we were no longer parodying. In fact, the foreign experiences – Egyptian, Western, Caribbean, Yemeni, Omani, Indian – were all partial, but never superficial: they rarely replaced our organic culture, but they also significantly contributed to our developing world view. I got into fights equally to defend my father's honour, as I did to proclaim Elvis supreme. This is the point. In fact "foreign" contact with our culture was formative and transformative and somehow real to our organic experience. Foreigners must have had substantive communicative devices, and counted upon and found a translation route with which to engage with our understanding. This is a rather different form of explanation from those offered by either diffusionist or cultural imperialist theorists. But why did this cultural contact happen?

It is also obvious that engagement with trivial teenage culture did not drive us away from our communities, then or later. Quite the contrary, it offered us a looking-glass through which we viewed those cultures more closely and compared them to our own. It is doubtful in any case that our sculptured teddy hairdos meant the same thing to us or were even the same act as when a white Manchester lad or Eden Kane did it. Most likely, once past the trivia, engagement with "foreign" cultures introduced us to arguments and literature that we later used to explore further and defend those distinctive and valuable aspects of our organic culture while learning from other cultures in the same way as it had complicated lives of prominent people like Fanon or Cabral. It gave us the language with which to promote those elements in our culture we recognized as unique because we compared them and focused on what was enduring about them and against imperialism. We partly absorbed or "indigenized" (Appadurai 1990: 295) this foreign culture because instinctively and experientially we knew this. However, once absorbed, aspects of the processed "foreign" cultures became ours, as much as they once were located elsewhere. Indeed despite my sculptured hairdo, I followed my mother around to anticolonial meetings (and picnics). But the teachers and the old folk failed to recognize the existence of a generational divide or the need to cope with new challenges and times, which demanded new engagements.

Using Ien Ang (1985) and Katz and Tamar (1985), Tomlinson (1991) underlines this paradoxical thinking by questioning the argument that the American media exploit and manipulate audiences. Watching *Dallas*, Arabs confirmed rather than abandoned their conventional views (1991: 48), a Moroccan Jew rejected Western decadence (1991: 49) and the material obviated underlying universal values. From which Tomlinson concludes that audiences are more active, critical, complex and responsive than media theorists think:

> their cultural values more resistant to manipulation and "invasion"... [with] a gap between how people rehearse their views of a text in public... and how they might "live" that experience of that text in the undisturbed and unmonitored flow of mundane existence.
>
> (1991: 49–50)

But this does not quite clinch it. Young Zanzibaris did more than "watch" European cultural icons and products, which in fact transformed their lives. They used them like so much change in their pockets to purchase extra excitement and power and maybe also like all other teenagers, to get up their parents' noses a little. Indeed, many people who watched *Dallas* were sufficiently influenced by it to copy its style in clothes. I think it would actually be fair to say that European culture profoundly affected my life and influenced my tastes. The point is, what does that actually mean? Furthermore, cannot the same now be said of young people in Britain with regard to African culture?

The tongue-in-cheek account and Tomlinson's comments raise important issues about the globalization of culture. Clearly the prima-facie evidence from our tale implies culture is exported. The point, however, is how can culture export be explained in terms of context, sharing of meaning, recovery of meaning and the internationalization of culture; how can we, in short, explain the pedagogic and formative properties of culture? (See also Giroux and McLauren 1994; Moharty 1994; and Gurnah, forthcoming.) Indeed, how do we explain cultural nationalism and imperialism in this context?

The fundamental tension in contemporary discussions about these problems lies between those who view the acquisition of a "foreign" culture as beneficial when shared "naturally" and willingly, and those who are watching out for bewitchment and domination. There is much literature under the banner of "modernization" and "popular culture" which fits in the first category (Gellner 1964; Tomlinson 1991), while the second category begins from the assumption that the introduction of foreign culture can only be achieved through manipulation, market penetration and imperial domination (de Kadt and Williams 1974; Nelson and Grossberg 1988). Culture here is used cynically by the powerful to reinforce and impose personal and class, national and imperial interest on other people, so they can exploit them economically and politically. The tension between the two positions probably represents the analytical separation of parallel processes, both of which are likely to happen concurrently, in sympathy, or in opposition.

While these are parallel and continuous processes tied together in a tense and complex relationship, they cannot be the only means of explaining the export of culture: the example of the young Zanzibari boy I described points to other possibilities. The export and import of culture cannot uncomplicatedly depend on "exchange" or "sharing", "domination" or "imperialism". Both sets of processes presume for their possibility, the pre-existence of profound social, cultural and especially linguistic common denominators, what Wittgenstein refers to as "finding one's feet with" (1953: 263), which can hardly be claimed to have existed in any significant way in the 1950s between the Indian Ocean and Anglo-American countries. Clearly, 400 years of colonization have left their mark on world relations (Frank 1969). But for these common denominators to drive this exchange or cultural imperialism they need to be deep and all consuming – they also need to be continuous and fragmented throughout the said culture and very difficult to isolate and remove by analytical surgery.

The third explanatory possibility must address the *nature* of the exchange itself and not concentrate simply on the agents or pressures which bring it about. We must also examine the *working* of that exchange both from the point of view of the subject – whether it is an individual or a group – and *how* that exchange affects subjective cultural modalities.

What made young Zanzibaris vulnerable to and participants in foreign cultures was, of course, partly the educational and commercial exposure they received from European tutors and partly the rationale of the colonial infrastructure and the glitz of dominant ideologies and lifestyles. But all could have been resisted and aspects were readily rejected by close adherence to local social life, especially in the heated nationalist context of Africa in the 1950s. What in my view made African people engage so enthusiastically with selected "imperialist" and other cultures, was an active desire to *construct* particular current and powerful cultural common denominators with the West and elsewhere. In our case, we were motivated to develop and be part of the young people's global culture. Taking an example from music and young culture, the phenomenon started emerging in a really big way in the 1950s with Frank Sinatra, Marlon Brando and the Everly Brothers and took off with Elvis, the Beatles, Jim Reeves and Ray Charles. The next question then is, why did Africans choose to be part of this global culture and so passionately love – of all people – Jim Reeves? In order to be "modernized"? Hardly.

Background to a Culture-Complex

Five considerations immediately spring to mind regarding the problem in Zanzibar. First, the commercialization and therefore internationalization of regional music through the radio – calypso or rhythm and blues or Congo jazz – and culture, in the 1950s and 1960s, and cheaper technology, which made access to them easier all round the world. With this appeared young people's assumptions that it was a "hoot" to imitate the "beautiful people"; so we did! Second, led by Ghana in 1957, many African countries gained their independence then or soon after. The experience of mounting campaigns and winning elections and/or armed struggles was immeasurably significant in the development of this African self-confidence. It increased people's willingness and desire to explore other cultures themselves, and not just accidentally bump into them. Third, many young people from the Third World were becoming highly politicized at a very early age and were motivated to seek better knowledge of imperialists and to learn arguments that contended against their ideologies, especially from radicals and those who were colonized themselves. The youth rebellions in imperialist countries were both amusing and appealing to them. Many sought, found and used effectively their political alliances with radical metropolitan intellectuals. Fourth, increased immigration to London, Paris and New York by young people from the colonies and ex-colonies increased their familiarity of the imperialist, but their presence there equally had a profound cultural and social impact on Western countries, which inclined young Third World intellectuals to absorb more from the West. Fifth, and most importantly, the politicized African middle classes and workers actively sought to create a knowledge-bridge and technology transfer from the West, in the belief that this would also bring them more excitement, wealth and political power. But they also worked just as hard to create effective barriers against Western economic and political exploitation. It proved to be a hopeless economic and political defence strategy, but a very powerful and productive cultural fusion. In short, they sought cultural exchange to enhance their lives, which was hardly the same as the search for "modernization" or "modernity" with its built-in evolutionary hierarchy. These factors together stimulated a powerful dynamic that enabled people to construct a new culture-complex with approaches that cannot be explained by diffusionist or imperialist models.

A foreign culture in this context is neither taken at face value nor mindlessly imposed. The processes that make up this culture-complex squeeze it for benefits, sieve it for relevance and partly reconstitute it before absorbing it. Geertz, dealing with very similar issues, talks of "control mechanisms – plans, recipes, rules, instructions (what computer engineers call 'programs') – for the governing of behaviour... [man is] most desperately dependent upon such extragenetic, outside-the-skin control mechanisms, such cultural programs, for ordering his behaviour" (1973: 44) and notes: "undirected by culture patterns – organized systems of significant symbols – man's behaviour would be virtually ungovernable, a mere chaos of pointless acts and exploding emotions, his experience virtually shapeless" (46) and people "would be unworkable monstrosities with very few useful instincts, fewer sentiments, and no intellect: mental basket cases" (49).

I shall return to this idea later when I discuss culture-complex in greater detail. For now I would simply point out that Geertz's "control mechanisms" fail to explain even what he is describing, which is dynamic and constantly moving.

The integration of a foreign Western culture into the body culture of the importing African communities, therefore, involves the reconstruction of the former, for in such an exchange there is an expectation that concessions have to be made by the exporting cultures too.

A political example from the 1950s and 1960s will clarify the point. The powerful impact of Western communism significantly transformed most Third World cultures and political ideas and institutions, regardless of whether they aspired to socialism or capitalism. Third World radical reformation of these ideas into "the Long March", "the Cultural Revolution", "Guerrilla Wars", "Ujamaa Villages and African Socialism" and so on, transformed Marx's and Engels' original ideas out of recognition, not least because these new ideas reflected much more the working of Chinese or Cuban or Tanzanian struggles and not nineteenth-century European working-class ones. And yet, powerfully though Marx's and Engels' influence on Third World people had been, the writings and thought of Mao Tse Tung, Ho Chi Minh, Fidel Castro, Che Guevara, Franz Fanon and Julius Nyerere too colonized the minds of young socialists and liberals in the West (and in the Third World); some adhered to the original just as strongly as the developments. The absorption of these new ideas by the thinking and seeking young intellectuals in Britain, France, Italy, Germany and the USA, made it possible for Third World intellectuals then to accept more ideas from Western communists.

These comments must not be taken to mean that there were not attempts by colonial governments or the USA to *impose* cultural (as well as economic and political) systems. Nor do I want to leave the impression that Africans did not parody Westerners in unhelpful ways which undermined emancipatory efforts of others. The point is, first, there is a tendency to read trivial parody into profound influences, such as sculptured hairdos or woollen socks in the tropics. Second, we must always try and remember that despite the colonial and imperial agenda, force and complete cynicism, African nationalists have wrestled considerable political and some economic freedom from colonial and resident white settlers and their agents. These comments, therefore, are not meant to make light of colonial/imperialist determination to continue to exploit and dominate. Rather, they are meant to point out what is too easily forgotten in radical rhetoric, that Africans were neither simply passively taking it all nor being influenced from a status of a deficit culture. The organic African cultures were and are as powerful as any others and as capable of selection and absorption as easily as they were of rejection. I shall return to some of these issues later.

In short, in the process of influencing other cultures, exporting cultures too make themselves comprehensible in order to *be understood*. Their signs and symbols become transparent, explicit and *charged*, to *read* and couple with those they aim to influence. Failure to do both reduces their ability immediately to connect with and influence the importer. But for the exporter to be more transparent the exporter also has to import ideas and thus understand the needs of importers. Unless the exporter also imports, the lines of communication dry up. Paradoxically, because good communication tends to be two-way it also in this case deletes the very *directional* distinction between importer and exporter. This is the fascinating context in which lie the processes of globalization and I hope my argument. And it is this aspect which diffusionist and cultural imperialist arguments neglect. Cultural stock inherited from parents, previous contacts, new contacts, all offer the *conductivity* for the development of an appropriate culture-complex. Of course the power carrying capacity of this new culture-complex signals both hope and danger. Individual or group cultural "recklessness" may lead to new findings, but it is also likely to trigger in other communities the need for caution and conservatism. The processes therein, which help to create new cultures, work in a continual paradoxical nexus: hermeneutic and educative, reassuring and challenging, at the same time familial and community developmental. But in the same way as Wittgenstein's "language games" do not, there is no reason to believe that these processes lead to "sameness" or cloning. Changing patterns in different cultures can *never* reproduce each other, for they are made up of different cultural raw materials forged in variant histories.

My description is not meant to replace the diffusionist and cultural imperialist explanations, but significantly to add to them. It does, however, emphasize aspects other than the viewing of culture as "custom" – something to be followed or passed on mindlessly – or as a symbolic given – a gift from nowhere – that we merely seek to interpret. It recognizes that an appropriation of own or other cultures is an active and intellectually intensive and demanding exercise which mobilizes rational and sensual faculties, always. But more importantly, our approach helps to explain *how* culture is in fact exported and "absorbed" and what motivates that in terms other than greed and trend. It calls for a *sociological* and *analytical* level of explanation, to what was previously mainly a descriptive (diffusionist) or political economic (cultural imperialist) explanation for globalization. [...]

The Culture-Complex

Culture is a repository of symbolic forms and social and individual experiences. It is the medium for personal, interpersonal and group exchange, expression and reception of ideas. Its mesh ties together personal ambitions and desires to a legitimate moral order and political action, authority and the economic system. Through culture, people create moral and epistemic parameters to control, yes, but also enhance their social and personal lives, in a way they can come close to and accept them as their own. It is a medium for the construction of meaning in those lives and a channel for transmitting and exchanging that meaning and knowledge – it is a "form of life", yes, but also a process for creating new lives and meanings and cultures. The culture-complex is the means for exchange, education and change. It is in this sense that it differs from Geertz's computer program, which is about control, not freeing of energy and creativity. I suspect Geertz would not disagree with this; his description of people's development attests to that (1973: 47–8). It is just that his nomenclature is out of step with those views.

When symbols representing individual and group experiences re-emerge or are imported from other cultures for our use and communication, they are always "screened" by us before reuse. To be *people* means precisely that every day, everyone of us, even the most confused and least informed amongst us, *never* accepts any representations, not even those constructed by ourselves, simply as naive copies of "reality" or as evidence of settled and agreed symbolic interactions without first personally screening them, regardless of whether we get it right or what we actually say theoretically. In this sense, to be a person is to be cultured. To be cultured is to stop playing a passive role in nature, or remain a cog in a regulated social machine. It is instead to be an active contributor in social interaction, change and development and to play a keen, active and integral part in social development, nature or in some of its parts. If there is a characteristic which is universally human then it is this need to check before use. Indeed, it is common to encounter non-professionals grappling with and forcefully forwarding *their* explanations for complex social and political events and representations. It makes no difference really whether their analysis is right or wrong to the reaffirmation of their humanity, that is confirmed by their participation in social life and their unwillingness to take anything for granted. This learning merely gives them tools to do it better – maybe. The idea of culture-complex provides the mechanism for this intellectual "testing", and "squeezing", this screening and selection process.

As I see it, the sole and integrative task of this culture-complex after selection is *to construct common cultural denominators within and between cultures.* [...]

So what is this culture-complex? It is a group of processes all of which motivate and cajole us to work with processes which screen, order, sieve, select and activate signs and symbols so that we make cultural encounters productive, meaningful and therefore possible. These processes are of cultural games, cultural recovery, cultural contrasting, cultural exchange, and cultural pedagogy and developments. Metaphorically speaking, these processes act through the concepts and cultural icons in such a way that later they may act rather like charged electrons in a chemical reaction. The "charge" then enables exchange between two or more fairly "stable" cultures when they make contact or "touch" each other. That is to say the charging processes – which are always there in every culture – stimulate communication between cultures by "energizing" their symbols and signs and "sensitize" their users to inter-action. Put prosaically, the contact raises people's curiosity to examine closely each other's mores and cultural products. The curiosity locks the people of the two cultures close together, encourages them to dig out permanent tunnels of communication between them, so that they can test and share each other's meanings, words, language and juxtapose their myths and histories. In short, this culture-complex makes it possible for cultural *common denominators to be constructed between cultures* by following specific rules.

But what stimulates the appearance of this cultural "charge" to energize cultural representations in encounters and ensure that all cultures involved are working from the same assumptions? Where do these processes in fact come from? I think the answer to the first question has to be that each instance is shaped by different stimuli which can only be isolated *a posteriori* through analysis similar to what we observed in the context of Africa. In that context I suggested there were at least five different reasons for the development of the stimuli, most of which were connected with change and a desire for a better life. If that is how the charge appears, what about the processes? I believe them to be implicit and practically immanent to an honest effort to create communication channels, but let me hasten to add there is nothing transcendental about them. And while better quality communications improves exchange, contra Habermas, there are no guarantees of emancipation here, though when that is induced it is always welcome.

Thus the acquisition of culture, even within one's own community, is neither a straightforward act of imitation, nor is it, as some will have it regarding language, merely a matter of training and usage. Training, usage and imitation are important aspects in the development of language and these are common denominators, especially at the beginning of the process. But more importantly, the acquisition of culture becomes possible when the culture-complex also comes into play. Following the stimulus, the culture-complex enables individuals and groups to play an active, forceful and permanent role in the continual construction of the common denominators, as an aspect of their routine participation in *any* cultural activities or framework.

The drive to construct these denominators comes from the impassioned human curiosity and obsession to experience and make sense and meaning, and maybe when people are in search of a little fun too. It is also to do with the character of aesthetic rationality (Gurnah and Scott 1992, ch. 6) and the implicit nature of the communication process itself, as Habermas would put it, truthfulness is implied in validity claims (1984). This said, however, it is precisely because the culture-complex can never work in a natural environment that we need to keep using it to get back to something like a "fairer" or less interest-bound interpretation of reality. In other words, though the culture-complex results from the sociological context, human curiosity and the process of communication, it is not due to some spontaneity – it is an active political act and interest-bound too.

"Cultural Games" and Rules for Cultural Common Denominators

As I envisage them, "cultural games", like language games, make exchange possible. They create movement in the system and make it possible for people to use their cultural products and experiences to specify their meaning as they relate and change their placement in different parts of the system or as they take up cultural products and experiences of new partners. Meaning emerges at each point of a continuous social movement: each point of interaction can be frozen into an image of the system's kaleidoscope in space and time, as it tumbles round to create new images and meanings.

Cultural games

In his later philosophy Wittgenstein suggests a device for viewing the status of language and its acquisition, which here I shall blend with the work of Lévi-Strauss to make sense of the process of cultural acquisition. Wittgenstein identifies the not unproblematic but still highly productive notion of language games to show how people acquire language and communicate. For him words are meaningful in their use in a social context where they become part of a language game (Kenny 1973: 14). They assume shared meaning and trigger people to recall their previous experiences. Thus, words and their behavioural surround make up language games. Thus by placing language games within the forms of life he sets up an internal association between linguistic competence, sociability and communication. Indeed, much of what Wittgenstein claims about language already has a respectable pedigree in sociology and anthropology (Nisbet 1976: x) and increases our understanding of how cultures work and how people use them to interrelate. But what Wittgenstein particularly offers me in this work is an analogy for viewing cultural acquisition and use in terms of cultural games. Here cultural practice and products too are internally linked to human association and cognition. Signs and symbols represent community meanings and values in a complex network that offers individuals the medium for self-expression and self-realization and, of course, self-correction and improvement.

For Wittgenstein, language is about *signs* and *symbols* learnt not only intellectually, but also through use (1975). Culture being symbolic too, I would argue, its use constitutes the social fabric and evidence for social analysis. For Durkheim (1995 [1912]) the study of religion (and therefore of culture) is not about internal and external *things*, but "rather, in what it does for the believer in his relation to the world, society and self" (Nisbet 1976: ix). Cassirer (1953, 1955, 1957) distinguishes people from animals by the fact that we live in the *symbolic* dimension of reality by our engagement with language, myth, art and religion as part of our universe: "They are the varied threads which weave the symbolic net, the tangled web of human experience. Instead of dealing with the things themselves man is in a sense constantly conversing with himself" (Cassirer 1944: 25). Then he observes, "instead of defining man as an *animal rationale*, we should define him as an *animal symbolicum* and assume that people are profoundly tied up in cultural forms" (25).

Working with something akin to the concept of "*animal symbolicum*", Lévi-Strauss (1966) develops his highly original anthropology which links the mind to cultural products and human communication, indeed, humanity itself (see Gurnah and Scott 1992, ch. 3). These arguments significantly tell us something about culture, its meaning for people and in short the use they make of it in order *to be* people. Culture is reality *sui generis*, thought Malinowski (see also Winch 1958:15).

In *Philosophical Investigations* Wittgenstein brings together language, rule following and a game, but does not distinguish any specific features of the "game" (1953, paragraphs 65–7). Rather, he points to "a complicated network of similarities and relationships overlapping and criss-crossing". He stresses that the way rules work in a game, is similar to how they work in a language. A language "is part of a communal activity, a way of living in a society a 'form of life'. It is through sharing in the playing of language-games that language is connected with our life" (Kenny 1973: 163). The games clarify meaning and define what makes sense. In games, words connect with other words and find purpose.

The way that cultures connect is rather similar. In a symbolic network, particular cultural products assume different meanings depending upon their placement in the system at a specific time and space and justification for their being there. In other words, the same cultural product will mean different things to the same person in varying contexts and to different people in the same context within the overall frame. This constitutes the general pattern of the "cultural game", shaped by aesthetic rationality – perspective of ordering – which defines use and meaning and conveys that to other participants in the system. When cultures which are foreign to each other come in contact, the energizing of cultural products and sensitizing of the people involved tentatively create the initial system for communication. The culture-complex then does its work here, and the initial fabric develops into a system of communication – a system of common denominators. Invariably this is a complex interaction whether it happens slowly or rapidly. Also inevitably, it is informed interaction whether recognized as such or not. People in all cultures habitually create these communication bridges within the narrow familial or community culture and expand them more widely to the nation and eventually the global systems.

Modalities of culture

In the example of the Zanzibari boy, cultural icons of rock and roll, foreign literature and music all formed part of the exciting mixture that brought enjoyment, instigated critical evaluation of home culture and helped to promote the search for liberty against colonial occupation. The motivation for the whole of the culture-complex here was also to dispose of colonialism, and that became the group focus, the modality of its culture. The motivation was powerful, successful and progressive. The raw material for that challenge came from both greater political awareness of and increasing familiarity with foreign cultures. What was internalized and used depended on individual experiences and interests, intelligence and also on luck; depending upon where and how individuals or groups entered the cultural game and what they took from it and chose to express by it. That combination for each individual that shared a "family resemblance" within the group modality, also expressed an individual modality or combination that distinguished her or his cultural preferences from the group.

To put it another way, regarding group cultural modality, our experience of Elvis was real, organic and selective. No doubt a point can be made about the black (African) influence in Elvis and rock 'n' roll, but, although quite valid, such an argument misses my present point. It is not fanciful to claim that rock and roll signified for us:

- collectively a link to the international youth movement, Western struggles and new heroes and at that time were as significant for us as Jesse Owen, Gamal Abdul Nasser or Che Guevara;
- our political distance from both the white colonial teachers and our parents and the development of our own political and cultural platform;
- emerging cultural common denominators that linked us to the knowledge in the West and paradoxically anti-imperialist struggles elsewhere;
- our opportunities culturally to manipulate situations for personal liberties that later linked us to the search for political liberties. (The same people who read

about Elvis later also read about Mao and Lenin. The ones who did not probably also continued to sing along in cafés);

- the absurdity of our situation, like nausea, highlighted our awareness of the liberties we took and offered a looking-glass that led to critical thinking.

The way the bits fit together is complex and requires much more detailed study and analysis. Furthermore, each individual version is influenced in different degrees and with variant subsequent identifications, leading to individual cultural modalities. This is an important issue, one which has in some ways motivated the writing of this piece. The idea of individual cultural modality explains why two members of the same family, with only a year or two difference in age, having received pretty much similar upbringing, should have in some ways quite different perceptions of their cultural identities. Such examples are pervasive in Zanzibar. Some see themselves as Westernized Afro-Arabs, while their brothers or sisters see themselves as Western-ized Arabized Africans. Some see themselves as Africans pure and simple, with foreign origins and influences. Others still hang on to their origins – Arabic, African, etc. – and view the influences as "interferences" caused by the misfortune of growing up in a foreign country or one contaminated by foreign influences. The permutations of identity are endless but their general experience, knowledge and expression of their culture has a family resemblance. This describes a very complex framework for moral legitimacy – all have the right to be Zanzibaris – and creates room, liberty and emancipation from group tyranny. Indeed, it creates this very desirable creative tension that *charges* the local community for internal communication and makes it available for communication with other cultures.

The general point made here is that such was a nexus for change and progressive thought. People are not led by their noses into other cultures' agendas, not even within the same culture group or family. If they enter these worlds in that fashion it is mainly out of choice – something there attracts them and becomes the most challenging world of learning and experimenting. This does not mean for the learners that they always make the right choices. I am sure the sculptured hair was on the margin of good taste, but great fun at the time. [...]

Conclusion

- Culture is globalized and it is not entirely or even mainly a negative experience. When Zanzibaris sing rock and roll or South Americans laugh at a Chaplin film we should be glad, particularly when we notice also English people are eating curries and reading African and Indian writers. This connotes a widening of human experiences and wisdom.
- The existence of group and individual cultural modalities ensures the confirmed existence and the workings of "family cultural resemblances" and individual choices. It helps to explain the internal struggles and accommodations within cultures (e.g. the old folk in Zanzibar and the young people). It also explains the meaning of "organic" culture, not as a collection of ossified traditions, but what a group or individuals come to construct and recognize as theirs and as life enhancing.

- Through this discussion I have in any case gained a greater understanding of how culture is shared and spread essentially not even mainly through brutality and mindless copying, but for positive reasons connected with human curiosity and the desire to improve and enrich our lives; it is the super highway for life-sustaining social knowledge and change.
- Cultural imperialism is often shorthand for identification of other struggles rather than clear explanation of cultural slavery. The cultural process is far too complex to be viewed in such a limited fashion. In cultural exchange both sides are affected for better or worse in the short term. Almost all imperializing nations end up civilizing and culturally broadening their own people through their attempts to occupy others.
- Imperialism of culture is a real enough experience, but not one which either lasts long or has a lasting *harmful* impact. For example the imposition of the English language on African people and Americanism on the Japanese both show the diabolical taking of liberties by imperialists. However, the people whose liberties were so grossly violated soon learnt to find ways to benefit from both.

The point is, a better understanding of cultural processes should pave the way for more intelligent cultural action and allow the processes of culture-complex to provide an efficient interrogation of cultural exchanges for greater knowledge and for obviating and keeping at bay mystifying immoralities.

As much as culture-complexes work between nations, they do so between classes, community groups and gender groups in the same nation. The working class and women are not passive receivers of ruling-class or high-culture domination. They do not, any more than do "immigrant" workers in European countries, merely *fight* and *resist* such cultural imperialism, but also play an important role in shaping and reshaping the dominant culture around them, and create new syntheses. These are some of the questions and issues that now require greater extrapolations via the culture-complex model.

REFERENCES

Ang, I. (1985) *Watching Dallas*, London: Matthews.

Appadurai, A. (1990) "Disjunction and difference in the global cultural economy" in M. Featherstone (ed.) *Global Culture: Nationalism, Globalization and Modernity*, London: Sage.

Bremmer, I. and Taras, R., (eds) (1993) *Nations and Politics in the Soviet Successor States*, Cambridge: Cambridge University Press.

Cassirer, E, (1944) *An Essay on Man*, New Haven: Yale University Press.

Cassirer, E. (1953/55/57) *The Philosophy of Symbolic Forms*, 3 volumes, translated by R. Manheim, New Haven: Yale University Press.

de Kadt, E. and Williams. G. (1974) *Sociology of Underdevelopment*, London: Tavistock Publications.

Durkheim, E. (1995) [1912] *The Elementary Forms of Religious Life*, translated by K. E. Fields, New York: The Free Press.

Frank, A. Gunder (1969) *Latin America: Underdevelopment or Revolution?*, New York: Monthly Review.

Geertz, C. (1973) *Interpretation of Cultures*, New York: Basic Books.

Gellner, E. (1964) *Thought and Change*, London: Weidenfeld and Nicolson.

Giroux, Henry A. and McLauren, P. (eds) (1994) *Between Borders: Pedogogy and the Politics of Cultural Studies*, London: Routledge.

Gurnah, A. (ed.) (forthcoming) *Culture for Social Renewal*, London: NIACE.

Gurnah, A. and Scott, A. (1992) *The Uncertain Science*, London: Routledge.

Habermas, J. (1984) *Theory of Communicative Action, Volume One: Reason and the Rationalization of Society*, translated by T. McCarthy, Cambridge: Polity Press.

Katz, E. and Tamar, L. (1985) "Mutual aid in decoding *Dallas*: preliminary notes from a cross-cultural study" in P. Drummond and R. Patterson (eds) *Television in Transition*, London: BFI.

Kenny, A. (1973) *Wittgenstein*, Harmondsworth: Penguin Books.

Lévi-Strauss, C. (1966) *The Savage Mind*, London: Weidenfeld and Nicolson.

Moharty, C. T. (1994) "On race and voice: challenge for liberal education in the 1990s" in Giroux and McLauren (eds) *Between Borders: Pedagogy and the Politics of Cultural Studies*, London: Routledge.

Nelson, C. and Grossberg, L. (eds) (1988) *Marxism and the Interpretation of Culture*, Basingstoke: Macmillan.

Nisbet, R. (1976) Introduction to Emile Durkheim's *The Elementary Forms of Religious Life*, London: Allen and Unwin.

Tomlinson, J. (1991) *Cultural Imperialism*, Leicester: Pinter Publishers.

Winch, P. (1958) *The Idea of a Social Science*, London: Routledge and Kegan Paul.

Wittgenstein, L., (1953) *Philosophical Investigations*, Oxford: Basil Blackwell.

Wittgenstein, L. (1975) *The Blue and Brown Books*, Oxford: Basil Blackwell.

From the Politics of Urban Place to a Politics of Global Displacement

Jonathan Raban pointed out, in pre-postmodern times, that when one first encountered a city, it was as a "hard city": a congeries of material features such as buildings, curbstones, and street grids. But the more time you spend in that city, the more you fill it with your own meanings. In the process, the hard city gradually melts into a "soft city" – a mental map marked by favorite restaurants, the corner where a lover was first encountered, and the office where a hateful job is worked. Given the many millions of residents within a city, inside every hard city are numerous soft cities. For all residents, their soft cities are of far greater importance than the hard city itself. Furthermore, the soft city does not remain entirely within the perceptions of each resident. Rather, every urbanite intervenes in the body of the hard city itself, by traveling certain routes and not others, or by putting built spaces to new uses. In innumerable small ways, these actions in turn remodel the material of the hard city itself. Thus, soft cities become hard, and people do not reside within the city so much as comprise it.

The link between the postmodern and the city, however, is not limited to the personal subjectivities of urban habitation. There is an epochal component, identifying (for instance) industrial restructuring as the radical break responsible for the emergence of a postmodern urban condition. As presented in Regulationist Theory and extended by Michael Storper and Allen Scott (Reading 20), restructuring consists of a shift away from Fordist mass-production by large vertically integrated companies. It has been replaced by post-Fordism (or flexible specialization), small-batch production undertaken by a diffuse network of numerous subcontractors. This change produced a new form of fast and loose capitalism, what Scott Lash and John Urry called "disorganized" capitalism, a shift in production strategies that carry a host of implications. City structures change from centralized industrial towns (e.g., Detroit) to polynucleated clusters of specialized industrial parks (e.g., portions of Southern California). Any step in the production process can be relocated regionally, nationally, and even globally with comparative ease, thus destabilizing localities as firms exercise the capacity to readily and quickly jettison particular peoples and places from productive operations.

Recent changes in global interconnectivity have further interwoven postmodernism and the urban. Faster and cheaper communications and transport technologies establish and maintain networks of connections between evermore widespread points on the planet's surface, permitting an unprecedentedly broad and rapid diffusion of peoples, artifacts, and information (the process of time–space compression). Insofar as these networks converge in large urban agglomerations, urban centers become condensers of people, networks, and commodities, but also of a growing plethora of world-views. The sudden juxtaposition of differing world-views within urban space requires, in turn, that these differences be acknowledged and negotiated. The subsequent proliferation of hybrids will cause the proliferation of new soft cities.

This diversifying confluence of soft cities, restructured cities, cities of flexibly specialized business and cities of mass immigration are not unidirectional phenomena. At the same time as multiple worlds, and indeed the world in general, is presencing itself in the city, the city is linking itself ever more tightly to others around the world. Disparate and distant places are presencing themselves within one another as cities continually swap pieces of themselves. Thus, cities become world cities, (in)forming a global urban system where neighborhoods become as diffuse as landsat phone calls and air travel will permit, predicated as much upon interests shared over wide distances as upon propinquity.

But exactly how is postmodern territory produced? Referring to the way landscapes can only be experienced from subjective perspectives, Arjun Appadurai identifies five globally-dispersed territories, or *'scapes*:

- ethnoscapes, the interconnections of social affinity groups;
- mediascapes, the capacity to disseminate information and mediated images to the world;
- technoscapes, the global configuration and flow of technologies;
- finanscapes, the shifting global disposition of capital; and
- ideoscapes, the global dispersion of political-ideological constructs, generally statist or counter-state, and couched in Enlightenment image-ideas of "freedom", "welfare", "democracy", etc.

According to Appadurai, individuals, families, diasporic communities, nations, and multinational institutions all experience these 'scapes, and experience them in different ways. Insofar as they are experienced differently, to different degrees, and in different combinations by differing actors, they comprise a variety of "imagined worlds." Imagined worlds propagate, run up against one another and, in the process, have the power to subvert the actual world they overlay. Consequently, the urbanism of postmodernity yields not just a restructured metropolis of intersecting soft cities, but also a shrinking planet of overlapping worlds. In other words, it is not just the city that goes soft, but the planet as well.

Postmodernism asserts that there are multiple versions of the city and the world at play in any one place. Each version has its own formative underpinning experiences, its own internal logic, and its own validity. In practice, some soft cities and some imagined worlds are more equal than others, and to the powerful go the spoils. Which world-view emerges as more dominant, however, is never a foregone conclusion. In the absence of a supreme metanarrative, the hegemony of any particular world-view is determined by often brutal battles for control over both discursive and material terrains. A postmodern soft planet of soft cities necessarily entails a postmodern (geo)politics which manifests itself as contests over who gets to structure discourse, who is permitted to materialize that discourse through bodily practice, and in who gets to control territory (cf. Reading 23).

Throughout the twentieth century, the unitary metanarrative structuring the play of politics was that of the nation-state. In the postmodern epoch, however, this long-standing primitive of the body politic is being repeatedly undermined, pierced, and superseded. Fluid global capital and waves of migration, sustained by networks of fast transportation and communication, have rendered the boundaries of the nation-state relentlessly porous. Simultaneously, the growing suspicion of metanarratives (and the vested interests they conceal) is increasingly delegitimizing the pronouncements and underlying axioms of the state. This may be seen at both the intranational and international levels.

Intranationally, postmodernity has witnessed the dissolution of hegemonic (often oppressive) regimes, increasing the audibility and influence of alternative, previously marginalized Others. The drive towards social polyvocality has in turn engendered a backlash, producing a conflicted domestic political landscape of mini-worlds and micro-nations. In the United States of the 1990s, for instance, the rap-musical group Public Enemy's "Black Planet," found opposition in the white supremacist "Aryan Nations," while both arrayed themselves against the gay activist-citizens of a "Queer Nation." Secession movements are rife, and local militia bands outlaw formal governments.

New immigration has heightened this fragmentation of the body politic. In sheer scale it is huge, abruptly reforging the streetscapes of major cities into world neighborhoods. In origin it is diverse, simultaneously drawn from an unprecedentedly wide array of locales scattered across the planet. And unlike in the past, when departures necessarily severed contact with homeland, rapid transport and communications technologies now permit the maintenance of active links with both the homeland and other widespread outposts of the diaspora. Thus systems of world neighborhoods become embedded within the system of world cities, abruptly bringing together "right here" a plentitude of the different worlds "out there."

Internationally, postmodernity has entailed the emergence and globalization of "quick-silver" capital and, with it, a chronic transgression of the nation-state's territorial boundaries. This is readily apparent in Deleuze and Guattari's claims about capitalism's tendency to "schizophrenize," to wrest all things free from fixed discursive and spatial coordinates and relationships. As capital becomes increasingly symbolic, traded not in the form of material such as land or machines but as an abstract thing in itself, it is transformed from an emplaced asset to a displaced flow. In the process, capital becomes deterritorialized and, in its capacity to flow with newfound freedom across territories and their administrative borders, deterritorializing. Thus, the territorial state's administrative organs are increasingly elided, dictated to, and, in many instances, purchased outright by the primary players in the international financial markets: transnational corporations (TNCs) and their shadowy twin, transnational criminal organizations (TCOs).

Nor are these two institutional categories so exclusive of each another as might be assumed. For example, TNCs and TCOs pass capital back and forth through often circuitous routes. They are also intimately bound up with immigration. Many TNCs, for instance, draw specialized personnel from certain globally mobile ethno-national groups (i.e., Filipino medical personnel, or electrical engineers from India's northeast), and many TCOs too are rooted in particular ethno-national formations. Finally, there exists no solid wall dividing transnational business enterprises, legitimate or otherwise, from the state itself. The revolving door between state organs and TNCs commonly enables legislators, bureaucrats, board members and CEOs to swap places at will. And a similar accessway is yawning wide between the state and TCOs, as exemplified by the speculative links between members of Mexico's former ruling party and narcotics barons, or by the participation of former members of the KGB in the new Russian *Mafiya*.

Faced with such punctures and compound fractures of the body politic, nation-states have adopted an arsenal of tactics to ensure their own bodily integrity. Some have advocated multiculturalism, the idea that a modern nation-state must encompass many nationalities and regulate their interactions; or economic neoliberalism, the notion that deregulated international trade enriches all while minimizing the possibility of war (except, apparently, war against those nation-states resistant to neoliberalism). Others have sought to shore up their dominant social order and economic autarchy by cracking down on minority dissent, militarizing their borders against migrants and contraband goods, and tightly delimiting who is entitled to citizenship and trade privileges. Often the same states have deployed these contradictory strategies simultaneously, as when the passage of the North American Free Trade Agreement (NAFTA) is accompanied by the installation of a steel palisade between San Diego and Tijuana.

Despite efforts to restabilize the territorial state and its constitutive boundaries, the survival of the modern nation-state remains debatable. Perhaps the most extreme example of this is Yugoslavia, where pressures brought to bear by external institutions combined with friction between internal nationalities to provoke the country's bloodily violent collapse. But more stable nations like the United States are no less immune, as citizen-militias take up arms in the heartland while affluent urbanites take flight to the privately administered precincts of walled and gated residential enclaves.

In response to the changing natures of cities and their global integration, recent geographical literature has tended to concentrate on the everyday street-level impacts of urban change, and on diversifying conceptions of the city itself. Simultaneously, newer writings on the urban condition have begun reconsidering the city as an entity extending beyond its municipal boundaries and, in the process, restructuring the region and the nation-state. Such administrative restructurings point, in turn, to a new body politic and a new realpolitik. The politics of postmodernity entail a global field with fluid demarcations. Upon this field, competing and incommensurable discourses wrestle with the very definititions of what constitutes legality and criminality, public and private, alien and citizen, foreign and domestic. Within this demobilization of politics-as-usual, geographers have taken up the task of examining their replacements: contingent coalitions of common interests, transnationalized localisms, a privatizing public sphere, and the proliferation of semi-formal state apparatuses densely interwoven with gangsterism and media-saturated disinformation. Two broad themes currently overarch this work. The first focuses upon the expression of minority claims, and how such claims conflict with one another and with the state's dominant social metanarratives. The second analyzes how the polity and territory of the state itself are no longer fundamental truths and material givens, but discursive pronouncements and materialized inventions.

We open this section with a snippet of a tale by Alasdair Gray, in which he very literally depicts the world not just as one city, but embodies that city in the form of a single, solitary, massively towering edifice. The following extract, by David Ley and Caroline Mills, is an investigation into the contentious on-going construction of the postmodern city. Ley and Mills dispel the notion that postmodernism is exclusively a novel aesthetic for the amusement of hegemonic classes, focusing on the mobilization of dissident groups within the city as a particularly postmodern resistance to elitist city-making (Reading 31). The contribution by Soja and Hooper takes a closer look at dissent through the lens of writings by Homi Bhabha, bell hooks, and other key thinkers about the "subaltern" and "subalterity" (or, less precisely, the subjugated). Soja and Hooper arrive at postcolonial insights into how the experiences, sensibilities, and lifeways of subaltern peoples empower them to seize space for themselves (Reading 32). The next two selections extend the territorial scale of the postmodern problematic by adopting an explicitly global focus. John Law and Kevin Hetherington reconceptualize globalization as a complex network of persons and artifacts (Reading 33). Asu Aksoy and Kevin Robins critique a specific subset of these network systems: those deployed by the state to execute and legitimize war (Reading 34). Complementing this critique, we end with a brief piece by a body on the localized receiving end of war-making networks. Subcomandante Marcos calls poetically for a devolution of decision making to the people and local places of the disenfranchised (Reading 35).

REFERENCES

Appadurai, A.: *Modernity at Large: Cultural Dimensions of Globalization*. University of Minnesota Press: Minneapolis 1996, pp. 27–46.

Deleuze, G. and Guattari, F.: *Anti-Oedipus: Capitalism and Schizophrenia*. University of Minnesota Press: Minneapolis 1983.

Lash, S. and Urry, J.: *The End of Organized Capitalism*. University of Wisconsin Press: Madison 1987.

Raban, J.: *Soft City*. E.P. Dutton: New York 1974.

Scott, A.: *Technopolis: High-Technology Industry and Regional Development in Southern California*. University of California Press: Berkeley 1993.

Unlikely Stories, Mostly

Alasdair Gray

The end of the Axletree

The emperor died, and his tomb was built in the centre of the capital city, then enlarged to enclose everything he had wanted. His suggestions for the name were also adopted. The inhabiters called it *the work*, outsiders called it *the axletree*. People travelling there saw it for a fortnight before arriving and I speak of the work itself, not the pillar of cloud overhead, creamy-gold on bright days, thunder-black on dull ones, and flickering with reflected orange light in the hours of darkness. As the traveller drew near the huge solitary bulk so filled his mind that sometimes he grew frightened and turned back before seeing the canals and merchant navies entering the artificial sea around the foundation. The roads bridged this by viaducts sloping up to market-gallery-level, a full mile above sea-level, yet rising so easily that blind travellers thought they were flat. It was a safe structure in those days and foreign kings bought shares in it as a way of banking their wealth. The construction company became the government of the empire – our emperors dropped their ancient title and were known as company chairmen. The first of these was a man of simple tastes who had a farm near the top of the work where he grew his own vegetables. He liked to feel he did not need the earth below, but everyone else in the axletree was fed off that. People in the nearest provinces usually looked thin and glum. It must also have been very depressing to live where half the world bent up to shut you out. Dwellers in remoter provinces saw us as a steep-sided mountain on the horizon, but to insiders we were not one thing but many: our living rooms and the rooms of friends, some connecting galleries lined with shops and parkland, the offices where we calculated or the scaffolding where we laboured. The simplest thing we knew was the world spread below like a map. Merchants, soldiers and tax-collectors had to visit that. Most of us were luckier.[...]

One evening I sat beside the professor of air, checking rockets at a table on the balcony of our office. This was in a low part of the work above a gate where the coalfleets sailed in, for one of our jobs was to superintend the nearby smoke station. We had found that smoke, enclosed in bags, could lift large weights, and had used this discovery to create a new transport system. My chief was testing the powder which made the rockets fly, I tested the fuses. Without raising my eyes I could see fat black

ships wallowing up the shining creek from a distant ocean. They docked directly under us but it would be a week before they unloaded. This was midsummer and a general holiday. All building had stopped, most fires were damped, the college had made a gale the night before and swept the sky clear and blue. The cries of children and picknickers came tiny and shrill, like birdnotes, from the green hills and valleys beside the creek. These smooth slopes had been made by giving ashbings a coat of soil and turf, and the lowest people liked to holiday on them. Even I had happy memories of playing there as a child. But the companies had started turning the old ashes into brick, and already half the green park had been scraped flat. The diggers had uncovered a viaduct of arches built two thousand years before by the old imperial construction company. The sight might have given me a melancholy sense of the booms and slumps of history but I was too excited. I was going to visit the height of the axletree.

The chief packed his rockets in a slingbag. I shouldered a light launching tube. We walked through our offices in the thickness of the outer wall and down some steps to the smokestation.

A two-seater lift was locked to our platform. We climbed in and arranged cushions round us while the bag filled up. It was a light blue bag with the college sign on the side: a yellow silk flame with an eye in the centre. The chief unlocked us and we swung into the hot oblique updraught used by very important people. We crossed the docks, the retorts and crucibles of the furnacemen and a crowded circus cheering a ball-game. We passed through the grate of an ancient portcullis, ascended a canyon between sewage cylinders with cedar forests on top, then swooped through a ventilator in the first ceiling. Within an hour we had pierced ceilings which separated six national companies, the customs officers leaping up to salute us on the lip of the ventilators as soon as they recognized the college colours. In solemn music we crossed the great canteen, rising into the dome as the foreman of the work, like a bright white bee, served the sacred food to a swarm of faithful on the floor below. The ventilator in the dome opened into a wind-cave where an international orchestra was distilling rain with bright instruments into an aquarium that was the head water of three national rivers. We lost the hot updraught here but the chief steered us into a current flowing up a slide of rubble where an ancient summit had been shaken down by earth-quakes during the first big slump. It was landscaped with heather, gorse and hunting lodges. Above that we entered the base of the tallest summit of all, ascending vertically through floors which were all familiar to me: hospitals, nurseries, schools, emporiums, casinos, banks, courts and boardrooms. Here we were stopped at a ventilator for the first time, since the highest inhabited parts of the tower belonged the military. The chief spent a long time proving that his rockets were not weapons but tools for testing the upper air, and even so he was only allowed through when I showed the examining colonel, by a secret sign, that I was not only a member of the college but an agent of his company. So we were allowed to rise up the glass funnel to the scaffolding. On every side we saw officers in neat identical clothes tending the huge steel catapults and firing pans poised to pour down thunderbolts and lightning on the other parts of the work, especially toward towers with co-operative connections. We passed through a builders' village, deserted except for its watchmen, then nothing surrounded us but a frame of slender rods and the deep blue blue blue of the gloaming sky. The thin cold air began to hurt my lungs. We stopped when our bag touched the highest platform. The chief slung the rockets from his shoulder and climbed a ladder to the very top. I followed him.

I had never known such space. The pure dark blueness was unstained by the faintest wisp of cloud. I lay flat on the planks with my head over the platform edge, trying to see the sunset on the horizon, but the golden shine of it was cut small by the web of bridges linking the summits lower down. I felt like a fly clinging to the tip of an arrow, the first of a flight of them soaring through infinite air. Lights were blinking on the tips of summits below. These were the signals of college men who would observe our experiments with lens and theodolite. The chief signalled back at them with a hand-lamp. He even blinked at the spiky summit of the great co-operative, which was nearest. This was a joke, because the co-operative pretended to ignore the work of our college, while watching it very closely.[...]

31 Can There be A Postmodernism of Resistance in the Urban Landscape?

David Ley and Caroline Mills

The city may well be different things to different people, but the built forms of the city clearly favor some people's urban visions at the expense of others'. While place-making is about how we represent and use space, it is also about how varied perspectives on "what space should be" contend with one another. Place-making, then, is inherently political. David Ley and Caroline Mills delineate the urban intersections of politics and postmodernity, providing critical distinctions that help us imagine a postmodern politics in the city. First they identify a politics *about* postmodernism, in which partisans argue over whether postmodernism empowers diverse resistances to the authoritarian city-making of the modern era, or merely fragments unified resistance while camouflaging authoritarian city-making beneath quaint aesthetic forms. Ley and Mills critically disassemble this latter assertion to derive a bifurcated postmodern urban politics. One face, they concede, is a coopted postmodernism of *reaction* that consists of a private retreat into cozy neotraditionalist preserves while the rest of the city burns. But the second face, a postmodernism of *resistance*, or reconstruction, permits multiple voices to retain their differences and yet join in opposition to any imposed single vision of what the city should be.

Rats, Posts and Other Pests...

The paradigmatic case of postmodern art is architecture, but within the architectural profession the reaction against postmodern design from established figures has frequently been vigorous. In 1981 Aldo van Eyck's Annual Discourse to the Royal Institute of British Architects under the title of "Rats, Posts and Other Pests" set the scene (and the level) for discussion in the early 1980s (Jencks, 1986, p. 11). It was soon to be followed by appellations of "transvestite architecture," "Charles Junk" (sic), and a 1983 debate generating such condemnations as "ephemeral, a throw-away, subject to the caprice of commercial culture and the exigencies of the marketplace" or "neofashion for the bored, the rich, the jaded, the blind" (AIA, 1983). As Christian Norberg-Schulz was to observe later, the vigor of these reprimands suggested that postmodernism was too important to ignore, its criticisms too central for an understated response. But the response, to the extent that it was substantive, was primarily aesthetic, concerned with the retention of what a corpus of professionals defined as good urban form.

In the social sciences as well, a common assessment of postmodern culture has been critical. An arsenal of conceptual hardware has been assembled: the "postmodern city" is assailed as a place of spectacle and surveillance, where aestheticisation and commodification lull the consumer into a quietism before the social control of a market-driven hegemony. This, of course, is the barest of skeletons, and arguments are assembled upon it in sometimes elegant and persuasive forms. There is, moreover, undoubtedly some truth to such a depiction. The important question then becomes, how complete is this truth, how adequate is the argument, both theoretically and empirically? Several observations appear relevant.

First, the imagery of the postmodern city employed by its critics is one of social control: superficial, garish, tasteless, deceitful and manipulative. It is notable how closely this vocabulary is shared with the Frankfurt School's condemnation of the culture industry, where the "reified false consciousness of industrialized mass culture has settled like a pall over history" (Brantlinger, 1983, p. 226). The protests of Horkheimer and Adorno a half-century ago as they contemplated cultural life in the *modern* city have a very current ring to them. A generic culture of "ready-made clichés to be slotted in anywhere" created an alienated consumer who "becomes the ideology of the pleasure industry, whose institutions he cannot escape" (Horkheimer and Adorno, 1972, pp. 154, 158). With little qualification these arguments are carried forward by influential authors like Debord (1973), Foster (1985) and Harvey (1989). Despite the sea change that we are told has led to the postmodern condition, a peculiarly modern theoretical model is sustained in its interpretation. Moreover, the discourse of the culture industry portrays an unusually claustrophobic world, where a homogeneous and tightly controlled public culture is projected unproblematically upon a passive citizenry.

This structural model has been criticized often enough before – not least in the realm of cultural geography – but some particular shortcomings bear repeating. Such models of hegemonic control present the consciousness of the masses as monolithic and unproblematic, passive and without the potential for resistance. The view of mass culture is distant and elitist. Soja's (1989) view of the surveillant state in Los Angeles, for example, is a view from on high; as the noose of total social control is drawn tightly around the city, we do not know if any member of the thousands of cultural worlds in that city has noticed, for no other voice or values are admitted other than those of the author. As in so much of the literature on cultural hegemony, the social control of consciousness is alleged but never proven. When we look for the voices of the manipulated masses we encounter in the text a gaping silence, a silence that encourages the disturbing thought that perhaps the manipulation of mass consciousness is accomplished also by the theorist, who as *spectator* him/ herself posits the existence of the spectacle as a source of confusion only for the undifferentiated Other. We might ask why the author-ial/-itarian I/eye does not take this criticism of a way of seeing in others more self-consciously (cf. Deutsche, 1991).

Second, and related, much of the discussion around postmodern design is characterized by what may be called a façadism which does not problematize the meaning of a building or a landscape. Totalizing views of a culture read off its impact upon an artifact under the assumption that the artifact expresses and reproduces mechanically the social relations imputed to the culture. This was the complaint directed against an earlier cultural geography which, in less sophisticated ways, treated dwellings as mere forms, carriers of an undifferentiated culture. Today, the dominant culture is represented as less harmonious and more conflict-strewn, but the treatment of landscape remains incomplete. Consider, for example, Harvey's (1990) reading of the redevelopment of Baltimore's Inner Harbor. While in important respects his interpretation rings true, it is rather too hermetically sealed, both theoretically and empirically, and its absences are as strategic as its presences. We accept his account of the remaking of the Inner Harbor and of the public investment that subsidized private development. Informed by his theoretical viewpoint, what has resulted is a "carnival mask," disguising the alienations of commodification, a quintessentially inauthentic "postmodern" landscape. But are there not also important absences, a depthlessness, *to this account?* Does the landscape not fit too closely the theoretical garb cast over it? If we treat the Inner Harbor less as the projection of a theoretical position and more fully as a historical-geographical landscape, other questions come to mind. Harvey does not say what alternative uses for a decaying industrial landscape he might propose, other than to rue the passing of a city fair in the early 1970s. He does not allow that the carnival might generate outcomes which are concealed by the hermetic concept of the spectacle. Mundanely, but importantly, what are the multipliers in the local economy and the job creation associated with them? What has been the effect on the city's tax base and its capacity to offer social services? May even the carnival be able to sustain practices which escape the imputed social control of spectacle? Is it not possible, for example, that the development of social and family relations among visitors might permit the advancement of the values of the lifeworld rather than "the impoverishment, the servitude and the negation of real life" (Debord 1973, paragraph 215; compare Ley and Olds, 1988)? These are all empirical questions to which we have no answer, but they are questions that must at least be asked and not concealed by the rhetoric of the spectacle.

Façadism, then, may lead to casual empirical study where buildings and landscapes are treated as conveniences for the outworking of a larger theoretical project.[...]

Toward a Postmodernism of Resistance?

We have argued with others that the cultural elitism of the modern project, its belief in the superior insight of the artist/architect, not only produced a self-referential aesthetic, but also implied an asymmetric politics which disenfranchised popular participation. From this criticism, a central element of a postmodern aesthetic is a dialogical model when conversations between the artist and local cultures should sustain intersubjective senses of identity and place. But such an aesthetic also has its political counterpart. Multiple voices can only be heard when they are empowered, when they are located in non-hierarchical political spaces. Thus if the tendencies of the modern movement are toward a politics of exclusion, the tendencies of the postmodern agenda are toward a politics of inclusion. Of course, whether or not such tendencies are fulfilled or deflected is a separate issue.

These general considerations provide a context for reviewing the social protests against the modern city in the 1960s and early 1970s. The vast modernization of the urban fabric during this period – urban renewal, new highway systems, urban redevelopment – represented a concentrated program of rebuilding after the inactivity of the Depression and World War Two. As Jacobs (1971) has noted, the idiom of reconstruction was the 1920s vision of the freeway, high-rise city. Resistance to this program was a resistance to both form and process, to both the alienating style of modernism and the destructive effects of modernization upon the existing urban landscape. The postmodern theme of contextuality redirected attention to "sensitive urban place-making" (Jencks, 1981, p. 82) and away from the "abstract universalism" (Rustin, 1987, p. 31) of modern spaces. What Rustin calls "a new particularism" has attempted over the past twenty years to re-establish the supportive integration of place and social identity (Robins, 1988). The animation of public space – where the models of the town square and "the short narrow street of the slum" have commonly been prototypes – has included the celebration of difference in the ethnic and lifestyle festivals of a postmodern urban culture, often sponsored by leftist city councils (Bianchini, 1987; Robins and Gillespie, 1988). New styles of social housing, the reclamation of the street from its modernist dedication to traffic circulation alone and enhanced attention to design and landscaping have been part of a larger program of planning in the 1970s and 1980s. Public art of a critical postmodernism has sought to lay bare the concealed meanings and social consequences accompanying the production of urban space (Deutsche, 1988), for example, in the ironic criticism of consumer culture coded in the design projects of the SITE partnership, where "comment is made on the soulless, exhausted, and ruined environment and indifferent nonarchitecture becomes striking antiarchitecture" (Fischer, 1985, p. 261).

Our argument is not, of course, that these objectives have been easily or even widely attained. The task is rather to show that a postmodernism of resistance is neither a theoretical nor a historical mirage. Locality is invariably contested and new urban landscapes are always outcomes of a contingent political process. Moreover, protests against the modern city have been directed against more than the built environment. They have also been concerned with a politics of inclusion – the claims of visible minorities and other marginalized groups to cultural recognition and political enfranchisement in civic administrations dominated by white, middle-class businessmen. Leadership of urban protests has been frequently coordinated by a growing segment of the middle class, social and cultural professionals often employed in the public or non-profit sectors who felt equally alienated from existing power bases and were joined by pre-professionals, particularly students, expressing what Peter Berger has called the demodernizing consciousness of the counter-culture (Berger et al., 1973, p. 208; also Offe, 1987). The same cohort has reappeared in other social movements: environmentalism, cultural nationalism and civil rights, including some feminist groups and the democracy movement. Here is the domain of a critical postmodern politics and each of these movements share important common themes in their resistance to modernization. Fundamental is a suspicion of the unconstrained power of both the state and the market. Calls for the diffusion of their influence and decentralization of their power are accompanied by a more plural set of societal goals and political voices than economic development and its attendant power elites. With modest revisions an alternative and critical social paradigm developed by environmentalists (Cosgrove and Duff, 1980) may be extended to some of these other domains. The core values of this paradigm recognize broader public interests than market forces or state power; they acknowledge the plurality of human and non-human rights in a complex society; they advocate more participatory and non-hierarchical political structures; they endorse small-scale and locally sensitive development and a more egalitarian society which is needs-driven; and they urge recognition of the limits of instrumental rationality and technical solutions. Because of their criticism of the postulates of modernism and modernization, such an alternative social agenda is said to be contained within a postmodern politics (Aronowitz, 1988; Betz, 1989; Mouffe, 1988).

This account, with its emphasis on the 1960s and 1970s, concurs with the periodization of both Huyssen (1984) and Jencks (1986), who see an initial critical positioning of the postmodern. But what happened after, say, 1975? Here they suggest a stage of cooptation and commodification which becomes increasingly strong into the 1980s, a view not very different from the critical assessments discussed earlier. A postmodernism of reaction becomes the cultural expression of neoconservative politics. But there is another all-too-obvious possibility. Jameson has made the simple point that "what matters in any defeat or success of a plan to transform the city is political power" (Stephanson, 1988, p. 15). The social movements of the 1960s successfully penetrated the state at different levels, and for a period adversarial politics seized an unprecedented share of the policy-making agenda. Not only was this period the high-water mark of the welfare state, but also a period of decentralist politics pursuing plural social objectives and showing successful signs of resistance in many cities to the alienations of continuing modernization in the image of modernism. For a variety of reasons the political coalitions of that period fell apart, and power recentralized. But this does not mean they are a spent force historically. In any case, the objective here is not to define a successful politics, but a *resistant* politics. Nor does it seem necessary to claim, as some authors do, that postmodern politics is a total politics completely redrawing past configurations. Clearly economic inequality will continue to be a major base of mobilization, though the claims to economic justice are now directed as much to state policy as to the labor contract. The potential for a new round of coalition-building remains; the populism of Jesse Jackson's Rainbow Coalition, for example, reached beyond conventional black politics to link a series of social movements, including environmentalism and feminism as well as civil rights. While electoral success remained concentrated in states with a large black population, primary victories in such unlikely places as Vermont and Alaska suggested that the coalition had broader support (Rogers, 1990). The radical capacity of such coalitions has been demonstrated most fully by the democracy movement in Eastern Europe, led by the cultural new class of professionals and intellectuals.

But the democracy movement raises a complication to this line of argument. Democracy does mean access to political enfranchisement and civil rights, but it also means access to full supermarket shelves. And so finally, and cautiously, we turn to the "debased" postmodernism of reaction.

Here, it should first be noted that the equivalence drawn between postmodern cultural forms and middle class privilege does not bear the *necessary* causality ascribed to it. For example, it has been noted that during the past decade postmodern design has been directed to such middle class icons as country houses, art museums, ski chalets and festival markets. This does not, however, reveal a necessary causal link with neoconservatism, for particular appropriations during the past decade do not exhaust a broader role for postmodernism itself. Indeed, as we shall see, social housing over the past twenty years has usually turned from austere modernism to more contextual postmodern motifs, but because there is so much less of it in a privatized era it does not have the same emblematic power as the designer locales of middle-class culture.

A second reflection on the so-called postmodernism of reaction is no doubt more tendentious. The landscapes of mass culture (and it is mass, not popular, culture that lies behind this conceptualization) are described in terms of consumer spaces of spectacle and the disneyesque and then dismissed in the convenient label of commodification, an overworked term which needs to be demystified. We are suggesting a more nuanced point which encompasses a more complex interpretation of the market, where what is hidden from consideration in the name of commodification reappears to line the shelves of supermarkets and bookstores. It is impossible to be unaware of the alienations of the market; this is a valid criticism as far as it goes and must be sustained, but it remains significantly incomplete. What the democracy movement reinforces is a perception that the market simultaneously *empowers*, albeit, and inherently, unequally. A fundamental resistance is a resistance to scarcity, a fundamental struggle is the struggle for survival. Access to goods (as basic as bread) is as much a facet of democratization as free elections and guarantees for the rights of the marginalized. Thus imperfectly and unequally the Janus face of commodification reveals also democratization; the hardback editions for the few become the paperback editions for the many. To this degree criticism of the consumption rights of others needs to be cautiously (and self-critically) shaped, and care taken that indiscriminate use of such terms as "disneyfication" is more than a statement of personal taste made possible by economic advantage (cf. Bourdieu, 1984). We suggest this conclusion may be a more general development of the point that Jameson is reaching for when he is pressed, but declines, to disqualify cultural postmodernism: "Think of its popular character and the relative democratization involved in various postmodernist forms...Postmodern architecture is demonstrably a symptom of democratization" (Stephanson, 1988, p. 12).

REFERENCES

AIA (American Institute of Architects) 1983 Postmodernism: Definition and Debate, *Journal of the American Institute of Architects* 72, 238–301.

Aronowitz, S. 1988 Postmodernism and Politics, in A. Ross (ed.), *Universal Abandon? The Politics of Postmodernism*. Minneapolis: University of Minnesota Press.

Berger, P., Berger, B. and H. Kellner 1973 *The Homeless Mind: Modernization and Consciousness*. New York: Random House.

Betz, H.G. 1989 Postmodern Politics and the New Middle Class: The Case of West Germany, unpublished paper, Department of Political Science, Marquette University.

Bianchini, F. 1987 Cultural Policy and Changes in Urban Political Culture: The "Postmodern Response" of the Left in Rome (1976–85) and London (1981–86), paper presented to the European Consortium for Political Research, Politics and Culture Workshop, Amsterdam, April.

Bourdieu, P. 1984 *Distinction*. London: Routledge & Kegan Paul.

Brantlinger, P. 1983 *Bread and Circuses: Theories of Mass Culture as Social Decay*. Ithaca, N.Y.: Cornell University Press.

Cosgrove, S. and A. Duff 1980 Environmentalism, Middle Class Radicalism and Politics, *Sociological Review*, 28, 333–51.

Debord, G. 1973 *Society of the Spectacle*. Detroit: Black and Red.

Deutsche, R. 1988 *Uneven Development: Public Art in New York City*. October, 47, 3–52.

Deutsche, R. 1991 Boys Town, *Society and Space*, 9, 5–30.

Fischer, V. 1985 SITE, in H. Klotz (ed.), *Postmodern Visions*. New York: Abbeville Press.

Foster, H. 1985 (Post)modern Polemics, in H. Foster (ed.), *Recodings: Art, Spectacle, Cultural Politics*. Port Townsend, WA: Bay Press.

Harvey, D. 1989 *The Condition of Postmodernity*. Oxford: Blackwell.

Harvey, D. 1990 Between Space and Time: Reflections on the Geographical Imagination, *Annals, Association of American Geographers*, 80, 418–34.

Horkheimer, M. and T. Adorno 1972 The Culture Industry: Enlightenment as Mass Deception, *Dialectic of Enlightenment*. New York: Herder and Herder.

Huyssen, A. 1984 Mapping the Postmodern, *New German Critique*, 33, 5–52.

Jacobs, J. 1971 *City Limits*. Ottawa: National Film Board 1971.

Jencks, C. 1981 *The Language of Post-Modern Architecture*. New York: Rizzoli.

Jencks, C. 1986 *What Is Post-Modernism?* New York: St. Martin's Press.

Ley, D. and K. Olds 1988 Landscape as Spectacle: World's Fairs and the Culture of Heroic Consumption, *Society and Space*, 6, 191–212.

Mouffe, C. 1988 Radical Democracy: Modern or Postmodern? in A. Ross (ed.), *Universal Abandon? The Politics of Postmodernism*. Minneapolis: University of Minnesota Press.

Offe, C. 1987 Challenging the Boundaries of Institutional Politics: Social Movements Since the 1960s, in C. Maier (ed.), *Changing Boundaries of the Political*. Cambridge: Cambridge University Press.

Robins, K. 1988 Reimagined Communities? European Image Spaces, Beyond Fordism. Unpublished paper, Centre for Urban and Regional Development Studies, University of Newcastle-Upon-Tyne.

Robins, K. and A. Gillespie 1988 Beyond Fordism? Place, Space and Hyperspace. Paper presented to the International Conference on Information, Technology and the New Meaning of Space, Frankfurt, May.

Rogers, A. 1990 Towards a Geography of the Rainbow Coalition, 1983–89, *Society and Space*, 8, 409–26.

Rustin, M. 1987 Place and Time in Socialist Theory, *Radical Philosophy*, 47, 30–36.

Soja, E. 1989 *Postmodern Geographies*. London: Verso.

Stephanson, A. 1988 A Conversation with Fredric Jameson, in A. Ross (ed.), *Universal Abandon? The Politics of Postmodernism*. Minneapolis: University of Minnesota Press.

32 The Spaces that Difference Makes: Some Notes on the Geographical Margins of the New Cultural Politics

Edward W. Soja and Barbara Hooper

Resistant politics remain possible in a postmodern era. But what makes a politics of resistance indicatively postmodern? In their survey of cultural criticism (and particularly of postcolonialist thinking), Soja and Hooper locate the difference in difference itself. Harkening back to this volume's earlier discussions of identity, the authors tell us that differences between people are hierarchically ordered, with those empowered to do the ordering pushing others to the margins of discourse and of physical space. To redress this subjugation, modernist politics prescribed discarding differences in order to rally about a singular commonality and thereby seize back the center. But Soja and Hooper identify something different: the formation at the margin of overlapping communities informed and empowered by their very differences, including (but certainly not limited to) race, class, gender, and culture. Note the similarities between Soja and Hooper's argument and that of Gillian Rose (Reading 27), in particular their shared presentation of discourse and the imaginary in spatial terms. The margins, they tell us, are no longer residual spaces defined by their enforced exclusion from the center and its authority. Instead, the margins are places in their own right, places of collective empowerment that actively refuse to shed their internal divisions so as to become an oppressive new center. In short, they become places that both displace and replace not just the center, but the very notion of centrality. Soja and Hooper thus provide a rich purview on postmodern politics, as the process whereby embodied identities, long silenced by reason of their appearance, practices and location, rise up to claim discursive and physical space for themselves locally, nationally, and globally.

On the Differences that Postmodernity Makes

The cultural politics of difference, whether old or new, arise primarily from the workings of power – in society and on space in both their material and imagined forms. Hegemonic power does not simply manipulate naïvely given differences between individuals and social groups, it actively *produces and reproduces difference* as a key strategy to create and maintain modes of social and spatial division that are advantageous to its continued empowerment. At the same time, those subjected, dominated, or exploited by the workings of hegemonic power and mobilized to resist by their putative postioning, their assigned "otherness", struggle against differentiation and division. This sociospatial differentiation, division and struggle is, in turn, cumulatively concretized and conceptualized historically and geographically as *uneven development*, a term which we use to describe the composite and dynamic spatio-temporal patterning of socially constructed differences at many different scales, from the local to the global.

Such differences as are ascribed to gender, sexual practice, race, class, region, nation, etc. are thus primarily "brute fashionings" (Cocks 1989: 20) which are neither transhistorical nor "natural" (in the sense of being naïvely or existentially given). This brute fashioning, as the social production (and strategic reproduction) of difference, is the catalyst for both hegemonic (conservative, order-maintaining) and counter-hegemonic (resistant, order-transforming) cultural and identity politics. That the historical process of uneven development is also intrinsically spatial as both medium and outcome gives to the (real and imagined) geography of cultural politics a particular significance.

Counter-hegemonic cultural politics has usually taken two broad forms, at least within Western capitalist societies. The first, rooted in the post-Enlightenment development of liberal humanism, has traditionally based its opposition on the assertion of universal principles of equality and democracy, seeking to reduce to a minimum the negative effects of difference whatever their origins. A second form of counter-hegemonic politics, not always completely separable from the first, arises from more radical contestation over the many axes along which socially constructed power differentials are polarized. Without excluding the liberal alternative entirely, what we define here as *modernist identity politics* refers primarily to this tradition of more radical subjectivity and resistance as it has developed since the mid-nineteenth century around such categories of cultural consciousness as class, race, ethnicity, nationality, colonial status, sexuality and gender.

Even when rejecting Marxian categories and explicitly revolutionary ideology, modernist identity politics and the various social and cultural movements associated with it have characteristically tended to develop along the lines charted out more than a century ago with respect to the formation of anticapitalist class-consciousness and the revolutionary struggle against exploitation. While varying greatly in their specificities, these movements have generally followed analogous trajectories based on a similar praxis of refusal and resistance that parallels the bipolar logic of class struggle: capital vs. labour, bourgeoisie vs. proletariat: a struggle defined around a deep structural dichotomy that "orders" differential power into two primary social categories, one dominant the other subordinate.

Each separate sphere of modernist identity politics has typically mobilized its version of radical subjectivity around a fundamentally epistemological critique of the binary ordering of difference that is particular to it: capital/labour, self/other, subject/object, colonizer/colonized, white/black, man/woman, majority/minority, heterosexual/homosexual. The critique is aimed at "denaturalizing" the origins of the binary ordering to reveal its social and spatial construction of difference as a means of producing and reproducing systematic patterns of domination, exploitation and subjection. As socially constructed, context-specific "technologies" of power (to use Foucault's term), these binary structures become subject to social and cultural transformation via a politics of identity that builds upon the empowerment of the "subaltern" against the "hegemon" (to use the most general terms covering the various oppositional forms of the cultural politics of difference).

Modernist identity politics characteristically projects its particular radical subjectivity, defined within its own oppressive binary structure, as overarchingly (and often universally) significant. Whether or not this totalization and essentialism is actually believed, its powerful mobilizing effect is used strategically in attempts to consolidate and intensify counter-hegemonic consciousness "for itself" and on its identified "home ground". In both theory and practice, therefore, a significant degree of closure and exclusiveness is embedded within the strategies and tactics of modernist identity politics. Even when one form avows its openness to alliance with others, it is usually open only on the former's terms and under its primary strategic guidance. The result has been the production of parallel, analogous, but rarely intersecting channels of radical political consciousness, each designed and primed to change their own discrete binary world of difference.

Under these ordered conditions, *fragmentation* (in the very real form of complex multiple subjectivities, with and without overlapping) becomes an endemic problem in modernist identity politics, especially for those social movements that theorize either a universalist encompassing of other radical subjectivities (e.g. substituting woman for women or the transcendental unity of an international working class for multiracial, multi-ethnic, and otherwise diverse men and women workers) or, alternatively, that recognize differences but none the less theorize and strategize from the assumption of the primacy and privileging of one or another set of agents in the process of radical social transformation. In the extreme case, as with most orthodox forms of modern Marxism and some forms of radical feminism and black nationalism, these essentialist tendencies abrogate any cross-cutting alliances of political significance by attributing "false consciousness" or subordinate identity to all radical subjectivities other than that emanating from the "primary" bipolarity.

When the primacy of one binary is viewed as competing with the privileging of another, the prospects for flexible and co-operative alliance and empathy are likely to be dim. While there have been fruitful dialogues between various radical movements (between Marxism and feminism, for example, and between both and those struggling against racism and colonial oppression), the deeply engrained essentialisms of modernist identity politics have tended to create a competitive exclusivity that resists, even rejects, seeing a "real" world populated by multiple subjects with many (often changeable) identities located in varying (and also changeable) subject positions. Hence, modernist identity politics, in its fear and rejection of a fragmented reality, has often tended to create and intensify political divisiveness rather than working toward a multiple, pluralized, and yet still radical conceptualization of agency and identity.

Modernist identity politics has always had to face reactionary hegemonic resistance and reformist liberal diversion. Over the past two decades, however, new theoretical and philosophical critiques (especially of taken-for-granted epistemologies and, in particular, the politically divisive tendencies toward master-narrative essentialism and binary totalization) and actual political events (ranging from the global restructurings of capital, labour, and ideology to the apparent defeat and retreat of governments inspired by modernist Marxism-Leninism and its dominant form of identity politics) have ushered in an extraordinary period of deep questioning that strikes more disruptively than ever before at the very foundations of modernist political practices – and simultaneously opens up new possibilities for radical resistance to all forms of hegemonic subordination.

There is no doubt that some who hasten to proclaim the death of modernism and announce the emergence of a new postmodern era from its ashes are motivated by the same old impulses of hegemonic re-empowerment and liberal diversion. But there is also emerging – in the postmodern blackness and post-colonialist critiques of bell hooks, Cornel West, Gayatri Spivak, Arjun Appadurai, Trinh T. Minh-Ha, Edward Said, Chandra Mohanty, Homi Bhabha; in the postmodern feminisms of Iris Marion Young, Jane Flax, Judith Butler, Diana Fuss, Meaghan Morris, Rosalyn Deutsche, Donna Haraway; and in the anti-essentialist critiques of various postmodern Marxist scholars such as Ernesto Laclau and Chantal Mouffe – a polyvocal postmodernism that maintains a commitment to radical social change while continuing to draw (selectively, but sympathetically) from the most powerful critical foundations of modernist identity politics. The intent behind this radical postmodernism of resistance is to deconstruct (not to destroy) the ebbing tide of modernist radical politics, to renew its strengths and avoid its weaknesses, and to reconstitute an explicitly postmodernist radical politics, a new cultural politics of difference and identity that moves toward empowering a multiplicity of resistances rather than searches for that one "great refusal", the singular transformation to precede and guide all others.

The *disordering* of difference from its persistent binary structuring and the reconstitution of difference as the basis for a new cultural politics of multiplicity and strategic alliance among all who are peripheralized, marginalized and subordinated by the social construction of difference (especially in its binary forms) are key processes in the development of radical postmodernism. Whether this revisioning of radical subjectivity requires a major transformation or merely a significant reform of modernist identity politics is still being contested. But it is clear that politics as usual can no longer be practised as it was in the past, at least among those who take seriously the conditioning effects of postmodernity.

In the wake of this continuing debate, a new breed of radical anti-postmodernists has emerged in force to "spin-doctor" the critical discourse toward reformist solutions and away from any deep deconstruction and reconstitution of modernist traditions. Given the intellectual elitism and neoconservative politics that have dominated so much of the postmodernist discourse, there is ample ammunition for the radical anti-postmodernist project. After all, the deconstructive challenge raised by postmodernism often sounds suspiciously like the same old hegemonic strategies of opposition, co-optation, and diversion; and the affirmedly prefixed "post" seems too literally to signal the irrevocable end of all progressive modernist projects rather than their potentially advantageous reconstitution. Moreover, to most modernist critics, the multiplicity of resistances continue to be seen as inevitably leading to a politically debilitating fragmentation and the abandonment of long-established forms of struggle. Under these presumed circumstances, the promise of eventual emancipatory reconstitution rings hollow, if not cruelly deceptive, especially at a time when nearly all radical modern movements are either in crisis or massive retreat.

The tendency to homogenize postmodernism and to totalize (i.e., ascribe to all postmodernisms) certain negative and oppressive political practices associated with postmodernity, makes the construction of a radical postmodern alternative even more difficult. Theoretically suggestive aphorisms arising from the postmodern and related post-structuralist critiques ("there is no reality outside the text", "the death of the subject", "anything goes") are now routinely set up as straw-objects to prove that all postmodern politics are abstract, unrelated to everyday life, inherently reactionary – and hence, immanently nihilistic with respect to real radical politics. A forbidding wall of categorical totems and taboos has thus been raised to hide the very possibility of radical postmodernism, making it all but invisible to outsiders, especially on the left.

In our view, this forbidding wall has materialized around the same modernist conditioning and rigid either/or logic that has become so central a target for contemporary cultural criticism and the new politics of difference: the infatuation with clean and orderly binary oppositions; the intolerance of ambiguity, disordering, multiplicity, fragmentation; the urge to unity enforced by epistemological closure and essentialism. The arguments we have outlined as a critique of modernist identity politics are thus a critique of the flourishing new anti-postmodernism. It is a critique that calls for a new way of looking at and making practical political sense of the precise circumstances of the contemporary moment, drawing insight from the realization that postmodernity has made more significant differences to our real and imagined political worlds than it has reinforced continuities with the past.

To turn what has thus far been a primarily deconstructive critique of modernism into a more reconstructive programme for a radical postmodernist cultural politics requires developing a more complex understanding of the key themes of disordering difference and empowering multiplicity. To work toward this understanding, our discussion takes a more explicitly spatial turn, into a subregion of the contemporary literature on the new cultural politics of difference that has begun to reconceptualize its discourse and critique around the spaces that difference makes. We suggest that it is here, in the creative spatialization arising from the broad field of cultural studies, that radical postmodernism is being most effectively conceptualized and made practically political.

The Spatial Turn in the New Cultural Politics of Difference

In *Yearning: Race, Gender, and Cultural Politics*, . . . bell hooks (1990) attempts to move beyond modernist binary oppositions of race, gender and class into the multiplicity of *other* spaces that difference makes; into a re-visioned spatiality that creates from difference new sites for struggle and for the construction of interconnected communities of resistance. In so doing, she opens up in these real and imagined "other spaces" the possibilities for a new cultural politics of difference and identity that is both radically postmodern and strategically spatialized from the start. This creative (re)spatialization is more than an appealing metaphor or abstraction. It is a vital discursive turn that both grounds the new cultural politics and facilitates its conceptual re-visioning around the empowerment of multiplicity, the construction of combinatorial rather than competitively fragmented and separated communities of resistance.[. . .]

hooks finds her place, positions herself (first of all as an African-American woman), by the simultaneously political and geographical act of *choosing marginality*. This positioning of identity is detached from the "narrow cultural nationalism masking continued fascination with the power of the white [and/or male] hegemonic order". Such an identification, hooks suggests, would not be choosing marginality but accepting its imposition by the more powerful, binary Other, a submission to the dominant, order-producing, and unremittingly modernist ideology and epistemology of difference. Instead, such an assertion of recentred identity "is evoked as a stage in a process wherein one constructs radical black subjectivity" (or what she has more recently called "wildness" (hooks 1992)). By extension and adjustment, choosing marginality can also become a critical turning point in the construction of other forms of counter-hegemonic or subaltern identity and more embracing communities of resistance.

As an initial stage, categorical identity as subaltern is crucial. But hooks' construction of radical black subjectivity pushes the process of identity formation beyond exclusionary struggles against white racism on to a new terrain, a "space of radical openness" where the key question of "who we can be and still be black" can be politically re-imagined. "Assimilation, imitation, or assuming the role of rebellious exotic are not the only options and never have been", hooks notes in rejecting the conventional choices that liberal modernist discourse has frequently imposed upon the activist black subject. Instead, she chooses a space that is simultaneously central and marginal (and purely neither at the same time), a difficult and risky place on the edge, in-between, filled with contradictions and ambiguities, with perils but also with new possibilities. [. . .]

This alternative process of choosing marginality reconceptualizes the problematic of subjection by deconstructing both margin and centre, while reconstituting in the restructured (recentred) margins new spaces of opportunity, the new spaces that difference makes. For hooks, and by extension and invitation, all others involved in this spatial disordering of difference, there is a "definite distinction between the marginality which is imposed by oppressive structure and that marginality one chooses as site of resistance, as location of radical openness and possibility" [. . .]

In choosing marginality as a space of radical openness, hooks contributes significantly to a powerful revisioning not only of the cultural politics of difference but also of our conceptualization of human geographies, of what we mean by the politics of location and geohistorically uneven development, of how we creatively combine spatial metaphor and spatial materiality in an assertively spatial *praxis*. By recontextualizing spatiality, she engages in a cognitive remapping of our many real and imagined worlds – from the most local confines of the body, the spatiality closest in, to the nested geographical worlds that are repeated again and again in an expanding sequence of scales reaching from the "little tactics of the habitat" to the "great strategies" of global geopolitics. For hooks, the political project is to occupy these (real and imagined) spaces on the margins, to reclaim them as locations of radical openness and possibility, and to make within them a place where one's radical subjectivity can be *seen* and practised in association with other radical subjectivities. It is thus a spatiality of inclusion rather than exclusion, a spatiality where radical subjectivities can multiply, connect and combine in polycentric communities of identity and resistance: the spatiality searched for but never effectively discovered in modernist identity politics. [...]

Remapping the city as a space of radical openness, a place where, like hooks' margin, ties are severed and subjection abounds but also, at the same time, a location for recovery and resistance, a meeting place where new and radical happenings can occur, has been a longstanding feminist project dating back at least to the fourteenth century. The feminist urban critique, led by architects, planners and geographers, broadened its base in the late 1970s around revealing analyses of the gendering of space (especially in the forms of the urban built environment) and the reproduction of this male-dominated gendering through the contextualizing effects of patriarchy.

For the most part, this expanded feminist critique and spatial remapping remained modernist, in the sense of channelling its critical power and emancipatory objectives around the gendered binary men/women. Urban spatiality thus came to be seen as oppressively gendered in much the same way that the city was shown to be structured by the exploitative class relations of capitalism and the discriminatory geographical effects of racism, the two other major channels of radical modernist urban critique developing over the same period. More recently, however, primarily through the development of an openly postmodern feminism, new directions are being taken that bring the feminist urban critique and remapping from its revealing recognition that space makes a difference into a creative exploration of the multiplicity of spaces that difference makes. What is new about this development, that is, how the postmodern feminist critique of urban spatiality can be distinguished from its modernist forms, brings us back to where we started, to "how and what constitutes difference, the weight and gravity it is given in representation", as Cornel West argued; into a more encompassing politics of difference and identity that opens new spaces for critical exchange and creative responses "to the precise circumstances of our present moment"; and into the strategic acts of disordering difference and choosing marginality.

In this growing literature, many new ways of looking at urban spatiality are explored. The body as the most intimate of spatialities is rediscovered and given a central place in the construction of real and imagined geographies of the city, while through this embodiment the city becomes charged with multiple sexualities. The alternative spaces of the visual and aesthetic imagination – in films, photography, advertising, fashion, museum exhibitions, murals, poems, novels, but also in shopping malls and beaches, factories and streets, motels and theme parks – are imaginatively evoked as ways of seeing the city; and in the works of such cultural critics as Rosalyn Deutsche and Meaghan Morris, the construction of these spaces (as *oeuvres*, works of art, as well as *produits*, manufactured products) is connected directly to the material dynamics of geographically uneven development and the political economy of contemporary capitalism. Iris Marion Young and Nancy Fraser, among others, have engaged effectively in deconstructing and reconstituting the ideology of urban community and the old modernist binary of public vs. private space in an explicitly radical postmodern and feminist politics of difference, while Donna Haraway has added nature and high technology to this ideological deconstruction and reconstitution.

Of particular importance here and now, in these "other" spaces and different geographies being opened up by the postmodern cultural critics, is the insight provided on how fragmentation, ruptures and discontinuities can be politically transformed from liability and weakness to opportunity and strength, a project which helps define the boundary between adaptive modernism and creative postmodernism. In the new postmodern cultural and geographical politics of difference, we position ourselves first by subjectively choosing *for ourselves* our primary "marginal" identities as feminist, black, radical socialist, anti-colonialist, gay and lesbian activist. But we do not remain rigidly confined by this "territorial" choice, as was usually the case in modernist identity politics. We seek instead to find more flexible ways of being other than we are while still being ourselves, of becoming open to combinations of radical subjectivities, to a multiplicity of communities of resistance, to what Trinh T. Minh-ha has called "the anarchy of difference" (Trinh 1991: 120; see also Trinh 1989).

Trinh develops a strategy of *displacement* (as opposed to a strategy of reversal), which adds significantly to hooks' reconceptualization of marginality. "Without a certain work of displacement", she writes, "the margins can easily recomfort the center in goodwill and liberalism." The margins are "our fighting grounds" but also "their site for pilgrimage... while we turn around and claim them as our exclusive territory, they happily approve, for the divisions between margins and center should be preserved, and as clearly demarcated as possible, if the two positions are to remain intact in their power relations". By actively displacing and disordering difference, by insisting that there are "no master territories", one struggles to prevent "this classifying world" from exerting its ordered, binary, categorical power.

Diana Fuss adds further insight to the caution needed and dangers involved in choosing marginality, and helps to defend this strategic choice against those who feel uneasy when persons of substantial power and status (bell hooks? Ed Soja?) subjectively position themselves in the margins. [...]

Gayatri Chakravorty Spivak faces the challenge of choosing marginality and the locational politics of difference through a similar deconstruction, displacement and repositioning. But more so than hooks and the urban feminists, Spivak and other key figures in what has come to be called postcolonial or subaltern studies, move beyond deconstruction and repositioning to begin another remapping, one of more explicitly global proportions. For Spivak, this remapping is a move "beyond a homogeneous internationalism, to the persistent recognition of heterogeneity", to a new "worlding of the world" (Spivak 1988a: 20; see also Spivak 1988b). She encapsules the difficulty of this task in the slow and careful labour of "un-learning our privilege as our loss", of "behaving as if you are part of the margin" but doing so by relinquishing the privileges that attach to choosing marginality as a space of radical resistance from the centre (Spivak 1990: 9, 30).

Thinking synchronically, in the precise (spatial) circumstances of the present (postmodern) moment, Spivak positions herself as a *bricoleur*, a preserver of discontinuities, an interruptive critic of the categorical logic of colonizer–colonized, elite–subaltern, global–local, centre–periphery, First World–Third World. [. . .]

Spivak's remapping (reworlding) disrupts the coherent spatiality of territorial imperialism, Eurocentrism, and spatial science – as well as the spatiality of modernist feminism and Marxism. And she does so with a strategic twist that brings "hegemonic historiography to crisis", a critique of Western historicism that becomes a vital turn in her reworlding project and in the larger spatialization of the new cultural politics of difference. [. . .]

From Modern Geography to Postmodern Geographies

The objectivist or materialist mode of spatial thinking and analysis has dominated modern geography throughout the twentieth century in a sequence that has shifted emphasis several times – from the simple contingencies of environmental determinism and possibilism, to the theoretically innocent description of the areal differentiation of human-environment relations, to the so-called quantitative and theoretical revolution of spatial science (which made more rigorous the accurate description of material geographies), to the radical redirection of spatial science in Marxist, feminist and other "critical" human geographies (seeking not simply more accurate description but "emancipatory" explanation, understanding and practice). The objects of analysis and explanation in all these phases are the concrete material forms of empirically "real" geographies seen as outcomes of what are typically presumed to be influential but usually non-spatial processes, such as those arising from the exigencies of societal cohesion, ecological adaptation, capitalist accumulation or the maintenance of patriarchal power.

A subjectivist or idealist geography has often arisen as a counterfoil to excessive objectivism, materialism and scientism, not unlike what has occurred in many other disciplines. Within the field, these subjectivist approaches, drawing deeply from humanistic, existential, phenomenological and cognitive or psycho-behavioural traditions, have tended to take on connotative aspects of the subaltern against the materialist hegemon. Except on very rare occasions, the material geographies remain the primary objects of explanation, understanding or interpretation, but the implied causality is seen as primarily ideational and subjective, formed in what are primarily "imagined" geographies rather than arising directly from objective material social (or other non-spatial) processes.

To borrow, with some modification, from Lefebvre, the first mode is fixed on the real "spaces of representation" while the second is focused on the imagined "representations of space". It is easy to say (as most geographers do) that both are important and should be combined in good geographical analysis, but too often in the history of geographic thought, subjectivism and objectivism, imagined and real geographies, have been placed in rigid opposition, especially when couched in extreme or essentialist forms of idealism or materialism. Philosophical and methodological critique in modern geography has tended to be dominated by this categorical opposition or by the struggles for intrabinary primacy between specific forms of materialist and ideational analysis, fostering a continuation of this divisive split and either/or competition.

Here is one point where the earlier discussion of binary orderings of difference and the critique of modernist identity politics becomes particularly relevant. In the new cultural politics of difference, the aim is neither simply to assert dominance of the subaltern over the hegemon in a rigidly maintained bipolar order, nor even to foster some specified combination of opposing traits and traditions. It is to break down and disorder the binary itself, to reject the simple structure of closed dualisms through a (sympathetic) deconstruction and reconstitution that allows for radical openness, flexibility and multiplicity. The key step is to recognize and occupy new and alternative geographies – a "thirdspace" of political choice – different but not detached entirely from the geographies defined by the original binary oppositions between and within objectivism and subjectivism.

For Lefebvre, this alternative geography is the socially produced spatiality wherein the directly experienced spaces of representation and the conceptual representations of space can strategically interrelate in the lived (*vécu*) contextuality of *spatial praxis*. Lefebvre always remained a Marxist and a materialist first, but his counter-hegemonic spatial praxis sought to recombine materialism and idealism and to reach beyond the parochialisms and illusions of both. He was able to achieve this recombinative simultaneity only by opening up a new terrain, by finding new sites for active resistance and critical dialogue. A similar thirdspace of political choice also figures prominently in Foucault's heterotopias, "formed in the very founding of society" as "something like counter-sites, a kind of effectively enacted utopia in which the real sites, all the other real sites that can be found within the culture, are simultaneously represented, contested, and inverted". Heterotopias, combining the real and imagined, are the "space in which we live, which draws us out of ourselves, in which the erosion of our lives, our time and our history occurs, the space that claws and gnaws at us."

We contend that the spatiality of bell hooks and others involved in the postmodern discourse on the new cultural politics can best be located and understood in this thirdspace of political choice – and inversely, that the explorers of this different spatiality cannot be appropriately seen and understood by those confined by the more traditional spatialities of modernism, whether trained as geographers or not. Hence our call for the development of *postmodern geographies* as a radical standpoint, perspective and positioning from which we can begin the process of re-visioning spatiality in a contemporary world where all real geographies are imagined and all imagined geographies are real.

Our final argument has to do with a more specific counter-hegemonic project that may be particularly suited to the marginal position occupied by the discipline of geography in the twentieth-century intellectual division of labour. The discipline can be described as having been doubly marginalized over most of the past century, first in conjunction with the modern social sciences and humanities (and for physical geography, within the physical sciences as well), with geography dwelling intellectually in an often forgotten periphery of utilitarian fact-gathering and map-making; and second, in the historical development of specifically social and political theory and philosophy, where the ontological and epistemological hegemony of history over geography, the temporal over the spatial, as well as the discipline of geography's own parochial spatialisms, further intensified the discipline's isolation and peripheralness. We suggest here that this peripheral positioning can now be used as a site of opportunity, another place of radical openness where new alternatives can be imagined and effectively practised by consciously and strategically disordering difference and choosing marginality.

We thus raise again the issue of *historicism* and hegemonic historiography. This privileging of the "making" of history and the critical historical imagination over the "making" of geographies and what should be the equally revealing and emancipatory power of the critical geographical imagination continues largely unquestioned and unacknowledged even among many postmodern cultural critics and geographers. The power engrained in the real and imagined spatiality of social life is recognized and creatively explored, but such exploration too often remains auxiliary to the superordinate significance of historical understanding and interpretation.

In identifying this alleged epistemological hegemony of historicism, it is difficult to avoid appearing simplistically antagonistic to the rich emancipatory insights of critical historiography: to be somehow "against" time and history and "for" space and geography. This is not the intention of the contemporary critique of historicism. Instead, the aim is to deconstruct and reconstitute the geographical and historical imaginations in a critical "trialectic" that revolves around the problematic interrelations between historicity, spatiality and sociality; or, more concretely and consciously political, the (social) making of histories, the (social) production of human geographies, and the (spatio-temporal) constitution of social practices and relations. Here again, the assertively spatialized discourse on the new cultural politics of difference vividly enters the debate, providing another way to clarify and redefine its meaning and intent: that from whatever disciplinary perspective we come from, to be critical thinkers we must all be historians, geographers and social analysts.

The critique of historicism can appropriately be seen, in this new light, as a critique of the constraining effects of an intellectually hegemonic historiography and an intellectually subordinated geography. Its tactics are not those of categorical inversion, constructing an essentialist spatialism in historicism's place, but of decentring the hegemonic subject, of disordering differences and creating a new terrain of reassembly, a common ground of multidisciplinarity, where we can be historical and spatial and critically social simultaneously and without a priori privileging of one or another viewpoint. This too is a space of openness, an "inclusive space where we recover ourselves", where one can be seen and be in contact with other sites of radical subjectivity and counter-hegemonic resistance. As bell hooks has said: Marginality is the space of resistance. Enter that space. Let us meet there.

REFERENCES

Cocks, J. (1989) *The Oppositional Imagination: Feminism, Critique and Political Theory*, London: Routledge, 20.

Fraser, N. (1990) "Rethinking the public sphere: a contribution to the critique of actually existing democracy". *Social Text* 25/26.

Haraway, D. (1991) *Simians, Cyborgs and Women: the Reconstruction of Nature*, New York: Routledge.

hooks, b. (1990) *Yearnings: Race, Gender and Cultural Politics*, Boston: South End Press.

—— (1992) *Black Looks: Race and Representation*, Boston: South End Press.

Spivak, G. C. (1988a) "Subaltern studies: deconstructing historiography", in R. Guha and G. C. Spivak (eds) *Selected Subaltern Studies*, New York: Oxford University Press.

—— (1988b) *In Other Worlds: Essay in Cultural Politics*, New York: Routledge.

—— (1990) *The Post-Colonial Critic: Interviews, Strategies, Dialogues*, New York: Routledge.

Trinh, T. Minh-Ha (1989) *Women, Native, Other: Writing Postcoloniality and Feminism*, Bloomington: Indiana University Press.

—— (1991) *When the Moon Waxes Red: Representation, Gender and Cultural Politics*, New York: Routledge.

Young, I. M. (1990) "The ideal of community and the politics of differences", in L. J. Nicholson (ed) *Feminism/Postmodernism*, London and New York: Routledge, 300–23.

33 Materialities, Spatialities, Globalities

John Law and Kevin Hetherington

The postmodern condition is often attributed to a compression of space and time, whereby our encounters with diverse and formerly distant ways of seeing the world increase in number and accelerate in frequency. These encounters undermine single-minded certainties of what the world is, of how we should be in the world. Space–time compression, however, must itself be accounted for, and to this end structural and technocentric factors are commonly invoked: the advent of "quicksilver capital" and international capital markets, the global spread of communication and transportation technologies, or simply something called "globalization." Confronted with the totalizing techno-economic logic of such a planetary structural juggernaut, can the spaces that difference makes survive on a global scale? John Law and Kevin Hetherington argue that there can indeed be such spaces, because globalization is not the monolithic structure it appears. They deconstruct globalization, revealing it as the aggregate of underlying relations between identifiable people and objects in identifiable locales. They claim that people and things enter into sustained relationships with one another, mutually coadapting to form hybrid network entities that extend across the planet and transform it. Globalization is therefore composed of innumerable connections that are subject to redirection, disruption, and collapse. In this way, Law and Hetherington demonstrate that space–time compression is not some faceless force of nature. It is the product of particular relationships within and between places, and eminently susceptible to intervention.

Global Visions Local Materialities

Six hundred years ago the world was divided into a series of different regions. Europe, the Arab world, China, Japan, the civilisations of the Indus, the Mayas and the Incas, various sub-Saharan civilisations, these and others existed apart from one another. Yes, there were some contacts. Arabs and Christians were engaged in a sustained trial of strength around the Mediterranean. The Chinese made periodic forays far from home. And there was a trade in luxuries between Europe and Asia. But there was no "world-system". Economic, social and cultural life subsisted almost independently in the separate regions of the world. Indeed, one might say that those different regions existed in different worlds.

Between the years 1400 and 1900 this all changed. A single world-system emerged as Europe colonised and came to dominate most of these other regions. The world entered a period of sustained economic growth which included revolutions in agricultural production, the harnessing of new energy sources, the growth of manu-facture and a world division of labour which depended on immeasurable improve-ments in transport and communications. At the same time, and as an inseparable part of this, a capitalist world order emerged. This was associated with huge increases in wealth and productivity. It was also characterised by massively unequal distributions in wealth, both within regions and to an even more marked extent, between core and peripheral regions. It was associated with the development of the European (subsequently the world-wide) nation state. And finally it was linked to the ever increasing importance of knowledge as a resource closely related to economic production – and more recently to consumption and cultural change.

Many of the formal trappings of the imperialist world order have now disap-peared. The past forty years has seen the virtual end of political colonialisation, and in certain respects the nation state appears to be under threat. But there is as much continuity as discontinuity. The nexus of capitalist enterprise, world trade, world division of labour, unequal division of resources, and growth in knowledge and communications has continued to develop apace. And it is clear that in terms of the flow of goods, information and people we live in many respects in an era that is both mobile and global. Networks of information, of sociation, span the world.

Marx notoriously observed – following Shakespeare's Prospero in *The Tempest* – that in capitalism all that is solid melts into air. He was thinking of old feudal loyalties – and more generally any forms of life which were irrelevant to the logic of capitalist economic accumulation. His aphorism still applies. Economic and cultural stabilities are more than ever elusive and ungraspable. The global economy with its information and capital flows is dominatory, generating asymmetries and distribut-ing and redistributing opportunities and miseries ever more rapidly. Social relations are disembedded from local contexts and stretched across time and space. The world is compressed and our links are distanciated at the same time. And, as a part of all this, cultural production is also more rapid than ever. Fragmented, its diasporic and hybrid character can be taken as a sign for the totality of a cultural shift.

In social science this story has been told in a number of different ways: as capitalist accumulation and world-domination; as a process of industrialisation; and, more recently, as a story about the networks of globalisation, and a shift from production to culture and consumption. Our brief sketch indeed reflects all of these, and this is a necessary context for what follows. But what we are most concerned with is the nexus of knowledge, space and economy as seen from one particular point of view: a concern with what we will what we will call materiality. So what does this mean? And where does it come from?

The most straightforward answer is that materiality is about stuff, the stuff of the world. Straightforwardly, we can imagine three kinds of stuff. First there are objects. Here, then, a concern with materiality is a concern with machines, houses and supermarkets. It is about satellite communications, military technologies, motorcars, the growth, the distribution and the consumption of tea and coffee. It is about the fancy corporate headquarters of the multinationals – or the favelas, the slums, of Rio de Janeiro. It is about the water supply in a Zimbabwe village, or the cable networks beneath the streets of London.

So stuff is about objects. But it is also about bodies too – for bodies are material. So it is about how bodies display themselves in clothes and cosmetics as objects of the gaze, come to embody their conditions of work, are added to or repaired by prostheses. It is about the conditions of childbirth or the embodiments of child-rearing. It is about blind bodies as they find their way around museums or try to get on and off the bus. It is about ability and disability.

So objects and bodies are stuff. They are material. But so too are information and media, and this is our third category of materiality. Texts such as this, newspapers, the pictures on the television at night, books in libraries, CD roms, maps, films, statistical tables, spreadsheets, musical scores, architect's drawings, engineering designs, all of these are information – but information in material form.

Until recently social science has had problems in thinking about materiality. Materials have usually been present in what's written because it's so obvious that the world and its relations are made of materials. But, at the same time, they have also been strangely absent from it – perhaps because it is so obvious that the world is made of materials that they've been taken-for-granted. And when they haven't been taken-for-granted sometimes the role of materials have been hyped up into some kind of drama in which we learn that technological changes determine how we live. The current candidate for this is the Web, though the same was said about the printing press, electricity and the electric telegraph. But this "technological determinism" is too simple. This is because technologies are shaped by social circumstances. The Web is a case in point. Its origins lie in the US military concern to create robust communication networks which would withstand Soviet nuclear attack. Had electronic communications developed under some other regime there is every reason to suppose that they would have been different in character. So instead of saying that technologies determine social life we need to say something more complicated, like: technologies-and-knowledge-about-technologies-and-a-good-deal-of-hard-work-and-capitalist-economic-relations together determine (parts of?) social life. Which catches fewer headlines, but is more realistic. And also reflects the way in which different materials – objects and technologies, bodies and texts are produced by and simultaneously produce social and economic relations.

So materials come in different shapes, forms, and kinds, and they interact together to reshape one another and produce effects. The implication of this argument is that if we want to understand phenomena such as global capital flows, the transmission of information, cultural hybridity, or economic inequality, it is also important to ask how the relations that produce these are materially brought into being and sustained in particular locations. This takes us back to the point about the invisibility of materiality. Thus for all the talk about globalisation, this is a phenomenon that also takes material form and does so in particular locations. And these are worthy of study. Indeed, if we want to understand how globalisation is achieved we have no choice: we have to look at the ways in which it is materially produced.

This takes us into questions to do with space. As is obvious, globalisation or world systems are spatial phenomena. They are made by materials which are in space – but which also have spatial effects. Some of those spatial effects have to do with inequality and domination. For instance, the literature on economics tells us that information is costly and that profit – indeed good decision-making – depends upon, is often almost indistinguishable from, superior information, quicker information, less distorted information. The better telegraph, the faster steamboat, the more powerful intranet, these are key tools in achieving advantage. So material arrangements generate information. They also generate rapidly moving information, which is why we say that they have spatial effects. In important respects the City of London is closer to Wall Street than it is to inner-city Salford. And this leads us to reflect on the character of spatiality itself. So we'll make the argument that spatiality isn't just about the Euclidean space of the globe, the space dealt with in physical geography. We'll argue that it is also about material networks which imply a different form of space. And then we'll go on to argue that the asymmetries of global capitalism, of information, may be understood in terms of the interaction between Euclidean and network spaces. That they are a consequence of what one might think of as spatial non-conformities.

Material Heterogeneity and Knowing Locations

To address global concerns it is often best to be local, specific and material. That is the assumption with which we start.

The place in which we might start is a managing director's office. It might be anywhere in a medium-sized enterprise. Actually it is the office of the director of Daresbury SERC Laboratory in the UK. It's furnished as one might expect. At one end, the end away from the door, there is a large desk and an office chair, a computer, a telephone and various other pieces of equipment. Then, at the other end of the table, nearer the door, there is a modest boardroom table, a table for meetings. It seats six, perhaps eight, people in comfortable upright chairs. Then there is a third area to one side, an informal area, with a coffee table, three or four easy chairs, a few magazines and scientific publications. This is where the director relaxes with high status guests. Where they may drink coffee and eat biscuits.

So where does the coffee come from? We might respond to this by talking about the global and link it with the local. By talking, say, of Andrew's office as the end point of a network associated with coffee beans produced in Columbia or Kenya. And this is not, of course, incorrect. However, for us this move already makes too many assumptions about the materiality of connections, and of how the global and the local are different in character. So we want to remain for the time being in Andrew's office without moving to sub-tropical plantations. In which case to find out where the coffee comes from we need to move through one of the doors into a large room where the secretaries work, typing, fielding phone calls, emails and visitors, keeping diaries, ordering up tickets, reports, and, yes, making coffee. Two rooms, then, with doors that lead also onto a corridor where people may wait to visit the managing director. A corridor where the trappings of power – the pile carpet, the décor – are suddenly absent.

The details don't matter. And in one way they are trivial. Everyone knows that power attracts trappings. But these are not just trappings. They are not idle. They are also performative. That is they act. And as they form part of a materially heterogeneous network of bits and pieces of all kinds, that participate in the generation of information, of power relations, of subjectivities and objectivities.

This is more obvious for some trappings than others. For instance Andrew, the managing director, is frowning at his computer. This is because he's discovered that the biggest project in the laboratory is seriously behind schedule, though it's only been going for a few months. But how does he know this? How has this been made visible? How has this information come into being? The answer is that he's got a spreadsheet up on the PC which tells him how much work time (they call it "manpower") has gone into the project so far. And he's comparing this with what they planned – and the two are very different. The project is a number of months behind schedule. Indeed, though this isn't obvious in any other way, it's used up most of its contingency time already.

We may think of Andrew, then, not just as a man but more specifically as a knowing location. Or a point of surveillance. But he's only a point of surveillance – he only knows – because he is at the right place in a network of materially heterogeneous elements. This is the argument, then, about material heterogeneity. We might number: his computer; its software; the figures typed into the spreadsheet; the process of collating those figures carried out by people in the finance department; the work of filling in the time sheets that is done (or supposedly done) on a monthly basis by all employees; the decisions that those employees have made about how to allocate their time (for in practice most work doesn't come in half-day blocks which is all the time sheets allow). And then we can extend the network: into the power company (no electricity, no surveillance), the work of the programmers both locally and at Microsoft, the decisions by previous directors to implement a time-booking system, the production of the time sheets; and then the car that Andrew drove to work; the fact that he and the other employees are paid; the telephone and the email that allow him to summon the other senior managers to an emergency meeting. For, yes, the point of this analysis is that the relations that produce knowing locations, information, are endless. That they are materially heterogeneous. And, one way or another, they all have to be in more or less working condition if there is to be such a thing as a "knowing location". We're saying, then, that knowing is a relational effect.

Let's state this more formally. In approaching knowledge in this way we're using what one might think of as a semiotics of materiality. It is about materiality for the reasons we have discussed: because knowledge, power, and subjectivities are all produced in circumstances that are materially heterogeneous. This means, inter alia, that the distinctions between human and non-human, between ideas and objects, between knowledge and infrastructure – that all of these are seriously overdrawn. And it is a semiotics because it assumes that what is produced, together with whatever goes to produce it, secures its significance, meaning, or status not because it is essentially this way or that, but rather because of how everything interacts together. So Andrew is a managing director not because this is given in the order of things, but because he is at the centre of a network. The spreadsheet is a spreadsheet because it relates to him, his computer, the power supply and everything else in a particular way. If something goes wrong then Andrew isn't a managing director any more – and the spreadsheet is similarly no longer a spreadsheet. A semiotics of materiality suggests that objects, materials, information, people and (one might add) the divisions between big and small or global and local, these are all relational effects. They are nothing more than relational effects. Which is why it is so important to study how they are produced.

Knowing at a Distance, Acting at a Distance

Here is another story about knowledge. It is more obviously about globalisation than the events in a laboratory, but it too is about material specificities. It's about the early stages of the imperialist expansion that we mentioned above, the early stages of the growth of the world system in the sixteenth century. It is about the Portuguese route to India.

Though there are a few exceptions, most of the histories of the Portuguese expansion mention their ships and navigational tools as important but essentially infrastructural items, means to the Portuguese end of seizing the spice trade from the Venetians and the Arabs, indulging in holy war, or discovering previously unknown sources of gold. Like the props for managing directors, powerful people and information-gatherers there is a division between social actors on the one hand and important but essentially uninteresting furniture on the other. But as we have just seen, a semiotics of materiality refuses this division and prior judgement about what is important or not, and says that if we want to understand how knowledge is produced we need to look at the whole set of heterogeneous elements, human and social on the one hand, and non-human and technical on the other. So how does this work for the Portuguese?

The quick answer is that the ship, its crew and its surroundings (or the navigator, his tables and instruments, and the sun or the stars) need to be seen as a continuous network. If the different parts stay in place, if their relations with their neighbours hold them in role, then the network as a whole generates knowledges. For instance, the Portuguese navigator together with his instruments, astronomical tables, and appropriate sightings of (say) the North Star, could determine the latitude of the vessel. The whole network of elements, arrayed together, produced that (vital) knowledge. Other physical effects might also result. The vessel itself, its equipment, its provisions and stores, its crew, knowledge of how to catch the winds, to take advantage of the currents, how to steer a course, knowledge of location, plus charts – these were parts of a network which helped (if all the parts successfully held one another in place) to sustain a watertight and seaworthy ship rather than (for instance) a collection of drowning mariners and a mess of wood splintered somewhere on a reef.

The argument once again is that knowledge, objects and people (or "subjects") are relational effects or emergent phenomena. Writer and philosopher Bruno Latour has a very particular way of saying this. He talks of immutable mobiles. In this way of talking, the immutable mobile is a network of elements that holds its shape as it moves. Indeed like a ship. Or, one might add, in cybernetic mode, like the electronic symbols, the bits and bytes of contemporary communication. So in this kind of account the vessel or the electronic symbol is a network that holds its shape and moves through Euclidean space But, we could add, so too is the navigator-chart-instrument-table network (or the electronic network). Or, indeed, the chart all by itself.

Do networks of relations hold their shape as they pass through geographical space? This is the crucial (if oversimplified) question which links knowledge with space. Or, restated, do (sub)networks insert themselves into larger networks of relations which are sufficiently stable so that they hold their shape and may pass through geographical space? These questions are ways of talking both about action at a distance or domination, and about knowledge at a distance or surveillance. For if the Portuguese were able to control the spice trade for nearly a century, if they were able to bombard the inhabitants of Calicut into submission, if they were able to get to India and get back, then this is because they succeeded by luck or good judgement in generating an array, a global network, within which immutable mobiles might circulate. Such that if a command was given in Lisbon, then war might be fought in India. Such that if a command was given in Lisbon it was both heard and enacted in India.

"Action at a distance". "Knowledge at a distance". A note is needed here about distance and about space. For this, as we noted in the introduction, is an important, indeed a vital, twist to the argument. We want to suggest that making action and knowledge at a distance not only makes action, knowledge and global asymmetry – though it certainly does all of these things. In addition we want, and somewhat counter-intuitively, to suggest that it also makes distance or space perform these into being. Which means that distances and space don't exist by themselves as part of the order of things. But rather that they are created.

That's a simple statement of a counterintuitive notion. But what does it mean? Let's start to answer by thinking empirically. Here the story is that before the Portuguese got to work, Lisbon and Calicut (in India) simply didn't exist for one another. They were in separate worlds. They existed (as we are saying) in different spaces. So it was through their efforts that the Portuguese turned Lisbon and India into places that, though they were distant from one another, were nevertheless in the same world, in the same space. Yes, it took many months to make the passage between the two in one of their vessels. Yes, it also took a lot of effort, time, skill and bravery to move from the Tagus to Calicut and back. It is because of this effort and the work involved in displacement that they were indeed distant from one another. But they were also distant because they were connected together in a single world rather than belonging to separate worlds.

We're saying, then, that locations which don't communicate with one another, which know nothing of one another, don't exist for one another, exist in entirely different worlds or spaces. Like the Incas and the Arabs who, so far as is known, never communicated, never knew of one another. The argument is that distance demands communication and interaction. Its very possibility, depends on communication or interaction. It depends on joining things up within – and thereby making – a single space. And if this is difficult to see – if, for instance, it seems that the Incas and the Arabs really belonged to a single world, existed within a single geographical space – this is because geographical space has somehow come to seem natural. As if it were given.

And because (for the case of the Incas and the Arabs) we have chosen to ignore the work of more recent historical geographers who have drawn them onto regions in a single world map. And because we have got so used to the work of the geographers together with the networks of trade, of air traffic control, of electronic links and all the rest, that we have come to experience the geographical space that it makes as if it were natural, something given in the order of things. Something that has to be that way. But we're saying that it isn't natural. Rather, geographical space, global space, is a material semiotic effect. It is something that is made.

Let's note that the same logic works for Andrew's office. It is linked to other locations on the globe, to be sure. It is located in a world-geographical space. But – and – this is because of the work involved in making and maintaining all the email, telephone and transport links which join it to other offices and laboratories around the globe. The work of keeping up the materially heterogeneous links which maintain the mobilities between places, and define their distances. The materially heterogeneous enactments and performances which create a global geographical space on the one hand and locations in that space such as Daresbury Laboratory on the other. Again, then, we want to say that the possibility of globality – and location in globality – is sustained in that work.

Capitalisation I

In this semiotics of materiality knowing, knowing at a distance, acting, acting at a distance, and the making of space, are all relational effects. And they are materially heterogeneous effects. Materials of all kinds are being disciplined, constituted, organised, and/or organising themselves to produce knowledges, subjects, objects, distances and locations. We might, with Foucault, note that this is the effect of a strategic ordering of elements. They could be ordered otherwise in which case knowing, location, and all the rest would be different. And then we'd need to add, again like Foucault, that strategy does not necessarily imply the presence of a self-conscious strategist. But this does not mean that there are not centres of accumulation. Places where surplus accrues. Places of profit. It does not mean, in other words, that what we are calling "capitalisation" does not take place. So, crucial questions in the context of globalisation are: what can be said about accumulation? and how are asymmetries between the centres of accumulation and the rest generated?

There are several responses. Responses that have to do with the configuration of the heterogeneous material elements which make up the network of relations.

One has to do with delegation. "Will you act as my agent at a distance? Will you stay reliable? Will you hold together? Or will you turn traitor, turn turtle, or go native?" In terms of a network logic of material relations these are the same questions. And they have the same logic as the immutable mobile. The issue is, will the configuration of bits and pieces that allow me to profit stay the same, or not? If the king issues an order to bombard Calicut, will it be followed through? Will the ships get there? Will the gunpowder stay dry? Will the crews follow their orders? Will they have avoided disease? If the answer to these questions is yes, then we are in the realm of immutable mobiles. If not, then not. And the same logic works for the laboratory too, albeit on a less dramatic geographical scale. Will the employees do as they are asked? Will their instruments, their computers, bend themselves to the project? Or will they not?

Delegation, then, may be understood in a semiotics of materiality as a way of talking about the immutable mobile. Delegation is sending something out which will hold its shape – so that the centre does not have to do the dirty work itself. Which is, to be sure, not simply a moral but also a practical matter. If the King of Portugal or Vasco da Gama had been obliged to subdue the Indians alone and with their bare hands they would not have been up to the task. Delegation, then, is also something which works through a series of tiers. It is an arrangement in which you push the levers and something happens, something that magnifies itself in the next stage, and then again. (Think of the tiers of simplification and delegation implied in building a spreadsheet). And, crucially, it is also something that happens in a play between different material forms. For delegation into non-human materials – cannon, prison walls, marching orders – is often particularly effective (though there are no guarantees, and the integrity of physical materials is, itself, a relational effect.)

But successful delegation, the successful creation of immutable mobiles, the capacity to know and act at a distance, has other asymmetry-relevant effects. Or it may be thought of in different ways. For instance, it may be thought of as the creation of what Michel Callon calls an obligatory point of passage. For the obligatory point of passage is the central node in a network of delegation, so to speak its panopticon. The place of privilege. This, then, is a second feature of material relations which creates asymmetries.

In what we have written we have already come across two obvious obligatory points of passage. On the one hand there is Andrew-and-his-spreadsheet. And on the other, there is the Portuguese state and some of its officials and traders. Here is the argument. Those caught up in one or other of these networks of relations have no choice: if they want to move, if they want to achieve their goals, then they have to do so by making a detour. A detour via Andrew-and-his spreadsheet. Or via Lisbon-and-its-spice-markets. So the pepper growers in India can't sell their crop to the Arabs any more. The network of the Portuguese – their guns, their money – have cut the old links. If they want to make money then they are necessarily enrolled into the Portuguese network. They, or more precisely, their crops, make the long detour via the Cape of Good Hope and Lisbon to get to the European market. They then become faithful delegates of the (newly distant) Portuguese centre, tributaries no doubt held in place by fear and need rather than love or affection. But this makes little difference from a semiotic point of view. For held in place they are. Contributing their ha'pennyworth to the network, buttressing it, and at the same time adding to, further performing, its centre as an obligatory point of passage. As a place of privilege. A centre of accumulation.

But the same is happening at Daresbury Laboratory. Employees do not, for the most part, turn up in Andrew's office in person to receive their orders. Instead immutable mobiles emerge from this obligatory point of passage, delegates that faithfully perform themselves across the space of the laboratory. Such that the elements which make up the network of the laboratory find that they are being displaced, moved to work on new projects, acting in ways that they would not otherwise have done. Being enrolled to act as clients of (what has therefore become) a centre, an obligatory point of passage, a privileged location that can see and act at a distance. That makes the distance and masters it, all at the same time. So Andrew does not bend the workings of the laboratory by himself. He delegates to (what he hopes will be) faithful emissaries. And into other material forms – for instance in the shape of minutes, memoranda and pay checks. Just like the Portuguese monarch. Which tells us, as we already noted, that "Andrew" (and the Portuguese monarch) is a heterogeneous relational effect rather than someone whose powers are given in his body.

Delegation and obligatory points of passage are crucial to capitalisation and its asymmetries. But these are also a play around scale effects. We've noted that distance is a product, an effect. Made and mastered in the creation of immutable mobiles. But delegation also makes spatial effects. For as we've hinted above, immutable mobiles passing to and from (and thereby creating) a centre also play havoc with scale. We will need to return to and revise the notion of scale below. But for the moment let's note that knowledge of distant events, distant actors, also implies that these are rendered small and simple. This is a version of the argument about power and delegation. Just as Andrew and the Portuguese monarch cannot do all the dirty work themselves, so they cannot know all about everything that goes on within their networks, know all about the dirty work. But, nevertheless, and this is one of the features of power, in some general sense they need to know about it. Knowing at a distance, then, necessarily implies pretty heroic simplifications and reductions. And it therefore also implies pretty heroic manipulations of scale. This means that that which is large in the geographical sense, spread out over time and over space, gets reduced to a report, to a map (and the development of mariners' maps counts as an exemplary case here) or, in the case of Andrew, to a set of figures in a spreadsheet. Everything – or representatives of everything – are being brought to one place, all at one time. That which was big is thereby being rendered small. And, as it is being rendered small, it generates a capacity to see far for the privileged centre. And, crucially, it also generates a capacity so see what would otherwise not have been visible – indeed what would in some sense not otherwise have existed. Which is, to be sure, where we came in: with Andrew-and-his-spreadsheet and the discovery/creation of a delay that would otherwise not have been visible. A Foucauldian point, one that derives from attention to a semiotics of materiality.

Delegation, the making of obligatory points of passage, and scale reversals – all these are configurational features of the asymmetrical networks of capitalisation which grow out of and produce immutable mobiles. Now we want to mention a fourth and final feature. This has to do with the production and concentration of discretion. To say it quickly: with the growth of action and representation at a distance there also grows discretion. To act, or not to act. To act in this way or, alternatively, to act in that. Empirically this is easiest seen for Andrew-and-his-spreadsheet. For he can see far enough – and he can successfully act in enough ways – that there are a variety of courses of action open to him. But how might we think of this in terms of the configurations of materially heterogeneous networks?

It has to do with the asymmetry generated between the centre (which becomes a centre because it is an obligatory point of passage for a series of tributaries) and those peripheral tributaries which are indeed peripheral precisely because they have no options, no choice. But, stood on its head, what this tells us is that it is probable (not certain) that because there are many tributaries to the centre, the centre correspondingly has many options. It has many alternative possibilities for acting at a distance, mobilising this rather than that tributary. The argument, then, has to do with redundancy. The centre enjoys the luxury of redundancy. For it, there are no obligatory points of passage in its heterogeneous networks. If one "circuit", if one set of immutable mobiles gets choked off, goes native, is turned into matchwood on a reef with drowned mariners, then it can always act through another. Send another vessel (which, since the shipping losses on the Portuguese route to India were heroic, was a very common occurrence). Which is not, to be sure, a recourse that is open to the client who is forced to pass through an obligatory point of passage. Like the unfortunate ruler of Calicut and his spice traders.

Our topic is knowledge and globalisation. But it is also capitalisation and power. As we have noted above, spatiality needs to be rethought. We have offered some suggestions about this – to do with scale and the making of distance. In this section, however, we have particularly attended to features of the logic of capitalisation or accumulation as seen from the point of view of such a material semiotics. In insisting on how it is that knowledges and actions get generated and distributed to particular locations in the social world, and noting how these may be understood as relational strategies or features of the shape of self-sustaining heterogeneous networks, we have identified four crucial moments: delegation (which may take material forms), the creation of obligatory points of passage, play with scale and size, and finally the far from even distribution of discretion.

Spatial Enactment

Distance, we have asserted, is made – and putatively mastered – all in the same moment. Lisbon and Calicut become places in a single space only when immutable mobiles such as ships shuttle between them – or, to bring the example up to date, with the growth of cartography, GIS, or the financial networks of the world. Until that moment they simply exist in different worlds. This is the crucial move if we are to understand spatiality – and the phenomena of globalisation – from the standpoint of a material semiotics. As we have argued above, space is made. It is a creation. It is a material outcome. Like objects, places, or obligatory points of passage it is an effect. It does not exist outside its performance. [...]

If we attend to a material semiotics and performed spatialities, to talk of "globalisation" is at best a risky short cut and at worst seriously misleading. It is a risky shortcut because it implies some kind of totality, some kind of global system, and some kind of overall space–time box within which the phenomena which we touched on at the beginning of this chapter are located. A "global society", a "global order". Even a global disorder. But this misses out, or so we have suggested, both on the enacted materiality of that order and also the complex spatialities implied in that enactment. These, or so we suggest, need to be understood if we are to make sense [of] asymmetries involved in making obligatory points of passage and the process of capitalisation.

REFERENCES

Callon, Michel (1986), "Some Elements of a Sociology of Translation: Domestication of the Scallops and the Fishermen of Saint Brieuc Bay", pages 196–233 in John Law (ed.), *Power, Action and Belief: a new Sociology of Knowledge? Sociological Review Monograph*, 32, London: Routledge and Kegan Paul.

Foucault, Michel (1979), *Discipline and Punish: the Birth of the Prison*, Harmondsworth: Penguin.

Latour, Bruno (1990), "Drawing Things Together", pages 19–68 in Michael Lynch and Steve Woolgar (eds), *Representation in Scientific Practice*, Cambridge, MA. MIT Press.

34 Exterminating Angels: Morality, Violence, and Technology in the Gulf War

Asu Aksoy and Kevin Robins

Already in this section, we have seen the postmodernisms of reaction and resistance at work in the urban landscape, and the role of localities and the localizable in producing the global. But can there be a postmodern politics of resistance/reaction on a global scale? Between the writing of Asu Aksoy and Kevin Robins on the one hand, and those of Subcomandante Marcos (Reading 35) on the other, it is apparent that both kinds of politics are globally in operation. Commenting on the Persian Gulf War, Aksoy and Robins note how the state rapidly deployed tightly regimented systems of data transmission and mass communications. These systems simultaneously permitted both the quick execution of field maneuvers and the demonization of the enemy. The ominous purpose of this, according to Aksoy and Robins, was a legitimization of state violence. The conflict was represented as an abstracted simulation, surgically precise and largely bloodless, carried out by a military force whose technological superiority bequeathed an aura of supernatural divinity and moral rectitude. Aksoy and Robins thus identify the inner workings of a postmodern geopolitics of reaction, as one side labored to maintain its hegemony though military might and control of geopolitical discourse. In revealing such techniques for the production and strategic representation of death, the authors themselves become part of a postmodern geopolitics of resistance.

The war in the Persian Gulf was cast as a global confrontation between humanity and bestiality, a battle between civilization and barbarism. This was a war to defend the priniciples of modernity and reason against the forces of darkness. It was in this cause that the "smart" weapons of the West meted out what was projected as a moral kind of violence. In this cause, the angels became exterminators.

Crusade Against the Evil Empire ⋅

When nearly two million men, 10,000 tanks, more than 5000 pieces of artillery, 3900 warplanes, 1800 helicopters and 175 warships were preparing for the conflict in the Gulf, President Bush declared to the US Congress that the ensuing war would be a "just" one: "I have resolved all moral questions in my mind: this is black versus white, good versus evil." America was "on the side of God". It had a "unique responsibility to do the hard work of freedom" against a criminal and a monster who dared to disturb the "moral order" of the world. The driving force behind the massive build-up of armaments was the notion that an aggressor "who uses force to replace the rule of law" must be punished. "We are ready," said Bush, "to use force to defend a new order emerging among the nations of the world, a world of sovereign nations living in peace." There was no question about the justness of this war. It was a matter of stopping "another Hitler" in time.

Bush's belief in the moral rightness of his crusade does not surprise us. What is notable, however, is the wider support that the Western cause received from most opposition parties and from much of the intellectual community in the West. Here, too, Saddam was demonized as a "new Hitler" poised to take over the world. Hans Magnus Enzensberger put it most bluntly: "The description of Saddam Hussein as the new Hitler is not merely journalistic licence, not the hyperbole of propaganda, but is actually deadly accurate . . . The behaviour of the new enemy of humanity is no different from that of his predecessor." Such an aggressor – this "enemy of the human race" – had to be "removed from the surface of the earth". [. . .]

Saddam Hussein was the Great Satan. Bush referred to Saddam's "immoral" and "unconscionable" brutality, to "rape, assassination, cold-blooded murder and rampant looting", and to the violation of every "civilized principle". Saddam was a violent monster who did not bat an eyelid when he was killing, whether it was the Iranians or the Kurds, the Saudis or the Palestinians, the Kuwaitis or the Israelis, or even his own unfortunate people. According to Bush and his publicists, Saddam's troops were supposed to have killed 300 premature babies by removing them from their incubators (though this accusation was subsequently proven to have no foundation). A "US girl Marine" prisoner was described by *The Sun* (1 February 1991), as being "at the mercy of the beast". According to the *Daily Star* (2 March 1991), "brutal Iraqi soldiers became real-life vampires during the occupation of Kuwait. They drained the blood of innocent civilians until their victims were dead." Almost any degree of force necessary to destroy Saddam was therefore seen as permissible. As *Newsweek* magazine (11 March 1991) put it, "The chain had to be pulled, to flush Saddam away."

It quickly became clear that Bush's war aims were more ambitious than just liberating Kuwait. The American generals were out there to go deep into Iraq, to destroy Saddam Hussein's "monstrous military machine", and maybe even to "take out" the man himself. As Edward Said has suggested, it was "as if an almost metaphysical need to rout Iraq had sprung forward", and this "because a small non-white country had disturbed or rankled a suddenly energised super-nation imbued with a fervour that can only be satisfied with compliance or subservience from 'sheikhs', dictators, and camel-jockeys". For Bush, the upstart Arab embodied the forces of irrationality and barbarism. And Bush was ready, in the name of civilization, in the name of reason and humanity, to discipline those alien forces, to defeat them "decisively and rapidly". That was the almost metaphysical dimension of the American crusade.

So convinced were the Western forces of the moral justness of their mission to "neutralize" Saddam that they were prepared to put no limits on the drive to accomplish this objective. In this just war against this new Evil Empire, all kinds of advanced weapons would be enlisted. Why, asked General Schwarzkopf, should the allied forces "have to stand up, allow ourselves to be shot, take on overwhelming numbers, and not use the weapons that we have available" when "the Iraqis are allowed to go out and do anything they want? They can gas innocent women and children, they can loft Scuds against civilian populations, they can use human shields." Why shouldn't they get a taste of their own medicine? This time the Western soldiers did not intend to go into battle, as they felt they had done in Vietnam, with one hand tied; this time they would use all the weapons they had available.

General Powell warned Saddam at the beginning of the war that "Iraq had not begun to see all the tools in the tool box that the US army brought". Through the course of the war it came to see just what the tools were in that box: the "daisy cutter" (America's biggest conventional bomb whose blast effect is comparable to that of a tactical nuclear weapon); fuel-air explosives (which have the same explosive capacity as a small atomic bomb, though without the same radioactive or political fallout); the cluster bomb; the Stealth bomber; the Tomahawk cruse missile; the Multiple Launch Rocket System; as well as more "conventional" weapons like B52 bombers which can carry up to fifty 500-pound bombs, each capable of devastating an area three miles long by half a mile wide. All of these were deployed in the Gulf. Through the use of their high-tech instruments of terror, the Western armies turned the war into a twenty-four-hour killing field from which nothing could escape.

Saddam Hussein's scuddish violence was always seen as vicious and brutal. His weapons appeared to be imprecise and undiscriminating as they were blindly launched against Israel and Saudi Arabia. In contrast, the allies were, paradoxically, able to project their bloody assault as clean and clinical. The desert was to be a theatre in which the Western forces would play out the fantasy of a war made bloodless through scientific and technological expertise. From the outset, the scientific warriors stressed that their aim was to "take out" legitimate targets through "professionally executed strikes" by allied aircraft using precision-guided munitions. Precision weapons would enable troops to identify and then remove chosen targets at will.

Moreover, these "super-sophisticated systems" – stealth weapons, sea-launched cruise missiles, SDI-like defences and space systems – would save the lives, not only of allied pilots, but also of ordinary Iraqis, "because they enable the kind of precision attack that limits civilian casualties". This was to be a "push-button, remote-control war", won without visible casualties. American accomplishments in science and technology would be used as instruments of targeted punishment. They would also serve to legitimate that punishment.

It was through this capacity to believe in a well-managed and rationally conducted war that the allies could come to have no moral qualms about the destructive and horrific power that they had unleashed. Even when it became clear that the "phe-nomenally accurate" weaponry could kill civilians in their hundreds and thousands, as happened with the allied bombing of the Al-Amiriya air-raid shelter in Baghdad, the moral certainty remained intact. As General Neal said after the bombing, "it belied logic" that the missile, which had been so well targeted at the bunker in order to destroy military communications equipment, could have led to the slaughter of so many civilians. "What were those civilians doing in the bunker at four in the morning?" Douglas Hurd was quick to emphasize that it was "Saddam Hussein who must take the blame if any civilians died accidentally"; it was "another devilish plot from Saddam". As General Neal commented, the air force planners continued to feel "very comfortable" with their choice of target.

Defending Civilization

But how could they be, and remain, so very comfortable? How was it that military high technology could be so closely associated with absolute virtue? How was it that "logic" could justify the technological violence that was bombing Iraq and its people "back into the dark ages"? These are the key questions. And it was not only the Western leaders who were disavowing responsibility and projecting guilt onto the "devilish" Other. The process of moral dissociation was a more general phenom-enon.

To different degrees it affected us all. As we were engulfed by images of the Western military machine, we seemed to forget how murderous and destructive those weapons were. It was as if our moral senses had been taken out and neutral-ized. The "smartness" or "brilliance" of computer-controlled rocket systems and of Tomahawk missiles seduced us into thinking that Iraq's murderous violence was being confronted by efficient and rational systems whose objectives were not to murder but simply to "clean out" enemy targets. As the allied bombing proceeded to fire the skies of Iraq with ammunition far exceeding the amount used during the whole of the Second World War, we in the West were being lured into a blind and complicit fascination with the high-tech arsenal.

Why did our moral sense not provoke a sense of outrage and shame? We became deaf, as John Berger declared, to the atrocities committed by our own civilization, and that deafness became exponential. We watched the war on our television screens, but our screen culture has come to sustain our moral blindness and moral passivity. "CNN is live and alive," one Turkish writer lamented, "as our humanity is about to die." We were expected to remain silent when we were told of the video tapes from the gun cameras of the Apache helicopter raids on Iraqi soldiers which revealed the horror of victims' deaths and showed how "they were cut down, one by one, by attackers they could not see", how "they were blown to bits by bursts of thirty-millimetre exploding cannon shells". How could we watch our civilization turning into a terminator? To ask these questions is to consider what the war can tell us about ourselves, and also what the war has done to us. It is also to consider the relationship between technology, violence and morality in Western culture.

The very distance of the campaign made it almost impossible to realize the awful truth of the carnage. We didn't see the suffering at the other end, and that made it difficult to identify with the sufferers. Those potentially subversive glimpses we were given of the human consequences of the "greatest aerial bombardment in history" were of faceless others. The enemy were objects, far removed from us, as Francis Fukuyama put it, "in a desolate Middle Eastern desert", and these objects were seen as undesirable. It seemed entirely reasonable, then, to apply Western techno-rationality to teach them their place in the world, their inferior place in our civilized world.

What emerged in most of the Western commentaries on the war was the belief that there was a profound moral difference between the violence of Saddam and that of Bush. After the war, Bush could declare that it had been "a victory for the UN, for all mankind, for the rule of law, and for what is right". Bush's deeds of violence were always assumed to be morally defensible; to be self-evidently just acts in defence of civilization, reason and sanity, and against the "dark practices" of an alien force. On what basis, we must ask, was it possible to sustain this belief and these assertions?

The key to this question is the polarization between Western civilization and its Other, represented in this episode by the endemic "barbarism" of Arab culture; the contrast between our enlightened modernity and their benighted Dark Ages. "Their twentieth century is not our's," wrote Alain Finkielkraut, "They have allowed honour to prevail over democracy, and force and machismo over freedom." According to Martin Woollacott, it was "the problem of irrationality and fantasy in Arab life"; there is an "Arab sickness" centred on the "failure of rational thought". Associated with this confrontation is a false dichotomy between the rational and the irrational. The choice, quite simply, is between reason and unreason. And, at the same time, the choice is then, implicitly, made between the moral and the immoral, for it is on the power of its reason and rationality that Western morality is reputedly grounded.

The symbolic damnation of Saddam reflected this logic: in positioning itself against the barbarity of "medieval practices", the USA solicited moral support. Insofar as its modern identity was defined against the irrationality and barbarism of the Other, it sought to legitimize its rationalized violence against what it is not in the name of civilized reason and progress. What had to be acknowledged, however, was that modernity sometimes has to proceed through violence. This legitimation was grounded in the belief that the allies' "modern" violence was of a different order from the "medieval practices" of Iraqi violence. It was "smart" violence. When "smart" means good", it becomes possible to maintain a distinction between good and bad kinds of weapon, and then to differentiate between morally right and wrong kinds of violence.

"Smart" therefore Good

The starkest expression of modernity and reason is technological rationality, and this rationality, in turn, becomes associated with the moral superiority of Western culture. This is because the very idea of rationality seems indissociable from the idea of worthwhile aims. It was on this basis, and only on this basis, that the awesome and devastating firepower of the Western war machine could actually seem to be an expression of moral virtue. It was on this basis that it could be assumed that the advanced nature of Western military technologies was in itself a guarantee of their moral rightness. According to Sidney Perkowitz, a military researcher,

> The allied forces' stated goal of minimising innocent casualties along with minimising casualties for our own soldiers, has moral weight. And it is the technical means to select targets that makes the moral decision possible, and therefore meaningful.

This researcher, like many others, honestly believed that he had "contributed to good technology". What the technology did was "to put a sharp spearpoint on war's bludgeon". The guilty feelings associated with being engaged in military research were then lifted as he "watched the breathtaking TV images of our missile attacks" and realized that these weapons were "smart"; they did not kill civilians. [. . .]

The clear message was that "smart" was good, and brilliant was virtuous. "Smart" weapons, it was being claimed, could actually save the lives of soldiers and civilians alike in the Gulf. To reduce error, to be so deadly accurate and efficient, was a reflection of the virtuous triumph of Western technology.

The Gulf War demonstrated that the power and the dominance of the techno-logical order had become so well secured that it is now the criterion of what is moral. The power of Western techno-rationality was not questioned. When the Al-Amiriya shelter was destroyed, or when an allied aircraft missed a targeted bridge during a bombing mission and devastated a shopping area in Falloujah instead, there was never any question of Western responsibility or guilt. "Bombs that veer off course is something that I have never seen before and something, to my knowledge, that has never happened before in this campaign," commented a certain Group Captain Irving. "There is no question of the crew being in error." (The inhabitants thought that the pilot "must have been Saudi".) We witnessed starkly that when morality is legitimated by efficiency, questions of efficiency tend to become a surrogate for ethical decisions and choices. And when efficiency fails there is no means to cope with the human and moral fallout. The technology is designed not to go wrong; it cannot be morally in the wrong.

On this basis, it became possible for the allies to dissociate themselves from the pain and death that their modern weapons brought about. Because the weapons were so "smart", it was possible to believe that they were delivering the Western forces from moral dilemmas. What they were doing in reality was to de-sensitize them and to de-link their actions from their human consequences. Smart technolo-gies allowed action "at a distance": soldiers pushed the buttons of Tomahawk missiles and then watched, if at all, the consequences of their action later on videotapes.

As Zygmunt Bauman has argued, "distance technologies" have "eliminated face-to-face contact between the actors and the objects of their actions, and with that neutralised their morally constraining impact". The causal connection between the act and its human consequences were broken, and the ultimate effects of actions remained invisible to the actors. One US military source admitted to having "abso-lutely no clue" about Iraqi casualities. It was as if the enemy had no human existence, as if they had become inhuman things.

But how different, really, was this modern violence of the Western military machine? What did the "smart" technologies actually deliver? As we now know, when the ground war started, "smart" quickly turned to hellish. With our very modern technologies we brought Armageddon to people we scarcely knew anything about. The horrific nature of the Western assault was exemplified as the allies "went in for the kill" at the start of the ground war and slaughtered the routed Iraqi army. The ensuing victory, as John Pilger has said, was "a one-sided bloodfest".

During the brief land war launched by Washington the allies shot thousands and thousands of fleeing Iraqi soldiers and civilians in the back. The shooting was described as being like "a giant hunt". The Iraqis were driven ahead, "like animals", by the allied air and land attacks. The American pilots were said to have likened their attack on the convoy to "shooting fish in a barrel". The retreating Iraqis were said to have presented a "bounty of targets". "We hit the jackpot," one pilot said. "It was like a turkey shoot." [...]

The killing that went on was no less violent than it had been at Dresden or in Vietnam. As a US Marine lieutenant conceded, in distress, "They had no air cover, nothing to defend themselves. It was not very professional at all." The American pilots had used Rockeye cluster bombs in the attack. Each Rockeye bomb dispersed 247 bomblets containing needle-sharp shrapnel designed for "soft" targets, in other words *people*. The "great victory" of the allied forces smelt of naked and brutal violence.... Where was the smartness in this? Where was the justice?

Reason and Violence

What we should learn from the experience of the Gulf War, once again, is how the "us good, them bad" logic hides the fears, anxieties and guilt that are buried deep in Western consciousness. Saddam was projected as a monster and a beast. Like Frankenstein's monster, he was an outcast from the "moral order" of the world; he was a "race apart". As in Mary Shelley's *Frankenstein*, the symbolic drama was between a "race of devils" and the "species of man". All the evil was projected outwards, into that "desert". In projecting all evil onto the monstrous alien, the Western psyche was seeking to protect the integrity of its own Reason and Rationality. As Bush made clear, it had to be black versus white, good versus evil.

Through this splitting process, the Western psyche was then able to avoid confronting the sources of its own violence. The fervour with which Saddam was accused of being criminal and bestial was fired by the desire to protect the "species of man", to absolve Western culture and civilization from the guilt associated with its own violence. It is difficult for us to acknowledge that violence and destruction, on both sides, are expressions of "rational" behaviour; that "reason" may be at the heart of violence.

As Franco Moretti has argued, the story of Frankenstein's monster is about a two-sided process in which formation entails deformation, in which civilization carries barbarism within itself. In this process, science and rationality contain the possibility of destructive violence. The monster – "the pedestal on which Frankenstein erects his anguished greatness" – turned out to be a distortion and "negation" of that greatness. The deformed monster then had to "become the object of an instinctive, elemental hatred; and 'men' need this hatred to counter-balance the force unleashed by the monster". This is what happened in the Gulf. Saddam's "monstrous military machine" was simply a distorting reflection of the West's anguished greatness. It was the West that created this "monster", and when the monster turned on its creator it had to be extinguished. And it was extinguished, as we now know, with a violence that surpassed that of the monster.

So the West was "on the side of God", and Saddam was in the camp of the devil, the "enemy of the human race". For that reason, the humiliation and destruction of Iraq seemed both desirable and inevitable. But there are those who don't now see this as a victory "for all mankind" and for "what is right". There are those who don't support the side of Bush's God. The journalist, James Buchan, described how, in Jalazan – a Palestinian refugee camp in Israel – "when the Scud missiles come over, everybody goes out on the roof to shout and dance". There are those who didn't see Saddam Hussein as "another Hitler". There were even those like the writer, Driss Chraibi, who found themselves applauding him, and doing this because "he defied the United States, and millions of people don't like what the United States stands for in the world."

Simone Weil wrote in her journal on 13 June 1940, as the German army marched into Paris, "This is a great day for the people of Indochina." As David Rieff comments,

> Weil reminded us that the history that we in the West care about . . . is neither the history of everywhere nor of everyone. She invites us to undertake that most uncomfortable of reasoning, the realisation that an event which for us is cause for mourning may be celebrated by other people every bit as decent as ourselves as the moment when hope first dawned.

REFERENCES

Bauman, Z. (1990) "Effacing the face: on the social management of moral proximity", *Theory, Culture and Society* 7.

Buchan, J. (1991) "The Arabs in the middle", *Independent on Sunday* 10 February.

Chraibi, D. (1991) "Vous avez dit libération?", *Libération* 15 February.

Enzensberger, H. M. (1991) "The second coming of Adolf Hitler", *The Guardian* 9 February.

Finkielkraut, A. (1991) "The Gulf of backwardness", *The Guardian* 1 March.

Fukuyama, F. (1990) "The world against a family", *The Guardian* 12 September.

Moretti, F. (1982) "The dialectic of fear", *New Left Review* 136.

Perkowitz, S. (1991) "The scientist at war", *The Guardian* 7 March.

Pilger, J. (1991) "A one-sided bloodfest", *New Statesman and Society* 8 March.

Rieff, D. (1990) "European time", *Salmagundi* 85/86.

Said, E. (1991) "Empire of sand", *The Guardian* (Weekend supplement) 12 January.

Woollacott, M. (1991) "Iraq was simply an especially extreme case of Arab sickness", *The Guardian* 4 March.

35

Old Antonio tells Marcos Another Story

Subcomandante Insurgente Marcos

Subcomandante Insurgente Marcos is the spokesperson for, and globally recognized face (or, more precisely, ski-mask) of, the uprising in the southern Mexican state of Chiapas. Technically, this is an uprising of impoverished indigenous peoples, predominantly Mayan and Zapotec, against the neoliberal land policies of an authoritarian state. But Marcos' writings, couched in literary forms that are themselves playful and hugely antiauthoritarian, make clear that the ultimate target of the uprising is the totalizing and exclusionary economic logic of "corporate globalization." His goal is a world where those who are different will not be disappeared, but instead sustained, respected, and empowered. In the meantime, the Chiapan rebels confront the postmodern Mexican war machine with few weapons of their own. And yet, the rebels have so far won major victories because of the way Marcos manipulated the political discourse surrounding the uprising – through television, children's books, and the Internet, instead of tanks and guns.

"Streams, when they begin to flow downhill, cannot turn back, except underground."
To the national weekly *Proceso*
To the national newspaper *La Jornada*
To the national newspaper *El Financiero*
To San Cristóbal de las Casas' local newspaper *El Tiempo*

May 28, 1994

Sirs,

Here comes a communiqué about the final goal – finally – of the consultations. Plus various letters with different destinations.

We are quite ... besieged. Resisting "heroically" the storm of reactions after the occurrence of May 15. The ever vigilant planes are now joined, as of three days ago, by helicopters. The cooks complain that there won't be enough pots if they all drop in on us at the same time. The superintendent argues that there is enough wood for a barbecue, so why don't we invite over some Argentinean journalists, because those people really know how to do barbecues.

I mull it over, and it's not right: the best Argentineans are *guerrilleros* (for example, el Ché), or poets (Juan Gelman, for example), or writers (for example, Borges), or artists (Maradona, for example), or *cronopios* (forever, Cortazar); there are no Argentinean barbecuers of lasting fame.

Some innocent proposes that we wait for the unlikely hamburgers of the CEU. Yesterday we ate the "*console*" and two microphones from station XEOCH; they had a rotten, rancid taste.

The medics are handing out slips of paper with jokes instead of painkillers – they say that laughter heals too. The other day I came upon Tacho and Moi crying... with laughter. "Why are you crying?" I asked. They couldn't answer because they were laughing so hard they couldn't breathe. A medic explained with some embarrassment: "It's because they've got terrible head-aches."

Day 136 of the siege... (sigh).

To top it off, Toñita asks me for a story. I'll tell her the story as it was told to me, by Old Antonio who wakes up in "Chiapas: The Southeast in Two Winds, a Storm, and a Prophecy..."

"When the world slept and didn't want to wake up, the great gods came together in their council to divide up the jobs and decided then to make the world and to make the men and women. And they reached a majority opinion on how to make the world and the people. They decided to make them very pretty and very durable, and so they made the first people out of gold, and the gods were very happy because the people they made were shiny and strong. But then the gods realized that the people made of gold didn't move. They were always sitting around, not walking and not working, because they were very heavy.

"And so the community of gods met to reach an agreement about how to solve that problem and so they reached an agreement to make other people. They made them from wood, and so these people were the color of wood. They worked a lot and walked a lot and the gods were happy again because now man worked and walked, and they were just about to go celebrate when they realized that the people of gold were making the people of wood carry them around and work for them. And then the gods saw that it was bad, what they had done, and so they searched for a good way to remedy the situation. And so it was that they decided to make the people of corn, the good people, the true men and women. Then they went off to sleep and the people of corn remained, the true men and women, coming to fix things because the gods went off to sleep. And the people of corn spoke the true language to reach agreements among them and went to the mountain to see that a good path was made for all the people."

Old Antonio told me that the people of gold were the rich people, the ones with white skin, and that the people of wood were the poor people, the ones with dark skin, who worked for the rich ones and always carried them around, and that the people of gold and the people of wood are waiting for the people of corn, the first with fear and the latter with hope. I asked Old Antonio what color skin the people of corn had and he showed me various kinds of corn, of a variety of colors, and told me that they were of all skins but nobody really knew, because the people of corn, the true men and women, didn't have faces...

Old Antonio died. I met him ten years ago, in a community deep in the jungle. He smoked like no one else and, when the cigarettes ran out, he would ask me for tobacco and make cigarettes with a corn leaf "roller"; he used to look curiously at my pipe, and once when I tried to loan it to him, he showed me the cigarette made with the "roller" in his hand, telling me without words that he preferred his own method of smoking.

About two years ago, in 1992, when I was making the rounds of the communities calling meetings to see whether or not we were to begin the war, I arrived at Old Antonio's town. Young Antonio caught up with me and together we walked through pastures and coffee groves. While the community discussed the matter of war, Old Antonio took me by the arm and led me to the river, some 100 meters below the center of the town. It was May and the river was green, with a barely discernible current. Old Antonio sat on a log and said nothing. After a while he spoke: "See? Everything is calm and clear, as if nothing were happening."

"Mmmm," I said, knowing that he didn't expect either a yes or a no. Then he pointed out the top of the nearest mountain; clouds were bedded down, gray, on the peak, and lightning bolts shattered the soft blue of the hills. A real storm, but it looked so far away and harmless that Old Antonio began to roll a cigarette and to look, in vain, for the lighter that he didn't have, which gave me enough time to pass him mine.

"When everything is quiet down below, there is a storm on the mountain; the streams begin to gather force and they head for the ravine," he said after taking a puff. "In the rainy season, this river is fierce, a dark brown whip, an earthquake, out of control; it is pure force. Its power doesn't come from the rain that falls on its banks, but from the streams that feed it as they come down from the mountain. Destroying the riverbed rebuilds the earth; its waters will be corn, beans, and brown sugar in the flats of the jungle. It's the same with our struggle," Old Antonio says to me and to himself. "The force is born on the mountain, but it can't be seen till it comes down." And, answering my question about whether he thinks that now is the time to start, he adds, "It is time now for the river to change color..."

Old Antonio falls silent and gets up, supporting himself on my arm. We go back slowly. He tells me, "You all are the streams and we are the river... it is time to come down now..." The silence continues and when we arrive at the village meeting place, it is already beginning to get dark. Young Antonio comes back after a while with the Act of Agreement, which says, more or less:

"The men and women and children met in the community school to examine in their hearts whether it is time to start the war for freedom and the three groups separated, that is, the women, the children, and the men, to discuss it and then later we met again in the little school and the majority had reached the point in their thinking that the war should begin because Mexico is being sold to foreigners and hunger is occurring, but it is not occurring that we are no longer Mexicans, and in the agreement 12 men and 23 women and 8 children who already have their thoughts clear came forward and those who know how signed and those who don't, put down their fingerprint."

I left before dawn. Old Antonio wasn't there: he had gone early to the river.

But I saw Old Antonio again a couple months ago. He didn't say anything when he saw me, and I sat down at his side and began to shuck ears of corn with him. "The river grew," he said after a while. "Yes," I said.

Later during the same visit I explained to Young Antonio about the consultation and handed over to him the documents with our demands and the government's responses. We talked about how it had gone with him in Ocosingo and, again before dawn, I left with the others to go back. In a bend of the road Old Antonio was waiting for me; I stopped at his side and took off my pack, looking for tobacco to offer him. "Not now," he said, waving away the bag I held out to him. He took me away from the line of marchers and took me to the foot of a silk-cotton tree. "Do you remember what I told you about the streams in the mountains and the river?" he asked. "Yes," I answered in the same murmur with which he had asked me. "There was something else I should have told you," he says, looking at his bare toes. I answered in silence. "The streams . . . ." he stops for the cough that wracks his body, takes a little breath, and continues, "The streams . . . when they begin to flow down . . ."

A new coughing attack makes me call the medic from the line, but he waves away the compañero with the red cross on his shoulder; the rebel looks at me and I signal to him to go back. Old Antonio waits until the medicine pack gets further away and, in the half-light, continues, "The streams . . . when they flow down . . . cannot turn back . . . except underground." He embraces me and quickly goes.

I stand there watching as his shadow moves away, lighting my pipe and hefting my pack onto my back. Once I'm on my horse again, I recall the scene. I don't know why, and it was very dark, but Old Antonio . . . seemed to be crying . . .

Now Young Antonio's letter reaches me with the village's response to the government's proposals. Young Antonio tells me that Old Antonio soon became very ill, that he didn't want them to let me know, and that he died that night. Young Antonio says that he only said: "No, I already told him what I had to tell him . . . leave him alone, he has a lot of work right now . . ."

When the story ends, Toñita, six years old and with holes in her teeth, says to me, with great solemnity, that she loves me but that she isn't going to give me kisses anymore because "it itches too much." Rolando says that when she has to go to sick bay, Toñita asks if the Sup is there. If they tell her that he is, she doesn't go to the infirmary, "Because that Sup wants nothing but kisses and it itches too much"; so says the inexorable logic of a six year old with holes in her teeth who from this side of the siege is named Toñita.

Here the first rains are beginning to make their presence known. All for the better, we were thinking we'd have to wait for the anti-riot trucks just to have water. Ana María says that the rain comes from the clouds that fight high in the mountains; they do it up there so that men and women can't see their squabbles. The clouds begin their fierce combat with what we call thunder and lightning; and there at the summit, armed to infinity with ingenuity, the clouds fight for the privilege of dying in rain to feed the earth. It's the same with us, without face like the clouds, like them without name, with no pay whatsoever... like them we fight for the privilege of being seeds in the earth.

Vale, salud, and a raincoat (for the rains and for the riots).

From the mountains of the Mexican Southeast
Subcomandante Insurgente Marcos
May 1994

Majority-which-disguises-itself-as-untolerated-minority P.S.: About this whole thing about whether Marcos is homosexual: Marcos is gay in San Francisco, black in South Africa, Asian in Europe, Chicano in San Isidro, Anarchist in Spain, Palestinian in Israel, Indigenous in the streets of San Cristóbal, bad boy in Neza, rocker in CU, Jew in Germany, ombudsman in the SEDENA, feminist in political parties, Communist in the post-Cold War era, prisoner in Cintalapa, pacifist in Bosnia, Mapuche in the Andes, teacher in the CNTE, artist without gallery or portfolio, housewife on any given Saturday night in any neighborhood of any city of any Mexico, *guerrillero* in Mexico at the end of the twentieth century, striker in the CTM, reporter assigned to filler stories for the back pages, sexist in the feminist movement, woman alone in the metro at 10 p.m., retired person in *plantón* in the Zócalo, campesino without land, fringe editor, unemployed worker, doctor without a practice, rebellious student, dissident in neoliberalism, writer without books or readers, and, to be sure, Zapatista in the Mexican Southeast. In sum, Marcos is a human being, any human being, in this world. Marcos is all the minorities who are untolerated, oppressed, resisting, exploding, saying "Enough." All the minorities at the moment they begin to speak and the majorities at the moment they fall silent and put up with it. All the untolerated people searching for a word, their word, which will return the majority to the eternally fragmented, us; all that makes power and good consciences uncomfortable, that is Marcos.

You're welcome, gentlemen of the PGR, I am here to serve you... with lead.

The Spaces of Representation

Perhaps the most frequently invoked term in the postmodern lexicon is "difference." Often, this term is regarded simply as the necessity to appreciate those characteristics distinguishing one from another. From a postmodern perspective, such appreciation includes a refusal to place differences, and the entities they define, in hierarchical relations of inferiority/superiority. In his early deployment of the term within the context of textual analysis, Derrida had something more in mind. Derrida's difference is translatable into English as "defference," a neologism marrying the words difference and defer. In this linguistic construction, it is the term "defer" that requires attention, since it encapsulates a broad critique of essence. According to Derrida, categorical classifications do not exist in their own right. Rather, humans produce, reproduce, modify, and abandon categorizations over time. Thus, categories are not extra-human, but constructed. When a category is constructed, it simultaneously excludes that which does not fit into the category. In this sense, every category contains within it the exclusions that generate the oppositional categories. Or, more simply, the construction of a category entails the simultaneous production of its "Other." The Other is commonly assigned a negative value, and is accordingly ill-treated. Derrida's reconceptualization of differences as reciprocally produced dismantles long-standing categorical "truths," dissolving both the essences as well as the supposedly inviolable boundaries that protect essences against contamination from one another.

The dismantling of categorical essences undermines hierarchically ranked divisions such as race and gender. But it also carries implications beyond the realm of human society. The assault upon essences necessarily assails the boundaries sectioning off "developed" culture from "exploitable" nature, "intelligent, cultured" people from "dumb, natural" animals, and both people and animals from their physical settings. Nor are such constructs limited to the realm of inter-human conceptualizations. John McPhee, in his essay "L.A. Against the Mountains," reveals the intricate system of check-dams, mud-flow diversion walls, concrete-lined seasonal rivers, and legions of civil engineers underpinning the supposedly idyllic ecology of Southern California. In so doing, he demonstrates how the very nature of what we take for natural is actually undergirded by a complex, expensive, and entirely human-made technological system straining (often unsuccessfully) to keep the powerful geological and geomorphological processes under control.

The dropping of borders among human, animal, and environment is part of an increasingly unavoidable consciousness of what Latour calls "hybrid phenomena." Hybrid phenomena are events that cannot be readily contained within a single category without running the risk of severely compromising one's perspective on those events. Is global warming, for instance, a natural phenomenon? Or a human product? Is it a scientific, a technological, or legislative issue? Is it a crisis for such supposedly distinct fields as public health, meteorology, wildlife preservation, or international development financing? Latour claims global warming is all of these things and, thus violates a host of categorical boundaries long taken for granted. Worse, global warming impacts the members and practices of every category and, if those categorical divisions are not breached to address the event, the impacts may well be catastrophic for all concerned.

This means that the categories we use to classify all sorts of phenomena do not, in any fundamental sense, exist. They are reified abstractions, our broadest representations of the world, and mistakenly presented as independently existing phenomena in their own right. Lacking any external necessity, such representations become contingent, porous, and modifiable. The biotechnology of genetically manipulated life-forms provides a particularly stark example. Is a tomato containing fish genes still a tomato? Is it vegetal, or animal, or something else entirely? Insofar as our fishified tomato is merely a new combination of previously existent genetic sequences, is this new creature artificial or natural? Or does it elide the divisions between fish and tomato, plant and animal, and artifice and nature entirely? If so, what exactly *is* it?

Biotechnology is one of a number of recent developments that indicate a collapse not just of the conceptual divide between humans and ecologies, but of the very idea of nature and culture, the natural and the artificial. These categorical terms, once regarded as essences with their own independent existences, are thus revealed as *signs* – as representations of material and symbolic spaces that we conflate with the represented spaces themselves and, through our actions, project back upon those spaces.

Originating in de Saussure's linguistics, the "sign" begins with the idea that no thing can be known in itself. Things in themselves can only be known through the signified (the perceptual representation of a thing) and its signifier (an externalizable, and hence communicable, symbol standing in for the signified). Together, the signified and signifier constitute the sign. Signs are the ever-present mediators of things, and indicate an irremediable distance between human comprehension and things themselves. So irremediable, in fact, that over time signs take on lives of their own while the things they refer to become increasingly unapprehendable and, therefore, largely ephemeral. This widening gap between things and "their" signs causes signs to float free from any underlying reality. Ultimately, in de Saussure's design, since all things come to exist in human understanding only as symbolic signs, the widening gap between things and signs produces a crisis of meaning: meaning is reduced to systems of symbols that interrelate with and point to one another without ever touching "real" ground.

Jean Baudrillard implicates the communications media's abstracted representations of the world as responsible for the crisis of meaning. As communications media become more comprehensive and pervasive, humans are increasingly precluded from experiencing any fixed reality at all. This does not imply that humans live solely in a state of utter confusion, unmoored from the world. Rather, human society comes to exist in a hyperreality comprised of mediated (soft) representations, a melange of predominantly electronically disseminated images that compose a broad consensual hallucination (the term is William Gibson's). In this waking dreamworld, what *is* and what it *means* are contingent upon what symbols are simultaneous in play at any given moment. Thus, the "real" becomes an impossibility, and is replaced by what Baudrillard calls "the simulacra," a copy of a simulation of an imaginary reality that, for all intents and purposes, need never have existed.

Baudrillard focuses on representation in the context of the increasingly omnipresent electronic communications media. But his ideas have serious repercussions for geographer's conceptions of spaces, both material and abstract. Simulacra do not remain in the realm of photons and neurons. They are concretely manifested in the remaking of places, simulating (mis)conceptions of originals that may never have been experienced. This is evident in commonplace spaces such as theme parks and shopping malls. There, simulacra are concretized through design strategies and technologies that render fantasy ever more experientially real. But let us not forget that, simultaneously, such places are subject to material practices of surveillance and control that ensure the exclusion of competing realities liable to contradict the carefully "imagineered" fantasy.

This drive towards electronically enabled simulation, surveillance, and control reaches its contemporary apogee in the on-going establishment of seemingly non-material realities such as the Internet. The Internet is indeed a "place," or a place of places. It is reliant upon servers and backbones sited in specific geographical locales. Yet experientially, the World Wide Web is simultaneously nowhere and everywhere, as long as you are hooked into a computer terminal with a reasonably reliable outside line. Increasingly, Baudrillard's simulacra are thus manifest spatially both in electronic spaces (or "cyberspace") that mimic and replace material places (or "meatspace"), and in the deepening theme-park-ification of material places themselves.

As signs such as "nature" and "culture," "real" and "artificial" separate from their underlying materiality and float free to recombine with one another, both signs and things become increasingly mutable. Much as nature is undergoing redefinition as sequences of adenine, guanine, cytozine, and thiamine, electronic virtuality becomes equatable with reality. The world thus becomes a metanarrative of infinitely manipulable binary codes, whether in the form of genetic base pairs or the zeros and ones of computer microprocessors. And we are redefining the world this way not only in our minds, but also through bodily practices of re-engineering. Thus, how we see is what we get, even if we may not be fully aware of what we are getting until well after the fact.

As the categorical walls among nature, society and space begin to crumble, humans become evermore enveloped in an emergent planetary hyperreality. For its part, geographical inquiry has followed suit by interrogating the spaces of the hyperreal and their intersections with the spaces of other realities. In the process, a host of new questions has emerged: how do representations of reality lead to spaces being reforged, reinvented? How have we gone about remaking spaces in the likeness of our images of them? And what are the concrete ramifications for human and nonhuman beings who occupy those spaces, and for the societies these lives comprise?

We begin addressing these questions with a François Boucq comic, which graphically depicts how a symbiosis between biological animals and mechanical animals satisfies the logistical needs most commonly ascribed to human animals. Following this are two extracts addressing the nature/human divide. The first, by K. J. Donnelly, considers how urbanites' changing perceptions of nature are resulting in efforts to bring "wilderness" in from the material and discursive edges of the city (Reading 36). The second, by Glen Elder, Jennifer Wolch, and Jody Emel, conjures up a mish-mash of misunderstandings about human–animal relationships. They show how ideas of what an animal is, and thus how it should be treated, are power-and value-laden inventions that vary enormously from culture to culture, and from place to place (Reading 37). The final two selections interrogate another important dividing line between the "real" and the "artificial." Anne Friedberg accompanies us into that ubiquitous "privately administered space of public agglomeration," the shopping mall. For her, the mall is undoubtedly a real material space but, at the same time, so thoroughly engineered – towards the image of consumption and the consumption of images – as to become indistinguishable from a virtual reality (Reading 38). For her part, Sherry Turkle engages virtual reality directly, taking on cyberspace's boosters and critics. In the process, she reveals how the space of virtuality is a contested terrain, rife with utopianism, opportunism, dissent, and subversion. In this sense, it is no less real than material space itself (Reading 39).

REFERENCES

Baudrillard, J.: (Glaser, S. F. trans.) *Simulacra and Simulation*. University of Michigan Press: Ann Arbor 1994.

Derrida, J.: (Spivak, G. C. trans.) *Of Grammatology*. Johns Hopkins University Press: Baltimore 1976.

Derrida, J.: (Bass, A. trans.) *Writing and Difference*. University of Chicago Press: Chicago 1978.

Latour, B.: (Porter, C. trans.) *We Have Never Been Modern*. Harvard University Press: Cambridge, MA 1993.

McPhee, J. A.: *The Control of Nature*. Farrar, Straus & Giroux: New York 1989.

de Saussure, F.: (Bally, C., Sechehaye, A. eds., with Reidlinger, A. Baskin, W. trans.) *Course in General Linguistics*. Fontana: London 1974.

Pioneers of the Human Adventure

Written and illustrated by François Boucq
Translated by Elizabeth Bell

PARIAHS OF NATURE

EIGHT O'CLOCK. ANOTHER DAY DRAWS TO A CLOSE. THE DYING EMBERS OF
THE SUN KINDLE A REDDISH GLOW ACROSS THE SAVANNAH, LENGTHENING THE SHADOWS TO INFINITY.

IT IS THE HOUR WHEN ANIMALS OF ALL SPECIES SEEK OUT THE WATERING HOLE TO
SLAKE THEIR THIRST AT THE END OF A TORRID DAY.

NIGHT SLOWLY UNFURLS ITS VAST MANTLE
OVER THE RUGGED TROPICAL VEGETATION
SCATTERED WITH TREES...

NOW THE STRAGGLERS ARE OFF TO THEIR
LAIRS TO SINK INTO THE ARMS OF
MORPHEUS.

IT IS NOT WISE TO TARRY
IN THESE PARTS AFTER
NIGHTFALL.

ONLY THE FAINT SOUND OF GIANT BAOBABS RELEASING THEIR
OXYGENATED BREATH STIRS THE VIBRANT DARKNESS... WHEN
SUDDENLY, FEROCIOUS GAZES PIERCE THE NIGHT !

A SAVAGE HORDE SPRINGS FROM NOWHERE AND RUSHES IN ON THE POND AS THOUGH GRIPPED BY SOME POTENT MAGNETISM.

IN THE MOONLIGHT, THE TRANQUIL SPOT SUDDENLY LOOKS LIKE A MONSTROUS FREAKSHOW...

NATURE'S PARIAHS, HER FORGOTTEN CHILDREN, GATHER WITH THEIR OWN KIND. CONCEALING THEMSELVES BY DAY, THESE MISSHAPEN CREATURES WAIT UNTIL THE EARTH IS IN SHADOW...

TO SHOW THEIR NIGHTMARE FACES!!

THERE ARE TIMES WHEN "THE CREATOR" MUST NOT FEEL VERY PROUD!

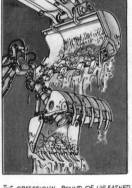

THE SPECTACLE HAS A SAVAGE BEAUTY, AND WORDS FAIL US IN THE EFFORT TO DESCRIBE ITS BEAUTEOUS SAVAGERY.

THE OBSESSIONAL ROUND OF UNLEASHED FRENZY GOES ON UNTIL MORNING...

AT DAWN, ONLY A STRUCTURE REMAINS, IMPUDENT, AS THOUGH THE CREATURES WHO ERECTED IT WISHED TO SHOUT THEIR BEING INTO THE WORLD'S EAR.

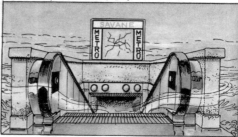

YET NOW, ON THE HORIZON, A CLOUD OF DUST RISES FROM A THOUSAND HAMMERING HOOVES...

THE GNUS ARE MIGRATING TO NEW PASTURELANDS.

WE TAKE OUR HATS OFF TO THE HUMBLE LABORERS IN THE SHADOWS WHO DO THEIR UTMOST TO MAKE LIFE ON THE SAVANNAH MORE COMFORTABLE.

36 A Ramble Through the Margins of the Cityscape: The Postmodern as the Return of Nature

K. J. Donnelly

The broadest and most fundamental distinction we, as humans, make is that between the natural and the artificial. Artifice, we believe, is that which is informed by human minds and produced by human hands. Nature, however, serves either as the raw material upon which humans act to create value (in an economic sense), or a realm outside culture that is both threateningly unpredictable and vulnerable to desecration by human intrusion. The city has long been the concretized representation of this discursive division. An artifact of artifacts, the buildings, streets, commodities, and administrative systems of much of the world's cities have traditionally been girdled with high walls. These walls served to exclude the wilderness beyond, holding it at bay while its mineral, animal, and agricultural resources were removed to the city within. By the beginning of the twentieth century, the city wall had largely become a historical curiosity but the discursive wall defining nature against the city was still in operation. Nonetheless, according to Donnelly, it is beginning to erode, and he offers explanations why. Primarily, Donnelly claims that rapprochement with nature is part and parcel of the critique of modernism, specifically the rejection of the modernist master-narrative of "progress" and its corollary ecosystemic disruption. But Donnelly also believes this critique informs (and is informed by) sympathetic media representations of extra-human ecologies such as forests and coral reefs, and the reappearance of flora and fauna in urban edges recently vacated by the closure of obsolete production facilities. He argues that the on-going reintegration of nature and culture, as represented in recent transformations of urban space, is rooted in the industrial restructuring, electronically mediated symbolic economy, and philosophical ontology of the postmodern.

Postmodernity evinces a changed relationship between humanity and nature. Postmodern visual culture has played an important part in the process of altering perception about nature, departing from modernism, which deemed the natural world unimportant. Indeed, ecological concern has to be seen as a fundamental postmodern phenomenon, a reaction to the modernist abuse, both ignorant and wilful, of the natural world. Actual changes in Britain have been mirrored and aided by a concrete perceptual shift, where in the cityscape and particularly its edges, modernist ideology has retreated, has been rolled back by a fundamentally changed attitude to the natural environment.

David Harvey's characterisation of postmodernity as an era where there is an acceleration in time and space compression (Harvey 1990: 284) applies to the natural environment in a concrete way, both physically as well as perceptually. The countryside has been partially pulled in to the cityscape, to some degree integrated, while perception of nature as a phenomenon that should be excluded from cities has waned. The distinctions between city and country are now, perhaps more than ever, dissolved as the boundaries between the two and their respective attributes have become less and less distinct. This is materially manifest in the migration of certain species of plant and animal to urban areas as well as behavioural changes that constitute an unprecedented transformation in the interactions between human and "natural" environments.

The collapse of industrial production has left gaps in the land-use in British cities, and whether landscaped or neglected, these have been colonised by animals and plants. Ecological concern and the green movement have helped enable this, and have to be approached as fundamentally postmodern, a reaction to modernism and its unbridled pollution and destruction of the natural world. They manifest Lyotard's characterisation of the postmodern condition as the collapse of belief in master discourses (Lyotard 1984: xxiv), and specifically that of "progress." If postmodernity demonstrates a change in the actual relationship between humans and the natural world, then this has been reflected as well as encouraged by the portrayal of nature on television. This change in attitude has to be seen as a wide-ranging reaction to modernist conceptions of nature as distinct from culture and an object for destruction. Thus the postmodern attitude allows for a seemingly contradictory embracing of the modern life and its accoutrements, while valuing the natural world as an integral element of life in postmodernity.

The city, and especially suburbia, has become a locus for this changed situation, with animals and plants acting in ways that would have been unheard of thirty years ago. On the one hand this can be partly attributed to postmodernity, where legacies of modernist ideology in terms of urban planning, pollution and control of the environment are now taking their toll. On the other hand, certain of these dramatic changes can be attributed to postmodernism and the changes in human attitudes that have marked the last twenty years or so.

The postmodern perspective on the association between humans and the natural is imbricated with the partial collapse and general disbelief in the master discourse of progress, one of the central tenets of modernist ideology. This is not to say that modernism is dead, it is alive and kicking in terms of much farming and road planning and yet is being consistently assailed by pressure groups that evince an antimodernist viewpoint.

Modernism should be defined as having as one of its central projects the control of nature. While this has been a trajectory that human beings have followed since the end of hunting and gathering communities, it has taken a dramatic turn since the industrial revolution. Modernism's human-centric view has allowed the heroic endeavours of human kind to triumph over the material world at whatever cost. This conception of culture as superior to nature has allowed a succession of events that have had hideous repercussions upon the natural world. The most conspicuous illustrations of these are pollution in all its aspects, ozone depletion, global warming, the removal of rain forests and wildlife habitats worldwide, desertification and the extinction of various animal and plant species.

The tokenistic event for the modernist desire to control the environment at any cost is the development of DDT. Embodying the modernist clarity of purpose, DDT was hailed at first as a panacea, yet another wonder of science. The pesticide allowed for the full destruction of crop pests and a maximisation of crop yield. However, its inability to degrade once inside a living organism means that not only are penguins and walruses in the Antarctic carrying particles that they have received through the food chain, but virtually all human beings must be carrying a deposit. The effects of this are still unclear. DDT sums up the modernist attitude – that the achievement is in itself of worth, and the consequences, if at all considered, will be dealt with later. The postmodern attitude declares that later is now.

Indeed, the general perception of agricultural practices has undergone a dramatic transformation over the last few years. While nature has been regulated by human beings since Neolithic times, with coppicing and pollarding of trees as well as crop cultivation, the attempt at full control, an industrialisation of agrarian production, is a recent phenomenon. The mechanisation of farms and the use of chemicals embody the modernist desire for maximisation of production through maximisation of control. While the "modern" farming process is still dominant – bumper output through factory farming and chemical application – there has been a significant increase in the amount of produce that is available from "organic" farming methods. This constitutes an attempted arresting of the modernist agrarian project through a denial of the progress of high production at a cost of perceived cruelty to animals and damage to the environment. [. . .]

In addition to this, farming methods have had a high degree of responsibility for changes in the landscape that have allowed the proliferation of certain types of plant at the expense of others, as well as the destruction of habitats that have maintained certain animals and plants (Shoard 1980: 9; Brown 1993:6). This has stimulated the colonising of urban (and suburban) spaces by certain flora and fauna, facilitated by the changes that have overtaken the towns and cities of Britain.

Postmodernity has seen the disintegration of city as it was conceived throughout the twentieth century, with the fragmenting of distinctions between urban domains and that of the natural. The modernist cityscape is a product of civic and industrial planning and demonstrates a desire to centre and regulate the system of the human living and working environment. Changes that have befallen British cities through-out the 1980s reveal a postmodern reconceptualisation of the city, with random patterns of development produced as a result of decentring or attempted recentring – and often seemingly unregulated – patterns of building. Overall, the modernist social project of the postwar period, a project of good quality housing for all, disintegrated in the 1980s. Central government blocked the building of new municipal housing and encouraged the selling off of those existing. This was bolstered by a policy of urban anti-sociality, where rich dockland fortresses endeavoured to keep the poor out and green belt destruction allowed the piecemeal development of suburbia among agrarian sites.

Since the 1970s the UK has witnessed the wholesale devastation of its green belts, the zones of countryside that set the bounds of urban development in previous years by ringing cities. This should be seen as the ending of the strict demarcation between the city and the countryside, which distinguished modernist planning. This tendency has at times allowed the interspersing of housing projects with open land as well as a blanket of new suburbs to be lain across the green fields of Britain. However, the building on green-field sites has become a principal battleground between conservation bodies and government-sanctioned business activity, with perhaps the prime example of this contestation being the Twyford Down controversy.

There has been a mirror to the 1980s urban regeneration in the impetus for developing public areas devoted to nature and animals in the heart of the city. Urban farms exist now in most large cities, where children are encouraged to meet farm animals rather than be shown the realities of the modern methods of farming. In Newcastle, landscaped slag heaps near the city's heart are fields now stocked with cows, to put a pastoral landscape within the urban. Added to the explosion of schemes like these and the commodification of nature in terms of trails and parks, the collapse of industry in large cities and the legacies of past industry have left large tracts of land to become wildlife havens, while wildlife corridors (disused canals and railway tracks) have allowed the movement of animals and plants into the heart of the city.

The far-reaching changes that have befallen flora and fauna have happened over the last twenty or more years and have affected both rural and urban areas of the UK. In terms of botanical species, we are now paying the price of cultivation with large tracts of the countryside having become nothing more than a limited repertoire of monocultures. Intensive farming has not only created a landscape of crops and green uniform fields of perennial ryegrass, but has changed the look of Britain through the destruction of hedgerows and the removal of woodland (Shoard 1980:25–6) [...]

The appearance of wild animals in cities has had rather more attention than the appearance of certain flora. Perhaps the most well-publicised immigrants to urban areas are foxes, who have adapted to urban living largely through becoming a scavenger of waste bins and thriving on our detritus. Large fox populations are common in almost any suburban environment. Portsmouth, for example, has a sizeable fox community centred on the railway tracks, despite being an island that is only accessible by bridges, and also despite being one of the most densely populated urban areas in Europe. Scorpions can be found in significant numbers in certain docks at the mouth of the Thames, while black widow spiders have been found living at south coast ports. Both of these species have been imported amongst consignments of food.

Birds have also started to colonise urban areas, although pigeons, seagulls and starlings started this process earlier in the century. More recent immigrants include kestrels and sparrowhawks that can prey on suburban garden birds and the feral pigeons and starlings that stock many city centres and nest in the tall buildings. Also, there have been significant incursions by magpies and crows, the former growing in such numbers that it has also been blamed for the devastation of suburbia's populations of small birds and may be culled in the near future. [...]

These adaptations to different environments and changes are significant. Within a relatively short period of time we have witnessed not only the adapting abilities of certain species, but the belated triumph of the natural world over the human through the appropriation of the margins of urban landscapes, areas that have heretofore been a symbol of humanity's ability to change and control its surroundings.

There has been a fundamental change in the way that we perceive our relationship with the environment and other living things. The growth of wildlife in cities and the awareness of the natural world within urban spaces is testified to by the proliferation of local projects and wildlife groups. Many of these are specialised, including bat and owl watching groups, organised toad crossings . . . This wave of concern for the natural is located within the traditionally urban space, and while reacting to the changes that were taking place in terms of the natural's relocation within the cityscape, these groupings worked to have an effect, both on the adaptation of urban margins to encourage nature and on education to foster approval rather than destruction.

Ecology's opposition to modernism and capital has been noted by a number of commentators (Harvey 1990:12; Hebdige 1988:230; Baudrillard 1983:61). Baudrillard identifies ecology as one of the "anti-universalist, anti-representative, tribalist, centripetal" impulses that is aiming to slow the implosion of modern civilisation (61), and indeed this seems to be one of its principal aims. The post-oil crisis collapse of industry in the UK corresponded roughly with the proliferation of ecological concern through international bodies like Greenpeace and Friends Of The Earth, which were founded in the late 1960s and early 1970s. These aspired to fight the DDT culture that had been a characteristic of modernist attitudes to nature, where scientific control and interference had been regarded in a totally positive light. In its place was offered a postmodern "dialogue" with the environment and a desire for science to redress imbalances in nature rather than create them.

The green movement and environmental awareness are specifically postmodern phenomena, fundamentally new attitudes to the natural environment. They are highly specific and cannot really be accounted for with reference to any precedents. It does not simply constitute a retrogressive and nostalgic attitude to the natural world, not a full "back to the land" approach. This is testified to by the fact that the green movement has far more support in cities than in rural areas. Green ideology has to be seen as fundamentally postmodern in its outlook as it is founded on the seeming contradiction of embracing both nature and the environmental concerns, and the technology of modern living. The green movement itself, while consisting of a number of international organisations as well as national Green Parties, cannot be seen as a homogenous unit in the sense of political parties or ideologies. It should more accurately be seen as a tendency that unites disparate groupings. There is no solid homogeneity to the green movement and its discourses. It is characterised by small scale and locally-geared action and organisation, which constitutes a negation of the mass politics that have been dominant in the twentieth century. The disintegration of the left-right spectrum of politics has induced this development, as a reaction to what Baudrillard describes as "The dwindling of the political . . . to the present scenario of neo-figuration, where the system continues under the same manifold signs but where these no longer represent anything" (Baudrillard 1983:19). The disillusionment with mass politics has encouraged the growth of the green movement and its techniques. It is a heterogeneous body that maximises its support through being a multiplicity of loose groupings (Lowe et al 1986:114), not explicitly centred on its political arm, the Green Party.

The green movement is utopian, and cannot be construed otherwise. Yet does its utopianism bear any resemblance to the utopianism of the project of modernity? It fails to embrace a full package of utopian aims and has only a vague overall project as any final objective. It is realistic and pessimistic, more concerned with small-scale aims, and posits a continual succession of small changes fought like a patient guerilla war. Indeed, green concerns can never really go all the way, can never be taken to a logical and final conclusion. The ideology is concerned with making a series of changes, with adapting the situation, sometimes fundamentally. Where would that lead if taken to a logical and utopian extreme? It is virtually impossible to consume food that is produced both organically and without exploitation, just as it is almost impossible to live in the modern world without producing waste: should green concern stop at the recycled paper on which ecological leaflets are printed? Overall then, the green ideology, a heterogeneous tendency at best, is utopian in the sense that it desires changes and a better future, but not in the sense of expounding a full programme of what that better world might be; it offers no integrated model and fully-fledged means of getting there.

While green ideology can accept contradiction, being a myriad of discourses, there is a dialectic between environmentalism and capital that has involved some level, a minor level perhaps, of synthesis in the form of green consumer goods. This is largely due to the ability of pressure groups rather than centralised executive bodies, change coming from below rather than above. Environmental concern presupposes a constant state of crisis, where even daily occurrences like the purchase of food or paper can involve a historicising of the object to be consumed rather than a simple and unproblematic consumption.

Visual culture has played a central role in this. Cinema of the 1970s portrayed a nature "gone strange" in films like *Picnic At Hanging Rock* (1975), *The Long Weekend* (1977), and perhaps even *Jaws* (1975). While these representations of nature as having broken its established relationship with humanity may be seen as reflecting the post-oil crisis uncertainty about the state of things, there is something of a cinematic tradition concerning changes in nature. In the 1950s films like *Tarantula* and *Them!* articulated a largely anti-science and anti-"progress" discourse. The most recent example of this is *Jurassic Park*, which, apart from being the ultimate simulated spectacle of the natural world, is primarily a cautionary tale about nonchalant interference in nature. While films have reflected the possibility of nature changing, television has actively been involved in changing the relationship between humans and flora and fauna.

The television set as the locus of postmodern visual culture has both reflected and been a conduit for changes in perception of the human's relation to its environment. While nature programming often embraces some form of environmental concern, it is primarily entertainment. This involves the packaging of the natural world as spectacle, offering action, visual splendour and little stories, and this procedure has had the net effect of not only integrating animals with the urban and the human, but has made animals in cities a signifier of television's version of nature.

The conversion of the natural world to a mainstay of televisual entertainment (Lowe et al 1986:118) has followed a small number of strategies. One of the central aspects involves a development of traditional anthropomorphism. It goes beyond the simple Victorian version of children's stories and teddy bears, into a construction of animals as different from yet profoundly similar to human beings. This is underlined by approaches that aim to "humanise" the animal through the delineation of distinct character traits added to the narrativisation of animal activities. The mundane events of the animals' everyday lives are converted into drama through engaging the techniques of television drama. These nature programmes are narratives of birth, sex, death, survival against the odds, races against time, familial relations, neighbourhoods, and dominance and submission; all in all the staple of television dramatic narrative, but replacing the human actors with animals.[. . .]

TV has effectively created an animal pantheon, where certain animals are highly evident while other parts of the natural world, such as plants, are neglected and become invisible. A visit to any video shop will illustrate this, with cats, sharks, big animals and furry animals proving to be the attractions while insects in particular are ignored. The net effect of the treatment of animals by nature programmes is that the reality of nature has become a signifier of TV's version of nature, following Baudrillard's description of the media's producing the hyperreal and destroying the real (Baudrillard 1983: 84–5) and Wakefield's description of Disneyland's animal simulacra as superior to the real (Wakefield 1990: 110). Television has to be seen as a prime mover in the changing of people's attitudes, through providing a perceptual blueprint for approaching the natural world as spectacle and narrative. Many who happily watch nature on television will not venture from their armchair to watch nature on their doorstep, and this is because the simulation is always superior to the real. Yet television nature programmes have become a significant and popular TV genre, mixing education, voyeurism, anthropomorphism and empathy to construct animals as relatives and neighbours rather than objects for the DDT spray.

In summary, postmodernity should be characterised as manifesting a changed relationship between humanity and nature, with concrete and dramatic changes having taken place in the fringes of Britain's cities over the last twenty years or so. While these have been partially facilitated by the retreat, in varying degrees, of modernist ideology, postmodern culture has played a primary role in the transformation of perception about the relationship between human beings and the environment. It has shadowed as well as nurtured concrete changes in Britain's natural scene, with television in particular acting as a conduit and a catalyst for this change in attitude, through the manifesting of that scene. Postmodernism has foregrounded discourses concerned with an interdependent relationship with nature, with ecological concern fostering a profoundly different attitude to wildlife in cities.

REFERENCES

Baudrillard, Jean. *In the Shadow Of The Silent Majorities*. New York: Semiotext(e), 1983.
Brown, Pat. "Town And Country" – on the publication of the Department Of The Environment report "Countryside Survey 1990." *The Guardian* 18 November 1993: 6.

Harvey, David. *The Condition Of Postmodernity: An Enquiry Into The Origins Of Cultural Change*. Oxford: Basil Blackwell, 1990.

Hebdige, Dick. *Hiding In The Light: On Images And Things*. London: Routledge, 1988.

Lowe, Philip, Graham Cox, Malcolm MacEwen, Tim O'Riordan, and Michael Winter. *Countryside Conflicts: The Politics Of Farming, Forestry and Conservation*. Aldershot: Gower, 1986.

Lyotard, Jean-François. *The Postmodern Condition: A Report On Knowledge*. Manchester: Manchester University Press, 1988.

Shoard, Marion. *Theft Of The Countryside*. London: Maurice Temple Smith, 1980.

Wakefield, Neville. *Postmodernism: The Twilight Of The Real*. London: Pluto, 1990.

37 La Pratique Sauvage: Race, Place, and the Human–Animal Divide

Glen Elder, Jennifer Wolch, and Jody Emel

As the categorical antipode of culture, nature is not just an innocent classification of that which is other than human. In valorizing the human, anthropocentricism devalues nature: as the location of the uncultured and the dehumanized, populated by animals and those animalistic less-than-humans referred to as "savages." It is the symbolic space to which others have long been consigned, and thereby represented as disordered and subrational, deserving of domination and exploitation. The time is fast passing when an hegemonic patriarchy could disparagingly equate women with nature, or when colonialist discourse could denigrate the colonized as animals in need of domestication. But to what extent have animals themselves been recipients of analogous exploitation and abuse? At one level, the answer to this question is self-evident, if we recall how much suffering humans inflict on animals simply because they want to eat, wear, experiment on, or simply kill them. However, in more nuanced analysis of cross-cultural contentions over what constitutes humane treatment of animals, Glen Elder, Jennifer Wolch, and Jody Emel demonstrate that the human/animal divide is indeed an arbitrary and malleable thing. They illustrate how an animal's status as food, friend, prey, or even spiritual intercessor varies from culture to culture. Thus what constitutes both "animal" and "nature" is not a "natural" fact but a matter of human representations in action – representations upon which the lives of innumerable sentient nonhuman beings hang. The authors deconstruct two popular notions: first, the assumption that there can be an appropriate way to exploit animals; and second, the idea that those who exploit animals differently from ourselves are savages.

Introduction

Animal practices are extraordinarily powerful as a basis for creating difference and hence racialization. This is because they serve as defining moments in the social construction of the human–animal divide. While universally understood in literal terms, the divide is a shifting metaphorical line built up on the basis of human–animal interaction patterns, ideas about hierarchies of living things (both human and nonhuman), and the symbolic roles played by specific animals in society. Certain sorts of animals (such as apes, pets, or revered species) become positioned on the human side of this metaphorical line, rendering some practices unacceptable. But other harmful practices are normalized, to reduce the guilt (or at least the ambivalence) associated with inflicting pain or death, and to justify them as defensible behaviors differentiated from the seemingly wanton violence observed in nonhuman nature.

Norms of legitimate animal practice are neither consistent nor universal. Instead, codes for harmful animal practices are heavily dependent on the immediate context of an event. Here, the critical dimensions of context include the animal species, human actor(s), rationale for and methods of harm, and site of action involved in the practice. And because animal practices emerge over long periods of time as part of highly variable cultural landscapes, place is also implicated in constructing the human–animal divide. When distinct, place-based animal practices are suddenly inserted into new locales by immigrants and are thus decontextualized, conflict erupts. Those newcomers who violate or transgress the many-layered cultural boundary between people and animals become branded as "savage," "primitive," or "uncivilized" and risk dehumanization, that is, being symbolically allocated to the far side of the human–animal divide. [. . .]

In this situation, racialization of those immigrants whose darker skin color feeds into entrenched racial ideologies, stereotypes, and discursive practices serves to demarcate the boundaries of national culture and belonging to place, and to exclude those who do not "fit." Conflicts over animal practices, rooted in deep-seated cultural beliefs and social norms, fuel ongoing efforts to racialize and devalue certain groups of immigrants. Animal practices have thus become tools of a cultural imperialism designed to delegitimize subjectivity and citizenship of immigrants under time–space conditions of postmodernity and social relations of postcoloniality. [. . .]

Postcolonial Animal Stories

We launch our arguments by telling a series of stories drawn from recent events in the US. Unlike colonial animal stories such as *Babar*, in which the animals are representations of colonists and "natives," these postcolonial stories focus on the treatment of animals by subaltern groups and the ways these practices are used to devalue them. Their practices, interpreted as "out of place" by dominant groups, serve to position them at the very edge of humanity – to racialize and dehumanize them through a complicated set of associations that measure their distance from modernity and civilization and the ideals of white America.

The rescue dog

Late in 1995, a three-month-old German shepherd puppy was beaten to death in a residential neighborhood of Fresno, one of the fastest growing urban regions in California's vast Central Valley.[1] The puppy death created a public furor. Neighbors complained to local authorities, and the man responsible for the dog's death was taken into custody on felony charges of animal cruelty. Later these charges were reduced to misdemeanor cruelty, to which the defendant pleaded guilty. The man charged in the case was Chia Thai Moua, a Hmong immigrant from Laos who had come to the United States in the 1970s. Moua was also what the press reports termed a "shaman." Curiously, his shaman's logic in turning to the puppy was precisely that of so many others who use dogs to serve people: he was trying to rescue another human (in this case, his wife). He explained that he had killed the dog in order to "appease an evil spirit" that had come to plague her in the form of diabetes. The sacrifice could drive out the spirit and effect a cure. According to Hmong beliefs, "a dog's night vision and keen sense of smell can track down more elusive evil spirits and barter for a sick person's lost soul." Other animals, such as chickens and pigs, are sacrificed first, but if the killing of such animals does not solve the problem, then, according to Moua, "If it is a serious case . . . I have no other choice" but to "resort" to a dog. Moua stated that each year he performs a special ceremony to release the souls of all the animals who have helped him, so that they can be reborn again. Thus, according to Moua, Hmong people from the highlands of Laos "are not cruel to animals . . . We love them . . . Everything I kill will be reborn again." [. . .]

Bambi's brother

One night in 1995, four men drove into the Angeles National Forest in southern California. One of the men proceeded to immobilize a deer with a spotlight, shoot the animal in the throat, and load the struggling creature into the trunk of the car. Back in town, the car was pulled over by a police officer, who, upon hearing thumping noises coming from the trunk, demanded that it be opened. There was the deer. Veterinarians were not able to save the deer, despite an emergency operation. All four men were arrested and charged with crimes; the shooter pleaded guilty to conspiracy for poaching and premeditated cruelty to an animal, and was sentenced to a year in jail, 100 hours of community service, and ordered to pay a $200 fine. The other three were convicted of lesser charges, for which one got a six-month jail sentence and all were ordered to perform community service and pay fines.[2]

The men involved in this case were Latinos: a photograph of all four appeared in the *Los Angeles Times* article covering the incident, and the images portray them as severe men with classically *indio* and *mestizo* features. [. . .]

The bowser bag

Two Long Beach men were charged with cruelty to animals for allegedly killing a German shepherd puppy and eating the dog for dinner on a March evening in 1989.

A Los Angeles area judge ruled that there was no law against eating dogs, and that the animal had not been killed in an inhumane fashion. The charges were therefore dropped.

The case did not die, however. Rather, it spurred the introduction of a law, signed by then-Governor George Deukmejian, making pet-eating a criminal misdemeanor, punishable by a six-month jail term and a $1000 fine. Pets are defined in this statute as any animal commonly kept as a pet. Killing and eating wildlife, poultry, livestock, fish, or shellfish remain legal since these sorts of creatures fall beyond accepted definitions of "pet."[3]

But all this is beside the point, which is that Americans eat hot dogs, not dogs. In fact, given the status of most pet dogs and cats as quasi-human members of the family, eating a dog or cat is much too close to cannibalism for comfort. Indeed, the puppy involved was killed in an apartment complex, at home, it was all in the family. But the two men above were not "American," they were refugees from Cambodia. Trying to minimize the backlash against his community, the head of the Cambodia Association of America claimed that "Cambodians don't eat dogs," but it is widely known that many people from various parts of Asia do. [...]

The blood of the lamb

In April 1987, a church practicing Santeria announced plans to open a house of worship in Hialeah, Florida. This announcement, along with a spate of angry calls from residents reacting to "whole piles of animals, stinking and with flies" that had been left behind following a sacrifice, prompted the Hialeah City Council to hold an emergency meeting in June. At that time, the council adopted a resolution noting that the Santeria religious group was potentially threatening public morals, peace, and safety, and passed an ordinance extending Florida's animal cruelty laws to cover ritual sacrifice, thus imposing criminal sanctions on the activity. The attorney general of Florida also expressed an opinion that religious animal sacrifice was not a "necessary" killing and so it was prohibited by state law. A few months later, the council adopted an ordinance that went further, prohibiting the possession, sacrifice, or slaughter of an animal with the intent to use such animal for food purposes. The prohibition applied, however, only if the animal was killed in any type of *ritual* regardless of whether the animal was in fact consumed for food. This left as legal the killing of animals in properly zoned and licensed establishments.[4] [...]

Ernesto Pichardo, founder and priest of Hialeah's Santeria church, located on a former used-car lot, took the city to court. In the face of protests by animal rights and humane society groups (as well as local Catholic and Baptist clergy), Pichardo argued that the city had violated the church's rights under the free exercise of religion clause of the Constitution's First Amendment. Santeria sacrifices were integral to key Santeria religious ceremonies (birth, death, marriage events) and were used to intervene with *orishas* or minor gods that are believed to have powers to help people with certain kinds of problems. An action for declaratory, injunctive, and monetary relief was filed in the US District Court, which ruled for the city on the grounds that the jurisdiction had a right to prevent health risks and emotional injury to children, protect animals from cruel and unnecessary killing, and restrict the slaughter of animals to areas zoned for slaughterhouses. The US Supreme Court, however, thought otherwise and on 11 June 1993 ruled that the city had not demonstrated a "compelling interest" in implementing the ban and had unfairly targeted a religious practice, sacrifice, used only by Santeros. The Court thus declared the ordinance void under the First Amendment.

This ruling was hardly surprising. To do otherwise could easily have opened up a Pandora's box for the Court and indeed the nation, since a finding of cruelty, for example, would have threatened such long-standing religious practices as Kosher slaughter, and could even have raised serious questions about the "humaneness" of conventional killing techniques practiced on the slaughterhouse floor. The visceral reaction at the local level thus necessarily faded away in the weighing of such national interests. [...]

Postcolonial Racialization and the Human–Animal Divide

Many forms of racialization have, in fact, long relied upon a discourse about human–animal boundaries, namely the dichotomous division of sentient beings into categories of "human" and "animal." The most basic and durable criteria used to fix the boundary have involved differences in *kind*. But although humans and animals do manifestly differ (a point that is universally recognized), the inter-specific divide is not solely a behavioral or biologically determined distinction. Rather, like so many other common categorizations (such as race or ethnicity), it is also a place-specific social construction subject to renegotiation over time. More-over, the reasons for assigning one human group to one side of the boundary or another may also change between times and places.

From its earliest beginnings, Christian theology identified the soul as the defining feature of humanity. Even with the advent of Enlightenment ideas about animals, such as Descartes' identification of animals with machines, the boundary rested on the presence/absence of souls. With the rise of a more secular Western science, the key differences in kind became biological and behavioral characteristics; criteria such as language or intentionality were employed to maintain the borders.[5] But Darwin's theory of evolution cast a fundamentally new light on the issue. The boundary distinguishing humans and animals was reinterpreted in the West to involve not only differences in kind but also differences in *progress* along an evolu-tionary path. This path began with "lower" life forms, proceeded through intermedi-ate stages inhabited by "higher" animals, and reached its pinnacle with (white) "man."

This scientific, evolutionary recasting fit squarely within an interconnected set of understandings about the human geography of the colonial world, in which the "discovery" of "races" raised complex questions of human taxonomy. Categorizing exotic-looking peoples from distant lands as lower on the evolutionary scale and thus closer to animals echoed and relied upon a myriad of similar divisions used to separate some humans from others: primitive versus modern, civilized versus savage, heathen versus Christian, cannibal versus noncannibal. In turn, the human–animal division construed as a continuum of *both* bodily form/function and temporal stage in evolutionary progress was used to reinforce these intrahuman categorizations and interpret them in temporal, evolutionary terms rather than in solely social or geographic ways. [...]

In postcolonial, Western capitalist space, the idea of a human–animal divide as reflective of both differences in kind and in evolutionary progress has retained its power to produce and maintain racial and other forms of cultural difference. The dominant uses of human–animal distinctions during the colonial epoch relied upon representations of similarity to animals to dehumanize and thus racialize particular cultural groups. Contemporary arguments, in contrast, are primarily characterized by a focus on animal practices employed by subdominant cultural groups as cruel, savage, criminal, and *inhuman:* the literal blood-letting of animals, the slicing up of their bodies. But although the precise terms of reference have shifted over time, the postcolonial moment is one that continues to use putative human–animal boundaries to inscribe totems of difference (savage, barbaric, heathen, or archaic versus civilized, Christian, or modern). [...]

Animals and the Body Politic

Racialization is far from a monolithic or static process but instead is situational and shaped by racial ideologies and stereotypes.[6] Exactly how and why does this postcolonial, postmodern form of racialization around animals occur? We argue that in the present instance, animal bodies have become one site of political struggle over the construction of cultural difference and maintenance of American white supremacy. By scrutinizing and interpreting subaltern practices on animal bodies (or simply "animal practices") through their own lenses, dominant groups in the US simultaneously construct immigrant others as uncivilized, irrational, or beastly, and their own actions as civilized, rational, and humane.

In general, animal bodies can be used to racialize, dehumanize, and maintain power relations in three key ways. First, animals serve as absent referents or models for human behavior.[7] Being treated "like an animal" is typically interpreted as a degrading and dehumanizing experience, and such treatment is therefore a powerful tool for subjugation of others.... The key aspect of such violent treatment that makes it dehumanizing, however, is not just the abuse or violation: it is the fact that victims are *objectified* and used like animals, who are commonly objectified and used without second thought.[8] Abusive treatment of slaves by masters, for example, was modeled on how people use animals without consideration of their subjectivity.[9]

Second, people are dehumanized by virtue of imputed similarities in behavior or bodily features and/or associations with the animal world in general or certain animals in particular. (Human identities also derive meaning and an enormous range of positive values from imputed similarities, of course, such as bravery, speed, and cunning.) Imputations are often made on the basis of associational representations of both humans and the animals to which they are being linked: colonial images of Africans as "ape-people" come readily to mind. Similarities can also be drawn on the basis of theories of human–animal continuity. For example, in Western thought, women's bodies have been deemed "like" animals due to their biological role, seemingly uncontrolled passions, and perceived irrationality. [...]

The third and least explored manner in which animals play a role in the social construction of racial difference, and the one which we argue characterizes the postcolonial, postmodern moment, involves specific human practices on animal bodies. Such practices have been used to construct other groups as well: in Medieval Europe, for instance, women who harbored feline "familiars" were often regarded as witches. And, as illustrated so vividly by Frederick Simoons,[10] taboos about which animal bodies to eat (and which body parts) are common amongst contemporary peoples, with the result that outsider groups not observing such taboos may be viewed with disgust and disdain. [...]

Animal Practices and Dehumanization

What makes one animal practice acceptable and another a potent symbol of savagery that can be used to dehumanize those who engage in it? We have argued that every human group defines the boundary between humans and other animals in part on the basis of their treatment of animal bodies or animal practices. Specific forms of human–animal interactions, legitimized and rationalized over time, are part and parcel of the repertoire of "civilized" behavior that defines the human–animal divide. Those who do not stay within this field fall over the human–animal boundary or at least into the netherworld of "savagery"; if the practices are too far over the line, they can be interpreted as cannibalism, the ultimate act of inhumanity. Policing the human–animal boundary through the regulation of animal practices is necessary to maintain identity as humans and, not coincidentally, to sustain the legitimacy of animal practices of dominant groups.

It is widely recognized that in most societies certain types of animal practices are taboo. Taboo practices involve sexual relations with animals (bestiality is rarely sanctioned, although sometimes tolerated). Beyond bestiality, the killing and eating of the "wrong" species or categories of animals (especially totemic species or those seen as too similar to humans) can also be forbidden. For example, the consumption of apes is widely interpreted as tantamount to cannibalism, since simians occupy an ambiguous position along the human–animal boundary. [...]

Despite the importance of animal species or category in determining which animal practices fall beyond the bounds of humanity in any given society, practices are rarely considered (un)acceptable on the basis of species alone. Species is only one part of the immediate context through which animal practices are interpreted. [...]

There are at least four other key elements of context which define the human–animal borderline. One is reason or rationale for harm. Was a specific harmful practice necessary for survival or to minimize human or animal pain/death? Few humans raise objections to killing and eating taboo animals if the alternative is starvation; the most commonly stated reason for killing laboratory animals (even "pet" species such as dogs and cats) is to prevent suffering or death; and "euthanasia" of companion animals is justified as a way to reduce animal suffering. When the rationale for harm is seen as unnecessary or irrational, or the results are defined as damaging, however, practices may be condemned. Just what is unnecessary or irrational or damaging varies from group to group.

Another important aspect of context is the social location of the perpetrator: was the person(s) involved in the harmful practice "appropriate"? For example, if an animal was killed for purposes of human consumption, did a butcher or slaughterhouse worker perform the act? Or if a companion animal was killed, was a veterinarian presiding? As our cases illustrate, problems arise when the human actor does not have the role and/or training deemed necessary by the dominant group to legitimize the act.... Similarly, where the actual killing of animals has become industrialized, professionalized, and removed from the course of everyday life, lay people have no legitimacy as animal killers.

A further contextual element revolves around the means or methods of harm: how was the harm inflicted? What techniques or tools were utilized, and did they fall within the range of local convention? Or were methods seen as archaic, barbaric, or brutally employed? A puppy can legitimately lose her head in a laboratory decapitator, but bludgeoning her to death is deemed too brutal. [...]

Lastly, the site of harm is perhaps the most crucial aspect of context in determining the legitimacy of an animal practice.... The issue of site has two dimensions. One is whether the harmful action is carried out in purpose-built quarters or reserved places (slaughterhouses, labs, shelters, forests during hunting season) or "out of site" in unspecialized spaces more typically used for other purposes or banned for the animal practice in question (residential areas, posted lands). A second site-related issue is whether the action occurs "out of sight" in abattoirs or factory farms banished from the city or in labs behind locked doors, or in highly visible places of everyday life such as homes, street corners, or church. [...]

Place and the Borders of Humanity

Human–animal borders and human practices on animals vary according to place. In representational politics that seek to dehumanize people by associating them with certain animals, place is often used to reinforce such associations.[11] Places are imbued with negative characteristics because they harbor (or are thought to harbor) certain feared or disliked animals, and then these places are linked to people who take on the dirty, polluted, or dangerous aspects of the place (and its animals). For example, "jungles" are dangerous places in the Western popular imagination, conjuring up images of dense foliage beneath which poisonous snakes slither and vicious beasts wait to pounce on unsuspecting humans. More concretely, marginalized groups such as gypsies are often relegated to residual places in urban areas (such as dumps), often inhabited by "dirty" and "disease-ridden" animals, for example, rats. Thus a "dirty–unsafe–rats–gypsies" association arises, linking a so-called pest-species to a particular subaltern group. This associational process has long been used to connect poor people, "dirty" animals, and dirt more generally.

In the case of animal practices, however, place plays both more straight-forward and more nuanced roles. At a basic level, specific repertoires of animal practices evolve and become normalized *in place*. Such repertoires are in part environmentally determined, since the diversity of animal species available to kill, eat, or otherwise use is shaped by environmental factors, as are particular modes of subsistence linked to specific animals (for example, pastoralism). In addition, however, cultural ideas about animals (like other aspects of culture) evolve in place over time due to social or technological change generated within a society, or by externally driven events such as migrations or invasions. Thus values and practices concerning cosmological, totemic, or companionate relations between people and animals, and the material uses of animals as food or clothing, medicines or aphrodisiacs, shift as a result of social dynamics, technological change, or culture contact. The result is a shifting but place-specific ensemblage of animals, valued and used according to particular, legitimized codes. Transgressions of such place-specific codes or boundaries of practice *by definition* situate an individual or group as "outsider," "savage," or "subhuman."

What happens when the coding of animal bodies and the codes of animal practice shared by people dominant in one place are broken or challenged by people from another place, who do not share these codes but share the same space? When people are uprooted and brought to new places, they encounter different human–animal boundary constructions and if they persist in their indigenous practices are much more likely to transgress the border than locals. During much of (pre)history, the pace of such culture contact was relatively slow, allowing both host and newcomer groups to adjust; in earlier international migration waves to the US, origins of immigrants were sufficiently similar to host populations that conflict on the basis of animal practices does not appear to have been rife. With the economic globalization, escalating geopolitical instabilities and conflicts, and vast international population flows that characterize the postmodern condition, the "empire" has come home. Newcomers from a wide variety of radically different environments and cultural landscapes are suddenly living cheek by jowl. Typically, immigrants must move into the territories of a more powerful host community. Adjustment possibilities are foreshortened; for the largest immigrant groups, the need to adjust may be obviated by the emergence of relatively self-contained immigrant districts, such as "ethnoburbs."[12] Thus in the contemporary US, immigrants whose indigenous animal practices clash with the codes of dominant society are at the greatest risk of racialization and dehumanization.

Nevertheless, non-immigrant people of darker (versus lighter) color can also be at risk on the basis of their animal practices. Here, place plays a more nuanced role, by exoticizing the imaginary places of origin of such groups. Risk in this case arises not only because dominant norms of animal practice are contravened, but also because of the deeply engrained evolutionary connotations of the primitive, exotic, racialized "homelands" lurking in the Western imagination just below the surface of contemporary race relations. Thus cock fighting among Native Americans or Chicanos, the adoption of Santeria on the part of many Chicanos and African Americans, or the keeping of aggressive, vicious dogs (or, worse, dog-fighting) among youth in inner-city communities of color can place such subaltern groups on the far side of the human–animal boundary. When problematic practices occur in racialized and marginalized places, such as "ghetto" areas that are already indirectly and sometimes even explicitly linked to Africa (by virtue of names like "The Jungle"), prospects of racialization on the basis of animal practices may rise still higher.

Lastly, there may be time–space displacement of one group's animal practices onto another group located in a different place. With globalization of environmental degradation and the rise of international efforts to prevent species extinction, local groups may risk racialization by virtue of animal practices occurring in their ancestral or natal-origin countries or regions rather than their *own* behavior toward animals. By a quick twist in the logic of postmodern hyperspace, they can in effect be held suspect while being thousands of miles away from the action. For example, the rhinoceros faces extinction due to poaching and the subsequent sale of their pulverized horns as an aphrodisiac to Asian consumers. Such practices contravene dominant Western environmental values as well as acceptable reasons for animal harm and may be used to devalue and dehumanize Asian Americans or Asian immigrants regardless of whether or not they support the market for such substances.

Toward *La Pratique Sauvage*

We are left with a dual challenge: how to break the links between animals and racialization, and stop the violence done to people racialized on the basis of their animal practices; and how to make the links between animals and people, and stop the violence directed at animals on the basis of their nonhuman status. [...]

What changes in human thought and practice does *la pratique sauvage* imply? One is that humans, especially dominant groups, accept rather than deny some of the vulnerability that animals have always known and reject the illusion that a devaluation of others (human or animal) either empowers or offers protection from harm. Another is that all humans need to abandon the drive for overarching control and instead choose a position of humility or marginality with respect to the Earth that balances needs for safety and security with consideration for the needs of other life-forms.... Finally, this sort of *pratique sauvage* implies that people must actively engage in a radically inclusive politics which considers the interests and positionality of the enormous array of animal life and lives, as well as the lives of diverse peoples.

NOTES

1   See Max Arax, "Hmong's Sacrifice of Puppy Reopens Cultural Wounds," *Los Angeles Times*, 16 December 1994, pp. A1,5; and Anonymous, "Sacrifice of Dog Highlights Clash of Cultures in Central Valley," *San Francisco Chronicle*, 19 December 1994, p.A22.

2   Frank B. Williams, "Four Men, Sentenced to Jail in Cruel Poaching of Deer," *Los Angeles Times*, 13 May 1994, pp. B1,2.

3   See David Haldane, "Culture Clash or Animal Cruelty?," *Los Angeles Times*, 13 March 1989, sect. II, p. 1; David Haldane, "Judge Clears Cambodians Who Killed Dog for Food," *Los Angeles Times*, 15 March 1989, sect. II, p. 1; Clay Evans, "Bill Outlawing Eating of Pets Clears Senate," *Los Angeles Times*, 29 August 1989, sect. I, p. 20; Paul Jacobs, "Governor Signs Pet Protection Bill But Opposes Penalties," *Los Angeles Times*, 19 September 1989, p. B3; Greg Lucas, "Governor Signs Bill Outlawing Dining on Pets," *San Francisco Chronicle*, 19 September 1989, p. A8; Katherine Bishop, "U.S.A.'s Culinary Rule: Hot Dogs Yes, Dogs No," *New York Times*, 5 October 1989, sect. A, p. 22.

4   The Santeria case is United States of America, *U.S. Supreme Court Reports*, 1993. Church of the Lukumi Babalu Aye, Inc., and Ernesto Pichardo v. City of Hialeah, 124 L Ed 472. Media reports include Paul M. Barrett, "Court to Test Religion Rights in Sacrifice Case," *Wall Street Journal* 18 October 1992, sect. B, pp. 1,7; Joan Biskupic, "Animal Sacrifices Ban Tests Religion Rights," *Washington Post*, 1 November 1992, sect. A, p.1, 8,9; Anonymous, "Santeria Priest Performs Sacrifices," *Sunday Telegram*, 27 June 1993, sect. A, p. 4. Earlier reports described Santeria in general (for example, Rick Mitchell, "Out of Africa: An Ancient Nigerian Religion Comes through Caribbean to the United States," *San Francisco Chronicle*, 1 May 1988, magazine 15, p. Z25); and the bans in Los Angeles and San Francisco are described in Anonymous, "L. A. Animal Torture-Killings Blamed on Sect," *San Francisco Chronicle*, 22 July 1988, sect. A, p. 14; Anonymous, "Ritualistic Animal Sacrifice Is Outlawed by L. A. Council," *San Francisco Chronicle*, 3 October 1990, sect. A, p. 17; Suzanne Espinosa, "Resistance to S. F. Ban on Animal Sacrifice," *San Francisco Chronicle*, 24 July 1992, sect. A, p. 24; Elaine Herscher, "Panel Compromises on Animal Sacrifice," *San Francisco Chronicle*, 19 August 1992, sect. A, p. 20.

5   Ann McClintock, *Imperial Leather: Race, Gender and Sexuality in the Colonial Contest*, New York: Routledge, 1994, p. 40.

6   Laura Pulido, "A Critical Review of the Methodology of Environmental Racism Research," *Antipode* 28, 1996, pp. 142–59.

7   See Carol J. Adams, *The Sexual Politics of Meat: A Feminist-Vegetarian Critical Theory*, New York: Continuum, 1990.

8   A long line of ethical reasoning, perhaps epitomized by Kantian theory, argues that humans have only indirect moral duties to animals because they lack subjectivity and thus can be treated like inanimate objects.

9   Marjorie Speigel, *The Dreaded Comparison: Human and Animal Slavery*, Denmark: Heretic Books, 1988.

10 See Frederick J. Simoons, *Eat Not This Flesh: Food Avoidances from Prehistory to the Present*, Madison: University of Wisconsin Press, 1994.

11 David Sibley, *Geographies of Exclusion*, London: Routledge, 1995.

12 See Wei Li, *Chinese Ethnoburbs of Southern California*, Ph. D. diss., Department of Geography, University of Southern California, 1997.

38 Window Shopping: Cinema and the Postmodern

Anne Friedberg

If the spaces of nature are the places to which we banish all that we mistrust, we also invent concomitant denatured spaces comprised of that which we wish to include as part of ourselves. Like the walls separating city from wilderness, the discursive divide excluding the uncontrollable, discomforting, and uncomfortably different simultaneously includes a controlled sanctuary well-stocked with the objects of our desires. In her analysis of the shopping mall, Anne Friedberg reveals that such sanctuaries exist not just as symbolic constructs, but as constructions of concrete, neon, and especially glass. For Friedberg, the mall is the postmodern imaginary made flesh. It is a place where the world's artifacts and experiences are excerpted from their space–time contexts, and then attractively arranged as juxtaposed fragments under a screen of glass for our delectation and consumption. Friedman identifies the mall as an archetypal space of representation, a place where we represent ourselves afresh by trying-on and consuming representations. In the process, the mall becomes a neon-lit twilight zone between the concrete and the imaginary. In this twilight zone, Friedberg observes how the unreal conventions of cinematic representation transform into physically experienced realities as the wandering shopper jump-cuts, fast-forwards, and slow-motions through a carefully edited montage of an imagined world outside.

Les Flâneurs/Flâneuse du Mall

"I just arrived in this *stupid suburb*. I have no friends, no money, no car, no license, and even if I did have a license all I could do was drive out to some *stupid mall* and maybe if I'm lucky play some fucking video games, smoke a joint and get stupid.

You see there's nothing to do anymore. Everything decent's been done. *All the great themes have been used up, turned into theme parks.* So I don't really find it exactly cheerful to be living in the middle of a totally like exhausted decade where there is nothing to look forward to and no one to look up to."

CHRISTIAN SLATER in the 1990 film, *Pump Up the Volume*[1] (emphasis added)

The ultimate extension of nineteenth-century urban artificial environments – parks, passageways, department stores, exhibition halls – is that contemporary urban "center," the shopping mall. If, for Benjamin, the arcade instantiated all of modernity, the shopping mall is an equally pivotal site, the key "topos," of postmodern urban space.

The nineteenth-century *passage* was readable to Benjamin while in its decline (*Verfall*). Perhaps, equally, the contemporary shopping mall now emerges as a comprehensible cultural space as it is threatened with its own obsolescence. (Electronic technologies now bring information, entertainment, products, and services into the home, the privatized public space of the shopping mall may soon be replaced by the "electronic mall" and the "home shopping network.") But whether or not life in the public realm diminishes, electronic flânerie further turns spaces into their virtual replacements, "conduits" that supplant the need for physical mobility. Just as the shift to a credit economy has relied on the virtual buying power of plastic, virtual realities, electronic "villages," and invisible "data highways" have become the new frontier. "Virtual" has entered the vernacular as the present predictive.

And yet for the moment, the dystopic aspects of urban flânerie are all too apparent. As homelessness becomes an increasingly visible consequence of the economies of obsolescence, the fluid subjectivity of the flâneur takes on a direct, if deplorable, implication. The all too familiar "street person" with shopping cart conducts a dire parody of a consumer culture gone awry. As a grim reminder of the excessive valuation of the perceptual mode of shopping-flânerie, the flâneuse as "bag lady" can stroll the "aisles" of a derelict urbanity, where shopping can be done without money, the "shelves" stocked with refuse and recyclable debris.

I will discuss the shopping mall as an architectural and social space. The cinema developed as an apparatus that combined the mobile with the virtual gaze and turned it into a commodifiable experience. I now argue a further alignment of the seemingly separate activities of shopping and tourism with cinema and television spectatorship. The shopping mall developed as a site for combining the speculative activity of shopping with the mobilities of tourism; the shopping mall "multiplex" cinema epitomizes both in a virtual form. And, as a mobilized gaze becomes more and more virtual, the physical body becomes a more and more fluid site: in this "virtual mobility" the actual body – gender-bound, race bound, ethnicity bound – becomes a veritable depot for departure and return. Hence, the changes in reception produced by multiplex cinemas, cable television, and VCRs will force us to challenge previous theoretical accounts of spectatorship, the body, and temporality.[...]

Let us retain the above epigraph from the 1990 film *Pump Up the Volume* to set our introductory tone. Even the most banal rhetoric of the fin de siècle pleads a certain exhaustion: a foreclosed sense of the future, where the only imaginable option is a turning back onto the past.

The Mall

The word *mall* is etymologically taken from *pall mall*, the protected grassy fairways for the eighteenth-century English sport called pall mall, a combination of golf and croquet. The game, one of many where a stick and a ball are exercised in the precision of eye-hand coordination, is played with a ball that is hit by a stick and aimed at a goal. But in the shopping mall the goal is less obvious. In the game of shopping mall consumerism, the ball is the consumer and the shop window the stick.

As a commercial form, the shopping mall is a distinctive sign of the global dissemination of late capitalist economies; it originated in North America, spread to Europe, Australia, Japan, Central and South America, and the Middle East. The United States led other developed capitalist countries in this form of consumer marketing. In 1957 there were three thousand shopping centers in the United States; by the mid 1970s seventeen thousand; by 1986 over twenty-six thousand. (Australia is second to the United States in number of shopping centers – and, in 1973, it had fewer than one hundred.[2]) The "shopping *center*" was a commercial concomitant to the demographic shifts produced by post-World War II urban populations decentered to the suburbs, its location a consequence of the automobile and more efficient highway systems.

Like the arcade in the 1830s and 1840s, by the mid-1970s the shopping mall had become a generic building type. As an architectural space, the mall derives its form both from the vaulted interiors of the nineteenth-century arcade and from the multistoried central well of the department store; both structures were designed to maximize the commercial effectiveness of a public interior.

The first fully enclosed two-level shopping mall was built in Edina, Minnesota, in 1956. Designed by Viénnese emigré architect Victor Gruen, it was the first shopping complex to turn the shops away from the parking lot and toward one another. (In Minnesota, of course, the bitter cold winter climate made this a wise design decision.) In this environmentally determined plan linking two "anchor" stores, Gruen's design for an indoor shopping center became a model for maximizing trading space via the multilevel enclosed mall. The "sales breed sales" logic of the department store was adapted to the shopping center where each store was still a separate (often competing) business. In the United States, the energy crisis of 1973 added the natural-light atrium as a new design element to the enclosed mall. Atrium malls invoke a more direct architectural quotation of a capacious nineteenth-century public space, with vaulted clerestory roof, indoor plants, wrought-iron railings, and tiled floors. If the energy crisis produced a disturbing sense of scarcity for the American consumer, the bounteous emporiums of the shopping mall provided a reassuring salve.

The mall encourages the perceptual mode of flânerie while instrumentalizing it for consumer objectives. Jon Jerde, the architect of a paradigmatic Los Angeles shopping mall, the Westside Pavilion, describes his concept of the American variation on flânerie:

> Urban and suburban Americans seldom stroll aimlessly, as Europeans do, to parade and rub shoulders in a crowd. We need a *destination, a sense of arrival* at a definite location. My aim, in developments such as Horton Plaza and the Westside Pavilion, *is to provide a destination that is also a public parade and a communal center.*[3] (emphasis added)

For Jerde, the speculative gaze of the shopper provides the motor for such flânerie.

Like the nineteenth-century train station, the shopping mall provides the "sense of arrival" and of departure; the shopper strolls distractedly past an assortment of

Figure I. "Europa Boulevard" in the West Edmonton Mall, 1992. Photograph © Anne Friedberg.

stores that promise consumerist digression. Zola described the department store as a "wonderful commercial machine"; the shopping mall is equally a selling machine designed to process shoppers through its cogs and pinions. Shopping mall planners employ a mechanist rhetoric to describe the circulation of consumers: magnet stores, generators, flow, pull. Escalators provide an illusion of travel, a mechanized mobility to the shopper's gaze in a serene glide through an entirely consumerist space.

Although architects and urban planners address the relation of the mall to its externals – its location in relation to the highway, the subdivision, the "metro-nucleation" of businesses clustered around the mall – the regional specificity of a shopping mall is not always considered. Many malls are planned as mini-theme parks – a mixed-use environment where the range of commodity-experiences "breeds sales." Such planning is a canny commercial synthesis of the activities of shopping and tourism, combining a wide variety of rationales for the mobile and virtual gaze of a shopper-spectator. Suburban mall planners rely on the logic of distraction to supply alternative vistas, a compensatory escape from drab suburbia and the imaginative parameters of its inhabitants. Enclosed malls that reclaim old market areas of cities (South Street Seaport in New York; Faneuil Hall in Boston; Ghiradelli Square in San Francisco) provide an equally canny combination of tourist destination with consumerist diversion. As we will see, multiplex cinemas fit ideally into this commercial mix.

The "world's largest" shopping mall in Edmonton, Alberta (constructed from 1981 until 1986), provides a suitably hyperbolic example. The West Edmonton Mall is, in Jerde's sense, a destination. Consumers travel from all over Alberta on a pilgrimage to what the mall's publicists call the "Eighth Wonder of the World." The West Edmonton Mall contains the world's largest indoor amusement park, a "wave pool" and five-acre waterpark with raging rapids, a fourteen-story-high triple-loop high-speed roller coaster, an ice rink, a saltwater dolphin tank, a full-size replica of the Columbus flagship *Santa Maria*, a fleet of submarines (larger than that of the Canadian Navy), a simulated "Europa" boulevard, a reconstituted "Bourbon Street," 110 eating establishments, and twenty-three cinemas. In addition, the attached Fantasyland Hotel has "fantasy rooms" that are thematic recreations of "ancient" Rome, a Hollywood nightclub, and a Polynesian catamaran. The West Edmonton Mall is a "world in miniature."

The mall is not a completely *public* place. Like the arcade before it, the street is made safely distant inside the mall. Like the department store – with shared pedestrian areas between various departments – the mall becomes a realm for consumption, effectively exiling the realm of production from sight. Like the theme park, the mall is "imagineered" with maintenance and management techniques, keeping invisible the delivery bays or support systems, concealing the security guards and bouncers who control its entrances. The mall is a contemporary phantasmagoria, enforcing a blindness to a range of urban blights – the homeless, beggars, crime, traffic, even weather. And, while the temperature-controlled environment of the indoor mall defies seasons and regional environments, the presence of trees and large plants give the illusion of outdoors. The mall creates a nostalgic image of the town center as a clean, safe, and legible place, but a peculiarly timeless place. As Barthes described the paradoxical "transported immobility" of tourism, the shopping mall imparts an inverse effect, a mobilized transportability: not psychic stasis, but psychic travel.

At the same time that malls are mixed-use heterotopias, they are also heterodystopias, the dialectical shadow of an Edenic ambulatory. In a marked discussion of the inner-city "Panopticon Mall," critic Mike Davis has underlined the dystopic aspects of this consumerized "public" space. Davis targets shopping mall developer Alexander Haagens who, borrowing "brazenly" from Bentham's prison model, has developed more than forty shopping centers (mostly in low-income neighborhoods) with closed-circuit video surveillance. The Haagens-designed Martin Luther King Center in Los Angeles is, for example, a fortress surrounded by eight-foot fences, with video cameras and motion detectors at every entrance. Based on the same "brutal dissymmetry" as the Bentham prison, this "security" system – designed to protect owners and managers – turns the shopping mall into a "seeing machine" reproducing the scopic regimes of power and visuality that Foucault found basic to modernity. The shopper becomes a direct analog to the prisoner who internalizes the surveillant gaze; but here the consumerist exercise of power (through looking; where purchase – not theft – is the sanctioned way to "having") becomes the internalized mode.[4] In a further Orwellian direction, a Denver company now markets a security device – "Anne Droid" – a mannequin with a camera in her eye and a microphone in her nose. A female mannequin empowered with a surveillant gaze "returns the look" as a deceptive decoy against consumer theft.[5] Seen in this light, the shopper is dialectically both the observer and the observed, the transported and confined, the dioramic and the panoptic subject.

"Malling" as cultural activity

> Individuals no longer compete for the possession of goods, they actualize themselves in consumption.
>
> JEAN BAUDRILLARD

> I've a mind to give up living and go shopping instead.
>
> PAUL BUTTERFIELD

In contemporary culture, the marketing of "commodity-experiences" has almost surpassed the marketing of goods. As *Fortune* magazine pronounced in 1986, there is "a new generation of consumers who crave experiences not goods... in the metaphysics of the market, only those who buy and sell truly exist."[6] Or, in the hyperbolic phrasing of Baudrillard, "we have reached the point where 'consumption' has grasped the whole of life." In Baudrillard's description of the landscape of accumulation and profusion, consumption is synecdochal behavior, marking one's subjective interpellation into "consumer society":

> Our markets, our shopping avenues and malls mimic a newfound nature of prodigious fecundity. Those are our Valleys of Canaan where flows, instead of milk and honey, streams of neon on ketchup and plastic – but no matter!

There exists an anxious anticipation, not that there may not be enough, but that there is too much, and too much for everyone: by purchasing a portion one in effect appropriates a whole crumbling pyramid of oysters, meats, pears or canned asparagus. *Our purchases the part for the whole.*[7]

The overwhelmed consumer "purchases the part for the whole." As if to echo Benjamin's description of the passage as a "world in miniature," Baudrillard asserts "a drugstore can become a whole city."[8] The "drugstore" – the French version of a shopping mall – captures in a "kaleidoscopic mode" the profusion of merchandise in display. The consumer must compute the "calculus of objects":

> The drugstore (or the new shopping malls) makes possible the synthesis of all consumer activities, not least of which are *shopping, flirting with objects, idle wandering, and all the permutations of these.*[9] (emphasis added)

William Kowinski's popular 1985 book, *The Malling of America*, provides a detailed descriptive account of "malling" as the "chief cultural activity in America." Kowinski is succinct in his claims for the shopping mall: "a new Main Street," "a virtual one-stop culture," "cathedrals of the postwar culture," "a utopia fashioned by the not-quite-invisible hand of merchandising."[10]

Figure 2. In *Dawn of the Dead* (George Romero, 1979), zombie-shoppers ride escalators in a lobotomized exaggeration of consumer robotics. Courtesy Museum of Modern Art, New York.

Despite the fact that the mall seems to embody the temperate and benign, it has figured as the site for a range of cultural extremes – from the dystopic locus of horror in films like George Romero's 1979 film *Dawn of the Dead* to the equally extreme claims of religious utopianists. In *Dawn of the Dead* zombie-shoppers ride the escalators in a lobotomized exaggeration of consumer robotics. In this film, the mall is a runaway machine; its escalators, fountains, videogames, and automated voice-announcements continue in endless repetition as the "back-from-the-dead" move with equally mechanical motions. "What are they doing? Where do they come from?" asks a terrorized shopper. Another shopper (as if recalling Benjamin's discussion of the passages as "residues of a dream world"[11] provides an incisive reply: "Part instinct, part memory, what they used to do. This was an important place in their lives.... These creatures are ... pure motorized instinct."

At the other extreme, in *The New Religious Image of Urban America: The Shopping Mall as Ceremonial Center*. Ira Zepp describes the mall as a sacred ceremonial center where "people are meeting their needs for renewal and reconnection." Whereas the mall serves as a locus of alienation in Romero's film. Zepp claims, "the need we have for solidarity with one another is a religious expression" (emphasis added).[12] In this argument, shopping becomes a ritual rejoinder to spiritual impoverishment. The commercial basis of the shopping mall "community" provides a tangential secondary gain.

With a more ideological valence, Meaghan Morris's study of shopping centers in Australia initiates a "feminist study" of shopping practices which implies the potential for shopping as a form of critique. "Like effective shopping," Morris argues, "feminist criticism includes moments of sharpened focus, narrowed gaze – of skeptical, if not paranoid, assessment."[13] As we have seen, the historical relation between feminism and female consumerism supports this analogy (made emphatic in Stanton's rallying cry: "GO OUT AND BUY!"). A recently sighted bumper sticker – "A Woman's Place Is in the Mall" – confirms the demographics: as one study maintains, at the mall, 85 percent of the shoppers are women.[14]

In this light, the shopping mall appears to be a historical endpoint of increasing female empowerment, a "Ladies Paradise" for the contemporary flâneuse. And yet, to embrace the practice of shopping as a form of protofeminist subjectivity will risk overlooking some notable liabilities. The prerogatives of the female shopper may be endorsed in the market (as in "the customer is always right"), but the relation between *looking* and *buying* is not an unmediated one.

First, the relation of female "spending power" to female "earning power" is a critical equation in a consumer economy. Shopping is more than a perceptual mode involving the empowered choices of the consumer, it – quite simply, quite materially – requires money. A credit-card economy may encourage the fantasy of *virtual* "spending power," but this imaginary diversion has a price. Veblen read female consumption as a "vicarious" sign of a husband's or father's wealth. Today's female consumer may be enacting a postmodern version of an equally "vicarious" empowerment; instead of deferring payment to husband or father, she defers payment to the bank.

Figure 3.   Car window tag. © 1987 H & L Enterprises, El Cajon, California.

And second, despite the illusion that shopping is about choice, the desires that activate these choices have been, in many cases, created by display techniques, advertising, and, often, by films themselves. It has been a staple of studies of consumer culture to describe the ways in which commodity-"fetishes" have been created and then displayed to prey upon a shopper's psychic needs, where consumer "choice" is only a reaction to a constructed desire.

The public space of the market is a contemporary arena for symptomatic pathologies. In this way, today's "compulsive shopper" – driven by an irresistible urge to buy – becomes a fitting contemporary equivalent to the nineteenth-century hysteric. Following Elaine Showalter's question about the relation of feminism to hysteria ("Was hysteria – the 'daughter's disease' – a mode of protest for women deprived of other social or intellectual outlets or expressive options?"), one might ask: Is compulsive shopping a mode of protest for the powerlessness felt in other social or intellectual arenas?

In a recent self-help book, *Women Who Shop Too Much*, Carolyn Wesson offers an eleven-step recovery program for "shopaholics" and "addicted shoppers" who seek to "escape other problems, relieve anxiety, and feel alive."[15]

Initially this analogy between hysteria and compulsive shopping may seem to neglect sexual etiology, but a further comparison of the theorization of hysteria and the psychic life of the shopper might provide support for conclusions about the fluid subjectivity of the spectator-shopper. As Jane Gallop suggests about the hysteric:

> Feminists' attraction to the case of Dora may be an attraction to hysteria itself. Freud links hysteria to bisexuality; the hysteric identifies with members of both sexes, cannot choose one sexual identity.... If feminism is the calling into question of constraining sexual identities, then the hysteric may be a proto-feminist.[16]

Like the hysteric, the shopper may be calling into question constraining identities – sexual, racial, class – but, to act out anxieties about identity in the realm of the market, one must believe in the commodity's transformative power.

The mall is open to anyone – of any race, class, or gender – no purchase required. If shopping activates the power of the consumer gaze, then the purchase asserts power over these objects. The shopper pays only a psychic penalty if nothing is purchased in the displeasure of unsated consumer desire. As a form of incorporation, shopping is not unlike identification: "I shop, therefore I am," but also "I am what I buy."[17]

The shopping mall as cinematic apparatus

We will shift here from our discussion of gender and the subjective experience of shopping, to a consideration of the temporal and spatial construction of consumerism. Like the department store, the shopping mall operates as a selling machine and, as I've suggested, the shopping mall "machine" also produces a sense of timelessness. To magnify this claim: the shopping mall propagates a form of subjectivity that is directly analogous to the subjectivity produced by cinematic spectatorship. And conversely, the cinematic apparatus, now arrayed in mall multiplexes (and at home in the VCR) is a machine that functions much like the consumer space of the shopping mall. The shopping mall has not replaced the movie theater: it has become its logical extension.

Kowinski asserts: "There are more shopping centers in the United States than movie theaters (and most movie theaters are now in shopping centers)."[18] Yet, in this piece of syllogistic accounting, Kowinski has not calculated the exact relation between the movie theater and the shopping center. He approaches an equation between them in the following epiphanic passage:

> I saw the white pools of light, the areas of relative darkness, the symmetrical aisles and gleaming escalator, the bracketed store facades, the sudden strangeness of live trees and plants indoors. It was as if I were standing on a balcony, looking down on a stage, waiting for the show to begin. That was it. This theatrical space. The mall is a theater.

But to Kowinski, it is not a movie theater:

> This sense of a special world – permits a kind of unity of experience within an effortless enclosure that is something like the classic theater's unities of time, place and action. It's all here, now. The mall concentrates drama, suspends disbelief.[19]

This grand equation "mall as theater" is suggestive, and Kowinski later asserts, "the mall always felt something like a movie," but he leaves the analogy undeveloped.[20] Unlike the theater, which still retains an "aura" of performance and the real, the technology of the cinema offers a less auratic, more uniformly repeatable experience.

Yet theorizing the shopper's subjectivity presents many of the same difficulties as theorizing cinematic spectatorship. The fact of purchase (number of items sold) does not adequately measure the psychic pleasures or anxieties of consumption, any more than box office statistics and television ratings tell us about the spectator subjectivity. Sales statistics can only reveal a limited amount about a commodity's subjective effect.

Shopping mall cinemas demand an expenditure. They provide the pleasure of purchase without yielding a tangible product. Instead they supply a commodity-experience – as do the virtual mobilities of tourism. Like tourism, which is prepared by mass publicity and cliché, the film industry prepares the contemporary spectator with auxiliary discourses of publicity – print advertising, television spots, preview trailers. Licensed movie tie-ins are reinforced in displays in mall stores.

The shopping mall – and its apparatical extension, the shopping mall cinema – offers a safe transit into other spaces, other times, other imaginaries. These "elsewheres" are available to the consumer in a theatrical space where psychic transubstantiation is possible through purchase. Douglas Gomery describes the strategy of multiplex exhibition:

> If a shopping mall of the 1970s offered a vast array of merchandise in its stores, Cineplex Odeon presented the customer with many more than the usual number of choices for its movie shows. . . . If mallgoers loved to browse and make "impulse" purchases for items from shoes to records, why shouldn't they be able to do the same thing for movies?[21]

Thought of in this way, the spectator-shopper tries on different identities – with limited risk and a policy of easy return. The cinema spectator can engage in a kind of identity bulimia. Leaving the theater, one abandons the garment, and takes only the memory of having worn it for a few hours – or having been worn by it.

Let us underline shopping as a powerful metaphor for spectatorship. Like cinematic spectatorship, the mall relies on a perceptual displacement; it defers external realities, retailing instead a controlled, commodified, and pleasurable substitution.

The 1991 Paul Mazursky film, *Scenes from a Mall*, provides a pertinent illustration. The film uses the shopping mall as its central stage – a public space where intimacy is more possible than in the domestic sphere of home or bedroom. The mall is an appropriate contemporary site for crises of identity because it is also a space where identity can so easily be transformed. But more than using a mall for its narrative setting, *Scenes from a Mall* becomes a Chinese-box metaphor for spectatorship; the mall itself is an analogic arena for shifts in identity and temporality that take place during the virtual flânerie of cinema spectatorship.

Scenes from a Mall, set in a generic mall space, uses the mall as a familiar and local idiom, the epitome of the everyday of everywhere. The Los Angeles viewer recognizes the exterior of a familiar and local mall space: the Beverly Center. Architect Charles Moore has captured the sense of the Beverly Center as the "brown hole" of Beverly Hills, describing it as "the most negative neutral brown-gray that human color sense has yet devised."[22] Its exterior hulk has the soft curves of a fifties coffee table; its shaved-off corners give the sense of a mammoth asymmetrical hat-box stamped with the pastel signet THE BEVERLY CENTER and the white letters of its anchor stores, BULLOCKS and THE BROADWAY.

After the characters Deborah Feingold-Fifer (Bette Midler) and her husband Nick Fifer (Woody Allen) drive their red Saab into the belly of this massive brown whale, and survive the congested gridlock of its digestive ramps, they abandon their automotive skin and enter the mall. With the magic of creative geography, the mall they enter is not the actual interior of the Beverly Center. They've crossed the continent and entered the interior of the Stamford, Connecticut, Town Center. It hardly matters: with so many national chains – such as The Limited and Sharper Image – the space of consumer culture is interchangeable.

The narrative of *Scenes* details the breakup and reunion of a marriage counselor and her sports lawyer husband. (The marriage counselor's self-help book, I DO, I DO, I DO, on reaffirming the marriage vow, is on display at the mall bookstore.) At the point when the couple's relationship is at its most anguished – Woody Allen is beginning to have a panic attack – the two enter a movie in the mall multiplex. It is here, in front of a screening of *Salaam Bombay*, that the couple's desire is rekindled. Inside the Beverly Center's bounteous theater of purchases, *Salaam Bombay* – a neorealist Indian film that details the unrelenting poverty of urban overpopulation on the streets of Bombay – becomes a twisted tourist escape, where the "life of the natives" serves only as an impoverished backdrop to excesses of passionate anniversary lovemaking. (We know from one of the jibes Midler delivers to Allen that, in their sixteen-year marriage, they have never made love without the TV being on. And we also know that Allen's favorite "program" is the home shopping channel.) In this film, shopping is not a form of erotic foreplay: sex is foreplay to the more fulfilling pleasures of shopping.

The mall serves as a regional center with a global cosmopolitan outreach. The couple can visit Mexico and drink margaritas, toast champagne in a faux France (the

Maison de Caviar), and buy Italian clothes that turn the couple into movie quotations. (Allen, as Marcello Mastroianni in a white jacket and dark glasses, cruises up the escalator to Nino Rota music as Bette Midler, as Guilietta-of-the-spirits-Masina, glides down the escalator in pumpkin chiffon.)

What seems striking here is not so much that a contemporary film uses the mall as locus for drama, but rather that, as a self-reflexive statement about spectatorship, *Scenes from a Mall* uses the multiplex cinema as the climactic (in all senses) site for a character transformation. No amount of shopping accomplished this. Only after cinematic spectatorship are the couple truly inspired as consumers, their shopping disorders magically cured.

As Mazursky's film suggests, the shopping mall is paradigmatic of the ever-shifting temporality of virtual flânerie. Commodity-experiences that offer such fantasies of transformation and displacement are now as much a part of the public sphere in the shopping mall as they are uniquely private at home with the television and the VCR. It is, I argue, the ubiquity of these simulated experiences that has fostered an increasingly derealized sense of presence and identity. At the same time, the mechanical (and now electronic) capacity to manipulate time and space, essential features of both cinematic and televisual apparatuses, has produced an increasingly detemporalized subjectivity. Film theory has traditionally examined the consequences of spatial displacement into an elsewhere, but it has paid scant attention to the subjective consequences of cinema's unique temporal displacement, the elsewhen.

NOTES

1   Christian Slater in *Pump Up the Volume* (written and directed by Allan Moyle, 1990).

2   Edgar Lion, *Shopping Centers: Planning, Development and Administration* (New York: John Wiley and Sons, 1976), 1–2.

3   Quoted in Leon Whiteson, "'This is Our Time': And Architect Jon Jerde Is Trying to Write a 'Different Urban Script' for L.A.," *Los Angeles Times*, January 20, 1988.

4   Mike Davis, *City of Quartz* (London and New York: Verso, 1990): 240–244. Foucault, *Discipline and Punish*, 195–228.

5   Dody Tsiantar, "Big Brother at the Mall," *Newsweek* (July 3, 1989): 44.

6   Quoted in "All Shopped Out?," *Utne Reader* (September–October 1989).

7   Jean Baudrillard, "Consumer Society" (1970) in *Jean Baudrillard: Selected Writings*, edited by Mark Poster (Stanford, Calif.: Stanford University Press, 1988), 30.

8   Walter Benjamin, "Paris of the Second Empire," 36–37 in Walter Benjamin (Rolf Tiedemann, ed.) *Passagen-Werk* volumes 1 and 2 (Frankfurt am Main: Suhrkamp, 1983); Baudrillard, "Consumer Society," 32. Baudrillard describes Parly 2, the planned community between Paris and Orly airport, which has a giant shopping center, tennis courts, pools, and library.

9   Baudrillard, "Consumer Society," 31.

10 William Kowinski, *The Malling of America* (New York: Morrow, 1985), 18, 22, 23.

11 Benjamin, "Paris–Capital of the Nineteenth Century," 176 in Benjamin, *Passagen-Werk*.

12 Ira G. Zepp, Jr., *The New Religious Image of Urban America: The Shopping Mall as Ceremonial Center* (Westminster, Md.: Christian Classics, 1986), 73.

13   Meaghan Morris, "Things to Do with Shopping Centres," *Center for Twentieth Century Studies*, working paper no. I (Fall 1988).

14   Ernest Hahn, "The Shopping Center Industry," in *Shopping Centers and Malls*, edited by Robert Davis Rathbun (New York: Retail Reporting, 1986), 6–7.

15   Carolyn Wesson, *Women Who Shop Too Much: Overcoming the Urge to Splurge* (New York: St. Martin's 1990).

16   Jane Gallop, "Nurse Freud: Class Struggle in the Family," unpublished paper quoted in Showalter, "Female Malady," 160.

17   "I Shop Therefore I Am" is the text on an untitled work by Barbara Kruger, 1987.

18   Kowinski, *Malling of America*, 20.

19   Ibid., 62.

20   Ibid., 376.

21   Douglas Gomery, "Thinking about Motion Picture Exhibition," *Velvet Light Trap* no. 25 (Spring 1990): 6.

22   Charles Moore, Peter Becker, and Regula Campbell, *The City Observed: Los Angeles* (New York: Vintage Books, 1984), 232.

39 Life on the Screen: Identity in the Age of the Internet

Sherry Turkle

Insofar as space is a product of our ordering of the concrete, every place is both a represented space and a space of representation. This is not to imply that space has no materiality: a forest-full of trees does not vanish in the absence of human conceptions of nature, just as a mall entails an architectural edifice packed with commodities (and their hidden production processes). But space *is* by virtue of how its materiality is rendered meaningful within a social context where representations are shared, negotiated, and instituted. "Real" space is therefore a highly contingent product of how the material and the symbolic are socially mediated. This mediation produces places that may be very much at odds with their apparent physical (im)materiality. Sherry Turkle's survey of "virtual" reality illustrates this point. The physical space of the Internet is one of transmission cables and silicon chips, not at all a humanly habitable terrain. Yet in her examination of Multi-User Dimensions and Multi-user dimensions Object Oriented (MUDs and MOOs), Turkle identifies something other than the strings of zeros and ones comprising these cybernetic locales, or the lines of text describing them to their habitués. In cyberspace, Turkle finds an unprecedented diversity of endlessly reconfigurable selves. Some of these selves bear little or no resemblance to the off-screen individuals they represent. Some, being literally sexless, or zoomorphic, or even deiform, can not possibly bear any resemblance to any off-screen individual. Any number of these selves may be avatars of the same off-screen individual. And others may have no off-screen presence whatsoever, being preprogramed automata of the computer itself. Yet these infinitely fluid selves occupy visceral spaces both liberating and dysfunctional: living rooms and dungeons, cafes and crime scenes, agoras and panopticons. Spaces that, although nowhere in particular, become real through the politics of their use and abuse. Thus, Turkle reminds us that while we must be attentive to how "the real" is inflected by the media through which it is embodied, reality remains located at the social intersection of the imaginary and the concrete. It is something we make, in places.

Introduction: Identity in the Age of the Internet

We come to see ourselves differently as we catch sight of our images in the mirror of the machine. A decade ago, when I first called the computer a second self, these identity-transforming relationships were almost always one-on-one, a person alone with a machine. This is no longer the case. A rapidly expanding system of networks, collectively known as the Internet, links millions of people in new spaces that are changing the way we think, the nature of our sexuality, the form of our communities, our very identities. [. . .]

In the story of constructing identity in the culture of simulation, experiences on the Internet figure prominently, but these experiences can only be understood as part of a larger cultural context. That context is the story of the eroding boundaries between the real and the virtual, the animate and the inanimate, the unitary and the multiple self, which is occurring both in advanced scientific fields of research and in the patterns of everyday life. From scientists trying to create artificial life to children "morphing" through a series of virtual personae, we shall see evidence of fundamental shifts in the way we create and experience human identity. But it is on the Internet that our confrontations with technology as it collides with our sense of human identity are fresh, even raw. In the real-time communities of cyberspace, we are dwellers on the threshold between the real and virtual, unsure of our footing, inventing ourselves as we go along. [. . .]

The development of windows for computer interfaces was a technical innovation motivated by the desire to get people working more efficiently by cycling through different applications. But in the daily practice of many computer users, windows have become a powerful metaphor for thinking about the self as a multiple, distributed system. The self is no longer simply playing different roles in different settings at different times, something that a person experiences when, for example, she wakes up as a lover, makes breakfast as a mother, and drives to work as a lawyer. The life practice of windows is that of a decentered self that exists in many worlds and plays many roles at the same time. In traditional theater and in role-playing games that take place in physical space, one steps in and out of character; MUDs, in contrast, offer parallel identities, parallel lives. The experience of this parallelism encourages treating on-screen and off-screen lives with a surprising degree of equality. Experiences on the Internet extend the metaphor of windows – now RL [Real Life] itself, as Doug said, can be "just one more window." [. . .]

As more people spend more time in these virtual spaces, some go so far as to challenge the idea of giving any priority to RL at all. "After all," says one dedicated MUD player and IRC user, "why grant such superior status to the self that has the body when the selves that don't have bodies are able to have different kinds of experiences?" When people can play at having different genders and different lives, it isn't surprising that for some this play has become as real as what we conventionally think of as their lives, although for them this is no longer a valid distinction. [. . .]

Today I use the personal computer and modem on my desk to access MUDs. Anonymously, I travel their rooms and public spaces (a bar, a lounge, a hot tub). I create several characters, some not of my biological gender, who are able to have social and sexual encounters with other characters. On different MUDs, I have different routines, different friends, different names. One day I learned of a virtual rape. One MUD player had used his skill with the system to seize control of another player's character. In this way the aggressor was able to direct the seized character to submit to a violent sexual encounter. He did all this against the will and over the distraught objections of the player usually "behind" this character, the player to whom this character "belonged." Although some made light of the offender's actions by saying that the episode was just words, in text-based virtual realities such as MUDs, words *are* deeds. [...]

So not only are MUDs places where the self is multiple and constructed by language, they are places where people and machines are in a new relation to each other, indeed can be mistaken for each other. In such ways, MUDs are evocative objects for thinking about human identity and, more generally, about a set of ideas that have come to be known as "postmodernism."

These ideas are difficult to define simply, but they are characterized by such terms as "decentered," "fluid," "nonlinear," and "opaque." They contrast with modernism, the classical world-view that has dominated Western thinking since the Enlightenment. The modernist view of reality is characterized by such terms as "linear," "logical," "hierarchical," and by having "depths" that can be plumbed and understood. MUDs offer an experience of the abstract postmodern ideas that had intrigued yet confused me during my intellectual coming of age. In this, MUDs exemplify a phenomenon we shall meet often in these pages, that of computer-mediated experiences bringing philosophy down to earth.

In a surprising and counter-intuitive twist, in the past decade, the mechanical engines of computers have been grounding the radically nonmechanical philosophy of postmodernism. The online world of the Internet is not the only instance of evocative computer objects and experiences bringing postmodernism down to earth. One of my students at MIT dropped out of a course I teach on social theory, complaining that the writings of the literary theorist Jacques Derrida were simply beyond him. He found that Derrida's dense prose and far-flung philosophical allusions were incomprehensible. The following semester I ran into the student in an MIT cafeteria. "Maybe I wouldn't have to drop out now," he told me. In the past month, with his roommate's acquisition of new software for his Macintosh computer, my student had found his own key to Derrida. That software was a type of hypertext, which allows a computer user to create links between related texts, songs, photographs, and video, as well as to travel along the links made by others. Derrida emphasized that writing is constructed by the audience as well as by the author and that what is absent from the text is as significant as what is present. The student made the following connection:

> Derrida was saying that the messages of the great books are no more written in stone than are the links of a hypertext. I look at my roommate's hypertext stacks and I am able to trace the connections he made and the peculiarities of how he links things together. . . . And the things he might have linked but didn't. The traditional texts are like [elements in] the stack. Meanings are arbitrary, as arbitrary as the links in a stack.

"The cards in a hypertext stack," he concluded, "get their meaning in relation to each other. It's like Derrida. The links have a reason but there is no final truth behind them."[1]

Like experiences on MUDs, the student's story shows how technology is bringing a set of ideas associated with postmodernism – in this case, ideas about the instability of meanings and the lack of universal and knowable truths – into everyday life. In recent years, it has become fashionable to poke fun at postmodern philosophy and lampoon its allusiveness and density. Indeed, I have done some of this myself. But in this book we shall see that through experiences with computers, people come to a certain understanding of postmodernism and to recognize its ability to usefully capture certain aspects of their own experience, both online and off.

In *The Electronic Word*, the classicist Richard A. Lanham argues that open-ended screen text subverts traditional fantasies of a master narrative, or definitive reading, by presenting the reader with possibilities for changing fonts, zooming in and out, and rearranging and replacing text. The result is "a body of work active not passive, a canon not frozen in perfection but volatile with contending human motive."[2] Lanham puts technology and postmodernism together and concludes that the computer is a "fulfillment of social thought." But I believe the relationship is better thought of as a two-way process. Computer technology not only "fulfills the post-modern aesthetic" as Lanham would have it, heightening and concretizing the postmodern experience, but helps that aesthetic hit the street as well as the seminar room. Computers embody postmodern theory and bring it down to earth.

As recently as ten to fifteen years ago, it was almost unthinkable to speak of the computer's involvement with ideas about unstable meanings and unknowable truths.[3] The computer had a clear intellectual identity as a calculating machine. Indeed, when I took an introductory programming course at Harvard in 1978, the professor introduced the computer to the class by calling it a giant calculator. Programming, he reassured us, was a cut and dried technical activity whose rules were crystal clear.

These reassurances captured the essence of what I shall be calling the modernist computational aesthetic. The image of the computer as calculator suggested that no matter how complicated a computer might seem, what happened inside it could be mechanically unpacked. Programming was a technical skill that could be done a right way or a wrong way. The right way was dictated by the computer's calculator essence. The right way was linear and logical. My professor made it clear that this linear, logical calculating machine combined with a structured, rule-based method of writing software offered guidance for thinking not only about technology and programming, but about economics, psychology, and social life. In other words, computational ideas were presented as one of the great modern metanarratives, stories of how the world worked that provided unifying pictures and analyzed complicated things by breaking them down into simpler parts. The modernist computational aesthetic promised to explain and unpack, to reduce and clarify. Although the computer culture was never monolithic, always including dissenters and deviant subcultures, for many years its professional mainstream (including computer scientists, engineers, economists, and cognitive scientists) shared this clear intellectual direction. Computers, it was assumed, would become more powerful, both as tools and as metaphors, by becoming better and faster calculating machines, better and faster analytical engines.

From a Culture of Calculation toward a Culture of Simulation

Most people over thirty years old (and even many younger ones) have had an introduction to computers similar to the one I received in that programming course. But from today's perspective, the fundamental lessons of computing that I was taught are wrong. First of all, programming is no longer cut and dried. Indeed, even its dimensions have become elusive. Are you programming when you customize your wordprocessing software? When you design "organisms" to populate a simulation of Darwinian evolution in a computer game called SimLife? Or when you build a room in a MUD so that opening a door to it will cause "Happy Un-Birthday" to ring out on all but one day of the year? In a sense, these activities are forms of programming, but that sense is radically different from the one presented in my 1978 computer course.

The lessons of computing today have little to do with calculation and rules; instead they concern simulation, navigation, and interaction. [...]

The meaning of the computer presence in people's lives is very different from what most expected in the late 1970s. One way to describe what has happened is to say that we are moving from a modernist culture of calculation toward a postmodernist culture of simulation.

The culture of simulation is emerging in many domains. It is affecting our understanding of our minds and our bodies. For example, fifteen years ago, the computational models of mind that dominated academic psychology were modernist in spirit: Nearly all tried to describe the mind in terms of centralized structures and programmed rules. In contrast, today's models often embrace a postmodern aesthetic of complexity and decentering. Mainstream computer researchers no longer aspire to program intelligence into computers but expect intelligence to emerge from the interactions of small subprograms. If these emergent simulations are "opaque," that is, too complex to be completely analyzed, this is not necessarily a problem. After all, these theorists say, our brains are opaque to us, but this has never prevented them from functioning perfectly well as minds. [...]

Sexual encounters in cyberspace are only one (albeit well-publicized) element of our new lives on the screen. Virtual communities ranging from MUDs to computer bulletin boards allow people to generate experiences, relationships, identities, and living spaces that arise only through interaction with technology. In the many thousands of hours that Mike, a college freshman in Kansas, has been logged on to his favorite MUD, he has created an apartment with rooms, furniture, books, desk, and even a small computer. Its interior is exquisitely detailed, even though it exists only in textual description. A hearth, an easy chair, and a mahogany desk warm his cyberspace. "It's where I live," Mike says. "More than I do in my dingy dorm room. There's no place like home."

As human beings become increasingly intertwined with the technology and with each other via the technology, old distinctions between what is specifically human and specifically technological become more complex. Are we living life *on* the screen or life *in* the screen? Our new technologically enmeshed relationships oblige us to ask to what extent we ourselves have become cyborgs, transgressive mixtures of biology, technology, and code.[4] The traditional distance between people and machines has become harder to maintain.

Writing in his diary in 1832, Ralph Waldo Emerson reflected that "Dreams and beasts are two keys by which we are to find out the secrets of our nature ... they are our test objects."[5] Emerson was prescient. Freud and his heirs would measure human rationality against the dream. Darwin and his heirs would insist that we measure human nature against nature itself – the world of the beasts seen as our forbears and kin. If Emerson had lived at the end of the twentieth century, he would surely have seen the computer as a new test object. Like dreams and beasts, the computer stands on the margins. It is a mind that is not yet a mind. It is inanimate yet interactive. It does not think, yet neither is it external to thought. It is an object, ultimately a mechanism, but it behaves, interacts, and seems in a certain sense to know. It confronts us with an uneasy sense of kinship. After all, we too behave, interact, and seem to know, and yet are ultimately made of matter and programmed DNA. We think we can think. But can *it* think? Could it have the capacity to feel? Could it ever be said to be alive?

Dreams and beasts were the test objects for Freud and Darwin, the test objects for modernism. In the past decade, the computer has become the test object for postmodernism. The computer takes us beyond a world of dreams and beasts because it enables us to contemplate dreams that do not need beasts. The computer is an evocative object that causes old boundaries to be renegotiated. [...]

In the spirit of Whitman's reflections on the child, I want to know what we are becoming if the first objects we look upon each day are simulations into which we deploy our virtual selves. In other words, this is not a book about computers. Rather, it is a book about the intense relationships people have with computers and how these relationships are changing the way we think and feel. Along with the movement from a culture of calculation toward a culture of simulation have come changes in what computers do *for* us and in what they do *to* us – to our relationships and our ways of thinking about ourselves.

In the past decade, the changes in the intellectual identity and cultural impact of the computer have taken place in a culture still deeply attached to the quest for a modernist understanding of the mechanisms of life. Larger scientific and cultural trends, among them advances in psychopharmacology and the development of genetics as a computational biology, reflect the extent to which we assume ourselves to be like machines whose inner workings we can understand. "Do we have our emotions," asks a college sophomore whose mother has been transformed by taking antidepressant medication, "or do our emotions have us?" To whom is one listening when one is "listening to Prozac"?[6] The aim of the Human Genome Project is to specify the location and role of all the genes in human DNA. The project is often justified on the grounds that it promises to find the pieces of our genetic code responsible for many human diseases so that these may be better treated, perhaps by genetic reengineering. But talk about the Project also addresses the possibility of finding the genetic markers that determine human personality, temperament, and sexual orientation. As we contemplate reengineering the genome, we are also reengineering our view of ourselves as programmed beings.[7] Any romantic reaction that relies on biology as the bottom line is fragile, because it is building on shifting ground. Biology is appropriating computer technology's older, modernist models of computation while at the same time computer scientists are aspiring to develop a new opaque, emergent biology that is closer to the postmodern culture of simulation.[8]

Today, more lifelike machines sit on our desktops, computer science uses biological concepts, and human biology is recast in terms of deciphering a code. With descriptions of the brain that explicitly invoke computers and images of computers that explicitly invoke the brain, we have reached a cultural watershed. The rethinking of human and machine identity is not taking place just among philosophers but "on the ground," through a philosophy in everyday life that is in some measure both provoked and carried by the computer presence.

We have sought out the subjective computer. Computers don't just do things for us, they do things to us, including to our ways of thinking about ourselves and other people. A decade ago, such subjective effects of the computer presence were secondary in the sense that they were not the ones being sought.[9] Today, things are often the other way around. People explicitly turn to computers for experiences that they hope will change their ways of thinking or will affect their social and emotional lives. When people explore simulation games and fantasy worlds or log on to a community where they have virtual friends and lovers, they are not thinking of the computer as what Charles Babbage, the nineteenth-century mathematician who invented the first programmable machine, called an analytical engine. They are seeking out the computer as an intimate machine.

NOTES

1 The student's association of Derrida and hypertext may be unsophisticated, but it is far from outlandish. See, for example, George P. Landow, *Hypertext: The Convergence of Critical Theory and Technology* (Baltimore: Johns Hopkins, 1992), pp. 1–34; and in George P. Landow and Paul Delany, eds., *Hypermedia and Literary Studies* (Cambridge, Mass.: MIT Press, 1991).

2 Richard A. Lanham, *The Electronic Word: Democracy, Technology, and the Arts* (Chicago: The University of Chicago Press, 1993), p. 51. George Landow sees critical theory and technology in the midst of a "convergence." See Landow, *Hypertext*.

3 I say almost unthinkable because a small number of postmodern writers had begun to associate their work with the possibilities of computer technology. See, in particular, Jean-François Lyotard, *The Postmodern Condition: A Report on Knowledge*, trans. Geoff Bennington and Brian Massumi (Minneapolis: University of Minnesota Press, 1984).

4 See, for example, Donna Haraway, "A Manifesto for Cyborgs: Science, Technology, and Socialist Feminism in the 1980s," *Socialist Review* 80 (March-April 1985): 65–107.

5 The quotation is from a journal entry by Emerson in January 1832. The passage reads in full, "Dreams and beasts are two keys by which we are to find out the secrets of our nature. All mystics use them. They are like comparative anatomy. They are out test objects." See Joel Porte, ed., *Emerson in His Journals* (Cambridge, Mass.: Belknap Press, 1982), p. 81.

6   Peter Kramer, *Listening to Prozac: A Psychiatrist Explores Mood-Altering Drugs and the New Meaning of the Self* (New York: Viking, 1993).

7   Nelkin and Lindee's *The DNA Mystique* documents the degree to which genetic essentialism dominates American popular culture today.

8   Evelyn Fox Keller, "The Body of a New Machine: Situating the Organism Between Telegraphs and Computers," *Perspectives on Science* 2, no. 3 (1994): 302–23.

9   For a view of this matter from the perspective of the 1980s, see Sherry Turkle, *The Second Self: Computers and the Human Spirit* (New York: Simon & Schuster, 1984).

Inconclusion: A Conversation ● ● ● ● ●

Michael J. Dear, Steven Flusty, and Django Sibley

I just parked the Snark outside the Doheny Library with a latte.

Is he Ok?

She seems fine! Didn't want to come to this meeting, though. Said that all she had to say on the matter of postmodernism was written down on the back of this envelope. Take a look.

Postmodernism is an ontology that composes a world of radically incommensurable viewpoints which give rise to a host of competing knowledges about that world. Postmodernity refers to the era of contemporary capitalism, the political, economic, and sociocultural conditions of our life and times. In both cases – the way we know ourselves, and the material conditions of our lives – we are in the process of a radical break from previous eras. As well as these philosophical and epochal breaks, however, be attuned to stylistic breaks too (in architecture, urban form, clothing, the way we do business), because these are the signs that enable us to witness the arrival of postmodernism/postmodernity.

Well, that's pretty straightforward. Did the Snark say anything about geography?

Yes, she wrote something on the back of the back of the envelope.

You mean the front of the envelope?

Shut up and read.

> Postmodern Geography deals with uncertainty and ambiguity. It is de-centered and de-centering, un-moored and un-navigable. And yet it remains, perforce, resolutely in place. It dares us to ground postmodern-ism/ity in discursive and material spaces. It dares us to recognize new and different geographies.

I thought that's what we were trying to do in this book, no?

Well, the Snark got a bit snarky on that point . . .

What do you mean?

She quite liked the first fit, said that deconstruction of human geography's last three-and-a-half decades of the twentieth century was pretty convincing – the groundwork of the 1960s and 1970s; the seeding that went on in the 1980s; and the splendiferous flowering of the 1990s. It's all there. You know, she had tears in her eyes when she talked about the spaces that postmodernity had opened up for critical voices.

Yes, but she also made the point that the excitement of postmodernism/ity (that's a bit hard to say as one word!) . . . she said that excitement shouldn't be used as ammunition to indiscriminately blow away the earlier traditions that got us to where we are today.

Fair enough. It's important to be able to trace geography's roots if we want to understand how the discipline developed into its current form.

But it's more than that, don't you see? The Snark insisted that all those old theories, ancient voices, had some merit. That we weren't so omniscient and potent that we could afford to toss out all that hard won experience and insight because of something new. If all viewpoints are potentially valid, this includes the viewpoints of the Ancient Ones, too.

A bit less of the "Ancient," if you don't mind! Most of the people in this book are alive and well!! But yes, in a sense, postmodernism/ity has a profound respect for histories. It permits intellectual forays and scavenger hunts across time. Part of its mission is to recover the earlier traditions, the voices of the past.

Nonetheless, postmodernism is hardly a done deal, is it? After all, it's still embattled in geography.

Actually, the war's just about over. And postmodernism's still here, and flourishing. I checked out the major geography journals from 1994 to the start of the new millennium, and counted over 250 articles that reflected postmodern themes.

Which journals did you look at? The Journal of Irreproduceable Results perhaps, maybe the Fortean Times...

Nothing quite so interesting, I'm afraid. Try: The Annals of the Association of American Geographers, The Professional Geographer, The Transactions of the Institute of British Geographers, Area *and* Society and Space.

So what sort of things were people writing about?

Well, apart from postmodernism/ity itself postcolonial themes were big, so was anything to do with culture, and nature–society relations.

And you think the authors of those articles would all call themselves "postmodernists"?

No. Many would undoubtedly, and even violently, resist being labeled with a term that eludes definition. However, much contemporary work done by geographers is clearly reflective of a context and consciousness that we can call "postmodern." But, many voices that have become elements of postmodern debates were being heard loud and clear before postmodernism/ity came on the disciplinary scene.

Such as feminism, for instance?

Exactly! Postmodernism can't take the credit for all the new ideas that have appeared since its inception. But when pomo hit, all these voices – existing and emerging – were tossed into a turbulent new space, which they molded and were molded by. We're still in that turbulent discursive space today. It's part of the postmodern condition.

What would a Snark say to that?

Nothing. I asked. She just kept pointing enigmatically at the book jacket. She's a big fan of Bill Viola's. Says he's probably the most important artist working in video today.

Care to translate?

Well, the Snark was suggesting that the cover's a perfect metaphor for the postmodern outlook this book tries to convey. Look, you've got two separate images being projected toward each other from opposite sides of a room. As the images pass through several veils they lose their clarity. Finally, after their passages through space and time, the images merge. At their confluence, they represent a new hybrid, even perhaps a totally original object. The Snark says this is what happens in postmodernism/ity.

So: objects are transformed by different ways of seeing, requiring new ways of understanding, a readiness to tolerate imprecision. It's like you have to walk into a seminar room naked.

Not going to happen!

But would you have a problem doing it if everyone else was naked too?

Depends on specifically who else everyone else is.

Just think of it as leaving your prejudices and ego on the table outside the seminar room. Take your openness and intelligence in with you, mind; just leave the other garbage behind.

I'll buy that, but I'm not sure readers of this Reader will. It's hard to resist the temptation to take your academic ego into the seminar room and let it bark at people. Besides, it's a helluva lot of work to read and understand all this stuff on the postmodern turn.

Well, that's where Ms. Snark chimed in again.

How so?

She said that the real challenge in this book comes in the Second Fit – how to reconstruct a practice of postmodern human geography? As the discipline's boundaries keep on melting, we're presented with almost infinite possibilities. And we've certainly strayed over the liquefying disciplinary line in putting the second part of this Reader together. But still, the Snark has opined (albeit genteelly) that we've only just begun to scratch the surface of this potential.

How depressing!

Not so! She said she'd help us through to the next steps by mapping out the terrain that we'd just passed through in the book.

Just wanted we need! Another blank Snark map!?

And for a territory we've just passed through?

Listen up, both of you. Snark's a bit of a witch really. She gave me a piece of magic. Sort of an ontological tarot reading.

Fantastic! Remind me to tell you a bit later what Harry Potter said about postmodernism.

Ignore him.

Thanks, I will. Look, every one of these cards she gave me has an idea from the Second Fit printed on it. The Snark said if I shuffle and deal them out, we'll get to understand the Reader Present, and a glimpse of a Reader Future.

So deal already!

POSTMODERNISM/ITY DEALS WITH
PLURAL/DIFFERENT WORLDS.

POSTMODERNISM/ITY RE-INSTATES THE
SUBJECT, THE BODY, AS ONE POINT OF
ANALYTICAL DEPARTURE.

POSTMODERNISM/ITY REINSTATES SPACE,
THE PRODUCTION OF PLACE, AS ONE POINT
OF ANALYTICAL DEPARTURE.

POSTMODERNISM/ITY CONCEDES THE
PARTIALITY OF ALL THEORIES, ALL WAYS OF
KNOWING, PLUS THE MERITS OF THOSE
DIFFERENT WAYS OF KNOWING.

*

THE CREATION OF SELF IN PLACE IS AKIN TO
SPINNING A WEAVING WEB OF NARRATIVES
FROM THE STUFF ABOUT YOU.

THE COLLECTION OF NARRATIVES
TOGETHER CONSTITUTE THE LIFESCRIPTS
OF SOCIETY.

NARRATIVES AND LIFESCRIPTS NORMALIZE;
THEY ENCOURAGE/ENFORCE CONFORMITY;
THEY PERMIT/ENABLE RESISTANCE.

ENDURING HYBRIDS FLOURISH IN LIMINAL
SPACES, AROUND THE MARGINS.

*

HARD CITY + SOFT CITY CONJOIN TO
PRODUCE LIFE EXPERIENCES.

HARD PLANET + SOFT PLANET CONJOIN TO
DEFINE THE LIMITS OF EXPERIENCE.

POSTMODERN GEOPOLITICS IS ABOUT THE
SURVIVAL OF HUMAN AND NONHUMAN
SPECIES.

POSTMODERN GEOPOLITICS ARE
NARRATIVES/LIFESCRIPTS OF
GLOBAL/LOCAL HYBRIDS.

EMERGENT LOCAL NATIONALISMS
CHALLENGE OBSOLETE
INSTITUTIONS/MODERNITIES OF THE
NATION-STATE.

EMERGENT GLOBALISMS – CORPORATE,
CRIMINAL, SUPRANATIONAL – CHALLENGE
EMERGENT NATIONALISMS.

POSTMODERN URBAN POLITICS IS
DIFFERENCE ON A LOCAL SCALE.

POSTMODERN URBAN POLITICS AND
POSTMODERN GEOPOLITICS CAN BE
HARNESSED FOR RESISTANT OR
REACTIONARY ENDS.

GLOBAL AND LOCAL ARE SEAMLESS IN
THEIR POSTMODERN CONNECTIVITIES.

*

DIFFERENCE AND ITS CATEGORIES ARE
SOCIALLY CONSTRUCTED AND
EXCLUSIONARY.

ADMITTING DIFFERENCE CONCEDES
REPRESENTATIONAL INDETERMINACY.

REPRESENTATIONAL INDETERMINACY IS
CONSTITUTIVE OF THE POSTMODERN
CONDITION.

IN A WORLD OF SIGNS, OF HYPER- AND
VIRTUAL-REALITY, REPRESENTATIONAL
INDETERMINACY IS HARNESSED TO
PRODUCE A WORLD OF SPECTACLE,
CONSUMPTION, AND IMAGINEERED
CONSCIOUSNESS.

POSTMODERN HYPERSPACE IS SOFT AND
HARD. IT REMAINS RESOLUTELY GROUNDED,
WITH ITS OWN DISTINCTIVE GEOGRAPHIES.

IN POSTMODERN HYPERSPACE, EVERYONE
CAN HEAR YOU SCREAM. THEY ARE ONLY
JUST LEARNING TO INTERPRET WHAT YOU
MEAN BY IT.

Wow! I'm not sure I understand all that. I'm not even sure I buy all that. But are you telling me that's where we've just been?

Well, I think Snark is saying that's where we've just arrived, here at the Reader Present. Plus, these are places we can go in the future.

And Geography, space, place – they're all part of the task?

So the Snark claims. And I believe her. Even though we're unsure about how it works, we *can* say that postmodern society is resolutely grounded, and that it is constituted through space. The terms and conditions of this groundedness, the constitutive processes . . . well, we simply haven't figured them out yet.

But we've made a start, no?

Yes. I think that's what this book is about.

What happens if you shuffle the cards?

The Snark says that you'll get a different perspective on the same issues. It's like forcing yourself to see differently, like wearing a different veil. Let's see what happens if I deal you two separate hands this time. How do your cards stack up?

Well, it's interesting! If you don't read the detailed propositions for a moment but instead think about the general topic that each card pinpoints, look at what you get:

SOFT	HARD
REPRESENTATION	REALITY
VIRTUAL	REAL
AUTHENTIC	SIMULATION
SIGN	SIMULACRA
SCREEN	TEXT
GLOBAL	LOCAL
BODY	SOCIETY
SUBJECT	OBJECT
NATURE	HUMAN
HYBRID	HOMOGENEITY
RESISTANCE	REACTION
.	.
.	.
.	.

Stop! This is getting to look like those lists that I've seen in other books. You know: This is modernity on one side, and these are the characteristics of postmodernity on the other. I hate these things, they force you into either/or choices.

I don't trust them either, but I think the Snark's cards are telling us something different.

It's not an either or situation. The cards are saying that we need both ends of the spectrum in postmodern work, no?

Exactly. These are not polar opposites. They're two ends of continua...

... or two addresses on a continuous n-dimensional figure...

... and each end...

... or address...

Can I finish please? As I was saying, both ends are necessary to grasp postmodern society. That's what a polyvocal discursive space is all about, isn't it?

I knew that! Go on, finish the deal.

No. You take the cards and keep playing. I'm going to check on the Snark...

Hey! These cards were printed in Zanzibar!! In the 1950s!!!

And so? I've got a deck from Calcutta that's about a hundred years old, and a far older one from Urumqi! What'd you expect, that there's only one Snark and she's all ours? There've been lots of other places and times when people've had to shack up with difference, polyvocality, radical uncertainty, and unresolvable contradiction. But it's certainly a new state of affairs for us moderns – or ex-moderns, or wuzmodernes, to be disrespectfully exact.

Who?

You know, citizens of overdeveloped societies, galumphing around with our univocal world-view pulled down tightly over our eyes and ears, and swinging our totalizing truths around like cudgels! But even though postmodernism may not be absolutely new – and some folk didn't need a modern period before it showed up! – it's definitely new, and definitely Post-the-Modern for us. And we're definitely playing it in original ways.

What's important, then, is that we keep on playing.

Right. Meantime, I'm going to check on the Snark.

Is she going to stay?

I don't think so. She's done all she can to help us unravel the mysterious spaces of postmodernity.

But people won't believe us, if she's not here to back us up.

Look, she's moving on. We've been very lucky; most people never get to see a Snark. What happens next is up to us.

Index